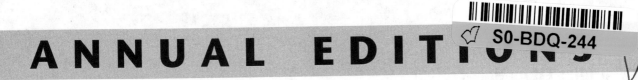

ANNUAL EDITIONS

Race and Ethnic Relations 09/10

Seventeenth Edition

EDITOR

John A. Kromkowski
Catholic University of America

John A. Kromkowski is the president of The National Center for Urban Ethnic Affairs in Washington, D.C., a nonprofit research, technical assistance, and educational institute that has sponsored programs and projects, and also published many books and articles on ethnic relations, urban affairs, and economic revitalization. He is also an undergraduate coordinator in the Department of Politics at the Catholic University of America. Dr. Kromkowski coordinates international seminars and internship programs in the United States, England, Ireland, and Belgium, activities between numerous scholarly institutes and a multivolume collection sponsored by the Council for Research in Values and Philosophy titled *Cultural Heritage and Contemporary Change*. He has served on national boards for the Baroni Institute, One American Foundation, Campaign for Human Development, U.S. Department of Education Ethnic Heritage Studies Program, White House Fellows Program, National Neighborhood Coalition, and American Revolution Bicentennial Administration.

Higher Education

Boston   Burr Ridge, IL   Dubuque, IA   New York   San Francisco   St. Louis
Bangkok   Bogotá   Caracas   Kuala Lumpur   Lisbon   London   Madrid   Mexico City
Milan   Montreal   New Delhi   Santiago   Seoul   Singapore   Sydney   Taipei   Toronto

The McGraw-Hill Companies

McGraw Hill | **Higher Education**

ANNUAL EDITIONS: RACE AND ETHNIC RELATIONS, SEVENTEENTH EDITION

Annual Editions® is a registered trademark of The McGraw-Hill Companies, Inc.

Annual Editions is published by the **Contemporary Learning Series** group within the McGraw-Hill Higher Education division.

1 2 3 4 5 6 7 8 9 0 QPD/QPD 0 9

ISBN 978–0–07–812762–5
MHID 0–07–812762–9
ISSN 1075–5195

Managing Editor: *Larry Loeppke*
Senior Managing Editor: *Faye Schilling*
Developmental Editor: *David Welsh*
Editorial Coordinator: *Mary Foust*
Editorial Assistant: *Nancy Meissner*
Production Service Assistant: *Rita Hingtgen*
Permissions Coordinator: *DeAnna Dausener*
Senior Marketing Manager: *Julie Keck*
Marketing Communications Specialist: *Mary Klein*
Marketing Coordinator: *Alice Link*
Project Manager: *Sandy Wille*
Design Specialist: *Tara McDermott*
Senior Production Supervisor: *Laura Fuller*
Cover Graphics: *Kristine Jubeck*

Compositor: Laserwords Private Limited
Cover Image: © Digital Vision/RF (inset); © Getty Images/RF (background)

Library in Congress Cataloging-in-Publication Data
Main entry under title: Annual Editions: Race and Ethnic Relations, 17/e.
 1. Race and Ethnic Relations—Periodicals. I. Kromkowski, John A., *comp.* II. Title: Race and Ethnic Relations.
658'.05

www.mhhe.com

Editors/Advisory Board

Members of the Advisory Board are instrumental in the final selection of articles for each edition of ANNUAL EDITIONS. Their review of articles for content, level, currentness, and appropriateness provides critical direction to the editor and staff. We think that you will find their careful consideration well reflected in this volume.

Preface

In publishing ANNUAL EDITIONS we recognize the enormous role played by the magazines, newspapers, and journals of the public press in providing current, first-rate educational information in a broad spectrum of interest areas. Many of these articles are appropriate for students, researchers, and professionals seeking accurate, current material to help bridge the gap between principles and theories and the real world. These articles, however, become more useful for study when those of lasting value are carefully collected, organized, indexed, and reproduced in a low-cost format, which provides easy and permanent access when the material is needed. That is the role played by ANNUAL EDITIONS.

The explosion of journalistic accounts, the growing legitimacy of ethnicity and race as relevant factors of political, economic, religious, and social affairs in the United States and throughout the world, rivet our attention to the topics addressed in collection. An accurate understanding of race and ethnicity begins with reviewing the experiences of particular places and people. Race and ethnicity are aspects of personal identity and the shared mentalities of groups, which are sustained within societies that are governed policies and practices embedded in historical narratives of meaning. The reader is invited to observe race and ethnicity in the United States, and to discern the development of regimes applied to race and ethnic relations in a modern, economically mobile, culturally pluralistic and immigrant-receiving country.

Nearly a hundred years after the U.S. Supreme Court declared that racial exclusion was unconstitutional, the Court returned to this question in *Brown v. Topeka Board of Education*. A decade later, in the mid-1960s, Congress passed civil and voting rights laws and immigration reform. By the mid-1960s, proclamation of the America Dream found new vigor, and engaged new challenges of pluralism and diversity. Though personal/individual rights are typically addresses in law, cultural rights are clearly associated with the participation of groups and the access of all to public, and social articulations of meaning derived from ethnic origins and traditions. Such access in America—given its size and embedded character of its historical legacies that included slavery, conquest, urbanization, and immigration—is necessarily a complex arena of continuities and changes. The contemporary reality of the United States remains rooted in the legacies of many cultures. America can be viewed as an ongoing drama of evocations of race and ethnicity that includes celebrations of tradition, proud proclamations of ethnic values, woeful lamentations

and righteous outrages, and claims for redress. In an age of ethnic and racial pluralism, such is the destiny of a large society consisting of many cultures. In America, race and ethnic relations occur at the boundaries of groups in a political order committed to personal liberties and civil rights. Thus, the issue and realities of racial and ethnic diversity are patently real, and are woven into the very nature of the country. Beyond the personal claims of liberties and rights stand other questions: How well are we negotiating relations among and between groups? How well are we shaping and sharing the burdens and benefits of social change and economic affluence? How we make such choices determines the quality of our common life.

This collection is designed to assist you in understanding ethnic and racial pluralism in the United States, in a global age. Unit 1, acquaints the reader with case-studies that are illustrative of the contemporary scene at the micro levels. Each case study reveals the specificity and particularity of race and ethnic intersections. Unit 2 reveals the foundational legal construction of diversity, and also traces the specific historical characteristics of American-diversity and its legal framework and aspirations for equality. The characteristics of American demography are broached in unit 3. The uniquely American expressions of indigenous groups are reviewed in unit 4. The two largest ethnic groups are treated in the selections found in units 5 and 6, which focus respectively on African Americans and Hispanic/Latino Americans.

Unit 7 explores the different dimensions of the Asian American experience. Unit 8 extends the discussion of ethnic identity to Americans of European and Mediterranean background, and offers comparative perceptions and perspectives of ethnic Americans on contemporary issues. Selections in unit 9 focus on the new horizons of race in the Presidential of 2008. Unit 10 is devoted to international aspects of ethnicity, and specific as well as grand-scale perspectives on possibilities for the resolution of ethnic conflict.

The intersection of the aspirations for inclusion and equality, and the realities of economic, gender, and racial claims reveal a pattern of cultural pluralism and contemporary challenges to the promise of American liberties. Each unit presents articles that help understand the origins of racialism. The religious and ethnic origins that shape the consciousness of group affinities and their interaction with political and governmental mobilizations are fundamental to understanding race and ethnic relations.

In addition to the annotated table of contents, this edition of *Annual Editions: Race and Ethnic Relations* contains a list of Internet References that can be used to further explore article topics and a Topic Guide to reference articles by subject. Readers may have input for the next edition of *Annual Editions: Race and Ethnic Relations* by completing and returning the prepaid article rating form in the back of the book. Thank you.

John A. Kromkowski
Editor

Contents

UNIT 1
Local Experiences of Racial and Ethnic Identity, Communities, and Diversity in America

The concepts in bold italics are developed in the article. For further expansion, please refer to the Topic Guide.

UNIT 2
The Legal Construction of Diversity and Disparity

Unit Overview   **28**

Section A

The concepts in bold italics are developed in the article. For further expansion, please refer to the Topic Guide.

UNIT 3
The Demography of Ethnicity

The concepts in bold italics are developed in the article. For further expansion, please refer to the Topic Guide.

UNIT 4
Indigenous Ethnic Groups

UNIT 5
African Americans

The concepts in bold italics are developed in the article. For further expansion, please refer to the Topic Guide.

UNIT 6
Hispanic/Latina/o Americans

UNIT 7
Asian Americans

The concepts in bold italics are developed in the article. For further expansion, please refer to the Topic Guide.

UNIT 8
European and Mediterranean Ethnics

The concepts in bold italics are developed in the article. For further expansion, please refer to the Topic Guide.

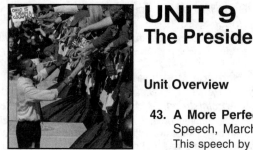

UNIT 9
The Presidential Election 2008

UNIT 10
Understanding International Aspects of Ethnic Relations

The concepts in bold italics are developed in the article. For further expansion, please refer to the Topic Guide.

The concepts in bold italics are developed in the article. For further expansion, please refer to the Topic Guide.

Correlation Guide

The *Annual Editions* series provides students with convenient, inexpensive access to current, carefully selected articles from the public press. **Annual Editions: Race and Ethnic Relations, 17/e** is an easy-to-use reader that presents articles on important topics such as *demography, immigration, local experiences,* and many more. For more information on *Annual Editions* and other *McGraw-Hill Contemporary Learning Series* titles, visit www.mhcls.com.

This convenient guide matches the units in **Annual Editions: Race and Ethnic Relations, 17/e** with the corresponding chapters in two of our best-selling McGraw-Hill Sociology textbooks by Aguirre/Turner and Kottak/Kozaitis.

Annual Editions: Race and Ethnic Relations, 17/e	American Ethnicity, 6/e by Aguirre/Turner	On Being Different, 3/e by Kottak/Kozaitis
Unit 1: Local Experiences of Racial and Ethnic Identity, Communities, and Diversity in America	**Chapter 4:** White Ethnic Americans **Chapter 5:** African Americans **Chapter 6:** Native Americans **Chapter 7:** Latinos **Chapter 8:** Asian and Pacific Island Americans **Chapter 9:** Arab Americans	**Chapter 4:** The Multicultural Society **Chapter 14:** Places and Spaces
Unit 2: The Legal Construction of Diversity and Disparity	**Chapter 1:** Ethnicity and Ethnic Relations	
Unit 3: The Demography of Ethnicity	**Chapter 1:** Ethnicity and Ethnic Relations **Chapter 2:** Explaining Ethnic Relations	**Chapter 13:** Class **Chapter 14:** Places and Spaces
Unit 4: Indigenous Ethnic Groups	**Chapter 6:** Native Americans	**Chapter 3:** Globalization and Identity
Unit 5: African Americans	**Chapter 5:** African Americans	**Chapter 5:** Ethnicity **Chapter 7:** Race: Its Social Construction **Chapter 15:** Linguistic Diversity
Unit 6: Hispanic/Latina/o Americans	**Chapter 7:** Latinos	**Chapter 5:** Ethnicity
Unit 7: Asian Americans	**Chapter 8:** Asian and Pacific Island Americans	**Chapter 5:** Ethnicity
Unit 8: European and Mediterranean Ethnics	**Chapter 4:** White Ethnic Americans **Chapter 9:** Arab Americans	**Chapter 5:** Ethnicity
Unit 9: The Presidential Election 2008		
Unit 10: Understanding International Aspects of Ethnic Relations	**Chapter 1:** Ethnicity and Ethnic Relations **Chapter 2:** Explaining Ethnic Relations	**Chapter 4:** The Multicultural Society **Chapter 17:** Conclusion

Topic Guide

This topic guide suggests how the selections in this book relate to the subjects covered in your course. You may want to use the topics listed on these pages to search the Web more easily.

On the following pages a number of Web sites have been gathered specifically for this book. They are arranged to reflect the units of this Annual Editions reader. You can link to these sites by going to *http://www.mhcls.com*.

All the articles that relate to each topic are listed below the bold-faced term.

African Americans
1. Cambridge Makes History
7. Mélange Cities
8. The Hotel Africa
9. The Fixer
11. *Dred Scott v. Sandford*
12. *Brown v. Board of Education of Topeka et al.*
27. Black History Month: February 2008
28. Who Is an African American?
29. That's a Bare-Knuckles Kiss
30. African American Philanthropy
31. For Black Politicians, a Rocky Road but a Steady Climb
41. Neither Natural Allies Nor Irreconcilable Foes: Alliance Building Efforts between African Americans and Immigrants
47. Is Obama the End of Black Politics?

Arab Americans
18. Ancestry 2000: Census 2000 Brief
19. Minority Population Tops 100 Million and More than 300 Counties Now "Majority-Minority"

Census
18. Ancestry 2000: Census 2000 Brief
19. Minority Population Tops 100 Million and More than 300 Counties Now "Majority-Minority"
29. That's a Bare-Knuckles Kiss

Civil rights
10. Racial Restrictions in the Law of Citizenship
11. *Dred Scott v. Sandford*
12. *Brown v. Board of Education of Topeka* et al.
14. 'Bakke' Set a New Path to Diversity for Colleges
15. *Shaare Tefila Congregation v. Cobb* and *Saint Francis College v. Al-Khazraji*

Community relations
1. Cambridge Makes History
2. Chicago and the Irish
3. 'Bursting with Pride' in Little Italy
4. Parishes in Transition: Holding on While Letting Go; Old Order Changing on South Bend's West Side
5. In Manassas, the Medium Is the Issue
6. In Brooklyn, an Evolving Ethnicity
7. Mélange Cities
35. To Be Asian in America
50. Never Underestimate the Power of Ethnicity in Iraq

Cultural conflict
2. Chicago and the Irish
3. 'Bursting with Pride' in Little Italy
5. In Manassas, the Medium Is the Issue
6. In Brooklyn, an Evolving Ethnicity
35. To Be Asian in America

Cultural continuity
3. 'Bursting with Pride' in Little Italy
35. To Be Asian in America

Cultural formation
1. Cambridge Makes History
3. 'Bursting with Pride' in Little Italy
6. In Brooklyn, an Evolving Ethnicity
7. Mélange Cities
13. How the GOP Conquered the South
32. Inventing Hispanics: A Diverse Minority Resists Being Labeled
35. To Be Asian in America
38. Miracle: American Polonia, Karol Wojtyła and the Election of Pope John Paul II
41. Neither Natural Allies Nor Irreconcilable Foes: Alliance Building Efforts between African Americans and Immigrants
42. The Study of Jewish American History and Dutch American History in Several Settings

Cultural pluralism
6. In Brooklyn, an Evolving Ethnicity
7. Mélange Cities
18. Ancestry 2000: Census 2000 Brief
35. To Be Asian in America

Culture
2. Chicago and the Irish
5. In Manassas, the Medium Is the Issue
6. In Brooklyn, an Evolving Ethnicity
7. Mélange Cities
35. To Be Asian in America

Culture change
4. Parishes in Transition: Holding on While Letting Go; Old Order Changing on South Bend's West Side
5. In Manassas, the Medium Is the Issue
6. In Brooklyn, an Evolving Ethnicity
7. Mélange Cities

Discrimination
1. Cambridge Makes History
10. Racial Restrictions in the Law of Citizenship
11. *Dred Scott v. Sandford*
12. *Brown v. Board of Education of Topeka et al.*
13. How the GOP Conquered the South
14. 'Bakke' Set a New Path to Diversity for Colleges
15. *Shaare Tefila Congregation v. Cobb* and *Saint Francis College v. Al-Khazraji*
16. Historical Discrimination in the Immigration Laws

Economy
34. Minority-Owned Firms More Likely to Export
36. Lands of Opportunity
37. Asian/Pacific American Heritage Month and Revenues for Asian-Owned Firms Up 24 Percent

Education
13. How the GOP Conquered the South
36. Lands of Opportunity

Ethnic issues
2. Chicago and the Irish
3. 'Bursting with Pride' in Little Italy

Internet References

The following Internet sites have been selected to support the articles found in this reader. These sites were available at the time of publication. However, because Web sites often change their structure and content, the information listed may no longer be available. We invite you to visit http://www.mhcls.com for easy access to these sites.

Annual Editions: Race and Ethnic Relations 17/e

General Sources

Library of Congress
http://www.loc.gov

Examine this extensive Web site to learn about resource tools, library services/resources, exhibitions, and databases in many different fields related to race and ethnicity.

Social Science Information Gateway
http://sosig.esrc.bris.ac.uk

Access an online catalog of thousands of Internet resources relevant to social science education and research at this site. Every resource is selected and described by a librarian or subject specialist.

Sociosite
http://www.pscw.uva.nl/sociosite/TOPICS/index.html

Open this enormous site of the University of Amsterdam's Sociology Department to gain insights into a number of social issues. A six-column alphabetical list provides links to activism, affirmative action, discrimination, poverty, race and ethnic relations, urbanization, women's issues, and much more.

UNIT 1: Local Experiences of Racial and Ethnic Identity, Communities, and Diversity in America

American Civil Liberties Union (ACLU)
http://www.aclu.org

This site contains links to the ACLU's archives of information about civil rights in the United States and around the world, now and historically. Consult the index to find discussions of such topics as racial equality and immigrants' rights.

Human Rights Web
http://www.hrweb.org

The history of the human-rights movement, text on seminal figures, landmark legal and political documents, and ideas on how individuals can get involved in helping to protect the rights of all peoples around the world can be found at this valuable site. Links to related sites can also be accessed here.

Supreme Court/Legal Information Institute
http://supct.law.cornell.edu/supct/index.html

Open this site for current and historical information about the Supreme Court. The archive contains many opinions issued since May 1990 as well as a collection of nearly 600 landmark decisions of the Court.

UNIT 2: The Legal Construction of Diversity and Disparity

U.S. Supreme Court Reports
http://bulk.resource.org/courts.gov/c/US/

U.S. Census Bureau
http://www.census.gov

Here is a link to the U.S. Census Bureau, which provides useful demographic research and statistics.

UNIT 3: The Demography of Ethnicity

U. S. Census Bureau
http://www.census.gov

The U.S. Census Bureau contains a wealth of information on topics such as populations and their breakdowns according to race, ethnicity, work status, etc.

Diversity.com
http://www.diversity.com

This site is an excellent source for recruiting job seekers from diverse ethnic cultures, life styles, life stages, creative persuasions, abilities, religious affiliations and gender. Diversity .com provides best-in-class recruitment advertising and diversity branding.

U. S. Bureau of Citizenship and Immigration Services
http://www.USCIS.gov/portal/site/uscis

Visit the home page of the USCIS to learn U.S. policy vis-à-vis immigrants, laws and regulations, and statistics.

UNIT 4: Indigenous Ethnic Groups

American Indian Science and Engineering Society (AISES)
http://www.aises.org

This AISES "Multicultural Educational Reform Programs" site provides a framework for learning about science, mathematics, and technology. There are useful links to programs for Native American education.

UNIT 5: African Americans

National Association for the Advancement of Colored People (NAACP)
http://www.naacp.org

Open this home page to explore the NAACP's stances regarding many topics in race and ethnic relations. Many links to other organizations and resources are provided.

Internet References

AIDs and Black New Yorkers
http://www.villagevoice.com/issues/0024/wright.php

This article, which is one of six, gives some understanding on the still growing death toll on the black community due to AIDs.

UNIT 6: Hispanic/Latina/o Americans

Latino American Network Information Center (LANIC)
http://lanic.utexas.edu

The purpose of this site is to offer Latinos sources of information on everything of importance. The site links to housing, employment, ethnicity, income, and political issues. It also offers the latest news of interest to Latinos and Hispanics.

National Council of La Raza (NCLR)
http://www.nclr.org

Explore NCLR's home page for links to health and education issues in the Hispanic community. Many other economic, political, and social concerns are also covered at this site.

UNIT 7: Asian Americans

Asian American Studies Center
http://www.aasc.ucla.edu/default.asp

Asian American for Equality
http://www.aafe.org

Asian-Nation
http://www.asian-nation.org/index.shtml

UNIT 8: European and Mediterranean Ethnics

Africa News Online
http://www.africanews.org

Open this site for *Africa News* on the Web. This source provides extensive, up-to-date information on all of Africa, with reports from Africa's newspapers and other sources.

Cultural Survival
http://www.culturalsurvival.org

This nonprofit organization works to defend and protect the human rights and cultural autonomy of indigenous peoples and oppressed ethnic minorities around the world. Learn about policies intended to avoid genocide and ethnic conflict.

The North-South Institute
http://www.nsi-ins.ca/ensi/index.html

Searching this site of the North-South Institute—which works to strengthen international development cooperation and enhance social equity—will help you find information on a variety of issues related to international race and ethnicity.

Order Sons of Italy in America
http://www.osia.org

This site encourages the study of Italian language and culture in American schools and universities.

The National Italian American Foundation
http://www.niaf.org

This is the website of The National Italian American Foundation. They are know as advocates in helping young Italian Americans with their educations and careers as well as strengthening cultural and economic ties between Italy and the U.S.

The Chicago Jewish News Online
http://www.chicagojewishnews.org

This site is an up-to-date news watch of what is happening in the Jewish community.

Polish American Congress
http://www.polamcon.org

At this site you can discover the current issues and recent events in the Polish community.

Polish American Journal
http://www.polamjournal.com

This is the site of the Polish American Journal, a monthly newspaper dedicated to the promotion and preservation of Polish American culture.

UNIT 9: The Presidential Election 2008

CNN Election Headquarters
http://www.cnn.com/ELECTION/2008/

Visit CNN's site for election coverage and results for the 2008 presidential and other races.

President-Elect Obama's Web Site
http://change.gov/

This site was set up to inform citizens of Barak Obama's agenda, his transition team, and other information.

UNIT 10: International Aspects of Ethnic Relations

Yale University Guide to American Ethnic Studies
http://www.library.yale.edu/rsc/ethnic/internet.html

This site, provided by Yale University, contains a list of resources regarding ethnic identity research and links to organizations that deal with ethnic identity.

American Indian Ritual Object Repatriation Foundation
http://www.repatriationfoundation.org

Visit this home page of the American Indian Ritual Object Repatriation Foundation, which aims to assist in the appropriate return of sacred ceremonial material.

Center for Research in Ethnic Relations
http://www.warwick.ac.uk/fac/soc/CRER_RC

This eclectic site provides links to a wealth of resources on the Internet related to race and ethnic relations.

The International Center for Migration, Ethnicity, and Citizenship
http://www.newschool.edu/icmec

The Center is engaged in scholarly research and public policy analysis bearing on international migration, refugees, and the incorporation of newcomers in host countries.

UNIT 1

Local Experiences of Racial and Ethnic Identity, Communities, and Diversity in America

Unit Selections

1. **Cambridge Makes History,** Chris Guy
2. **Chicago and the Irish,** Tom Deignan
3. **'Bursting with Pride' in Little Italy,** Kelly Brewington
4. **Parishes in Transition: Holding on While Letting Go and Old Order Changing on South Bend's West Side,** Jessica Trobaugh Temple and Erin Blasko
5. **In Manassas, the Medium Is the Issue,** Nick Miroff
6. **In Brooklyn, an Evolving Ethnicity,** Delizia Flaccavento
7. **Mélange Cities,** Blair A. Ruble
8. **The Hotel Africa,** G. Pascal Zachary
9. **The Fixer,** Adam Matthews

Key Points to Consider

- Explore the racial and ethnic diversity of neighborhoods, towns, and counties that are within your experience and compare them to the accounts presented in these articles.

- In what positive and negative respects do local newspapers define perceptions of race and ethnic relations?

- Does the rise of ethnic marketing foster widespread interest in new immigrants among existing populations?

- What opinions do you have about the religious practices of ethnic groups?

- Does the economic climate of a particular place and in a particular time period significantly influence race and ethnic relations?

- How are politics and ethnicity influential?

- Has the celebration or the revival of ethnic tradition increased?

- What variables seem to influence positive and negative views and attitudes among ethnic groups?

- Are some persons utterly inattentive to ethnic variety?

- Why do some persons feel threatened by public emphasis on ethnicity and race?

- What approaches to inter-group relations seem to be successful?

Student Web Site

www.mhcls.com

Internet References

American Civil Liberties Union (ACLU)
http://www.aclu.org
Human Rights Web
http://www.hrweb.org

Supreme Court/Legal Information Institute
http://supct.law.cornell.edu/supct/index.html

© ImageState Royalty Free/Alamy

A new generation of American leaders is increasingly comfortable with racial and ethnic diversity. They continually challenge the country and its institutions of cultural formation to discard the "melting pot" ideology and to replace it with the universalism of law, due process, and equal protection for all. This effort could be easily claimed in legislation, but the stubborn facts of social practices are embedded in patterns of regional diversity and mobility. The economic limitations faced in the process of urbanization and social development as well as a political potential and competitive edge that could be achieved by pandering the passions of fear, hatred, and prejudice created a web of contradictions that would define race and ethnic relations as follows: the singular isolation and exclusion of persons whose ancestry was rooted in American slavery and consciousness of color; the mentalities and constraints of a unique American form of shared consciousness derived from the dichotomous mentality of Anglo-conformists and their logic, practices of social division, and divisiveness; the urban immigrant and ethnic enclave experiences that demanded a new evocation of cultural pluralism beyond the insularity, isolation, and racialist mentalities; and institutions of governance derived from the rural foundations of states in the Anglo-Scot-Irish American culture that lacked mechanisms of metropolitan governance.

Ethnic and racial identities are social constructions of culture. The articles in this unit present contemporary accounts of local experiences that suggest that modern forms of identity and communities are formed by shared symbols and meanings that constitute bonds of union among persons. Such modern bonds are self expressed in various ways as types of ethnic and race relations. Such behaviors are not simply primordial givens. On the contrary, they are dynamic and changing cultural forms. They are fashioned from relationships among persons and the constitutions of groups, and they are significantly—if not essentially—shaped by the willful orchestration of leaders intent on explanations and actions within social, economic, and cultural institutions.

Dr. Thaddeus C. Radzilowski, president of the Piast Institute, argues that ethnicities are derived from and cultivated in local communities. Thus, localism is a feature of race and ethnic relations experienced in specific residential communities and in the bonds of shared values—traditions—that are formative of personal consciousness and group identity. Radzilowski's view on this approach to ethnic and race relations is grounded in the argument expressed in the following three points:

- Ethnicity is one of the deepest and most enduring of human identities because it is based on language, religion, culture, family, common history, and local community. It can have political salience and as such play both negative and positive roles. However, political or public salience is not necessary for its survival. It can be the basis of community formation and a generous pluralism on one hand, or divisiveness and prejudice on the other.

- Ethnicity in America has been a creative adaptation to life in the New World by immigrants, both free and coerced. It was an attempt by newcomers to make themselves at home in a new place, often under difficult and challenging conditions. By this process came cultures born out of preservation, adaptation, direct borrowing, and invention—often reinforced by prejudice and interest. Successful ethnicities have kept the ability to change themselves in order to meet new conditions, as well as to modify the dominant society in which they are embedded, and to affect other ethnic cultures with whom they exist.

- Ethnic adaptation to preserve core values and to mobilize group members in times of difficulty has happened with remarkable speed given the usual leisurely pace of historical change. To be able to anticipate and use ethnicity in ways beneficial to the evolution of our society requires a clear understanding of recent history and current prospects.

Articles in this unit present a sample of case studies. This sampling, like the many thousands of weekly profiles of ethnics, immigrants, and enclave populations that appear in your local papers and magazines provides access to distinctive locations and their particular qualities. In composite, they are the pieces of pluralism within our social fabric, our consciousness of human variety and the values rooted in rural and various national traditions that are a part of the American reality. The challenges and opportunities of contemporary race and ethnic relations in America are shaped within the framework of social, political, economic, and cultural institutions. Contemporary trends that include current opinions and attitude are influenced by significant events and communications, as well as by imaginative portrayals, which is at times called 'literary ethnicity'. Such social processes are woven into porous configurations of local, regional, and national relationships. Viewed from this perspective, a significant facet of what constitutes the American reality is derived from fundamentally localized demography. To adopt this perspective requires attention to the variety of populations, their settlement patterns, and the movement and succession of groups and cultures from old neighborhoods to new neighborhoods. This social and analytical approach, invites the observer to examine the American reality, as a dynamic process involving the shifting clustering of racial and ethnic groups and their renegotiation of relationships in new places, in new ways, and with new opportunities and challenges that are endemic to American pluralism.

These articles recount experiences of ethnic populations in specific situations and places. They portray unresolved dilemmas related to American pluralism. Ethnic clustering was driven in part by the "creative destructiveness" of economic growth and the bonds of group affinity—their choices, opportunities, and challenges experienced in both turbulent group relations and the hopeful processes of recovering viable urban communities. The pivotal significance of terrorism on immigration is particularly salient for the entire country. Yet the process of forging new relations among communities reveals the development of new strategies and the formation of shared values derived from various traditions, and articulated as each group negotiates the pathway from being an immigrant to an ethnic American group. Thus "becoming American" occurs in the ongoing process of addressing challenges and opportunities. This shift in consciousness, regarding race and ethnic relations along with the technological capacity, and data explosion, produces new models and explanations of society and culture, and further increases awareness of ethnicity and race.

Settlement patterns and economic differences within societies, and the arrangements of economic production are usually explained in terms of the theories of progressive development or of class conflicts. Unlike such structural causes and determinants, current social practice and new modes of explanation appear to be motivated by a new horizon of cultural values and the collective aspirations of ethnic groups. We have come to discover that the forces reconstructing social realities are the products of creativity, imagination, and religion. Each of these factors appears to be influenced by and interrelated to contemporary articulation of racial and ethnic relations. Consciousness of the pluralism expressed in ethnic, racial, religious, and cultural diversity have emerged throughout the world. Various social science and humanistic disciplines are recasting models and calibrating variables to account for these powerful forces of cultural, religious, and ethnic cohesion, as well as for the forms of conflict that erupt from time to time.

Cambridge Makes History

Racial strife in the past, city picks first African-American mayor.

CHRIS GUY

This Eastern Shore city has elected its first African-American mayor, four decades after images of an angry clash here between black protesters and white police played across the nation's television screens.

Victoria Jackson-Stanley, deputy director of the Dorchester County Department of Social Services, said her victory over two-term incumbent Cleveland Rippons left her humbled at breaking racial and gender barriers.

"As a woman and an African-American, I'm overwhelmed," said Jackson-Stanley, 54. "I think it shows just how much things have changed in Cambridge since the 1960s."

Jackson-Stanley's victory in Tuesday's election was confirmed yesterday after officials counted hundreds of absentee ballots.

The city of roughly 11,000 people, known for its seafood, historic buildings and views of the Choptank River, is just slightly more than 50 percent black.

"From what I understand it, many of her voters crossed racial lines," said Carl Snowden, director of Maryland's Office of Civil Rights.

"This election is an important signal that the Eastern Shore has changed," he said. "Cambridge is at a crossroads."

It was a tumultuous time nationally when, in 1967, H. Rap Brown, chairman of the Student Nonviolent Coordinating Committee, gave a speech here that led to an outburst of protest that white authorities characterized as a riot.

The clash between black residents and white police officers was for years the main thing many outsiders knew about Cambridge.

"I was a very young teenager then, and no one who was there will forget," Jackson-Stanley said.

In recent years, town leaders have been working to revitalize the downtown, which like many small Shore towns has been struggling.

Cambridge officials have approved nearly a dozen projects aimed at revitalizing the once-vibrant manufacturing and canning center. The town has many new residents who have moved here from the Baltimore and Washington areas to restore Victorian-era homes in the city's West End.

Developers have begun restoring a mix of residential buildings, along with commercial ventures that have revamped signature department stores.

The effort suffered a setback when two turn-of-the-century brick storefronts were destroyed by fire in January, but town leaders have said they will go forward with the help of state aid.

Yesterday's final tally showed that Jackson-Stanley won the nonpartisan election 1,383 to 1,231.

A social worker for more than 30 years, the wife, mother and grandmother said she will remain in her state job and run the city as a part-time mayor, collecting $12,000 a year for a post that is designed to be part-time.

She said during the campaign that the city should hire "competent department heads" to run the day to day affairs of the city.

Rippons, a two-time mayor who clashed frequently with city employees and slow-growth advocates, said race became an issue in the mayoral campaign.

"This city is split almost evenly—of course race was a part of it," said Rippons, also 54. "Either consciously or unconsciously, race is an issue every day."

But town Councilman Gibert Cephas, who lost his bid for a second term, said race was of little interest to many voters who supported Jackson-Stanley. "Rippons has led with an iron fist for eight years, and that attitude was what voters have rejected," Cephas said.

Rippons upset many downtown preservationists when he pushed for Cambridge to annex farmland outside town to allow the development of a huge resort community near the Blackwater National Wildlife Refuge.

The project was eventually scaled back significantly in the wake of protests statewide from environmentalists.

Chicago and the Irish

TOM DEIGNAN

Before he was the trailblazing Democratic nominee for president, Barack Obama was an ambitious young politician who learned a valuable lesson thanks to the Chicago Irish.

The year was 1999. Obama, a state senator, announced he was going to challenge Congressman Bobby L. Rush, a legend in the working-class African-American wards of Chicago's South Side. Decades earlier, the South Side was heavily Irish. It was the world that James T. Farrell recreated in his famous Studs Lonigan trilogy of novels from the 1930s.

In fact, for all the changes in Chicago, the same rules have always applied when it comes to politics: you have to pay your dues before you challenge a veteran.

Meanwhile, though it's true that the district that Obama hoped to win was 65 percent black, it also had "several relatively affluent Irish-American neighborhoods," as *The New York Times* noted recently.

Obama (himself Irish on his mother's side) was ultimately trounced in the South Side race, and learned that when it came to Windy City politics, he still had some dues to pay.

Obama's loss illustrates key facts about the Chicago Irish experience. First, the Irish have been playing a crucial political role in Chicago for over 150 years. Furthermore, the Irish have always had to build coalitions among other racial, ethnic and religious groups. Often, they did so successfully, though other times, the result was tension and violence.

Either way, from Studs Lonigan, Michael Flatley and Mrs. O'Leary's infamous cow to Comiskey Park and O'Hare International Airport, the Irish have left a deep impression upon Chicago.

"City on the Prairie"

Unlike Boston, New York or Philadelphia, Chicago was not settled until the 1800s. So the Chicago Irish did not face the worst kind of anti-Catholic, anti-Irish bigotry from established, native-born elites. This also allowed early Irish immigrants to, in a sense, get in on the ground floor of Chicago.

"For the Irish, Chicago's emergence as the nascent city on the prairie was timely," writes John Gerard McLaughlin in his book *Irish Chicago*. "The construction of the Illinois and Michigan Canal, which would connect the Great Lakes to the Mississippi River, began in 1836, drawing Irish laborers. . . . The completion of the canal in 1848 coincided with the mass emigration from Ireland caused by the Great Famine."

Kerry native Dr. William Bradford was among the earliest boosters of Chicago and the opportunities presented by the canal's construction. Bradford, a physician, was also one of Chicago's earliest successful real estate speculators.

Canal work brought hordes of additional laborers—as well as class tension and cries for unionization. It also meant that when the Great Hunger struck Ireland, some Chicago laborers were able to send money, food and other materials back to Ireland.

"Depraved, Debased, Worthless"

Although Chicago was spared the anti-Irish violence of other large American cities, there was no lack of rabid anti-Irish sentiment. The *Chicago Tribune,* edited by Joseph Medill (a descendant of Scotch-Irish Presbyterians), regularly dismissed the Irish as lazy and shiftless.

"Who does not know that the most depraved, debased, worthless and irredeemable drunkards and sots which curse the community are Irish Catholics?" the *Tribune* sneered. This came even as Irish laborers worked feverishly to complete Chicago's stately St. Patrick's church at Adams and Desplaines Streets in the mid-1850s.

Besides Dr. Bradford, another example of Chicago's Irish rising class was Cork native James Lane. In this city which would lead the nation in meat production, Lane is said to have opened Chicago's first meat market in 1836. He marched in the city's first St. Patrick's Day parade in 1843—and was still doing so five decades later, in the 1890s.

Meanwhile, decades before Jane Addams and Hull House became synonymous with Chicago charity, Carlow native Agatha O'Brien and nuns from the Mercy Sisters worked in hospitals, schools and asylums caring for victims of cholera and other diseases.

By the 1870s, the Irish-born population of Chicago was approaching 70,000—over 25 percent of the people. Then came a calamity which transformed the city forever.

The Great Fire

According to legend, the Great Chicago Fire was started by Mrs. O'Leary's cow. The immigrant family was ultimately exonerated, but the O'Learys were subjected to awful harassment. The fire scorched large swaths of Chicago, including a dressmaking business owned by Cork native and future labor leader Mary Harris "Mother" Jones, who entered the labor movement soon after the fire. The newly rebuilt city saw further upward mobility for the Irish.

A priest at St. John's parish on the South Side, Father Woldron, watched "in sorrow as hundreds of beloved families surrendered their humble homes and moved."

By the 1880s, 30 percent of Chicago's police force and other civil service jobs were held by Irish Americans. Many of Chicago's Irish Americans now earned enough money to move to neighborhoods such as Englewood, where (much to the dismay of local Protestants) they laid foundations for working- or middle-class parishes such as St. Bernard's.

Politics, Labor and Religion

The Irish, as they did in many other cities, proved adept at politics, as well as parish life.

Again, Chicago is unique in that, while the Irish were the largest immigrant minority group in other large cities, they were just one of many in Chicago. Germans, Poles, Jews and other Eastern Europeans flocked to Chicago in large numbers.

"Second generation Chicago Irishmen assumed the role of buffers between the strange speaking newcomers and the native, older residents," Paul M. Green has written.

Affairs in Ireland were also profoundly important to the Chicago Irish. The revolutionary group Clan na Gael had a strong presence in the city, where support was strong for controversial measures such as the London bombing campaign of the 1880s, meant to draw attention to the cause of freedom for Ireland. This became a tougher stance to defend, however, in the wake of the infamous Haymarket Square bombing of 1886, when Irish nationalists in Chicago struggled to draw distinctions between anti-British nationalism and homegrown American anarchism.

Meanwhile, Irish pride in Chicago was not merely confined to the continued struggle against the British.

According to Ellen Skerrit: "Since the 1890s, the city's Irish have played a leading role in the cultural revival of traditional music and dance."

Cork native Francis O'Neill, a police chief, was one of the driving forces behind reviving traditional Irish music in the Chicago area.

Meanwhile, as Charles Fanning has noted, Chicago writer Finley Peter Dunne created one of the great voices in American letters at the turn of the century: Mr. Dooley, the saloon keeper/philosopher with the exaggerated brogue who was beloved by millions in nationwide newspapers and books.

Finally, early 1900s labor leaders included Margaret Haley, president of the Chicago Teachers Federation, and John Fitzpatrick, leader of Chicago's Federation of Labor.

Gangsters and "Studs"

There was also a dark side to Chicago Irish life, painted most memorably in the 1930s Studs Lonigan trilogy of novels by James T. Farrell. Particularly disturbing is the racism, violence and narrow-mindedness we see among Studs, his family and friends. It should be added, however, that Farrell also wrote another series of novels about a youth named Danny O'Neill, who escaped Chicago and chased his dreams. Chicago groups such as the Catholic Interracial Council also showed that some Chicago Irish were promoters of racial justice.

Meanwhile, by the 1920s, though many Chicago Irish moved into the American mainstream, another group chose a very different path. This was evident on the morning of February 14, 1929—Valentine's Day—when two men dressed as police officers ushered six gangsters into a garage on Chicago's North Side. A hail of bullets followed.

The famous massacre had been ordered by Al Capone. He was gunning for Bugs Moran, but the Irish crime boss had escaped. The St. Valentine's Day massacre was the culmination of Irish-Italian turf wars which dominated the 1920s. Prohibition, and competition over the sale of illegal booze, led to these gang wars, and Chicago was the center of Irish organized crime. (Jimmy Cagney's electrifying film *The Public Enemy*, from 1931, was set in the Windy City.)

Deanie O'Banion was the era's most prominent Irish gangster. He grew up in a notorious neighborhood known as Little Hell. Even when he became a full-time murderer, O'Banion sported a rosary in his pocket and a carnation in his jacket. In fact, O'Banion so loved flowers that he opened a flower shop on North State Street, which was where he was killed in 1924, after he had swindled members of Capone's crew.

The Daley Dynasty

All in all, Chicago has had a dozen Irish mayors. Early city leaders include John Comiskey (father of White Sox baseball owner Charles Comiskey), John Coughlin, "Foxy" Ed Cullerton and Johnny Powers. Later, in 1979, Irish-American Jane Byrne was the first woman to serve as Chicago mayor.

The most powerful Irish-American mayor ever was Richard J. Daley, who ran Chicago for over 20 years, beginning with his 1955 election. Daley was a humble, devout Catholic who raised his family not far from the South Side Irish enclave where he grew up. As a multi-ethnic town, Chicago required a mayor who knew how to reward all ethnic groups, a task which Daley mastered.

Daley became such a key figure in the Democratic Party that he was known as a "president-maker," whose support was needed to nominate any White House candidate.

Daley's image was tarnished by the violent events of the 1968 Chicago Democratic convention. But in the mayoral election of 1971, Daley received nearly 60 percent of the vote. He died while in office in 1976. Fittingly, his son, Richard M. Daley, was later elected Chicago mayor in 1989.

The New Chicago Irish

By the 1980s, many Chicago Irish had been in the city three or four generations. But a whole new wave of immigrants then arrived, escaping an Ireland which was still struggling economically.

These immigrants breathed new life into Chicago's Irish-American life and culture. A daughter of immigrants, Liz Carroll is a Chicago native who is one of today's top Irish fiddlers. Then, of course, there is *Riverdance* star Michael Flatley. A native of the South Side, Flatley reinvented Irish dance and brought it to the international masses.

Dance is not something we would expect to arise from the streets once stalked by Studs Lonigan and his band of roughs. But history shows us that, when it comes to the Chicago Irish, there is one thing you should expect: the unexpected.

'Bursting with Pride' in Little Italy

'Little Nancy' Pelosi and her political family remembered fondly.

KELLY BREWINGTON

Around the narrow streets of Baltimore's Little Italy yesterday, the O'Malley and Ehrlich placards were still hanging proudly in the windows of restaurants and Formstone rowhouses.

But no one was talking about the men who duked it out in the race to become Maryland's next governor. Instead, neighbors were buzzing with pride about one of their own, Nancy Pelosi, who is likely to become the nation's first female speaker of the House.

They remembered the shy girl who wasn't allowed on a date without one of her five brothers along as chaperone. They recalled the gracious teenager who never assumed she was better than any of the other neighborhood kids just because her father was Thomas J. D'Alesandro Jr., a legendary Baltimore mayor.

And they marveled that "Little Nancy," who they said took after her iron-willed mother, also known as Nancy, is poised to ascend to the post that is third in line for the presidency.

"I ate chocolate pudding with Nancy and watched Howdy Doody at night," said Mary Ann Campanella, 65, who still lives two blocks from the D'Alesandro home, which is at 245 Albemarle St. "That's how far back I go with Nancy."

The families actually go back further. In 1930, Pelosi's father was the best man in the wedding of Campanella's parents, she said, holding up a sepia-toned wedding portrait. The ceremony was held at St. Leo's Roman Catholic Church, which has been the center of tight-knit Little Italy.

"I'm bursting with pride for Nancy," said Campanella, president of the Little Italy Community Organization. "To have her out of this small community, an Italian-American female to hold the third-largest position in our country, I want to say it's breathtaking to me."

When Campanella learned that Pelosi, 66, a married mother of five and grandmother of five who represents San Francisco, was likely to become House speaker, she was in awe.

"I turned to my husband and said, 'A little girl from Little Italy, could you believe it'?"

The tiny neighborhood with its score of Italian restaurants draws tourists and local residents. And to Little Italy natives, the D'Alesandro family is as much a fixture as St. Leo's, summertime bocce tournaments and the Feast of St. Gabriel.

Two Mayors

Pelosi's father, known as "Tommy the Elder," was a congressman, then Baltimore's mayor from 1947 to 1959. Her brother, Thomas J. D'Alesandro III, "Tommy the Younger" was Baltimore's mayor from 1967 to 1971. And her mother, Annunciata, ran a tight ship raising six children while serving as the unofficial power in the family Democratic machine.

Pelosi was the youngest child and only daughter in a family that seemed to always be the community's center of attention.

"You could just open their door and walk in and socialize," said Angie Guerriero, 74, who grew up several blocks from the D'Alesandro home. "Or they were at our house. We shared jokes. In those days, there wasn't much else to do. They were just fine people."

Guerriero and her husband, John, who live a block from St. Leo's, are Pelosi supporters and offer moral and financial support for her political campaigns.

John Guerriero happily displayed a photo taken at a St. Leo's function two years ago showing him standing beside Pelosi.

"We just believed in her," he said. "She's just a beautiful, charismatic person. You just couldn't not believe in her."

John Guerriero's first call yesterday morning was to congratulate Pelosi's brother Thomas J. D'Alesandro III.

"She deserved it," he said, "She'll do a heck of a job."

D'Alesandro said he talked to his sister three times Tuesday night as the votes were being counted around the country and political power was shifting to the Democrats, meaning she is likely to become House speaker.

"She was so thrilled, and I was so proud of her," he said yesterday. "She's a trailblazer. And you have to understand, she brings to the table a set of credentials that are not matched by many in Congress."

D'Alesandro said Pelosi was a polite child who developed a head for politics as an adolescent, along with the rest of the family.

'Strict Taskmaster'

When she was growing up, a first-floor room of the family home was converted into a constituent office for Tommy the Elder, and each child took turns at the desk for two hours a day. Failure to report for duty meant that "you were replaced," D'Alesandro said. "My mother was a strict taskmaster."

Pelosi thrived in the position.

"When Nancy turned 13, she took over," he said. "She was just perfect. She loved it."

Pelosi was also remembered outside Little Italy at the Institute of Notre Dame, where Pelosi graduated. The school is the alma mater of another prominent politician from Baltimore, Sen. Barbara A. Mikulski.

Sister Mary Fitzgerald, president of the Institute of Notre Dame, said students there have been inspired by the legacy left by the two politicians.

"It's truly an honor to have two women in such outstanding positions in the U.S. Congress," she said. "It's not every day that a school has that. We are very proud."

Charles Sudano, 64, who lives on High Street, around the corner from the D'Alesandro home, said he was not only proud, but also impressed at the quiet girl who grew up to become a political powerhouse. He said his sister Jackie and Pelosi were "inseparable."

"My father used to scare the heck out of her," he said. "He'd say, 'Nancy eat more pizza. You're too skinny.'"

'She's Tough Now'

"She was real timid, a real nice girl," he said. "She was a little princess. But she's strong now. She's tough now."

In a neighborhood where loyalty mattered, "she never had that thing, you know, 'My father's the mayor' thing. She didn't have that snobby thing," Sudano said. "Besides, we would never let her get away with that."

Parishes in Transition
Holding on While Letting Go

Parishioners face momentous mission in joining their distinctive traditions.

JESSICA TROBAUGH TEMPLE AND ERIN BLASKO

Riding a pink two-wheeler bike, a young Hispanic girl cruises the sidewalk in front of St. Adalbert Catholic Church.

Outside the building's heavy front doors, she pauses and cranes her head, looking for something.

Unsatisfied, she takes off again. But as she rounds the corner, she finds what she's been seeking. She hops from the bicycle seat and kicks down the stand.

Trucks and motorcycles rev and basses boom at the four-way stop on the corner of Olive and Huron streets, but the girl pays them no notice.

She kneels on the cement, folds her hands and with lifted gaze utters her prayers before a figure of Jesus, who greets her with lowered arms and bowed head.

She knows nothing of the church whose statue this is. Its heritage, its service times or whether Masses are said in Polish or Spanish. She's come simply looking for Christ.

Parishioners of St. Stephen, St. Adalbert and St. Casimir Catholic churches in South Bend may similarly find themselves resting on their commonality of Christianity.

On April 27, St. Stephen Catholic Church, South Bend's first Hungarian-founded parish that now serves a predominantly Spanish-speaking congregation, learned that it will close on May 31 and merge with the traditionally Polish St. Adalbert.

St. Adalbert will become part of a "parish community" by sharing two Congregation of Holy Cross priests, the Rev. David Porterfield and the Rev. Christopher Cox, with St. Casimir, another Polish parish.

As parishioners of churches with distinct cultural heritages and practices, they and clergy are faced with the challenge of meshing those cultures while preserving each one's special character.

During a session of the transition committee, which formed late last year and includes members of each parish and ethnic group, Porterfield created a subcommittee on ethnic traditions.

"It'll take education" for each group to understand and appreciate one another's religious traditions and practices, Porterfield said.

"Participation and education," added St. Adalbert member Tim Hudak.

But the group has the added challenge of holding tight to this task while weeding through a tangle of suggestions, concerns and logistical issues that comes with such a drastic and disorienting move.

St. Casimir parishioner Ann Marie Sommers mentioned carrying the Blessed Sacrament around the church building on Easter as one example of a cherished ritual in her parish not practiced at all Catholic churches.

But new liturgical rules might require a change in that, noted Monsignor J. William Lester, who earlier this week relinquished his duties as St. Adalbert's administrator.

Another parishioner suggested to Lester, however, that the Stations of the Cross in St. Stephen, which are statuaries, take the place of the portrait-style Stations in St. Adalbert.

While many agreed the fixtures are beautiful and would be a nice element to carry over from St. Stephen, questions of wall placement and mounting challenges arise. And what of the Stations at St. Adalbert? "We have to first find out if some family donated them," Lester said.

A statue of Our Lady of Guadalupe and some pictures will make the move, Porterfield said. But the sensitive issue of what will happen to the pews, stained-glass windows and ornate wood altar remains to be decided and will depend on whether or not the local diocese chooses to preserve the structure.

The possibility of a joint bulletin for St. Adalbert and St. Casimir came up for discussion, too. But, Porterfield pointed out, in the early stages of the transition most Hispanic activities will take place in St. Adalbert.

One committee member suggested that including the events in the St. Casimir bulletin would help Hispanics feel more welcome at the church. A second member agreed and said the inclusion would advance the effort "to be one big community."

ANNUAL EDITIONS

But Porterfield offered up a sobering fact. "Given that people really don't want this, I think we should hold off on that for a while."

The issue of English Masses also arose for debate. On any given Sunday, people clog the aisles and spill out the doors during the two Spanish Masses at St. Stephen. Parishioners registered there, most of them Spanish speaking, number 6,500. Church rolls at St. Adalbert list roughly 1,300 and at St. Casimir, 550 parishioners. Both churches will add Spanish Masses.

Though Mass times haven't been officially hammered out, the group unanimously agreed on one Sunday English Mass per church. "I'm just thinking that if one church has two (English Masses), then the other will have to also," Porterfield said.

And though letters of welcome from St. Casimir and St. Adalbert appeared in the St. Stephen bulletin on Sunday, Guadalupe Salazar of St. Stephen tearfully mentioned one unpleasant encounter with a member of St. Adalbert. "She said she felt the Hispanics would push them out," Lopez said. "And it hurt: Because we're not coming to this church because we want to. We have no choice."

And because there is no other choice, Louis Ciesielski of St. Adalbert said, the transition will have to be accepted by everyone who intends on remaining with the parishes.

"My brother, who used to attend St. Stephen, said that the older Hispanic women would get on their knees and walk on them to their pews. They showed great devotion. I hope some of that devotion will rub off on us, too," Ciesielski said: "We are a Catholic church. . . . We must open our arms to everyone."

But St. Stephen member Irene Egry, whose parents married in the church, said she doubts she'll make the move to St. Adalbert.

She and her baby sister made their First Communion at St. Stephen. They graduated from the grade school and every Sunday walked to Mass with their father—their mother attended a later Mass.

She grew up hearing her father sing in the men's choir, and every year she and her sister dressed up in their traditional Hungarian garb and danced in the St. Stephen Day street festival. Today, she's still a member of the St. Theresa Society.

In her west-side home, stacks of church memorabilia sit at her fingertips: memory books, photos, sheet music to Polish hymns. From beside her chair she picks up a pocket-size volume with a creased and faded cover—her father's prayer book.

"I like old things," she says.

It will be hard letting go.

Old Order Changing on South Bend's West Side

ERIN BLASKO

A return visit to South Bend in 2002 confirmed a Polish sociologist/anthropologist's prediction about South Bend's Polish community.

When Janusz Mucha visited South Bend in 1990 he hadn't anticipated writing about the Polish community here. In fact, he didn't know it existed.

Mucha, a professor of sociology and anthropology from Krakow, Poland, served as a visiting professor at Indiana University South Bend.

After learning of the Polish community on the city's west side, Mucha began to study and take part in many of the community's activities.

His research led him to write "Everyday Life and Festivity in a Local Ethnic Community," published in 1996 by Columbia University Press. In the book he suggests that the once strong community will decline.

In August 2002, Mucha returned to South Bend as a visiting Fulbright professor at IUSB. Once here, he learned his prediction had been correct.

"Now the article is about the Polish community *and* the Latinos," he said, referring to the large number of Hispanics who have moved to South Bend's west side in the last several years.

"The area is actually an area in transition," he said. "First it was to black, and now it is to Hispanic."

In 1990, Poles made up 21 percent of the west-side population and Hispanics made up 4.3 percent, Mucha pointed out. In contrast, the 2000 census showed Poles dropping to 11 percent and Hispanics rising to 14 percent.

"It's a process of ethnic succession," Mucha said. "One population is moving out, and another one is coming in."

"Ten years ago there were many Polish businesses" on the west side, he said, "and now they are nearly gone. Many are Hispanic now."

The ethnic succession of the west side is unique because the Poles are not being forced out but are leaving on their own, Mucha said.

"In reality, it's first that the Poles move out and leave vacant stores," he said. "And then the Hispanics take over the vacant stores."

But why are all of the Polish residents leaving?

According to Mucha, it has to do with education.

"Educated professionals are moving out of the neighborhood," he said. "And the old population is dying out . . . or going to nursing homes."

10

Besides Polish people and businesses leaving the west side, the local Polish Catholic parishes also are going through a period of change.

Because of smaller congregations and a shortage of priests, many of the old Polish parishes are either sharing priests or merging with other parishes.

"St. Hedwig's and St. Patrick's (have) one pastor," Mucha said. "St. Casimir has the same pastor with St. Stephen's, and St. Stanislaus merged with another parish."

And he cited the merger between St. Stephen and St. Adalbert Catholic churches.

Currently, St. Stephen, originally a Hungarian parish, is predominantly Hispanic, while St. Adalbert remains predominantly Polish.

As early as 1990, west-side parishioners were offered at least two Polish Masses a week. The Masses are mostly in English now.

Now St. Hedwig and St. Adalbert have only one Polish Mass a month. "There are not many people during these Polish Masses. And most of them are elderly," Mucha said.

Despite the decline in Polish parishes, Mucha said the churches are decorated with many Polish symbols and at least one Polish carol is included in Christmas services.

"There also are some other Polish religious traditions in the Masses," he added. "But it's shrinking."

Not only is the Polish language disappearing from the church, it is also disappearing from daily life.

"The Polish language is gone" from the South Bend Polish community, Mucha said. "Only old people know Polish now."

"After World War II, the schools stopped using Polish as the language of instruction. The younger generations know some phrases and use some phrases, but nothing more."

Although the Polish neighborhood and language are in decline, many Poles still gather for important Polish events throughout the year, including Mucha.

"I attended the Polish Heritage Month Dinner at the very beginning of November," he said, "and also the Polish Oplateck" on Christmas Eve.

The Oplateck, explained Mucha, is "a very thin wafer that is shared with others with wishes of all the best."

According to Mucha, the Polish Heritage Month Dinner was attended by fewer than 200 people, and the Polish Oplateck attracted about 300.

Mucha described the crowd at both events as "mostly elderly."

Although the decline of South Bend's Polish community is evident, Mucha said it will be quite a while before it completely dies out.

Mucha pointed to the continued existence of Polish organizations such as the Achievement Forum and the Chopin Fine Arts Club as evidence of the staying power of many Polish traditions.

"They don't care much about language," Mucha said of the Polish clubs, "but they like to socialize with people who care about Polish traditions."

Staff writer **Jessica Trobaugh Temple**: jtemple@sbtinfo.com (574) 235–6173 and **Erin Blasko**: eblasko@sbtinfo.com

In Manassas, the Medium Is the Issue

Nick Miroff

In Manassas's quaint, red-brick Old Town neighborhood, a giant billboard greets visiting tourists and commuters, but it was not put there by the city or Chamber of Commerce.

"PWC and Manassas the National Capital of Intolerence," it declares, in hand-painted, none-too-subtle red and blue block lettering. The sign, 40 feet long and 12 feet high, sits on the property of Gaudencio Fernandez, 47, a contractor who immigrated to the United States from Mexico in 1979.

What follows is a rambling indictment of Prince William County and Manassas, likening efforts to target illegal immigrants in the jurisdictions with slavery, Jim Crow laws and the Ku Klux Klan. "We demand equality and justice for all," Fernandez's broadside concludes. "We will not be your slaves of the 21st century."

Since it first appeared last fall, the billboard, called "The Liberty Wall" by Fernandez's supporters because of its address at 9500 Liberty St., has become a political symbol and a rallying point for those who see it as a truth-to-power act of defiance. The sign's text has changed a few times, but its message has essentially remained the same: Latino immigrants have been exploited by ungrateful, racist white residents who took advantage of their labor and now want them to leave.

To many residents and business owners, "The Sign," as they call it, is an ugly diatribe and galling eyesore. Comparing tougher immigration enforcement with genocide and slavery is offensive, insulting and wildly exaggerated, they said.

Local editorials and letters to Manassas officials have urged the city for months to remove the sign. Vandals with less patience have attacked the structure on several occasions, including one failed attempt to destroy it with a firebomb last year.

Despite the public pressure, Manassas officials have proceeded cautiously. With a Justice Department investigation into unfair housing practices pending against the city, as well as an unresolved lawsuit accusing the city of discrimination, Manassas officials are wary of further litigation and racial criticism. For the most part, city staff and council members have been silent or circumspect in discussing Fernandez and his sign, eager to avoid an escalation. Instead, they have prodded Fernandez to obtain a building permit for the sign or remove the billboard, but so far he has rebuffed them, citing the right to freedom of speech.

A standoff has set in, and next week, the city will take Fernandez to court. It recently sent police to his home to serve a summons to him and his wife, who is listed on the deed. City Manager Lawrence D. Hughes said Manassas is simply upholding city regulations, and that while Fernandez's billboard has offended many residents, its content is not the issue.

Fernandez could write anything he wanted on an existing, permitted structure because the city has no anti-sign ordinance, Hughes said. City officials said, however, that because the sign is mounted on the remaining wall of a house that burned down in 2006, and Fernandez reinforced the sign with a wooden base, he should have applied for a building permit.

"If anyone can build anything they want where they want, then we don't have a building code," Hughes said. "We've balanced the issue of free speech with the need to enforce the building code."

City zoning inspectors have also cited Fernandez for failing to keep the property in good order, accusing him of using it as a junkyard and providing a "habitat for undesirable wildlife," including rats and snakes.

Not true, Fernandez said.

Seeing the city's efforts as a ruse to silence him, Fernandez insists he will not remove the sign, nor allow it to be removed. Instead—and this is where the standoff takes an especially strange twist—Fernandez plans to enlarge the structure, having spent $1,500 on architectural drawings for a new, bigger, L-shaped wall, 140 feet by 61 feet, that would span the length of the property.

The new sign, Fernandez said, would feature painted murals and captions depicting the history of American racial injustice. "I really want the community to see what has been done to us people of color these last 500 years," said Fernandez, whose message to the "European Americans" of Manassas considers Latino immigrants to be "Native Americans" with a historical right to live in the United States.

To build such an installation on his property, Fernandez would need to apply to the city for a special-use permit because the property is zoned residential. Hughes said he considers the billboard a commercial use, even though its owner is trying to make a political statement, not a profit.

Fernandez said he bought the house and the property in 2003, and the original structure dates to the 1880s. Its location on Liberty Street puts it at the end of a block that is the last remnant of what was once Manassas's historically African American neighborhood. The house was not considered a historic property, Hughes said, because so many alterations and additions had been made to it over the decades.

In June 2006, the house was gutted in a fire that investigators traced to an improperly used extension cord. Fernandez was renting the house to tenants at the time, and a fire marshal's inquiry also found the house was in disrepair and in poor upkeep at the time of the blaze. The property remained in its damaged state until Fernandez began tearing it down last year.

It was about then that supervisors in Prince William County launched an enforcement campaign against illegal immigrants, sparking protests and unleashing the raw emotions of residents on both sides of the issue. Web sites and blogs erupted with angry comments and verbal attacks, and the county was thrust into the national spotlight.

That was when Fernandez launched his eye-catching, more old-fashioned kind of blog. Before then, Fernandez said, he was just a "regular person" who had not taken much interest in politics. He moved to the Manassas area seven years ago from the New York suburbs and enrolled his three children in Manassas public schools. With his centrally located, highly visible parcel as a soapbox, Fernandez left one wall of the ruined house intact and hung a banner from it that read: "Prince William Co. Stop Your Racism to Hispanics!"

The message quickly became a lightning rod. The banner was torn apart by vandals not long after it was put up, but Fernandez responded with a new message and sturdier materials. He also began hosting community cultural and political gatherings on his property.

"Mr. Fernandez's sign reflects the frustration he and others in the immigrant community have been feeling over the past year that their voices have not been heard," said Nancy Lyall, spokeswoman for the immigrant advocacy group Mexicans Without Borders, which has rallied behind Fernandez.

The group did not help Fernandez craft his politically charged statement, but Lyall said it supports his right to keep the sign because it does not use the language of "hate speech."

"We perhaps would have chosen some modification of the wording had it been a Mexicans Without Borders message," she said. "But the important thing is we understand Mr. Fernandez's heart. His sign represents the disappointment and pain that this country has inflicted on the immigrant community."

Many business owners and merchants in the Old Town district of Manassas say the sign is a disappointment. "It's like a dark cloud," said Joanne Wunderly, president of the Manassas Old Town Business Association. Her fine-arts and crafts store, "The Things I Love," is about 100 yards from Fernandez's billboard.

The structure has grown so notorious, Wunderly said, that when she explains her shop's location to visitors from other areas, they treat it like a city landmark and say, "Oh, that's where the sign is."

After spending millions of dollars trying to enhance the neighborhood's historic charm, it was not the kind of image the city bargained for, Wunderly said. "It's such a negative thing," she said. "When you see something calling you a racist, it takes away from the positive image you're trying to portray."

Lawrence "Buck" Buchanan, 82, sees Fernandez's sign every day from the house across the street where he has lived since 1947. He remembers when the city's African American community was much larger and when segregation was the reigning social order. Jim Crow laws in Manassas were not as rigid as they were in other parts of Northern Virginia, he said, recalling that his doctor had a common waiting room for patients.

The gatherings Fernandez has held around the sign do not bother him, Buchanan said, and there is a lot to the message that is true. Buchanan said, however, that he does not want to be confronted with the sign's loaded imagery every day.

"You put KKK up there and you bring blood up in my face," he said, shaking his head. "Why are you trying to bring that old stuff up again?"

At a Crossroad

In Brooklyn, an Evolving Ethnicity

The Italian immigrants who came to Brooklyn, New York, in the mid-twentieth century are gradually aging and moving away. The Federation of Italian-American Organizations in Brooklyn is hoping to cultivate their cultural identity with new Italian language programs and community centers.

DELIZIA FLACCAVENTO

The streets of Bensonhurst, a Brooklyn neighborhood in New York City, are dotted with pasticcerie, paesani clubs, pizzeria, barber shops and tailors—examples of how Italian immigrants overcame homesickness by incorporating the food and habits of the old country into their new neighborhood's daily rhythms.

But, as the last wave of these immigrants from the 1950s, 1960s, and 1970s ages, these last bastions of their culture are disappearing. Faced with watching their heritage fade away, some Brooklyn residents are using language, athletic, and social programs as modern methods of preserving their heritage and attracting young Italian Americans back to the neighborhoods their parents left.

"First-generation Italian Americans struggled and they succeeded in order to survive. That time is gone," says Brooklyn resident G. Jack Spatola, chairman of the Federation of Italian-American Organizations in Brooklyn, which represents 44 local associations. "A new generation has been brought up, an American generation that is proud of its Italian heritage but wants more than a few tables and decks of cards to be motivated to come together and share their common roots."

The Neighborhood

Things have changed considerably since the days when 18th Avenue between 65th and 75th Streets was an Italian "enclave" where newcomers could speak Italian to shop and socialize. Today, more recent Chinese and Russian immigrants are buying the businesses and houses that once belonged to Italians.

In the early 1980s, there were more than 600,000 Italian Americans in Brooklyn, according to research by sociologist Jerome Krase, a professor at Brooklyn College of the City University of New York. Less than 200,000 remain, according to the 2000 U.S. Census. Rising real estate costs coupled with the desire for better schools and a less urban lifestyle have led second-generation Italian Americans to relocate to Staten Island, New Jersey and Long Island, New York.

As has already happened on Mulberry Street in Manhattan, this part of New York City is losing much of its Italian cultural identity. Although Brooklyn still has a number of pasticcerie where one can smell and taste centuries of culinary tradition, the neighborhood is changing. In the streets, the sight of elderly men wearing tailored topcoats, cuffed trousers, and coppolas—traditional Sicilian floppy berets with short visors—reinforces the awareness that a way of life is fading away.

"People in a sense, they're nostalgic," said Brooklyn resident Jim Grundy, an employee of the Federation. "They see the change and they wish it could always stay the same, but it never is that way of course."

On 18th Avenue, 86th Street and in downtown Brooklyn near the port, there are many clubs of paesani—immigrants born in the same city, town, or village—such as the Society of the Citizens of Pozzallo, and the Sciacca, Vizzini, Militello and Palermo. Membership in these clubs is dwindling.

Emanuele Tumino, a retired carpenter who has lived in Brooklyn for nearly 45 years, spends his days talking of the old days, drinking coffee and playing cards at the Societá Figli di Ragusa on 18th Avenue, a social club for immigrants born in the Sicilian town of Ragusa. "In those times, there was nothing in Italy, otherwise would we ever have come to America?" he said in January, explaining both the impetus that drove him to the United States and his longing for the old country's way of life.

"The immigrants, mostly from the South and from Sicily, were poor and unskilled and had a real need for the assistance and the comfort of the paesani societies, which also helped them maintain a feeling of closeness to home," explained Bay Ridge resident Frank Susino.

But despite their once-vital role, many of these social clubs are losing membership, acknowledged Salvatore Fronterré, director of the Patronato Ital-Uil, a Brooklyn office funded by the Italian government that helps first-generation Italian Americans with bureaucratic problems and pensions. "Many clubs are closing down and nothing can really be done to stop history from taking its course," he said.

Saint Dominic's Roman Catholic Church on 20th Avenue in Bensonhurst is one of the very few churches still offering daily masses in Italian. Although Sunday services are full, Father Ellis Tommaseo predicts that won't last much longer. "I came to the U.S. less than one year ago; people were so happy and excited to hear that a priest would be assigned here from Italy," he said in January. "I found a very warm environment, but we are already fewer than we were when I got here. In less than 15 years, there will be nobody left."

Creating a Change

Father Tommaseo strongly believes that language is the key to preserving cultural heritage and, outside the church, has joined the Federation of Italian-American Organizations of Brooklyn language program. He teaches today's Italian to adults who know only old dialects and children who want to connect with their heritage.

Similarly, Federation members are working to attract young Italian Americans now scattered across New York City back to traditionally Italian communities.

"The community is concerned because the young people are not staying," said Grundy. "They're moving out to the suburbs and things like that."

Spatola says the disappearance of Brooklyn's Italian soul can be avoided only if the Italians remaining in the area unite to invest in leisure and cultural centers. Therefore, paesani social clubs could be replaced by Italian-American community centers offering athletic and leisure facilities, language and cooking classes, libraries, art galleries and movie screening spaces.

In May, the Federation was in the final negotiations to purchase a property in Bensonhurst for the area's first such Italian-American community center. An estimated $6 million is needed to build the center, much of which could come from the New York City government, said Grundy, the Federation's project coordinator.

The Federation plans to open a two-story structure and gradually add two more stories, creating a full-fledged community center with gymnasium, swimming pool, community meeting center and classrooms, Grundy said. Eventually, the center would house all of the disparate youth outreach, language, and soccer programs now offered by the Federation all over Brooklyn.

Such programs can also provide support to the children of Italian immigrants. Born in Brooklyn to Sicilian parents, Salvina Barresi, 23, often feels trapped between the American drive to do what is best for the individual and the Italian pressure to do what is best for the family. She still cannot answer whether she is Italian, American, or both. "During my last trip to Italy, I was Sicilian in Rome, American in Sicily and Sicilian again in New York," she said.

Salvina's mother, Giovanna, said she considers herself an Italian living in America. Many immigrants feel similarly, but in at least one borough, some are carving out a place where their children can have the best of both worlds.

Mélange Cities

The disruption that immigrants bring is often a benefit.

BLAIR A. RUBLE

T
enstions and conflict get the headlines when peoples make contact, but historically migration is not a singular event tied always to a "crisis." Migrants of all sorts—immigrants, emigrants, refugees, displaced persons, guest workers—have become a significant presence in cities around the world. According to the UN Human Settlements Program, there are approximately 175 million official international migrants worldwide, not including those without complete documentation. Even this massive movement of people is not unprecedented. During the past 500 years, Europeans began to inhabit the rest of the world and nearly 10 million African slaves were forced to migrate to the Americas; another 48 million people left Europe for the Americas and Australia between 1800 and 1925. That is not to mention the tens of millions of people who have migrated across other national boundaries, continental divides, and oceans during the past half-century. Migration is simply part and parcel of human existence. And it has always brought fruitful encounters as well as conflict.

The transformative power of today's migration is easiest to see not in established "mélange cities" such as New York but in traditionally more insular communities such as Washington, D.C., and Montreal, which were long divided by race, language, culture, religion, ethnicity, or class. Once split along single fault lines between two core groups—whites and blacks in Washington, French-speakers and English-speakers in Montreal—these urban centers have become new mélange cities, and the evidence suggests that we should view such transformations with more hope than fear.

Montreal offers the clearest example in North America of the creative disruption wrought by new immigrants. In that city divided—and defined—for decades by conflicts between Francophones and Anglophones, a curious story appeared in the press a couple of years ago. During the depths of a typically harsh Quebec February, it was reported that Filipino and Hispanic parents were trekking with their sick children through snow-filled streets to a small apartment complex in the fringe neighborhood of St.-Laurent, where they desperately beseeched an iconlike portrait of the Virgin Mary to cure them. Abderezak Mehdi, the Muslim manager of the low-rise building, claimed to have discovered the Virgin's image in the garbage. According to Mehdi and Greek Melkite Catholic priest Michel Saydé, the Virgin shed tears of oil that could cure the ill and tormented.

Michel Parent, the chancellor of the Roman Catholic archdiocese of Montreal, cautioned skepticism, noting that "while it is true that nothing is impossible for God, historically, that is not how God acts."

This small and almost comically inclusive multicultural scene of healing, which unfolded in a dreary neighborhood built at a time when Montreal was starkly divided between speakers of French and of English, captures some of the positive aspects, as well as some of the tensions, of a change that has occurred over the past three decades or so, as immigrants and their Canadian-born children have grown to number more than a quarter of the city's population.

Immigrants are not the only force for change. Montreal's growth into a sprawling metropolitan region laced by freeways that provide a new organizing structure of daily life has rendered many old cultural and geographical boundaries meaningless. The Internet is likewise no friend to the old order. But it is the newcomers, who have no stake in the city's past divisions, who have had a singular impact on its political life. The once-powerful Francophone *sovereigntiste* movement, which long pressed for the secession of the entire province of Quebec from Canada, has lost momentum in considerable measure because of opposition from immigrant groups. Those groups were an essential component of the very narrow majority that defeated the last referendum on Quebec sovereignty in 1995, 50.6 percent to 49.4 percent. Pro-sovereignty politicians have since been looking for ways to court the immigrant vote. The communally based populism that once dominated Montreal politics is giving way, slowly but surely, to a new pragmatism more suited to a world in which communities compete for investment and bond ratings.

M
ontreal maybe further along the road to true cultural diversity than most North American cities, but its experience is hardly unique. Metropolitan Washington, D.C., another historically divided city, was the United States' fifth largest recipient of legal migrants during the 1990s, and it is beginning to experience some of the same sort of change affecting Montreal.

Twenty-first-century Washington is already dramatically different from the "Chocolate City, Vanilla Suburbs" days of the 1970s. New arrivals from El Salvador and Ukraine, Ethiopia and Vietnam, Brazil and India, and dozens of other countries, as well as other areas of the United States, have fanned out across an expanding metropolitan region that extends from Frederick, Maryland, 50 miles to the west, to the shores of the Chesapeake Bay and beyond to the east; from north of Baltimore more than 100 miles south to Fredericksburg, Virginia. The region as a whole is an incredible polyglot blend. The neighborhoods in the inner-ring Virginia suburb of South Arlington defined by zip code 22204, as well as zip code 20009 in the city's trendy Adams Morgan–Mt. Pleasant area, are each home to residents from more than 130 different countries, according to a group of Brookings Institution analysts led by Audrey Singer. Yet not very many Americans or even Washingtonians appear aware that their capital has become a mélange city.

New arrivals from El Salvador, Ukraine, Ethiopia, Vietnam, Brazil, India, and many other countries have made America's capital a mélange city.

After Congress gave up its direct oversight of the capital city and reinstated partial home rule in the 1970s, local affairs quickly came to be dominated by the politics of race. As children of the civil rights battles of the 1960s, many of Washington's first elected officials appeared to view local politics as a new version of the nation's great racial struggle, and symbolic politics took precedence over pragmatic city management. This civil rights regime began to flay as the city's financial and management problems grew, and by the time Mayor Marion Barry was arrested in 1990 on charges of smoking crack cocaine, the dream of the city's activist leadership to transform D.C. into a showcase for their values and policies had been shattered. Congress essentially placed the city in receivership by appointing a financial control board in 1995.

The collapse of local government prompted a new generation of neighborhood leaders to enter local politics, shifting attention to pragmatic concerns about city services and neighborhood quality of life—a focus that began to allow immigrants into the city's political mix even as their presence became a subject of debate. During his 2002 reelection campaign, for example, Mayor Anthony Williams stirred controversy by proposing that noncitizens should be allowed to vote in local elections. Arriving in large numbers just at the moment of municipal regime shift, immigrants helped mold a new, broader political environment in which race yielded its preeminence to more pragmatic concerns. When the first major issue of the new era emerged in 2004 in the form of a controversy over the financing of a new baseball stadium, most local observers were not prepared for the spectacle of a raging city council debate waged virtually without any reference to race.

In other new mélange cities, the story plays out in different ways. The Latinization of Denver's population and voter base has encouraged both political parties to reach out to minority voters. Once-sleepy Charlotte, North Carolina, has been transformed by, among other things, a 932 percent increase in its Hispanic population between 1980 and 2000. The country's second-largest city, Los Angeles, elected Antonio Villaraigosa in 2005 as its first Hispanic mayor since it was a village of 6,000 people, back in 1872.

Similar shifts are occurring throughout the world. In the Ukrainian capital of Kyiv, immigrants from Vietnam, China, Pakistan, and the Middle East are blunting the force of a nationwide population decline, and officials are beginning to speak of migration as a long-term answer to the country's economic and demographic decline.

Even as seemingly homogenous a society as Japan has felt the impact of immigration. Japan's shrinking population and economic uncertainty are helping to drive companies to relocate factories abroad. Japan's reputation for homogeneity is not unearned, and national policies do not encourage immigration, but local leaders in some cities have decided that the best way to keep their local economies healthy is to actively seek out migrants from abroad.

Few cities anywhere in the world have been as aggressive in pursing international migrants as Hamamatsu. A city of more than half a million located half way between Tokyo and Osaka, Hamamatsu boasts major Honda, Yamaha, and Suzuki factories. Realizing that the city would lose its economic base without new residents, municipal officials began to recruit workers from Japanese migrant communities in Brazil and Peru. The officials assumed—rather naively, it would seem to American eyes—that given their Japanese heritage, the immigrants would easily fit into local neighborhoods and workplaces. In fact, the migrants were descendants of Japanese who had left the home islands as much as a century before. They were Brazilian and Peruvian more than they were Japanese.

As a result, Hamamatsu—like Montreal, Washington, and many other mélange cities—is no longer the community it was. There are four Portuguese newspapers, four Brazilian schools and a Peruvian school, Portuguese and Spanish community centers, and numerous samba nightclubs. City hall now publishes local laws and regulations in several languages, and municipal leaders have learned to embrace Brazilian holidays as their own, often using them as launching pads for local political campaigns.

Other cities in Japan have been changing as well. Osaka, long the home of Japan's largest Korean community, publishes city documents in nearly a half-dozen languages. Sapporo and other communities on the island of Hokkaido post street signs in Russian. Tens of thousands of city residents of all ages and races turn out for Kobe's annual samba festival.

Migrants, though still few in number, have brought significant change to Japan. Some of that change is measurable and lamentable, such as increasing income inequality, rising crime rates, and enervated traditional institutions. Other changes that cannot be measured neatly may be creating opportunities for communities to escape dysfunctional institutions and patterns of life. One unexpected effect of the search by Hamamatsu and other Japanese cities for labor from abroad has been pressure from below on the traditionally hyper-centralized Japanese state to cede some central control over immigration policy.

How should we weigh the negative and positive impacts of immigration? Is all change for the worse? Heightened anxiety over international terrorism has cast suspicion on cities themselves as a social form and on migration as a social phenomenon. The impulse to withdraw into a cocoon of homogeneity increasingly undermines the acceptance of difference. The experiences of mélange cities such as Montreal, Washington, and Hamamatsu show us another course. Voluntarily or not, such cities have come to represent lively alternatives to a 21st-century metropolitan future in which everyone seeks protection from others unlike themselves. Despite the new mélange cities' obvious imperfections, their enormous intercultural vitality provides the basis for successful strategies for a 21st century in which people's movement around the world remains a fact of human existence.

BLAIR A. RUBLE is the director of the Wilson Center's Kennan Institute and its Comparative Urban Studies Program. His most recent book, *Creating Diversity Capital* (2005), examines the impact of transnational migrants on Montreal, Washington, and Kyiv.

The Hotel Africa

A growing number of Africans are arriving in the United States in search of a better life. But even as these immigrants learn to negotiate a complex new culture, they cannot forget the beloved and blighted lands that sent them forth, yet call them back.

G. Pascal Zachary

I dread phone calls from Africa.

A sister is having a baby, her fifth, and wants us to send cash before the birth. An aunt calls on Christmas Day, hoping to tap our holiday spirit. Can't we pay for human traffickers to sneak her into the United States? The price is "only" $5,000, which strikes me as suspiciously low. My father-in-law rings just long enough to ask for a return call. Another aunt calls to announce that, tired of waiting for us to send money, she's changed her name from Patience to Joy. She really has. Then there is the distant relative phoning for the first time, asking us to pay his rent, his children's school fees, anything.

These people telephone because my wife, Chizo, is an African living in America. To be precise, Chizo is a Nigerian living in northern California. The telephoners are Nigerians too. They don't know California from the Carolinas, but they are poor, needy, and, by comparison with Chizo, in dire straits. They want her help, and usually help means sending cash. Chizo is a hair braider, working long hours for low pay and earning nothing when there are no heads to braid. Her mother and father live in Nigeria's second-largest city, where they can afford to rent only a small, windowless room with no running water, bathroom, or kitchen. Chizo regularly sends money to her parents, her six siblings, and her favorite aunts. She also supports a daughter in Togo, whom we are preparing to bring to America.

No matter how much money Chizo sends, her African relatives are never satisfied, and she feels that her obligations to them remain unmet. She is haunted by Africa, haunted by requests for money and her great distance from the motherland. From all of 8,000 miles away, she misses Africa, and the ache in her heart is not diminished by her support of family members.

When Chizo came to California three years ago, she joined an estimated one million African immigrants living in the United States, many of whom have come in recent years because of changes in U.S. immigration laws. Before 1980, African immigrants overwhelmingly moved to Europe, in part because its former colonial powers left more doors open. That year,

Congress made it easier to enter the United States as a refugee, and in 1990 it created visa "lotteries" for high school graduates from nations historically underrepresented in the United States, such as Ghana and Nigeria. "This lottery," notes Salih Omar Eissa, a child of Sudanese parents who has studied immigration law, "quickly became the primary method by which Africans immigrated" to the United States.

As a result of these changes, the African-born population has boomed. More than half of the sub-Saharan, or black, Africans living in the United States today have arrived since 1990. Hailing from Nigeria, my wife is part of the largest single African contingent. More immigrants—an estimated 150,000—have come to the United States from Nigeria than from any other sub-Saharan country. Newcomers from Ghana rank second, Ethiopians third, Liberians fourth, Somalis and Kenyans fifth and sixth. Though these numbers reflect both legal and illegal immigration, they seem to undercount Africans in the United States. No matter what the actual number is, Africans are a tiny part, a mere 2.8 percent, of the foreign-born population legally in the United States, according to the U.S. Census Bureau.

Yet the significance of these new African immigrants eclipses their relatively small number, for it highlights the enormous changes in American society over the past 40 years while reminding us that for centuries Africans came to this country in chains. "More Africans Enter U.S. Than in Days of Slavery," *The New York Times* headlined a front-page article last year. Because of the central role of slavery in American history and the still-vexing problem of black-white relations, African immigrants are worth watching.

To be sure, generalizing about Africans is tricky. Africa south of the Sahara is highly diverse. The term "African" is a construction open to gross misunderstanding. (George W. Bush, during his first presidential campaign, compared Africa to Mexico, as if both were countries.) Travel within sub-Saharan Africa is frequently difficult, and people from different parts of the region often do not display any immediate solidarity, racial or otherwise. I was reminded of Africa's great diversity when I attended a private party recently at an Oakland nightclub, not far from where Chizo and I live. The guests were mainly from Cameroon and spoke French. In the same club, in the next room, a group of Ethiopians were also partying. The two groups ate different foods, listened to different music, dressed differently, danced differently—and carried on separately. No wonder. Paris and Moscow are much closer to each other than Lagos and Addis Ababa.

Years abroad haven't diminished Ike Nwadeyi's sense of identity. "You can't put a Nigerian in your pocket," he says.

Despite such differences and a tendency to stick close to their own, African immigrants in the United States have much in common. They tend to be highly educated and to come from relatively privileged backgrounds. More than four in 10 hold university degrees; an astonishing 98 percent reportedly have completed high school. One-third of African women and 38 percent of African men hold professional and managerial jobs. Because of their education and because Africans generally live in the largest American cities, where wages tend to be highest, both sexes earn about 20 percent more than the median pay of all American workers. African immigrants are younger than other immigrants. Only 2.6 percent are over 65, the lowest percentage of any immigrant group; more than 70 percent are between 25 and 54.

I talk with Africans regularly in my frequent visits to Africa and in the United States, and so I meet them in Africa dreaming about coming to America and meet them in America dreaming of returning to or saving their motherland. The principal challenge for recently arrived Africans in America is not succeeding in the United States—they are—but realizing their desire to maintain a dynamic relationship with Africa. Their attachment to the motherland arises at least partly from a belief that the enormous outflow of talent from Africa, however understandable given the hardships of life there, poses a great developmental handicap. "Africans are doing incredible things in the U.S.," says Derrick Ashong, a Ghanaian-born Harvard graduate who lives in New York City and is building an African media company. "Would our countries be underdeveloped if our energies were applied back home?" So long as Africa suffers under the burden of poverty and inequity, war and disease, Ashong's question is both a challenge and a reproach to Africans in America.

Ike Nwadeyi is a stickler for manners. He wants his daughter to greet him each day with the words, "Good morning, sir." When she lived in America with him, she told him, "Hi, Daddy." He angrily replied, "You don't tell me, 'Hi, Daddy.' "

This breakfast banter explains why Nwadeyi's seven-year-old daughter is growing up in Nigeria while he works in Washington, D.C., and obtains his American citizenship. "America will spoil my daughter," he insists. "Children have no manners here. By growing up in Nigeria, she'll know what I mean by respect."

Nwadeyi's daughter lives with his wife, a geologist working for Chevron in oil-rich Nigeria. Her job is too well paying and too interesting for her to abandon. So she stays in Nigeria, while Nwadeyi lives in the United States and drives a taxi. "There's no enjoyment in this country," he says. "Nothing. This country has no life." But working in America affords him the chance to visit Nigeria for long stretches when he wishes. His presence in the United States and his American citizenship give his family an insurance policy against the instability that always threatens Nigeria, but he is typical of the many Africans who leave their young children behind in Africa so they can be raised properly.

Before Nwadeyi came to the United States, he lived in Thessalonica, where he studied business at a Greek university. His many years in Europe and the United States, however, have not diminished his sense of identity. "You can't hide a Nigerian," he says. "We are loud. It is natural. You can't put a Nigerian in your pocket."

Nwadeyi's straddle of two worlds is typical of recent African immigrants. "Africans represent a new type of immigrant," writes Sylviane A. Diouf, a scholar of African migration who is a researcher at the Schomburg Center for Research in Black Culture in New York City. "They are transnationals, people who choose to maintain their separateness in the host country and retain tight links to their community of origin." Drawing strength from migration, Diouf observes, "they generally view their American experience as transitory, the most effective way to construct a better future at home for themselves and their relatives."

Of course, Diouf's description of Africans might be applied to many immigrant groups. Filipinos, Koreans, Central Americans, Mexicans, Russians, Chinese, and Indians maintain strong ties to their countries of origin. What sets Africans apart is the undeniable marginalization of their homeland. Sub-Saharan Africa is the only major region of the world that has grown poorer over the past several decades and that has seen a dramatic decline in the job market for highly skilled workers. The development arcs of Mexico, China, India, South Korea, and most other countries exporting people to the United States are traveling in the opposite direction. These countries are increasingly sophisticated, wealthy, and accommodative of the needs of talented people. Indeed, in some parts of India and China and elsewhere, job opportunities are now far better than in the United States.

Only in black Africa, among the world's regions, have conditions deteriorated, and not just for the elite. Because of the plights of their home countries, Africans are forced to create a distinctive relationship with both America and Africa. In short, no other immigrant group carries anything like the baggage that Africans carry—a homeland that is a source of embarrassment but also offers an unparalleled opportunity to give back.

Africans feel that the quickest route to becoming "super-empowered" individuals capable of giving back to the motherland is success in the United States. The pull of their homeland paradoxically drives them to greater heights in America. "They are fast learning how to live the American dream," wrote Joseph Takougang, a professor of African history at the University of Cincinnati, in a recent survey. "They are becoming involved in their communities, starting small businesses, and participating in local politics."

As people of African origin have gained visibility in America in recent years, their sometimes-troubled relations with African Americans have belied Americans' monolithic views of race. Many white Americans as well as African Americans have assumed that African immigrants are natural allies of African Americans, and are surprised when tensions surface.

One figure who has put the spotlight on Africa is Illinois senator Barack Obama, son of a Kenyan. In his 2004 senatorial campaign, he had to establish his "blackness" in the eyes of the African-American electorate because he had been raised by a white mother. Even his Africanness was considered attenuated. In his memoir, *Dreams From My Father: A Story of Race and Inheritance (1995),* Obama symbolically reclaims his Africanness by traveling to Kenya. None of these gymnastics in the establishment of identity makes sense in an African context. In the United States, Obama's carefully constructed identity is critical to his public career.

The friction between African immigrants and African Americans is perhaps starkest in applications of affirmative action policies. Often, hiring preferences work to the advantage of people who have just arrived in the United States. Because many African immigrants are highly educated, they can compete for jobs that might otherwise to go to African Americans. Tensions between the two groups are exacerbated by African insensitivity. "Too many Africans are dismissive of African Americans in a general way," says Victor Mallet, a Ghanaian who works with black small-business owners in Philadelphia. He notes that Africans fear being lumped together with African Americans as second-class citizens. They also harbor some of the same stereotypes of African Americans held by many whites.

To be sure, Africans in America experience racism and outrages, such as the death of Amadou Diallo, an unarmed New York street vendor from Guinea who was shot by police in 1999. Events such as the Diallo killing promote a common understanding of what it means to be black in America by reminding Africans that black people still face sometimes-fatal racial prejudice. Mallet, who grew up in Africa with a white mother and a black father, feels obliged to sympathetically hear out African-American objections to mainstream American society. "More Africans need to look past the appealing notion that America is a meritocracy and that there is equal opportunity for all," says Mallet, who first came to the United States to attend the Massachusetts Institute of Technology in the 1990s. "While Africans are right not to hide behind the excuse of racial bias, they also must comprehend the history of African-American exclusion—and how racial awareness continues to distort American life today."

The core division between Africans and African Americans is rooted in radically different notions of identity, and is therefore unlikely to vanish anytime soon. For Africans, ethnic identification—what was once known as tribe—trumps race. When my wife first came to California, she did not view black people as natural allies, but sought help from West Africans, people reared close to her home turf. She visited braiding shops, looking for casual work and new friends, and joined a shop managed by two Cameroonian women and staffed by braiders from Senegal and Gabon. The braiders became Chizo's best friends and the shop a virtual Africa that helped ease her transition to a new and alien country.

My wife is the only Nigerian in the braiding shop, but she found many nearby, even members of her own ethnic group, the Igbo. A local grocery story, run by an Igbo man, sells her favorite foods from home: *gari* (cassava), dried fish, fresh yams, plantains, and an exotic spice called *ugba*. A community of Igbo Catholics holds a monthly Mass in her native language. In our living room, she hangs a Nigerian flag (and the flags of the United States and Ghana, where she and I first met).

Too great an attachment to one's community of origin can encourage provincial thinking, of course. Chizo's own fellow Igbos are quite clannish, and of the scores I have met in America, not one is married to a non-Igbo, and certainly not a white American. To the Igbos I meet, my wife is somewhat suspect. They question why she would marry, not outside her race, but outside her ethnic group. Possessing pride born partly from their communal suffering during the Biafran war, Igbos have the kind of ethnic solidarity found in Armenian, Jewish, and Kosovar communities.

Africans have no monopoly on ethnic narcissism. More striking, actually, is their openness to wide currents and their willingness to draw on materials not indigenous to Africa. A young African writer, Taiye Tuakli-Wosornu, a Yale graduate living in New York, has coined the term "Afropolitan" to highlight the benefits of blending a cosmopolitan outlook with continuing participation in one's African community. "Perhaps what most typifies the Afropolitan consciousness is this . . . effort to understand what is ailing Africa alongside the desire to honor what is uniquely wonderful," Tuakli-Wosornu writes.

Economic, social, and technological forces are driving Africans in America toward playing a larger role in their home countries.

The Afropolitans must succeed in America, but in a manner that pushes them toward Africa, not away from it. The emergence of a new generation of African writers, who succeed first in the United States and then gain an audience in Africa, illustrates this pattern. In his short-story collection *The Prophet of Zongo Street* (2005), Mohammed Naseehu Ali, who lives in Brooklyn and has spent 17 years in the United States since arriving at the age of 18 to attend university, rescues the rich folk stories of his Hausa forebears in Ghana and Nigeria. Ensconced in America, by day he works at the database company Lexis-Nexis, and at night he emerges in Brooklyn as a troubadour of the wisdom of his ancestors. "I have great hope for Africa," he says.

Like a number of African writers, Ali published first in the United States and is preoccupied with the African experience, home and away. Uzodinma Iweala, who last year published a celebrated short novel, *Beasts of No Nation,* also draws on African sources in his tale about child soldiers. Shuttling between D.C. and Lagos, he is now building a literary reputation in Nigeria on the strength of his American success. "You can't ever escape being a Nigerian," he told an interviewer in the United States recently, adding:

> If you try to say, 'No, I am not Nigerian,' people say, 'What are you talking about? I know where your father is from. I know the village. There is no way that you can tell me you are not Nigerian.' In fact, if you don't come back and maintain the ties, people start asking questions. It's not as if when you leave you are looked down upon for leaving your country. Most Nigerians that you speak to here expect to return to Nigeria at some point in time—whether or not that will actually happen is not important. It's the mentality.

In the past, many new immigrants to America said they would maintain tight links to their countries of origin, but over time they—and their children and grandchildren—have not. Fidelity to Africa, so intensely felt by most immigrants, may also fade over time. "Are they [African immigrants] going to melt into the African-American population?" historian Eric Foner asked in an article in *The New York Times* last year. "Most likely yes."

The opposite could well happen. Economic, social, and technological forces are driving Africans in America toward playing a larger role in their home countries in the years ahead. The spread of cell phones in Africa and the rise of Internet telephony in the United States make calling back to Africa—once an expensive and tedious task often requiring many connection attempts—inexpensive and easy. Flights to all parts of sub-Saharan Africa, while not cheap, are more frequent than ever. And private companies operating in Africa are beginning to see the pool of skilled Africans working in the United States as a source of managerial and professional talent. Though Africa's brain drain continues, a small but significant number of people are returning to the continent to take jobs or start businesses.

Demographic forces are at play too. As the first big wave of African immigrants from the 1980s approaches retirement, some look homeward. No statistics are kept on Africans who move back for good. But some members of all immigrant groups do return home and always have, even before the days of easy travel, telephone calls, and money transfers. Roughly half of all Italian immigrants to the United States before World War I returned home permanently. Today, because documentation is essential for crossing borders, legal immigrants must first acquire a green card and then, usually, a U.S. passport. Once in possession of papers, an African who leaves the United States invariably will

come back to it, if only to work. As they age, some Africans are retiring to their home countries, funding an African lifestyle with American dollars. So many Ghanaians are repatriating, for instance, that a Texas homebuilder has an operation in Ghana that has constructed hundreds of houses for returnees.

Africans commonly travel back and forth, motivated as much by opportunity and nostalgia as by a kind of survivor's guilt. My wife often expresses nagging doubts about the fairness of living affluently in America while her family lives in deprivation back home. "Why did I escape the poverty of Africa," she asks. "What kind of God chooses paradise for me and misery for my loved ones?"

The cries of Africans left behind are difficult to drown out, and they shape the aspirations of Africans in America. Consider the choices made by my friend Guy Kamgaing, an engineer from Cameroon who arrived in the United States to attend graduate school 11 years ago. Now 35, he has built a successful career in Los Angeles in the burgeoning field of mobile telephony. He holds a green card, is married (to another Cameroonian, an accountant), and has two children. He is living, in short, the American dream, and the corruption and difficulty of doing business in Cameroon make him reluctant to return full time. Yet Kamgaing maintains a big African dream. He is renovating a hotel in the Cameroon port city of Douala that his father, now 72 and still living in the city, built and ran through good times and bad. The 160-room hotel is a relic—sprawling, decrepit, a nuisance, and, until recently, shuttered.

One morning, I met Kamgaing on the roof of the hotel. He has opened a café there, and the waiter served us café au lait and croissants. I could see for miles: the Atlantic Ocean, the forests ringing the city, the crowded streets. It was the rainy season, the air was heavy, and I could feel the two of us moving back in time, to 40 years ago, soon after independence, when Cameroon was wealthy thanks to abundant timber, oil, and agricultural production; it was home to tens of thousands of French people; and the future looked bright. The hotel, called the Beausejour Mirabel, is a means by which Kamgaing can honor his father and revive his country.

The task is difficult. He has renovated the lobby and is repairing rooms floor by floor. Soon he will reopen the long-empty pool on the roof. He knows that the project is a drain, robbing him of capital he might invest in his American life, but he finds it irresistible. "Sometimes when I think about this hotel, it brings tears to my eyes," he says. "I am resurrecting my father's pride and joy." The hotel even boasts wireless Internet access, which not even its poshest competitors in Douala offer. Kamgaing wants to establish a mid-priced hotel, but the odds are against him because the city's few foreign visitors usually want luxury, not nostalgia and value.

The cries of Africans left behind are difficult to drown out, and they shape the aspirations of Africans in America.

Back in northern California recently, Kamgaing visited my house for dinner. While he spooned up my wife's goat meat and pepper soup, he admitted that perhaps he has gone slightly mad in reviving the old hotel. But he's proving that he hasn't forsaken the land of his birth.

My wife has yet to find her Hotel Africa. I was reminded of the delicacy of her search one night not long ago, when she and I dined with a Jewish friend and his father, approaching 85, who was visiting from Long Island. As a child living near the home of Anne Frank in Amsterdam, the father had been snatched by the Nazis and sent to a death camp. Chizo told him that his ordeal and that of the Jewish people in Europe reminded her of the suffering of her own people, the Igbo, who tried to secede from Nigeria some 35 years ago and form their own nation, Biafra. Her older brother and sister, then infants, died during the war that followed—along with a million other Nigerians. "Every people suffer," she said. The old survivor smiled.

The persistence of suffering in Africa may bind African immigrants to their homeland in unexpected ways. Perhaps Africans will never forget, and will be defined by memory, just as Jews have been.

G. Pascal Zachary, a former foreign correspondent for *The Wall Street Journal,* often writes on African affairs. His books include *The Diversity Advantage: Multicultural Identity in the New World Economy* (2003), and he is currently working on a memoir of his marriage to an African.

The Fixer

Why is this man fighting to end affirmative action in higher education? Inside Ward Connerly's state-by-state campaign to end racial quotas.

ADAM MATTHEWS

A short while ago, Ward Connerly, the indefatigable anti-affirmative-action crusader, was visiting Kevin Johnson, the former guard for the Phoenix Suns. Johnson is a Democrat who runs the St. Hope Academy, which helps at-risk kids. He is also running for mayor of Sacramento. "I was making my database available to him to get contributions," Connerly recalls. "And I'm walking out and this attractive black woman looked at me and said, 'Are you who I think you are?'"

"And I said, 'Who do you think I am?' 24'"

"Ward Connerly?" the woman replied, her face registering her shock.

"That's who I am."

"What are you doing here?" she asked him.

"And I said, 'I'm supporting my friend.'"

For Connerly, 69, widely credited with halving the black student population at the University of California at Berkeley, the encounter carried great significance. Here, a man who has dedicated the better part of his life to dismantling affirmative action suddenly felt pigeonholed. "Why do we put people into these boxes and say that they're monolithic of thought?" he says now, reclining in his chair at the Westin hotel in Washington, D.C. "The general notion is that I just want to take away opportunities for minorities rather than [that] I don't think what we're doing now works. There is a better way to solve the problem."

Ward Connerly is seated comfortably in a dining room that opens onto a rear patio of the cushy Westin. He seems at ease in these environs, attired in the uniform of a middle-aged man of means: chinos, a white-and-blue-checked button-down, a navy blazer, sensible loafers. A neat moustache frames his mouth. He has high cheekbones, significant jowls, and straight salt-and-pepper hair that rings a prominent bald spot. His default expression is skepticism. A few tense moments earlier, his face creased and his eyes bore into mine. He was trying to figure out if he was being set up for another hit piece.

As the most vilified conservative black man since Clarence Thomas, Ward Connerly has grown tired of defending himself. He has walked off the stage when confronted by hostile college students, and said no to many interviews. He has built a career on taking stances unpopular with both blacks and conservatives, and expects the criticism, he says, to an extent. "I'm no right-wing extremist," he maintains. "How can you characterize a guy who sides with gays on marriage as a right-wing extremist?"

In the 12 years that he's been campaigning against racial quotas in higher education, he's been called much worse. He's been dismissed as a "house negro" by his opponents, who tirelessly chronicle his every move through a network of labor, civil-rights, and legal-advocacy groups. His supporters, meanwhile, feel he's championing the idea of a post-racial society, one in which merit trumps skin color and socioeconomics are a primary issue.

Connerly came to the fore of the affirmative-action debate in 1996. As a University of California regent—one of the 26 governing members of the state's university system—Connerly championed a ballot initiative called Proposition 209, the biggest blow to the use of racial quotas in college admissions since, well, ever. Fifty-four percent of California's electorate ultimately voted for Prop 209, which banned the consideration of race in public hiring, contracting, and admissions to the University of California, the largest state-run university system in the world. But Connerly didn't stop there. Two years later, he championed I-200, a similar ballot initiative in Washington State, and then in 2000 he helped Florida's Governor Jeb Bush push an affirmative-action ban through the state legislature.

If all three of Connerly's new ballot initiatives were to pass into law, it would be a precedent-setting assault on the nationwide effort to preserve affirmative action.

Now, he is taking the effort nationwide. Through his American Civil Rights Institute, a nonprofit that he founded with Thomas L. "Dusty" Rhodes in 1996, Connerly has sponsored eight major anti-affirmative action initiatives. In 2006, his initiative banning affirmative action was passed by a 16-point margin in Michigan, and the last year he embarked on his most ambitious campaign to date: Super Tuesday for Equal Rights, a well-organized, well-funded drive to end sex- and race-based preferences in public universities, hiring, and contracting in five states—Oklahoma, Missouri, Nebraska, Colorado, and Arizona. If all those initiatives were to pass into law, it would be a precedent-setting assault on the nationwide effort to preserve affirmative action.

So far, Connerly has seen mixed results: The ACRI didn't gather enough signatures to get the measure on the Oklahoma and Missouri ballots; it landed on the Colorado ballot, but may not remain there, as it is being challenged in Denver district court; in early July, it made it onto the ballot in Nebraska and Arizona.

What I am working on is getting rid of preferences based on race . . . The other thing is I think we need to change is how black people are viewed.

"What I am working on is getting rid of preferences based on race, and trying to force my country into the position of going with affirmative action based on socioeconomics," he says. "You know it would be naïve for anyone to believe that we have totally climbed to the mountaintop with Obama's nomination, [that] all racism is over. It's not. There is still a lot of stuff to be done, but I think we have to do it in a different way."

In Connerly's world, the racial playing field began to even out in the 1970s, and has been getting better ever since. For him quotas, at this point, are beside the point. As for what exactly he is proposing, his suggestions are less concrete. "The other thing I think we need to change," he says, "is how black people are viewed."

Wardell Anthony Connerly has lived long enough to see a shift in America's perception of black people. He was born in Leesville, Louisiana, just over the Texas line. His father abandoned the family when he was 2; he was 4 when his mother died. Shortly after that, Ward came north to live with his grandmother in Washington State; he later moved in with an aunt and uncle in Sacramento.

For the better part of his early years, Connerly lived in Del Paso Heights, a mixed, working-class neighborhood where options for higher education were limited. "There were only about four black kids in my neighborhood who wanted to go to college," he says. "And one of them had the wheels." He followed the kid with the car to American River Junior College. By the time he graduated, he was student-body president.

In 1959, Connerly transferred to Sacramento State University, where he again became student-body president, as well as chairing the committee against housing discrimination

and becoming the first black member of his fraternity. While he was there, he formed close relationships with key faculty members, in particular a political-theory professor named John Livingston. "Dr. Livingston would end his lectures often by saying 'We shall overcome,' " Ward recalls. "Not in a Black Panther style but just a suggestion of revving people up. And I once asked him, 'How will we know if we've overcome?' " He gave Connerly three measures: "Number one, when a white girl can bring her [black] fiancé home to mom and dad and the dad not become apoplectic; second, when any white, no matter how lowly, is willing to walk in the shoes of any black, no matter how successful; the third test was when a black man could be seriously considered for President of the United States. I think by his definition we have overcome."

After graduating, in 1962, Connerly proved to be an adept networker. He spent four years in the office of state legislator Pete Wilson, who urged him to start Connerly & Associates, a land-use planning company. Their relationship was symbiotic: Wilson drove business his way; Connerly became a big Republican donor and a key ally. By 1991, Wilson had become governor of California. He appointed Connerly to the University of California Board of Regents.

Connerly's crusade to end affirmative action is powered by a complex money web that connects the same handful of conservative heavyweights.

Since then, Connerly has remained close to the right-wing power structure. His crusade to end affirmative action is powered by a complex money web that connects the same handful of conservative heavyweights—something that isn't lost on the progressive watchdogs who proliferate online. He has received money from Rupert Murdoch (he's also a Fox News darling), the Bradley Foundation (the same folks who funded *The Bell Curve,* the book that posits that black people are intellectually inferior to whites and Asians), the Coors family, and the now-defunct John M. Olin Foundation (which gave research money to libertarian ABC reporter John Stossel), to name a few.

The money trail bothers his critics, but not as much as some of Connerly's other strategies—particularly his portrayal of Super Tuesday as a series of grassroots campaigns that sprang up organically in states where he's sponsored the ballots. "It's all driven from out-of-state money and out-of-state ideology," says Craig Hughes, a Denver political consultant who is battling the Colorado ballot initiative. "There hasn't been any clamoring in the state of Colorado to ban equal-opportunity programs." Connerly claims he chose five states where there was popular support for repealing affirmative action. But look a little closer and the so-called "local" supporters—Arizona's Goldwater Institute, the Nebraska Association of Scholars, and Colorado's Independence Institute—and you'll see they're all connected to the same deep right-wing pockets as the ACRI.

Connerly is also paid handsomely for his crusade—a factor his critics think is his true motivation. He makes no apologies for his salary. When he's asked if reports that he makes as much as $400,000 per year are accurate, he flashes a quick smile and says ambiguously, "I hope it's more than that." As it turns out, it's much more. In 2003, he earned more than $1 million in compensation—the same year he was fined $95,000 by the California Fair Political Practices Commission for not disclosing who funded a proposed California ballot initiative. In his defense, the Heritage Foundation's Becky Norton Dunlop has said, "Most people who donate to causes such as this, that are controversial, recognize that talented and effective leaders must be compensated or they'll find other ways to make a living. Connerly's . . . willingness to speak out on the issue has had national impact." In other words, he's invaluable to the cause.

To critics like Shanta Driver, who heads an organization called the Coalition to Defend Affirmative Action, Integration, And Fight for Equality By Any Means Necessary (known as BAMN), it's unimaginable that a black man born in the Jim Crow South can in good conscience take money from opponents of the 1964 Civil Rights Acts like the Coors family. Driver thinks the real intent of Connerly's ballots is far more dire. She charges that his aim is to "resegregate higher education in America and through that to really restructure American society in a way that is once again aimed at preserving white privilege."

But Connerly feels unfairly targeted. "We are promoting a change in the system," he says. "They have the luxury of hanging back and throwing their barbs. I understand some of that, but there is no equality there. People don't ask them the same question. They never ask the NAACP or the ACLU 'Where do you get your funding?'"

Since Proposition 209, the first large-scale affirmative action rollback, three of the four largest state university systems in the country—California, Florida, and Texas—have adopted similar programs. During this time, according to a graph trotted out by the American Civil Rights Institute, there has been an impressive increase in minority enrollment across the nine-campus University of California system. "We had this huge retention gap, a huge gap in the graduation rate, that is now beginning to close as people are going where they are academically competitive," Connerly says.

But the ACRI's data often clashes with dismal stats showing drops in black and Latino enrollment at the best schools in the system—like UCLA and Berkeley—according to a study the University of California published in 2008. ACRI data also doesn't account for California's demographic shifts: In 1989, underrepresented minorities (blacks, Latinos, American Indians, and Pacific Islanders) comprised 30 percent of all California high school graduates and 21 percent of freshman admitted to the university system. In 2006, that same group had grown to comprise 46 percent of high school graduates, but the number admitted to UC schools remained nearly the same.

The now-banned affirmative action system has been replaced with other official policies. There is the Connerly-championed "comprehensive review," which takes a holistic view of students.

"We look at what school a student attended, what courses were offered, what courses you took, your socioeconomic conditions, whether you had a parent go to college," Connerly explains. Also, the top 4 percent of California high school graduates who have taken the required courses are guaranteed admission to the UC system. In schools that are de facto racially segregated, diversity will be achieved in a way that doesn't use quotas and is more palatable to conservatives. A third Connerly-backed pathway to the UC schools, through California's community colleges, is supposed to further mitigate the effects of the ban.

Affirmative action might help a handful of [middle-class] black kids go to Berkeley with a heavy hand on the scale, rather than San Francisco State University on their own.

Still, the numbers don't quite add up. At UC schools, blacks still have the lowest system-wide admission rates of any ethnic group. The community-college pathway is also producing the lowest return for black students and for Latinos as well. And while admittance rates for blacks have skyrocketed at the university's least-competitive campuses—Riverside, Merced, and Santa Cruz—they've halved at the more prestigious Berkeley and UCLA. By this, Connerly seems unmoved. "Affirmative action might help a handful of [middle-class] black kids go to Berkeley with a heavy hand on the scale, rather than San Francisco State University on their own," he says.

With anti-affirmative-action efforts making it onto the ballots in Arizona, Colorado, and Nebraska, Connerly's opponents fear similar effects on those student bodies.

Much of the debate between Connerly and his detractors revolves around the term "affirmative action" itself. Connerly draws a distinction between two phases of affirmative action. The first phase, which began with John F. Kennedy's Executive Order 10925 and was later bolstered by the landmark 1964 Civil Rights Act, made sure that the government did not discriminate. The second phase, proactively helping minorities, began in the mid-1960s, and can be summed up in the words of Lyndon Johnson, who once said, "You do not take a person who, for years, has been hobbled by chains and liberate him, bring him up to the starting line in a race and then say, 'You are free to compete with all the others,' and still justly believe that you have been completely fair."

In practice, says Connerly, Johnson's is a policy that "[gives] certain groups of Americans what one can call preferential treatment—lower standards for college admission, contracts that are set aside . . . in the interest of diversity. I was in favor of LBJ's version at that moment in time. And I think we're beyond that point." Connerly says the shift occurred somewhere in the mid-1970s, when the notion "that black people needed a heavy hand on the scale in order to enter the mainstream of American life began to change."

Now Connerly wants the ACRI's ballot initiatives to enforce the precise language of the Civil Rights Act. But to the average person, the term "affirmative action" connotes specific diversity goals, not a general antidiscrimination statute. It's a language game conservatives play well, and Connerly is no exception. "The more you can say 'affirmative action' and 'equal-opportunity programs' in the ballot language, the better chance you have of winning," says Shanta Driver. "The more the question is posed as 'preferences,' the better chance the Connerly people have of winning. There's a real [debate] about how you pose questions, a real language fight."

This language fight has already landed one of Connerly's local proxies in hot water. During the 2006 Michigan Civil Rights Initiative, the United States District Court found that the Michigan chapter of the ACRI engaged in "systematic voter fraud" by telling voters that they were signing a petition supporting affirmative action. (Ultimately, since the court found that "the MCRI appears to target all Michigan voters by deception without regard to race," it was not found to be in violation of the Voting Rights Act.) And there is credible evidence the ACRI used similar tactics during 2008's five-state signature-gathering drive for the Super Tuesday initiative.

With signature gathering complete in all five states, the stakes have remained high. Connerly charges that "union thugs" were being paid to prevent his people from circulating petitions in Missouri. But opponents from a broad-based coalition called We Can Missouri say they were only conducting voter education.

The group Colorado Civil Rights Initiative, meanwhile, faces similar charges. It turned in 129,000 signatures in support of the anti-affirmative-action ballot initiative in the state, almost double the required number. But the validity of more than half of those signatures is now being challenged in court. Its opponents would need to prove about 53,000 are false to have the petition disqualified. "We are challenging signatures like 'Jesus' and 'the Lord Jesus' as obviously not current registered voters in Colorado," says Craig Hughes.

Connerly, for his part, claims no real knowledge of the alleged fraud, saying that circulators are paid per petition—nothing to do with his campaign. For canvassers, he says, "it's not a matter of what they believe, it's a matter of how much money can they get. . . . Any time you attach a profit to it, the [potential for fraud] is unavoidable."

With all the back-and-forth bickering, the blood feud between Connerly and his opponents has no end in sight. Even as November nears, it seems clear that no matter the outcome in those five states, neither side will accept it quietly.

With Connerly's side claiming to have gathered enough signatures, Driver is preparing a lawsuit in Arizona to keep the initiative off the ballot there. In Colorado, Craig Hughes's lawsuit to have Connerly's signatures nullified also proceeds. And in Nebraska, David Kramer, the former chairman of the Nebraska Republican party, is leading a bipartisan measure to challenge the validity of the signatures gathered.

To Connerly, however, they are just delaying the inevitable: "The notion that we can use race as the entry point to solve social problems—that's dead," he says, looking past me, his eyes fixed on the hotel's patio. "And I'm not talking just race preferences. Race-based decision-making is dead."

UNIT 2

The Legal Construction of Diversity and Disparity

Unit Selections

Key Points to Consider

- In the late 1960s, proposals that sought to depolarize race issues argued for a policy of benign neglect, meaning that although equal protection and opportunity were essential, economic and education policy should focus on the needs of persons, groups, and regions regardless of their race. What can be said in support of such criteria? What does this philosophy of public policy contribute to our understanding of race and ethnic relations?

- Comment on the view that the American political process has relied too extensively on the Supreme Court. What policies or initiatives related to race relations do you support?

- The U.S. Congress is the lawmaking institution, which authorized national policies of equal protection that are constitutionally guaranteed to all. What explains the disparity between the patently clear proclamation of equality and the painfully obvious practices of racial/ethnic discrimination?

- In your experience, does the argument against affirmative action, which claims that its beneficiaries are stigmatized and thus made objects of disdain and scorn ring true?

- Why has the constitutional penalty of reducing the number of representatives in Congress stated in Article 14, Section 2, not been applied?

- In your opinion, are the issues related to slavery and the history of the South—particularly the impact of large-scale plantation slavery—ongoing influences, and thus relevant to contemporary public issues?

- Does the grouping of people into categories and divisions such as black or white have the same meaning in all regions of this country? Are such categories relevant for self-identification? For government policy? For the law? For understanding pluralism in America?

- What stereotypes of American regions have you encountered? Explain and discuss the question of regional and universal values.

- Does the historical archaeology of your personal identity shape your view on race and ethnicity? What significance does the past have on your current personal and social interaction?

Student Web Site
www.mhcls.com

Internet References

U.S. Census Bureau
http://www.census.gov

U.S. Supreme Court Reports
http://bulk.resource.org/courts.gov/c/US/

© Library of Congress Prints and Photographs Division [LC-DIG-ppmsca-08102]

The legal framework established by the U.S. Constitution illustrates the way the American Founders handled ethnic pluralism. In most respects, they ignored the cultural and linguistic variety within and between the 13 original states, adopting instead a legal system that guaranteed religious exercise free from government interference, due process of law, and freedom of speech and the press. The founders, however, conspicuously compromised their claims of unalienable rights and democratic republicanism with regard to the constitutional status of Africans in bondage and indigenous Native Americans. Even after the Civil War—with the inclusion of constitutional amendments that ended slavery, which provided for political inclusion of all persons and specifically mandated the loss of representation in the House of Representatives for those states that denied equal protection of the laws to all—exclusionary practices continued. Decisions by the U.S. Supreme Court helped to establish a legal system in which inequality and ethnic discrimination—both political and private—were legally permissible. The Supreme Court's attempt to redress the complex relationship between our constitutional system and the diverse society it governs is mediated by a political leadership that has not persistently sought "equal justice under the law" for all.

Moreover, the history of American immigration legislation, from the Alien and Sedition Laws at the founding, to the most recent statutes, reveals an ambiguous legacy. This legal framework continues to mirror the political forces that influence the definition of citizenship and the constitution of ethnic identity and ethnic groups in America.

The legacies of African slavery, racial segregation, and ethnic discrimination established by the Constitution and by subsequent court doctrines are traced in the following abbreviated U.S. Supreme Court opinions.

- In *Dred Scott v. Sandford* (1856), the Supreme Court addressed the constitutional status of an African held in bondage who had been moved to a state that prohibited slavery. U.S. Supreme Court Chief Justice Roger B. Taney attempted to resolve the increasingly divisive issue of slavery by declaring that the "Negro African race"—whether free or slave—was "not intended to be included under the word 'citizens' in the Constitution, and can therefore claim none of the rights and privileges that instrument provides for and secures to citizens of the United States." Contrary to Taney's intentions, however, the *Dred Scott* decision further fractured the nation, ensuring that only the Civil War would resolve the slavery issue.

- In *Plessy v. Ferguson* (1896), the Supreme Court upheld the constitutionality of "Jim Crow" laws that segregated public facilities on the basis of an individual's racial ancestry. The Court reasoned that this "separate but equal" segregation did not violate any rights guaranteed by the U.S. Constitution, nor did it stamp "the colored race with a badge of inferiority." Instead, the Court argued that if "this be so, it is not by reason of anything found in the act but solely because the colored race chooses to put that construction upon it." In contrast, Justice John M. Harlan's vigorous dissent from the Court's Plessy opinion contends that "our Constitution is color-blind, and neither knows nor tolerates classes among citizens." The history of the Courts' attention to citizenship provides a view of a culturally embedded character of color consciousness and the strict textual dependence of the Justices that interpreted the Constitution. Another perspective, however, emerges from the congressional debate that occurred, when a civil rights law ensuring equal protection and voting rights was passed shortly after the Civil War. That legislative history is cited extensively in Shaare Tefila/Al-Khasraji (1987). This expansive view of protection for all ethnic groups cited in these decisions, and the origin of these views in congressional intention voiced by elected legislators are indications of the Court's new directions. The Court's dependence on statutes rather than on the exercise of constitutional authority as the judiciary, and thus as a policymaker and initiator, appears to be waning. Moreover, the Court, under the influence of a color-blind doctrine, seems ready to challenge policies that significantly rely on race and ethnicity, thus changing the landscape as well as the discussion of race and ethnicity, inviting all of us to reexamine both the intentions and outcomes of all legislation in this field.

- In *Brown v. Board of Education of Topeka* (1954), the Supreme Court began the ambitious project of dismantling state-supported racial segregation. In Brown, a unanimous Court overturned *Plessy v. Ferguson,* arguing that "in the field of public education the doctrine of 'separate but equal' has no place," because "separate educational facilities are inherently unequal."

However, this era of civil rights consensus, embodied in the landmark actions of the Supreme Court, has been challenged by contemporary plaintiffs who have turned to the Court for clarification regarding specific cases related to the significance of race and ethnic criteria in public affairs. The lack of popular support for the administration and implementation of policies and the judicial leadership of those policies in California emerged in Proposition 209. This issue of popular concern was played out in the referendum, which was supported by the electorate, but their decision will be played out in the Court as the country braces itself for another cycle of tension and acrimony between the will of the people in a particular state and the rule and supremacy of national law. The mediation between law and popular expression, and the political nexus of state and federal legitimacy, will no doubt be challenged by these contentions.

Nearly a generation after the Civil Rights Era, the national public understanding of the thrust of that period can be regained by reviewing the Congressional deliberation in support of the Civil Rights Act and its goal of equal protection and equality before the law. Contemporary legal arguments and the current judicial politics pose a far more complex set of considerations. Careful analysis of our legal foundations and our expectations for the next epoch of equality with the legal tradition will emerge from these reconsiderations and the new search for remedies.

The implementation of desegregation remedies, voting rights remedies, and affirmative action have been challenged in the judicial rulings as well as by the decision to avoid court action that might compromise hard won gains for minority populations. The politics of affirmative action includes advocates and opponents that have become more strident and competitive for rewards and benefits. Thus the privileging of claims and all that is implied in such argumentation has massively shifted public discourse, and even the most popular accounts of race in the American legal tradition have been changed and revalued in the crucible of persistent racism and ongoing political and media manipulation of racialist passion in pursuit of remedies and privilege.

Racial Restrictions in the Law of Citizenship

Ian F. Haney López

The racial composition of the U.S. citizenry reflects in part the accident of world migration patterns. More than this, however, it reflects the conscious design of U.S. immigration and naturalization laws.

Federal law restricted immigration to this country on the basis of race for nearly one hundred years, roughly from the Chinese exclusion laws of the 1880s until the end of the national origin quotas in 1965.[1] The history of this discrimination can briefly be traced. Nativist sentiment against Irish and German Catholics on the East Coast and against Chinese and Mexicans on the West Coast, which had been doused by the Civil War, reignited during the economic slump of the 1870s. Though most of the nativist efforts failed to gain congressional sanction, Congress in 1882 passed the Chinese Exclusion Act, which suspended the immigration of Chinese laborers for ten years.[2] The Act was expanded to exclude all Chinese in 1884, and was eventually implemented indefinitely.[3] In 1917, Congress created "an Asiatic barred zone," excluding all persons from Asia.[4] During this same period, the Senate passed a bill to exclude "all members of the African or black race." This effort was defeated in the House only after intensive lobbying by the NAACP.[5] Efforts to exclude the supposedly racially undesirable southern and eastern Europeans were more successful. In 1921, Congress established a temporary quota system designed "to confine immigration as much as possible to western and northern European stock," making this bar permanent three years later in the National Origin Act of 1924.[6] With the onset of the Depression, attention shifted to Mexican immigrants. Although no law explicitly targeted this group, federal immigration officials began a series of round-ups and mass deportations of people of Mexican descent under the general rubric of a "repatriation campaign." Approximately 500,000 people were forcibly returned to Mexico during the Depression, more than half of them U.S. citizens.[7] This pattern was repeated in the 1950s, when Attorney General Herbert Brownell launched a program to expel Mexicans. This effort, dubbed "Operation Wetback," indiscriminately deported more than one million citizens and noncitizens in 1954 alone.[8]

Racial restrictions on immigration were not significantly dismantled until 1965, when Congress in a major overhaul of immigration law abolished both the national origin system and the Asiatic Barred Zone.[9] Even so, purposeful racial discrimination in immigration law by Congress remains constitutionally permissible, since the case that upheld the Chinese Exclusion Act to this day remains good law.[10] Moreover, arguably racial discrimination in immigration law continues. For example, Congress has enacted special provisions to encourage Irish immigration, while refusing to ameliorate the backlog of would-be immigrants from the Philippines, India, South Korea, China, and Hong Kong, backlogs created in part through a century of racial exclusion.[11] The history of racial discrimination in U.S. immigration law is a long and continuing one.

As discriminatory as the laws of immigration have been, the laws of citizenship betray an even more dismal record of racial exclusion. From this country's inception, the laws regulating who was or could become a citizen were tainted by racial prejudice. Birthright citizenship, the automatic acquisition of citizenship by virtue of birth, was tied to race until 1940. Naturalized citizenship, the acquisition of citizenship by any means other than through birth, was conditioned on race until 1952. Like immigration laws, the laws of birthright citizenship and naturalization shaped the racial character of the United States.

Birthright Citizenship

Most persons acquire citizenship by birth rather than through naturalization. During the 1990s, for example, naturalization will account for only 7.5 percent of the increase in the U.S. citizen population.[12] At the time of the prerequisite cases, the proportion of persons gaining citizenship through naturalization was probably somewhat higher, given the higher ratio of immigrants to total population, but still far smaller than the number of people gaining citizenship by birth. In order to situate the prerequisite laws, therefore, it is useful first to review the history of racial discrimination in the laws of birthright citizenship.

The U.S. Constitution as ratified did not define the citizenry, probably because it was assumed that the English common law rule of *jus soli* would continue.[13] Under *jus soli*, citizenship accrues to "all" born within a nation's jurisdiction. Despite the seeming breadth of this doctrine, the word "all" is qualified because for the first one hundred years and more of this country's history it did not fully encompass racial minorities. This is the import of the *Dred Scott* decision.[14] Scott, an enslaved man, sought to use the federal courts to sue for his freedom.

However, access to the courts was predicated on citizenship. Dismissing his claim, the United States Supreme Court in the person of Chief Justice Roger Taney declared in 1857 that Scott and all other Blacks, free and enslaved, were not and could never be citizens because they were "a subordinate and inferior class of beings." The decision protected the slave-holding South and infuriated much of the North, further dividing a country already fractured around the issues of slavery and the power of the national government. *Dred Scott* was invalidated after the Civil War by the Civil Rights Act of 1866, which declared that "All persons born . . . in the United States and not subject to any foreign power, excluding Indians not taxed, are declared to be citizens of the United States."[15] *Jus soli* subsequently became part of the organic law of the land in the form of the Fourteenth Amendment: "All persons born or naturalized in the United States, and subject to the jurisdiction thereof, are citizens of the United States and of the state wherein they reside."[16]

Despite the broad language of the Fourteenth Amendment—though in keeping with the words of the 1866 act—some racial minorities remained outside the bounds of *jus soli* even after its constitutional enactment. In particular, questions persisted about the citizenship status of children born in the United States to noncitizen parents, and about the status of Native Americans. The Supreme Court did not decide the status of the former until 1898, when it ruled in *U.S. v. Wong Kim Ark* that native-born children of aliens, even those permanently barred by race from acquiring citizenship, were birthright citizens of the United States.[17] On the citizenship of the latter, the Supreme Court answered negatively in 1884, holding in *Elk v. Wilkins* that Native Americans owed allegiance to their tribe and so did not acquire citizenship upon birth.[18] Congress responded by granting Native Americans citizenship in piecemeal fashion, often tribe by tribe. Not until 1924 did Congress pass an act conferring citizenship on all Native Americans in the United States.[19] Even then, however, questions arose regarding the citizenship of those born in the United States after the effective date of the 1924 act. These questions were finally resolved, and *jus soli* fully applied, under the Nationality Act of 1940, which specifically bestowed citizenship on all those born in the United States "to a member of an Indian, Eskimo, Aleutian, or other aboriginal tribe."[20] Thus, the basic law of citizenship, that a person born here is a citizen here, did not include all racial minorities until 1940.

Unfortunately, the impulse to restrict birthright citizenship by race is far from dead in this country. Apparently, California Governor Pete Wilson and many others seek a return to the times when citizenship depended on racial proxies such as immigrant status. Wilson has called for a federal constitutional amendment that would prevent the American-born children of undocumented persons from receiving birthright citizenship.[21] His call has not been ignored: thirteen members of Congress recently sponsored a constitutional amendment that would repeal the existing Citizenship Clause of the Fourteenth Amendment and replace it with a provision that "All persons born in the United States . . . of mothers who are citizens or legal residents of the United States . . . are citizens of the United States."[22] Apparently, such a change is supported by 49 percent of Americans.[23] In addition to explicitly discriminating against fathers by eliminating their right to confer citizenship through parentage, this proposal implicitly discriminates along racial lines. The effort to deny citizenship to children born here to undocumented immigrants seems to be motivated not by an abstract concern over the political status of the parents, but by racial animosity against Asians and Latinos, those commonly seen as comprising the vast bulk of undocumented migrants. Bill Ong Hing writes, "The discussion of who is and who is not American, who can and cannot become American, goes beyond the technicalities of citizenship and residency requirements; it strikes at the very heart of our nation's long and troubled legacy of race relations.[24] As this troubled legacy reveals, the triumph over racial discrimination in the laws of citizenship and alienage came slowly and only recently. In the campaign for the "control of our borders," we are once again debating the citizenship of the native-born and the merits of *Dred Scott*.[25]

Naturalization

Although the Constitution did not originally define the citizenry, it explicitly gave Congress the authority to establish the criteria for granting citizenship after birth. Article I grants Congress the power "To establish a uniform Rule of Naturalization."[26] From the start, Congress exercised this power in a manner that burdened naturalization laws with racial restrictions that tracked those in the law of birthright citizenship. In 1790, only a few months after ratification of the Constitution, Congress limited naturalization to "any alien, being a free white person who shall have resided within the limits and under the jurisdiction of the United States for a term of two years."[27] This clause mirrored not only the de facto laws of birthright citizenship, but also the racially restrictive naturalization laws of several states. At least three states had previously limited citizenship to "white persons": Virginia in 1779, South Carolina in 1784, and Georgia in 1785.[28] Though there would be many subsequent changes in the requirements for federal naturalization, racial identity endured as a bedrock requirement for the next 162 years. In every naturalization act from 1790 until 1952, Congress included the "white person" prerequisite.[29]

The history of racial prerequisites to naturalization can be divided into two periods of approximately eighty years each. The first period extended from 1790 to 1870, when only Whites were able to naturalize. In the wake of the Civil War, the "white person" restriction on naturalization came under serious attack as part of the effort to expunge *Dred Scott*. Some congressmen, Charles Sumner chief among them, argued that racial barriers to naturalization should be struck altogether. However, racial prejudice against Native Americans and Asians forestalled the complete elimination of the racial prerequisites. During congressional debates, one senator argued against conferring "the rank, privileges, and immunities of citizenship upon the cruel savages who destroyed [Minnesota's] peaceful settlements and massacred the people with circumstances of atrocity too horrible to relate."[30] Another senator wondered "whether this door [of citizenship] shall now be thrown open to the Asiatic population," warning that to do so would spell for the Pacific coast "an end to republican government there, because it is very well ascertained that those people have no appreciation of that form of government; it seems to be obnoxious to their very nature; they seem to be incapable either of understanding or carrying it out."[31] Sentiments such as these ensured that even after the Civil War, bars against Native American and Asian naturalization would continue.[32] Congress opted to maintain the "white person" prerequisite, but to extend the right to naturalize to "persons of African nativity, or African descent."[33] After 1870, Blacks as well as Whites could naturalize, but not others.

During the second period, from 1870 until the last of the prerequisite laws were abolished in 1952, the White-Black dichotomy in American race relations dominated naturalization law. During this period, Whites and Blacks were eligible for citizenship, but others, particularly those from Asia, were not. Indeed, increasing antipathy toward Asians on the West Coast resulted in an explicit disqualification of Chinese persons from naturalization in 1882.[34] The prohibition of Chinese naturalization, the only U.S. law ever to exclude by name a particular nationality from citizenship, was coupled with the ban on Chinese immigration discussed previously. The Supreme Court readily upheld the bar, writing that "Chinese persons not born in this country have never been recognized as citizens of the United States, nor authorized to become such under the naturalization laws."[35] While Blacks were permitted to naturalize beginning in 1870, the Chinese and most "other non-Whites" would have to wait until the 1940s for the right to naturalize.[36]

World War II forced a domestic reconsideration of the racism integral to U.S. naturalization law. In 1935, Hitler's Germany limited citizenship to members of the Aryan race, making Germany the only country other than the United States with a racial restriction on naturalization.[37] The fact of this bad company was not lost on those administering our naturalization laws. "When Earl G. Harrison in 1944 resigned as United States Commissioner of Immigration and Naturalization, he said that the only country in the world, outside the United States, that observes racial discrimination in matters relating to naturalization was Nazi Germany, 'and we all agree that this is not very desirable company.'"[38] Furthermore, the United States was open to charges of hypocrisy for banning from naturalization the nationals of many of its Asian allies. During the war, the United States seemed through some of its laws and social practices to embrace the same racism it was fighting. Both fronts of the war exposed profound inconsistencies between U.S. naturalization law and broader social ideals. These considerations, among others, led Congress to begin a process of piecemeal reform in the laws governing citizenship.

In 1940, Congress opened naturalization to "descendants of races indigenous to the Western Hemisphere."[39] Apparently, this "additional limitation was designed 'to more fully cement' the ties of Pan-Americanism" at a time of impending crisis.[40] In 1943, Congress replaced the prohibition on the naturalization of Chinese persons with a provision explicitly granting them this boon.[41] In 1946, it opened up naturalization to persons from the

Philippines and India as well.[42] Thus, at the end of the war, our naturalization law looked like this:

The right to become a naturalized citizen under the provisions of this Act shall extend only to—

1. white persons, persons of African nativity or descent, and persons of races indigenous to the continents of North or South America or adjacent islands and Filipino persons or persons of Filipino descent;
2. persons who possess, either singly or in combination, a preponderance of blood of one or more of the classes specified in clause (1);
3. Chinese persons or persons of Chinese descent; and persons of races indigenous to India; and
4. persons who possess, either singly or in combination, a preponderance of blood of one or more of the classes specified in clause (3) or, either singly or in combination, as much as one-half blood of those classes and some additional blood of one of the classes specified in clause (1).[43]

This incremental retreat from a "Whites only" conception of citizenship made the arbitrariness of U.S. naturalization law increasingly obvious. For example, under the above statute, the right to acquire citizenship depended for some on blood-quantum distinctions based on descent from peoples indigenous to islands adjacent to the Americas. In 1952, Congress moved towards wholesale reform, overhauling the naturalization statute to read simply that "[t]he right of a person to become a naturalized citizen of the United States shall not be denied or abridged because of race or sex or because such person is married."[44] Thus, in 1952, racial bars on naturalization came to an official end.[45]

Notice the mention of gender in the statutory language ending racial restrictions in naturalization. The issue of women and citizenship can only be touched on here, but deserves significant study in its own right.[46] As the language of the 1952 Act implies, eligibility for naturalization once depended on a woman's marital status. Congress in 1855 declared that a foreign woman automatically acquired citizenship upon marriage to a U.S. citizen, or upon the naturalization of her alien husband.[47] This provision built upon the supposition that a woman's social and political status flowed from her husband. As an 1895 treatise on naturalization put it, "A woman partakes of her husband's nationality; her nationality is merged in that of her husband; her political status follows that of her husband."[48] A wife's acquisition of citizenship, however, remained subject to her individual qualification for naturalization—that is, on whether she was a "white person."[49] Thus, the Supreme Court held in 1868 that only "white women" could gain citizenship by marrying a citizen.[50] Racial restrictions further complicated matters for noncitizen women in that naturalization was denied to those married to a man racially ineligible for citizenship, irrespective of the woman's own qualifications, racial or otherwise.[51] The automatic naturalization of a woman upon her marriage to a citizen or upon the naturalization of her husband ended in 1922.[52]

The citizenship of American-born women was also affected by the interplay of gender and racial restrictions. Even though under English common law a woman's nationality was unaffected by marriage, many courts in this country stripped women who married noncitizens of their U.S. citizenship.[53] Congress recognized and mandated this practice in 1907, legislating that an American woman's marriage to an alien terminated her citizenship.[54] Under considerable pressure, Congress partially repealed this act in 1922.[55] However, the 1922 act continued to require the expatriation of any woman who married a foreigner racially barred from citizenship, flatly declaring that "any woman citizen who marries an alien ineligible to citizenship shall cease to be a citizen."[56] Until Congress repealed this provision in 1931,[57] marriage to a non-White alien by an American woman was akin to treason against this country: either of these acts justified the stripping of citizenship from someone American by birth. Indeed, a woman's marriage to a non-White foreigner was perhaps a worse crime, for while a traitor lost his citizenship only after trial, the woman lost hers automatically.[58] The laws governing the racial composition of this country's citizenry came inseverably bound up with and exacerbated by sexism. It is in this context of combined racial and gender prejudice that we should understand the absence of any women among the petitioners named in the prerequisite cases: it is not that women were unaffected by the racial bars, but that they were doubly bound by them, restricted both as individuals, and as less than individuals (that is, as wives).

Notes

1. U.S. COMMISSION ON CIVIL RIGHTS, THE TARNISHED GOLDEN DOOR: CIVIL RIGHTS ISSUES IN IMMIGRATION 1–12 (1990).

2. Chinese Exclusion Act, ch. 126, 22 Stat. 58 (1882). *See generally* Harold Hongju Koh, *Bitter Fruit of the Asian Immigration Cases,* 6 CONSTITUTION 69 (1994). For a sobering account of the many lynchings of Chinese in the western United States during this period, *see* John R. Wunder, *Anti-Chinese Violence in the American West, 1850–1910,* LAW FOR THE ELEPHANT, LAW FOR THE BEAVER: ESSAYS IN THE LEGAL HISTORY OF THE NORTH AMERICAN WEST 212 (John McLaren, Hamar Foster, and Chet Orloff eds., 1992). Charles McClain, Jr., discusses the historical origins of anti-Chinese prejudice and the legal responses undertaken by that community on the West Coast. Charles McClain, Jr., *The Chinese Struggle for Civil Rights in Nineteenth Century America: The First Phase, 1850–1870,* 72 CAL. L. REV. 529 (1984). For a discussion of contemporary racial violence against Asian Americans, *see* Note, *Racial Violence against Asian Americans,* 106 HARV. L. REV. 1926 (1993); Robert Chang, *Toward an Asian American Legal Scholarship: Critical Race Theory, Post-Structuralism, and Narrative Space,* 81 CAL. L. REV. 1241, 1251–58 (1993).

3. Act of July 9, 1884, ch. 220, 23 Stat. 115; Act of May 5, 1892, ch. 60, 27 Stat. 25; Act of April 29, 1902, ch. 641, 32 Stat. 176; Act of April 27, 1904, ch. 1630, 33 Stat. 428.

4. Act of Feb. 5, 1917, ch. 29, 39 Stat. 874.

5. U.S. COMMISSION ON CIVIL RIGHTS, *supra,* at 9.

6. *Id. See* Act of May 19, 1921, ch. 8, 42 Stat. 5; Act of May 26, 1924, ch. 190, 43 Stat. 153.

7. U.S. COMMISSION ON CIVIL RIGHTS, *supra,* at 10.

8. *Id.* at 11. *See generally* JUAN RAMON GARCIA, OPERATION WETBACK: THE MASS DEPORTATION OF MEXICAN UNDOCUMENTED WORKERS IN 1954 (1980).

9. Act of Oct. 2, 1965, 79 Stat. 911.

10. Chae Chan Ping v. United States, 130 U.S. 581 (1889). The Court reasoned in part that if "the government of the United States, through its legislative department, considers the presence of foreigners of a different race in this country, who will not assimilate with us, to be dangerous to its peace and security, their exclusion is not to be stayed." For a critique of this deplorable result, *see* Louis Henkin, *The Constitution and United States Sovereignty: A Century of Chinese Exclusion and Its Progeny,* 100 HARV. L. REV. 853 (1987).

11. For efforts to encourage Irish immigration, *see, e.g., Immigration Act of 1990, § 131, 104 Stat. 4978 (codified as amended at 8 U.S.C. § 1153 (c) [1994]).* Bill Ong Hing argues that Congress continues to discriminate against Asians. *"Through an examination of past exclusion laws, previous legislation, and the specific provisions of the Immigration Act of 1990, the conclusion can be drawn that Congress never intended to make up for nearly 80 years of Asian exclusion, and that a conscious hostility towards persons of Asian descent continues to pervade Congressional circles."* Bill Ong Hing, Asian Americans and Present U.S. Immigration Policies: A Legacy of Asian Exclusion, *ASIAN AMERICANS AND THE SUPREME COURT: A DOCUMENTARY HISTORY 1106, 1107 (Hyung-Chan Kim ed., 1992).*

12. Louis DeSipio and Harry Pachon, Making Americans: Administrative Discretion and Americanization, *12 CHICANO-LATINO L. REV. 52, 53 (1992).*

13. CHARLES GORDON AND STANLEY MAILMAN, IMMIGRATION LAW AND PROCEDURE § 92.03[1][b] (rev. ed. 1992).

14. Dred Scott v. Sandford, 60 U.S. (19 How.) 393 (1857). For an insightful discussion of the role of *Dred Scott* in the development of American citizenship, see *JAMES KETTNER, THE DEVELOPMENT OF AMERICAN CITIZENSHIP, 1608–1870, at 300–333 (1978);* see also *KENNETH L. KARST, BELONGING TO AMERICA: EQUAL CITIZENSHIP AND THE CONSTITUTION 43–61 (1989).*

15. Civil Rights Act of 1866, ch. 31, 14 Stat. 27.

16. U.S. Const. amend. XIV.

17. 169 U.S. 649 (1898).

18. 112 U.S. 94 (1884).

19. Act of June 2, 1924, ch. 233, 43 Stat. 253.

20. Nationality Act of 1940, § 201(b), 54 Stat. 1138. See generally *GORDON AND MAILMAN, supra,* at § 92.03[3][e].

21. Pete Wilson, Crack Down on Illegals, *USA TODAY,* Aug. 20, 1993, at 12A.

22. H. R. J. Res. 129, 103d Cong., 1st Sess. (1993). An earlier, scholarly call to revamp the Fourteenth Amendment can be found in PETER SCHUCK and ROGER SMITH, CITIZENSHIP WITHOUT CONSENT: ILLEGAL ALIENS IN THE AMERICAN POLITY (1985).

23. Koh, *supra,* at 69–70.

24. Bill Ong Hing, Beyond the Rhetoric of Assimilation and Cultural Pluralism: Addressing the Tension of Separatism and Conflict in an Immigration-Driven Multiracial Society, *81 CAL. L. REV. 863, 866 (1993).*

25. Gerald Neuman warns against amending the Citizenship Clause. Gerald Neuman, Back to *Dred Scott? 24 SAN DIEGO L. REV. 485, 500 (1987)*. See also *Note*, The Birthright Citizenship Amendment: A Threat to Equality, *107 HARV. L. REV. 1026 (1994)*.

26. U.S. Const. art. I, sec. 8, cl. 4.

27. Act of March 26, 1790, ch. 3, 1 Stat. 103.

28. KETTNER, *supra, at 215–16*.

29. One exception exists. In revisions undertaken in 1870, the "white person" limitation was omitted. However, this omission is regarded as accidental, and the prerequisite was reinserted in 1875 by "an act to correct errors and to supply omissions in the Revised Statutes of the United States." Act of Feb. 18, 1875, ch. 80, 18 Stat. 318. See *In re Ah Yup, 1 F.Cas. 223 (C.C.D.Cal. 1878) ("Upon revision of the statutes, the revisors, probably inadvertently, as Congress did not contemplate a change of the laws in force, omitted the words 'white persons.' ")*.

30. Statement of Senator Hendricks, 59 CONG. GLOBE, 42nd Cong., 1st Sess. 2939 (1866). See also *John Guendelsberger*, Access to Citizenship for Children Born Within the State to Foreign Parents, *40 AM. J. COMP. L. 379, 407–9 (1992)*.

31. Statement of Senator Cowan, 57 CONG. GLOBE, 42nd Cong., 1st Sess. 499 (1866). For a discussion of the role of anti-Asian prejudice in the laws governing naturalization, see generally *Elizabeth Hull,* Naturalization and Denaturalization, *ASIAN AMERICANS AND THE SUPREME COURT: A DOCUMENTARY HISTORY 403 (Hyung-Chan Kim ed., 1992)*.

32. The Senate rejected an amendment that would have allowed Chinese persons to naturalize. The proposed amendment read: "That the naturalization laws are hereby extended to aliens of African nativity, and to persons of African descent, and to persons born in the Chinese empire." BILL ONG HING, MAKING AND REMAKING ASIAN AMERICA THROUGH IMMIGRATION POLICY, 1850–1990, at 239 n.34 (1993).

33. Act of July 14, 1870, ch. 255, § 7, 16 Stat. 254.

34. Chinese Exclusion Act, ch. 126, § 14, 22 Stat. 58 (1882).

35. Fong Yue Ting v. United States, 149 U.S. 698, 716 (1893).

36. Neil Gotanda contends that separate racial ideologies function with respect to "other non-Whites," meaning non-Black racial minorities such as Asians, Native Americans, and Latinos. Neil Gotanda, "Other Non-Whites" in American Legal History: A Review of *Justice at War, 85 COLUM. L. REV. 1186 (1985). Gotanda explicitly identifies the operation of this separate ideology in the Supreme Court's jurisprudence regarding Asians and citizenship. Neil Gotanda,* Asian American Rights and the "Miss Saigon Syndrome," *ASIAN AMERICANS AND THE SUPREME COURT: A DOCUMENTARY HISTORY 1087, 1096–97 (Hyung-Chan Kim ed., 1992)*.

37. Charles Gordon, The Racial Barrier to American Citizenship, *93 U. PA. L. REV. 237, 252 (1945)*.

38. MILTON KONVITZ, THE ALIEN AND THE ASIATIC IN AMERICAN LAW 80–81 (1946) (citation omitted).

39. Act of Oct. 14, 1940, ch. 876, § 303, 54 Stat. 1140.

40. Note, The Nationality Act of 1940, *54 HARV. L. REV. 860, 865 n.40 (1941)*.

41. Act of Dec. 17, 1943, ch. 344, 3, 57 Stat. 600.

42. Act of July 2, 1946, ch. 534, 60 Stat. 416.

43. Id.

44. Immigration and Nationality Act of 1952, ch. 2, § 311, 66 Stat. 239 (codified as amended at 8 U.S.C. 1422 [1988]).

45. Arguably, the continued substantial exclusion of Asians from immigration not remedied until 1965, rendered their eligibility for naturalization relatively meaningless. "[T]he national quota system for admitting immigrants which was built into the 1952 Act gave the grant of eligibility a hollow ring." Chin Kim and Bok Lim Kim, Asian Immigrants in American Law: A Look at the Past and the Challenge Which Remains, *26 AM. U. L. REV. 373, 390 (1977)*.

46. *See generally Ursula Vogel,* Is Citizenship Gender-Specific? *THE FRONTIERS OF CITIZENSHIP 58 (Ursula Vogel and Michael Moran eds., 1991)*.

47. Act of Feb. 10, 1855, ch. 71, § 2, 10 Stat. 604. Because gender-based laws in the area of citizenship were motivated by the idea that a woman's citizenship should follow that of her husband, no naturalization law has explicitly targeted unmarried women. GORDON AND MAILMAN, *supra, at § 95.03[6] ("An unmarried woman has never been statutorily* barred from naturalization.").

48. PRENTISS WEBSTER, LAW OF NATURALIZATION IN THE UNITED STATES OF AMERICA AND OTHER COUNTRIES 80 (1895).

49. Act of Feb. 10, 1855, ch. 71, § 2, 10 Stat. 604.

50. Kelly v. Owen, 74 U.S. 496, 498 (1868).

51. GORDON AND MAILMAN, *supra* at § 95.03[6].

52. Act of Sept. 22, 1922, ch. 411, § 2, 42 Stat. 1021.

53. GORDON AND MAILMAN, *supra* at § 100.03[4][m].

54. Act of March 2, 1907, ch. 2534, § 3, 34 Stat. 1228. This act was upheld in MacKenzie v. Hare, 239 U.S. 299 (1915) (expatriating a U.S.-born woman upon her marriage to a British citizen).

55. Act of Sept. 22, 1922, ch. 411, § 3, 42 Stat. 1021.

56. *Id.* The Act also stated that "[n]o woman whose husband is not eligible to citizenship shall be naturalized during the continuance of the marriage."

57. Act of March 3, 1931, ch. 442, § 4(a), 46 Stat. 1511.

58. The loss of birthright citizenship was particularly harsh for those women whose race made them unable to regain citizenship through naturalization, especially after 1924, when the immigration laws of this country barred entry to any alien ineligible to citizenship. Immigration Act of 1924, ch. 190, § 13(c), 43 Stat. 162. *See, e.g.,* Ex parte (Ng) Fung Sing, 6 F.2d 670 (W. D. Wash. 1925). In that case, a U.S. birthright citizen of Chinese descent was expatriated because of her marriage to a Chinese citizen, and was subsequently refused admittance to the United States as an alien ineligible to citizenship.

Dred Scott v. Sandford

December term 1856.

Mr. Chief Justice Taney delivered the opinion of the court.

This case has been twice argued. After the argument at the last term, differences of opinion were found to exist among the members of the court; and as the questions in controversy are of the highest importance, and the court was at that time much pressed by the ordinary business of the term, it was deemed advisable to continue the case, and direct a reargument on some of the points, in order that we might have an opportunity of giving to the whole subject a more deliberate consideration. It has accordingly been again argued by counsel, and considered by the court; and I now proceed to deliver its opinion.

There are two leading questions presented by the record:

1. Had the Circuit Court of the United States jurisdiction to hear and determine the case between these parties? And
2. If it had jurisdiction, is the judgment it has given erroneous or not?

The plaintiff in error, who was also the plaintiff in the court below, was, with his wife and children, held as slaves by the defendant, in the State of Missouri; and he brought this action in the Circuit Court of the United States for that district, to assert the title of himself and his family to freedom.

The declaration is in the form usually adopted in that State to try questions of this description, and contains the averment necessary to give the court jurisdiction; that he and the defendant are citizens of different States; that is, that he is a citizen of Missouri, and the defendant a citizen of New York.

The defendant pleaded in abatement to the jurisdiction of the court, that the plaintiff was not a citizen of the State of Missouri, as alleged in his declaration, being a negro of African descent, whose ancestors were of pure African blood, and who were brought into this country and sold as slaves.

To this plea the plaintiff demurred, and the defendant joined in demurrer. The court overruled the plea, and gave judgment that the defendant should answer over. And he thereupon put in sundry pleas in bar, upon which issues were joined; and at the trial the verdict and judgment were in his favor. Whereupon the plaintiff brought this writ of error.

Before we speak of the pleas in bar, it will be proper to dispose of the questions which have arisen on the plea in abatement.

That plea denies the right of the plaintiff to sue in a court of the United States, for the reasons therein stated.

If the question raised by it is legally before us, and the court should be of opinion that the facts stated in it disqualify the plaintiff from becoming a citizen, in the sense in which that word is used in the Constitution of the United States, then the judgment of the Circuit Court is erroneous, and must be reversed.

It is suggested, however, that this plea is not before us; and that as the judgment in the court below on this plea was in favor of the plaintiff, he does not seek to reverse it, or bring it before the court for revision by his writ of error; and also that the defendant waived this defence by pleading over, and thereby admitted the jurisdiction of the court.

But, in making this objection, we think the peculiar and limited jurisdiction of courts of the United States has not been adverted to. This peculiar and limited jurisdiction has made it necessary, in these courts, to adopt different rules and principles of pleading, so far as jurisdiction is concerned, from those which regulate courts of common law in England, and in the different States of the Union which have adopted the common-law rules.

In these last-mentioned courts, where their character and rank are analogous to that of a Circuit Court of the United States; in other words, where they are what the law terms courts of general jurisdiction; they are presumed to have jurisdiction, unless the contrary appears. No averment in the pleadings of the plaintiff is necessary, in order to give jurisdiction. If the defendant objects to it, he must plead it specially, and unless the fact on which he relies is found to be true by a jury, or admitted to be true by the plaintiff, the jurisdiction cannot be disputed in an appellate court.

Now, it is not necessary to inquire whether in courts of that description a party who pleads over in bar, when a plea to the jurisdiction has been ruled against him, does or does not waive his plea; nor whether upon a judgment in his favor on the pleas in bar, and a writ of error brought by the plaintiff, the question upon the plea in abatement would be open for revision in the appellate court. Cases that may have been decided in such courts, or rules that may have been laid down by common-law pleaders, can have no influence in the decision in this court. Because, under the Constitution and laws of the United States, the rules which govern the pleadings in its courts, in questions of jurisdiction, stand on different principles and are regulated by different laws.

This difference arises, as we have said, from the peculiar character of the Government of the United States. For although it is sovereign and supreme in its appropriate sphere of action, yet it does not possess all the powers which usually belong to the sovereignty of a nation. Certain specified powers, enumerated in the Constitution, have been conferred upon it; and neither the legislative, executive, nor judicial departments of the Government can lawfully exercise any authority beyond the limits marked out by the Constitution. And in regulating the judicial department, the cases in which the courts of the United States shall have jurisdiction are particularly and specifically enumerated and defined; and they are not authorized to take cognizance of any case which does not come within the description therein specified. Hence, when a plaintiff sues in a court of the United States, it is necessary that he should show, in his pleading, that the suit he brings is within the jurisdiction of the court, and that he is entitled to sue there. And if he omits to do this, and should, by any oversight of the Circuit Court, obtain a judgment in his favor, the judgment would be reversed in the appellate court for want of jurisdiction in the court below. The jurisdiction would not be presumed, as in the case of a common-law English or State court, unless the contrary appeared. But the record, when it comes before the appellate court, must show, affirmatively, that the inferior court had authority under the Constitution, to hear and determine the case. And if the plaintiff claims a right to sue in a Circuit Court of the United States, under that provision of the Constitution which gives jurisdiction in controversies between citizens of different States, he must distinctly aver in his pleading that they are citizens of different States; and he cannot maintain his suit without showing that fact in the pleadings.

This point was decided in the case of *Bingham v. Cabot,* (in 3 Dall., 382,) and ever since adhered to by the court. And in *Jackson v. Ashton,* (8 Pet., 148,) it was held that the objection to which it was open could not be waived by the opposite party because consent of parties could not give jurisdiction.

It is needless to accumulate cases on this subject. Those already referred to, and the cases of *Capron v. Van Noorden,* (in 2 Cr., 126) and *Montalet v. Murray,* (4 Cr., 46,) are sufficient to show the rule of which we have spoken. The case of *Capron v. Van Noorden* strikingly illustrates the difference between a common-law court and a court of the United States.

If, however, the fact of citizenship is averred in the declaration, and the defendant does not deny it, and put it in issue by plea in abatement, he cannot offer evidence at the trial to disprove it, and consequently cannot avail himself of the objection in the appellate court, unless the defect should be apparent in some other part of the record. For if there is no plea in abatement, and the want of jurisdiction does not appear in any other part of the transcript brought up by the writ of error, the undisputed averment of citizenship in the declaration must be taken in this court to be true. In this case, the citizenship is averred, but it is denied by the defendant in the manner required by the rules of pleading, and the fact upon which the denial is based is admitted by the demurrer. And, if the plea and demurrer, and judgment of the court below upon it, are before us upon this record, the question to be decided is, whether the facts stated in the plea are sufficient to show that the plaintiff is not entitled to sue as a citizen in a court of the United States. . . .

We think they are before us. The plea in abatement and the judgment of the court upon it, are a part of the judicial proceedings in the Circuit Court, and are there recorded as such; and a writ of error always brings up to the superior court the whole record of the proceedings in the court below And in the case of the *United States v. Smith,* (11 Wheat., 172) this court said, that the case being brought up by writ of error, the whole record was under the consideration of this court. And this being the case in the present instance, the plea in abatement is necessarily under consideration; and it becomes, therefore, our duty to decide whether the facts stated in the plea are or are not sufficient to show that the plaintiff is not entitled to sue as a citizen in a court of the United States.

This is certainly a very serious question, and one that now for the first time has been brought for decision before this court. But it is brought here by those who have a right to bring it, and it is our duty to meet it and decide it.

The question is simply this: Can a negro, whose ancestors were imported into this country, and sold as slaves, become a member of the political community formed and brought into existence by the Constitution of the United States, and as such become entitled to all the rights, and privileges, and immunities, guarantied by that instrument to the citizen? One of which rights is the privilege of suing in a court of the United States in the cases specified in the Constitution.

It will be observed, that the plea applies to that class of persons only whose ancestors were negroes of the African race, and imported into this country, and sold and held as slaves. The only matter in issue before the court, therefore, is, whether the descendants of such slaves, when they shall be emancipated, or who are born of parents who had become free before their birth, are citizens of a State, in the sense in which the word citizen is used in the Constitution of the United States. And this being the only matter in dispute on the pleadings, the court must be understood as speaking in this opinion of that class only, that is, of those persons who are the descendants of Africans who were imported into this country, and sold as slaves.

The situation of this population was altogether unlike that of the Indian race. The latter, it is true, formed no part of the colonial communities, and never amalgamated with them in social connections or in government. But although they were uncivilized, they were yet a free and independent people, associated together in nations or tribes, and governed by their own laws. Many of these political communities were situated in territories to which the white race claimed the ultimate right of dominion. But that claim was acknowledged to be subject to the right of the Indians to occupy it as long as they thought proper, and neither the English nor colonial Governments claimed or exercised any dominion over the tribe or nation by whom it was occupied, nor claimed the right to the possession of the territory, until the tribe or nation consented to cede it. These Indian Governments were regarded and treated as foreign Governments, as much so as if an ocean had separated the red man from the white; and their freedom has constantly been acknowledged, from the time of the first emigration to the English colonies to the present day, by the different Governments which succeeded each other. Treaties have been negotiated with them, and their alliance sought for in war; and the people who compose these Indian political communities have always been treated as foreigners not living under our Government. It is true that the course of events has brought the Indian tribes within the limits of the United States under subjection to the white race; and it has been found necessary, for their sake as well as our own, to regard them as in a state of pupilage, and to legislate to a certain extent over them and the territory they occupy. But they may, without doubt, like the subjects of any other foreign Government, be naturalized by the authority of Congress, and become citizens of a State, and of the United States; and if an individual should leave his nation or tribe, and take up his abode among the white population, he would be entitled to all the rights and privileges which would belong to an emigrant from any other foreign people.

We proceed to examine the case as presented by the pleadings.

The words "people of the United States" and "citizens" are synonymous terms, and mean the same thing. They both describe the political body who, according to our republican institutions, form the sovereignty and who hold the power and conduct the Government through their representatives. They are what we familiarly call the "sovereign people," and every citizen is one of this people, and a constituent member of this sovereignty. The question before us is, whether the class of persons described in the plea in abatement compose a portion of this people, and are constituent members of this sovereignty? We think they are not, and that they are not included, and were not intended to be included, under the word "citizens" in the Constitution, and can therefore claim none of the rights and privileges which that instrument provides for and secures to citizens of the United States. On the contrary, they were at that time considered as a subordinate and inferior class of beings, who had been subjugated by the dominant race, and, whether emancipated or not, yet remained subject to their authority, and had no rights or privileges but such as those who held the power and the Government might choose to grant them.

It is not the province of the court to decide upon the justice or injustice, the policy or impolicy, of these laws. The decision of that question belonged to the political or law-making power; to those who formed the sovereignty and framed the Constitution. The duty of the court is, to interpret the instrument they have framed, with the best lights we can obtain on the subject, and to administer it as we find it, according to its true intent and meaning when it was adopted.

In discussing this question, we must not confound the rights of citizenship which a State may confer within its own limits, and the rights of citizenship as a member of the Union. It does not by any means follow, because he has all the rights and privileges of a citizen of a State, that he must be a citizen of the United States. He may have all of the rights and privileges of the citizen of a State, and yet not be entitled to the rights and privileges of a citizen in any other State. For, previous to the adoption of the Constitution of the United States, every State had the undoubted right to confer on whomsoever it pleased the character of citizen, and to endow him with all its rights. But this character of course was confined to the boundaries of the State, and gave him no rights or privileges in other States beyond those secured to him by the laws of nations and the comity of States. Nor have the several States surrendered the power of conferring

these rights and privileges by adopting the Constitution of the United States. Each State may still confer them upon an alien, or any one it thinks proper, or upon any class or description of persons; yet he would not be a citizen in the sense in which that word is used in the Constitution of the United States, nor entitled to sue as such in one of its courts, nor to the privileges and immunities of a citizen in the other States. The rights which he would acquire would be restricted to the State which gave them. The Constitution has conferred on Congress the right to establish a uniform rule of naturalization, and this right is evidently exclusive, and has always been held by this court to be so. Consequently, no State, since the adoption of the Constitution, can by naturalizing an alien invest him with the rights and privileges secured to a citizen of a State under the Federal Government, although, so far as the State alone was concerned, he would undoubtedly be entitled to the rights of a citizen, and clothed with all the rights and immunities which the Constitution and laws of the State attached to that character.

It is very clear, therefore, that no State can, by any act or law of its own, passed since the adoption of the Constitution, introduce a new member into the political community created by the Constitution of the United States. It cannot make him a member of this community by making him a member of its own. And for the same reason it cannot introduce any person, or description of persons, who were not intended to be embraced in this new political family which the Constitution brought into existence, but were intended to be excluded from it.

The question then arises, whether the provisions of the Constitution, in relation to the personal rights and privileges to which the citizen of a State should be entitled, embraced the negro African race, at that time in this country or who might afterwards be imported, who had then or should afterwards be made free in any State; and to put it in the power of a single State to make him a citizen of the United States, and endue him with the full rights of citizenship in every other State without their consent? Does the Constitution of the United States act upon him whenever he shall be made free under the laws of a State, and raised there to the rank of a citizen, and immediately clothe him with all the privileges of a citizen in every other State, and in its own courts?

The courts think the affirmative of these propositions cannot be maintained. And if it cannot, the plaintiff in error could not be a citizen of the State of Missouri, within the meaning of the Constitution of the United States, and, consequently, was not entitled to sue in its courts.

It is true, every person, and every class and description of persons, who were at the time of the adoption of the Constitution recognised as citizens in the several States, became also citizens of this new political body; but none other; it was formed by them, and for them and their posterity, but for no one else. And the personal rights and privileges guarantied to citizens of this new sovereignty were intended to embrace those only who were then members of the several State communities, or who should afterwards by birthright or otherwise become members, according to the provisions of the Constitution and the principles on which it was founded. It was the union of those who were at that time members of distinct and separate political communities into one political family, whose power, for certain specified purposes, was to extend over the whole territory of the United States. And it gave to each citizen rights and privileges outside of his State which he did not before possess, and placed him in every other State upon a perfect equality with its own citizens as to rights of person and rights of property; it made him a citizen of the United States.

It becomes necessary, therefore, to determine who were citizens of the several States when the Constitution was adopted. And in order to do this, we must recur to the Governments and institutions of the thirteen colonies, when they separated from Great Britain and formed new sovereignties, and took their places in the family of independent nations. We must inquire who, at that time, were recognised as the people or citizens of a State, whose rights and liberties had been outraged by the English Government; and who declared their independence, and assumed the powers of Government to defend their rights by force of arms.

In the opinion of the court, the legislation and histories of the times, and the language used in the Declaration of Independence, show, that neither the class of persons who had been imported as slaves, nor their descendants, whether they had become free or not, were then acknowledged as a part of the people, nor intended to be included in the general words used in that memorable instrument. . . .

Supreme Court of the United States, 1856.

Brown et al. v. Board of Education of Topeka et al.

347 U.S. 483 (1954).

Mr. Chief Justice Warren delivered the opinion of the Court.

These cases come to us from the States of Kansas, South Carolina, Virginia, and Delaware. They are premised on different facts and different local conditions, but a common legal question justifies their consideration together in this consolidated opinion.[1]

In each of the cases, minors of the Negro race, through their legal representatives, seek the aid of the courts in obtaining admission to the public schools of their community on a non-segregated basis. In each instance, they had been denied admission to schools attended by white children under laws requiring or permitting segregation according to race. This segregation was alleged to deprive the plaintiffs of the equal protection of the laws under the Fourteenth Amendment. In each of the cases other than the Delaware case, a three-judge federal district court denied relief to the plaintiffs on the so-called "separate but equal" doctrine announced by this Court in *Plessy v. Ferguson,* 163 U.S. 537. Under that doctrine, equality of treatment is accorded when the races are provided substantially equal facilities, even though these facilities be separate. In the Delaware case, the Supreme Court of Delaware adhered to that doctrine, but ordered that the plaintiffs be admitted to the white schools because of their superiority to the Negro schools.

The plaintiffs contend that segregated public schools are not "equal" and cannot be made "equal," and that hence they are deprived of the equal protection of the laws. Because of the obvious importance of the question presented, the Court took jurisdiction.[2] Argument was heard in the 1952 Term, and reargument was heard this Term on certain questions propounded by the Court.[3]

Reargument was largely devoted to the circumstances surrounding the adoption of the Fourteenth Amendment in 1868. It covered exhaustively consideration of the Amendment in Congress, ratification by the states, then existing practices in racial segregation, and the views of proponents and opponents of the Amendment. This discussion and our own investigation convince us that, although these sources cast some light, it is not enough to resolve the problem with which we are faced. At best, they are inconclusive. The most avid proponents of the post–War Amendments undoubtedly intended them to remove all legal distinctions among "all persons born or naturalized in the United States." Their opponents, just as certainly, were antagonistic to both the letter and the spirit of the Amendments and wished them to have the most limited effect. What others in Congress and the state legislatures had in mind cannot be determined with any degree of certainty.

An additional reason for the inconclusive nature of the Amendment's history, with respect to segregated schools, is the status of public education at that time.[4] In the South, the movement toward free common schools, supported by general taxation, had not yet taken hold. Education of white children was largely in the hands of private groups. Education of Negroes was almost nonexistent, and practically all of the race were illiterate. In fact, any education of Negroes was forbidden by law in some states. Today, in contrast, many Negroes have achieved outstanding success in the arts and sciences as well as in the business and professional world. It is true that public school education at the time of the Amendment had advanced further in the North, but the effect of the Amendment on northern States was generally ignored in the congressional debates. Even in the North, the conditions of public education did not approximate those existing today. The curriculum was usually rudimentary; ungraded schools were common in rural areas; the school term was but three months a year in many states; and compulsory school attendance was virtually unknown. As a consequence, it is not surprising that there should be so little in the history of the Fourteenth Amendment relating to its intended effect on public education.

In the first cases in this Court construing the Fourteenth Amendment, decided shortly after its adoption, the Court interpreted it as proscribing all state-imposed discriminations against the Negro race.[5] The doctrine of "separate but equal" did not make its appearance in this Court until 1896 in the case of *Plessy v. Ferguson, supra,* involving not education but transportation.[6] American courts have since labored with the doctrine for over half a century. In this Court, there have been six cases involving the "separate but equal" doctrine in the field of public education.[7] In *Cumming v. County Board of Education,* 175 U.S. 528, and *Gong Lum v. Rice,* 275 U.S. 78, the validity of the doctrine itself was not challenged.[8] In more recent cases, all on the graduate school level, inequality was found in that specific benefits enjoyed by white students were denied to

Negro students of the same educational qualifications. *Missouri ex rel. Gaines v. Canada,* 305 U.S. 337; *Sipuel v. Oklahoma,* 332 U.S. 631; *Sweatt v. Painter,* 339 U.S. 629; *McLaurin v. Oklahoma State Regents,* 339 U.S. 637. In none of these cases was it necessary to reexamine the doctrine to grant relief to the Negro plaintiff. And in *Sweatt v. Painter, supra,* the Court expressly reserved decision on the question whether *Plessy v. Ferguson* should be held inapplicable to public education.

In the instant cases, that question is directly presented. Here, unlike *Sweatt v. Painter,* there are findings below that the Negro and white schools involved have been equalized, or are being equalized, with respect to buildings, curricula, qualifications and salaries of teachers, and other "tangible" factors.[9] Our decision, therefore, cannot turn on merely a comparison of these tangible factors in the Negro and white schools involved in each of the cases. We must look instead to the effect of segregation itself on public education.

In approaching this problem, we cannot turn the clock back to 1868 when the Amendment was adopted, or even to 1896 when *Plessy v. Ferguson* was written. We must consider public education in the light of its full development and its present place in American life throughout the Nation. Only in this way can it be determined if segregation in public schools deprives these plaintiffs of the equal protection of the laws.

Today, education is perhaps the most important function of state and local governments. Compulsory school attendance laws and the great expenditures for education both demonstrate our recognition of the importance of education to our democratic society. It is required in the performance of our most basic public responsibilities, even service in the armed forces. It is the very foundation of good citizenship. Today it is a principal instrument in awakening the child to cultural values, in preparing him for later professional training, and in helping him to adjust normally to his environment. In these days, it is doubtful that any child may reasonably be expected to succeed in life if he is denied the opportunity of an education. Such an opportunity, where the state has undertaken to provide it, is a right which must be made available to all on equal terms.

We come then to the question presented: Does segregation of children in public schools solely on the basis of race, even though the physical facilities and other "tangible" factors may be equal, deprive the children of the minority group of equal educational opportunities? We believe that it does.

In *Sweatt v. Painter, supra,* in finding that a segregated law school for Negroes could not provide them equal educational opportunities, this Court relied in large part on "those qualities which are incapable of objective measurement but which make for greatness in a law school." In *McLaurin v. Oklahoma State Regents, supra,* the Court, in requiring that a Negro admitted to a white graduate school be treated like all other students, again resorted to intangible considerations: ". . . his ability to study, to engage in discussions and exchange views with other students, and, in general, to learn his profession." Such considerations apply with added force to children in grade and high schools. To separate them from others of similar age and qualifications solely because of their race generates a feeling of inferiority as to their status in the community that may affect their hearts and minds in a way unlikely ever to be undone. The effect of this separation on their educational opportunities was well stated by a finding in the Kansas case by a court which nevertheless felt compelled to rule against the Negro plaintiffs:

"Segregation of white and colored children in public schools has a detrimental effect upon the colored children. The impact is greater when it has the sanction of the law; for the policy of separating the races is usually interpreted as denoting the inferiority of the negro group. A sense of inferiority affects the motivation of a child to learn. Segregation with the sanction of law, therefore, has a tendency to [retard] the educational and mental development of negro children and to deprive them of some of the benefits they would receive in a racial[ly] integrated school system."[10]

Whatever may have been the extent of psychological knowledge at the time of *Plessy v. Ferguson,* this finding is amply supported by modern authority.[11] Any language in *Plessy v. Ferguson* contrary to this finding is rejected.

We conclude that in the field of public education the doctrine of "separate but equal" has no place. Separate educational facilities are inherently unequal. Therefore, we hold that the plaintiffs and others similarly situated for whom the actions have been brought are, by reason of the segregation complained of, deprived of the equal protection of the laws guaranteed by the Fourteenth Amendment. This disposition makes unnecessary any discussion whether such segregation also violates the Due Process Clause of the Fourteenth Amendment.[12]

Because these are class actions, because of the wide applicability of this decision, and because of the great variety of local conditions, the formulation of decrees in these cases presents problems of considerable complexity. On reargument, the consideration of appropriate relief was necessarily subordinated to the primary question—the constitutionality of segregation in public education. We have now announced that such segregation is a denial of the equal protection of the laws. In order that we may have the full assistance of the parties in formulating decrees, the cases will be restored to the docket, and the parties are requested to present further argument on Questions 4 and 5 previously propounded by the Court for the reargument this Term.[13] The Attorney General of the United States is again invited to participate. The Attorneys General of the states requiring or permitting segregation in public education will also be permitted to appear as *amici curiae* upon request to do so by September 15, 1954, and submission of briefs by October 1, 1954.[14]

It is so ordered.

Notes

1. In the Kansas case, *Brown v. Board of Education,* the plaintiffs are Negro children of elementary school age residing in Topeka. They brought this action in the United States District Court for the District of Kansas to enjoin enforcement of a Kansas statute which permits, but does not require, cities of more than 15,000 population to maintain separate school facilities for Negro and white students. Kan. Gen. Stat. §72–1724 (1949). Pursuant to that authority, the Topeka Board of Education elected to establish segregated elementary schools. Other public schools in the community, however, are operated on a nonsegregated basis.

In the South Carolina case, *Briggs v. Elliott,* the plaintiffs are Negro children of both elementary and high school age residing in Clarendon County. They brought this action in the United States District Court for the Eastern District of South Carolina to enjoin enforcement of provisions in the state constitution and statutory code which require the segregation of Negroes and whites in public schools. . . .

In the Virginia case, *Davis v. County School Board,* the plaintiffs are Negro children of high school age residing in Prince Edward County. They brought this action in the United States District Court for the Eastern District of Virginia to enjoin enforcement of provisions in the state constitution and statutory code which require the segregation of Negroes and whites in public schools. . . .

In the Delaware case, *Gebhart v. Belton,* the plaintiffs are Negro children of both elementary and high school age residing in New Castle county. They brought this action in the Delaware Court of Chancery to enjoin enforcement of provisions in the state constitution and statutory code which require the segregation of Negroes and whites in public schools. . . .

2. technical footnote deleted.

3. technical footnote deleted.

4. technical footnote deleted.

5. technical footnote deleted.

6. technical footnote deleted.

7. technical footnote deleted.

8. technical footnote deleted.

9. technical footnote deleted.

10. technical footnote deleted.

11. K. B. Clark, Effect of Prejudice and Discrimination on Personality Development (Midcentury White House Conference on Children and Youth, 1950); Witmer and Kotinsky, Personality in the Making (1952), c. VI; Deutscher and Chein, The Psychological Effects of Enforced Segregation: A Survey of Social Science Opinion, 26 *J. Psychol.* 259 (1948); Chein, What Are the Psychological Effects of Segregation Under Conditions of Equal Facilities?, 3 *Int. J. Opinion and Attitude Res.* 229 (1949); Brameld, Educational Costs, in Discrimination and National Welfare (MacIver, ed., 1949), 44–48; Frazier, The Negro in the United States (1949), 674–681. And see generally Myrdal, An American Dilemma (1944).

12. technical footnote deleted.

13. technical footnote deleted.

14. technical footnote deleted.

Supreme Court of the United States, 1954.

How the GOP Conquered the South

MICHAEL NELSON

The greatest change in American national politics of the past 60 years has been the transformation of the South from the most solidly Democratic to the most solidly Republican region of the country. In the 1930s and 1940s, Democrats enjoyed a strong advantage in presidential elections because they could count on winning the 127 electoral votes cast by the 11 states of the old Confederacy. Congress was almost always Democratic because Democrats owned all 22 Southern seats in the Senate and all but a couple of the South's 105 seats in the House of Representatives. In other words, the Democrats began every election nearly halfway to the finish line.

Consider how much has changed. In 2004 John F. Kerry ran up a 252–133 electoral-vote lead over George W. Bush outside the South but lost the election because the South went 153–0 for Bush. In the current Congress, although Democrats from non-Southern states outnumber Republican non-Southerners by 41–37 in the Senate and 154–150 in the House, the GOP has converted its Southern majorities—82–49 in the House and 18–4 in the Senate—into control of both chambers. The South not only switched parties from the 1940s to 2000, but it also became, because of rapid population growth, a bigger political prize.

The 2004 election was no fluke. The GOP has won seven of the last 10 presidential elections (interestingly, the three Democratic victories belonged to Southerners, Jimmy Carter of Georgia in 1976 and Bill Clinton of Arkansas in 1992 and 1996), and it has controlled both houses of Congress since 1994, the longest period of Republican legislative dominance since the 1920s. John Roberts's confirmation as chief justice of the United States is just the latest example of how control of the presidency and the Senate has also enabled the Republicans to populate the third branch of government, the judiciary. Since 1968 Republican presidents have made 10 of 12 Supreme Court appointments, along with 65 percent of all federal appeals-court appointments and 62 percent of all district-court appointments.

The new Republican majority did not come about through a sudden and dramatic realigning election like the ones in 1860 and 1932. Instead, there has been what Karl Rove calls a "rolling" (or, to use a preferred term of political scientists, a "secular") realignment in which the GOP has gradually become home to the great majority of Southern white voters of all social and economic classes.

The tale of how the South's secular Republican realignment came about can be understood in large part through three recent books, each of them by or about a major southern GOP leader: *Strom: The Complicated Personal and Political Life of Strom Thurmond*, by Jack Bass and Marilyn W. Thompson; *Here's Where I Stand: A Memoir*, by Jesse Helms; and *Herding Cats: A Life in Politics*, by Trent Lott. The well-researched Thurmond biography is illuminating because of—and Helms's and Lott's self-serving memoirs despite—what the authors have to say.

The story of the South's Republican transformation begins in 1948, even though the national Democratic majority that Franklin D. Roosevelt built in the 1930s was then in the midst of winning its fifth consecutive presidential election, and the Republicans weren't competitive in a single Southern state. FDR's New Deal coalition was a complex assemblage, constituted differently in different parts of the country. In the North, it rested on the support of groups that Roosevelt himself had helped to attract into the Democratic fold: blue-collar workers, Roman Catholic and Jewish voters, ideological liberals, and African-Americans.

The Southern part of the New Deal coalition—essentially, every white voter in a region where, in most counties, only whites could vote—was one that Roosevelt inherited. The South was solidly Democratic because of the antipathy Southern whites had developed during Reconstruction toward the occupying Republicans and their agenda of civil rights for the newly freed slaves. Thurmond, Helms, and Lott were heirs to this tradition. Each of them was a politically active Democrat before he became a Republican.

Despite the Democrats' majority status, a fault line ran through their coalition: The interests of integrationist blacks and segregationist Southern whites were clearly not harmonious. As long as African-Americans did not press a civil-rights agenda on the federal government, this fault line remained unexposed and, therefore, politically insignificant. But in the aftermath of World War II, returning black veterans who had fought against racism and tyranny abroad increasingly demanded federal protection for their civil rights at home. Northern liberals and labor-union leaders supported those demands.

Forced to choose between the Northern and Southern wings of his party, President Harry S. Truman reluctantly accepted a strong civil-rights plank in the 1948 Democratic platform. He won the election, but only at the price of a crack appearing in the solidly Democratic South. From 1932 to 1944, FDR had carried every Southern state in all four elections. In 1948, however, Georgia stayed with Truman, but the other four Deep South states—Alabama, Louisiana, Mississippi, and South Carolina—cast their electoral votes for Democratic Gov. Strom Thurmond of South Carolina, the nominee of the rebellious Southern Democrats who had walked out of their party's pro-civil-rights convention and formed the States' Rights Party, or Dixiecrats.

Curiously, Thurmond had risen through the ranks of South Carolina politics as a strong advocate for improving the public schools that served both races, so much so that Bass and Thompson title their chapter on his governorship "Progressive Outlook, Progressive Program, Progressive Leadership." As a public-school teacher and, at age 26, the winner of an election that made him the youngest county superintendent of education in the state, Thurmond crusaded for adult literacy, especially among African-Americans. But the educational improvements Thurmond wanted to make were to schools that he insisted remain segregated. Truman's 1948 civil-rights program not only took Thurmond by surprise—he had actually endorsed Truman for re-election the year before—but also spurred him to run against the president.

In 1954, after the Supreme Court ruled segregated public schools unconstitutional in *Brown v. Board of Education,* Thurmond ran a write-in campaign for senator. He won, the only write-in candidate in the history of Congress ever to do so, and soon established himself as the South's angriest face of opposition to civil rights. "Listen to ol' Strom," said South Carolina's other senator, the Democrat Olin Johnston, as Thurmond waged a 24 hour and 18 minute filibuster against the rather weak 1957 Civil Rights Act. "He really believes all that shit."

All of the Deep South states that Thurmond carried returned to the Democratic fold in the 1952 and 1956 presidential elections, when the party muted its commitment to civil rights for the sake of unity. But by then a new crack had appeared in the Democratic South, this one along economic lines. The Republican candidate in both elections, Dwight D. Eisenhower, did well in the six states of the Peripheral South—Arkansas, Florida, North Carolina, Tennessee, Texas, and Virginia—where racial issues mattered somewhat less and, as metropolitan areas began to grow rapidly after World War II, the GOP's pro-business policies mattered more. Eisenhower carried all of the Peripheral South states except Arkansas and North Carolina both times he ran.

The Republican breakthroughs in the South proved to be enduring. In 1960 the GOP presidential candidate, Richard M. Nixon, lost the election but carried half of the Peripheral South. Four years later Sen. Barry Goldwater of Arizona, a prominent opponent of the Civil Rights Act of 1964, won all five Deep South states, including, with Thurmond's

strong support, South Carolina. (The only other state Goldwater carried in losing overwhelmingly to President Lyndon B. Johnson was Arizona.) Thurmond not only campaigned for Goldwater but became a Republican, leading an exodus into the GOP that many of his fellow white Southerners joined. Starting with Goldwater in 1964, the Republican nominee has outpolled his Democratic opponent among Southern white voters in every presidential election.

The 1968 election took place in a changed political environment. Because of the 1964 Civil Rights Act and the Voting Rights Act of 1965, both championed by President Johnson, African-Americans in the South were newly enfranchised and enjoyed federal protection against many forms of racial discrimination. In reaction, a strong Southern Democratic opponent of civil rights, Alabama governor George C. Wallace, bid for the support of Southern whites in hopes of denying both major party candidates a majority of electoral votes and throwing the election into the House of Representatives. Polls showed him leading Nixon, the GOP nominee, and Democratic Vice President Hubert H. Humphrey in every Southern state. Thurmond, however, stood solidly by Nixon, touring the South to argue that "a vote for Wallace is a vote for Humphrey." "Strom killed us," Bass and Thompson quote Wallace's campaign manager, Tom Turnipseed, as saying. Although Wallace carried most of the Deep South, Nixon carried South Carolina and nearly all of the Peripheral South, enough to win the election.

During his first term as president, Nixon labored to bring Wallace's supporters into his 1972 re-election coalition. His efforts to use issues such as law and order and opposition to school busing to graft white support from all parts of the South onto the traditional Midwestern Republican base were rewarded on election day. Nixon swept the South, carrying every state in the region by majorities ranging from 65 percent to 78 percent.

The success of Republican presidential candidates in the South began to be echoed in other Southern elections. The infusion of millions of loyally Democratic African-American voters into the Southern electorate in the late 1960s made the party more liberal and drove many conservative whites into the GOP in Congressional and state as well as presidential elections. The number of Republican senators in the 22-member Southern delegation rose from 0 as recently as 1960 to 3 in 1966, 7 in 1972, 11 in 1982, 13 in 1994, and 18 in 2004. Similar gains occurred in Southern elections to the House, where the Republican ranks grew from 7 percent of Southern members in 1960 to 22 percent in 1966, 29 percent in 1982, 51 percent in 1994, and 63 percent in 2004. In elections to state office, the number of Republican governors increased from 0 to 7 of 11 from 1960 to 2004. Republicans did not control a single Southern state legislative house as recently as the late 1960s; they now control half of them.

Two of the Southern Republicans who rode Nixon's 1972 coattails into Congress were Helms, the first Republican elected to the Senate from North Carolina since Reconstruction, and Lott, the first post-Reconstruction Republican from Mississippi to win a seat in the House. Like Thurmond, Helms and Lott were active Democrats before they migrated into the Republican Party—indeed, each had worked in Washington for one of his state's conservative Democratic legislators. "I'm tired of the Muskies and the Kennedys and the Humphreys and the whole lot," Lott said when he publicly announced his conversion.

Once in the Republican fold, each in his way helped to solidify the GOP's hold on Southern white voters. The rough-edged, goggle-eyed Helms, who quickly became the Senate's leading conservative gadfly on issues like defunding the National Endowment for the Arts, resisting the creation of the Martin Luther King holiday, and keeping the Panama Canal in U.S. hands, led the Republican campaign to win rural and blue-collar support based on these and other cultural and religious appeals. Lott, the blow-dried (he has a chapter in Herding Cats called "Hair: An Issue for Our Time") veteran of fraternity politics at Ole Miss, used his growing influence as House minority whip and Senate majority leader to promote conservative economic policies that reinforced Republican loyalties among the South's business and professional classes.

Helms based his 1972 Senate candidacy less on his erratic career as a newspaper and radio reporter in Raleigh, staff member for conservative Democratic Sen. Willis Smith, executive director of the North Carolina Bankers Association, and news director of WRAL-TV in Raleigh than on the enemies he had attacked during 12 years of nightly five-minute editorials that aired on WRAL and, through syndication, on many of the state's radio stations. The University of North Carolina was one of Helms's favorite editorial targets. As far as he was concerned, UNC was an arrogant bastion of Northern radicalism on issues like civil rights and communism. "The word from Chapel Hill," he said in one broadcast, "is: Send money and shut up. That is the measure of 'academic freedom' as it is practiced there." Another recurring theme of Helms's editorials was "the harm being done to relations among neighbors of different races by the militant intrusion of outsiders."

As a first-term senator, Helms harnessed his ambitions to former governor of California Ronald Reagan's high-risk challenge to President Gerald R. Ford for the 1976 Republican presidential nomination. The gamble paid off. Reagan's candidacy was floundering because, as Helms rightly points out in Here's Where I Stand, the conservative candidate was listening to "self-declared experts" advising him to "tone down his conservatism and make himself appear more 'mainstream.'" After losing the first five primaries to Ford, Reagan won North Carolina by following Helms's advice to fan the flames of populist resentment engendered by the president's proposal to deed the Panama Canal to Panama. Reagan's primary victory enabled him to carry the fight for the nomination to the convention and, although he narrowly lost, to move to the front of the Republican pack in 1980.

Race as a defining element of Southern politics won't stay under the Republican rug any more than it did when the South was solidly Democratic.

Helms also came to the rescue of Southern Republicanism after the setback of Carter's victory over Ford in the general election. Carter carried 10 Southern states, partly on the basis of regional pride and partly because, as a born-again Southern Baptist, he won the support of most evangelical Christian voters. Forced to the left as president by the liberal Democrats who dominated Congress, however, Carter alienated his home region and many of his coreligionists. Helms stepped forward to help rouse white evangelicals, who had not been especially active in politics during most of the 20th century, to organize in opposition when the Carter administration proposed to withdraw tax-exempt status from the mostly white Christian schools to which many of them sent their children.

Reagan capitalized on that development, as well as on a stagnant economy and a decline in American power abroad, when he challenged Carter's bid for re-election in 1980. His strong rhetoric opposing abortion and upholding traditional values appealed to white Southern Christians across class lines. Helms again spurred him on. In a chapter called "Hot-Button Issues," Helms lays bare the political issues that mattered most to him, then and since: the liberal media ("men and women who certainly have a smug contempt for American ideals and principles"), the NEA (financing "decadent people" with "a militant disdain for the moral and religious sensibilities of the majority of the American people"), school prayer ("in its place has been enshrined a sort of permissiveness in which the drug culture has flourished, as have pornography, crime, and fornication"), and abortion (a "holocaust, by another name").

Helms's most famous election came in 1990, when he was challenged by the African-American mayor of Charlotte, Harvey Gantt. Trailing in the polls, Helms ran a television ad that showed a white hand crumpling a rejection letter from an employer. "You needed that job and you were the best qualified," the announcer intoned. "But they had to give it to a minority because of a racial quota. Is that really fair? Harvey Gantt says it is." In Here's Where I Stand, Helms denies that his campaign was "about Mr. Gantt being black; it was always and only about him being a liberal." But Helms's own words belie his claim. One of the first things he tells us about Gantt is that he "had taken advantage of a minority preference to gain an available television license" in Charlotte. As a measure of just how successful Helms's long-term political strategy was, however, he won stronger support from the state's poorest and least-educated white voters than from any other group.

L ike Helms, Lott grew up in a blue-collar family and rode a strong high-school record to college and a professional career. Interestingly, Lott devotes not a single word to academics in *Herding Cats's* chapter on "The Legacy of Ole Miss." Instead, he dwells lovingly on membership in Sigma Nu and, through it, as bass-baritone in a vocal quartet he formed and as head cheerleader at Ole Miss football games. Those positions helped wire him into the campus's leadership network—no small thing at a school that, Lott notes, has traditionally produced all of Mississippi's governors and other statewide officials.

Lott stayed at Ole Miss for law school, joined Pascagoula's leading firm, and, after spending four years as Democratic Congressman William Colmer's administrative assistant, ran as a Republican when Colmer retired in 1972. He won, with Colmer's support, and concentrated his efforts in the House on "fiscal responsibility and a strong national defense." As his party's whip from 1981 to 1988, Lott continued to stress economic issues. His major achievement was to woo enough conservative Democratic support in the Democratically controlled House to pass Reagan's massive 1981 tax cuts and domestic spending reductions. One favorite tactic was to look up "the names of [their] key contributors and supporters" and rouse those mostly wealthy conservatives to put pressure on their Democratic representatives in Washington.

Truman won the 1948 election, but only at the price of a crack appearing in the solidly Democratic South.

Elected to the Senate in 1988 against a Democrat who tried to brand him (in Lott's phrase) "as an over-dressed elitist—a country-club Republican," Lott networked his new colleagues with Sigma Nu aplomb, forging a brother-pledge style of coalition that included young GOP conservatives like Phil Gramm of Texas and John Ashcroft of Missouri with "some of the 'old bulls,' like Jesse Helms [and] Strom Thurmond." In 1994 they chose him as Senate GOP whip; two years later, when the GOP's Senate leader, Bob Dole, resigned to run for president, Lott was easily elected to take his place.

Although Lott was insider to Helms's outsider and emphasized mainstream economic conservatism rather than Helms-style cultural conservatism, both men were strong supporters of President Bush. (Helms awards Bush his ultimate accolade: "I know Ronald Reagan would be proud of this man.") The president's tax cuts and strongly pro-business tax and regulatory policies gladdened Lott's heart, as well as those of the South's white business and professional classes. To Helms's delight and that of working-class and rural white Southerners, Bush also identified himself and his party as the chief defenders of traditional social values, both by what he upheld (religious faith, flag-waving patriotism, marriage between a man and a woman, restrictions on abortion) and what he opposed (gay marriage, sexual permissiveness, gun control).

As the Democratic pollster Stanley Greenberg points out, Republicans "don't say, 'Vote for us because we're making progress.' They say, 'Vote for our worldview.'" Therein lies a source of enduring Republican strength in the South and, increasingly, in the other red states. Voters who support a party because they share its values are much less likely to abandon it than voters whose support is based on how well things are going in the economy or the world.

Republicans pride themselves on the progress they have made in the South by stressing conservative economic policies and Christian values. Appeals based on race, they like to think, are a thing of the past. After all, no one figured out more quickly than Thurmond what it meant in the late 1960s when Southern blacks became enfranchised: "It means you can't win any longer just by cussin' the niggers," Bass and Thompson quote him telling an aide. Thurmond hired the first African-American staff member of any Southern senator, became a champion in Washington of his state's traditionally black colleges, and voted for the King holiday and the Voting Rights Act of 1982. Even Helms makes much in his memoirs of his recent crusade to end AIDS in Africa, an effort in which he and U2's Bono have been famous if unlikely bedfellows.

But race as a defining element of Southern politics won't stay under the Republican rug any more than it did when the South was solidly Democratic. The first and last chapters of Lott's book deal with the incident for which he always will be most remembered, his remarks at Strom Thurmond's 100th birthday party on December 5, 2002. Harking back to the 1948 election, in which Thurmond made his national debut as the candidate of the segregationist Dixiecrats, Lott said, "Mississippians voted for him. And if the rest of the country had followed our lead, we wouldn't have had all these problems over the years either."

In *Herding Cats,* Lott explains his remark in terms of personal compassion (Thurmond "slipped easily into bouts of depression. I often rushed over to lighten his mood") and historical ignorance ("I was only 7 when Strom was barnstorming the South"). Besides, Lott writes, "he was already 87 years old when I came to the Senate in 1989, and by then he was fully committed to the minorities in his native South Carolina." Few others had any trouble remembering Thurmond's crusading segregationist past, and some pointed out that Lott had lavished nearly identical praise on Thurmond's 1948 candidacy in a speech he gave in 1980, long before Thurmond needed any special cheering up.

In the firestorm that followed Lott's thoughtless remarks, the story of Thurmond's racist past was retold in the present, Lott's friend Bush cut him loose, and by the end of the month, Lott had been replaced as Senate majority leader by Bill Frist. As far as Lott is concerned, the whole thing was personal—the president "blasted me . . . in a tone that was booming and nasty," and Frist engaged in "a personal betrayal." Lott could not very well claim to be a victim of prejudice against Southerners, of course—Bush is a Texan and Frist a Tennessean.

"In its grand outlines," wrote the political scientist V.O. Key in his classic 1949 book *Southern Politics in State and Nation,* "the politics of the South revolves around the position of the Negro." To be sure, African-Americans now can vote in the South, and many have been elected to local office, especially in the region's increasingly black cities. But one thing hasn't changed: The South's dominant political party, Democratic in Key's time, Republican now, is essentially all white.

MICHAEL NELSON is a professor of political science at Rhodes College. His book *The Politics of Gambling: State Policy Innovation in the American South,* written with John Lyman Mason, is scheduled to be published by Louisiana State University Press in 2007.

'Bakke' Set a New Path to Diversity for Colleges

30 years after the ruling, academe still grapples with race in admissions.

PETER SCHMIDT

Thirty years ago, Justice Lewis F. Powell Jr. sent the nation's selective colleges down a path where few had ventured before.

In the U.S. Supreme Court's landmark ruling in *Regents of the University of California v. Bakke,* he wrote that colleges were legally justified in giving some modest consideration to their applicants' race, so long as they were motivated by a desire to attain the educational benefits of diversity.

Before *Bakke,* selective colleges regarded race-conscious admissions policies mainly as a way to remedy past societal discrimination against black, Hispanic, and Native American applicants. The *Bakke* ruling declared that justification off limits, replacing a rationale grounded in history with one grounded in educational theory.

The approaching 30th anniversary of that Supreme Court decision, announced on June 23, 1978, finds many in higher education wondering where Justice Powell's guidance has gotten them—and what, exactly, lies ahead.

His rationale for race-conscious policies may have ensured their long-term survival in the courts, by linking them to a common educational concern that is unlikely to go away anytime soon. But the decision also limited the reach of such policies, forcing colleges to consider race only as a "plus factor." They had to abandon quests for enrollments that reflected society's racial composition in favor of having enough minority students to ensure a variety of perspectives.

The Supreme Court upheld Justice Powell's reasoning in 2003, in a case involving a challenge to the race-conscious admissions policies of the University of Michigan's law school. But the argument that such policies have educational benefits has not protected them from political challenges. Michigan's residents subsequently voted to ban the use of affirmative action by public colleges and other state and local agencies. Similar measures were adopted by California and Washington State in the 1990s and are seen as likely to pass in Arizona, Colorado, and Nebraska if critics of affirmative action succeed in getting them on the ballot this fall.

Some advocates for minority students express frustration that the educational-diversity rationale has led colleges to seek out all different types of students rather than focusing on trying to increase their black, Hispanic, and Native American enrollments. At the end of the day, the advocates argue, pursuing diversity for educational purposes is not the same thing as pursuing racial equality and social justice—and is not nearly enough.

"There are some of us who still believe there is a strong remedial justification for affirmative action," says William L. Taylor, chairman of the Citizens' Commission on Civil Rights, a Washington-based group that monitors the federal government's compliance with civil-rights laws. Mr. Taylor, a leading civil-rights lawyer since 1954, says he holds the view that Justice Harry A. Blackmun expressed in a dissenting opinion in *Bakke,* that "in order to get beyond racism, we must first take account of race."

The Missing Motive

In *Bakke,* the court affirmed a lower court's decision that Allan P. Bakke had to be admitted to a University of California medical school because it had discriminated against him because he was white.

But the path that Justice Powell chose for colleges in his *Bakke* opinion was so new that the Supreme Court's eight other justices had not seen it at all. They were evenly divided over the only two options they thought they had: Letting colleges continue to use affirmative action to remedy societal discrimination, or telling colleges that they could not use such preferences at all.

Certainly the court and the nation's colleges had considered the idea that diversity might have educational benefits. In the Supreme Court's pivotal 1950 *Sweatt v. Painter ruling,* calling for the desegregation of the University of Texas law school, the majority opinion talked of "the interplay of ideas and the exchange of views" found in classrooms with students from different backgrounds.

But when selective colleges adopted race-conscious admissions policies in the late 1960s, their leaders said little about educational benefits. Instead they argued that such policies were needed for two other reasons: to remedy societal discrimination and to send a clear signal—during a time of devastating urban riots—that the "establishment" many black Americans were fighting was in fact open to them.

In the *Bakke* case, the University of California said little about the educational benefits of diversity in opposing the lawsuit that Mr. Bakke had filed after twice being rejected by the medical school on its Davis campus. Its lawyers argued that such policies provided minority students with educational opportunities that societal discrimination might otherwise deny them.

The ruling that was being appealed by the university—a California Supreme Court decision striking down the medical school's admissions policy—held that the educational benefits of diversity were irrelevant.

The argument that campus diversity has educational benefits was introduced into the case through friend-of-the-court briefs.

Columbia, Harvard, and Stanford Universities and the University of Pennsylvania joined in arguing that diversity "makes the university a better learning environment," and that many faculty members reported "that the insights provided by the participation of minority students enrich the curriculum, broaden the teachers' scholarly interests, and protect them from insensitivity to minority perspectives."

Early Obstacles

The educational-diversity rationale offered in *Bakke* may have been untried, but the social-justice rationale already was showing signs of serious wear.

Within just a few years of adopting race-conscious admissions, selective colleges began scaling back their efforts to enroll black students from poor urban settings, concluding that many were too academically unprepared.

At the same time, many began expanding the scope of their affirmative-action programs to include Native Americans as well as Hispanic people—some of whom were Cuban immigrants or otherwise came from backgrounds that made it difficult for them to argue their families had historically experienced oppression on U.S. soil.

By the mid-70s, the fledgling neoconservative movement had developed a critique of race-conscious admissions steeped in the civil-rights movement's own rhetoric, stressing individual rights and colorblindness.

The legal threats to race-conscious policies were real enough by 1977 to prompt the Carnegie Council on Policy Studies in Higher Education to urge colleges to consider minority students' experiences, rather than simply their race or heritage, in the admissions process, because not all "have special characteristics that we believe warrant consideration."

One thing selective colleges showed little interest in doing was acknowledging any past discrimination on their own part. The Davis medical school was exceptional in how divorced it was from American higher education's history of discrimination. The school opened in 1966 and reserved seats for minority applicants almost from the start. Minority groups had urged the University of California not to appeal the case to the Supreme Court, because they thought the policy would be hard to justify.

When the Supreme Court finally ruled in the *Bakke* case, its nine members were so divided they issued six different opinions, with Justice Powell in the tie-breaker role. He sided with the four justices who said the university's use of quotas amounted to illegal discrimination. And he joined the same four in rejecting the use of social policies to remedy societal discrimination, saying the government should not be in the business of trying to sort out which segments of society owed what to whom.

Justice Powell was reluctant, however, to cause upheaval in higher education, and therefore he refused to go along with the four conservatives in holding that colleges should give up all consideration of applicants' race for purposes other than court-ordered desegregation. Unwilling to embrace the liberal faction's views on the need to remedy societal discrimination, he instead put forward an educational rationale for considering race as a "plus factor" in admissions. His opinion spoke approvingly of the policy that Harvard described in its friend-of-the-court brief.

Birth of a Buzzword

Because no other justices signed on to Justice Powell's opinion stating an educational rationale for race-conscious admissions, legal scholars and federal judges would later argue that his view on the matter did not represent the holding of the court. That debate was largely laid to rest in 2003, however, when a five-member Supreme Court majority embraced Justice Powell's thinking in upholding the University of Michigan law school's admissions policies in *Grutter v. Bollinger.*

Certainly the confusion over how to interpret the *Bakke* decision did not deter higher education—or, for that matter, the business sector and much of the rest of society—from adopting the term "diversity" as both a buzzword and goal. Academics used it in calling for the college curriculum to accommodate movements such as Afrocentrism, feminism, and multiculturalism. Businesses went from talking about the need to have more black and Hispanic employees to saying they needed to employ a wide spectrum of people to reflect the diversity of society and position themselves to compete globally.

John A. Payton, president of the NAACP Legal Defense and Educational Fund, credits the *Bakke* decision with creating an environment in which colleges proudly list their minority enrollments on their Web sites as a measure of their quality. "They actually compete on that basis," he says. "And that has resulted in higher education being pretty diverse, and that has been to the benefit of higher education and the whole country."

So broad was the imprint left by Justice Powell's reasoning in *Bakke* that Justice John Paul Stevens would later remark, in a speech delivered three months after the *Grutter* decision, that he had argued to his fellow justices that rejecting the diversity rationale would cause a "sea change" in American society.

Truth be told, however, many college administrators still describe race- and ethnicity-conscious admissions policies as tools for improving black and Hispanic access to their institutions.

Relatively few colleges have done any research showing that their policies produce favorable educational outcomes.

Arthur L. Coleman, a veteran higher-education lawyer now at Education-Counsel, a for-profit law and policy center, says many people "still don't get" that "we are looking at issues of diversity in a fundamentally educationally oriented way." In advising colleges, he says, he does not use the term "affirmative action," and he warns that focusing on enrollment numbers or talking about promoting social justice is "at core a mistake."

Roger B. Clegg, president of the Center for Equal Opportunity and a leading opponent of race-conscious admissions policies, says he hears talk of remedying past discrimination pop up in the statements of judges and lawyers who know that such justifications fall outside *Bakke*.

He cites Justice Sandra Day O'Connor's statement in the Supreme Court's *Grutter* decision that colleges will not need race-conscious admissions policies in 25 years, or the Democratic presidential candidate Barack Obama's belief that this daughters should not be given extra consideration in admissions because of the privileges they had growing up.

Better Law than Politics?

Some higher-education leaders believe that the Supreme Court's *Grutter* decision broadened the legal rationale for race-conscious admissions. In writing for the five-member *Grutter* majority, Justice O'Connor said colleges must ensure that the path to positions of leadership is "visibly open to talented and qualified individuals of every race and ethnicity."

William G. Bowen, a former president of Princeton University and co-author of several books on with college admissions, says Justice O'Connor's opinion made clear that the government's interest in allowing such policies "is not just about better learning environments on campuses."

Mr. Coleman says he believes the *Grutter* majority established a "strong foundation for arguing" such a rationale, even though it is unclear whether the courts will go along. But Sheldon E. Steinbach, a lawyer at the Dow Lohnes law firm, in Washington, and a former general counsel at the American Council on Education, says a college that expands its race-conscious admissions policies on the basis of such an interpretation of the law places itself at "more than reasonable" legal risk.

Also open to debate is the question of whether Justice Powell's rationale for race-conscious admissions policies has left them more, or less, vulnerable to political challenge.

Some leading opponents of affirmative-action preferences argue that the public is unswayed by assertions that such policies have educational benefits. "People are losing jobs, and their kids are not getting into colleges, and they want to know why," says Terence J. Pell, president of the Center for Individual Rights, a Washington-based group that has provided legal assistance to plaintiffs in several major challenges to race-conscious admissions. "Someone needs to explain this with a political rationale and not a legal rationale that barely makes sense in the political sphere."

But Mr. Payton, of the NAACP Legal Defense and Educational Fund, says the political campaigns against such policies have succeeded mainly by convincing large numbers of people—wrongly, he believes—that there is no longer any need to remedy past racial discrimination.

Mr. Coleman says having an educational rationale for such policies has helped rally higher education and business leaders around them, and has enabled defenders of such policies to argue that "it is not about us versus them. It is about benefits to all students."

Shaare Tefila Congregation v. Cobb and *Saint Francis College v. Al-Khazraji*

Shaare Tefila Congregation v. Cobb

Cite as 107 S.Ct. 2019 (1987).

Justice White delivered the opinion of the Court.

On November 2, 1982, the outside walls of the synagogue of the Shaare Tefila Congregation in Silver Spring, Maryland, were sprayed with red and black paint and with large anti-Semitic slogans, phrases and symbols. A few months later, the Congregation and Federal District Court, alleging that defendants' desecration of the synagogue had violated 42 U.S.C. §§ 1981, 1982, 1985(3) and the Maryland common law of trespass, nuisance, and intentional infliction of emotional distress. On defendants' motion under Fed. Rule Civ.Proc. 12(b)(1) and (6), the District Court dismissed all the claims. The Court of Appeals affirmed in all respects. 785 F.2d 523 (CA4 1986). Petitioners petitioned for writ of certiorari. We granted the petition, 479 U.S. _____, 107 S.Ct. 62, 93 L.Ed.2d 21 (1986), and we now reverse the judgment of the Court of Appeals.

[1] Section 1982 guarantees all citizens of the United States, "the same right . . . as is enjoyed by white citizens . . . to inherit, purchase, lease, sell, hold, and convey real and personal property." The section forbids both official and private racially discriminatory interference with property rights, *Jones v. Alfred H. Mayer Co.,* 392 U.S. 409, 88 S.Ct. 2186, 20 L.Ed.2d 1189 (1968). Petitioners' allegation was that they were deprived of the right to hold property in violation of § 1982 because the defendants were motivated by racial prejudice. They unsuccessfully argued in the District Court and Court of Appeals that Jews are not a racially distinct group, but that defendants' conduct is actionable because they viewed Jews as racially distinct and were motivated by racial prejudice. The Court of Appeals held that § 1982 was not "intended to apply to situations in which a plaintiff is not a member of a racially distinct group but is merely *perceived* to be so by defendants." 785 F.2d, at 526 (emphasis in original). The Court of Appeals believed that "[b]ecause discrimination against Jews is not racial discrimination," *id.,* at 527, the District Court was correct in dismissing the § 1982 claim.

[2] We agree with the Court of Appeals that a charge of racial discrimination within the meaning of § 1982 cannot be made out by alleging only that the defendants were motivated by racial animus; it is necessary as well to allege that defendants' animus was directed towards the kind of group that Congress intended to protect when it passed the statute. To hold otherwise would unacceptably extend the reach of the statute.

[3–5] We agree with petitioners, however, that the Court of Appeals erred in holding that Jews cannot state a § 1982 claim against other white defendants. That view rested on the notion that because Jews today are not thought to be members of a separate race, they cannot make out a claim of racial discrimination within the meaning of § 1982. That construction of the section we have today rejected in *Saint Francis College v. Al-Khazraji,* _____ U.S., at _____, 107 S.Ct., at _____. Our opinion in that case observed that definitions of race when § 1982 was passed were not the same as they are today and concluded that the section was "intended to protect from discrimination identifiable classes of persons who are subjected to intentional discrimination solely because of their ancestry or ethnic characteristics." At _____, 107 S.Ct., at 2028. As *St. Francis* makes clear, the question before us is not whether Jews are considered to be a separate race by today's standards, but whether, at the time § 1982 was adopted, Jews constituted a group of people that Congress intended to protect. It is evident from the legislative history of the section reviewed in *Saint Francis College,* a review that we need not repeat here, that Jews and Arabs were among the peoples then considered to be distinct races and hence within the protection of the statute. Jews are not foreclosed from stating a cause of action against other members of what today is considered to be part of the Caucasian race.

The judgment of the Court of Appeals is therefore reversed and the case is remanded for further proceedings consistent with this opinion.

Saint Francis College v. Al-khazraji

Cite as 107 S.Ct. 2022 (1987).

Justice White delivered the opinion of the Court.

Respondent, a citizen of the United States born in Iraq, was an associate professor at St. Francis College, one of the petitioners here. In January 1978, he applied for tenure; the Board of Trustees denied his request on February 23, 1978. He accepted a 1-year, nonrenewable contract and sought administrative reconsideration of the tenure decision, which was denied on February 6, 1979. He worked his last day at the college on May 26, 1979. In June 1979, he filed complaints with the Pennsylvania Human Relations Commission and the Equal Employment Opportunities Commission. The State agency dismissed his claim and the EEOC issued a right to sue letter on August 6, 1980.

On October 30, 1980, respondent filed a *pro se* complaint in the District Court alleging a violation of Title VII of the Civil Rights Act of 1964 and claiming discrimination based on national origin, religion, and/or race. Amended complaints were filed, adding claims under 42 U.S.C. § § 1981, 1983, 1985(3), 1986, and state law. The District Court dismissed the 1986, 1985(3) and Title VII claims as untimely but held that the § § 1981 and 1983 claims were not barred by the Pennsylvania 6-year statute of limitations. The court at that time also ruled that because the complaint alleged denial of tenure because respondent was of the Arabian race, an action under § 1981 could be maintained. Defendants' motion for summary judgment came up before a different judge, who construed the pleadings as asserting only discrimination on the basis of national origin and religion, which § 1981 did not cover. Even if racial discrimination was deemed to have been alleged, the District Court ruled that § 1981 does not reach claims of discrimination based on Arabian ancestry.[1]

The Court of Appeals rejected petitioners' claim that the § 1981 claim had not been timely filed. Under the Court of Appeals' holding in *Goodman v. Lukens Steel Co.,* 777 F.2d 113 (CA 2 1985), that the Pennsylvania 2-year statute of limitations governed § 1981 cases, respondent's suit would have been barred. The Court of Appeals, however, relying on *Chevron Oil Co. v. Huson,* 404 U.S. 97, 92 S.Ct. 349, 30 L.Ed.2d 296 (1971), held that *Goodman* should not be retroactively applied and that this suit was timely under its pre-*Goodman* cases which had borrowed the State's 6-year statute.

Reaching the merits, the Court of Appeals held that respondent had alleged discrimination based on race and that although under current racial classifications Arabs are Caucasians, respondent could maintain his § 1981 claim.[2] Congress, when it passed what is now § 1981, had not limited its protections to those who today would be considered members of a race different from the race of the defendant. Rather, the legislative history of the section indicated that Congress intended to forbid "at the least, membership in a group that is ethnically and physiognomically distinctive." 784 F.2d 505, 517 (CA 3 1986). Section 1981, "at a minimum," reaches "discrimination directed against an individual because he or she is genetically part of an ethnically and physiognomically distinctive sub-grouping of *homo sapiens.*" *Ibid.* Because respondent had not had full discovery and the record was not sufficient to determine whether he had been subjected to the sort of prejudice § 1981 would redress, respondent was to be given the opportunity to prove his case.[3]

We granted certiorari. 479 U.S. _____, 107 S.Ct. 62, 93 L.Ed.2d 21 (1986), limited to the statute of limitations issue and the question whether a person of Arabian ancestry was protected from racial discrimination under § 1981, and now affirm the judgment of the Court of Appeals.

I

[1] We agree with the Court of Appeals that respondent's claim was not time barred. *Wilson v. Garcia,* 471 U.S. 261, 105 S.Ct. 1938, 85 L.Ed.2d 254 (1985), required that in selecting the applicable state statute of limitations in § 1983 cases, the lower federal courts should choose the state statute applicable to other personal injury torts. Thereafter, the Third Circuit in *Goodman* held that *Wilson* applies to § 1981 cases as well and that the Pennsylvania 2-year statute should apply. The Court of Appeals in this case, however, held that when respondent filed his suit, which was prior to *Wilson v. Garcia,* it was clearly established in the Third Circuit that a § 1981 plaintiff had six years to bring an action and that *Goodman* should not be applied retroactively to bar respondent's suit.

Insofar as what the prevailing law was in the Third Circuit, we have no reason to disagree with the Court of Appeals. Under controlling precedent in that Circuit, respondent had six years to file his suit, and it was filed well within that time. See 784 F.2d, at 512–513. We also assume but do not decide that *Wilson v. Garcia* controls the selection of the applicable state statute of limitations in § 1981 cases. The Court of Appeals, however, correctly held that its decision in *Goodman* should not be retroactively applied to bar respondent's action in this case. The usual rule is that federal cases should be decided in accordance with the law existing at the time of decision. *Gulf Offshore Co. v. Mobil Oil Corp.,* 453 U.S. 473, 486, n. 16, 101 S.Ct. 2870, 2879, n. 16, 69 L.Ed.2d 784 (1981); *Thorpe v. Durham Housing Authority,* 393 U.S. 268, 281, 89 S.Ct. 518, 526, 21 L.Ed.2d 474 (1969); *United States v. Schooner Peggy,* 1 Cranch 103, 110, 2 L.Ed. 49 (1801). But *Chevron Oil Co. v. Huson, supra,* counsels against retroactive application of statute of limitations decision in certain circumstances. There, the Court held that its decision specifying the applicable state statute of limitations should be applied only prospectively because it overruled clearly established circuit precedent on which the complaining party was entitled to rely, because retroactive application would be inconsistent with the purpose of the underlying substantive statute, and because such application would be manifestly inequitable.

The Court of Appeals found these same factors were present in this case and foreclosed retroactive applications of its decision in *Goodman*. We perceive no good reason for not applying *Chevron* where *Wilson* has required a Court of Appeals to overrule its prior cases. Nor has petitioner persuaded us that there was any error in the application of *Chevron* in the circumstances existing in this case.

II

Section 1981 provides:

> "All persons within the jurisdiction of the United States shall have the same right in every State and Territory to make and enforce contracts, to sue, be parties, give evidence, and to the full and equal benefit of all laws and proceedings for the security of persons and property as is enjoyed by white citizens, and shall be subject to like punishment, pains, penalties, taxes, licenses, and exactions of every kind, and to no other."

[2] Although § 1981 does not itself use the word "race," the Court has construed the section to forbid all "racial" discrimination in the making of private as well as public contracts. *Runyon v. McCrary,* 427, U.S. 160, 168, 174–175, 96 S.Ct. 2586, 2593, 2596–2597, 49 L.Ed.2d 415 (1976). The petitioner college, although a private institution, was therefore subject to this statutory command. There is no disagreement among the parties on these propositions. The issue is whether respondent has alleged *racial* discrimination within the meaning of § 1981.

[3] Petitioners contend that respondent is a Caucasian and cannot allege the kind of discrimination § 1981 forbids. Concededly, *McDonald v. Sante Fe Trail Transportation Co.,* 427 U.S. 273, 96 S.Ct. 2574, 49 L.Ed.2d 493 (1976), held that white persons could maintain a § 1981 suit; but that suit involved alleged discrimination against a white person in favor of a black, and petitioner submits that the section does not encompass claims of discrimination by one Caucasian against another. We are quite sure that the Court of Appeals properly rejected this position.

Petitioner's submission rests on the assumption that all those who might be deemed Caucasians today were thought to be of the same race when § 1981 became law in the 19th century; and it may be that a variety of ethnic groups, including Arabs, are now considered to be within the Caucasian race.[4] The understanding of "race" in the 19th century, however, was different. Plainly, all those who might be deemed Caucasian today were not thought to be of the same race at the time § 1981 became law.

In the middle years of the 19th century, dictionaries commonly referred to race as a "continued series of descendants from a parent who is called the *stock*," N. Webster, An American Dictionary of the English Language 666 (New York 1830) (emphasis in original), "[t]he lineage of a family," N. Webster, 2 A Dictionary of the English Language 411 (New Haven 1841), or "descendants of a common ancestor," J. Donald, Chambers's Etymological Dictionary of the English Language 415 (London 1871). The 1887 edition of Webster's expanded the definition somewhat: "The descendants of a common ancestor; a family, tribe, people or nation, believed or presumed to belong to the

same stock." N. Webster, Dictionary of the English Language (W. Wheeler ed. 1887). It was not until the 20th century that dictionaries began referring to the Caucasian, Mongolian and Negro races, 8 The Century Dictionary and Cyclopedia 4926 (1911), or to race as involving divisions of mankind based upon different physical characteristics. Webster's Collegiate Dictionary 794 (1916). Even so, modern dictionaries still include among the definitions of race as being "a family, tribe, people, or nation belonging to the same stock." Webster's Third New International Dictionary Mass.1870 (1971); Webster's Ninth New Collegiate Dictionary 969 (Springfield, Mass. 1986).

Encyclopedias of the 19th century also described race in terms of ethnic groups, which is a narrower concept of race than petitioners urge. Encyclopedia Americana in 1858, for example, referred in 1854 to various races such as Finns, vol. 5, p. 123, gypsies, 6 *id.,* at 123, Basques, 1 *id.,* at 602, and Hebrews, 6 *id.,* at 209. The 1863 version of the New American Cyclopaedia divided the Arabs into a number of subsidiary races, vol. 1, p. 739; represented the Hebrews as of the Semitic race, 9 *id.,* at 27, and identified numerous other groups as constituting races, including Swedes, 15 *id.,* at 216, Norwegians, 12 *id.,* at 410, Germans, 8 *id.,* at 200, Greeks, *id.,* at 438, Finns, 7 *id.,* at 513, Italians, 9 *id.,* at 644–645 (referring to mixture of different races), Spanish, 14 *id.,* at 804, Mongolians, 11 *id.,* at 651, Russians, 14 *id.,* at 226, and the like. The ninth edition of the Encyclopedia Britannica also referred to Arabs, vol. 2, p. 245 (1878), Jews, 13 *id.,* at 685 (1881), and other ethnic groups such as Germans, 10 *id.,* at 473 (1879), Hungarians, 12 *id.,* at 365 (1880), and Greeks, 11 *id.,* at 83 (1880), as separate races.

These dictionary and encyclopedic sources are somewhat diverse, but it is clear that they do not support the claim that for the purposes of § 1981, Arabs, Englishmen, Germans and certain other ethnic groups are to be considered a single race. We would expect the legislative history of § 1981, which the Court held in *Runyon v. McCrary* had its source in the Civil Rights Act of 1866, 14 Stat. 27, as well as the Voting Rights Act of 1870, 16 Stat. 140, 144, to reflect this common understanding, which it surely does. The debates are replete with references to the Scandinavian races, Cong.Globe, 39th Cong., 1st Sess., 499 (1866) (remarks of Sen. Cowan), as well as the Chinese, *id.,* at 523 (remarks of Sen. Davis), Latin, *id.,* at 238 (remarks of Rep. Kasson during debate of home rule for the District of Columbia), Spanish, *id.,* at 251 (remarks of Sen. Davis during debate of District of Columbia suffrage) and Anglo-Saxon races, *id.,* at 542 (remarks of Rep. Dawson). Jews, *ibid.,* Mexicans, see *ibid.,* (remarks of Rep. Dawson), blacks, *passim,* and Mongolians, *id.,* at 498 (remarks of Sen. Cowan), were similarly categorized. Gypsies were referred to as a race. *Ibid.,* (remarks of Sen. Cowan). Likewise, the Germans:

> "Who will say that Ohio can pass a law enacting that no man of the German race . . . shall ever own any property in Ohio, or shall ever make a contract in Ohio, or ever inherit property in Ohio, or ever come into Ohio to live, or even to work? If Ohio may pass such a law, and exclude a German citizen . . . because he is of the German nationality or race, then may every other State do so." *Id.,* at 1294 (Remarks of Sen. Shellabarger).

There was a reference to the Caucasian race, but it appears to have been referring to people of European ancestry. *Id.,* at 523 (remarks of Sen. Davis).

The history of the 1870 Act reflects similar understanding of what groups Congress intended to protect from intentional discrimination. It is clear, for example, that the civil rights sections of the 1870 Act provided protection for immigrant groups such as the Chinese. This view was expressed in the Senate. Cong.Globe, 41st Cong., 2d Sess., 1536, 3658, 3808 (1870). In the House, Representative Bingham described § 16 of the Act, part of the authority for § 1981, as declaring "that the States shall not hereafter discriminate against the immigrant from China and in favor of the immigrant from Prussia, nor against the immigrant from France and in favor of the immigrant from Ireland." *Id.,* at 3871.

[4–6] Based on the history of § 1981, we have little trouble in concluding that Congress intended to protect from discrimination identifiable classes of persons who are subjected to intentional discrimination solely because of their ancestry or ethnic characteristics. Such discrimination is racial discrimination that Congress intended § 1981 to forbid, whether or not it would be classified as racial in terms of modern scientific theory.[5] The Court of Appeals was thus quite right in holding that § 1981, "at a minimum," reaches discrimination against an individual "because he or she is genetically part of an ethnically and physiognomically distinctive sub-grouping of *homo sapiens.*" It is clear from our holding, however, that a distinctive physiognomy is not essential to qualify for § 1981 protection. If respondent on remand can prove that he was subjected to intentional discrimination based on the fact that he was born an Arab, rather than solely on the place or nation of his origin, or his religion, he will have made out a case under § 1981.

The Judgment of the court of Appeals is accordingly affirmed.

Notes

1. technical footnote deleted.
2. technical footnote deleted.
3. technical footnote deleted.
4. There is a common popular understanding that there are three major human races—Caucasoid, Mongoloid, and Negroid. Many modern biologists and anthropologists, however, criticize racial classifications as arbitrary and of little use in understanding the variability of human beings. It is said that genetically homogeneous populations do not exist and traits are not discontinuous between populations; therefore, a population can only be described in terms of relative frequencies of various traits. Clear-cut categories do not exist. The particular traits which have generally been chosen to characterize races have been criticized as having little biological significance. It has been found that differences between individuals of the same race are often greater than the differences between the "average" individuals of different races. These observations and others have led some, but not all, scientists to conclude that racial classifications are for the most part sociopolitical, rather than biological, in nature.
5. technical footnote deleted.

Supreme Court of the United States, 1987.

Article 16

Historical Discrimination in the Immigration Laws

The Early Years

During the formative years of this country's growth, immigration was encouraged with little restraint. Any restrictions on immigration in the 1700s were the result of selection standards established by each colonial settlement. The only Federal regulation of immigration in this period lasted only 2 years and came from the Alien Act of 1798, which gave the President the authority to expel aliens who posed a threat to national security.[1]

Immigrants from northern and western Europe began to trickle into the country as a result of the faltering economic conditions within their own countries. In Germany, unfavorable economic prospects in industry and trade, combined with political unrest, drove many of its nationals to seek opportunities to ply their trades here.[2] In Ireland, the problems of the economy, compounded by several successive potato crop failures in the 1840s, sent thousands of Irish to seaports where ships bound for the United States were docked.[3] For other European nationals, the emigration from their native countries received impetus not only from adverse economic conditions at home but also from favorable stories of free land and good wages in America.[4]

The Nativist Movements

As a result of the large numbers of Catholics who emigrated from Europe, a nativist movement began in the 1830s.[5] It advocated immigration restriction to prevent further arrivals of Catholics into this country. Anti-Catholicism was a very popular theme, and many Catholics and Catholic institutions suffered violent attacks from nativist sympathizers. The movement, however, did not gain great political strength and its goal of curbing immigration did not materialize.

Immigrants in the mid-19th century did not come only from northern and western Europe. In China, political unrest and the decline in agricultural productivity spawned the immigration of Chinese to American shores.[6] The numbers of Chinese immigrants steadily increased after the so-called Opium War, due not only to the Chinese economy, but also to the widespread stories of available employment, good wages, and the discovery of gold at Sutter's Mill, which filtered in through arrivals from the Western nations.[7]

The nativist movement of the 1830s resurfaced in the late 1840s and developed into a political party, the Know-Nothing Party.[8] Its western adherents added an anti-Chinese theme to the eastern anti-Catholic sentiment.[9] But once again, the nativist movement, while acquiring local political strength, failed in its attempts to enact legislation curbing immigration. On the local level, however, the cry of "America for Americans" often led to discriminatory State statutes that penalized certain racially identifiable groups.[10] As an example, California adopted licensing statutes for foreign miners and fishermen, which were almost exclusively enforced against Chinese.[11]

In the mid-1850s, the Know-Nothing Party lost steam as a result of a division over the question of slavery, the most important issue of that time.[12] The nativist movement and antiforeign sentiment receded because of the slavery issue and the Civil War. It maintained this secondary role until the Panic of 1873 struck.

Chinese Exclusion

The depression economy of the 1870s was blamed on aliens who were accused of driving wages to a substandard level as well as taking away jobs that "belonged" to white Americans. While the economic charges were not totally without basis, reality shows that most aliens did not compete with white labor for "desirable" white jobs. Instead, aliens usually were relegated to the most menial employment.[13]

The primary target was the Chinese, whose high racial visibility, coupled with cultural dissimilarity and lack of political power, made them more than an adequate scapegoat for the economic problems of the 1870s.[14] Newspapers adopted the exhortations of labor leaders, blaming the Chinese for the economic plight of the working class. Workers released their frustrations and anger on the Chinese, particularly in the West.[15] Finally, politicians succumbed to the growing cry for exclusion of Chinese.

Congress responded by passing the Chinese Exclusion Act of 1882.[16] That act suspended immigration of Chinese laborers for 10 years, except for those who were in the country on November 17, 1880. Those who were not lawfully entitled to reside in the United States were subject to deportation. Chinese immigrants were also prohibited from obtaining United States citizenship after the effective date of the act.

The 1882 act was amended in 1884 to cover all subjects of China and Chinese who resided in any other foreign country.[17] Then in 1888, another act was enacted that extended the suspension of immigration for all Chinese except Chinese officials, merchants, students, teachers, and travelers for pleasure.[18] Supplemental legislation to that act also prohibited Chinese laborers from reentering the country, as provided for in the 1882 act, unless they reentered prior to the effective date of the legislation.[19]

Senator Matthew C. Butler of South Carolina summed up the congressional efforts to exclude Chinese by stating:

> [I]t seems to me that this whole Chinese business has been a matter of political advantage, and we have not been governed by that deliberation which it would seem to me the gravity of the question requires. In other words, there is a very important Presidential election pending. One House of Congress passes an act driving these poor devils into the Pacific Ocean, and the other House comes up and says, "Yes, we will drive them further into the Pacific Ocean, notwithstanding the treaties between the two governments."[20]

Nevertheless, the Chinese exclusion law was extended in 1892[21] and 1902,[22] and in 1904 it was extended indefinitely.[23]

Although challenged by American residents of Chinese ancestry, the provisions of these exclusion acts were usually upheld by judicial decisions. For example, the 1892 act[24] mandated that Chinese laborers obtain certificates of residency within 1 year after the passage of the act or face deportation. In order to obtain the certificate, the testimony of one credible white witness was required to establish that the Chinese laborer was an American resident prior to the passage of the act. That requirement was upheld by the United States Supreme Court in *Fong Yue Ting v. United States*.[25]

Literacy Tests and the Asiatic Barred Zone

The racial nature of immigration laws clearly manifested itself in further restrictions on prospective immigrants who were either from Asian countries or of Asian descent. In addition to extending the statutory life of the Chinese exclusion law, the 1902 act also applied that law to American territorial possessions, thereby prohibiting not only the immigration of noncitizen Chinese laborers from "such island territory to the mainland territory," but also "from one portion of the island territory of the United States to another portion of said island territory."[26] Soon after, Japanese were restricted from free immigration to the United States by the "Gentleman's Agreement" negotiated between the respective governments in 1907.[27] Additional evidence would be provided by the prohibition of immigration from countries in the Asia-Pacific Triangle as established by the Immigration Act of 1917.[28]

During this period, congressional attempts were also made to prevent blacks from immigrating to this country. In 1915 an amendment to exclude "all members of the African or black race" from admission to the United States was introduced in the Senate during its deliberations on a proposed immigration bill.[29] The Senate approved the amendment on a 29 to 25 vote,[30] but it was later defeated in the House by a 253 to 74 vote,[31] after intensive lobbying by the NAACP.[32]

In 1917 Congress codified existing immigration laws in the Immigration Act of that year.[33] That act retained all the prior grounds for inadmissibility and added illiterates to the list of those ineligible to immigrate, as a response to the influx of immigrants from southern and eastern Europe. Because of a fear that American standards would be lowered by these new immigrants who were believed to be racially "unassimilable" and illiterate, any alien who was over 16 and could not read was excluded. The other important feature of this statute was the creation of the Asia-Pacific Triangle, an Asiatic barred zone, designed to exclude Asians completely from immigration to the United States. The only exemptions from this zone were from an area that included Persia and parts of Afghanistan and Russia.

The 1917 immigration law reflected the movement of American immigration policy toward the curbing of free immigration. Free immigration, particularly from nations that were culturally dissimilar to the northern and western European background of most Americans, was popularly believed to be the root of both the economic problems and the social problems confronting this country.

The National Origins Quota System

Four years later, Congress created a temporary quota law that limited the number of aliens of any nationality who could immigrate to 3 percent of the United States residents of that nationality living in the country in 1910.[34] The total annual immigration allowable in any one year was set at 350,000. Western Hemisphere aliens were exempt from the quota if their country of origin was an independent nation and the alien had resided there at least 1 year.

The clear intent of the 1921 quota law was to confine immigration as much as possible to western and northern European stock. As the minority report noted:

> The obvious purpose of this discrimination is the adoption of an unfounded anthropological theory that the nations which are favored are the progeny of fictitious and hitherto unsuspected Nordic ancestors, while those discriminated against are not classified as belonging to that mythical ancestral stock. No scientific evidence worthy of consideration was introduced to substantiate this pseudoscientific proposition. It is pure fiction and the creation of a journalistic imagination. . . .
>
> The majority report insinuates that some of those who have come from foreign countries are non-assimilable or slow of assimilation. No facts are offered in support of such a statement. The preponderance of testimony adduced before the committee is to the contrary.[35]

Notwithstanding these objections, Congress made the temporary quota a permanent one with the enactment of the 1924 National Origins Act.[36] A ceiling of 150,000 immigrants per year was imposed. Quotas for each nationality group were 2 percent of the total members of that nationality residing in the

United States according to the 1890 census.[37] Again, Western Hemisphere aliens were exempt from the quotas (thus, classified as "nonquota" immigrants). Any prospective immigrant was required to obtain a sponsor in this country and to obtain a visa from an American consulate office abroad. Entering the country without a visa and in violation of the law subjected the entrant to deportation without regard to the time of entry (no statute of limitation). Another provision, prohibiting the immigration of aliens ineligible for citizenship, completely closed the door on Japanese immigration, since the Supreme Court had ruled that Japanese were ineligible to become naturalized citizens.[38] Prior to the 1924 act, Japanese immigration had been subjected to "voluntary" restraint by the Gentleman's Agreement negotiated between the Japanese Government and President Theodore Roosevelt.

In addition to its expressed discriminatory provisions, the 1924 law was also criticized as discriminatory against blacks in general and against black West Indians in particular.[39]

The Mexican "Repatriation" Campaign

Although Mexican Americans have a long history of residence within present United States territory,[40] Mexican immigration to this country is of relatively recent vintage.[41] Mexican citizens began immigrating to this country in significant numbers after 1909 because of economic conditions as well as the violence and political upheaval of the Mexican Revolution.[42] These refugees were welcomed by Americans, for they helped to alleviate the labor shortage caused by the First World War.[43] The spirit of acceptance lasted only a short time, however.

Spurred by the economic distress of the Great Depression, Federal immigration officials expelled hundreds of thousands of persons of Mexican descent from this country through increased Border Patrol raids and other immigration law enforcement techniques.[44] To mollify public objection to the mass expulsions, this program was called the "repatriation" campaign. Approximately 500,000 persons were "repatriated" to Mexico, with more than half of them being United States citizens.[45]

Erosion of Certain Discriminatory Barriers

Prior to the next recodification of the immigration laws, there were several congressional enactments that cut away at the discriminatory barriers established by the national origins system. In 1943 the Chinese Exclusion Act was repealed, allowing a quota of 105 Chinese to immigrate annually to this country and declaring Chinese eligible for naturalization.[46] The War Brides Act of 1945[47] permitted the immigration of 118,000 spouses and children of military servicemen. In 1946 Congress enacted legislation granting eligibility for naturalization to Pilipinos[48] and to races indigenous to India.[49] A Presidential proclamation in that same year increased the Pilipino quota from 50 to 100.[50] In 1948 the Displaced Persons Act provided for the entry of approximately 400,000 refugees from Germany, Italy, and

Austria (an additional 214,000 refugees were later admitted to the United States).[51]

The McCarran-Walter Act of 1952

The McCarran-Walter Act of 1952,[52] the basic law in effect today, codified the immigration laws under a single statute. It established three principles for immigration policy:

1. the reunification of families,
2. the protection of the domestic labor force, and
3. the immigration of persons with needed skills.

However, it retained the concept of the national origins system, as well as unrestricted immigration from the Western Hemisphere. An important provision of the statute removed the bar to immigration and citizenship for races that had been denied those privileges prior to that time. Asian countries, nevertheless, were still discriminated against, for prospective immigrants whose ancestry was one-half of any Far Eastern race were chargeable to minimal quotas for that nation, regardless of the birthplace of the immigrant.

"Operation Wetback"

Soon after the repatriation campaigns of the 1930s, the United States entered the Second World War. Mobilization for the war effort produced a labor shortage that resulted in a shift in American attitudes toward immigration from Mexico. Once again Mexican nationals were welcomed with open arms. However, this "open arms" policy was just as short lived as before.

In the 1950s many Americans were alarmed by the number of immigrants from Mexico. As a result, then United States Attorney General Herbert Brownell, Jr., launched "Operation Wetback," to expel Mexicans from this country. Among those caught up in the expulsion campaign were American citizens of Mexican descent who were forced to leave the country of their birth. To ensure the effectiveness of the expulsion process, many of those apprehended were denied a hearing to assert their constitutional rights and to present evidence that would have prevented their deportation. More than 1 million persons of Mexican descent were expelled from this country in 1954 at the height of "Operation Wetback."[53]

The 1965 Amendments

The national origins immigration quota system generated opposition from the time of its inception, condemned for its attempts to maintain the existing racial composition of the United States. Finally, in 1965, amendments to the McCarran-Walter Act abolished the national origins system as well as the Asiatic barred zone.[54] Nevertheless, numerical restrictions were still imposed to limit annual immigration. The Eastern Hemisphere was subject to an overall limitation of 170,000 and a limit of 20,000 per country. Further, colonial territories were limited to 1 percent of the total available to the mother country (later raised to 3 percent or 600 immigrants in the 1976 amendments). The Western Hemisphere, for the first time, was subject to an overall limitation of 120,000 annually, although no individual per country limits were imposed. In place of the national origins system, Congress created a seven category preference system giving immigration priority to relatives of United States residents and immigrants with needed talents or skills.[55] The 20,000 limitation per country and the colonial limitations, as well as the preference for relatives of Americans preferred under the former selections process, have been referred to by critics as "the last vestiges of the national origins system" because they perpetuate the racial discrimination produced by the national origins system.

Restricting Mexican Immigration

After 1965 the economic conditions in the United States changed. With the economic crunch felt by many Americans, the cry for more restrictive immigration laws resurfaced. The difference from the 19th century situation is that the brunt of the attacks is now focused on Mexicans, not Chinese. High "guesstimates" of the number of undocumented Mexican aliens entering the United States, many of which originated from Immigration and Naturalization Service sources, have been the subject of press coverage.[56]

As a partial response to the demand for "stemming the tide" of Mexican immigration, Congress amended the Immigration and Nationality Act in 1976,[57] imposing the seven category preference system and the 20,000 numerical limitation per country on Western Hemisphere nations. Legal immigration from Mexico, which had been more than 40,000[58] people per year, with a waiting list 2 years long, was thus cut by over 50 percent.

Recent Revisions of the Immigrant Quota System

Although the annual per-country limitations have remained intact, Congress did amend the Immigration and Nationality Act in 1978 to eliminate the hemispheric quotas of 170,000 for Eastern Hemisphere countries and 120,000 for Western Hemisphere countries. Those hemispheric ceilings were replaced with an overall annual worldwide ceiling of 290,000.[59]

In 1980 the immigrant quota system was further revised by the enactment of the Refugee Act. In addition to broadening the definition of refugee, that statute eliminated the seventh preference visa category by establishing a separate worldwide ceiling for refugee admissions to this country. It also reduced the annual worldwide ceiling for the remaining six preference categories to 270,000 visas, and it increased the number of visas allocated to the second preference to 26 percent.[60]

Notes

1. Ch. 58, 1 Stat. 570 (1798).
2. Carl Wittke, *We Who Built America* (rev. 1964), p. 67.
3. Ibid., pp. 129–33.
4. Ibid., pp. 101–10.
5. Ibid., pp. 491–97.
6. Li Chien-nung, *The Political History of China, 1840–1928* (1956), pp. 48–49; Stanford Lyman, *Chinese Americans* (1974), pp. 4–5.
7. Mary Roberts Coolidge, *Chinese Immigration* (1909), pp. 16–17.
8. Wittke, *We Who Built America*, pp. 497–510.
9. Coolidge, *Chinese Immigration*, p. 58.
10. Ibid., pp. 69–82. Some municipalities also adopted ordinances that discriminated against Chinese. As an example, a San Francisco municipal ordinance, subsequently held unconstitutional in Yick Wo v. Hopkins, 118 U.S. 356 (1886), was enacted regulating the operation of public laundries but in practice was enforced almost exclusively against Chinese.
11. Ibid., pp. 33–38, 69–74.
12. Wittke, *We Who Built America*, pp. 509–10.
13. As one author noted, "[b]efore the late 1870's the Chinese engaged only in such work as white laborers refused to perform. Thus the Chinese not only were noninjurious competitors but in effect were benefactors to the white laborer." S.W. Kung, *Chinese in American Life: Some Aspects of Their History, Status, Problems, and Contributions* (1962), p. 68.
14. Carey McWilliams, *Brothers Under the Skin* (rev. 1951), pp. 101–03.
15. Coolidge, *Chinese Immigration*, p. 188.
16. Ch. 126, 22 Stat. 58 (1882).
17. Ch. 220, 23 Stat. 115 (1884).
18. Ch. 1015, 25 Stat. 476 (1888).
19. Ch. 1064, 25 Stat. 504 (1888).
20. 19 Cong. Rec. 8218 (1888).
21. Ch. 60, 27 Stat. 25 (1892).
22. Ch. 641, 32 Stat. 176 (1902).
23. Ch. 1630, 33 Stat. 428. (1904).
24. Ch. 60, 27 Stat. 25 (1892).
25. 149 U.S. 698 (1893).
26. Ch. 641, 32 Stat. 176 (1902).
27. The Gentleman's Agreement of 1907, U.S. Department of State, *Papers Relating to the Foreign Relations of the United States 1924* (1939), vol. 2, p. 339.
28. Ch. 29, 39 Stat. 874 (1917).
29. 52 Cong. Rec. 805 (1914).
30. *Id.* at 807.
31. *Id.* at 1138–39.
32. See *Crisis,* vol. 9 (February 1915), p. 190.
33. Ch. 29, 39 Stat. 874 (1917).
34. Ch. 8, 42 Stat. 5 (1921).
35. As reprinted in the legislative history of the INA [1952] U.S. Code Cong. and Ad. News 1653, 1668.
36. Ch. 190, 43 Stat. 153 (1924).
37. That act provided, however, that:

   The annual quota of any nationality for the fiscal year beginning July 1, 1927, and for each fiscal year thereafter, shall be a number which bears the same ratio to 150,000 as the number of inhabitants in continental United States in 1920 having that national origin (ascertained as hereinafter provided in this section) bears to the number of inhabitants in continental United States in 1920, but the minimum quota of any nationality shall be 100.

Ch. 190, 43 Stat. 153, 159, § 11(b).

38. Early congressional enactments restricted eligibility for naturalization to free white persons (ch. 3, 1 Stat. 103 (1790)) and to persons of African nativity or descent (Rev. Stat. §2169 (1875)). But when Congress passed the Naturalization Act of June 29, 1906 (ch. 3592, 34 Stat. 596), persons of Japanese ancestry began submitting petitions to become naturalized citizens under the procedures established by that act. The Supreme Court, however, held that the 1906 act was limited by the prior congressional enactments and thus Japanese were ineligible for naturalization. Ozawa v. United States, 260 U.S. 178 (1922).

39. "West Indian Immigration and the American Negro," *Opportunity,* October 1924, pp. 298–99.

40. Under the Treaty of Guadalupe Hidalgo, many Mexican citizens became United States citizens after the annexation of territory by the United States following the Mexican War. Leo Grebler, Joan W. Moore, and Ralph C. Guzman, *The Mexican American People* (1970), pp. 40–41. The Treaty of Guadalupe Hidalgo is reprinted in Wayne Moquin, *A Documentary History of the Mexican Americans* (1971), p. 183.

41. Grebler, Moore, and Guzman, *The Mexican Americans People,* pp. 62–63.

42. Ibid.

43. Ibid., p. 64.

44. Ibid., pp. 523–26.

45. Moquin, *A Documentary History of the Mexican Americans,* p. 294.

46. Ch. 344, 57 Stat. 600 (1943).

47. Ch. 591, 59 Stat. 659 (1945).

48. 60 Stat. 1353.

49. Ch. 534, 60 Stat. 416 (1946).

50. Presidential Proclamation No. 2696, [1946] U.S. Code Cong. and Ad. News 1732.

51. Ch. 647, 62 Stat. 1009 (1948).

52. Ch. 477, 66 Stat. 163 (1952).

53. Grebler, Moore, and Guzman, *The Mexican American People,* pp. 521–22. Mark A. Chamberlin *et al.,* eds., "Our Badge of Infamy: A Petition to the United Nations on the Treatment of the Mexican Immigrant," in *The Mexican American and the Law* (1974 ed.), pp. 31–34.

54. Pub. L. No. 89–236, 79 Stat. 911 (1965).

55. The 1965 amendments to the Immigration and Nationality Act provided the following seven category preference system:

First preference: unmarried sons and daughters of U.S. citizens. (20 percent)

Second preference: spouses and unmarried sons and daughters of lawful resident aliens. (20 percent plus any visas not required for first preference)

Third preference: members of the professions and scientists and artists of exceptional ability and their spouses and children. (10 percent)

Fourth preference: married sons and daughters of U.S. citizens and their spouses and children. (10 percent plus any visas not required for first three preferences)

Fifth preference: brothers and sisters of U.S. citizens and their spouses and children. (24 percent plus any visas not required for first four preferences)

Sixth preference: skilled and unskilled workers in occupations for which labor is in short supply in this country, and their spouses and children. (10 percent)

Seventh preference: refugees. (6 percent)

Spouses and minor children of American citizens are exempt from the preference system.

56. "6–8 million," *New West Magazine,* May 23, 1977; "4–12 million," *Los Angeles Times,* Aug. 7, 1977.

57. Pub. L. No. 94–571, 90 Stat. 2703 (1976).

58. In 1976 there were 57,863 immigrants from Mexico; in 1975, 62,205. U.S., Immigration and Naturalization Service, *Annual Report 1976,* p. 89.

59. Pub. L. No. 95–412, 92 Stat. 907 (1978).

60. Refugee Act of 1980, Pub. L. No. 96–212 (to be codified in scattered sections of 8 U.S.C.). The Refugee Act also increased the allocation of refugee visas to 50,000 annually for the first three fiscal years under the statute and provided that the number of refugee admissions in the following years would be determined by the President after consultation with Congress.

From *The Tarnished Golden Door,* September 1980.

The Diversity Visa Lottery—
A Cycle of Unintended Consequences
in United States Immigration Policy

ANNA O. LAW

Each year since 1988, the federal government of the United States runs an unusual lottery—not a lottery that awards cash, but one that awards 50,000 visas to nationals of a special list of designated countries that are deemed "underrepresented" in the current legal immigration system. The lucky winners of the visa lottery are granted a visa to enter the United States, lawful permanent residence status (the coveted green card), and the recipients eventually qualify for naturalization. Many immigration analysts and others in the public may have heard by now of this small and obscure provision.[1] What is not known is the true origin of the provision including the impetus for its creation, and how far the program has strayed from its originally intended purpose. How did such a bizarre program that contradicts the philosophy of American immigration admissions become a temporary, and then later a permanent part of the Immigration and Nationality Act?

This article argues that the factors that created the push for the diversity lottery in existence today had its roots in the changed immigration patterns wrought by the Immigration Act of 1965. The diversity lottery idea actually dates much further back in time than the late 1980s when the program first met with legislative success. This article further argues that the chain of unanticipated consequences emanating from the 1965 Act led to the creation of the diversity lottery, a policy which itself, spawned further unintended consequences in the shifting group of beneficiaries. Using Congressional hearing reports, other government documents, and personal interviews with actors who took part in creating and implementing the diversity lottery, this article traces the creation and evolution of the lottery and the role of several key Congressmen who sought to create a policy to benefit their ethnic constituents in the time honored practice of pork barrel politics.

Impact of the 1965 Act

To truly understand the reason for the existence of the diversity lottery today, one must understand the impetus for the policy that dates back to the passage of the Immigration Act of 1965

because today's lottery is actually a direct response to these changes.[2] The present lottery system is also a cobbling together of different concepts and strategies devised by many different Congressmen over the years who were responding to the changed immigration patterns.

The Immigration Act of 1965 was viewed as a watershed act and one of the most liberal and expansive reforms to the American system because of its abolition of race, ethnicity and national origin from the immigration selection process.[3] The 1965 Act revamped the entire immigration selection system by replacing national origin considerations with a seven-category preference system. This preference system prioritized immigrant admissions based primarily on close family relationships to a United States citizen or a lawful permanent resident (a green-card holder), and secondarily on considerations for employment skills. The 1965 Act completely abolished race, ethnicity and national origin as criteria for immigrant admissions and replaced it with the neutral preference system and a 20,000 per country limit within the Eastern Hemisphere, which also had an overall hemisphere limit of 170,000. Originally, the 1965 Act did not place per country limits on the Western Hemisphere, although the region was capped at 170,000. In 1978, Congress passed a law without controversy that brought the Western Hemisphere countries under a worldwide cap and imposed a 20,000 per country limit on all countries worldwide. With this change, the reforms begun in 1965 were finally complete.[4]

As will become clear, the call for the creation of the diversity lottery arose from a group of politically well-situated Irish and Italian-American Members of Congress who sought to benefit their ethnic constituents by rigging the immigration system in favor of these ethnic groups. To comprehend why these two particular groups led the charge, one needs to understand some of the unforeseen circumstances that resulted from the overhaul of the immigration system in 1965 and their connection to the movement to create the diversity lottery in the late 1980s.

Unanticipated Results of the 1965 Act and Early Remedies

One major unforeseen, and certainly unintended, result of the 1965 Act was that it precipitated a huge shift in the ethnic and racial composition of the immigrant flow. Architects of the 1965 Act expected Europeans to be the main beneficiaries of the new preference system since it was expected that the groups who were already in the United States in large numbers would be the ones to petition for their relatives and not the small numbers of racial minorities like the Asians and Africans, for example. In a Department of Justice form letter sent to members of the public who wrote to the Johnson Administration regarding the 1965 Act and also in an informal briefing book sent out to Congressional staff, the Administration addressed the racists' and xenophobes' charge that "the bill would let in hordes of Africans and Asiatics"

> The bill would not let in hordes from anywhere at all. Persons from Africa and Asia would continue to be in effect, quota immigrants, as they were under present law, but would be treated like everyone else ... but immigrants will have to compete and to qualify to get in, and immigration will not be predominantly from Asia and Africa ... The simple fact is that nations differ greatly in the number of their people who have occupational attainment, or the family ties in the United States, to obtain a preference ... Indeed very few people from certain areas could even pay the cost of tickets to come here.[5]

The statement shows that the Administration and authors of the 1965 Act did not anticipate the shift in the national origin composition of immigrants that happened after the 1965 reforms.[6] Whereas the previous immigrant flow was largely from Northern and Western Europe, the 1965 Act led to a modest increase in Eastern and Southern immigration, but an explosion in immigration from Asia and Latin America. By 1975, immigrants from Asia and Latin America accounted for about two-thirds of the immigration to the United States.[7]

Lottery supporters have often cited the empirically observable shift as justification for their approach to distributing immigration visas, the logic being that older immigrant groups like the Italians and Irish were being shut out of the system due to the shift toward Asian and Latino admissions that was facilitated by the 1965 changes. While Asian and Latino immigration rose, immigration from Ireland went on a steep decline after 1965, and Italy developed large waiting lists in family preference categories. The *INS Statistical Yearbook* reports that while immigration from Ireland was an average of 4,836 per year in the decade 1951–1960, and 8,597 per year in 1961–1970, the numbers decreased precipitously in 1971–1980 to 1,149 per year. By 1985, on the eve of the debate over the first version of the lottery provision legal immigration from Ireland numbered 1,397.[8]

However, to focus on the observable increase in numbers of legal immigrants from Asia and Latin America, and the decline of Irish immigrants and the growing demand for Italian immigration, is to focus on the symptoms of the phenomena and not the root causes. Two particular provisions in the 1965 Act directly caused the drop in Irish and Italian immigration as well as backlogs[9] under the fifth family preference (brothers and sisters of United States citizens): the labor certification requirement and the lack of a preference system governing Western Hemisphere immigration after the 1965 changes. In finding solutions to these problems that plagued Irish and Italian immigration in the late 1960s, several enterprising Congressmen devised initial approaches to benefiting their ethnic constituents that lay the groundwork for what is the diversity lottery today.

The Irish and Labor Certification

The connection between the labor certification requirement which was created by the 1965 Act and the rise of the diversity visa movement is a little known fact.[10] Prior to the labor certification requirement created by the 1965 Act, the labor certification was a negative requirement; an alien was ineligible for immigration only if the Secretary of Labor determined that qualified United States workers were available for the job or the alien's employment would adversely affect American workers in the same line of employment. Under this system, it was rare for the Secretary of Labor to take this type of action and the labor certification "requirement" was not really any kind of screen on immigration at all. After the passage of the 1965 Act that amended section 212(a)(14) of the Immigration and Nationality Act, the labor certification requirement (which was a last minute addition to the Act) became an affirmative requirement. An alien could immigrate only if he/she obtained, *prior to the issuance of their visa,* the Secretary of Labor's pre-clearance that they would not adversely affect the job market for United States workers.[11]

The pre-1965 system also had a loose version of the preference system in place before and after 1965. Under this system, there was a "non-preference" category of immigrants to which no percentage was assigned, but who would receive all the unused numbers of the preference categories. For countries with high immigration in comparison to their quota, the non-preference route was foreclosed. For instance, Italy with its pre-1965 annual quota of 5,600 always had more demand for immigration than supply of visas so there were no non-preference numbers left. The case in Ireland however was very different. It was a high quota country with a demand for immigration that was below the supply of visas. Most Irish immigrants utilized this non-preference category to get to the United States. The procedure for non-preference immigrants to get a visa was fairly simple and "pretty much any Irish man or woman who wanted to immigrate could just pick up and do so, with relative ease."[12]

In fact, for most of the Irish, the non-preference route to immigration was the only route available to them. The majority of the Irish who wanted to immigrate had only distant relatives in the United States (cousins, aunts, uncles) and none close enough to petition for them.[13] Those who had no relatives to petition for them could theoretically obtain a visa by qualifying through one of the employment preferences, but few of the Irish possessed the skills and education to qualify via an employment preference. The last nail in the coffin was that now the new "affirmative" labor certification requirement was in place and the requirement applied fully to non-preference immigrants. The labor certification requirement devastated Irish non-preference immigration. With no close relatives to petition for them, unskilled, semi-skilled, and even some skilled workers had great difficulty qualifying under the employment preferences.[14]

The Department of Labor pre-clearance requirement prevented many Irish intending immigrants from coming to the United States, which led to a drastic decline in admission numbers from 1968 forward. From 1971 forward, Ireland ranked among the highest of the countries that did not use up their annual quotas and among the countries that had a huge gap in the number of immigrants the country was actually sending and the number of visas allotted annually to that country. In his testimony before the House Immigration Subcommittee in 1973, John P. Collins, on behalf of the American Irish National Immigration Committee,[15] testified to that effect when he noted that individuals who were seeking to escape the civil unrest in Ireland were prevented from doing so by the immigration laws:

> These individuals, not yet large in number, have aunts, uncles and cousins in the United States. Lacking sisters and brothers who are U.S. citizens, they cannot qualify for fifth preference visas. Nor can they meet the requirement of the other family related preferences. The stringent application of labor clearance makes it impossible for them to qualify for a nonpreference, third preference, or sixth preference visa. Their only hope is to seek asylum here and obtain status as a refugee.[16]

Collins' also offered anecdotes and documents from the INS in his testimony indicating that the Irish attempts at applying for political asylum were by and large being rejected. One of the letters to his client from the INS that Collins quoted noted that the Irishman was ineligible for asylum because he was not coming from a Communist country. Collins' testimony fits the pattern of United States asylum policy before the 1980 reforms in which asylum policy was an extension of United States cold war foreign policy, where almost any and all applicants for asylum from Communist countries were successful and few nationals from non-Communist countries were successful.

The labor pre-clearance policy created by the 1965 Act prevented many Irish from immigrating through the formerly heavily utilized non-preference category, effectively cutting off the most popular way of legally immigrating to the United States. In an earlier appearance before Congress, Collins also confirmed the direct effect of the labor certification requirement on Irish immigration, "there is no doubt that section 212(a)(14) of the Act has caused a decrease in Irish immigration to the United States, as many Irish visa applicants are unskilled or semi-skilled workers, they are unable to qualify."[17]

As a byproduct of their inability to qualify for family, employment, or non-preference immigration, a large number of Irish entered the United States under temporary, nonimmigrant visas and overstayed their visas with the implicit consent of the United States consulate. In his 17 June 1973 testimony before the House Subcommittee on Immigration, Collins was asked what he thought about the large number of Irish "tourists" who were coming to the states. The questioning went as follows:

> Mr. Cline. We understand, Mr. Collins that there are approximately 20,000 visitor visas issued in the Republic of Ireland each year. I wonder whether there is intent to immigrate rather than a temporary visit, if they know they could apply somehow for 234(h) and stay deportation. If so, would many people from the six counties come to Southern Ireland and attempt to obtain visitor visas?
>
> Mr. Collins. That is possible. The fact that there are 20,000 visitors coming to this country from Ireland, I think is one of the problems inherent in the present law. I think, we would be kidding ourselves and this committee be kidding itself, if it believed that all these 20,000 coming here from Ireland were just coming here, in fact, just as visitors.[18]

Collins and the members of Congress were aware of the growing illegal Irish population in the United States and seemed to look the other way. Another source also confirmed that the United States consulate in Ireland was "issuing nonimmigrant visas left and right."[19] The American consulate personnel appeared complicit in creating an undocumented Irish population in the United States. The growth and presence of this illegal Irish population would eventually be another source of pressure for the creation of the diversity lottery.

The Italians and the Fifth Preference Backlog

Italian migration patterns under the changes created by the 1965 Act were quite different from the Irish. The problem plaguing Italian immigration was oversubscribed categories that led to backlogs, especially in the fifth preference (brothers and sisters of United States citizens).[20] Prior to 1965, Italy had an annual quota of 5,600, which was heavily oversubscribed.[21] When the 1965 Act was passed, the people on the waiting list simply got transferred over to the new waiting list. The new system prescribed by the 1965 Act did not actually take full effect until 1968. In the interim, there was a transitional system where the old quotas remained, but unused quota numbers were assigned to a pool that would go toward clearing backlogs. There was "an expectation" that the Italian backlog numbers would go down during the transition period. However, this did not happen and by 1 July 1968, there were still about 100,000 Italians on the fifth preference waiting list.[22]

By 1970, there was a call to "do something for the Italians," the rationale being that the system was not working as intended to reduce backlogs, and that Italian families should not be kept apart. Rev. Joseph Cogo, representing the American Committee on Italian Migration, appeared as a witness to testify about the fifth preference backlog and other immigration issues relating to the Italians. In 1973, he appeared before the House Subcommittee on Immigration to testify in favor of the preference system (like the one already in place in the Eastern hemisphere) being imposed on the Western Hemisphere. While endorsing many of the changes created by the 1965 Act, Cogo explained why he supported a preference system for the Western Hemisphere.

> We fully support the establishment of a preference system for natives of the Western Hemisphere. The present 18-month backlogs experienced by qualified applicants from the Western Hemisphere are deplorable. Moreover, to treat all applicants subject to the numerical limitation identically without regard to closeness of family ties or job skills inflicts great hardship upon applicants.[23]

Cogo was referring to Italy's backlogs in the fifth preference that existed from 1970 to a portion of 1973 and voicing his support for a preference system that would at least prioritize the clearing of the backlog. Without a preference system, all intending immigrants were granted visa priority dates according to a first come first serve basis, not based on the closeness of ties to relatives in the United States.

Although the rhetoric emphasized the urgent need to "do something for the Italians," the fact was that many Italians eventually lost interest in immigrating to the United States by the early 1970s. The Department of State (DOS) visa office tried to show the distinction between people on the backlog waiting list and those whose turn had been reached but not yet issued a visa. From the visa office's point of view, the application was valid indefinitely, or for as long as the relationship between the United States petitioner and Italian beneficiary existed. The DOS had no idea why people were not responding when they got the call that their priorities date had been reached. Some could have moved without a forwarding address, others could have died, but whatever the case, many of the eligible immigrants who were contacted by the DOS were not responding.[24] One might suspect this drop in interest was due to the improving economic conditions in Italy (and in Europe more generally) and the fact that Italy was an original member of the European Community (later the European Union), thus making it easier for their nationals to travel to other parts of Europe rather than come to the United States.

In any event, the demand for Italian visas dropped considerably and at a 1976 hearing, Congressman Joshua Eilberg (D-PA) expressed gratification that the backlog in the fifth preference for Italy was no longer a problem. He asked Reverend Cogo to explain the reason for the clearance of the backlog. Cogo responded:

> In my opinion, the primary reason for the tremendous fallout under fifth preference is the fact that the American citizen is more anxious to give his counterpart Italian brother or sister a chance to migrate here than the Italian is actually to come. . . . Another great factor for the fallout is the present uncertain situation of the American economy and the poverty of job opportunities.[25]

Cogo too realized that the demand for immigration from Italy was decreasing. While he was a frequent witness at Congressional hearings on immigration to press the Italian cause (appearing nine times before Congress between 1970 and 1989) the reality was that by 1970 many of the Italians had lost interest in coming. Yet, the *idea* of continuing to admit Italian immigrants

had taken on a life of its own. When the DOS visa office tried to explain that their letters offering American visas were not being answered, their efforts to explain "fell on deaf ears, and, in fact, simply infuriated many people, both because the explanation was complicated" and because it was a politically unpopular idea that the Italians simply had no interest in coming.[26] So the efforts to "do something for the Italians" continued.

Joining Forces and the Rhetoric of "Reform"

The Irish had the labor certification problem and the Italians, for a while, had the backlog problem. They decided to join forces to increase their political strength and because the two groups' goals were very similar—to amend the Immigration and Nationality Act specifically to benefit nationals from Italy and Ireland. The two groups also faced the same political and public relations problems of justifying the rigging of the system to benefit certain countries, which in fact constituted a return to the national origins principle that the 1965 Act had both wiped out and renounced.

At this point, several policy entrepreneurs[27] stepped in to champion the causes of the Irish and Italians. One of the first was William "Frits" Ryan (D-NY), a member of the House immigration subcommittee, who repeatedly attempted from 1968 to 1973 to introduce bills to benefit the Irish, but without success. H.R. 165 introduced in 1969 is an example of one of Ryan's bills. This bill attempted to place a floor on the level of immigration for each country in the Eastern Hemisphere of which Ireland was a part. The floor would be computed as 75 percent of the average annual number of immigrant visas made available to each country during the 10-year period preceding the 1965 Act. If a country after 1965 did not use up its annual allotment, the difference between that number and the floor would result in extra visas outside of the numerical limit of 20,000 per country and would be exempted from the labor certification requirement.[28] In so doing, Ryan was attempting to address the low usage of Irish visa numbers and deal directly with the source of the problem by eliminating the labor certification requirement that was preventing the majority of the Irish from immigrating.

While Ryan was trying to help the Irish, Peter Rodino (D-NJ) tried to pass bills to benefit the Italians and Irish, first in 1968, again in 1969 and several times after that. Examples of his attempts were H.R. 10618 and H.R. 2118, both introduced in 1968. This bill would be a three-year temporary measure, not a permanent measure like the one Ryan was suggesting. The approach Rodino took was to authorize the utilization of available but unused visa numbers for a three-year period beginning in 1968. These additional visas would also be exempt from the labor certification requirement. H.R. 10618 though intended to aid the Irish and Italians, was neutral in language, and it sought to confer benefits on any other "disadvantaged countries" who did not use up their annual allotment of visas in 1968. These extra visas would be issued on a first come first serve basis, not by country. Rodino argued that without this legislation, the unused numbers would simply be lost.[29] The Irish interest groups however, favored Ryan's bill citing the temporary nature of Rodino's bill as insufficient to alleviate the Irish problem in the long run.

In the late 1960s and through the 1970s, Ryan, Rodino and Emmanuel Celler (D-NY)[30] wrote bills to benefit the Irish and Italians. These seasoned politicians realized that to argue for additional visas for a group of what could be generally characterized as unskilled, not well educated workers, and with no close family ties to those in the United States, but who wished to immigrate, was not a politically savvy or viable move. Instead they adopted two rhetorical strategies to champion their cause. One was to introduce the concept of "new seed immigrants," an idea that was largely Celler's invention.[31] "New seed immigrants" or "independent immigrants" were young, single immigrants who would be allowed to immigrate under a "new seed" visa category and who would be exempt from labor certification. Using the concept was a clever way to distract from the fact that these immigrants had neither close family ties to the United States nor qualifying job skills, and otherwise did not qualify for immigration. Celler and others argued that a number of seed immigrants should be admitted each year because there was something valuable in someone who simply wanted to come to the United States not because of family relations or work skills, but because of their pioneering spirit and immigrant work ethic.

A related rhetorical strategy was to wax nostalgic about the great contributions to this country by the earliest immigrant groups. For example, in one of his appearances before Congress, Collins catalogued the Irish and their historical contributions in the American Revolution, the Civil War, and of Andrew Jackson, the first American President of partial Irish extraction. Collins added:

> If the handiwork of the Irish were painted green, the average American city would be splashed in all sides with emerald hues. . . . It is safe to say that all the Irish have done for America has never been fully told . . . but despite these facts we now find that the restrictive new immigration law has drastically reduced the issuance of immigration visas to Ireland.[32]

Similarly, Edward J. Sussman, National Secretary of the Steuben Society of America[33] stated:

> We cannot conceive that Congress or the people want a law which would all but "dry up" immigration from all of northern Europe. It is inequitable and unjust to those components of the American people who contributed most generously to the founding and building of the nation.[34]

The rhetoric of "seed immigrants" fused with the "we built this country" rhetoric became the verbal strategy of the Irish and Italian pro-immigration forces.

The champions of the diversity lottery also used a third rhetorical strategy, one of a claim of discrimination against these two groups. This strategy was to present the observable decline in Irish and Italian immigration as *prima facie* evidence that the post-1965 system constituted discrimination (intentional or not) against these two groups, even if the 20,000 per country limit was designed to guard against national origin discrimination. Some of this language of discrimination rose to the level of hyperbole, comparing the present immigration laws to the Chinese Exclusion Acts. Philip O'Rourke, Chairman of the California branch of the American Irish Immigration Committee asserted, "Having corrected such past inequities as the 'Chinese Exclusion Act,' it surely was not the intent of Congress that there be an 'Irish Exclusion Act' contained in the present law."[35] What the language of "new seed," "we built this country" and "discrimination" had in common was simply that the rhetoric was a calculated way to gain support for what was purely pork barrel politics and to mask the reality of a return to a national origins based system which privileged some countries over others in the immigration system.

The rhetorical efforts and other political maneuvering by the pro-Irish and Italian immigration congressmen culminated in a House bill that was passed on 17 March 1973, not coincidentally, on St. Patrick's Day. The bill contained specific provisions to benefit the Irish and Italians. The plan was to take a historical average of the number of visas that adversely affected countries that had been issued prior to 1965, and then to restore those visa numbers to make up for the drop off in numbers in the post-1965 period.[36] However, the bill got no further than the House. Sen. James Eastland (D-MS), then chair of the Senate Judiciary committee, a staunch foe of increased immigration and a supporter of national origins quotas, was not about to let another immigration bill remain active in wake of the results of the 1965 Act. Between 1966 and 1976, Eastland did not hold a single hearing on any immigration bill and any bill that was sent to his committee got bottled up there and died.[37]

The 1980s and the Immigration Reform and Control Act of 1986 (IRCA)

The issue lay untouched for many years after Ryan's death in 1976 and was not taken up again until the mid 1980s. No bills came to the floor in the 1980s to address the Italian and Irish question because the nation's attention had by then turned to the question of illegal immigration.[38] There was no movement on the Irish/Italian immigration until the swirl of politics involving the passage of IRCA in 1986.

By the mid 1980s, the Italians had thoroughly lost interest in immigrating but the Irish had not due in large part to the sizeable illegal population in the United States seeking legal status and the worsening economic conditions in Ireland. Representative Brian J. Donnelly (D-MA) and others stepped in and took over Frits Ryan's role as champion of Irish immigration. These new advocates of Irish and Italian immigration adopted such concepts as "new seed immigration," "adversely affected countries," and "discrimination" from the late 1960s and 1970s and worked them into their bills. Donnelly's program called NP-5, sought to amend section 314 of the Immigration and Nationality Act.[39] The Donnelly amendment provided 10,000 visas for nationals of "adversely affected countries." Edward Kennedy (D-MA) filed companion legislation in the Senate.

Donnelly and Kennedy's efforts also received an important and timely boost from then Speaker of the House, Tip O'Neal. As Speaker, he had great influence over the House Rules Committee that determines which bills would be allowed to the floor for debate. When Rodino, chair of the Judiciary Committee, went to see O'Neal about scheduling IRCA for floor debate, O'Neal told Rodino that the before the bill came out of committee there had better be something in the bill for the Irish or the bill would never see floor action.[40] Rodino agreed and allowed the Donnelly/Kennedy amendment to remain, O'Neal waived the necessary points of order, and the Donnelly/Kennedy provision became part of the law when IRCA eventually passed. From a timely *quid pro quo* was born the first incarnation of the diversity visa lottery.

Donnelly's NP-5 program benefited persons from "adversely affected countries." A list of "adversely affected countries" would be generated with such a country defined as any country that did not use more than 25 percent of its 20,000 annual allotment of visas. The Department of State was charged with compiling the statistics to determine which countries were the top thirty-six "adversely affected countries." After crunching the numbers, these countries were designated as "adversely affected": Albania, Algeria, Argentina, Austria, Belgium, Bermuda, Canada, Czechoslovakia, Denmark, Estonia, Finland, France, The Federal Republic of Germany, the German Democratic Republic, Great Britain and Northern Ireland, Guadeloupe, Hungary, Iceland, Indonesia, Ireland, Italy, Japan, Latvia, Liechtenstein, Lithuania, Luxembourg, Monaco, the Netherlands, New Caledonia, Norway, Poland, San Marino, Sweden, Switzerland, and Tunisia.[41] Nationals of these predominantly European and African countries would be allowed to submit their names and the first 10,000 applicants who were drawn based on their applications' arrival time in the mail would obtain immigration visas.

The Department of State received a whopping 1.4 million applications for the NP-5 program during a seven-day registration period in January 1987! The NP-5 results showed that, the countries that benefited the most from the program and the respective number of lottery winners were: Ireland (3,112), Canada (2,078), and Great Britain (1,181).[42] The high success rate of the Irish was due to their well-planned and coordinated efforts that involved that country chartering planes and literally depositing the applications in post office boxes on Capitol Hill.[43]

Donnelly, like previous proponents before him argued that there was a great need for such a program because certain countries, especially Ireland, were being "shut out" under the current admission system. Donnelly gave three reasons for introducing the visa lottery. First he noted, "our Nation must reintroduce into the immigrant stream those countries that have been determined to be adversely affected by the reform act of 1965 and face the same barriers with the passage of the 1986 reform bill." Second, he added that the NP-5 program held out the possibility of legal immigration for those who would normally come illegally (or who were presently illegally residing in the United States). Third, Donnelly noted that NP-5 would allow for natives of the adversely affected thirty-six countries to compete in a more "equitable" manner with other nationalities.

Donnelly agreed that the goal of the 1965 Act was admirable in ending discrimination against immigrants based on national origins and added that it was "a principle I would not wish to change." However, Donnelly asserted that "the southern and eastern Europeans who are expected to benefit from the 1965 law are now effectively excluded from the immigrant pool on an equal basis with residents of northern and western Europe."[44] In his rhetoric, Donnelly simply drew from and adopted the ideas of Ryan, Celler and Cogo that had been floating around for a while and until then, had not met with legislative success.

After the NP-5 program and during the debate leading up to the Immigration Act of 1990 (IMMACT '90) Donnelly was counseled to add the diversity concept as a political tactic to gain the support of Asian and Latino ethnic groups and employers who were all lobbying for different provisions to be included in IMMACT '90.[45] These groups were not at all fooled by the politically correct language, as evident in their testimonies before Congress.[46] Of course the politics surrounding the entire diversity lottery itself, going back to its origins in the late 1960s, cast serious doubt on the sincerity and commitment of the provisions supporters of true diversity. Perhaps by utilizing the term "diversity" Donnelly and his supporters hoped to tap into the popularity and influence of the multicultural movement that was in vogue in the 1980s. But the use of the terms "diversity," "independent immigrant" and "new seed immigrant" to describe the NP-5 and its progeny, glossed over the real return to national origin considerations represented in these programs.

The Immigration Act of 1990 (Immact '90)

After major legislation concerning illegal immigration was enacted in the Immigration Reform and Control Act of 1986, Congress turned its attention to legal immigration. Legal or permanent immigration became an issue for two reasons. First, there was concern over the imbalance between the overwhelming majorities of immigrants admitted on family reunification track as opposed to the number of "independent immigrants." The diversity lottery in the 1990s was partially a response to the claim that Asians and Latinos have a "lock" on the family-based preferences. Others have raised the accusation that the diversity lottery actually had more sinister intentions to carefully calibrate the lottery to minimize Mexican and Asian migration while maximizing the migration of European and African immigrants.[47] I found no evidence that this was the case, although the strange classification of Mexico as a country in South/Central America rather than North America was curious.

Second, there was concern over the backlogs under the family-based immigration petition preference system, specifically the second preference (spouses, and minor children of permanent residents; and also unmarried sons and daughters of lawful permanent residents); and the fifth preference (brothers and sisters of United States citizens). This time, the backlogs were hurting Asian and Latino families and intending immigrants.

Reflecting these concerns, the primary focus on IMMACT '90 was the numerical limits and preference systems that regulate the current permanent legal immigration admission system.

IMMACT '90 established a three track preference system for the admission of immigrants: family-sponsored, employment-sponsored, and an independent track. Highlights of IMMACT '90 included an increase in the worldwide cap, an increase in employment-based visas from 54,000 to 140,000, and a *permanent* provision for the diversity lottery.[48]

Many different interest groups in addition to the Irish and Italians organized to affect the outcome of IMMACT '90, including Asians and Latinos. While Asian and Latino interests found the diversity lottery idea repugnant because of its clear return to national origin considerations, potentially the most damaging proposals in IMMACT '90 from these groups' point of view were proposals to cut back on numbers on the second preferences (spouses, children and unmarried sons and daughters of lawful permanent residents) and to eliminate altogether the fifth preference (brothers and sisters of United States citizens). These were and continue to be the admissions preferences most heavily used by Asians and Latinos. The rationale for cutting back on these two categories was to minimize "chain migration." In particular, some Congressmen argued that brothers and sisters and adult children were not nuclear family members and that the system should not allow an immigrant to bring "extended" family members.[49]

It is necessary to understand how important the family preference issues were to Asian and Latino interests and how much they had at stake because the battles over these provisions eventually eclipsed their efforts to defeat the diversity provision, thus allowing the lottery to eventually pass. Asian and Latino interests were victorious in preventing the constriction of the family preferences and the second and fifth preferences remained intact. However, despite their opposition (and others) to the diversity lottery, the provision became a part of IMMACT '90.

Legislative History of the "Diversity Lottery" in Immact '90

The diversity lottery that is in existence today was a relatively obscure provision buried in a huge omnibus immigration bill. The diversity lottery, being neither a family nor employment-based policy, was classified under the independent immigration track. It is precisely because the lottery was neither family nor employment based that made the provision extremely controversial. The fact that such a provision was even under consideration at all was highly unusual given the primary goals of American immigration to reunify families and secondarily to address employment needs of the country. Even during the era of national origins and Chinese exclusion, American immigration policy had always operated on the understanding that this nation purposefully and deliberately selects immigrants based on their family ties to those already in the country and based on the jobs skills they will contribute. But the lottery approach to immigration admissions dispenses with the affirmative selection of immigrants by introducing a random selection process.

In effect, there were two diversity programs. One program was a transitional program that ran in fiscal years 1991 to 1994. This transitional program provided for 40,000 visas for each fiscal year. At this point, the program was changed from a first come first serve basis to a true lottery where applications received would be assigned a number and a computer would randomly draw numbers from the total applications received. As testament to the influence of the bill's architects, during the transitional programs, *40 percent (18,000) of the 40,000 visas for each fiscal year 1992 through 1994 would be reserved for Ireland.* Beginning in fiscal year 1995, 50,000 visas would be allotted each year for the diversity lottery with the top ten countries that have contributed the most immigrants to the United States (after the 1965 reforms), excluded from eligibility. These ineligible countries are China, Taiwan, Colombia, Dominican Republic, India, Jamaica, Korea, Mexico, Philippines, Great Britain, Guyana, and Haiti. The only requirements of lottery applicants was that they have either a high school education or at least two years of work experience in an occupation which requires two years of training or experience. Applicants would be selected randomly by computer and would have to re-register each year if not selected.[50]

In the debate leading up to the passage of IMMACT '90 in 1987, Congressman Donnelly again introduced legislation that sought to make the visa lottery a permanent part of the immigration system since the NP-5 program was to expire after the 1988 fiscal year. Donnelly further justified the need for the permanent lottery system citing the tremendous response to the NP-5 program, especially from natives of "older sources of immigration" such as Canada, Ireland, Italy, and other nations in Europe. In a 1987 Congressional hearing before the subcommittee on Immigration, Donnelly stated:

> The cumulative effect of the policy for the last twenty years has been to discriminate against any of the peoples who have traditionally made up our immigrant stock . . . Today we have an opportunity to correct these imbalances in immigration and open our doors once again to legal immigration slammed shut on those nations that enjoy long historic and family ties with our country.[51]

In the question and answer period following Donnelly's testimony, Chairman Romano Mazzolli (D-NY) probed Donnelly on his motivation for introducing the lottery and asked whether there were many illegals on the Eastern seaboard. Donnelly admitted that the program was intended as a backdoor amnesty program for the Irish when he answered:

> [B]ecause we were unable to extend the amnesty program, they would still have an undocumented illegal status like any other—most especially I think you are indicating the young Irish undocumented workers . . . of which I have in my constituency alone over 10,000.[52]

Even if his illegal constituents could not vote, Donnelly as an elected official was in the position to help them in a direct way through creative law making.

On the Senate side, the main supporters of the lottery approach to visa allocation were Senators Edward Kennedy (D-MA) and Daniel P. Moynihan (D-NY); and Senator Alfonse D'Amato (R-NY), all with considerable seniority and influence. In addition, Senator Kennedy was a member of the Judiciary Subcommittee on Immigration, Refugees, and International

Affairs. Senator Kennedy introduced companion legislation to the House bill to redress the "unforeseen problems" posed by the 1965 Act that inadvertently restricted immigration from "old seed sources of our heritage."[53] Meanwhile, Senator Moynihan argued, "fairness is at issue" and added "we need to help the descendants of our forefathers, to open the doors to opportunity for them also."[54] Senator D'Amato, another supporter of the lottery, charged that the current visa system dominated by Asian and Latin American countries "is an injustice which I believe we should work to correct . . . it is simply not fair to penalize so many countries, and it is not in our self-interest."[55] Again, the same mantras of discrimination, new seed immigration, and nostalgia for the past permeated their rhetoric, divorced from the reality of the pork barrel politics that was going on.

While Donnelly took the initiative in creating the NP-5 program, the move to make it a permanent part of the immigration system required the lottery provision to be passed as part of an overall immigration act. Enter Congressman Bruce Morrison (D-CT) who was then the first term chairman of the Judiciary's Subcommittee on Immigration, Refugees and International Law. Morrison has been credited as the author and "prime architect" of IMMACT '90. Although he worked closely with Senators Edward Kennedy and Alan Simpson (R-WY) Morrison reportedly "galled some of his colleagues by his single-handed steering of the legislation." Morrison saw to it that when his bill was being scaled back that the lottery provision remained intact. Opponents of the measure dubbed the lottery provision the "Irish Amnesty Provision."[56]

But this time, the pro-Irish lobby met not opposition in the form of a James Eastland, but in other ethnic interests. Asians and Latinos, through their interest group representatives, vigorously protested against the lottery system arguing that it would represent a backsliding in immigration policy and a reintroduction of discriminatory national origins considerations into immigrant admissions policy. In a statement before the Senate Judiciary Committee, a representative of the Mexican American Legal Defense [and Education] Fund (MALDEF) said:

> If Congress lends its imprimatur to the legislation, it will signal a major reversal of policy in which national origins will once again play a role in determining which persons can be admitted into the United States.[57]

Many other groups joined MALDEF and individuals in their protest against the lottery provision or any point system that would award extra points for English language ability, and award extra points to nationals from "adversely affected countries." *La Raza,* the Asian American Legal Defense Fund, Organization of Chinese Americans, and Japanese American Citizens League were other ethnic lobbies that protested against both the lottery system and a point system that would favor Europeans.

The Asian and Latino interests were not the only groups that objected to the diversity lottery. Other non-Latino and non-Asian groups and individuals found the diversity lottery equally objectionable on principle, even if they did not have a personal stake in the matter. Also posing objections to the lottery were the American Immigration Lawyers Association,

Doris Meissner (of the Carnegie Endowment for International Peace and former INS Commissioner) and Lawrence Fuchs of Brandeis University, a well-known scholar of American immigration. Fuchs asserted that the visa lottery made no sense because it was based on the idea that "nations and countries immigrated, rather than individuals." Reminding the committee of the progress made in the abolition of national origins by the 1965 Act he said, "we should seek them as immigrants because they are desirable for their attributes as persons, and not because of their national origins backgrounds."[58] Fuchs underscored a fact that the lottery proponents were trying to conceal, that "the Filipino, Mexican, or Chinese who lacked employment skills or close relatives were in the same predicament as the Irish and Italian"—any bias in the system was not nation specific but specific to the individual circumstances of the intending immigrant.[59] Like many other observers, Fuchs realized that the lottery was an attempt to legalize the illegal Irish population since many of the illegal Irish had missed the eligibility cutoff date for the 1986 amnesty program, a second chance amnesty and a throwback to national origins based immigration.[60]

Despite objections from many sectors, the diversity lottery passed and remains a part of today's immigration system. Several factors contributed to the lottery's legislative success. The first, was the leadership of Morrison who was in a key position of power as the Immigration Subcommittee Chair, and the tireless efforts of Donnelly and the support of other senior members of Congress. The second, was the neutralizing of the opposition in Asian and Latino interests who had their hands full fighting the cutbacks on family preferences. Despite attempts to cut back on the second and fifth preferences, those preferences remained untouched in IMMACT '90. The Asian and Latino communities considered this development a huge victory for them since they had all along viewed the preservation of these preferences as their first priority in the IMMACT '90 debate. When these provisions of the law remained untouched or when their "piece of the pie" was given back they were willing to stomach the passage of the diversity lottery. Finally, the relatively small number of visas (44,000 for the first three years, and 50,000 thereafter) as well as the temporary nature of the pro-Irish bias made the lottery more palatable.

Post Immact '90—Variation on a Theme of Unintended Consequences

After the passage of IMMACT '90, interest in the diversity lottery issue seemed to fade from the political radar screen.[61] There were no further hearings on the subject after 1990 and there were no serious efforts to remove the provision from the immigration law. By 1996, the attention of the policy and immigrant communities had again shifted to much larger issues such as the preservation of alien welfare rights and the fate of criminal aliens as Congress debated and eventually passed the [Illegal] Immigration Reform and Immigrant Responsibility Act (IIRIRA), Anti-Terrorism and Death [Effective] Penalty Act (AEDPA), and sweeping welfare reform legislation in the Personal Responsibility and Work Opportunity Reconciliation

Act (PRWORA). Later, in 2001, the Bush Administration's discussion of the possibility of another amnesty or "regularization" for approximately 3 million illegal immigrants from Mexico (and potentially other groups) took center stage. The amnesty proposal was in turn eclipsed by the terrorist attacks on 11 September 2001. These two events relegated the comparatively insignificant 50,000 diversity visas to the back burner for policymakers.

Eventually, the Irish also lost interest in the visa lottery that was created for them. The economic situation in Ireland greatly improved by 1995. The *Financial Times* reported, "Ireland's crippling unemployment problem eased sharply in 1994–95 as the economy created 49,000 new jobs, the biggest annual increase since 1972." The same article also noted that the improved economy in Ireland had slowed the flow of emigration, "The recent economic recovery has also stemmed the flow of net migration, which reached a peak of 43,900 in 1989."[62] Also, because Ireland was admitted to the European Union in 1973, their nationals, like the Italians are now able to travel and work in other parts of Europe which may in turn have further cut down on Irish emigration to the U.S. After the improved economy beginning in 1995, the Irish abandonment of the diversity lottery was clear and the stark statistics tell the story. As late as 1994, the last year of the diversity lottery transition program, a total of 16,344 Irish immigrated via the diversity lottery. But by 1996, the number dropped to 963, by 1997 it was 359 and by 1998 the number was 318![63]

Perhaps one of the strangest footnotes to the diversity lottery odyssey is that the lottery unintentionally came to benefit many more nationalities than its original target beneficiaries. The neutral mathematical formula devised by the Department of State to determine which were the adversely affected countries produced a list that in addition to Italy and Ireland included many African and European countries, and a few Asian countries. Although the largest beneficiaries were the Irish in the NP-5 program and transitional programs, the most recent Immigration and Naturalization statistics from 1996 through 1998 show that the latest beneficiaries of the lottery have been largely the nationals of other European and African nations. More specifically, in fiscal year 1996 nationals from Nigeria, Ghana, Bangladesh, Ethiopia, and Poland were the most successful in the lottery. In fiscal year 1997, the top diversity visa receiving countries were Albania, Poland, Bangladesh, Ethiopia and Nigeria. And in fiscal year 1998 (the most recent and complete set of INS statistics available) the top diversity visa receiving countries were: Albania, Nigeria, Bulgaria, Bangladesh, and Romania.[64] Although the official numbers are not yet available for the 1999 and 2000 lotteries, *This Day,* a Nigerian newspaper in Lagos, reported that Nigerian nationals received approximately 6,000 visas in the fiscal year 2000 visa lottery, a number up from the approximately 4,000 figure in 1999.[65] These numbers place Nigeria as first or second among diversity visa receiving countries in 1999 and 2000. A program that was created by and intended for the Irish and Italians and then abandoned by those two groups has become a permanent part of the immigration system benefitting entirely different groups of individuals.[66]

Conclusion

The story of policy making in general, and American immigration policy in particular, is often marked by unintended consequences that flow from previously implemented policies. The diversity lottery is an example of the efforts of a group of policy entrepreneurs who had the will and the way to mitigate the unintended effects of the 1965 Act that had foreclosed using national origins as a selection criterion. The end result of their efforts led to even more unpredictable outcomes. The unanticipated consequences emanating from the Immigration Act of 1965 begot the diversity lottery which in turn, went on autopilot, and begot an unanticipated group of beneficiaries. Perhaps the biggest irony of the diversity visa lottery is that the lottery, conceived for less than principled purposes, is in fact producing a stream of immigrants from countries that are very different than the ones that currently dominate the immigration system.

Notes

I wish to thank Sandy Levinson, Cara Wong, Lawrence Fuchs, Gary Freeman, and the anonymous reviewer(s) who read earlier drafts of the essay and provided helpful suggestions. I am also indebted to Cornelius "Dick" Scully, Arthur "Skip" Endres, Brett Endres, and Edward Skerrett for providing me with information crucial to the essay.

1. See for example Stephen Legomsky, *Immigration and Refugee Law and Policy,* 2nd ed. (New York, 1997), pp. 204–211, Walter Jacob, "Note: Diversity Visas: Muddled Thinking and Pork Barrel Politics," *Georgetown Immigration Law Journal* (June 1992) and numerous articles in the print media and ethnic media. Jacob attributes the origin of the diversity lottery idea to the recommendations of the Select Commission on Immigration and Refugee Policy that existed in the mid-1980s.

2. I am very grateful to Cornelius "Dick" Scully for pointing out to me that the roots of the lottery go much further back than the late 1980s.

3. David Reimers, *Still the Golden Door—The Third World Comes to America.* (New York, 1985), pp. 80–81.

4. David Reimers, "An Unintended Reform: The 1965 Immigration Act and Third World Immigration to the United States," *Journal of American Ethnic History,* 3 (Fall 1983): 80, 87, 89.

5. Letter in Q & A form from Norbert A. Schlei, Assistant Attorney General, Office of Legal Counsel to "Fellow Citizens" in response to the public writing in about the immigration act. Also published in the *Congressional Record* of the 89th Congress, 28 April 1965. "Legislative Background Immigration Law 1965" Box 1. Folder "Road to Final Passage" Lyndon Baines Johnson Presidential Library, Austin, Texas.

6. See also Reimers, "An Unintended Reform." Reimers lays out in detail how the unintended shift in the ethnicity in immigrants came about.

7. U.S. Immigration and Naturalization Service, *Statistical Yearbook of the Immigration and Naturalization Services, 1994* (Washington, D.C., 1996), p. 12.

8. U.S. Immigration and Naturalization Service, *Statistical Yearbook of the Immigration and Naturalization Service, 1994* (Washington, D.C., 1996), pp. 27–28.

9. Due to the implementation of the 20,000 per country limit for immigrant admissions, some countries had developed large backlogs in certain family petition categories because there are more people who wish to immigrate per year than there are available visa numbers. For example, U.S. citizens petitioning for their unmarried brothers and sisters in the Philippines or China must wait 18–20 years before their brothers and sisters will have a current visa priority date that would allow them to enter the United States and obtain permanent residence (get a greencard). Some argued that these lengthy backlogs undermine the credibility of the system.

10. Dick Scully explained in detail what this connection was. Cornelius "Dick" Scully, telephone conversation with author, 28 June 2001.

11. Cornelius "Dick" Scully, telephone conversation with the author, 28 June 2001 and email communication to the author, 26 July 2001. Mr. Scully (now retired) was a career civil servant at the Department of State between 1968 and 1997. He was for many years, the Director of the Office of Legislation, Regulations and Advisory Assistance, which was the technical section of the visa office at State. While at his position, Mr. Scully was responsible for writing all the regulatory orders to implement all the various lotteries, including the current one. Given the many years he was at the Department of State's visa section, Mr. Scully is truly the institutional memory of the place.

12. Additionally, the process for immigrating under the non-preference quota was quick. One simply wrote a letter to the consular officer stating their desire to immigrate; the officer would send them a biographical information form to fill out. Upon receipt of the form the officer would check whether there were actual numbers available for the non-preference applicant. If there were, which was always the case in Ireland, the applicant was sent information to prepare for a visa interview. If the interview went smoothly, the visa would be issued on the spot and the applicant could travel to the US. (Scully, email communication to author 26 July 01.)

13. Under U.S. immigration law, only close relatives such as spouses, sons and daughters, and brothers/sisters have petitioning rights—not more distant relatives like cousins, aunts, uncles or grandparents.

14. David Reimers "An Unintended Reform," pp. 73–74 and Scully, telephone interview with author 28 June 2001.

15. This umbrella organization was composed of members of all the major Irish American organizations in the U.S. including the Ancient Order of Hibernians, the Knights of Equity, and the Gaelic Athletic Association.

16. Testimony of John P. Collins, House Subcommittee on Immigration, *Western Hemisphere Immigration Hearing on H.R. 981,* 93rd cong., 1st session, 1973, p. 324.

17. Testimony of John P. Collins. Subcommittee No. I of the Committee on the Judiciary, House of Representatives, *The Effect of the Act of October 5, 1965, on Immigration From Ireland and Northern Europe,* 91st cong., 1st session, 1969, p. 15.

18. Testimony of John P. Collins, House Subcommittee on Immigration, *Western Hemisphere Immigration Hearings on H.R. 981,* 93rd cong., 1st sess., 1973, p. 323.

19. Arthur "Skip" Endres, phone interview with author, 11 July 2001. Mr. Endres was Chief Counsel to Congressman Peter Rodino (D-NJ) when Rodino was first Chair of the House Immigration Subcommittee and then Chair of the full Judiciary Committee. Rodino and his staff played active leadership roles in the passage of the 1986 Immigration Reform and Control Act and the Immigration Act of 1990.

20. Backlogs result when more persons than 20,000 wish to immigrate each year to a particular country. If the 20,000 slots are already used up that year, the persons must wait on a wait list until the year a slot opens up for them.

21. Dick Scully reports that at one point, there were well over 100,000 registrants on the Italian waiting list for brothers and sisters of U.S. citizens. (Scully, email communication to author 26 July 2001.)

22. Scully, email communication to author, 26 July 2001.

23. Testimony of Rev. Joseph A. Cogo, *Western Hemisphere Immigration,* 1975, p. 313. Reimers notes the Italians were also in favor of the 20,000 per country limit even though it meant an increase in backlogs because the general feeling at the time was that no country should dominate the immigration system and a set per country limit would be the fairest way to ensure that goal. (Reimers, "An Unintended Reform," p. 74.)

24. Scully, email communication to author, 26 July 2001. Scully adds that in the late 1960s the U.S. government took the extraordinary step of instructing the Italian postal service to find the persons whom the visa approval letters had been sent to and get them into the immigration process.

25. Testimony of Rev. Joseph A. Cogo, House Immigration Subcommittee Hearing on H.R. 981, *Western Hemisphere Immigration,* 1973, p. 320.

26. Scully, email communication to author, 26 July 2001.

27. In the political science literature, policy entrepreneurs are described as "advocates who are willing to invest their resources—time, energy, reputation, and money—to promote a position in return for anticipated future gain in the form of material, purposive or solidary benefits." Kingdon further articulates three common qualities of such entrepreneurs. They have some claim to a hearing as a representative of a group or an "authoritative decision-making position; they are known for their political connections and negotiating skills, and they are persistent and tenacious." John Kingdon, *Agendas, Alternatives, and Public Policies,* (New York, 1995), pp. 179–181. One will see that Kingdon's description of policy entrepreneurs quite aptly describes the Members of Congress who negotiated previous and present versions of the diversity lottery.

28. Opening statement of Michael Feighan, Hearings of the U.S. House, Committee on the Judiciary, Subcommittee No. 1, *The Effect of the Act of October 3, 1965 on the Immigration from Ireland and Northern Europe,* 91st cong., 1st sess., 1969, pp. 2–3.

29. Opening remarks of Peter Rodino. *The Effect of the Act of October 3, 1965 on the Immigration from Ireland and Northern Europe,* 1969, pp. 4–5, 8–9.

30. Celler, and later Rodino, served first as chair of the House Immigration Subcommittee then the House Judiciary committee.

31. Endres, telephone interview with author, 11 July 2001.

32. Testimony of John P. Collins, Hearings of the U.S. House Committee on the Judiciary, Subcommittee, *The Effect of the Act of October 3, 1965 on the Immigration from Ireland and Northern Europe,* 1969, pp. 11–12.

33. The society is a national organization of American citizens wholly or in part of Germanic origin and who have been actively interested in U.S. immigration issues.

34. Testimony of Edward J. Sussman, U.S. House, Committee on the Judiciary, Subcommittee on Immigration, *The Effect of the Act of October 3, 1965 on the Immigration from Ireland and Northern Europe.* 1969, pp. 26–27.

35. Statement of Philip O'Rourke, U.S. House, Committee on the Judiciary, Subcommittee No. 1, *The Effect of the Act of October 3, 1965 on the Immigration from Ireland and Northern Europe,* 1969, p. 30.

36. Endres, phone interview with author, 11 July 2001.

37. Scully, email communication to author, 26 July 2001. Scully speculated that Eastland bottled up all immigration legislation because he felt he would lose control of an immigration bill if it went to the floor.

38. Endres, telephone interview with author, 11 July 2001.

39. House Report 100-1038, *Immigration Amendments of 1988,* Document submitted by Peter Rodino to accompany H.R. 5115.

40. Endres, telephone interview with author, 11 July 2001. Mr. Endres, as chief counsel of the Judiciary, was present at the meeting between O'Neal and Rodino when this deal transpired.

41. 52 *Federal Register* 1,449 (1987).

42. U.S. Senate, Committee on the Judiciary, *Diversity Lottery Program, 1987: Hearings on S. 161,* 101st cong., 1st sess., 1987, p. 4.

43. Endres, telephone interview with author, 11 July 2001. It was clear that the Irish government took a very active interest in this lottery given the depressing economic situation in that country. Endres reports that during the events leading up to the passage of IRCA, he asked Donnelly whether the Irish are interested in the provision and why Rodino had not heard from the Irish consulate. Rodino received a call the following day from the Irish Prime Minister.

44. Testimony of Brian J. Donnelly, U.S. House, Subcommittee on Immigration, Refugees, and International Law, 100th cong., 2nd sess., 1988, p. 7.

45. Walter Jacob, "Note: Diversity Visas," p. 313. Jacob writes that Harris Miller, the chief lobbyist for the Irish Immigration Reform Movement told him that the diversity language was used to gain support from the other interest groups.

46. See the statements of objection to the diversity provision in the testimonies from representatives from the Organization of Chinese Americans, La Raza, Mexican American Legal Defense Fund, and the Japanese American Citizens League among others in U.S. Senate, Subcommittee on Immigration, *Hearings on S 161—the Diversity Lottery Program,* 101st cong., 1st sess., 1987.

47. Scully pointed out that no Administration had ever treated Mexico as anything but a North American country. (Scully, telephone interview with author 28 June 2001) The gerrymandering of Mexico into South/Central America seems to lend credence to the charge that the current lottery is a reaction against Latino migration. With Mexico in another hemisphere, the only three countries left in the Northern Hemisphere are the U.S., Canada and the Bahamas. Under the present diversity lottery rules, each hemisphere has a cap and each country has a cap. Moving Mexico to another hemisphere would free up more visas for the remaining countries in North America.

48. Joyce Vialet and Larry Eig, *Immigration Act of 1990* (P.L. 101-649) Congressional Research Service report to Congress, 1990 (no. 90–601), pp. 1–2.

49. Asian and Latino interests strenuously fought the proposals that would cut back on family preferences. Both these groups criticized the proposal's definition of "nuclear family" as Eurocentric and culturally insensitive. Asian interest groups also argued that it was too soon to cut back on these preferences especially when their communities had just recently begun to enjoy the benefits of the liberalized immigration laws provided by the 1965 Act after they had been discriminated for so long under the Asia-Pacific Triangle system.

50. U.S. Department of State, *Visa Bulletin Number* 2a Volume VII, p. 3.

51. Statement of Brian Donnelly, U.S. House, Subcommittee on Immigration, *Hearings on S. 161, Diversity Lottery Program,* 101st cong., 1st sess., 1987, p. 52.

52. Statement of Brian Donnelly, U.S. House, Subcommittee on Immigration, Refugees, and International Law of the Committee on the Judiciary House of Rep., 100th cong., 2nd sess., 1988, p. 11. The Immigration Reform and Control Act (IRCA) in 1986 granted amnesty to illegal aliens who were residing in the country but most of the illegal Irish missed the cut-off date for eligibility because the economic problems in Ireland that precipitated a large number of illegals coming to the U.S. occurred *after* the amnesty cut-off date. Since IRCA was intended as a one-time only amnesty opportunity that could not be repeated, the diversity lottery was designed as a "back door amnesty" for the Irish illegals.

53. Statement of Edward Kennedy, U.S. House, Subcommittee on Immigration, Refugees, and International Law of the Committee on the Judiciary, 100th cong., 2nd sess., 1988, p. 2.

54. Statement of Patrick Moynihan, U.S. House, Subcommittee on Immigration, Refugees, and International Law of the Committee on the Judiciary, 100th cong., 2nd sess., 1988, pp. 37, 40.

55. Statement of Alfonse D'Amato, U.S. House, Subcommittee on Immigration, Refugees, and International Law of the Committee on the Judiciary. 100th cong., 2nd sess., 1988, p. 41.

56. Dick Kirschten, "Opening the Door," *National Journal* (1990): 2003.

57. Statement of MALDEF. U.S. House, Subcommittee on Immigration, Refugees, and International Law of the Committee on the Judiciary, 100th cong., 2nd sess., 1988, p. 519.

58. Testimony of Lawrence Fuchs, U.S. House, Subcommittee on Immigration, Refugees, and International Law of the Committee on the Judiciary, 100th cong., 2nd sess., 1988, p. 180.

59. I have elsewhere written about Fuchs' objection to the provision and the logic inconsistencies of the lottery defenders' arguments. Anna O. Law, "Race, Ethnicity and National Origins in Public Policy—When Should it Matter?" *Georgetown Immigration Law Journal* (1986) vol. 10: 71, 75.

60. Lawrence Fuchs, telephone interview with the author, 13 March 1998. Fuchs added that there was no illusion on the part of the sponsors of the bill that the lottery provision could be justified on principle. All the rhetoric about diversity was "just window dressing."

61. Scully's view was that by the time IMMACT '90 passed, the interest groups and the policy community were more generally worn out over the battle and gave up on attacking the lottery. He notes that even the Federation for American Immigration Reform, a restrictionist group, has stopped attacking the diversity lottery (email communication with author 19 July 2001). Between 1996 and the present, the *New York Times* ran fewer than a dozen stories on the diversity lottery. Most of these stories were about the effects of the lottery on individuals' lives or on neighborhoods and communities. However, I suspect the lottery received far more coverage in the ethnic media, especially in countries that were meeting with high rates of success with the lottery.

62. John Murray Brown, "Irish economic recovery brings biggest rise in jobs since 1972," *Financial Times* (London, 25 October 1995).

63. U.S. Immigration and Naturalization Service, *Statistical Yearbook of the Immigration and Naturalization Service, 1994* (Washington, D.C.,) (1994, p. 44, 1996, p. 46, 1997, p. 44, 1998, p. 32) INS Statistical Yearbooks for 1999–2000 are not yet available.

64. U.S. Immigration and Naturalization Service, *Statistical Yearbook of the Immigration and Naturalization Service, 1994* (Washington, D.C.,) (1996, pp. 46–47, 1997, p. 44–45 1998, 32–33) INS Statistical Yearbooks for 1999–2000 are not yet available.

65. Chidi Uzor, "US Embassy Issues 3000 Diversity Visas to Nigerians," *This Day,* (Lagos, Nigeria) 5 April 2001.

66. It is unclear whether there is a constituency supporting the diversity lottery today and who that constituency may be because there has been no serious policy discussion about the lottery since 1990. However, one might suspect that new interest groups (other than the Irish and Italian ones) would emerge to defend the lottery if the provision was under attack.

ANNA O. LAW is a Ph.D. candidate in the Department of Government at the University of Texas at Austin (Austin, TX 78712). She is currently completing her dissertation on the effects of institutional norms (such as legal principles, cognitive structures, and institutional arrangements) on the judicial behavior of Supreme Court and Federal Circuit court judges in immigration cases. Her research interests include United States immigration law and policy, constitutional law, American political development, and the effects of race and ethnicity in American politics. Prior to returning to graduate school, she was an analyst at the United States Commission on Immigration Reform.

UNIT 3

The Demography of Ethnicity

Unit Selections

Key Points to Consider

- Given the tabulation of multiple race and ethnic identifications, can you calculate the number of combinations and permutations of race and ethnic identity?

- In what senses are these combinations of self-identification reflective of American attitudes toward self-identification?

- Are ethnic interest groups really representative of their constituencies? What does representation mean?

- With respect to the nature of geographic boundaries, what positive and negative impacts are associated with the concentration of ethnic groups into nearly homogenous enclaves?

- Does public attention to race and ethnicity reinforce mentalities that are deeply formative of race and ethnic identities and relationships among persons and organizations?

- Do such mentalities foster negative stereotypes and positive prototypes of race and ethnicites?

- In what respect does the attention to the history of slavery and immigration shape contemporary consciousness?

Student Web Site
www.mhcls.com

Internet References

U.S. Census Bureau
http://www.census.gov
Diversity.com
http://www.diversity.com
U.S. Bureau of Citizenship and Immigration Services
http://www.USCIS.gov/portal/site/uscis

© John Kershaw/Alamy

The history of immigration and ethnic group diversity is embedded in the history of America from its earliest times. The material in this unit reveals the ongoing process of peopling America and the experiences of new immigrants. These articles illustrate the accessibility and attractiveness of economic opportunities, the impact of new technologies, and the development of new partnerships and collaborations. The specific dynamics of group isolation and integration point to the complexity generated by public policy—most importantly—the designations available for racial and ethnic identity offered for the first time in the 2000 U.S. Census. The plentitude of resources and the social imagination of community leaders, as well as specific characteristics of race and ethnic populations—their size, scale, and scope—and the range of governmental policies determine race and ethnic relations.

Because of the considerable fluidity of immigrant experiences, the complex processes of cultural identity, and the political use of cultural symbols such as race and ethnicity, the search for more analytical rigor in the field of race and ethnic relations is far from complete. A guide to discernible and measurable features of ethnic phenomena and characteristics that are attributes of ethnicity that was developed in to a fine collection of materials on this topic, lists the following markers of ethnic groups: common geographic origin; migratory status; language/dialect; religious faith(s); ties

that transcend kinship, neighborhood, and community boundaries; shared traditions, values, symbols, and literature; folklore; music; food preferences; settlement and employment patterns; special interests in regard to politics in the homeland and in the United States; institutions that specifically serve and maintain the group; and an internal as well as external sense of distinctiveness. The contributions and concerns of various ethnic immigrant groups over many generations provide a deeply woven pattern of information along with a complex social history of America. From the 1850s to the 1870s, immigrants to America came predominantly from Britain and northern Europe. To these European, and perhaps to some Asian immigrants, America represented freedom to enter the economic struggle without constraints of state- and status-bound societies, whose limits could not be overcome except through emigration. Yet this historical pathway to liberty, justice, and opportunity came to be perceived as a "tarnished door," when the deep impulses of exclusion and exclusivity came to the forefront. The victims were aliens who, ironically, achieved the American promise but were denied the reward of acceptance and incorporation into the very culture they helped to fashion. This unit's articles describe the immigrants' experience, and once again, raise the issues that every large-scale multiethnic regime must address: How can unity and diversity be channeled into political, economic, and cultural well-being?

Ancestry 2000
Census 2000 Brief

ANGELA BRITTINGHAM AND G. PATRICIA DE LA CRUZ

Ancestry is a broad concept that can mean different things to different people; it can be described alternately as where their ancestors are from, where they or their parents originated, or simply how they see themselves ethnically. Some people may have one distinct ancestry, while others are descendants of several ancestry groups, and still others may know only that their ancestors were from a particular region of the world or may not know their ethnic origins at all. The Census Bureau defines ancestry as a person's ethnic origin, heritage, descent, or "roots," which may reflect their place of birth, place of birth of parents or ancestors, and ethnic identities that have evolved within the United States.

This report is part of a series that presents population and housing data collected by Census 2000, where 80 percent of respondents to the long form specified at least one ancestry. (About one-sixth of households received the long form.) It presents data on the most frequently reported ancestries and describes population distributions for the United States, including regions, states, counties, and selected cities.[1] The listed ancestries were reported by at least 100,000 people, and the numbers cited in this report represent the number of people who reported each ancestry either as their first or second response.

The question on ancestry first appeared on the census questionnaire in 1980, replacing a question on where a person's parents were born. The question on parental birthplace provided foreign-origin data only for people with one or both parents born outside the United States. The current ancestry question allows everyone to give one or two attributions of their "ancestry or ethnic origin" (Figure 1), and in doing so, enables people to identify an ethnic background, such as German, Lebanese, Nigerian, or Portuguese, which was not otherwise identified in the race or Hispanic-origin questions.

The ancestries in this report also include the groups covered in the questions on race and Hispanic origin, such as African American, Mexican, American Indian, and Chinese. For these groups, the results from the ancestry question and the race and Hispanic-origin questions differ, but the latter are the official sources of data for race and Hispanic groups. In some cases, the totals reported on the ancestry question are lower than the numbers from the race or Hispanic-origin question. For

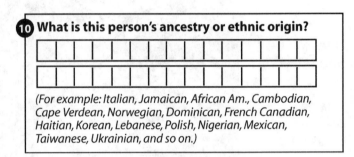

10 What is this person's ancestry or ethnic origin?

(For example: Italian, Jamaican, African Am., Cambodian, Cape Verdean, Norwegian, Dominican, French Canadian, Haitian, Korean, Lebanese, Polish, Nigerian, Mexican, Taiwanese, Ukrainian, and so on.)

Figure 1 Reproduction of the Question on Ancestry from Census 2000.

Source: U.S. Census Bureau, Census 2000 questionnaire.

instance, nearly 12 million fewer people specified "African American" as their ancestry than gave that response to the race question. One reason for this large difference is that some people who reported Black or African American on the race question reported their ancestry more specifically, such as Jamaican, Haitian, or Nigerian, and thus were not counted in the African American ancestry category. Similarly, more than 2 million fewer people reported Mexican ancestry than gave that answer to the Hispanic-origin question.[2] In other cases, the ancestry question produced higher numbers, such as for Dominicans, whose estimated totals from the ancestry question were over 100,000 higher than from the Hispanic-origin question, where many Dominicans may have reported a general term (like Hispanic) or checked "other" without writing in a detailed response.[3]

More than four out of five people specified at least one ancestry.

In 2000, 58 percent of the population specified only one ancestry, 22 percent provided two ancestries, and 1 percent reported an unclassifiable ancestry such as "mixture" or "adopted." Another 19 percent did not report any ancestry at all, a substantial increase from 1990, when 10 percent of the population left the ancestry question blank (Table 1).

Table 1   Ancestry Reporting: 1990 and 2000

Ancestry	1990[1]		2000		Change, 1990 to 2000	
	Number	Percent	Number	Percent	Numerical	Percent
Total population	248,709,873	100.0	281,421,906	100.0	32,712,033	13.2
Ancestry specified	222,608,257	89.5	225,310,411	80.1	2,702,154	1.2
Single ancestry	148,836,950	59.8	163,315,936	58.0	14,478,986	9.7
Multiple ancestry	73,771,307	29.7	61,994,475	22.0	−11,776,832	−16.0
Ancestry not specified	26,101,616	10.5	56,111,495	19.9	30,009,879	115.0
Unclassified	2,180,245	0.9	2,437,929	0.9	257,684	11.8
Not reported	23,921,371	9.6	53,673,566	19.1	29,752,195	124.4

(Data based on sample. For information on confidentiality protection, sampling error, nonsampling error, and definitions, see www.census.gov/prod/cen2000/doc/sf3.pdf)

[1] 1990 estimates in this table differ slightly from 1990 Summary Tape File 3 in order to make them fully consistent with data from Census 2000.

Source: U.S. Census Bureau, Census 2000 Summary File 3 and 1990 special tabulation.

Nearly one of six people reported their ancestry as German.

In 2000, 42.8 million people (15 percent of the population) considered themselves to be of German (or part-German) ancestry, the most frequent response to the census question (Figure 2).[4] Other ancestries with over 15 million people in 2000 included Irish (30.5 million, or 11 percent), African American (24.9 million, or 9 percent), English (24.5 million, or 9 percent), American (20.2 million, or 7 percent), Mexican (18.4 million, or 7 percent), and Italian (15.6 million, or 6 percent).

Other ancestries with 4 million or more people included Polish, French, American Indian, Scottish, Dutch, Norwegian, Scotch-Irish, and Swedish.

In total, 7 ancestries were reported by more than 15 million people in 2000, 37 ancestries were reported by more than 1 million people, and 92 ancestries were reported by more than 100,000 people (Table 2).

The largest European ancestries have decreased in population, while African American, Hispanic, and Asian ancestries have increased.

The highest growth rates between 1990 and 2000 occurred in groups identified by a general heritage rather than a particular country of ancestry. For example, the number of people who reported Latin American, African, or European all more than quadrupled (Latin American increased from 44,000 in 1990 to 250,000 in 2000, African grew from 246,000 to 1.2 million, and European rose from 467,000 to 2.0 million). Other general heritage groups that at least doubled in size included Western European, Northern European, Asian, Hispanic, and White.

The three largest ancestries in 1990 were German, Irish, and English. In 2000, these groups were still the largest European ancestries, but each had decreased in size by at least 8 million and by more than 20 percent (Table 2). As a proportion of the

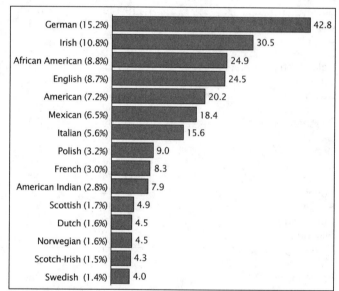

Figure 2   Fifteen Largest Ancestries: 2000.   (In millions. Percent of total population in parentheses. Data based on sample. For information on confidentiality protection, sampling error, nonsampling error, and definitions, see www.census.gov/prod/cen2000/doc/sf3.pdf).

Source: U.S. Census Bureau, Census 2000 special tabulation.

population, German decreased from 23 percent in 1990 to 15 percent in 2000, while Irish and English decreased from 16 percent to 11 percent, and from 13 percent to 9 percent, respectively. Several other large European ancestries also decreased over the decade, including Polish, French, Scottish, Dutch, and Swedish.

The number of people who reported African American ancestry increased by nearly 1.2 million, or 4.9 percent, between 1990 and 2000, making this group the third largest ancestry. However, the proportion of African Americans decreased slightly over the decade, from 9.5 percent to 8.8 percent.

The population of many ancestries, such as Mexican, Chinese, Filipino, and Asian Indian, increased during the decade, reflecting sizable immigration, especially from Latin America and Asia. Several small ancestry populations, including Brazilian, Pakistani, Albanian, Honduran, and Trinidadian and Tobagonian, at least doubled.

Table 2 Ancestries with 100,000 or More People in 2000: 1990 and 2000

Ancestry	1990		2000		Change, 1990 to 2000	
	Number	Percent of total population	Number	Percent of total population	Numerical	Percent
Total population	248,709,873	100.0	281,421,906	100.0	32,712,033	13.2
African*	245,845	0.1	1,183,316	0.4	937,471	381.3
African American*[1,2]	23,750,256	9.5	24,903,412	8.8	1,153,156	4.9
Albanian	47,710	–	113,661	–	65,951	138.2
American*	12,395,999	5.0	20,188,305	7.2	7,792,306	62.9
American Indian*	8,689,344	3.5	7,876,568	2.8	−812,776	−9.4
Arab*	127,364	0.1	205,822	0.1	78,458	61.6
Armenian	308,096	0.1	385,488	0.1	77,392	25.1
Asian*	107,172	–	238,960	0.1	131,788	123.0
Asian Indian	569,338	0.2	1,546,703	0.5	977,365	171.7
Austrian	864,783	0.3	730,336	0.3	−134,447	−15.5
Belgian	380,403	0.2	348,531	0.1	−31,872	−8.4
Brazilian	65,875	–	181,076	0.1	115,201	174.9
British	1,119,140	0.4	1,085,718	0.4	−33,422	−3.0
Cambodian[2]	134,955	0.1	197,093	0.1	62,138	46.0
Canadian	549,990	0.2	638,548	0.2	88,558	16.1
Chinese	1,505,229	0.6	2,271,562	0.8	766,333	50.9
Colombian	351,717	0.1	583,986	0.2	232,269	66.0
Croatian[1]	544,270	0.2	374,241	0.1	−170,029	−31.2
Cuban	859,739	0.3	1,097,594	0.4	237,855	27.7
Czech	1,296,369	0.5	1,258,452	0.4	−37,917	22.9
Czechoslovakian	315,285	0.1	441,403	0.2	126,118	40.0
Danish	1,634,648	0.7	1,430,897	0.5	−203,751	−12.5
Dominican[1,2]	505,690	0.2	908,531	0.3	402,841	79.7
Dutch	6,226,339	2.5	4,541,770	1.6	−1,684,569	−27.1
Ecuadorian[1]	197,374	0.1	322,965	0.1	125,591	63.6
Egyptian	78,574	–	142,832	0.1	64,258	81.8
English	32,651,788	13.1	24,509,692	8.7	−8,142,096	−24.9
European*	466,718	0.2	1,968,696	0.7	1,501,978	321.8
Filipino	1,450,512	0.6	2,116,478	0.8	665,966	45.9
Finnish	658,854	0.3	623,559	0.2	−35,295	−5.4
French	10,320,656	4.1	8,309,666	3.0	−2,010,990	−19.5
French Canadian[1,2]	2,167,127	0.9	2,349,684	0.8	182,557	8.4
German[1]	57,947,171	23.3	42,841,569	15.2	−15,105,602	−26.1
Greek	1,110,292	0.4	1,153,295	0.4	43,003	3.9
Guatemalan	241,559	0.1	463,502	0.2	221,943	91.9
Guyanese	81,665	–	162,425	0.1	80,760	98.9
Haitian[1,2]	289,521	0.1	548,199	0.2	258,678	89.3
Hawaiian	256,081	0.1	334,858	0.1	78,777	30.8
Hispanic*	1,113,259	0.4	2,451,109	0.9	1,337,850	120.2
Hmong	84,823	–	140,528	–	55,705	65.7
Honduran	116,635	–	266,848	0.1	150,213	128.8
Hungarian	1,582,302	0.6	1,398,702	0.5	−183,600	−11.6
Iranian	235,521	0.1	338,266	0.1	102,745	43.6
Irish[1]	38,735,539	15.6	30,524,799	10.8	−8,210,740	−21.2
Israeli	81,677	–	106,839	–	25,162	30.8
Italian[1,2]	14,664,189	5.9	15,638,348	5.6	974,159	6.6
Jamaican[1,2]	435,024	0.2	736,513	0.3	301,489	69.3
Japanese.	1,004,622	0.4	1,103,325	0.4	98,703	9.8
Korean[1,2]	836,987	0.3	1,190,353	0.4	353,366	42.2
Laotian	146,947	0.1	179,866	0.1	32,919	22.4
Latin American*	43,521	–	250.052	0.1	206,531	474.6
Lebanese[1,2]	394,180	0.2	440,279	0.2	46,099	11.7
Lithuanian	811,865	0.3	659,992	0.2	−151,873	−18.7

(See footnotes on next page)

(continued)

Table 2 Ancestries with 100,000 or More People in 2000: 1990 and 2000 (continued)

Ancestry	1990 Number	1990 Percent of total population	2000 Number	2000 Percent of total population	Change, 1990 to 2000 Numerical	Change, 1990 to 2000 Percent
Mexican[1,2]...............	11,580,038	4.7	18,382,291	6.5	6,802,253	58.7
Nicaraguan...............	177,077	0.1	230,358	0.1	53,281	30.1
Nigerian[1,2]...............	91,499	–	164,691	0.1	73,192	80.0
Northern European*.........	65,993	–	163,657	0.1	97,664	148.0
Norwegian[2]..............	3,869,395	1.6	4,477,725	1.6	608,330	15.7
Pakistani.................	99,974	–	253,193	0.1	153,219	153.3
Panamanian...............	88,649	–	119,497	–	30,848	34.8
Pennsylvania German.......	305,841	0.1	255,807	0.1	−50,034	−16.4
Peruvian.................	161,866	0.1	292,991	0.1	131,125	81.0
Polish[1,2].................	9,366,051	3.8	8,977,235	3.2	−388,816	−4.2
Portuguese..............	1,148,857	0.5	1,173,691	0.4	24,834	2.2
Puerto Rican.............	1,955,323	0.8	2,652,598	0.9	697,275	35.7
Romanian................	365,531	0.1	367,278	0.1	1,747	(NS)
Russian.................	2,951,373	1.2	2,652,214	0.9	−299,159	−10.1
Salvadoran...............	499,153	0.2	802,743	0.3	303,590	60.8
Scandinavian.............	678,880	0.3	425,099	0.2	−253,781	−37.4
Scotch-Irish..............	5,617,773	2.3	4,319,232	1.5	−1,298,541	−23.1
Scottish.................	5,393,581	2.2	4,890,581	1.7	−503,000	−9.3
Serbian..................	116,795	–	140,337	–	23,5422	0.2
Slavic...................	76,923	–	127,136	–	50,213	65.3
Slovak[1].................	1,882,897	0.8	797,764	0.3	−1,085,133	−57.6
Slovene.................	124,437	0.1	176,691	0.1	52,254	42.0
Spaniard................	360,858	0.1	299,948	0.1	−60,910	−16.9
Spanish.................	2,024,004	0.8	2,187,144	0.8	163,140	8.1
Swedish.................	4,680,863	1.9	3,998,310	1.4	−682,553	−14.6
Swiss...................	1,045,492	0.4	911,502	0.3	−133,990	−12.8
Syrian...................	129,606	0.1	142,897	0.1	13,291	10.3
Taiwanese[1,2].............	192,973	0.1	293,568	0.1	100,595	52.1
Thai[1]..................	112,11	–	146,577	0.1	34,460	30.7
Trinidadian and Tobagonian ..	76,270	–	164,738	0.1	88,468	116.0
Turkish..................	83,850	–	117,575	–	33,725	40.2
Ukrainian[1,2].............	740,723	0.3	892,922	0.3	152,199	20.5
United States*.............	643,561	0.3	404,328	0.1	−239,233	−37.2
Vietnamese..............	535,825	0.2	1,029,420	0.4	493,595	92.1
Welsh..................	2,033,893	0.8	1,753,794	0.6	−280,099	−13.8
West Indian*.............	159,167	0.1	147,222	0.1	−11,945	−7.5
Western European*........	42,409	–	125,300	–	82,891	195.5
White*..................	1,799,711	0.7	3,834,122	1.4	2,034,411	113.0
Yugoslavian..............	257,986	0.1	328,547	0.1	70,561	27.4
Other ancestries..........	3,989,728	1.6	4,380,380	1.6	390,652	9.8

(Data based on sample. For information on confidentiality protection, sampling error, nonsampling error, and definitions, see www.census.gov/prod/cen2000/doc/sf3.pdf)

– Rounds to 0.0.

*General response which may encompass several ancestries not listed separately (i.e., African American includes Black and Negro). NS Not statistically different from zero at the 90-percent confidence level.

[1]Included in the list of examples on the census questionnaire in 1990.

[2]Included in the list of examples on the census questionnaire in 2000.

Notes: Because of sampling error, the estimates in this table may not be significantly different from one another or from other ancestries not listed in this table. People who reported two ancestries were included once in each category. The estimates in this table differ slightly in some cases from the estimates in other data products due to the collapsing schemes used. For example, here German does not include Bavarian. Some groups correspond to groups identified separately in the race and Hispanic-origin questions. The race item provides the primary source of data for White, Black, American Indian, Alaska Native, Asian groups, Native Hawaiian, and Pacific Islander groups. The Hispanic-origin question is the primary identifier for Mexican, Puerto Rican, Cuban, and other Hispanic groups.

Source: U.S. Census Bureau, 1990 Census and Census 2000 special tabulations.

Seven percent of the U.S. population reported their ancestry as American.

The number who reported American and no other ancestry increased from 12.4 million in 1990 to 20.2 million in 2000, the largest numerical growth of any group during the 1990s.[5] This figure represents an increase of 63 percent, as the proportion rose from 5.0 percent to 7.2 percent of the population.

The Geographic Distribution of Ancestries

In each of the four regions, a different ancestry was reported as the largest.

Among the four regions, the largest ancestries in 2000 were Irish in the Northeast (16 percent), African American in the South (14 percent), German in the Midwest (27 percent), and Mexican in the West (16 percent, see Table 3).[6]

At the state level, 8 different ancestries were each the largest reported in 1 or more states. German led in 23 states, including every state in the Midwest, the majority of states in the West, and 1 state in the South. In 3 of those states, German was reported by more than 40 percent of the population: North Dakota (44 percent), Wisconsin (43 percent), and South Dakota (41 percent).

The other leading ancestries at the state level were African American in 7 contiguous states from Louisiana to Maryland and in the District of Columbia (also notably high at 43 percent); American in Arkansas, Tennessee, Kentucky, and West Virginia; Italian in Connecticut, New Jersey, New York, and Rhode Island; Mexican in 4 states from California to Texas; English in Maine, Utah and Vermont; Irish in Delaware, Massachusetts and New Hampshire; and Japanese in Hawaii.

Many other ancestries were not the largest ancestry in any state but represented more than 10 percent of a state's population, including American Indian in Oklahoma (12 percent) and Alaska (11 percent); Filipino (18 percent) and Hawaiian (16 percent) in Hawaii; French in Maine (14 percent), Vermont (15 percent), and Rhode Island (11 percent); French Canadian in New Hampshire (10 percent); and Norwegian in North Dakota (30 percent), Minnesota (17 percent), South Dakota (15 percent), and Montana (11 percent, see Table 3).

Other ancestries not noted above were among the 5 largest in a state but represented less than 10 percent of the state's population. Examples include Chinese in Hawaii (8.3 percent), Czech in Nebraska (4.9 percent), Danish in Utah (6.5 percent), Eskimo in Alaska (6.1 percent), Polish in Michigan (8.6 percent), Portuguese in Rhode Island (8.7 percent), Spanish in New Mexico (9.3 percent), and Swedish in Minnesota (9.9 percent).

Twenty-four different ancestries were the largest in at least one county in the United States.

German was the leading ancestry reported in many counties across the northern half of the United States, from Pennsylvania to Washington, as well as some counties in the southern half. Mexican was the leading ancestry along the southwestern border of the United States, and American and African American were the most commonly reported ancestries in many southern counties, from Virginia to eastern Texas.

Several ancestries that did not predominate in any state were the most common within one or more counties. Examples include Aleut and Eskimo in some counties of Alaska; American Indian in counties in Alaska, Arizona, California, Montana, Nebraska, Nevada, New Mexico, North Carolina, Oklahoma, Oregon, South Dakota, Washington, and Wisconsin; Finnish in several counties in the Upper Peninsula of Michigan; French in counties in Connecticut, New York, Maine, New Hampshire, Vermont, and Louisiana; French Canadian in counties in Maine; Dutch in several counties in Michigan and Iowa; Norwegian in counties in Iowa, Minnesota, Montana, North Dakota, and Wisconsin; Polish in one county in Pennsylvania; and Portuguese in one county each in Massachusetts and Rhode Island.

African American and Mexican were the most commonly reported ancestries in the ten largest cities in the United States.

In 2000, African American was the most frequently reported ancestry in New York City, Chicago, Philadelphia, and Detroit (Table 4).[7] Mexican was the leading ancestry in Los Angeles, Houston, Phoenix, San Diego, Dallas, and San Antonio.

Additional Findings
What Combinations Were the Most Common among Respondents Who Reported Two Ancestries?

The most common ancestry combinations in 2000 were German and Irish (2.7 percent of the population), German and English (1.7 percent), and Irish and English (1.4 percent).

What Other Ancestries Were Reported?

Overall, about 500 different ancestries were reported during Census 2000. The category "Other ancestries" in Table 2 consists of all ancestries with fewer than 100,000 people (such as Venezuelan, Samoan, or Latvian) as well as all religious identifications (which are not tabulated).[8]

Table 3 Largest Ancestries for the United States, Regions, States, and for Puerto Rico: 2000

Ancestry	Total population	Ancestry	Percent	Ancestry	Percent	Ancestry	Percent	Ancestry	Percent	Ancestry	Percent
United States	281,421,906	German	15.2	Irish	10.8	African Am.	8.8	English	8.7	American	7.2
Region											
Northeast	53,594,378	Irish	15.8	Italian	14.1	German	13.6	English	8.3	African Am.	6.5
Midwest	64,392,776	German	26.6	Irish	11.8	English	8.4	African Am.	7.8	American	6.5
South	100,236,820	African Am.	14.0	American	11.2	German	10.0	Irish	8.8	English	8.4
West	63,197,932	Mexican	16.0	German	13.3	English	9.9	Irish	9.0	American	4.1
State											
Alabama	4,447,100	African Am.	19.9	American	16.8	English	7.8	Irish	7.7	German	5.7
Alaska	626,932	German	16.6	Irish	10.8	Am. Indian	10.5	English	9.6	Eskimo	6.1
Arizona	5,130,632	Mexican	18.0	German	15.6	English	10.4	Irish	10.2	Am. Indian	6.1
Arkansas	2,673,400	American	15.7	African Am.	11.9	Irish	9.5	German	9.3	English	7.9
California	33,871,648	Mexican	22.2	German	9.8	Irish	7.7	English	7.4	African Am.	5.1
Colorado	4,301,261	German	22.0	Irish	12.2	English	12.0	Mexican	9.0	American	5.0
Connecticut.	3,405,565	Italian	18.6	Irish	16.6	English	10.3	German	9.8	Polish	8.3
Delaware	783,600	Irish	16.6	German	14.3	African Am.	14.0	English	12.1	Italian	9.3
District of Columbia	572,059	African Am.	43.4	Irish	4.9	German	4.8	English	4.4	Salvadoran	2.3
Florida	15,982,378	German	11.8	Irish	10.3	English	9.2	African Am.	8.6	American	7.8
Georgia	8,186,453	African Am.	21.6	American	13.3	English	8.1	Irish	7.8	German	7.0
Hawaii	1,211,537	Japanese	20.7	Filipino	17.7	Hawaiian	16.3	Chinese	8.3	German	5.8
Idaho	1,293,953	German	18.8	English	18.1	Irish	10.0	American	8.1	Mexican	5.5
Illinois	12,419,293	German	19.6	Irish	12.2	African Am.	11.5	Mexican	8.2	Polish	7.5
Indiana	6,080,485	German	22.6	American	11.8	Irish	10.8	English	8.9	African Am.	6.5
Iowa	2,926,324	German	35.7	Irish	13.5	English	9.5	American	6.6	Norwegian	5.7
Kansas	2,688,418	German	25.8	Irish	11.5	English	10.8	American	8.7	Mexican	4.7
Kentucky.	4,041,769	American	20.7	German	12.7	Irish	10.5	English	9.7	African Am.	5.7
Louisiana	4,468,976	African Am.	25.5	French	12.2	American	10.0	German	7.0	Irish	7.0
Maine	1,274,923	English	21.5	Irish	15.1	French	14.2	American	9.3	Fr. Canadian	8.6
Maryland.	5,296,486	African Am.	20.5	German	15.7	Irish	11.7	English	9.0	American	5.6
Massachusetts ..	6,349,097	Irish	22.5	Italian	13.5	English	11.4	French	8.0	German	5.9
Michigan	9,938,444	German	20.4	African Am.	11.0	Irish	10.7	English	9.9	Polish	8.6
Minnesota.	4,919,479	German	36.7	Norwegian	17.3	Irish	11.2	Swedish	9.9	English	6.3
Mississippi	2,844,658	African Am.	28.3	American	14.0	Irish	6.9	English	6.1	German	4.5
Missouri	5,595,211	German	23.5	Irish	12.7	American	10.4	English	9.5	African Am.	8.8
Montana	902,195	German	27.0	Irish	14.8	English	12.6	Norwegian	10.6	Am. Indian	7.4
Nebraska	1,711,263	German	38.6	Irish	13.4	English	9.6	Swedish	4.9	Czech	4.9
Nevada.	1,998,257	German	14.1	Mexican	12.7	Irish	11.0	English	10.1	Italian	6.6
New Hampshire .	1,235,786	Irish	19.4	English	18.0	French	14.6	Fr. Canadian	10.3	German	8.6
New Jersey.	8,414,350	Italian	17.8	Irish	15.9	German	12.6	African Am.	8.8	Polish	6.9
New Mexico	1,819,046	Mexican	16.3	Am. Indian	10.3	German	9.8	Hispanic	9.4	Spanish	9.3
New York	18,976,457	Italian	14.4	Irish	12.9	German	11.2	African Am.	7.7	English	6.0
North Carolina ..	8,049,313	African Am.	16.6	American	13.7	English	9.5	German	9.5	Irish	7.4
North Dakota ...	642,200	German	43.9	Norwegian	30.1	Irish	7.7	Am. Indian	5.1	Swedish	5.0
Ohio	11,353,140	German	25.2	Irish	12.7	English	9.2	African Am.	9.1	American	8.5
Oklahoma	3,450,654	German	12.6	Am. Indian	12.1	American	11.2	Irish	10.3	English	8.4
Oregon	3,421,399	German	20.5	English	13.2	Irish	11.9	American	6.2	Mexican	5.5
Pennsylvania ...	12,281,054	German	25.4	Irish	16.1	Italian	11.5	English	7.9	African Am.	7.4
Rhode Island ...	1,048,319	Italian	19.0	Irish	18.4	English	12.0	French	10.9	Portuguese	8.7
South Carolina ..	4,012,012	African Am.	22.8	American	13.7	German	8.4	English	8.2	Irish	7.9
South Dakota ...	754,844	German	40.7	Norwegian	15.3	Irish	10.4	Am. Indian	8.2	English	7.1
Tennessee	5,689,283	American	17.3	African Am.	13.0	Irish	9.3	English	9.1	German	8.3
Texas	20,851,820	Mexican	22.6	German	9.9	African Am.	8.7	Irish	7.2	American	7.2
Utah	2,233,169	English	29.0	German	11.5	American	6.6	Danish	6.5	Irish	5.9
Vermont	608,827	English	18.4	Irish	16.4	French	14.5	German	9.1	Fr. Canadian	8.8
Virginia	7,078,515	African Am.	14.9	German	11.7	American	11.2	English	11.1	Irish	9.8
Washington	5,894,121	German	18.7	English	12.0	Irish	11.4	Norwegian	6.2	American	5.2
West Virginia ...	1,808,344	American	18.7	German	14.0	Irish	11.0	English	9.7	Am. Indian	4.4
Wisconsin	5,363,675	German	42.6	Irish	10.9	Polish	9.3	Norwegian	8.5	English	6.5
Wyoming	493,782	German	25.9	English	15.9	Irish	13.3	American	6.4	Am. Indian	4.7
Puerto Rico	**3,808,610**	**Puerto Rican**	**69.0**	**American**	**2.5**	**Spaniard**	**2.1**	**Dominican**	**1.7**	**Hispanic**	**0.8**

(Data based on sample. For information on confidentiality protection, sampling error, nonsampling error, and definitions, see www.census.gov/prod/cen2000/doc/sf3.pdf)

Notes: Because of sampling error, the estimates in this table may not be significantly different from one another or from other ancestries not listed in this table.

People who reported two ancestries were included once in each category. Some groups correspond to groups identified separately in the race and Hispanic-origin questions. The race item provides the primary source of data for White, Black, American Indian, Alaska Native, Asian groups, Native Hawaiian, and Pacific Islander groups. The Hispanic-origin question is the primary identifier for Mexican, Puerto Rican, Cuban, and other Hispanic groups.

About Census 2000

Why Census 2000 Asked about Ancestry

Information about ancestry is required to enforce provisions under the Civil Rights Act that prohibit discrimination based upon race, sex, religion, and national origin. More generally, these data are needed to measure the social and economic characteristics of ethnic groups and to tailor services to accommodate cultural differences.

Data about ancestry assist states and local agencies on aging to develop health care and other services tailored to address the language and cultural diversity of various groups.

Under the Public Health Service Act, ancestry is one of the factors used to identify segments of the population who may not be receiving medical services.

Accuracy of the Estimates

The data contained in this report are based on the sample of households who responded to the Census 2000 long form. Nationally, approximately 1 out of every 6 housing units was included in this sample. As a result, the sample estimates may differ somewhat from the 100-percent figures that would have been obtained if all housing units, people within those housing units, and people living in group quarters had been enumerated using the same questionnaires, instructions, enumerators, and so forth. The sample estimates also differ from the values that would have been obtained from different samples of housing units, people within those housing units, and people living in group quarters. The deviation of a sample estimate from the average of all possible samples is called the sampling error.

In addition to the variability that arises from the sampling procedures, both sample data and 100-percent data are subject to nonsampling error. Nonsampling error may be introduced during any of the various complex operations used to collect and process data. Such errors may include: not enumerating every household or every person in the population, failing to obtain all required information from the respondents, obtaining incorrect or inconsistent information, and recording information incorrectly.

In addition, errors can occur during the field review of the enumerators' work, during clerical handling of the census questionnaires, or during the electronic processing of the questionnaires.

Nonsampling error may affect the data in two ways: (1) errors that are introduced randomly will increase the variability of the data and, therefore, should be reflected in the standard errors; and (2) errors that tend to be consistent in one direction will bias both sample and 100-percent data in that direction. For example, if respondents consistently tend to underreport their incomes, then the resulting estimates of households or families by income category will tend to be understated for the higher income categories and overstated for the lower income categories. Such biases are not reflected in the standard errors.

While it is impossible to completely eliminate error from an operation as large and complex as the decennial census, the

Table 4   Largest Ancestry for the Ten Cities with the Highest Population: 2000

| City | Total population | Largest ancestry | | | |
		Ancestry	Number of people	Percent of population	90-percent confidence interval
New York, NY	8,008,278	African American	922,116	11.5	11.4–11.6
Los Angeles, CA	3,694,834	Mexican	983,157	26.6	26.5–26.8
Chicago, IL	2,895,964	African American	804,053	27.8	27.6–27.9
Houston, TX	1,954,848	Mexican	467,213	23.9	23.7–24.1
Philadelphia, PA	1,517,550	African American	493,177	32.5	32.3–32.8
Phoenix, AZ	1,320,994	Mexican	320,092	24.2	24.0–24.5
San Diego, CA	1,223,341	Mexican	237,867	19.9	19.2–19.7
Dallas, TX	1,188,204	Mexican	306,072	25.8	25.5–26.0
San Antonio, TX	1,144,554	Mexican	472,324	41.3	41.0–41.6
Detroit, MI	951,270	African American	599,667	63.0	62.7–63.4

(Data based on sample. For information on confidentiality protection, sampling error, nonsampling error, and definitions, see *www.census.gov/prod/cen2000/doc/sf3.pdf*)

Notes: Because of sampling error, the estimates in this table may not be significantly different from one another or from other ancestries not listed in this table. People who reported two ancestries were included once in each category. Some groups correspond to groups identified separately in the race and Hispanic-origin questions. The race item provides the primary source of data for White, Black, American Indian, Alaska Native, Asian groups, Native Hawaiian, and Pacific Islander groups. The Hispanic-origin question is the primary identifier for Mexican, Puerto Rican, Cuban, and other Hispanic groups.

Source: U.S. Census Bureau, Census 2000 special tabulation.

Census Bureau attempts to control the sources of such error during the data collection and processing operations. The primary sources of error and the programs instituted to control error in Census 2000 are described in detail in *Summary File 3 Technical Documentation* under Chapter 8, "Accuracy of the Data," located at www.census.gov/prod /cen2000/doc/sf3.pdf.

All statements in this Census 2000 Brief have undergone statistical testing and all comparisons are significant at the 90-percent confidence level, unless otherwise noted. The estimates in tables, maps, and other figures may vary from actual values due to sampling and nonsampling errors. As a result, estimates in one category may not be significantly different from estimates assigned to a different category. Further information on the accuracy of the data is located at www.census.gov/prod/ cen2000/doc/sf3.pdf. For further information on the computation and use of standard errors, contact the Decennial Statistical Studies Division at 301-763-4242.

For More Information

The Census 2000 Summary File 3 data are available from the American Factfinder on the Internet (factfinder.census.gov). They were released on a state-by-state basis during 2002. For information on confidentiality protection, nonsampling error, sampling error, and definitions, also see www.census.gov /prod/ cen2000/doc/sf3.pdf or contact the Customer Services Center at 301-763-INFO (4636).

Information on population and housing topics is presented in the Census 2000 Brief series, located on the Census Bureau's Web site at www.census.gov/population/www/cen2000/briefs. html. This series presents information on race, Hispanic origin, age, sex, household type, housing tenure, and social, economic, and housing characteristics, such as ancestry, income, and housing costs.

For additional information on ancestry, including reports and survey data, visit the Census Bureau's Web site on at www.census.gov /population/www/ancestry.html. To find information about the availability of data products, including reports, CD-ROMs, and DVDs, call the Customer Services Center at 301-763-INFO (4636), or e-mail webmaster@census.gov.

Notes

1. The text of this report discusses data for the United States, including the 50 states and the District of Columbia. Data for the Commonwealth of Puerto Rico are shown in Table 3.

2. The estimates in this report are based on responses from a sample of the population. As with all surveys, estimates may vary from the actual values because of sampling variation or other factors. All statements made in this report have undergone statistical testing and are significant at the 90-percent confidence level unless otherwise noted.

3. For more information about race and Hispanic groups, see Census 2000 Briefs on Hispanic, American Indian and Alaska Native, Asian, Black, Native Hawaiian and Pacific Islander, White, and Two or More Races populations, available on the Census Bureau Web site at www.census.gov/prod/cen2000/index.html.

4. The estimates in Figure 2 and Table 2 in some cases differ slightly from the estimates in other data products due to the collapsing schemes used. For example, here German does not include Bavarian.

5. American was considered a valid ancestry response when it was the only ancestry provided by a respondent.

6. The Northeast region includes the states of Connecticut, Maine, Massachusetts, New Hampshire, New Jersey, New York, Pennsylvania, Rhode Island, and Vermont. The Midwest region includes the states of Illinois, Indiana, Iowa, Kansas, Michigan, Minnesota, Missouri, Nebraska, North Dakota, Ohio, South Dakota, and Wisconsin. The South region includes the states of Alabama, Arkansas, Delaware, Florida, Georgia, Kentucky, Louisiana, Maryland, Mississippi, North Carolina, Oklahoma, South Carolina, Tennessee, Texas, Virginia, West Virginia, and the District of Columbia, a state equivalent. The West region includes the states of Alaska, Arizona, California, Colorado, Hawaii, Idaho, Montana, Nevada, New Mexico, Oregon, Utah, Washington, and Wyoming.

7. Census 2000 showed 245 places in the United States with 100,000 or more population. They included 238 incorporated places (including 4 city-county consolidations) and 7 census designated places that were not legally incorporated. For a list of places by state, see www.census.gov/population/www/cen2000/phc-t6.html.

8. Smaller groups are listed at www.census.gov/population/www/ ancestry.html.

From *U.S. Census Bureau*, June 2004, pp. 1–10.

Minority Population Tops 100 Million and More than 300 Counties Now "Majority-Minority"

Minority Population Tops 100 Million

The nation's minority population reached 100.7 million, according to the national and state estimates by race, Hispanic origin, sex and age released today by the U.S. Census Bureau. A year ago, the minority population totaled 98.3 million.

"About one in three U.S. residents is a minority," said Census Bureau Director Louis Kincannon. "To put this into perspective, there are more minorities in this country today than there were people in the United States in 1910. In fact, the minority population in the U.S. is larger than the total population of all but 11 countries."

The population in 1910 was 92.2 million. On Oct. 17, 2006, the Census Bureau reported that the overall population had topped 300 million.

California had a minority population of 20.7 million—21 percent of the nation's total. Texas had a minority population of 12.2 million—12 percent of the U.S. total.

There were other milestones reached as well during the July 1, 2005, to July 1, 2006, period: The nation's black population surpassed 40 million, while the Native Hawaiian and Other Pacific Islander group reached the 1 million mark.

Hispanic remained the largest minority group, with 44.3 million on July 1, 2006—14.8 percent of the total population. Black was the second-largest minority group, totaling 40.2 million in 2006. They were followed by Asian (14.9 million), American Indian and Alaska Native (4.5 million), and Native Hawaiian and Other Pacific Islander (1 million). The population of non-Hispanic whites who indicated no other race totaled 198.7 million in 2006.

With a 3.4 percent increase between July 1, 2005, and July 1, 2006, Hispanic was the fastest-growing minority group. Asian was the second fastest-growing minority group, with a 3.2 percent population increase during the 2005–2006 period. The population of non-Hispanic whites who indicated no other race grew by 0.3 percent during the one-year period.

Four states and the District of Columbia are "majority-minority." Hawaii led the nation with a population that was 75 percent minority in 2006, followed by the District of Columbia (68 percent), New Mexico (57 percent), California

(57 percent) and Texas (52 percent). No other state had a minority population exceeding 42 percent of the total.

Highlights for the various groups:

Hispanic

- Hispanics accounted for almost half (1.4 million) of the national population growth of 2.9 million between July 1, 2005, and July 1, 2006.
- California had the largest Hispanic population of any state as of July 1, 2006 (13.1 million), followed by Texas (8.4 million) and Florida (3.6 million). Texas had the largest numerical increase between 2005 and 2006 (305,000), with California (283,000) and Florida (161,000) following. In New Mexico, Hispanics comprised the highest proportion of the total population (44 percent), with California and Texas (36 percent each) next in line.
- The Hispanic population in 2006 was much younger, with a median age of 27.4 compared with the population as a whole at 36.4. About a third of the Hispanic population was younger than 18, compared with one-fourth of the total population.

Black

- The black population increased by 1.3 percent, or 522,000, between 2005 and 2006.
- New York had the largest black population in 2006 (3.5 million), followed by Florida (3 million) and Texas (2.9 million). Texas had the largest numerical increase between 2005 and 2006 (135,000), with Georgia (101,000) and Florida (86,000) next. In the District of Columbia, the black population comprised the highest percentage (57 percent); Mississippi (37 percent) and Louisiana (32 percent) were next.
- The black population in 2006 was younger, with a median age of 30.1, compared with the population as a whole at 36.4. About 31 percent of the black population was younger than 18, compared with 25 percent of the total population.

Asian

- The Asian population rose by 3.2 percent, or 460,000, between 2005 and 2006.
- California had the largest Asian population on July 1, 2006 (5 million), as well as the largest numerical increase during the 2005 to 2006 period (114,000). New York (1.4 million) and Texas (882,000) followed in population; Texas (43,000) and New York (34,000) followed in numerical increase. In Hawaii, Asians made up the highest proportion of the total population (56 percent), with California (14 percent) and New Jersey and Washington (8 percent each) next.
- The Asian population in 2006 was younger with a median age of 33.5, compared with the population as a whole at 36.4.

American Indian and Alaska Native

- The American Indian and Alaska Native population rose by 1 percent or 45,000, from 2005 to 2006.
- California had the largest population of American Indians and Alaska Natives (689,000) on July 1, 2006, with Oklahoma (397,000) and Arizona (331,000) next. Arizona had the largest numerical increase (8,000) since July 1, 2005, followed by Texas (7,000) and Florida (4,000). In Alaska, American Indians and Alaska Natives made up the highest proportion of the total population (18 percent), with Oklahoma and New Mexico, at 11 percent each, next.
- The American Indian and Alaska Native population in 2006 was younger, with a median age of 31, compared with the population as a whole at 36.4. About 28 percent of the American Indian and Alaska Native population was younger than 18, compared with 25 percent of the total population.

Native Hawaiian and Other Pacific Islander

- The Native Hawaiian and Other Pacific Islander population rose by 1.7 percent, or 17,000, from 2005 to 2006.
- Hawaii had the largest population (275,000), followed by California (260,000) and Washington (49,000); California had the largest numerical increase (3,400) of people of this group, with Texas (2,000) and Florida (1,500) next. In Hawaii, Native Hawaiians and Other Pacific Islanders comprised the largest proportion (21 percent) of the total population, followed by Utah (1 percent) and Alaska (0.9 percent).
- The Native Hawaiian and Other Pacific Islander population in 2006 was younger, with a median age of 28.6, compared with the population as a whole at 36.4. About 30 percent of the Native Hawaiian and Other Pacific Islander population was younger than 18, compared with 25 percent of the total population.

Non-Hispanic White

- The non-Hispanic, single-race white population, which represented 66 percent of the total population, accounted for less than a fifth (18 percent) of the nation's total population growth.
- California, New York and Texas had the largest population of this group (15.7 million, 11.7 million and 11.4 million, respectively), but Texas experienced the largest numerical increase (104,000), followed by North Carolina (91,000) and Arizona (78,000). Maine and Vermont had the highest proportion of single-race non-Hispanic whites (96 percent each), followed by West Virginia (94 percent).
- The non-Hispanic, single-race white population in 2006 was older than the population as a whole: The respective median ages were 40.5 and 36.4. About 21 percent of the population of this group was younger than 18, compared with 25 percent of the total population.

Also released today were tabulations by age, which showed:

- There were 37.3 million people 65 and older in 2006, accounting for 12 percent of the total population. In 2005, this group numbered an estimated 36.8 million.
- The number of people 85 and older reached 5.3 million, up from 5.1 million in 2005.
- In 2006, working-age adults (18 to 64) totaled 188.4 million, which was 63 percent of the population. A year earlier, the total was 186.2 million.
- The number of preschoolers (younger than 5) in the United States in 2006 was estimated at 20.4 million, up slightly from 20.3 million.
- The number of elementary school-age (5 through 13) children was 36.1 million, with high-school age (14 through 17) children numbering 17.2 million.
- States with the highest percentages of older people (65 and older) include Florida (16.8 percent), West Virginia (15.3 percent) and Pennsylvania (15.2 percent). States with the lowest percentages were Alaska (6.8 percent), Utah (8.8 percent) and Georgia (9.7 percent).
- States with the highest percentages of preschoolers include Utah (9.7 percent), Texas (8.2 percent) and Arizona (7.8 percent). States with the lowest percentages were Vermont (5.3 percent), Maine (5.3 percent) and New Hampshire (5.6 percent).

Unless otherwise specified, the data refer to the population who reported a race alone or in combination with one or more other races. The detailed tables show data for both this group and those who reported a single race only. Censuses and surveys permit respondents to select more than one race; consequently, people may be one race or a combination of races. Hispanics may be any race.

The federal government treats Hispanic origin and race as separate and distinct concepts. In surveys and censuses, separate questions are asked on Hispanic origin and race. The question on Hispanic origin asks respondents if they are Spanish, Hispanic or Latino. Starting with Census 2000, the question on race asked respondents to report the race or races they consider themselves to be. Thus, Hispanics may be of any race. (See U.S. Census Bureau Guidance on the Presentation and Comparison of Race and Hispanic Origin Data.)

These data are based on estimates of U.S. population for July 1, 2006. The Census Bureau estimates population change from the most recent decennial census (Census 2000) using annual data on births, deaths and international migration. More detailed information on the methodology used to produce these estimates can be found at http://www.census.gov/population/www/socdemo/compraceho.html.

Editor's Note—The embargoed data can be accessed at http://www.census.gov/Press-Release/www/releases/archives/embargoed_releases/index.html. After the release time, go to http://www.census.gov/popest/estimates.php.

More than 300 Counties Now "Majority-Minority"

Nearly one in every 10 of the nation's 3,141 counties has a population that is more than 50 percent minority. In 2006, eight counties that had not previously been majority-minority pushed the national total to 303, the U.S. Census Bureau reported today.

The two largest counties passing this threshold between July 1, 2005, and July 1, 2006, are Denver County, Colo., and East Baton Rouge Parish, La., with total populations of 566,974 and 429,073, respectively. Three other counties were in Texas (Winkler, Waller and Wharton), with one each in Montana (Blaine), New Mexico (Colfax) and Virginia (Manassas Park, an independent city and considered a county equivalent).

Los Angeles County, Calif., had the largest minority population in the country in 2006. At 7 million, or 71 percent of its total, Los Angeles County is home to one in every 14 of the nation's minority residents. The county's minority population is higher than the total population of 38 states, with the largest population of Hispanics, Asians, and American Indians and Alaska Natives in the country. It also has the second largest population of blacks and Native Hawaiians and Other Pacific Islanders.

Harris County, Texas, gained 121,400 minority residents between 2005 and 2006, which led the nation. Harris (Houston is its largest city) now has a minority population of 2.5 million, comprising 63 percent of its total. Its minority population ranks third nationally, not far behind second place Cook County, Ill. (Chicago).

Based on total population, Starr County, Texas, located on the Mexican border, had the highest proportion of all counties that was minority, at 98 percent. Among the nation's 25 most populous counties, Miami-Dade County, Fla., had the highest proportion minority, at 82 percent.

Highlights for the various groups:

Hispanic

- Los Angeles County had the largest Hispanic population (4.7 million) in 2006, followed by Harris County, Texas, and Miami-Dade (1.5 million each). (See table.)
- Maricopa County, Ariz. (home of Phoenix), had the biggest numerical increase in the Hispanic population (71,000) since July 2005, followed by Harris County, Texas (63,000).

- Starr County, Texas had the highest Hispanic proportion of its total population in 2006, at 97 percent. In fact, each of the 11 counties with the highest Hispanic proportion of its total population was in Texas.

Black

- Cook County had the largest black population (1.4 million) in July 2006, followed by Los Angeles County (1 million).
- Harris County had the largest numerical increase (52,000) between 2005 and 2006, with East Baton Rouge Parish next (19,000).
- Claiborne County, Miss., had a population that was 85 percent black in 2006, which led the nation. All 50 countries with the highest percentage black population were in the South.

Asian

- Los Angeles County had the largest Asian population (1.4 million) in 2006, with Santa Clara County, Calif. (home of San Jose) the runner-up (556,000).
- Santa Clara County had the largest numerical increase (17,600) from 2005 to 2006, followed by Los Angeles (15,700).
- Honolulu County, Hawaii, led the nation with a population that was 59 percent Asian. One other county—Kauai, Hawaii—was also majority Asian. San Francisco County, Calif., led the continental United States, with 34 percent of its population Asian.

American Indian and Alaska Native

- Los Angeles County had the largest population of American Indians and Alaska Natives in 2006 (150,000) with Maricopa County, Ariz., ranking second (95,000).
- Maricopa County had the largest numerical increase between 2005 and 2006 (3,700), followed by Riverside County, Calif. (1,600).
- Shannon County, South Dakota led the country in 2006, with 88 percent of its total population of 13,800 being a member of this group in 2006. Shannon was first of 10 counties/county equivalents that were majority American Indian and Alaska Native.

Article 19. Minority Population Tops 100 Million and More than 300 Counties Now "Majority-Minority"

Native Hawaiian and Other Pacific Islander

- Honolulu County had the largest population of this race (177,000) in 2006, with Los Angeles County (59,000) second.
- Hawaii County, Hawaii and Clark County, Nev. (home of Las Vegas) had the largest numerical increases in this race since July 2005, around 900.

Non-Hispanic White Alone

- Los Angeles County had a nation-leading 2.9 million residents who were part of this group in 2006, with Cook, Ill., second at 2.4 million.
- The largest numerical increase from 2005 to 2006 belonged to Maricopa County, Ariz. (35,500). Wake, N.C. (home of Raleigh), ranked second, gaining 18,700.
- Magoffin County, Kentucky, with an estimated 13,400 total residents, and Mitchell County, Iowa, with an estimated 10,900 total residents, led the nation with 98.9 percent of their population being non-Hispanic white alone in 2006.

Tabulations by age released today showed:

- The 10 counties with the highest proportion of people 65 and older is dominated by Florida which contributed four counties to the list, led by Charlotte County at 31.2 percent.
- Georgia, Alaska and Colorado combined accounted for seven of the 10 counties with the lowest proportion of people 65 and older.

Chattahoochee

- County, Ga.—home of the Army's Fort Benning—had the lowest percentage in the country at 2.6 percent.
- Seven of the 10 counties with the highest proportion of their population younger than 5 were in Texas, South Dakota or Utah. Webb County, Texas (home of Laredo), topped the list at 13.1 percent.

The minority population is defined as anyone who indicated that they were either Hispanic or a race other than white alone. The percent rankings for race, Hispanic origin, and age are based on counties with population in 2006 of 10,000 or more in 2006.

Unless otherwise specified, the data refer to the population who reported a race alone or in combination with one or more other races. The detailed tables show data for both this group and those who reported a single race only. Censuses and surveys permit respondents to select more than one race; consequently, people may be one race or a combination of races. Hispanics may be any race.

The federal government treats Hispanic origin and race as separate and distinct concepts. In surveys and censuses, separate questions are asked on Hispanic origin and race. The question on Hispanic origin asks respondents if they are Spanish, Hispanic or Latino. Starting with Census 2000, the question on race asked respondents to report the race or races they consider themselves to be. Thus, Hispanics may be of any race. (See U.S. Census Bureau Guidance on the Presentation and Comparison of Race and Hispanic Origin Data.) More detailed information on race and Hispanic origin can be found at http://www.census.gov/population/www/socdemo/compraceho.html.

These data are based on estimates of U.S. population for July 1, 2006. The Census Bureau estimates population change from the most recent decennial census (Census 2000) using annual data on births, deaths and international migration. More detailed information on the methodology used to produce these estimates can be found at http://www.census.gov/popest/topics/methodology/2006_st_char_meth.html.

Editor's Note—The embargoed data can be accessed at http://www.census.gov/Press-Release/www/releases/archives/embargoed_releases/index.html. After the release time, go to http://www.census.gov/popest/estimates.php.

From *U.S. Census Bureau*, 2006.

Irish-American Heritage Month (March) and St. Patrick's Day (March 17) 2008

Originally a religious holiday to honor St. Patrick, who introduced Christianity to Ireland in the fifth century, St. Patrick's Day has evolved into a celebration for all things Irish. The world's first St. Patrick's Day parade occurred on March 17, 1762, in New York City, featuring Irish soldiers serving in the English military. President Truman attended the parade in 1948, a proud moment for the many Irish whose ancestors had to fight stereotypes and prejudice to find acceptance in America. Congress proclaimed March as Irish-American Heritage Month in 1995, and the president issues a proclamation each year.

Population Distribution

36 million
Number of U.S. residents who claim Irish ancestry. This number is almost nine times the population of Ireland itself (slightly more than 4 million). Irish is the nation's second most frequently reported ancestry, trailing only German.[1]

24%
Percent of Massachusetts residents who are of Irish ancestry. This compares with a corresponding rate of 12 percent for the nation as a whole.[2]

Irish-Americans Today

31%
Percentage of people of Irish ancestry, 25 or older, who had a bachelor's degree or more education. In addition, 91 percent of Irish-Americans in this age group had at least a high school diploma. For the nation as a whole, the corresponding rates were 27 percent and 84 percent.[3]

$54,531
Median income for households headed by an Irish-American, higher than the $48,451 for all households. In addition, 9 percent of people of Irish ancestry were in poverty, lower than the rate of 13 percent for all Americans.[4]

38%
Percentage of employed civilian Irish-Americans 16 or older who work in management, professional and related occupations. Additionally, 28 percent work in sales and office occupations;

15 percent in service occupations; 10 percent in production, transportation and material moving occupations; and 9 percent in construction, extraction, maintenance and repair occupations.[5]

72%
Percentage of householders of Irish ancestry who own the home in which they live, with the remainder renting. For the nation as a whole, the homeownership rate was 67 percent.[6]

Trade with the "Old Sod"

$22.9 billion
The value of U.S. imports from Ireland for January to September 2007. Meanwhile, the United States exported $6.6 billion worth of goods to Ireland.[7]

Places to Spend the Day

4
Number of places in the United States named Shamrock, the floral emblem of Ireland. Mount Gay-Shamrock, W.Va., and Shamrock, Texas, were the most populous, with 2,623 and 1,855 residents, respectively. Shamrock Lakes, Ind., had 159 residents and Shamrock, Okla., 124. (Statistic for Mount Gay-Shamrock is from Census 2000; the other statistics are 2006 estimates.)[8]

9
Number of places in the United States that share the name of Ireland's capital, Dublin. Since Census 2000, Dublin, Calif., has surpassed Dublin, Ohio, as the most populous of these places (41,840 compared with 36,565, respectively, as of July 1, 2006).

If you're still not into the spirit of St. Paddy's Day, then you might consider paying a visit to Emerald Isle, N.C., with 3,716 residents.[9]

The Celebration

42.1 billion and 2.6 billion
U.S. beef and cabbage production, respectively, in pounds, in 2006. Corned beef and cabbage is a traditional St. Patrick's Day dish. The corned beef that celebrants dine on may very well have originated in Texas, which produced 6.8 billion pounds worth of beef, while the cabbage most likely came from

California, which produced 607 million pounds worth, or New York (462 million pounds).[10]

$42 million

Value of potted florist chrysanthemum sales at wholesale in 2006 for operations with $100,000 or more sales. Lime green chrysanthemums are often requested for St. Patrick's Day celebrations.[11]

Notes

1. Sources: 2006 American Community Survey http://factfinder.census.gov and International Data Base http://www.cso.ie/releasespublications/documents/population/current/popmig.pdf

2. Source: 2006 American Community Survey http://factfinder.census.gov

3. Source: 2006 American Community Survey http://factfinder.census.gov

4. Source: 2006 American Community Survey http://factfinder.census.gov

5. Source: 2006 American Community Survey http://factfinder.census.gov

6. Source: 2006 American Community Survey http://factfinder.census.gov

7. Source: Foreign Trade Statistics http://www.census.gov/foreign-trade/www/

8. Sources: American FactFinder http://factfinder.census.gov and population estimates http://www.census.gov/Press-Release/www/releases/archives/population/010315.html

9. Sources: American FactFinder http://factfinder.census.gov and population estimates www.census.gov/Press-Release/www/releases/archives/population/010315.html

10. Source: USDA National Agricultural Statistics Service http:www.nass.usda.gov/index.asp

11. Source: USDA National Agricultural Statistics Service http://www.nass.usda.gov/index.asp

Editor's note—The preceding data were collected from a variety of sources and may be subject to sampling variability and other sources of error. Facts for Features are customarily released about two months before an observance in order to accommodate magazine production timelines. Questions or comments should be directed to the Census Bureau's Public Information Office: telephone: 301-763-3030; fax: 301-763-3762; or e-mail: pio@census.gov.

From *U.S. Census Bureau*, February 25, 2008.

A Profile of Today's Italian Americans

A Report Based on the Year 2000 Census Compiled by the Sons of Italy

Report Highlights

I. Ethnicity

- Over 15.7 million people in the United States identify themselves as Italian Americans. They constitute nearly six percent (6%) of the U.S. population.
- Italian Americans are the nation's fourth largest European ancestry group after the Germans, Irish and English.

German	43,000,000	15%
Irish	30,600,000	11%
English	24,500,000	9%
Italian	15,700,000	6%

- Despite being in the U.S. for more than 120 years, Italian Americans still strongly identify with their Italian roots.

  The number of people who identified themselves as Italian American in the Year 2000 Census increased by 1,000,000 people or seven percent (7%) compared to the 1990 census.
- Italian Americans are the only European group whose population has increased since the 1990 census.

  In fact, the number of Americans claiming German, Irish, English and Polish descent decreased nearly 19 percent collectively–dropping from 128 million in 1990 to 108 million.
- Italian is the fourth European language most spoken in U.S. homes.

II. Demographic Information

Median Age:	34 years old
Marital Status:	married
Family Size:	one child
Median Income:	$61,300/year (in 1999) [National Median Income: $50,000/year]
Education:	High School Graduates: 29% [National Percentage: 28.5%]
	College Graduates: 18.5% [National Percentage: 15.5%]
Advanced Degrees:	Master's Degree: 7% [National Percentage: 6%]
	Professional Degree: 2% [National Percentage: 2%]
	Doctorate Degree: 0.85% [National Percentage: 0.95%]
Occupation:	White Collar workers: 66% [National Percentage: 64%]
	Blue Collar workers: 34% [National Percentage: 36%]

III. Geographic Information

A. The Ten States with the Most Italian Americans

New York	2,700,000
New Jersey	1,500,000
California	1,450,000
Pennsylvania	1,400,000
Florida	1,001,000
Massachusetts	860,000
Illinois	745,000
Ohio	676,000
Connecticut	634,000
Michigan	451,000

B. States with 15% or More Italian Americans or More than One Million Italian Americans

State	# of Italian Americans	% of Population
California	1,450,000	4%
Connecticut	630,000	19%
Florida	1,004,000	6%
New Jersey	1,500,000	18%
New York	2,700,000	14%
Pennsylvania	1,420,000	12%
Rhode Island	200,000	19%

C. The Ten Metro Areas with Most Italian Americans

Metro Area	# Italian Americans	# Total Population
New York	3,400,000	21,200,000
Philadelphia	886,000	6,189,000
Boston	801,000	5,800,000
Chicago	637,000	9,158,000
Los Angeles	568,000	16,373,000
San Francisco	423,000	7,039,000
Washington/ Baltimore	378,000	7,600,000
Pittsburgh	358,000	2,359,000
Detroit	321,000	5,456,000
Cleveland	278,000	2,946,000

D. The Ten Cities with the Most Italian Americans

City	# of Italian Americans	# Total Population
New York	692,800	8,008,300
Philadelphia	140,000	1,517,600
Chicago	101,900	2,896,000
Los Angeles	95,300	3,695,000
Phoenix	58,600	1,321,000
San Diego	55,800	1,223,400
Boston	49,000	589,100
San Jose, CA	43,200	893,900
Pittsburgh, PA	40,000	335,000
San Francisco	39,200	776,800

Demographic Chart
United States Census Analysis
U.S. Italian American Demographics vs. Total Population Demographics*
Figures Rounded to the nearest 100

	Italian American Population	Total U.S. Population
Total Population	15,723,000	281,422,000
Male	49.5% (7,789,000)	48% (137,916,000)
Female	50.5% (7,935,000)	52% (143,506,000)
Population 17 and under	14% (2,240,000)	13% (37,007,000)
Median Age	33.8	35.4
Male	33.1	34.1
Female	34.6	36.6
Marital Status (Population 15 and over)		
Male: Never Married	32% (1,916,000)	30% (32,381,000)
Female: Never Married	27% (1,665,000)	24% (27,532,000)
Male: Now Married	57% (3,375,000)	59% (62,692,000)
Female: Now Married	54% (3,296,000)	55% (62,309,000)
Male: Divorced	8% (468,000)	8.5% (9,255,000)
Female: Divorced	10% (623,000)	11% (12,305,000)
Family		
Number of Families	3,948,000	72,262,000
Average Family size	3.08	3.14
Median Income In 1999 Living Environment	$61,297	$50,046
Urban	88% (13,809,000)	79% (222,358,000)
Rural	12% (1,914,000)	21% (59,064,000)
Place of Birth		
U.S. Native	96% (15,119,000)	89% (250,314,000)
Foreign Born	4% (604,000)	11% (31,108,000)
Foreign Born: % from Europe	76% (459,000)	16% (4,916,000)
Naturalized Citizen	2.5% (409,000)	4.5% (12,543,000)
Not a Citizen	1.2% (195,000)	6.5% (18,565,000)
Education (Population 25 and Over)	9,853,000	182,212,000
High School Graduate	29% (2,893,000)	28.5% (52,169,000)
Bachelor's Degree	18.5% (1,843,000)	15.5% (28,318,000)
Master's Degree	7% (691,000)	6% (10,771,000)
Professional School Degree	2% (229,000)	2% (3,620,000)
Doctorate Degree	0.85% (84,000)	0.95% (1,754,000)
Occupation (Employed 16 years and older)		
Total In Workforce	49% (7,692,000) /(15,700,000)	46% (129,722,000) /(281,422,000)
White Collar Occupations	66% (5,081,000) /(7,692,000)	64% (82,472,000) /(129,722,000)
Blue Collar Occupations (Includes farmers, police officers & fire fighters)	34% (2,611,000) /(7,692,000)	36% (7,205,000) /(129,722,000)

Italian American Population of the U.S. All 50 States and the District of Columbia*

State	# of Italian Americans	Of State
Alabama	56,220	1.3%
Alaska	17,944	2.9%
Arizona	**224,795**	**4.4%**
Arkansas	34,674	1.3%
California	**1,450,884**	**4.3%**
Colorado	**201,787**	**4.7%**
Connecticut	**634,364**	**18.6%**
Delaware	**72,677**	**9.3%**
District of Columbia	12,587	2.2%
Florida	**1,003,977**	**6.3%**
Georgia	**163,218**	**2.0%**
Hawaii	22,094	1.8%
Idaho	34,553	2.7%
Illinois	**744,274**	**6.0%**
Indiana	**141,486**	**2.3%**
Iowa	49,449	1.7%
Kansas	50,729	1.9%
Kentucky	62,383	1.5%
Louisiana	**195,561**	**4.4%**
Maine	58,866	4.6%
Maryland	**267,573**	**5.1%**
Massachusetts	**860,079**	**13.5%**
Michigan	**450,952**	**4.5%**
Minnesota	**111,270**	**2.3%**
Mississippi	40,401	1.4%
Missouri	**176,209**	**3.1%**
Montana	28,031	3.1%
Nebraska	42,979	2.5%
Nevada	**132,515**	**6.6%**
New Hampshire	**105,610**	**8.5%**
New Jersey	**1,503,637**	**17.9%**
New Mexico	43,218	2.4%
New York	**2,737,146**	**14.4%**
North Carolina	**181,982**	**2.3%**
North Dakota	5,328	0.8%
Ohio	**675,749**	**6.0%**
Oklahoma	49,970	1.4%
Oregon	**111,462**	**3.3%**
Pennsylvania	**1,418,465**	**11.6%**
Rhode Island	**199,077**	**19.0%**
South Carolina	81,377	2.0%
South Dakota	7,541	1.0%
Tennessee	94,402	1.7%
Texas	**363,354**	**1.7%**
Utah	57,512	2.6%
Vermont	**38,835**	**6.4%**
Virginia	**257,129**	**3.6%**
Washington State	**191,442**	**3.2%**
West Virginia	69,935	3.9%
Wisconsin	**172,567**	**3.2%**
Wyoming	15,286	3.1%

State-By-State Percentages of Italian Americans*
All States and the District of Columbia

State	# of Italian Americans	% of Population
Rhode Island	199,077	19.0%
Connecticut	634,364	18.6%
New Jersey	1,503,637	17.9%
New York	2,737,146	14.4%
Massachusetts	860,079	13.5%
Pennsylvania	1,418,465	11.6%
Delaware	72,677	9.3%
New Hampshire	105,610	8.5%
Nevada	132,515	6.6%
Vermont	38,835	6.4%
Florida	1,003,977	6.3%
Ohio	675,749	6.0%
Illinois	744,274	6.0%
Maryland	267,573	5.1%
Colorado	201,787	4.7%
Maine	58,866	4.6%
Michigan	450,952	4.5%
Louisiana	195,561	4.4%
Arizona	224,795	4.4%
California	1,450,884	4.3%
West Virginia	69,935	3.9%
Virginia	257,129	3.6%
Oregon	111,462	3.3%
Wisconsin	172,567	3.2%
Washington State	191,442	3.2%
Montana	28,031	3.1%
Wyoming	15,286	3.1%
Missouri	176,209	3.1%
Alaska	17,944	2.9%
Idaho	34,553	2.7%
Utah	57,512	2.6%
Nebraska	42,979	2.5%
New Mexico	43,218	2.4%
North Carolina	181,982	2.3%
Indiana	141,486	2.3%
Minnesota	111,270	2.3%
District of Columbia	12,587	2.2%
Georgia	163,218	2.0%
South Carolina	81,377	2.0%
Kansas	50,729	1.9%
Hawaii	22,094	1.8%
Iowa	49,449	1.7%
Tennessee	94,402	1.7%
Texas	363,354	1.7%
Kentucky	62,383	1.5%

*Listed in alphabetical order. States in bold have percentages of Italian Americans five percent or above or more than 100,000 Italian Americans.

(continued)

State	# of Italian Americans	% of Population
Oklahoma	49,970	1.4%
Mississippi	40,401	1.4%
Alabama	56,220	1.3%
Arkansas	34,674	1.3%
South Dakota	7,541	1.0%
North Dakota	5,328	0.8%

*Listed in order of Percentage of the Population.

The 50 U.S. Metropolitan Areas with the Most Italian Americans

Rank	Area	Italian Population	Total Population
1	New York—Northern NJ—Long Island	3,394,397	21,199,865
2	Philadelphia—Wilmington, DE—Atlantic City	886,102	6,188,463
3	Boston—Worcester—Lawrence, MA	801,020	5,819,101
4	Chicago—Gary, IN–Kenosha, IL	646,399	9,157,540
5	Los Angeles—Riverside—Orange County, CA	568,153	16,373,645
6	San Francisco—Oakland—San Jose, CA	422,969	7,039,362
7	Washington, DC—Baltimore, MD	377,893	7,608,070
8	Pittsburgh, PA	358,317	2,358,695
9	Detroit—Ann Arbor—Flint, MI	321,443	5,456,428
10	Cleveland—Akron, OH	277,628	2,945,831
11	Miami—Fort Lauderdale, FL	206,119	3,876,380
12	Providence—Fall River—Warwick, RI	200,626	1,188,613
13	Tampa—St. Petersburg—Clearwater, FL	199,457	2,395,997
14	Hartford, CT	191,676	1,183,110
15	Buffalo—Niagara Falls, NY	190,038	1,170,111
16	Rochester, NY	183,815	1,098,201
17	Phoenix—Mesa, AZ	158,959	3,251,876
18	Albany—Schenectady—Troy, NY	148,073	875,583
19	San Diego, CA	133,304	2,813,833
20	Seattle—Tacoma—Bremerton, WA	127,106	3,554,760
21	Denver—Boulder—Greeley, CO	123,553	2,581,506
22	St. Louis, MO	117,754	2,603,607
23	Syracuse, NY	115,057	732,117
24	New Orleans, LA	109,710	1,337,726
25	Atlanta, GA	109,023	4,112,198
26	Scranton—Wilkes-Barre—Hazelton, PA	107,307	624,776
27	West Palm Beach—Boca Raton, FL	106,774	1,131,184
28	Dallas—Fort Worth, TX	106,287	5,221,801
29	Houston—Galveston—Brazoria, TX	105,645	4,669,571
30	Las Vegas, NV	102,708	1,563,282
31	Orlando, FL	99,033	1,644,561
32	Sacramento—Yolo, CA	96,515	1,796,857
33	Youngstown—Warren, OH	86,968	594,746
34	Minneapolis—St. Paul, MN	81,803	2,968,806
35	Columbus, OH	77,307	1,540,157
36	Portland—Salem, OR	76,540	2,265,223
37	Milwaukee—Racine, WI	75,977	1,689,572
38	Cincinnati—Hamilton, OH	75,698	1,979,202
39	Allentown—Bethlehem—Easton, PA	69,671	637,958
40	Norfolk—Virginia Beach—Newport News, VA	62,854	1,569,541
41	Springfield, MA	61,640	591,960
42	Utica—Rome, NY	59,015	299,896
43	Kansas City, MO—KS	57,191	1,776,062
44	Jacksonville, FL	44,953	1,100,491
45	New London—Norwich, CT	44,279	293,566
46	Daytona Beach, FL	42,719	493,175
47	Sarasota—Bradenton, FL	41,407	589,959
48	Raleigh—Durham—Chapel Hill, NC	41,033	1,187,941
49	Charlotte—Gastonia—Rock Hill, NC—SC	40,998	1,499,293
50	Harrisburg—Lebanon—Carlisle, PA	39,258	629,401

The 50 U.S. Cities with the Most Italian Americans*

Rank	Area	Italian Population	Total Population
1	New York city, NY	692,739	8,008,278
2	Philadelphia City, PA	140,139	1,517,550
3	Chicago City, IL	101,903	2,895,964
4	Los Angeles City, CA	95,263	3,694,834
5	Phoenix City, AZ	58,578	1,320,994
6	San Diego City, CA	55,764	1,223,341
7	Boston City, MA	49,017	589,141
8	San Jose City, CA	43,165	893,889
9	Pittsburgh City, PA	39,632	334,563
10	San Francisco City, CA	39,144	776,733
11	Yonkers City, NY	36,907	196,086
12	Columbus city, OH	35,236	711,644
13	Buffalo City, NY	34,379	292,648
14	Las Vegas City, NV	32,124	478,868
15	Houston City, TX	31,899	1,954,848
16	Cranston City, RI	27,359	79,269
17	Toms River, NJ	27,250	86,452
18	Jacksonville city, FL	25,385	735,503
19	Waterbury City, CT	24,476	107,271
20	Providence City, RI	23,960	173,618
21	Virginia Beach City, VA	23,949	425,257
22	Metairie, Louisiana	23,259	145,852
23	Rochester City, NY	22,077	219,766
24	Cleveland City, OH	22,053	478,393
25	Seattle City, WA	21,754	563,375
26	San Antonio City, TX	21,697	1,144,554
27	Syracuse City, NY	20,778	147,326
28	Worcester City, MA	19,950	172,648
29	Stamford City, CT	19,873	117,083
30	Portland City, OR	19,810	529,025
31	Tucson City, AZ	19,636	486,591
32	Warwick City, RI	19,549	85,808
33	Denver City, CO	19,333	554,636
34	Omaha City, NE	18,716	390,112
35	Baltimore City, MD	18,492	651,154
36	Levittown, NY	18,020	53,063
37	Mesa City, AZ	17,724	397,215
38	Charlotte City, NC	17,676	542,131
39	Revere City, MA	17,662	47,283
40	Milwaukee City, WI	17,499	596,956
41	Indianapolis City, IN	17,442	782,414
42	Medford City, MA	17,390	55,765
43	Scottsdale City, AZ	17,283	202,744
44	Tampa City, FL	17,096	303,512
45	St. Petersburg City, FL	16,736	247,793
46	Albuquerque City, NM	16,721	448,627
47	Coral Springs City, FL	16,709	117,482
48	Colorado Springs City, CO	16,692	360,798
49	Sterling Heights City, MI	16,556	124,471
50	Norwalk City, CT	16,397	82,951

*Based on Year 2000 U.S. Census.

The Order Sons of Italy in America

- The **Order Sons of Italy in America (OSIA)** is the largest and oldest national organization of Italian American men and women in the United States.
- Founded in 1905, OSIA now has 600,000 members and supporters and a network of more than 700 chapters coast to coast.
- Originally established as a mutual aid society for the early Italian immigrants, today OSIA is the leading service and advocacy Italian American organization.
- OSIA promotes the study of Italian language and culture in American schools and universities; conducts research on Italian American traditions, culture, history and heritage; and encourages closer cultural relations between Italy and the United States.
- The **Sons of Italy Foundation (SIF)** is a private, grant-making philanthropic institution established by OSIA in 1959. To date, the **SIF has given more than $83 million** to scholarships, medical research, cultural preservation, disaster relief and other projects.
- The **Commission for Social Justice (CSJ)** is the anti-defamation arm of OSIA. The CSJ is committed to fighting racism, prejudice, and the stereotyping of all races, religions and cultures.
- OSIA's national headquarters is in Washington, D.C. near Capitol Hill.

Bibliography

For extensive bibliographies on Italian American history, literature and culture, visit OSIA's Web site at www.osia .org see "Italian American Culture and History—Research and Reports" or the American Italian Historical Association at www.mobilito.com/aiha.

Italians In America: A Celebration **Gay Talese, editor.**

An illustrated history of Italian Americans that begins with the 15th century explorers, and traces the Italians in America from the American Revolution to the present day.

Available through the ORDER SONS OF ITALY at a discount. For details, call: 202/547-2900 or see www.osia.org at "Market Place"

Blood of My Blood **by Richard Gambino. New York: Anchor Books, 1975.**

Landmark study on the Italian America experience.

The Children of Columbus **by Erik Amfitheatrof. Boston: Little Brown, 1973.**

Perhaps the most intelligently written study on what Italian immigrants found in "la Merica."

The Italian American Experience: An Encyclopedia **LaGumina, Cavaioli, Primeggia and Varacalli, eds. New York: Garland Press, 1999.**

Excellent reference book on Italian American history, literature, culture and issues.

The Italian American Reader **Bill Tonelli, editor; William Morrow & Co.**

The first hardcover, mainstream press anthology of Italian American writing, this collection of 68 fiction and non-fiction pieces presents three generations of Italian American writers.

WOP! A Documentary History of Anti-Italian Discrimination **by Salvatore J. LaGumina. Toronto: Guernica, 1999.**

Documents the prejudice and discrimination the early Italian immigrants faced through citing newspaper articles, speeches and political cartoons of the late 19th and early 20th centuries.

Polonia in Numbers

How Many of Us Are out There?

Official census numbers show almost a million increase in the population of Poles in the United States in only 5 years. That's a 9% increase. Poles make up, on estimate, 3.1% of the population of the United States.

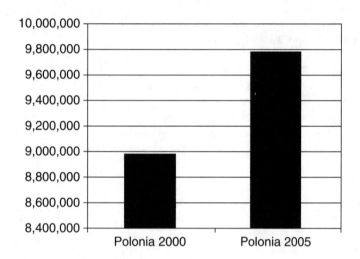

Most Polish Metropolitan Areas in 2000

Chicago	831,774
Detroit	479,659
Philadelphia	288,440
New York	268,228
Buffalo—Niagara Falls, NY	209,303
Pittsburgh, PA	209,032
Milwaukee—Waukesha, WI	190,076
Cleveland-Lorain-Elyria, OH	186,571
Minneapolis-St. Paul, MN-WI	148,876
Los Angeles	122,680
Boston	120,245
Newark	120,193
Bergen-Passaic, NJ	95,403
St. Louis, MO	67,084
Houston	59,254
Omaha, NE	32,132
Jersey City, NJ	27,673

Top 13 Polish States

78% of all Poles live in the 13 states with the highest Polish populations.

State	2000 Census	2005 ACS	Rate of Change
New York	986,106	997,987	+1%
Illinois	932,996	995,445	+7%
Michigan	854,844	919,007	+8%
Pennsylvania	824,146	885,218	+7%
New Jersey	576,473	572,918	−1%
Wisconsin	497,726	533,787	+7%
California	491,325	530,733	+8%
Florida	**429,691**	**523,162**	**+22%**
Ohio	433,016	474,569	+10%
Massachusetts	323,210	325,663	+1%
Connecticut	284,272	303,047	+7%
Minnesota	240,405	265,706	+11%
Texas	228,309	261,511	+15%

As shown by the above table, only one of the 13 states noticed a decline in the Polish population, and that decrease was quite insignificant—only one percent. All the other states noticed an increase in the population of the Poles, with ten states getting 7% and above.

We Are Educated

National statistics show that 80% of the total population (over 25 years old) of the United States are High School graduates. 88% of Poles are High School graduates. National statistics also show that 24% of the total population of America holds a Bachelor's degree or higher. 33% of Poles hold Bachelor's degree or higher.

We Are Houseowners

National statistics demonstrate that 73% of Poles are houseowners, while 27% rent their housing unit. Only 66% of all the people in America own their house, and 34% rents. Therefore, 7% more Poles own their house than an average American.

We Are Doing Quite Well

Only 6% of Poles live below the poverty level, that is a half of the national average. Median income of a Polish family exceeds the average one by $11,589 (Polish—$61,635 compared to the Average—$50,046). Median value of a Polish housing unit is $137,300, which exceeds the national average by $17,700.

Poles in Michigan

Michigan, too, experienced a significant increase in the Polish population. The number of Poles rose from 854,815 to 919,007. That's an 8% jump. Poles make up, on estimate, 7% of the Michigan population.

Michigan Poles are also more educated than an average Michigander. 87% of Poles over 25 years old are High School graduates and 24% hold a Bachelor's degree or higher. The state average is, respectively, 83% and 22%.

Michigan Polish population also is more likely to own a house than an average person. 81% of Poles are house owners, while 19% rent. On average, only 74% of the people own their home.

Only 6% of the Poles are currently below the poverty level. That's 4% less than a state average. Median income of Polish families also exceeds the average one by $7,565 (Polish—$61,022, Average—$53,457).

Also, a median value of the Polish housing unit exceeds the average one by $11,200.

Tri-County Polish Population

In terms of the Tri-County Poles, we see similar trends as state and nationwide. In Wayne County more Poles are house owners than the average (82% to 67%). Also, more people are High School graduates and hold higher education diplomas (83% and 18% to, respectively, 77% and 17%). Only 5% of the Poles live below the poverty level, compared to the average of 16%.

Also, Polish median family income is much greater than average—$61,500 compared to $48,805. The average value of the Polish home is also much greater than average and it amounts to $118,100 compared to $99,400.

In Macomb County more Poles are house owners than the average (84% to 79%). Also, more people are High School graduates (86% as compared to 83%). The number of

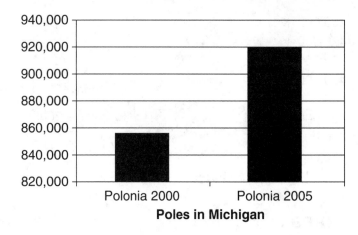

Poles in Michigan

highly educated people is the same—17%. Only 4% of the Poles live below the poverty level, compared to the average of 6%.

Polish median family income is greater than average—$65,341 compared to $62,816. The average value of the Polish home is slightly smaller than average though—$137,800 compared to $139,200.

In Oakland County more Poles are house owners than the average (81% to 75%). Also, more people are High School graduates and hold higher education diplomas (93% and 41% to, respectively, 89% and 38%).

Only 4% of the Poles live below the poverty level, compared to the average of 5%. Also, Polish median family income is much greater than average—$83,401 compared to $75,540.

The average value of the Polish home is also much greater than average—$189,300 compared to $181,200.

Poles in Ohio

The number of people of Polish ancestry in Ohio increased from 433,016 in the year 2000 to 474,569 in 2005. That's a 10% increase. Poles make up, on estimate, 4% of the Ohio population.

The Ohio Poles exhibit the same patterns as the rest of the Polonia nationwide. 76% of the Poles are house owners, compared to 69% of the statistical Ohioan. Poles are also more educated, with 89% high school graduation rate and 27% completing higher education, compared to 83% average high school graduation rate and 21% of the population completing an institution of higher learning (the numbers apply to people 25 years old and above). In terms of poverty, only 6% of Poles in Ohio live below the poverty level, which is 4% lower than the state average of 10%.

Also, Polish median family income exceeds the average one by almost $8,000 (compare $58,301 to $50,037). The average value of the Polish home also exceeds the average one by over $10,000 (compare $115,900 to $103,700).

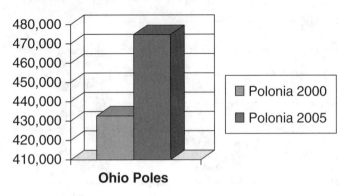

Ohio Poles

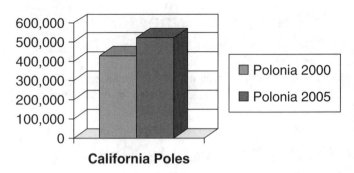

California Poles

Poles in Florida

The Polish population of Florida increased from 429,691 in 2000 to 523,162 in 2005. That's almost 100,000 more Polish people (22%) in only a period of 5 years. Poles make up, on estimate, 3% of the Florida population.

The Florida Poles exhibit the same characteristics as Poles nationwide. More Poles are house owners than average Florida residents (78% compared to 70%). Poles are also better educated, with 88% holding High School diplomas, and 28% holding Bachelor's degree or higher.

The state average is 80% high school graduates and 22% Bachelor degree holders. In terms of median family income, the Florida Poles beat the statistical Floridian by 17%! (Compare $53,270 to $45,625). Considering poverty, only 6% of the Polish-Americans in Florida live below the poverty level, compared to 12% state statistic. Also, the average value of a Polish house exceeds the average value of a housing unit by $13,600 (compare $119,100 to $105,500).

Poles in California

The Poles make up roughly 1.4% of the total California population. Their number increased from 491,325 in 2000 to 530,733 in 2005. That is an 8% increase. The Polish population of California displays the same patterns as the Polonia throughout the country.

Poles are more likely to be house owners than the average Californian (compare 64% to 60%). Poles are also much more educated—94% of Poles finished High School and 44% holds a Bachelor's degree or higher. Only 76% of the California population are High School graduates, and only 27% hold a Bachelor's degree or higher (the numbers apply to the population 25 years old and above).

In terms of poverty, only 6% of Poles live below the poverty level, compared to 14% of the average Californians! Poles also make much more money—average family income for Poles is $75,502, while the statistical California family earns $53,025. The median value of the Polish home is also significantly higher than the average Californian—compare $270,900 to $211,500.

Poles in Georgia

The Poles of Georgia make up 1% of their state's population. In Georgia, as elsewhere, there has been a growth of the Polish population between the 2000 Census and the 2005 American Community Survey. The population rose from 82,765 to 103,061. That's a 25% increase!

It is not surprising that the Polish population of Georgia exhibits the same trends as the Poles in California, Michigan, and other states. 71% of the Poles own their house, compared to 67% of the average Georgians. Poles are also much better educated, with 95% holding High School diplomas and 46% holding Bachelor's degrees or higher. In the total Georgia population, only 76% of the people graduated from High School and only 24% hold a Bachelor's degree or higher (the total population refers to people 25 years of age and older). Also, only 5% of the Poles live below the poverty level, compared to 13% of the total population. Georgia Poles also make more money than the average Georgians—compare $73,135 median Polish family income to the average $49,280. The median value of the Polish home ($158,400) also exceeds that of the average Georgia home ($111,200).

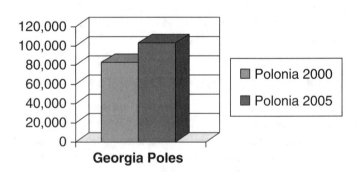

Georgia Poles

Poles in Missouri

The Polish population in Missouri increased by 20% between the 2000 U.S. Census and the 2005 American Community Survey. Poles make up 2% of the population of the state.

Characteristics	Polish Population of St. Louis	Total Population of St. Louis
Percentage of the population owning their home	57	47
Percentage of the population 25 years old and over who graduated from High School	83	71
Percentage of the population 25 years old and over who hold a Bachelor's degree or higher	36	19
Percentage of the population living below the poverty level	12	24
Median family income	$49,551	$32,585
Median value of the home	$78,200	$63,900

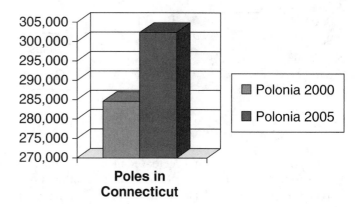

Poles in Connecticut

Just like the Poles in other corners of the United States, Missouri Polish population is "above the average." 74% of the Poles are house owners, compared to 70% of the total population. In terms of education, 90% of the Poles 25 years old and above graduated from High School and 33% hold a Bachelor's degree or higher (compared to 81% High School and 22% Bachelor's degree in the total population).

Poles also tend not to live below the poverty level, since only 6% of the Polish population experiences such hardships, compared to 11% of the total population. In material terms, Poles also exhibit "above the average" trends. Median family income of the Polish family exceeds the average one by over $10,000 (Polish—$57,515; Missouri Average—$46,044). Also, the median value of the Polish home exceeds the average one by over $22,000 ($112,000 vs. $89,900).

The Independent City of St. Louis shows the same patterns. Poles make up 2% of the population of the city, but the increase of the population between 2000 and 2005 was minimal—the Polish population rose by 5 people (the total population of the city, on the contrary, decreased by 15,000 people).

Poles in Connecticut

Poles make up 9% of the population of the state of Connecticut. The Polish population increased by 7% in five years, growing from the number of 284,272 in year 2000 to 303,047 in year 2005.

Not surprisingly, the Poles of Connecticut are not worse from their friends in other states. 75% of the Polish population are house owners, compared to 67% state average. 87% of Poles above the age of 25 are High School graduates and 31% hold a Bachelor's degree or higher. In the general population 25 years old and over, 84% are High School graduates and 31% hold a Bachelor's degree. The percentage of Poles in poverty is half of the state average (4% compared to 8%). Polish median family income exceeds the average state one by $2,000 (compare Polish $68,553 to State—$65,521). However, the average median value of the Polish home is lower than the state average by almost $10,000 (compare Polish—$156,700 to State—166,900).

Poles in Illinois

Poles make up 8% of the population of Illinois. The Polish population increased from 932,996 to 995,445 in just five years. That's a 7% increase.

As a historic place of Polish significance, the Illinois Polonia is not disappointing. The average house ownership in the state—67% is exceeded by Poles by 9% (76% of Poles are house owners). Illinois Poles are also better educated, with 86% holding a High School diploma (compared to 81% state average) and 28% holding a Bachelor's degree or higher (with 26% state average). Only 4% of Poles live below the poverty level, compared to 10% state average.

Economically speaking, Poles also exceed the average by all means. Median family income of a Polish family is $66,001 compared to $55,545 state average. Average median value of a Polish home also exceeded the state average (compare $165,000 to $130,800).

The Windy City has always been associated with the Poles. And the Polish population of the city follows the same patters than Poles everywhere else in the United States.

97

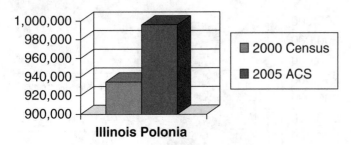

Illinois Polonia

	Polish Population of Chicago	Total Population of Chicago
Characteristics		
Percentage of the population owning their home	60	43
Percentage of the population 25 years old and over who graduated from High School	77	72
Percentage of the population 25 years old and over who hold a Bachelor's degree or higher	26	25
Percentage of the population living below the poverty level	8	19
Median family income	$54,154	$42,724
Median value of the home	$152,700	$132,400

Source: Census 2000 and 2005 American Community Survey.

The population of Polonia decreased in size over the last five years (from 210,421 to 184,621), just like the entire population of the city did. However, the Poles still make up almost 7% of the city's population.

Increase of the population between 2000 and 2005 was minimal—the Polish population rose by 5 people (the total population of the city, on the contrary, decreased by 15,000 people).

Still Unmelted after All These Years[1]

JOHN DAVID KROMKOWSKI

A re Polish Americans or Italian Americans or African Americans uniformly distributed through the United States? No; in fact, America is stunningly "unmelted". Just look. MAPS 1-4 Distribution by State of Polish, Italian, Irish, and "American".

A bowl of raw meat and uncooked potatoes, celery, carrots and onions is not per se appetizing. But even in a well simmered and tasty soup or stew, you can tell by looking that there are carrots, potatoes, celery, onions and meat. So let's not despair. Let's investigate.

The Ancestry Question on the US Census has produced a stunning array of information about how Americans self-describe themselves. The self-describing aspect of the US Census, especially The Ancestry Question is an highly important feature of data collection in a pluralistic democracy. Unlike the Race Question on the US Census which was constitutionally and historically imposed and rooted in pseudo-scientific and political assumptions of exclusion, the Ancestry Question emerged from a more current understanding[2] of ethnicity and its organic character and growth through the self-determined iterations rooted in the person, family, household and neighborhoods that constitute the American experience of immigration, urbanization and the attendant cultural pluralism of democratization and freedom fostered by a wide range of forces that accompanied American political development especially for the past seven decades. These social economic, political, and personal dynamics make the demography of ethnicity in America seem messy. Indeed, the ostensible messiness of immigration, the articulation of ancestry and identity rooted in ethnicity may well explain the slow evolutionary process and the significant impediments to collection of demographic information. Uniform data would be achieved by replacing the variety of Race and Ethnic Origin Questions associated with Hispanic, Asian, Indigenous Peoples with a single Ancestry question and the tabulation of the multiple responses that are clearly evident in America. Nonetheless, now that Ancestry data has been collected for the last three Censuses and the computer driven computational revolution is firmly in place, demographic analysis can employ standard protocols and verifiable methods that enable a fresh look at the data and thus establish connections, patterns and places and further discussion, interpretations and a scientific understanding of American pluralism.

Legend

Data Classes
Percent
- ☐ 0.0–2.5
- ▨ 2.7–5.2
- ▦ 6.7–9.3

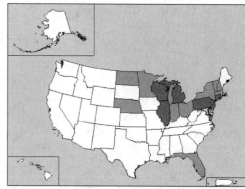

TM-PCT037. Percent of Persons of Polish Ancestry: 2000.
Universe: Total population.
Data Set: Census 2000 Summary File 3 (SF 3)—Sample Data
United States by State.

Source: U.S. Census Bureau, Census 2000 Summary File 3, Matrices P1, and PCT18.

Legend

Data Classes
Percent
- ☐ 0.2–3.9
- ▨ 4.3–9.3
- ▦ 11.6–19.0

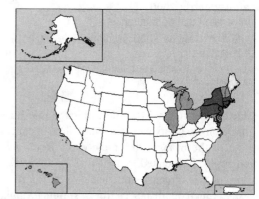

TM-PCT034. Percent of Persons of Italian Ancestry: 2000.
Universe: Total population.
Data Set: Census 2000 Summary File 3 (SF 3)—Sample Data
United States by State.

Source: U.S. Census Bureau, Census 2000 Summary File 3, Matrices P1, and PCT18.

This article investigates one such method: State Similarity Scores. A Similarity Score investigates the "distance" between States. Consider three cities: Baltimore, MD; Washington, DC and Chicago, IL. Baltimore is about a 40 mile drive from Washington. The driving distance between Washington and

Legend

Data Classes
Percent
☐ 0.1–7.9
▨ 9.3–13.5
■ 14.8–22.5

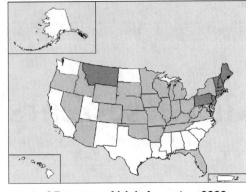

TM-PCT033. Percent of Persons of Irish Ancestry: 2000.
Universe: Total population.
Data Set: Census 2000 Summary File 3(SF 3)—Sample Data
United States by State.

Source: U.S. Census Bureau, Census 2000 Summary File 3, Matrices P1, and PCT18.

Legend

Data Classes
Percent
☐ 1.4–6.8
▨ 7.5–12.0
■ 13.5–20.9

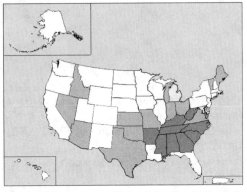

TM-PCT047. Percent of Persons of United States or American Ancestry: 2000.
Universe: Total population.
Date Set: Census 2000 Summary File 3 (SF 3)—Sample Data
United States by State.

Source: U.S. Census Bureau, Census 2000 Summary File 3, Matrices P1, and PCT18.

Chicago is roughly 710 miles. Chicago is 720 miles from Baltimore on the interstates. Knowing these distances, we can conceive of the triangle that these cities form and how they are geographically related.

In the two dimensional space of a map, a computer can now easily crunch out distances from a simple formula derived from Phythagoras.

$$Distance^2 = a^2 + b^2 \text{ or}$$
$$Distance = \sqrt{(a^2 + b^2)}$$

For example, using latitude and longitude to get the distance between Chicago and Baltimore, we find the difference between Chicago's latitude and Baltimore's latitude and the difference between Chicago's longitude and Baltimore's longitude.

$$a = Lat_{Chicago} - Lat_{Baltimore} \text{ and } b = Long_{Chicago} - Long_{Baltimore}$$

$$So, \ Distance = \sqrt{\left(Lat_{Chicago} - Lat_{Baltimore}\right)^2 + \left(Long_{Chicago} - Long_{Baltimore}\right)^2}$$

In three dimensions, we'd add c^2, to handle perhaps altitude for Google Earth. The theorem isn't limited to our spatial definition of distance. It can apply to any orthogonal dimensions: space, time, movie tastes, colors, temperatures, and even ancestry responses. There is no limit to the number of variables. The focus, however, of this research is race, ethnicity and ancestry data form the US Census 2000. Appropriately, this type of investigation is also known as Nearest Neighbor Analysis. To find out how closely related any two states in terms of ethnicity, our equation would look like this:

$$Distance = \sqrt{\begin{array}{l}\left(Ancestry1_{State\ 1} - Ancestry1_{State\ 2}\right)^2 \\ + \left(Ancestry2_{State\ 1} - Ancestry2_{State\ 2}\right)^2 \\ + \cdots + \left(Ancestry\ N_{State\ 1} - Ancestry\ N_{State\ 2}\right)^2\end{array}}$$

For this paper I used 56 of the largest ethnicities[3] as orthogonal dimensions: Asian Indian, Asian Multiple Response, American Indian, "American", Arab, Austrian, Black or African American, Belgian, British, Canadian, Chinese, Cuban, Czech, Czechoslovakian, Danish, Dutch, English, Finnish, French excluding Basque, Filipino, French Canadian, German, Greek, Guamanian and/or Chamorrian, Jamaican, Japanese, Korean, Hawaiian, Hispanic or Latino Other, Hungarian, Irish, Lithuanian, Mexican, Native Not Specified, Norwegian, "Others", Other Asian, Other Pacific Islander, Puerto Rican, Polish, Portuguese, Russian, Samoan, Scandinavian, "Scotch Irish", Scottish, Slovak, Slovene, "Some Other Race", Sub Saharan African, Swedish, Ukrainian, Vietnamese, Welsh, and West Indian.[4]

For any two states, we can calculate a measure of similarity. A measure of 0, would mean that the two states are identical, i.e. they have exactly the same percentage of Polish American, Italian Americans, Irish Americans, African Americans, etc. The largest "distance" between two states was between DC and North Dakota at 91.429. The closest "distance" between two states was between Tennessee and Arkansas 3.720. Table 1 shows each state's "nearest cultural neighbors" and the "distance" metric.

If we look at only the closest connection for each of state, some distinct networks or groupings emerge. The largest of these clusters happens to correspond roughly to "The South".

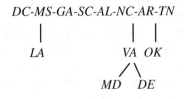

Table 1 Nearest Neighbors along 56 dimensions of Ethnicity/Ancest

	First Closest			Second Closest			Third Closest	
AL	SC	5.947	GA	7.213	NC	7.639
AK	WA	12.354	OK	12.893	CO	15.157
AZ	NV	9.405	TX	16.69	CO	17.233
AR	TN	3.720	NC	7.809	VA	8.382
CA	TX	10.344	AZ	19.1	NM	21.128
CO	WA	9.759	OR	9.958	KS	12.213
CT	MA	11.011	RI	14.181	NJ	14.499
DC	MS	33.68	LA	37.691	GA	40.758
DE	VA	10.625	MI	12.782	NJ	12.936
FL	NY	10.115	VA	10.430	NJ	11.253
GA	SC	4.179	AL	7.213	MS	9.648
HI	CA	47.499	NM	49.38	TX	51.121
ID	OR	7.619	WY	9.058	WA	10.961
IL	NJ	13.474	MI	13.955	DE	14.214
IN	MO	5.327	OH	6.3	KS	7.847
IA	NE	8.916	MT	13.289	WI	13.514
KS	IN	7.847	MO	8.337	OR	8.670
KY	WV	6.661	TN	13.896	IN	14.001
LA	MS	12.163	SC	13.077	GA	13.124
ME	VT	4.781	NH	7.475	RI	19.544
MD	VA	12.451	SC	12.606	GA	13.117
MA	RI	7.942	CT	11.011	NH	16.286
MI	OH	10.340	MO	10.977	PA	11.927
MN	SD	11.895	WI	13.981	IA	15.716
MS	GA	9.648	SC	9.947	LA	12.163
MO	OH	4.801	IN	5.327	KS	8.337
MT	WY	9.427	IA	13.289	OR	14.668
NE	IA	8.916	WI	11.648	WY	15.914
NV	AZ	9.405	CO	13.675	IL	14.786
NH	VT	4.607	ME	7.475	MA	16.286
NJ	NY	6.026	FL	11.253	DE	12.936
NM	CA	21.128	TX	23.53	AZ	27.923
NY	NJ	6.026	FL	10.115	DE	14.651
NC	VA	5.9	AL	7.639	AR	7.809
ND	SD	17.030	MN	17.407	WI	24.532
OH	MO	4.801	IN	6.3	PA	6.692
OK	AR	12.557	AK	12.893	FL	14.080
OR	WA	4.784	ID	7.619	KS	8.670
PA	OH	6.692	MO	10.27	IN	10.718
RI	MA	7.942	CT	14.181	NH	16.638
SC	GA	4.179	AL	5.947	NC	9.094
SD	MN	11.895	WI	14.146	IA	14.527
TN	AR	3.720	NC	9.043	VA	9.934
TX	CA	10.344	AZ	16.69	NV	18.018
UT	ID	14.655	OR	20.362	WA	21.495
VT	NH	4.607	ME	4.781	MA	17.455
VA	NC	5.9	AR	8.382	TN	9.934
WA	OR	4.784	CO	9.759	KS	10.921
WV	KY	6.661	IN	14.056	MO	17.644
WI	NE	11.648	IA	13.514	MN	13.981
WY	OR	8.960	ID	9.058	MT	9.427

Other networks also emerged, when considering only the first closest connection:

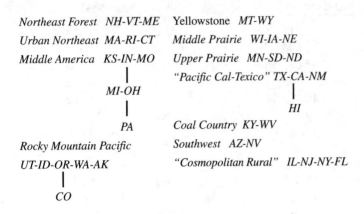

Northeast Forest *NH-VT-ME* Yellowstone *MT-WY*

Urban Northeast *MA-RI-CT* Middle Prairie *WI-IA-NE*

Middle America *KS-IN-MO* Upper Prairie *MN-SD-ND*

|
MI-OH

|
PA

Rocky Mountain Pacific

UT-ID-OR-WA-AK

|
CO

"Pacific Cal-Texico" *TX-CA-NM*

HI

Coal Country *KY-WV*

Southwest *AZ-NV*

"Cosmopolitan Rural" *IL-NJ-NY-FL*

"Ethnic Distance" to US

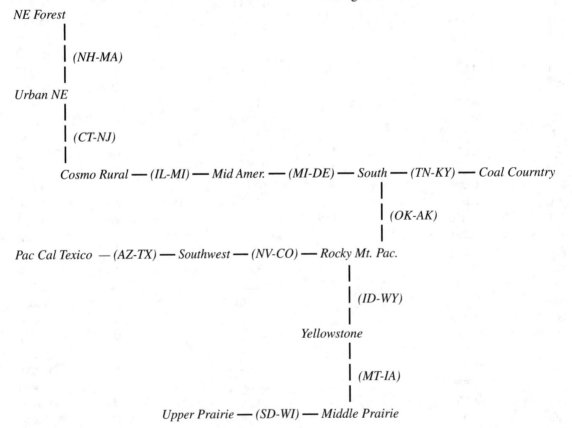

Figure 1   "Ethnic Distance" to US.

We can also connect all of the States with the minimum possible distance among states, i.e a "minimum spanning tree", as follows:

Finally, we can also measure the distance of each State to the United States as a whole. Illinois and Florida are very similar to the entire US, while North Dakota, DC and Hawaii are furthest in "distance" from the US in our 56 dimensional ethnic space. See Figure 1.

NE Forest

| *(NH-MA)*

Urban NE

| *(CT-NJ)*

Cosmo Rural — *(IL-MI)* — *Mid Amer.* — *(MI-DE)* — *South* — *(TN-KY)* — *Coal Courntry*

| *(OK-AK)*

Pac Cal Texico — *(AZ-TX)* — *Southwest* — *(NV-CO)* — *Rocky Mt. Pac.*

| *(ID-WY)*

Yellowstone

| *(MT-IA)*

Upper Prairie — *(SD-WI)* — *Middle Prairie*

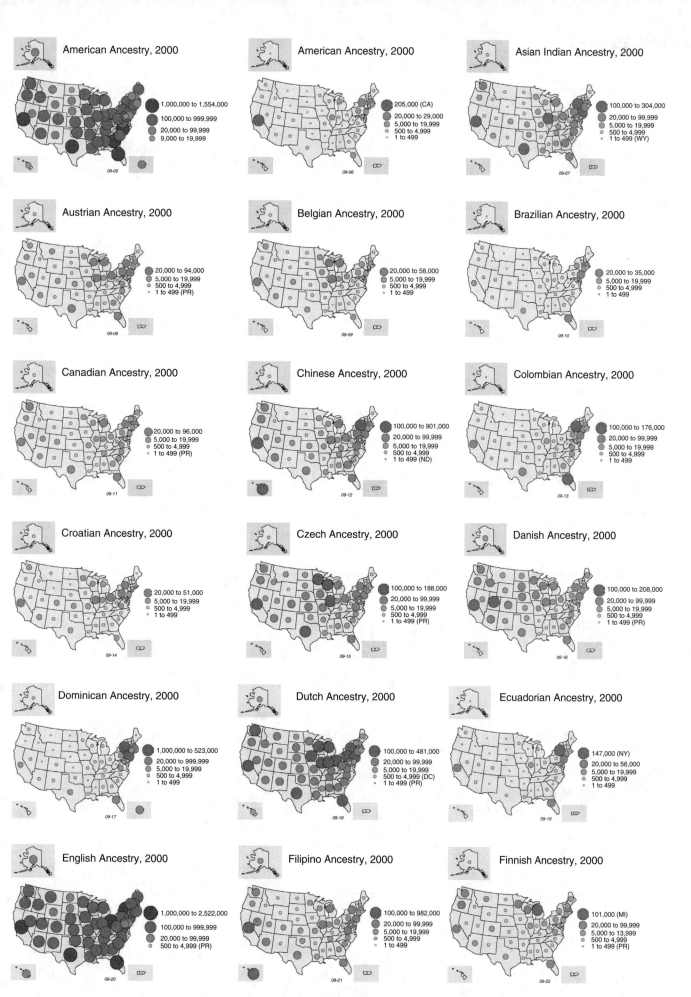

American Ancestry, 2000

1,000,000 to 1,554,000
100,000 to 999,999
20,000 to 99,999
9,000 to 19,999

09-05

American Ancestry, 2000

205,000 (CA)
20,000 to 29,000
5,000 to 19,999
500 to 4,999
1 to 499

09-06

Asian Indian Ancestry, 2000

100,000 to 304,000
20,000 to 99,999
5,000 to 19,999
500 to 4,999
1 to 499 (WY)

09-07

Austrian Ancestry, 2000

20,000 to 94,000
5,000 to 19,999
500 to 4,999
1 to 499 (PR)

09-08

Belgian Ancestry, 2000

20,000 to 58,000
5,000 to 19,999
500 to 4,999
1 to 499

09-09

Brazilian Ancestry, 2000

20,000 to 35,000
5,000 to 19,999
500 to 4,999
1 to 499

09-10

Canadian Ancestry, 2000

20,000 to 96,000
5,000 to 19,999
500 to 4,999
1 to 499 (PR)

09-11

Chinese Ancestry, 2000

100,000 to 901,000
20,000 to 99,999
5,000 to 19,999
500 to 4,999
1 to 499 (ND)

09-12

Colombian Ancestry, 2000

100,000 to 176,000
20,000 to 99,999
5,000 to 19,999
500 to 4,999
1 to 499

09-13

Croatian Ancestry, 2000

20,000 to 51,000
5,000 to 19,999
500 to 4,999
1 to 499

09-14

Czech Ancestry, 2000

100,000 to 188,000
20,000 to 99,999
5,000 to 19,999
500 to 4,999
1 to 499 (PR)

09-15

Danish Ancestry, 2000

100,000 to 208,000
20,000 to 99,999
5,000 to 19,999
500 to 4,999
1 to 499 (PR)

09-16

Dominican Ancestry, 2000

1,000,000 to 523,000
20,000 to 999,999
5,000 to 19,999
500 to 4,999
1 to 499

09-17

Dutch Ancestry, 2000

100,000 to 481,000
20,000 to 99,999
5,000 to 19,999
500 to 4,999 (DC)
1 to 499 (PR)

09-18

Ecuadorian Ancestry, 2000

147,000 (NY)
20,000 to 56,000
5,000 to 19,999
500 to 4,999
1 to 499

09-19

English Ancestry, 2000

1,000,000 to 2,522,000
100,000 to 999,999
20,000 to 99,999
500 to 4,999 (PR)

09-20

Filipino Ancestry, 2000

100,000 to 982,000
20,000 to 99,999
5,000 to 19,999
500 to 4,999
1 to 499

09-21

Finnish Ancestry, 2000

101,000 (MI)
20,000 to 99,999
5,000 to 13,999
500 to 4,999
1 to 499 (PR)

09-22

103

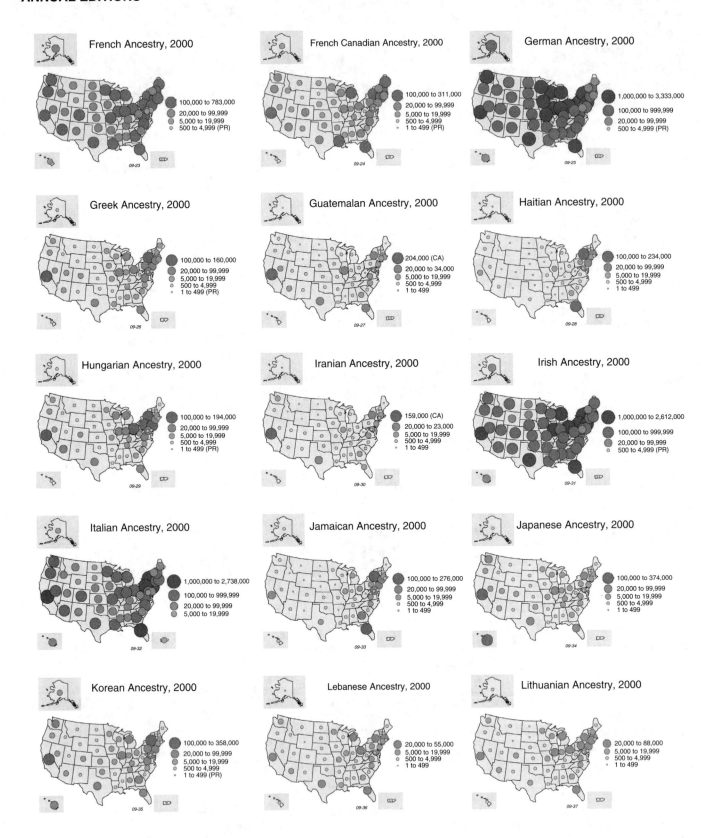

French Ancestry, 2000
09-23

100,000 to 783,000
20,000 to 99,999
5,000 to 19,999
500 to 4,999 (PR)

French Canadian Ancestry, 2000
09-24

100,000 to 311,000
20,000 to 99,999
5,000 to 19,999
500 to 4,999
1 to 499 (PR)

German Ancestry, 2000
09-25

1,000,000 to 3,333,000
100,000 to 999,999
20,000 to 99,999
500 to 4,999 (PR)

Greek Ancestry, 2000
09-26

100,000 to 160,000
20,000 to 99,999
5,000 to 19,999
500 to 4,999
1 to 499 (PR)

Guatemalan Ancestry, 2000
09-27

204,000 (CA)
20,000 to 34,000
5,000 to 19,999
500 to 4,999
1 to 499

Haitian Ancestry, 2000
09-28

100,000 to 234,000
20,000 to 99,999
5,000 to 19,999
500 to 4,999
1 to 499

Hungarian Ancestry, 2000
09-29

100,000 to 194,000
20,000 to 99,999
5,000 to 19,999
500 to 4,999
1 to 499 (PR)

Iranian Ancestry, 2000
09-30

159,000 (CA)
20,000 to 23,000
5,000 to 19,999
500 to 4,999
1 to 499

Irish Ancestry, 2000
09-31

1,000,000 to 2,612,000
100,000 to 999,999
20,000 to 99,999
500 to 4,999 (PR)

Italian Ancestry, 2000
09-32

1,000,000 to 2,738,000
100,000 to 999,999
20,000 to 99,999
5,000 to 19,999

Jamaican Ancestry, 2000
09-33

100,000 to 276,000
20,000 to 99,999
5,000 to 19,999
500 to 4,999
1 to 499

Japanese Ancestry, 2000
09-34

100,000 to 374,000
20,000 to 99,999
5,000 to 19,999
500 to 4,999
1 to 499

Korean Ancestry, 2000
09-35

100,000 to 358,000
20,000 to 99,999
5,000 to 19,999
500 to 4,999
1 to 499 (PR)

Lebanese Ancestry, 2000
09-36

20,000 to 55,000
5,000 to 19,999
500 to 4,999
1 to 499

Lithuanian Ancestry, 2000
09-37

20,000 to 88,000
5,000 to 19,999
500 to 4,999
1 to 499

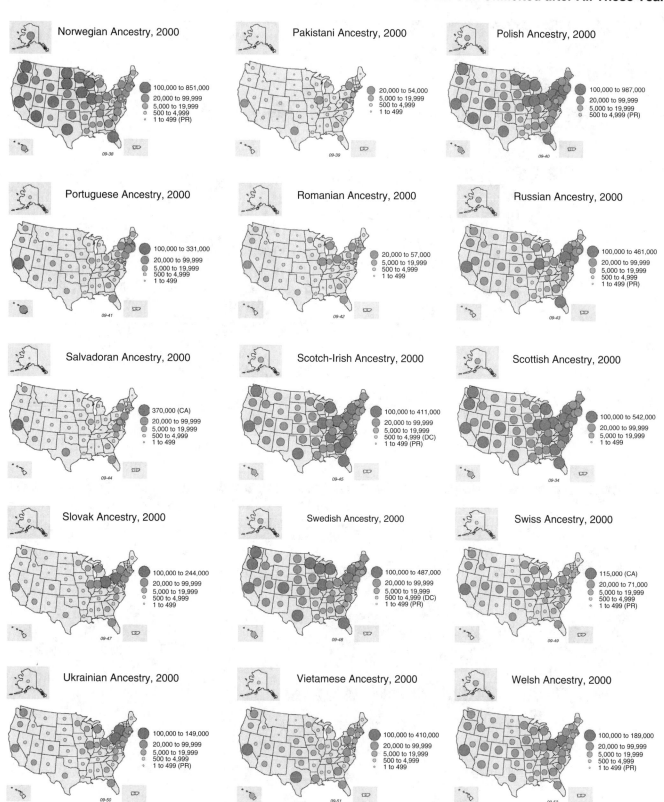

Norwegian Ancestry, 2000
100,000 to 851,000
20,000 to 99,999
5,000 to 19,999
500 to 4,999
1 to 499 (PR)
09-38

Pakistani Ancestry, 2000
20,000 to 54,000
5,000 to 19,999
500 to 4,999
1 to 499
09-39

Polish Ancestry, 2000
100,000 to 987,000
20,000 to 99,999
5,000 to 19,999
500 to 4,999 (PR)
09-40

Portuguese Ancestry, 2000
100,000 to 331,000
20,000 to 99,999
5,000 to 19,999
500 to 4,999
1 to 499
09-41

Romanian Ancestry, 2000
20,000 to 57,000
5,000 to 19,999
500 to 4,999
1 to 499
09-42

Russian Ancestry, 2000
100,000 to 461,000
20,000 to 99,999
5,000 to 19,999
500 to 4,999
1 to 499 (PR)
09-43

Salvadoran Ancestry, 2000
370,000 (CA)
20,000 to 99,999
5,000 to 19,999
500 to 4,999
1 to 499
09-44

Scotch-Irish Ancestry, 2000
100,000 to 411,000
20,000 to 99,999
5,000 to 19,999
500 to 4,999 (DC)
1 to 499 (PR)
09-45

Scottish Ancestry, 2000
100,000 to 542,000
20,000 to 99,999
5,000 to 19,999
1 to 499
09-34

Slovak Ancestry, 2000
100,000 to 244,000
20,000 to 99,999
5,000 to 19,999
500 to 4,999
1 to 499
09-47

Swedish Ancestry, 2000
100,000 to 487,000
20,000 to 99,999
5,000 to 19,999
500 to 4,999 (DC)
1 to 499 (PR)
09-48

Swiss Ancestry, 2000
115,000 (CA)
20,000 to 71,000
5,000 to 19,999
500 to 4,999
1 to 499 (PR)
09-49

Ukrainian Ancestry, 2000
100,000 to 149,000
20,000 to 99,999
5,000 to 19,999
500 to 4,999
1 to 499 (PR)
09-50

Vietamese Ancestry, 2000
100,000 to 410,000
20,000 to 99,999
5,000 to 19,999
500 to 4,999
1 to 499
09-51

Welsh Ancestry, 2000
100,000 to 189,000
20,000 to 99,999
5,000 to 19,999
500 to 4,999
1 to 499 (PR)
09-52

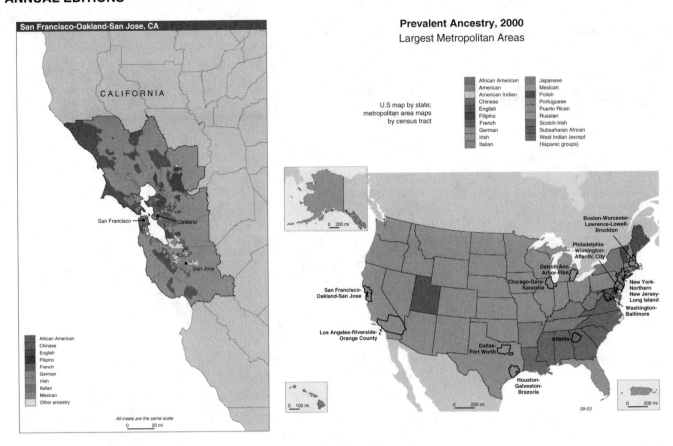

Prevalent Ancestry, 2000
Largest Metropolitan Areas

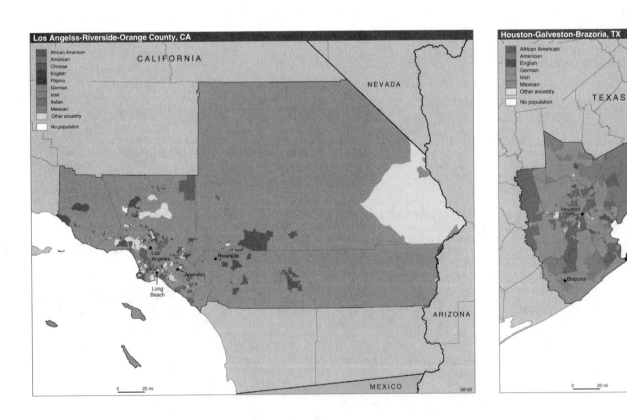

Notes

1. With acknowledgments to Michael Novak, The Rise of the Unmeltable Ethnics (1972) and Paul Simon's 1975 album and song.

2. Although, in some ways the Ancestry Question is arguably back to the future. See *Saint Francis College v. al-Khazraji*, 481 U.S. 604 (1987). A unanimous Court held that that persons of Arabian ancestry were protected from racial discrimination under Section 1981. The history of the definitions of "race", presented by the Court, is well worth reading because it shows how prior to the 20th century "race" and "ancestry" were synonymous concepts. After outlining the history and usage of the term "race", Justice White and the Court rejected the claim that "a distinctive physiognomy" is essential to qualify for 1981 protection and concluded: "We have little trouble in concluding that Congress intended to protect from discrimination identifiable classes of persons who are subjected to intentional discrimination solely because of their **ancestry or ethnic characteristics.**" William J. Brennan, Jr., in a separate concurrence, added that "Pernicious distinctions among individuals based solely on their **ancestry** are antithetical to the doctrine of equality upon which this nation is founded." (Emphasis supplied).

3. Some of these categories also come from the Race and Hispanic origin questions of the Census. Even though the Ancestry Question captures ethnic responses like Japanese, Korean, Cuban, Mexican and Black or African American, the Census Bureau sanitizes its Ancestry data, so that these responses are only readily available from the Race and Hispanic origin questions.

4. Older analysis of ethnic disimilarity differs from this method because it grouped ancestry responses into larger but far fewer categories such as "Old Stock", "Eastern and Southern European", "Asian", etc. Calculating similarity in 56 dimensional space was simply not possibly with hand calculations employed by previous researchers.

UNIT 4
Indigenous Ethnic Groups

Unit Selections

Key Points to Consider

- The history of relations between Native Americans and the U.S. government can be described in various ways. How much of the past is significant and consequential?

- Preservation of languages and heritage is on the agenda of many ethnic groups. Discuss the relevance of such activities, and the related matter of acquiring a second and third language and a second and third cultural competency. Should schools for such activities be supported by the ethnic groups? Public funds? Philanthropies?

- Gambling/gaming has attracted a large-scale tourist-driven economic foundation for Native American reservations. Are the benefits of such development fairly distributed to the entire tribe of Native Americans in the nation?

- Could the National Museum of the American Indian be funded without the capital generated from the gaming industry and profitable casinos?

- Does the widespread practice of evoking and using Native American symbols and rituals in high school, university, and professional athletics constitute ethnic defamation?

- Will the strides of the current Native American community allow the next generation to enter the middle class mainstream of America? Should that be a goal? Does improving economically, and in terms of other quality-of-life indicators, mean the denial of traditional cultural values and practices?

Student Web Site
www.mhcls.com

Internet Reference

American Indian Science and Engineering Society (AISES)
http://ww.aises.org

The contemporary issues of Native Americans as well as the descendants of all conquered indigenous peoples add their weight to the claims for cultural justice, equal protection, and due process in our hemisphere. But, in fact, this is a worldwide phenomenon. The United Nations provides a forum for attention to indigenous populations, and nongovernmental organizations (NGOs) committed to human rights address global economic interests regarding the protection of human and physical ecologies. The post-World War II end of colonialism and the emergence of new nations in Asia and Africa pointed not only to the development of new states, but also to the problems of nation building in the context of extreme ethnic variety. Even the new empires of the former Soviet Union became engaged in the plethora of nations and ethnic populations of Central Asia and Eastern Europe. Only during the last decade have social and political scientists been able to view these widespread phenomena from a perspective, which now enables us to see the full implications of ethnic and race relations as foundational issues for political and economic order.

In the United States, indigenous peoples were at one time marginalized and isolated. Their cultures were articulated in folkloric and turistic ways when interaction with mainstream America occurred. Such traditional relations were challenged during the Civil Rights Era of the 1960s. Moreover, the celebration of the Bicentennial of the American Revolution in 1976, and the reorganization of native Americans in ways that claimed their empowerment over the dominance of the Bureau of Indian Affairs, and their victories in the courts and in legislative authority, produced a new threshold from where the renegotiation of relationships could begin.

With new cultural confidence and economic capacity—most notably gained from involvement in the gaming industry—the descendants of native peoples entered a new epoch of American pluralism. While some may argue that the reclamation and revival of tradition and power are unique social and political events, a wider view suggests that they are but another manifestation of ethnicity and ethnic group articulation of its agenda within the contexts of the American legal and economic order. Acute popular consciousness of indigenous peoples was heightened when attempts of cultural entrepreneurs to celebrate the 500th anniversary of Christopher Columbus's voyage of discovery encountered strong resistance from Native American advocates. On the international level, another front of resistance emerged in the struggle against apartheid in South Africa. Many Americans viewed the South African situation through the simplistic lens of color consciousness—as if South Africa was an extension of "black power." However, the large arena of ethnic multiplicity among indigenous people in South Africa eventually became ever so apparent when the transitional South African regime increased awareness of its array of indigenous people. The exploration of roots and new remedies for the conquest that

© Nancy G. Photography/Alamy

turned many into permanent underclass citizens have awakened indigenous people; and a code of international conduct in protection of cultural rights has entered international law.

The following articles present data and a few accounts of the current experience of indigenous ethnic groups, their adaptation of the new high-tech world, the environmental and cultural effects of rapid change, and the challenges in renewing their traditions. The indigenous ethnic populations invite us to recall their struggles, to find ways of shaping and sharing the new sense of pluralism offered within the American experience, and the spiritual sources of ethnic identity that people encounter as the legitimacy of ancient practices widens.

Indigenous ethnic communities have encountered a complex array of historical, social, cultural, and economic forces. As a result, in the late twentieth century, the traditions of indigenous ethnic groups have been renegotiated by yet another generation.

The North and South American economies and pluralistic cultures, as well as those of other continents, are a challenging stage for their quest for self-sufficiency as well as their aspirations for the preservation of a unique cultural legacy. Current indigenous ethnic leaders challenge past perceptions. They find it increasingly difficult to strike a balance between traditional values and new demands. Native Americans have increasingly interfaced with the American legal system at the state level, on issues of land use and gaming, which represent part of this current redefinition. Finally, however, they are challenging themselves to be themselves; and examples of indigenous self-help reveal insights into how personal leadership and community weave the social fabric of civil society.

Novel approaches toward the peaceful reconciliation of conflict should be explored more thoroughly. For example, unlike conflict among ethnic groups in the United States, conflict between the United States and Native Americans is regulated by treaties. The struggle over claims regarding the rights of nations and the interests of the U.S. government and its citizens is no longer at the margin of public affairs. Does the definition of this conflict as an issue of foreign and not domestic policy provide a meaningful distinction? Should the claims of ethnic groups in defense of culture, territory, and unique institutions be honored and protected by law and public policy?

Ethnicity is built upon the truth and strength of a tradition. Sense of family and community, and an unwillingness to give up, have led to standoffs with many forces within America. From this perspective, this unit details ways in which an ethnic group retrieves its rights and heritage in order to preserve an ancient culture from amnesia and extinction.

The expansion and profitability of Native American gambling casinos, their attendant impact on state and local economies, and the tax exemptions enjoyed by these ventures appear to be headed toward contentions that may spill over into new issues of public order. On the international level, the discussion of human and cultural rights of peoples guaranteed in the United Nations, and the traditional mode of state sovereignty indicates that a fragile accommodation between indigenous people and the mainstream societies at whose margins they exist may be entering a new phase. Their unequal relationship began with the consolidation of large, territorial political and economic regimes. Under scrutiny are personal rights and group rights, pluralistic realms that ensure transnational solidarity, and cultural and religious challenges to those in authority fueled by the passion for power at those intersections between modernity and tradition—the large-scale institutional versus the local and culturally specific community.

In 2004, the National Museum of the American Indian held the grand opening of a new institution on the Mall in Washington, D.C. This institutionalization of the Native American guiding spirit signified that pluralism among the Native American peoples had entered a new phase of cultural development, one that would engage the American experience alongside and within the framework of a civil culture.

Who Is a Native American?

PETER ORTIZ

George Armstrong Custer predicted Native Americans soon would be extinct before he ordered his soldiers to kill them at the Battle of Little Bighorn in 1876. Just as Custer discovered in his fatal encounter with Lakota and Cheyenne warriors, the native tribes proved resilient in surviving impossible odds.

More than 4 million U.S. citizens in 2003 identified as Native Americans, either alone or in combination with another race. This is a little more than 1 percent of the total 294 million people living in the United States, far fewer than the 10 to 25 million believed to be living in North America when European settlers arrived about 500 years ago. Those settlers spread fatal diseases, imposed genocide, forced assimilation, stole land, broke treaties, destroyed cultures and committed other crimes that ravaged indigenous societies.

Centuries of dehumanization resulted in the educational, economic and health disparities evidenced by Native Americans today. But refusal to succumb also nurtured a strong will embodied by many Native Americans who now comprise more than 560 federally recognized tribes and nations spread across 34 states and 140 more tribes applying for federal recognition.

That strong will has empowered Native-American entrepreneurs and those in the corporate world to thrive in a society where mainstream values sometimes run counter to their traditional beliefs. Yet Jackie Gant's frustration is clear when she speaks of how many people only envision slot machines and blackjack tables when they think of Native Americans as an economic force.

Gant, national executive director of the Native American Business Alliance, met Bush administration officials in the White House in September to let them know of the 10,000 Native-American-owned businesses listed in her database. Her organization's mission is to create networking opportunities and promote Native-American businesses as suppliers to corporate America and government agencies. Her group has the support of corporate sponsors including United Parcel Service, Ford Motor Co., General Motors, DaimlerChrysler, Toyota, The Coca-Cola Co., General Mills, Target and The Walt Disney Co. At the meeting, she tried to convey the strength of a people who saved the first white settlers from starvation and influenced the founding fathers in shaping the Constitution. Gant is a member of the Oneida Nation of the Thames, Canada, and Munsee-Delaware Nation.

"As I stood, I felt the weight of Indian country on my shoulders and I knew the words I spoke needed to be heard," Gant says.

Gant and other Native Americans have made great strides in dispelling myths and bringing attention to their issues, but the widespread ignorance of their history still pervades the highest levels of leadership, up to and including the president himself. President Bush displayed a lack of knowledge on the most crucial issue facing Native Americans—sovereignty—when he was asked in August what tribal sovereignty in the 21st century meant to him.

"You are a . . . you have been given sovereignty, and you are viewed as a sovereign entity," Bush told journalists of color gathered in Washington, D.C.

Bush's response rang hollow and was reminiscent of the countless false promises many white men have made to Native Americans over centuries. Sovereignty speaks to the right of Native Americans to control their own land where they are free to shape their economic and spiritual destiny and maintain their traditions and culture. The lack of substance and depth in Bush's answer typified the harmful perceptions, attitudes and actions that have persisted for centuries among white leaders.

Those who say that the wrongs of the past are history and that it is time to move forward frustrate Native Americans, for it is the ignorance of history that defines their present situation and continues to threaten their future. Forgetting and ignoring the past is not an option, but Native Americans live in a white man's world. Their challenge lies in enlightening non-Natives about their history, traditions, cultures and rights as distinct governments, while creating a prosperous future on their own terms.

Entrepreneurial Spirit

Entrepreneurs, such as Margaret Rodriguez, demonstrate the strong desire of Native Americans to succeed. A member of the Salt River Pima-Maricopa Indian community in Arizona, Rodriguez started her company, Au Authum Kí, 12 years ago when bankers refused to lend her money. Her company generated $24 million in revenue for 2003. Au Authum Kí translates into "the people's home."

Rodriguez's projects have ranged from a $1.9-million contract for rebuilding a high-tech structure to house a weather squadron at a Tucson Air Force Base to having her workers camp within the Grand Canyon, where they installed portable classrooms on the Havasupai reservation. She also started a charity last year that builds homes for members of her tribal community who can't afford them.

Table 1 Top 10 Native-American States by Population

California	683,922
Oklahoma	394,831
Arizona	327,547
Texas	239,907
New Mexico	202,529
New York	186,024
Washington	164,642
North Carolina	139,223
Florida	134,036
Michigan	123,322

Source: U.S. Census Bureau.

The entrepreneurial spirit isn't unique to Rodriguez as the economic muscle of Native Americans continues to grow, according to the Selig Center for Economic Growth and the U.S. Census Bureau. Americans who identified themselves solely as Native Americans and Alaska Natives numbered 2.4 million and 4.1 million when they identified with one or more races, according to the 2000 census. Most Native Americans, 43 percent, lived in the West, while 11 states comprised 62 percent of the Native-American population.

Despite their small population, Native Americans are expected to see their buying power jump from $47.7 billion in 2004 to $65.6 billion in 2009. Native Americans will account for 0.6 percent of total U.S. buying power in 2009, up from 0.5 percent in 1990, according to the Selig Center.

The 2001 Survey of Minority Owned Business Enterprises by the Census Bureau reported 197,300 Native-American- and Alaska-Native-owned businesses in the United States that employed 298,700 people. From 1992 to 1997, their numbers increased 84 percent, compared with 7 percent for all U.S. businesses.

But even with successes such as Rodriguez, much of the attention remains focused on gaming. Gant, a Harvard University graduate, credits some casinos for pulling tribal members out of poverty when little economic opportunity existed. About 201 of the 562 federally recognized tribes are engaged in gaming, but most are small operations that provide a few jobs to members in dire need of work. Casinos and gaming operations must be located on tribal lands, and federal law dictates that tribes use gaming revenue to fund services, such as education, law enforcement, tribal courts, health care, social services and infrastructure improvements.

Native Americans must live in a white man's world. Their challenge lies in enlightening non-Natives about their history, traditions, cultures and sovereign rights, while creating a prosperous future on their own terms.

Casinos also have helped spur new small businesses. But the reality is that most Native Americans don't benefit from casinos. About 60 percent live outside of reservations, with the rest living on tribal lands or bordering rural areas. A report by the National Congress of American Indians shows Native Americans ranking last or near last on nearly all social, health, education and economic barometers. Their poverty rate from 2001 to 2003 was 23 percent, similar to that for African Americans and Latinos, while the poverty rate for whites and Asian Americans was about 10 percent. About one-third of the Native-American population on reservations live in poverty. From 2001 to 2003, Latinos, at 32.8 percent, were the only group to surpass Native Americans, 23.8 percent, for those without health coverage.

Native Americans also continue to struggle because of the federal government's early attempts to educate them with a total disregard for their culture. Children were prevented from speaking their language, practicing traditional customs and wearing indigenous dress. Native Americans were not taught the reading, writing and math skills of their white peers and instead were steered toward trades that did not guarantee a secure job because of racial barriers.

About 75 percent of Native Americans 25 years and older earned a high-school degree or more, compared with 84 percent of the U.S. population in 2002. About 14 percent of Native Americans 25 years and older earned at least a bachelor's degree or higher, compared with 27 percent for the overall population.

Maggie Necefer remembers when she was forbidden to speak her language as a student in the 1960s. Necefer's Navajo nation established the first tribal college in 1968 and is now among 34 tribal colleges in the United States. She serves as academic vice president at Dine College, which offers 17 degree programs and includes Navajo language and Navajo studies degrees.

"They paid missionaries to put up these schools and the whole intent was to proselytize, to kill the savage and save the man," Necefer recounts of her border school experience. "Oftentimes, we had missionaries come into the schools and tell us what god to believe in."

Necefer kept her language and culture, thanks to her family, and later completed bachelor's, master's and doctoral programs. She represents a model for students; in her, they can see that a Native American can survive from an imposed educational system and retain their culture.

"It is just taking ownership of our own education and what education should be for our people," Necefer says. "We validate the cultural identity and cultural piece interspersed with Western knowledge to prepare balanced individuals who can live in both worlds."

Corporate America's Gap

Much of corporate America, like society itself, does not understand Native Americans. When corporate America is focused on diversity, rarely are Native Americans mentioned in the same breath as African Americans, Latinos and Asian Americans, Gant says.

"We are able to compete like any other non-Native organizations, provided we are given the opportunity to do so by corporate America," Gant says.

Table 2 Median Income from 2001 to 2003

Asian Americans	$55,089
Whites	$47,957
Native Americans and Alaska Natives	$34,740
Latinos	$33,913
African Americans	$29,987

Source: U.S. Census Bureau.

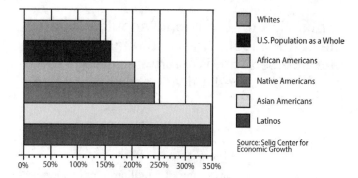

Figure 1 Native-American Buying Power. Projected rate of increase 1990–2009.

Source: Selig Center for Economic Growth.

Stormy Hicks, 58, heeded the advice from his father when he told the then 8-year-old that he was of the Shawnee Nation, but to keep that a secret between the two. Thomas Hicks took pride in his native heritage, regaling his son with stories of relatives dressed in buck skin and visiting him near his tribe's reservation in West Virginia. But Native Americans in the early 1900s often were denied jobs and faced discrimination.

Hicks is president of ITT Automotive Industries, a company that generates $500 million to $600 million a year in sales and makes fuel and brake lines as well as various plastic parts. For 20 years, he worked at Ford, where he started as a design engineer and ran manufacturing plants in Brazil and Mexico. He retired from Ford as executive director in charge of worldwide logistics and transportation in 1998.

For many years, Hicks kept his Native-American heritage a secret, even when some in corporate America realized the value that people of color brought to their ranks.

"I wasn't embarrassed by it," Hicks says. "In the corporate world, they wanted senior executives who were minorities and I never wanted to give that to the corporations I worked for. I just kept it to myself."

Hicks' wife Elizabeth, who was inducted as a non-native member of his tribe, researched her husband's lineage and urged him to acknowledge his heritage to everyone. He took her advice 10 years ago and regrets not doing it sooner.

"She started to realize there was something missing from my life," Hicks says.

Hicks kept true to his Native-American values even as he remained silent. His struggle speaks to the experiences of many Native Americans who must balance two worlds that have historically clashed from the time European settlers arrived. A legendary chief from Hicks' Shawnee tribe, Tecumseh, echoed the anger of Native Americans when he tried to rally them against white land invasion in the early 1800s.

Hicks did not face the life-and-death choice Tecumseh and many Native Americans grappled with in their fight. But Tecumseh not only called for Native Americans to stand up to white injustice, he also showed compassion by not killing noncombatants. He urged other Native Americans to emulate the same humane treatment. His example survived in future generations.

"I've labored with it throughout my whole career whenever I've had to make big layoffs," Hicks says. "I think as part of

Native-American culture, one of our teachings is you always take care of your people, and I'm not sure corporate America does that all the time."

Hicks' success did not come from conforming to the corporate culture, but rather adopting a Native-American approach. He avoided hiring excess employees and trained them in different skills so they could increase their chances of staying employed if layoffs were necessary. Hicks clashed with his supervisors and figures he could be in a higher position if he just played the corporate game.

"I worked with a very senior guy . . . who told me that sometimes I thought more of the people than the bottom line," Hicks recalls. "My response was the people are the bottom line and if you treat them right, they will produce the bottom line you need."

Hicks urges Native Americans entering or in corporate America to find strength in their traditions. "I would tell them to be true to themselves and to their heritage, that the native way does not have to be subjugated by the corporate way," he says.

Tracy Stanhoff, president of the American Indian National Chamber of Commerce, says corporate America and government contractors need to do better to inform Native-American businesses about opportunities and mentorships. Her organization started two years ago and represents the 12-member chamber of commerce nationwide, she says.

Stanhoff is a member of the Prairie Band Potawatomi Nation out of Kansas. She sees her organization supporting mentoring opportunities that she did not have when she started her advertising and graphics design business in 1988 at age 26.

"There are lots of issues that have to do with a lack of outreach from corporate America and their diversity departments," Stanhoff says. "We need to step up and say, 'Hey, don't forget about us.'"

Business on the Reservation

Lois Taylor and Barbara Poley steered clear of corporate America when they joined a nonprofit group to help jump-start tribal businesses on their Hopi reservation. The Hopi Foundation has helped the Hopi realize their entrepreneurial spirit without having to compromise traditions by leaving the reservation.

> "Education for our people should validate the cultural identity and cultural piece interspersed with Western knowledge to prepare balanced individuals who can live in both worlds."
>
> —Maggie Necefer, Dine College

The Hopi reservation occupies 1.5 million acres in northeastern Arizona and many of its residents live in remote areas. The idea for one business, Native Sun, sprung from the objections of many Hopi who did not want a power company's electrical grid crossing over sacred cultural land. Many choose instead to use kerosene lamps and battery-operated lights.

"They did not want to be subservient to a company that would provide them electricity," he adds. "They are staunchly independent."

The Hopi Foundation in 1988 helped start Native Sun, a Hopi-run business that sells solar panels, batteries and equipment. Two years ago, the company became a limited corporation with a majority Hopi board. Hopi living in remote areas are able to harness the sun's energy via solar panels placed on top or near their homes. When banks denied loans to families who could not afford the solar panels, the foundation started a revolving loan fund and maintained "one of the lowest default rates of any institution," Taylor says.

Like many tribes on reservations, the challenges of high unemployment, poor health and inadequate educational opportunities are a daily reality. In some Hopi villages, unemployment can reach as high as 55 percent. Reservations were created by the federal government with the promise of sovereignty and protection. In exchange, Native Americans had to relinquish land as white settlers hungered for more property. The reservations often consisted of the worst land, but today, Hopi and other Native Americans refuse to leave, saying the reservation serves as the spiritual connection to their ancestral roots.

"The Hopi people have a year-long religious calendar . . . and one of the key and important principles was for us to work with micro-enterprises that were compatible with the Hopi lifestyle," Taylor says.

Out of that desire, another business, Gentle Rain Designs, was born. Hopi women already sewing from their homes created the cooperative and now design fleece items ranging from jackets and vests to pillows and purses, all from recycled plastic. The women operate a small shop on the reservation and sell their clothing to boutiques outside the reservation, allowing them to work around their tribal ceremonies.

"If we are going to have survival on our own reservations, we have to build up the capacity and sustainability with businesses we produce on the reservation," Poley says.

Fred DuBray does not dwell on monetary gain when he talks about the growth of the InterTribal Bison Cooperative he directs in South Dakota. DuBray, a member of the Cheyenne River Sioux Tribe, watched the cooperative grow from 1,000 bison in 1990 to 15,000 today with 53 tribes from 18 states participating.

Cultural Competency: Understanding Native Americans in Business Dealings

The great divide between Native-American and corporate culture doesn't mean the two sides can't find common ground to conduct business.

One of Patty Dimitrious missions is helping non-Natives understand proper social and business etiquette when dealing with Native Americans. Dimitriou 35, is a member of the Dine (Navajo) Nation and owner of Alternatives/Alternativos, a multicultural advertising agency in Phoenix, Ariz., specializing in Native American and Latino marketing communications. She offers the following suggestions to clients who do business in "Indian Country."

Making your presence known through direct eye contact or a strong handshake can be interpreted as disrespectful and dominating in Native American circles. Dimitriou advises a more modest tack that does not boast of your presence. It's also a good idea to let your Native-American contact know more about your own family background and personal interests. "It's really important to understand each others' roots and background so that we know how to communicate with each other," Dimitriou says. "By sharing where you and your family are from, you support the Native-American custom of building a sense of relatedness."

Dimitriou decided to pursue a degree in communications after leaving her Navajo Nation, in part to help her better understand how to succeed in a dominant white culture. She since has advised non-Natives who are concerned that they might have offended Native Americans at business encounters.

"Say, for example, a developer goes to meet with a tribal council and he really wants to close the deal, so he is . . . trying to be direct and engaging in the type of behavior white America would say is assertive and knowledgeable," Dimitriou says. "But with his conduct, he is coming across as very combative, aggressive and very disrespectful and he creates the exact opposite outcome he is seeking."

And don't be surprised if you stay long at a tribal council business meeting. Dimitriou has heard of visitors who expected to present at a 5 p.m. meeting and waited until 1 a.m. the next morning. But she encourages clients to appreciate the cultural reasons for longer meetings. "One of the things I think is wonderful about Native-American communication is that everyone is invited to speak freely and express themselves without someone cross-talking them," she says. "The most important things are that everyone is in agreement and that everyone has a chance to share."

—Peter Ortiz

The buffalo provide a healthy food source that could help alleviate some of the serious health problems that afflict many Native Americans.

"The most important aspect . . . is recognition that buffalo is such an important and vital part of Indian culture," DuBray says. "If we can't allow them to exist, we probably can't exist as a people."

White settlers knew of the spiritual bond between the buffalo and Native Americans when they systematically tried to wipe out the animal. Native Americans treated the buffalo and other animals with respect and thanked the animals they slaughtered for providing for their families. That concept was foreign to many whites who only hunted the buffalo for food, profit or to further destroy the Native-American way of life.

A big challenge faced by the cooperative is avoiding the idea of domesticating animals, a concept white settlers brought to the Americas. Native Americans viewed themselves, as well as other living beings, as temporary tenants of land that owned them. DuBray says buffalo need to roam freely, as their ancestors did, and that this is necessary to strengthen the spiritual bond they share with the animal.

"We are working toward restoring them as a wildlife resource, not as a commodity," DuBray says. "For them to provide a healthy source of food, they need a healthy source of food themselves like medicinal plants."

DuBray, 54, acknowledges that individual tribes must make tough decisions about how to use limited land. The Native-American way of raising buffalo requires lots of space that some tribal members may want to use for other economic projects. He has 100 buffalo, while his tribe owns several thousand. But despite the success of the cooperative, suspicion remains of the federal government or real-estate interests wanting to take over the land.

"There are still people out there developing ingenious ways to strip away what is left, so we can't let our guard down," DuBray says. "The only promise the white man kept is the promise to take our land. He took it."

American Indian and Alaska Native Heritage Month: November 2008

The first American Indian Day was celebrated in May 1916 in New York. Red Fox James, a Blackfeet Indian, rode horseback from state to state, getting endorsements from 24 state governments, to have a day to honor American Indians. In 1990, President George H.W. Bush signed a joint congressional resolution designating November 1990 as "National American Indian Heritage Month." Similar proclamations have been issued every year since 1994. This Facts for Features presents data for American Indians and Alaska Natives, as this is one of the six major race categories.

Note: Unless otherwise specified, the data in the "Population" section refer to the population who reported a race alone or in combination with one or more other races.

Population

4.5 million
As of July 1, 2007, the estimated population of American Indians and Alaska Natives, including those of more than one race. They made up 1.5 percent of the total population.[1]

8.6 million
The projected population of American Indians and Alaska Natives, including those of more than one race, on July 1, 2050. They would comprise 2 percent of the total population.[2]

44,803
Increase in the nation's American Indian and Alaska Native population from July 1, 2006, to July 1, 2007. The population of this group increased by 1 percent during the period.[3]

30.3
Median age of the single-race American Indian and Alaska Native population in 2007, younger than the median of 36.6 for the population as a whole. About 27 percent of American Indians and Alaska Natives were younger than 18, and 8 precent were 65 and older.[4]

689,120
The American Indian and Alaska Native population in California as of July 1, 2007, the highest total of any state. California was followed by Oklahoma (393,500) and Arizona (335,381).

About 8,300 American Indians and Alaska Natives were added to Texas' population between July 1, 2006, and July 1,

2007. That is the largest numeric increase of any state. Georgia (3.4 percent) had the highest rate of increase during the period.[5]

5
Number of states where American Indians and Alaska Natives were the largest race or ethnic minority group in 2006. These states are Alaska, Montana, North Dakota, Oklahoma and South Dakota.[6]

11
Number of states with more than 100,000 American Indian and Alaska Native residents on July 1, 2007. These states were California, Oklahoma, Arizona, Texas, New Mexico, New York, Washington, Florida, North Carolina, Michigan and Alaska. Combined, these states were home to 62 percent of the nation's American Indian and Alaska Native residents.[7]

18%
The proportion of Alaska's population identified as American Indian and Alaska Native as of July 1, 2007, the highest rate for this race group of any state. Alaska was followed by Oklahoma (11 percent) and New Mexico (10 percent).[8]

146,500
The number of American Indians and Alaska Natives in Los Angeles County, Calif., as of July 1, 2007. Los Angeles led all of the nation's counties in the number of people of this racial category.

Maricopa County, Ariz., added about 2,300 people to this group between July 1, 2006, and July 1, 2007, leading the nation's counties in this category.[9]

10
Among counties or equivalents with total populations of 10,000 or more, number that were majority American Indian and Alaska Native, as of July 1, 2007. Shannon, S.D., led the way, with 87 percent of its population being a member of this race group.[10]

Families and Children

537,500
The number of American Indian and Alaska Native families in 2007. Of these:

- 314,900 were married-couple families, including those with children.
- 146,400 were married couples with their own children, under the age of 18.[11]

3.57

Average number of people in an American Indian and Alaska Native family in 2007. This was larger than the national average size for all families (3.2 people).[12]

Housing

56%

The percentage of American Indian and Alaska Native households who own their owned home in 2007.[13]

$116,700

Median value of homes owned by American Indians and Alaska Natives.[14]

Languages

27%

Percentage of American Indians and Alaska Natives 5 and older who spoke a language other than English at home.[15]

Education

76%

The percentage of American Indians and Alaska Natives 25 and older who had at least a high school diploma. Also, 13 percent had at least a bachelor's degree.[16]

61,976

Number of American Indians and Alaska Natives 25 and older who have a graduate or professional degree.[17]

Businesses

$26.9 billion

Receipts for American Indian- and Alaska Native-owned businesses in 2002. These businesses numbered 201,387.

20,380

Number of American Indian- and Alaska Native-owned firms in the Los Angeles-Long Beach-Riverside combined statistical area, making that area number one in the metro category. Among counties, Los Angeles had the highest number of firms (13,061).

38,125

Number of American Indian- and Alaska Native-owned firms in California, which led the states. Oklahoma, Texas, New York and Florida followed.

Nearly 3 in 10

Number of American Indian- and Alaska Native-owned firms that operated in construction and other services (such as personal services, and repair and maintenance).

24,498

Number of American Indian- and Alaska Native-owned firms that had paid employees. These businesses employed 191,270 people.

3,631

Number of American Indian- and Alaska Native-owned firms with receipts of $1 million or more. These firms accounted for nearly 2 percent of the total number of American Indian- and Alaska Native-owned firms and more than 64 percent of their total receipts.

178

Number of American Indian- and Alaska Native-owned firms with 100 or more employees. These firms generated nearly $5.3 billion in gross receipts—24 percent of the total revenue for American Indian- and Alaska Native-owned employer firms.

New York; Los Angeles; and Gallup, N.M.

The three cities with the largest number of American Indian- and Alaska Native-owned firms, with 7,134; 5,767; and 2,642, respectively.[18]

Jobs

25%

The percentage of civilian employed American Indian and Alaska Native people 16 and older who worked in management, professional and related occupations. In addition, 23 percent worked in sales and office occupations and about the same percentage worked in service occupations.[19]

Caregivers

54%

Percentage of American Indians and Alaska Natives 30 and older who lived with grandchildren and were responsible for caring for their care. The corresponding rate for the population as a whole was 40 percent.[20]

Veterans

165,200

The number of American Indian and Alaska Native veterans of the U.S. armed forces.[21]

Income and Poverty

$35,343

The 2007 median income of households where the householder reported being American Indian and Alaska Native and no other race.[22]

25.3%

The 2007 poverty rate of people who reported they were American Indian and Alaska Native and no other race.[23]

Health Insurance

32.1%

The percentage of people who reported they were American Indian and Alaska Native and no other race who lacked health insurance coverage, based on a three-year average (2005-2007).[24]

Notes

1. Source: Population estimates http://www.census.gov/Press-Release/www/releases/archives/population/011910.html

2. Source: Population projections http://www.census.gov/Press-Release/www/releases/archives/population/012496.html

3. Source: Population estimates http://www.census.gov/Press-Release/www/releases/archives/population/011910.html

4. Source: Population estimates http://www.census.gov/Press-Release/www/releases/archives/population/011910.html

5. Source: Population estimates http://www.census.gov/Press-Release/www/releases/archives/population/011910.html

6. Source: Population estimates http://www.census.gov/Press-Release/www/releases/archives/population/011910.html

7. Source: Population estimates http://www.census.gov/Press-Release/www/releases/archives/population/011910.html

8. Source: Population estimates http://www.census.gov/Press-Release/www/releases/archives/population/011910.html

9. Source: Population estimates http://www.census.gov/Press-Release/www/releases/archives/population/012463.html

10. Source: Population estimates http://www.census.gov/Press-Release/www/releases/archives/population/012463.html

11. Source: 2007 American Community Survey for the American Indian and Alaska Native alone population. http://factfinder.census.gov

12. Source: 2007 American Community Survey for the American Indian and Alaska Native alone population. http://factfinder.census.gov

13. Source: 2007 American Community Survey for the American Indian and Alaska Native alone population. http://factfinder.census.gov

14. Source: 2007 American Community Survey for the American Indian and Alaska Native alone population. http://factfinder.census.gov

15. Source: 2007 American Community Survey for the American Indian and Alaska Native alone population. http://factfinder.census.gov

16. Source: 2007 American Community Survey for the American Indian and Alaska Native alone population. http://factfinder.census.gov

17. Source: 2007 American Community Survey for the American Indian and Alaska Native alone population. http://factfinder.census.gov

18. Source for data in this section: *American Indian- and Alaska Native-Owned Firms: 2002* http://www.census.gov/Press-Release/www/releases/archives/business_ownership/007013.html

19. Source: 2007 American Community Survey for the American Indian and Alaska Native alone population. http://factfinder.census.gov

20. Source: 2007 American Community Survey for the American Indian and Alaska Native alone population. http://factfinder.census.gov

21. Source: 2007 American Community Survey for the American Indian and Alaska Native alone population. http://factfinder.census.gov

22. Source: Income, Earnings, and Poverty Data from the 2007 American Community Survey http://www.census.gov/Press-Release/www/releases/archives/income_wealth/010583.html

23. Source: Income, Earnings, and Poverty, Data from 2007 American Community Survey http://www.census.gov/Press-Release/www/releases/archives/income_wealth/012528.html

24. Source: *Income, Poverty, and Health Insurance Coverage in the United States: 2007,* http://www.census.gov/Press-Release/www/releases/archives/income_wealth/010583.html

Editor's note—The preceding data were collected from a variety of sources and may be subject to sampling variability and other sources of error. Facts for Features are customarily released about two months before an observance in order to accommodate magazine production timelines. Questions or comments should be directed to the Census Bureau's Public information Office: telephone: 301-763-3030; fax: 301-763-3762; or e-mail: pio@census.gov.

From *U.S. Census Bureau*, November 2007.

Tribal Philanthropy Thrives

DANIEL GIBSON

A merican Indian tribes all have social values that encourage sharing with those in need. Historically, a deer, tapir or walrus brought in by hunters would be split among tribal members or families. Corn, squash and beans from the fields usually went into a common larder. Work was often divided up into group tasks. The emphasis was on survival of all, common goals and a communal spirit. Today those same values are guiding the gifting of millions of dollars each year from tribes benefiting from gaming income to their surrounding non-Indian communities and to non-gaming tribes. Tribes understand what difficult times are all about, and they are stepping up to the plate in a major fashion to aid and assist those less fortunate.

In 2006 alone, tribal governments nationwide gave more than $150 million to charitable causes, according to the National Indian Gaming Association.

Examples abound across the nation. In California, the **Morongo Band of Mission Indians** near Banning has set up a scholarship program open to all California Native students. In recent years, the tribe has also supported programs of the Special Olympics, the Boy Scouts of America, San Gorgonio Memorial Hospital, the Riverside Sheriffs' Association Relief Fund, the local Little League, the American Cancer Society, Big Brothers/Big Sisters, the YMCA, the AIDS Assistance Program, the American Red Cross and the Juvenile Diabetes Association.

In the Southwest, many tribes are generously providing financial assistance to nearby communities and home states. The **Pascua Yaqui Tribe** near Tucson, Arizona donated more than $1.1 million in 2006 and 2007, including $338,000 to the City of Tucson to purchase land for affordable housing, parks and recreation programs; $150,000 for cultural programs and tourism endeavors in the Town of Guadalupe; and $50,000 to the Tucson School District. "The Pascua Yaqui Tribe is committed to investing in the future of our state," notes former tribal chairwoman Herminia Frias.

In fact, when Arizona voters passed Proposition 202 in 2002, which clarified the legal status of Indian gaming in the state, the legislation called for the gaming tribes to donate substantial revenue to the state. Of these funds, 12 percent goes directly to Arizona cities, towns and counties, while the other 88 percent is divided up among a handful of state departments and programs. Of the latter revenue stream, in 2007 alone Arizona tribes provided more than $46 million to the state's Instructional Improvement Fund for charter schools, $23 million to the Trauma & Emergency Services Fund, $6.5 million for the Arizona Office of Tourism, $6.5 million to the Arizona Game & Fish Department's Wildlife Conservation Fund, $8 million to the Arizona Department of Gaming and $1.8 million to the Arizona Office of Problem Gambling.

The **Soboba Band of Luiseño Indians** in southern California has been a good neighbor to its surrounding towns in Riverside County. In June 2003, the tribe gave $400,000 to the City of Hemet Public Library, but that was just one of its many large contributions in the area in recent years. A room at the tribal hall is filled with plaques of appreciation from local youth sports organizations. The tribe has gifted $60,000 in donations to six local football programs, and some 600 other local kids are benefiting from contributions ranging from $10,000 to $20,000 per year to the local parks and recreation program. The Ramona Outdoor Play, a production incorporating local history held annually in Hemet, is now sponsored by the tribe. When the Vietnam Veterans Memorial Moving Wall visited San Jacinto, it was due to a grant from the tribe. Local chamber of commerce events are sponsored by the tribe, which also provides space and staff for the chamber's annual community fair.

"It comes from a lot of years of local people giving us things," explained vice chairwoman Rosemary Morillo in an article in the Riverside *Press-Enterprise* a few years ago. "People would donate oranges, candy and toys for our kids at Christmas. Now we're able to return that gesture." In the same article, tribal administrator Andrew Masiel stated, "We've always had the desire (to contribute to local community events and charitable causes) but not the resources. But now it's different."

The **Forest County Potawatomi** tribe of Wisconsin is actively helping to fund many programs and projects outside of its reservation. Each year in August, the tribe's Community Foundation selects 20 children's charities from Milwaukee, Waukesha, Washington, Racine and Ozaukee counties to receive at least $50,000 each. This August will mark the 15th anniversary of the program, which has provided more than $7 million to date. The funds are derived from the Potawatomi Bingo Casino on Canal Street in Milwaukee, which hosts special Miracle on

Canal bingo games, a two-night dinner and auction, and an annual golf event.

The tribe also is active in funding medical programs. Last December, it donated $45,000 to the Medical College of Wisconsin for research and educational programs focused on diabetes treatment and prevention. It was just the most recent gift in a relationship going back several years. "It's a goal of the tribe to be at the forefront when it comes to eliminating this debilitating disease," says Tom Bolter, the executive director of the tribe's Foundation Enterprise Fund. All told, the tribe has given away tens of millions of dollars since its foundation was established in 1999.

The **Confederated Tribes of the Umatilla Indian Reservation** of Oregon established the Wildhorse Foundation in 2001, which is funded by a set percentage of the Wildhorse Resort and Casino's net income. As the resort's business grows, so do the foundation's annual grants. In 2001, grants totaled $294,000; in 2002, $230,000; in 2003, $470,000; in 2004, $503,000; in 2005, $507,000; in 2006, $589,000; and in 2007, $655,000.

Grants range from $500 to $20,000 and are focused on projects and programs in Umatilla, Union, Morrow and Wallowa counties. For instance, in 2007 the tribe gave a $10,000 grant to provide orthodontic and dental treatment to local children through the nonprofit Advantage Smiles for Kids program; $500 for the Cancer Society Relay for Life; $12,000 for the Pendleton Parks Department for new lifeguard chairs; and $10,000 to the Arts Council of Pendleton for public art exhibitions. Other funds were directed to the City of Ukiah and the City of Echo, the Blue Mountain Nordic Club, Eastern Oregon University, Homestead Youth and Family Services, Oregon Historical Society, St. Andrews Mission and Pilot Rock Fire District.

Perhaps the most generous tribe in the nation is the **Shakopee Mdewakanton Sioux Community** of Prior Lake, Minnesota (see Sept./Oct. 2002 issue). Since the tribe opened its first bingo hall in October 1982, it has given away more than $115 million, and in the fiscal year ending last Sept. 30 it hit an annual high mark of $26 million.

"We need to give back—it's the nature of the Dakota people," explains Bill Rudnicki, the tribal administrator for the past 15 years. So far, the tribe has resisted putting a cap on annual donations. "It's gone up every year," says Rudnicki. "The more you help, the more you see the need out there. It's such a good feeling when we get notes from kids, for example, stating that they wouldn't have had textbooks that year if it weren't for our efforts. It really hits home."

The tribe also donates regularly to the American Red Cross, the American Cancer Society, the American Diabetes Association and the American Heart Association, and recently provided $500,000 over a two-year period to the local hospital. It gives more than $200,000 a year at Christmas to some 44 social service organizations in the Twin Cities to buy toys, clothing, food and other gifts. Contributions can be relatively small but play an important role—such as the $1,000 given to

Soboba Leader Honored

In April, the chairman of the Soboba Band of Luiseño Indians, Robert Salgado, was recognized for his leadership abilities with the presentation of the Wendell Chino Humanitarian Award from the National Indian Gaming Association. Salgado spent nearly two decades guiding his tribe from obscurity to a high-profile position in southern California's political and economic life.

The tribe has an active program of donating funds to local and regional causes (see main story), but Salgado says perhaps his greatest contribution to his tribe and the region was forging a water-rights pact with the Metropolitan Water District of Southern California and the Eastern Municipal Water District, which came after decades of litigation.

He also oversaw the transformation of his reservation from a pocket of poverty to relative affluence, largely due to revenue derived from the Soboba Casino and the Country Club at Soboba Springs. In 2006, the tribe refurbished The Oaks resort, which included construction of a football stadium for the reservation's Noli Indian High School. A semi-professional football team owned by Salgado also uses the facility, revealing another passion of the chairman. Salgado is still widely remembered in the area for his record-setting role on the local high school football team as a kicker, and later roles as a coach for San Jacinto High School and Mt. San Jacinto College.

the Emily, Minnesota Police Department to acquire and train a German shepherd drug dog. Or they can be huge. On Oct. 19, 2007, the tribe delivered a check for $10.4 million to the University of Minnesota to fund construction of a new stadium, and has committed $2.5 million for university scholarships.

Despite these major gifts that benefit the general Minnesota populace, "The bulk of what we give is actually to other tribes, to specific programs and projects when we hear of unmet needs," Rudnicki notes. Between 1997 and 1998, the tribe created a formal process for annual donations to other tribes. Last year, 19 tribes were on the receiving end of the Shakopees' generosity.

The Red Lake Band of Chippewa of northern Minnesota—scene of a terrible student shooting in March 2005—is one tribal beneficiary. The Red Lake Boys & Girls Club has also been the recipient of $1 million in Shakopee funding. The Red Lake government wanted to restore its once-famous and lucrative walleye fisheries, and with the help of the Shakopees and the state government, they are now undergoing a strong recovery. "I'm really proud of the tribe's being ahead of the times, in terms of funding 'green' initiatives," says Rudnicki.

In January 2008, the Flandreau Santee Sioux Tribe of South Dakota received a $1 million grant to fund construction of an eldercare center. In February, the Spirit Lake Nation of North Dakota was gifted $1 million to build a new courthouse and undertake other building maintenance and improvement projects. And in March, the Kiowa Tribe of Oklahoma received a $1 million grant to purchase and operate a nearby tourist attraction, Indian City USA.

The tribe is also active in providing loans to tribal governments for economic development and social projects. From 2004 to 2007, $67 million was loaned.

Programs that benefit a wide range of Indian people have also received assistance. For instance, the American Indian College Fund was given $1.8 million over a six-year period. "We've been blessed, and we're grateful for the opportunity to help others," concludes the Shakopee tribal chairman, Stanley Crooks. Details on the tribe's philanthropic program can be found at ccsmdc.org/donations.html.

DANIEL GIBSON has been the editor of *Native Peoples* since February 2001. His most recent book is *Pueblos of the Rio Grande: A Visitor's Guide* (Rio Nuevo Publishers).

UNIT 5
African Americans

Unit Selections

Key Points to Consider

- Characterize relationships between ethnic and racial groups on your campus.

- What are the most compelling issues that face African American communities?

- In what respects are desegregation, integration, discrimination, and prejudice woven into the discussion of contemporary issues related to African Americans?

- What role will new African immigrants play in the African American community?

- What social, economic, and political conditions have supported the expansion of an African American middle class?

- What factors explain the persistence of an African American underclass? In what respect is this question related to integration?

- In what respect is attention to education an answer to economic and social integration of African Americans?

Student Web Site
www.mhcls.com

Internet References
National Association for the Advancement of Colored People (NAACP)
http://www.naacp.org
AIDs and Black New Yorkers
http://www.villagevoice.com/issues/0024/wright.php

© Purestock/PunchStock

Revisiting the legislative history of the civil rights era can shed new light on our national public understanding of the thrust of that period. By reviewing the congressional deliberation in support of the Civil Rights Act and its goal of equal protection and equality before the law and then juxtaposing the contemporary legal arguments and current politics of equal protection, the reader will discover a complex set of considerations. A careful analysis of the moral foundations of our legal system and its expectations and attention to the practical consequence of defining and achieving an epoch of equality and the limits of legal remedies will emerge from these re-considerations and the attendant search for new remedies and assurance of fairness and non-exclusionary practices.

This unit's glimpses of the African American reality, its struggles for freedom, its tradition and community, its achievements, and the stresses of building bridges between worlds reveal a dense set of problems. More importantly, they suggest pieces of authentic identity rather than stereotype. Becoming a healthy ethnic society involves more than the end of ethnic stereotyping. The basis of ethnic identity is sustained by authentic portrayals

of positive personal and group identity. The cultivation of ethnicity that does not encourage disdain for and self-hatred among members and groups is an important psychological and social artifice. Progress on issues of race involves examination of complex historical, social, cultural, and economic factors. Analysis of this sort requires assessment of the deep racism in the American mentality, that is, the cultural consciousness, and the institutions whose images and practices shape social reality. These patterns of change within African American populations compel discussion of the emerging black middle class. The purpose and influence of the historically black university, the reopening of the discussion of slavery and the separate-but-equal issue, and the renewed attention to Afro centric education are clear evidence of the ambivalence and ambiguity inherent in the challenges of a multi-cultural society. Earlier dichotomies—slave/free, black/white, poor/rich—are still evident, but a variety of group relations based on historical and regional as well as institutional agendas to preserve cultural and racial consciousness have complicated the simple hope for liberty and justice that was shared by man.

Black History Month: February 2008

To commemorate and celebrate the contributions to our nation made by people of African descent, American historian Carter G. Woodson established Black History Week. The first celebration occurred on Feb. 12, 1926. For many years, the second week of February was set aside for this celebration to coincide with the birthdays of abolitionist/editor Frederick Douglass and Abraham Lincoln. In 1976, as part of the nation's bicentennial, the week was expanded into Black History Month. In 2000, President Clinton proclaimed February as National African American History Month.

Population Distribution

40.2 million
As of July 1, 2006, the estimated population of black residents in the United States, including those of more than one race. They made up 13.4 percent of the total U.S. population. This figure represents an increase of half a million residents from one year earlier.[1]

61.4 million
The projected single-race black population of the United States for July 1, 2050. On that date, according to the projection, blacks would constitute 14.6 percent of the nation's total population.[2]

18
Number of states with an estimated black population on July 1, 2006, of at least 1 million. New York, with 3.5 million blacks, led the way. The 17 other states on the list were Alabama, California, Florida, Georgia, Illinois, Louisiana, Maryland, Michigan, Mississippi, New Jersey, North Carolina, Ohio, Pennsylvania, South Carolina, Tennessee, Texas and Virginia.[3]

37%
Percentage of Mississippi's population that is black, highest of any state. Blacks also make up more than a quarter of the population in Louisiana (32 percent), Georgia (30 percent), Maryland (30 percent), South Carolina (29 percent) and Alabama (27 percent). They comprise 57 percent of the population in the District of Columbia.[4]

135,000
The increase in Texas' black population between July 1, 2005, and July 1, 2006, which led all states. Georgia (101,000), Florida (86,000) and North Carolina (41,000) also recorded large increases.[5]

22
Number of states in which blacks are the largest minority group. These states are Alabama, Arkansas, Delaware, Georgia, Illinois, Indiana, Kentucky, Louisiana, Maryland, Michigan, Minnesota, Mississippi, Missouri, New York, North Carolina, Ohio, Pennsylvania, South Carolina, Tennessee, Virginia, West Virginia and Wisconsin. (Note: Minorities are part of a group other than single-race non-Hispanic white.)[6]

1.4 million
The number of blacks in Cook County, Ill., as of July 1, 2006. Cook led all the nation's counties in the number of people of this racial category. Los Angeles County, Calif., also topped the 1 million mark. Harris County, Texas, had the largest numerical increase in the black population between July 1, 2005, and July 1, 2006 (52,000), followed by East Baton Rouge Parish, La. (19,000).[7]

Among counties with total populations of at least 10,000, all 50 with the highest percentage black population were in the South. Claiborne County, Miss., which was 85 percent black, led the country.[8]

31%
The proportion of the black population younger than 18 as of July 1, 2006. At the other end of the spectrum, 8 percent of the black population was 65 and older.[9]

Note: Unless otherwise noted, the estimates in this section refer to the population that is either single-race black or black in combination with one or more other races.

Serving Our Nation

2.4 million
Number of black military veterans in the United States in 2006. More military veterans are black than any other minority group.[10]

Education

81%
Among blacks 25 and older, the proportion who had at least a high school diploma in 2006.[11]

18%
Percentage of blacks 25 and older who had a bachelor's degree or higher in 2006.[12]

1.3 million

Among blacks 25 and older, the number who had an advanced degree in 2006 (e.g., master's, doctorate, medical or law). In 1996, 683,000 blacks had this level of education.[13]

2.3 million

Number of black college students in fall 2005. This was an increase of roughly 1 million from 15 years earlier.[14]

Note: 2005 and 2006 data in this section pertain to single-race blacks.

Businesses

$88.6 billion

Revenues for black-owned businesses in 2002. The number of black-owned businesses totaled nearly 1.2 million in 2002. Black-owned firms accounted for 5 percent of all nonfarm businesses in the United States.

129,329

The number of black-owned firms in New York in 2002, which led all states. New York City alone had 98,080 such firms, which led all cities.

10,716

The number of black-owned firms operating in 2002 with receipts of $1 million or more. These firms accounted for 1 percent of the total number of black-owned firms in 2002 and 55 percent of their total receipts, or $49 billion.

969

The number of black-owned firms with 100 or more employees in 2002. Firms of this size accounted for 24 percent of the total revenue for black-owned employer firms in 2002, or $16 billion.[15]

Income, Poverty and Health Insurance

$31,969

The annual median income of single-race black households in 2006. In constant dollars, this is up from $26,468 in 1986.[16]

$34,770 & $30,352

The 2006 median earnings of single-race black men and women, respectively, 15 and older who worked full time, year-round.[17]

24.3%

Poverty rate in 2006 for single-race blacks. This rate was down from 31.1 percent in 1986.[18]

20.5%

The percentage of single-race blacks lacking health insurance in 2006, up from 19 percent in 2005.[19]

Families and Children

Note: The first two statements in this section pertain to households with a householder who is single-race black.

64%

Percentage of black households that contained a family. There were 8.4 million black family households.[20]

45%

Nationally, the percentage of black families containing a married-couple family.[21]

1.2 million

Number of single-race black grandparents living with their own grandchildren younger than 18. Of this number, 51 percent were also responsible for their care.[22]

Homeownership— the American Dream

46%

Nationally, the percentage of black households that lived in owner-occupied homes. The rate was higher in certain states, such as Mississippi, where it reached 58 percent.[22]

Note: Data in this section pertain to households with a householder who is single-race black.

Jobs

26%

The percentage of single-race blacks 16 and older who work in management, professional and related occupations. There are 44,900 black physicians and surgeons, 80,000 postsecondary teachers, 48,300 lawyers, and 52,400 chief executives.[23]

Notes

1. Source: Population estimates http://www.census.gov/Press-Release/www/releases/archives/population/010048.html
2. Source: Population projections http://www.census.gov/Press-Release/www/releases/archives/population/001720.html
3. Source: Population estimates http://www.census.gov/Press-Release/www/releases/archives/population/010048.html
4. Source: Population estimates http://www.census.gov/Press-Release/www/releases/archives/population/010048.html
5. Source: Population estimates http://www.census.gov/Press-Release/www/releases/archives/population/010048.html
6. Source: Population estimates http://www.census.gov/Press-Release/www/releases/archives/population/010048.html
7. Source: Population estimates http://www.census.gov/Press-Release/www/releases/archives/population/010482.html
8. Source: Population estimates http://www.census.gov/Press-Release/www/releases/archives/population/010482.html
9. Source: Population estimates http://www.census.gov/Press-Release/www/releases/archives/population/010048.html
10. Source: 2006 American Community Survey http://factfinder.census.gov. Data pertain to single-race blacks.

11. Source: Educational Attainment in the United States: 2006 http://www.census.gov/Press-Release/www/releases/archives/education/009749.html

12. Source: Educational Attainment in the United States: 2006 http://www.census.gov/Press-Release/www/releases/archives/education/009749.html

13. Source: Educational Attainment in the United States: 2006 http://www.census.gov/Press-Release/www/releases/archives/education/009749.html

14. Source: School Enrollment—Social and Economic Characteristics of Students: October 2005 http://www.census.gov/Press-Release/www/releases/archives/education/007909.html

15. Source: Black-Owned Firms: 2002 http://www.census.gov/prod/ec02/sb0200csblk.pdf

16. Source: Income, Poverty, and Health Insurance Coverage in the United States: 2006 http://www.census.gov/Press-Release/www/releases/archives/income_wealth/010583.html

17. Source: Income, Poverty, and Health Insurance Coverage in the United States: 2006 http://www.census.gov/Press-Release/www/releases/archives/income_wealth/010583.html

18. Source: Income, Poverty, and Health Insurance Coverage in the United States: 2006 http://www.census.gov/Press-Release/www/releases/archives/income_wealth/010583.html

19. Source: Income, Poverty, and Health Insurance Coverage in the United States: 2006 http://www.census.gov/Press-Release/www/releases/archives/income_wealth/010583.html

20. Source: 2006 American Community Survey http://factfinder.census.gov

21. Source: 2006 American Community Survey http://factfinder.census.gov

22. Source: 2006 American Community Survey http://factfinder.census.gov

23. Source: 2006 American Community Survey http://factfinder.census.gov

24. Sources: 2006 American Community Survey and Upcoming Statistical Abstract of the United States: 2008 http://factfinder.census.gov and http://www.census.gov/compendia/statab/

Editor's note—The preceding data were collected from a variety of sources and may be subject to sampling variability and other sources of error. *Facts for Features* are customarily released about two months before an observance in order to accommodate magazine production timelines. Questions or comments should be directed to the Census Bureau's Public Information Office: telephone: 301-763-3030; fax: 301-763-3762; or e-mail: pio@census.gov.

From *U.S. Census Bureau,* January 24, 2008.

Who Is an African American?

Yoji Cole

To answer the question in 21st-century America, look back to 17th-century British America and the colony of Virginia:

"In the early 1620s slave traders captured a man in Angola, gave him the name Antonio, and brought him to the Americas, where he was sold to a colonist in Virginia. During these early days in British North America, before the system of slavery was strictly codified, some bound Africans were treated much like indentured servants and were freed after a period of servitude . . . By [1650] Antonio, a free man known as Anthony Johnson, was the owner of . . . about 250 acres and the family held servants of their own . . . When Anthony died in 1670 . . . A white planter was allowed to seize the Virginia land because, the court said, as a black man, Anthony Johnson was not a citizen of the colony."

—Hard Road to Freedom: The Story of African America

Johnson's story illustrates the life Africans faced after they were forcibly brought to this country, stripped of any connection to their families or cultures and forced to eke out an existence at the whim of people who considered them second-class human beings or sometimes less than human. Out of this system, enslaved Africans created a set of socially acquired values, beliefs, language, music, food and rules of conduct that created today's African Americans.

It is poetic justice that African-American culture has come to define the United States as much as the nation's white culture. Throughout their years in this country and through personal and cultural name changes, African Americans have shunned mainstream stereotypes and conventions, redefining their culture through music, fashion and educational and economic attainment.

"The United States has a two-category system, white and non-white, that comes out of the slave code," says Robert Allen, professor of ethnic and African-American studies at the University of California, Berkeley. "Race is a political category and not a biological category."

While biology only recognizes one race—the human race— politics recognizes several. The United States has been mired in racial politics since the 17th century, when the Virginia colony created laws that made slavery a birthright of black people. This construct remains today as Americans are asked to check off boxes to reveal their racial heritage.

The Evolution of Blackness

The creation of the African-American community, known during different times in history as the Negro, colored and black community, is conjoined with the evolution of whiteness in the United States. Around 1676, laws were enacted that separated African slaves from European indentured servants. Slavery not only became inheritable for "Negroes," but black people were punished more harshly for crimes and poor whites were given new rights and opportunities, including jobs as overseers to police slaves. As the importance of slavery grew, colonial laws that conflated being "white" with freedom created a culture based on white privilege and black subjugation. The Transatlantic Slave Trade was the first system in which all slaves shared similar physical characteristics and thus provided slave owners, legislators and judges a "race"-based reason to justify forced, life-long service.

Those mores became the basis of national law. For example, the U.S. Naturalization Law of March 26, 1790, mandated that states only could confer citizenship on aliens who were "free white persons." Citizenship was not extended to African slaves, indentured servants and most women, according to the U.S. Citizenship and Immigration Services.

"Race is a political category and not a biological category."

—Robert Allen, University of California, Berkeley

"The nation's answer to the question 'Who is black?' has long been that a black is any person with any known African black ancestry," wrote F. James Davis, author of *Who is Black?: One Nation's Definition.* He continues, "This definition reflects the long experience with slavery and later with Jim Crow segregation. In the South it became known as the 'one-drop rule,' meaning that a single drop of 'black blood' makes a person black."

The "one-drop rule" made it impossible for the racially mixed children of an African slave and a white slave owner to claim they were white and, therefore, free. Most half-black and half-white children had black mothers. English law stipulated that a child's human status depended on the status of the father. In the course of the 17th century, however, the Virginia colony

Percent of U.S. Population

15%
12
9
6
3
0
1980 2004 2020

Where They Live
by Region

West 8.6%
Northeast 18.1%
Midwest 18.1%
South 55.3%

States Where 60% of Blacks Live

NY
MI
IL
MD
CA
VA
GA
TX LA
FL

How They Spend

$1,000 billion
800
600
400
200
0
1990 2000 2004 2009

Share of Nation's Buying Power

10%
8
6
4
2
0
1990 2004 2009

Professionals Who Are Black

Managers, Professionals
Doctors
Engineers
Lawyers
0 1 2 3 4 5 6%

How They Score

Mean scores, SAT 2004   ■ Verbal   ■ Math

Black Men
Black Women
White Men
White Women
Asian-American Men
Asian-American Women
Latino Men
Latinas

0 100 200 300 400 500 600

Educational Attainment

High School Degrees
Asian Americans
Whites
Blacks
Latinos

Bachelor's Degrees
Asian Americans
Whites
Blacks
Latinos

0 20 40 60 80 100%

Graduate or Professional Degrees
Asian Americans
Whites
Blacks
Latinos

0 1 2 3 4 5%

Figure 1 African-American Statistics.

changed that law so that mixed children inherited the status of their black mothers. Then the Supreme Court legitimized the "one-drop rule" nationally with its ruling in *Plessy v. Ferguson* (1896), effectively establishing that whiteness meant no link to African blood.

Laws that defined who was white and black corralled black people into one non-white category that did not allow many opportunities for success. The Jim Crow era (beginning around 1877 and continuing into the 1960s) that created separate facilities for blacks and whites further entrenched the notion in the nation's collective conscious that people who had African blood were inferior to people who were white. Such laws and judicial decisions, along with a legal system that kept people captive based on their African features and lineage, effectively created the Negro community—today, the African-American community.

African Americans have been defining and redefining who they are since the abolition of slavery provided the freedom to do so—remember, Antonio changed his name to Anthony Johnson once he became free. As with Anthony Johnson, the

128

constant renaming of the community is indicative of a people seeking to define themselves on their own terms. Historically, African Americans fought for their rights from the time they were enslaved. That struggle became the community's signature cause with the civil-rights movement, which largely was organized and led by the African-American church.

"The church was the only independent black institute and [the] only place where black folk could assemble that white folk couldn't control," says the Rev. Walter A. McCray, associate pastor of the Chicago-based First Baptist Congregational Church and president of the National Black Evangelical Association. "So the church became the hub of life in the black experience in America."

It should come as no surprise that the African-American community's most influential leaders came out of organized religion, whether it's the Christian church with leadership such as the Rev. Martin Luther King Jr. and the Rev. Jesse Jackson or the Nation of Islam with leaders such as Malcolm X.

"Black males who wanted a leadership role found it in the church, while white society precluded black males from that," says McCray.

Segregation was dealt a severe blow in 1954 with the Supreme Court's decision in *Brown v. Board of Education of Topeka.* That ruling made illegal all segregation in public schools, effectively overturning *Plessy v. Ferguson.* The African-American community continued to demand equality, however, and in 1964, President Johnson signed the most comprehensive civil-rights act to date. The act finally killed segregation by prohibiting discrimination in voting, education and the use of public facilities.

Names and Notes of Pride

As African Americans gained power, the community again sought a name that identified its pride. The term "black" rapidly replaced "Negro" in general usage in the United States as the Black Power Movement peaked toward the end of the 1960s. And, in the 1980s, "African American" became popular as leaders such as the Rev. Jesse Jackson felt its ethnic label ascribed a culture to black people. Today, there is more support in the African-American community for the term "African American," 23 percent to 15 percent, but most, 59 percent, say it does not matter if people use the term "African American" or "black," according to a survey conducted by Gallup Poll News Service June 12–18, 2003. Immigration and intermarriage have made "black" a more universal term for Americans of color, many of whom may have no direct African ancestry.

"Black males who wanted a leadership role found it in the church, while white society precluded black males from that."

—The Rev. Walter McCray,
First Baptist Congregational Church

African-American culture, which always was a curiosity to whites, has become more accessible. The vanguard culture of the 1940s and 1950s was jazz; white jazz fans would drive to the African-American sections of cities to listen to African-American jazz musicians. But now the vanguard culture is hip hop, which is characterized as multicultural.

"Almost everything we have in the United States is African-derived, especially popular culture," says Jacqueline Cogdell DjeDje, professor of ethnomusicology and director of UCLA's ethnomusicology archive.

"African-derived," DjeDje explains, connotes traits such as improvisation and ornamentation, melody in music and pitches used by African-American musicians in the jazz, blues and gospel genres. Africans emphasize multipart rhythms; in an African drum ensemble, individuals layer their play so the sounds interact with one another. In West and Central Africa, where many enslaved Africans originated, the cultures emphasize group traditions where drum ensembles improvise together, switching parts throughout the cadence. Such elements are intrinsic in jazz and bebop, which encourage improvisation from its musicians.

Jazz is defined by *The Columbia Encyclopedia* as: "The most significant form of musical expression of African-American culture and arguably the most outstanding contribution the United States has made to the art of music."

The improvisation implicit in African-American music is "different from other cultures where the emphasis is not on creating culture but on how well you can duplicate what happened before," says DjeDje, a piano major in college who remembers having to duplicate Bach. "But when I played gospel music, no one wanted to hear me play gospel the way other musicians did; they wanted me to tell my story."

To illustrate how African-American music has influenced all forms of American culture, DjeDje contrasts the relationship between rock performers with their audiences and classical performers and their audiences.

"When you go to a rock concert, the people in the audience are jumping up and responding to what they see on stage—that's very African and creating a dialogue between the performer and the audience," says DjeDje. "Go to a symphony and they're playing Beethoven and everyone is quiet and the emphasis is on the individual."

African-American music also is known for its soul. Soul was born out of the Negro spirituals, once the defining music of the African-American church. Spirituals infused elements of African music, such as syncopation, polyrhythmic structure, the pentatonic scale and a responsive rendition of text with patient, profound melancholy. Such elements of sound and mood reflected the feeling of oppression and evolved into soul. It is common for people who feel oppressed to relate with the music and the despair in the lyrics and melodies of spirituals, blues and gospel. For example, the African-American gospel standard "We Shall Overcome" was sung by thousands in Suhl, East Germany as the Berlin Wall that separated East and West Germany was torn down in 1989. Now, hip hop is considered popular music and, according to Nielsen Soundscan, counts whites as 70 percent of its consumers, making African-American artists legitimate pop-culture idols.

"Almost everything we have in the United States is African-derived, especially popular culture."

—Jacqueline Cogdell DjeDje,
University of California, Los Angeles

It is not uncommon when traveling abroad to see an African-American celebrity plastered on billboards throughout foreign countries to sell products.

"A few years ago, I went to Hong Kong for my birthday and I was amazed that in every mall I was confronted by a life-size cutout of Michael Jordan," says Edward Rutland, executive vice president of New York-based Matlock Advertising and Marketing. "I knew he was popular, but to see a cutout of someone looking like me hawking sports apparel in China was a mind-blower."

African-American culture has increasing influence over corporate America and its decisions on how to market products, says Rutland.

Consider this: In New York City, a 2004 advertising campaign for clothing company Akademiks plastered on city buses a picture of a thin girl in briefs on her knees with books all around her. The caption read: "Read Books, Get Brain." It seemed to be a G-rated use of sexuality combined with a positive message of developing intellect through reading. However, African-American slang connoted "getting brain" with receiving oral sex. Akademiks, a hip-hop clothing line, was well aware of the slang meaning but hoodwinked city administrators who vowed to pull the ads.

African-American street slang influences major advertising campaigns because white kids are paying attention to what African-American kids consider cool. This relationship evolved throughout the nation's history, but in the past 15 years, as more African Americans integrated white neighborhoods, the taboos each racial group has held for one another have almost completely disappeared.

"It's very clear that African Americans today set many of the trends in consumer behavior," says Harvard Business School Professor David A. Thomas, who investigates the role social identity, family circumstances and developmental relationships play in careers.

Thomas sees African Americans now entering corporate America with enthusiasm as companies seek to diversify their employee pool in response to the African-American community's increasing size, influence and economic largess.

"As I look at corporate America today, you're hard-pressed to find, at least at entry level, an industry that African Americans are absent from," says Thomas.

African-American educational attainment is rising and, along with buying power, has made African Americans stakeholders in corporate America.

African Americans are achieving throughout corporate America as well. Notable African-American CEOs include Richard Parsons, chairman and CEO of Time Warner; Stanley O'Neal, president, chairman, COO and CEO of Merrill Lynch; and Ken Chenault, chairman and CEO of American Express. Such success is motivating more African Americans to consider careers in corporate America, says Thomas.

"If you survey a set of students today and you ask them what occupations they want to go into, you don't find much difference between what African-American students say and what white students say," says Thomas. "Go back 30 years to when I was in college, [and] the majority of bright African Americans saw their futures in the professions such as law, medicine and dentistry as opposed to corporations."

Thomas, who has studied the results of companies creating diverse work groups, says recruiting African Americans is creating a culturally competent work force. He cautions, however, that African Americans should not be hired to only service African-American communities. African-American executives usually fare better among groups of white clients than white executives do among groups of clients of color. That's because African-American executives come from a culture that has learned how best to deal with white culture through its history.

One of the best results of employing a diverse group of employees is that white employees who work in an office that features a racially diverse work force learn the cultural competencies that make them effective in addressing consumers outside of their white ethnic group, says Thomas.

"Cultural competency is learned through the transfer of knowledge among colleagues in the workplace and that's when diversity becomes a dynamic resource to the company," says Thomas. "We shouldn't draw the picture that people can't sell across racial lines."

Besides joining corporate America, African Americans are launching private businesses in record numbers. African Americans are 50 percent more likely than others to forgo a traditional 9-to-5 career to go into business for themselves. Seventy-six percent of African Americans say they want to own their own business, compared with 53 percent of whites, according to the Ewing Marion Kauffman Foundation.

"As with the culture, it's a strive for freedom," says Rutland. "It's about self-expression and self-reliance."

While African Americans are enjoying new levels of success, preconceived notions based on antiquated racial stereotypes still persist. For example, African Americans on average struggle with achieving high scores on standardized tests, such as the Scholastic Aptitude Test (SAT), created in the 1930s to admit white males to Harvard. The test has become the standard by which a high school student's ability is judged. And, an increasing number of businesses are requiring college graduates to submit their high-school SAT scores as a means to gauge an applicant's future employment success.

Research into the SAT has revealed, however, that African Americans fare better on its harder questions since hard questions are based on classroom knowledge, while easier questions use language that is susceptible to different interpretation depending on the English dialect used in the person's community. This finding is up for debate by the College Board, which distributes the SAT and contends it does everything in its power to ameliorate racial bias. At any rate, using the SAT, which is taken in one's junior or senior year of high school, to judge the future success of an applicant rather than only judging the applicant's college record or job experience places African Americans at a disadvantage because of the test's cultural gaps.

Including communities of color is this nation's secret weapon. African Americans, because of their unique history in this country, sometimes feel like stepchildren whose past everyone wants to forget. To do so would be to ignore the results, both positive and negative.

". . . The African-American community in this country has made major sacrifices for people all over the world," says James Jennings, professor of urban and environmental policy and planning at Tufts University. "People from all over the world can come to this country and thrive because the civil-rights struggle, led by the African-American community, challenged this country's apartheid."

That's a Bare-Knuckles Kiss

**Gesture by Obama and his wife is 'dap,' short for 'dignity and pride.'
It's a black thing, at least for now.**

JILL ROSEN

When Barack Obama clinched the Democratic nomination Tuesday night, in his victory moment he didn't merely turn to his wife for a perfunctory, sterile hug. Nor did the two engage, like Al and Tipper Gore, in an awkward make-out session.

The Obamas dapped.

That is, in a move that has electrified African-Americans and young people nationwide, the couple faced each other, looked into each other's eyes, formed fists and then tapped knuckles.

Dap!

If the nomination of the first African-American candidate for president is itself a historic moment, that little gesture, for many, punctuated the occasion with ethnic style and inherent coolness.

"For me, it was something special," says Mark Anthony Neal, a Duke University professor who specializes in black popular culture. "It's clear that Bill and Hillary wouldn't have given each other dap. John McCain wasn't giving his wife dap. It speaks to the uniqueness of the moment."

The move might have perplexed some political commentators, but it enchanted bloggers and more youthful pundits. Thousands have watched it again and again on YouTube, many dropping approving comments.

"That was the coolest and easiest fist bump 'ever' !" one viewer gushed.

Another person declared: "One of the best moments in the campaign. . . . I damn near teared up."

"That was my favorite part of the evening," someone else wrote. "Keep it real, Barack!"

The fist bump or pound is a greeting of sorts that carries more familiarity than a handshake and more panache than an embrace.

Though it was born in the black community, some say during the 1960s black power movement, most people—of any color—who haven't made it too far past their 40s have probably given, taken or at least borne witness to some friendly dap. Its name is an abbreviation of the phrase *dignity and pride.*

Gene Demby, a blogger with PostBourgie, a site that discusses issues of politics and race, says he knew as soon as he saw fist meet fist that Obama's gesture would likely separate the culturally with-it from the without.

"A lot of people were like 'Whaa?' and a lot of people were like 'That's really dope," the 27-year-old says approvingly. "It's why so many young people have flocked to his campaign. It just seemed like a very authentic moment.' "

Neal likes to throw a little dap at his 9-year-old daughter. If she does well in school, or wins a track meet, or even just to say goodbye, it's reason enough for a fist touch.

"It's a way to acknowledge our relationship when she's getting out of the minivan," he says. "It's a way to express a certain kind of unique intimacy. It's a way to maintain your personality in a public form, something that speaks to who we are."

When Barack and Michelle Obama did it, Neal considered it a revealing personal moment in the black vernacular, as if they were saying to each other, "Let's give each other a little dap to acknowledge the success of the journey."

Writer Ta-Nehisi Coates tagged an item on his blog about Obama's gesture with the line: "The sacred art of giving dap."

"I think it says so much," says Coates, who's originally from Baltimore. "I really wonder how many white viewers caught that."

Neal thinks Obama's candidacy, from the beginning, has brought aspects of black culture to parts of society that, until now, have been largely, so to speak, dap-free.

Obama shoots hoops to relax, he doesn't embarrass himself when dancing on Ellen DeGeneres' show, he references iconic rap stars.

Ethelbert Miller absolutely loved it when Obama, in an April debate, borrowed a move from Jay-Z's "Dirt Off Your Shoulder?" video, brushing away imaginary shoulder dust to show how he's handling attacks on his campaign.

"I liked that better than the bump," Miller says. "There's a real coolness that I feel that he exhibits."

Marc Lamont Hill, a Temple University professor who writes about hip-hop culture and considers himself a "hard-core critic" of Obama, found the politician's gesture surprisingly genuine and "an unequivocal display of black cultural literacy."

"This seemed like a genuine act," Hill says. "Furthermore, the move showed a level of love, partnership and commitment that is rarely shown in public space, particularly among African-American couples.

"Given Barack's star power, and the historical role that black culture has played in broader American culture, expect many people to mimic their dap."

African American Philanthropy
A Deep-Rooted Tradition Continues to Grow

PONCHITTA PIERCE

At a time when African-American philanthropy proudly bears the distinctive stamp of its origins—notably, the key role traditionally played by black churches—it is also being transformed by a new class of ultra-wealthy donors. "We're about to see an enormous breakthrough in philanthropic institutions being created by African Americans," predicts Dr. Emmett D. Carson. "We may not be there yet, but we are poised," says Carson, who heads the Silicon Valley Community Foundation, which has $1.9 billion in assets and a mission to "strengthen the common good, improve quality of life and address the most challenging problems" throughout California's San Mateo and Santa Clara counties.

Pioneering industrialists John D. Rockefeller, Andrew Carnegie, and Henry Ford made a dynamic difference while they were alive, Carson observes, yet their posthumous impact, particularly through the foundations and other institutions they created, including Carnegie Corporation of New York, has been even more dramatic. Carson singles out Oprah Winfrey, Bill Cosby, and a host of athletes, and entertainers as the first generation of what he calls "African-American affluents."

Carson has been especially taken with money manager and chair of Fletcher Asset Management Alphonse Fletcher, who operated below the publicity radar until 2004, on the 50th anniversary of the Supreme Court's 1954 Brown v. Board of Education decision, when he gave $50 million, to be awarded over a number of years, to endow scholarships that will advance the ideals of the decision. Fletcher has formed a committee, which includes Henry Louis Gates, Jr., director of the W. E. B. Du Bois Institute for African and African American Research at Harvard, to help him decide on the most effective ways to disburse the funds. Fletcher intends for a portion of the money to support established institutions such as the Howard University School of Law, the NAACP and the NAACP Legal Defense Fund, but individuals doing innovative and committee work on improving race relations and related issues will likely benefit, as well. "Fletcher is the future," says Carson, and he should know: when it comes to research on African-American philanthropy, Dr. Emmett Carson is the gold standard.

For African Americans, Carson explained during the course of a conversation with this reporter, philanthropy has been "a survival mechanism" almost from the beginning. At first, African-American philanthropy was characterized by aid from friends and neighbors during periods of crisis: a house that burned down, a passenger seeking safe haven on the Underground Railroad, a school or bank hungry for seed money. "These direct services were often channeled through the churches," Carson notes. "At many points in our history we lacked access to the capital of mainstream society, so we have had to cultivate our own charitable resources to fuel our civic efforts. We have really had to do things on our own."

Carson defines the second stage in the evolution of African-American philanthropy as taking shape in the late 1960s and 70s as represented by the National Black United Fund, which was founded in 1972 "to provide a viable, systematic, and cost efficient mechanism for black Americans to make charitable contributions to black American organizations engaged in social change, development, and human services." For the first time, people were systematically donating money to causes and institutions that were not necessarily known to them personally, but that they believed would benefit the African American community as a whole.

"Now fast-forward to the year 2000 or 2001," Carson continues, "and you see the third stage in the evolution, where wealthy African Americans are beginning to serve as donor advisors through community foundations—or even setting up philanthropic foundations of their own. Now consider what a difference it would make if only a fraction of wealthy African-Americans were to ask in the course of their estate planning, 'How do I want to continue to be generous when I'm no longer here?'" Carson notes that since "wealthy people share an information network that differs from that of others" and have more access to financial advisors, it may be that today, distinctions among groups of people are based much more on class, than race, which may also be a contributing factor in planning for a philanthropic legacy.

Assessing the trends he sees emerging in African American philanthropy, Carson is thoughtful, suggesting that, "We have not used black philanthropy in the modern period to support social change nearly to the extent that we did in our earlier years." Why is that? Carson suggests that perhaps it's because in the past, blacks in America saw themselves as an oppressed community, and so their philanthropy reflected that sense—but today, successful Americans of every race have benefited from the nation's economic progress and so, in many cases, seem less focused on systemic reform.

When asked if the problem, then, is that African Americans aren't giving enough, Carson says, "I tell charitable organizations, 'If people aren't giving to you, it's not because of them—it's because of you.' People today are generous, but charities must be more accountable: for instance, does your staff reflect the diversity of the broader community?" Citing specific examples, Carson points to a study of teen pregnancy in Newark, New Jersey that showed, despite the high teen pregnancy rates, Planned Parenthood lacked an office in that city. "How can you mount a campaign when you're absent from the community?" he asks. And, "Heart disease is a leading cause of death for black men," he notes, "but how many times have you seen an African American talking about heart disease on a billboard or a TV commercial?"

When asked about his own clear-eyed view of charitable giving, Carson, who has urged black philanthropists not to limit themselves exclusively to supporting black organizations or causes, explains, "My father always said, 'You've got to rake the neighbors' leaves, you've got to shovel their snow.' By his own actions—helping the elderly neighbors on both sides—he demonstrated that voluntarism is just as sturdy a pillar of African-American philanthropy as giving money. Although I started working in philanthropy only later in my life, my father showed me that I had been a philanthropist all my life."

How does it feel for someone so thoroughly steeped in the psychology of philanthropy to donate money from his own pocket? "It gives me a sense of satisfaction," Carson replied without hesitation. "It's comforting to think that a kid from the South Side of Chicago could become secure enough in his professional development—and in his family's financial future—to support a cause he cares about without having to worry about eating the next day."

Of Social Networking and Net Worth

The setting was casual yet elegant: a summer dinner party in upscale Sag Harbor, on the shores of New York's Long Island Sound. Japanese lanterns lit the garden and threw soft highlights on a pair of handsome Vietnamese vases while jazz played in the background and hot food beckoned from the buffet table. Many of the guests that evening were African Americans of achievement who knew one another from Manhattan. Eager to trade the hustle and bustle of the city for a weekend in the Hamptons, the partygoers seemed intent on relaxing and enjoying themselves.

I was among the partygoers. As I stood talking to friends, I heard someone ask, "Are you coming to my benefit?" The speaker was Reggie Van Lee, senior vice president in the New York office of Booz Allen Hamilton, and he was referring to the Evidence Dance Company, which holds two benefits—one in Bridgehampton and the other in New York City—each year. The next event, which was to be held in a week's time, would feature a special program: a fusion of ballet, contemporary and African dance performed by Evidence's eight-member dance troupe.

Building Blocks of Black Philanthropy

Among the keystone organizations that aim to institutionalize Black philanthropy, these are a few of the notables that have either emerged in recent years or endured for decades:

- Association of Black Foundation Executives, founded in 1971, focuses on promoting "effective and responsive philanthropy in Black communities." The organization supports initiatives aimed at strengthening "the effectiveness of philanthropic professionals and institutions whose priorities include addressing issues facing communities of the Black diaspora."
- The Twenty-First Century Foundation was created in 1971 as an endowed, national philanthropic institution that supports the civil rights, economic empowerment, and grassroots leadership of the African American community in the United States through its grantmaking and donor services. Its mission is to facilitate "strategic giving for black community change. Specifically, 21CF works with donors to invest in institutions and leaders that solve problems within black communities nationally."
- The National Black United Fund was founded in 1972 with a focus on the areas of "health, education, children, criminal justice, economic development, discrimination, and other systemic needs that shaped the quality of life for Black Americans." Among its current concerns: "A restoration of philanthropic values must be introduced to a young Black American wealthy and affluent class, and systematic models and channels for philanthropic giving must be created for both traditional and new generations of Black American philanthropists."
- National Center for Black Philanthropy "conducts National Conferences on Black Philanthropy, which began in Philadelphia in 1997." Today, the conferences feature "on average, over forty workshops, panels and plenary sessions exploring black participation in grant making, fundraising, individual giving, and faith-based philanthropy through the Historically Black Church."

Van Lee confided his hope that the benefit performance would raise $250,000 to $300,000—nearly quadruple the $80,000 the benefit had netted five years previously. He was expecting 400 benefit-goers, up from 75 just four years ago.

"In truth," Van Lee told me, "I use every opportunity I get to plug my favorite cause."

He wasn't alone. Earlier that evening, I had heard Charlynn Goins reminding guests that her New York City Health and Hospitals Corporation theater benefit would be held later in the fall. Starring Sarah Jones, who took home a Tony for her one-woman Bridge and Tunnel show, the benefit had an ambitious fundraising goal of $300,000. Sponsors aimed to get there by charging

$100 to $125 for the performance only, and a lofty $600 for cocktails, dinner, and the show. To anyone expressing interest in the event, Goins handed an envelope containing more details.

"I'm no fundraiser," Goins told me, laughing. "I'm chairing this benefit because I couldn't get anybody else to do it."

Her words were an apt précis of what I was about to discover in the course of investigating the dynamics—and mechanics—of African-American philanthropy (or any other type of giving, for that matter): Whether you're trying to get people to donate their money or their time, persuading them to step up to the plate can be a difficult task indeed.

During a weekend that summer in which cultural events competed with political fundraisers for African American support, I also visited the East Hampton home of well-connected Carl and Barbaralee Diamonstein, who were raising money for Congressman Charles B. Rangel (D-Harlem) and his political action committee. Still several months in the future was the Democratic groundswell that would sweep the Democrats back into power in Congress and hand Representative Rangel the reins of the House Ways and Means Committee, making him the most powerful African American on the national political scene. Even so, I was surprised at the sparse African American turnout at the fundraiser—and disappointed by the low percentage of black attendees who actually broke out their checkbooks.

I had come to the Hamptons as the weekend guest of Loida Nicolas Lewis, widow of Reginald Lewis, the financial guru whose nearly $1 billion leveraged buyout of TLC Beatrice had galvanized Wall Street in 1987. Not long after that coup, Lewis was being hailed as the wealthiest black man in America. It was a wealth tempered by generosity: among the many educational efforts Reginald Lewis undertook during his lifetime was to provide a $3 million endowment to the Harvard Law School, which named its international law center after him.

When a brain tumor felled Lewis prematurely at age 50, American finance and philanthropy lost a role model for African Americans all across the socioeconomic spectrum. The torch then passed to Philippine-born Loida Nicolas Lewis, who had married Reginald Lewis in 1968. It was time for Mrs. Lewis to make her own mark in the field.

Determined to keep her husband's memory alive, Loida and her two daughters, Leslie Lewis Sword and Christina S. N. Lewis, pledged $5 million to the Museum of Maryland African American History and Culture in Baltimore, where Reginald Lewis had been born; it was renamed the Reginald F. Lewis Museum. The $5 million in private seed money donated by the Reginald F. Lewis Foundation ultimately helped to leverage $30 million in public funds from the state of Maryland. Indeed, since its doors opened in 2005, the museum has become a signature destination for city visitors—and an archetype of African American philanthropy.

"My husband taught me how to give," Loida Lewis told me in the magnificent Fifth Avenue apartment she once shared with Reginald Lewis. There wasn't much money in the early years of their marriage, Lewis recalled, but even then her husband insisted on sending Harvard an annual check for $10. As the Lewises prospered, those contributions—not only to Harvard, but to other institutions as well—steadily grew.

Today, Loida Lewis continues on as a philanthropist in her own right. One fundraiser she attended, a gala to benefit the Studio Museum in Harlem, brought out what Lewis dubs the "crème de la crème" of African American society. Thanks largely (but hardly exclusively) to the patronage of America's black corporate elite—among them, American Express chairman and chief executive officer Kenneth Chennault; former chairman of the board and chief executive officer of Merrill Lynch, E. Stanley O'Neal; and Richard Parsons, chairman of the board and former CEO of Time-Warner—the benefit raised more than $1.5 million in the course of a single evening. "Wow, it broke a record!" she said, her pride and sense of achievement shining through. "That kind of thing is going to happen more and more," she told me, noting that the audience was more than 90 percent African American.

From Citrus Grove to Capital Management

In Baltimore, I met another African-American philanthropist, investor Eddie C. Brown, and his wife, Sylvia. My visit to the elegant row house that holds the offices of Brown Capital Management told a tale of understated financial success. Peering out through one window, I caught a glimpse of the ultramodern Brown Center, the beneficiary of a $6 million contribution the Browns made to the Maryland Institute College of Art (MICA) in 2003. The college contributed the remaining $14 million in costs.

"We don't believe in buildings so much as in education," Sylvia Brown told me with a shy smile. "I think I would have preferred for that gift to remain anonymous." On the other hand, there is pride in the fact that this stellar building—a new city landmark—stands as a reminder to all city residents, minority children among them, of just how much a black man can achieve.

The source of that symbolism is Eddie Brown, a modest man who began his career as a portfolio manager and vice president at T. Rowe Price Associates in 1973. Nine years later, he launched his eponymous investment company. Today, Brown handles investments with a minimum entry of $20 million—all this accomplished by a man born to an unwed mother 66 years ago, then raised by his grandparents in a Florida farmhouse with no hot water or plumbing. Although Brown helped his grandfather pick oranges and grapefruits on the farm, his grandmother correctly sensed that better days lay ahead for her sharp young grandson. On a trip to Orlando, she pointed out to young Eddie every man she saw wearing a suit and tie. Education, she told him, was the ticket that would take him from the citrus groves to an office job.

The Browns' business success has enabled them to establish a considerable art collection, with a primary focus on African American artists. In 2002, for example, they gave a partial gift of Henry Ossawa Tanner's Bishop Benjamin Tanner to the Baltimore Museum of Art. In Brown's office hangs another Tanner, The Three Wise Men, alongside an arresting sculpture by Edmonia Lewis, Rebecca at the Well, Edward Bannister's Woodland Interior and Jacob Lawrence's Genesis Series.

Oprah and Others

An African American donor particularly distinguished by both her wealth and her generosity is Oprah Winfrey, the television host who once famously opined that "The benefit of making money is to give it away." When Winfrey traveled to South Africa in 2002 to deliver gifts to 50,000 children, she wound up adopting 10 children, ages 7 to 17, who had no parents or family. She placed them in private boarding schools and told readers she had hired caretakers to look after them.

Then she went to visit them—unannounced.

As Oprah related the scene in the December 2006 edition of her namesake magazine, she was shocked by what she saw of their newly adopted lifestyles: "When I sat them down in the living room for a conversation, everyone's cell phone kept going off—the latest 'razr' model that costs about $500. That inner spark I was used to seeing in their eyes was gone, replaced by their delight in rooms full of things."

Immediately, Oprah said, she realized she had given them too much. And she had not helped to instill the proper values to help them appreciate those gifts. "What I now know for sure," she revealed in the pages of her magazine, "is that a gift isn't a gift unless it has meaning. Just giving things to people, especially children, creates the expectation of more things."

That disappointment didn't prevent Winfrey from traveling to South Africa in January 2007 to open the $40 million Oprah Winfrey Leadership Academy for Girls in the hamlet of Henley-on-Klip, south of Johannesburg. The school received 3,500 applications for the 152 spaces available, but will eventually make room for 450 girls. Later in the year, Winfrey was reportedly devastated by the news that a dorm matron at the school had been arrested for abusing some of the students. Winfrey flew to South Africa to meet with school officials and parents, and many praised her for directly confronting the problem. Writing in the Lexington Herald-Leader, columnist Merlene Davis said, "The good coming out of this . . . is that those girls, who all have come from extreme poverty, have some idea of what a powerful woman looks like and what she stands for. So do those who no longer work at the academy."

Another prominent African American donor is music impresario and entrepreneur Russell Simmons, who has contributed more than $10 million to various charities. He tells family and friends that he hopes his tombstone will say, "Here lies a philanthropist." Yet another noted figure in the African American community, Tiger Woods, receives countless requests to donate his golf earnings to worthy causes, but he has opted to focus on building a learning center in California and another in Washington, D.C. where young people will find tools to further their education.

Magnanimity Enshrined in Arts and Culture

On September 26, 2007, the Smithsonian Institution, partnering with IBM, announced the opening of the National Museum of African American History and Culture, the Smithsonian's 19th and newest museum. Perhaps the most interesting thing about the museum—in its current incarnation—is that it's a virtual institution, existing at the moment only online, at http://nmaahc .si.edu. The physical museum—created by an Act of Congress in 2003—will be built on the National Mall in Washington, D.C. and is scheduled for completion in 2014. Its collections and educational programming will focus on slavery, post-Civil War Reconstruction, the Harlem Renaissance, and the Civil Rights movement, among other issues and events.

Historian, author, curator and educator, Lonnie G. Bunch, III is the founding director of the museum, and is deeply involved in developing the museum's mission, coordinating its fundraising and membership campaigns, and establishing its collections and cultural partnerships. If Bunch feels burdened by that responsibility, he doesn't let on in person. On a balmy September morning not too long ago, I walked across the Mall in Washington, D.C., the gravel of the wide walkways crunching noisily beneath my feet, to visit Bunch in his office near the museum. Bunch's ever-present smile and spontaneous bear hug embodied his contagious determination. He feels confident, for example, that in support of the museum, he is about to tap into a new, younger source of African American philanthropy. "If my parents gave to the church," he told me, "and my wife and I give to education, then my daughters—following their own interests—will cast their net even wider."

If that's the case, it may signal a marked departure from the experience, for example, that independent producer Margo Lion had fifteen years ago when she tried to raise money for "Jelly's Last Jam," starring Gregory Hines and directed by George Wolfe of the Joseph Papp Public Theater/New York Shakespeare Festival. The musical brought to life the controversial turn-of-the-century New Orleans jazz musician Ferdinand "Jelly Roll" Morton, yet Lion was able to attract very few African American investors. Seeing investment in the theater as a barometer for raising money, she told me, "I'm interested in where African American philanthropists—or perhaps I should say those in a position to be philanthropic—feel their money could best be applied. What projects are they most interested in supporting?"

We were speaking in Lion's cozy office at the St. James Theater on New York's Theater Row. The office overflowed with mementos of her many stage successes, among them "Hairspray," "Elaine Stritch at Liberty," "Angels in America," and "The Crucible." In her latest coup, Lion brought the August Wilson play "Radio Golf" to Broadway in May 2007.

For all her obvious éclat, Lion has found it challenging to raise large contributions from African American donors. "Broadway is always risky," she muses, "but August Wilson was a great figure in the history of dramatic literature, and 'Radio Golf' had received great reviews all over the country. Wilson was writing for all America, but the fact remains that this is a play abut black Americans, and I was frustrated by the lack of support for it." Lion acknowledges that there might not be a rich history of theatergoing among African Americans—the 2002 National Endowment for the Arts Survey of Public Participation in the Arts reported African American attendance at non-musical plays at under seven percent—but she feels that the financial barriers to that particular cultural tradition are falling. "Surely there are many African Americans who have the money, no?"

Grassroots Giving

Does all this high-profile activity mean that only well-known players are making an impact in the world of African American philanthropy? Far from it. Individual donors—including those with modest lifetime earnings—can make a difference, and often a disproportionate one. For example, there is Oseola McCarty, the 87-year-old laundress, who gave her life savings of $150,000 to the University of Mississippi for scholarships. She said of her gift, "I'm giving it away so the children won't have to work so hard, like I did." In many ways, McCarty reflects the bedrock role that African American women have long played in philanthropy, whether it was enacted by the Links, a membership organization of 12,000 professional women of color that also supports programs and services aimed at improving the quality of life for African Americans; the Delta Sigma Theta sorority, founded in 1913 by twenty-two collegiate women at Howard University to promote academic excellence and to provide assistance to persons in need, and which, with a current membership of over 200,000, continues to work toward advancing human welfare; or the National Council of Negro Women, "a voluntary nonprofit membership organization helping women of African descent to improve the quality of life for themselves, their families and communities."

As Emmett Carson likes to point out, "It's not the amount you have—it's focusing that resource on what you care about."

Numerous studies seem to back up that notion: low-income people tend to give a larger percentage of their disposable income to charitable organizations than do the rich. America, in particular, seems to have developed what Carnegie Corporation of New York president Vartan Gregorian has termed "a culture of giving." A recent study by the Center on Philanthropy at Indiana University adds more evidence, reporting that the average American donates 2.6 percent of his or her income. When it comes to giving by blacks specifically, a Chronicle of Philanthropy report reveals that blacks give 25 percent more of their discretionary income to charity than do whites. For instance, blacks who make between $30,000 and $50,000 give an average of $528 annually, compared with $462 donated by whites in the same income range.

That model of grassroots generosity is one familiar to many African Americans. It certainly underlies the story Charlynn Goins, chairperson of the board of directors for the New York City Health and Hospitals Corporation, told me about her husband's dream of attending medical school. After confiding those hopes to his own physician, Dr. Aurelious King, Warren Goins was admitted to Howard University Medical School in 1959. Goins worked his way through all four years on what he thought were academic scholarships. In his second year of medical school he found out through documents the school had sent him that Dr. King was paying those tuition bills.

That story is readily understood by Loida Lewis, who remarks that the "sub-rosa generosity" of African-Americans often renders it invisible to larger or different communities. For example, "The white community probably did not—could not—fully understand the community where my husband grew up," she observes. "African Americans have always been giving—but not necessarily in a very public manner. They've sent their nieces or nephews to school, or they've paid the overdue rent for an uncle or aunt or best friend. There's a similar dynamic at work in the Philippine-American community, where philanthropy is spontaneous, small-scale, and not splashily publicized. Because it takes place beneath the radar, the philanthropic associations tend to discount it. But the fact of the matter is that giving is going on in the African American community."

Charity Begins at . . . College?

A more typical historical target of African-American fundraising has been the educational institution, often singled out by individual donors. At board meetings for Xavier University of Louisiana in New Orleans—which, among other accomplishments, is distinguished by its high number of outstanding pharmacy graduates—I listened as the college's development officer described Xavier's struggle to raise enough money to cover its annual budget of around $90 million. In 1999-2000, the university received major grants from the Kresge and the Southern Education foundations to enhance their development program. In 2006, Xavier received a $4 million grant from Carnegie Corporation of New York to help revitalize higher education in New Orleans after Hurricane Katrina. (Tulane and Dillard universities received Corporation funding for the same purpose.)

In December 2006, the Presidential Medal of Freedom—the nation's highest civilian award—was conferred on Dr. Norman C. Francis, who has served as president of Xavier for more than 40 years, for his "steadfast dedication to education, equality, and service to others," and in recognition of his work as Chairman of the Louisiana Recovery Authority, in which he played "a vital role in helping the people of the Gulf Coast rebuild their lives in the aftermath of Hurricane Katrina."

In a wide-ranging conversation, Dr. Francis constantly touched on the moral responsibility of raising money to help the university achieve its educational mission. His face lit up as he retraced the last half-decade—banner years for Xavier University in terms of alumni giving. "My parents and the families around us had to focus their time and resources on raising children and holding down jobs," Dr. Francis remarked. "Today's college graduates have different priorities. A crucial dimension of their lives is to give back to the institutions that played a significant part in their growth and development. I'm thrilled to see Xavier graduates responding to our needs; [their contributions] tell me black philanthropy is flourishing."

Making a Leap of Faith

Although a handful of naysayers continued to contend that philanthropy has yet to gain serious traction within the black community, it's a matter of historical record that African Americans have always generously supported their churches, their schools, and their families.

"When I was growing up," Norman Francis recalls, "I watched people with very small incomes give to their churches. Religion was close to them. If there was one sustainable part of their lives, they knew it had to be their church. 'God will take care of you in times of need,' they believed. 'The bread you give up today will come back to you tomorrow.' My Neighbor is not just that person next door—he is any human being in need."

Indeed, writes LaTasha Chaffin in "Philanthropy and the Black Church,"* "Historically, the Black church has been a core institution for African-American philanthropy. The Black church does not only serve as a faith-based house of worship, but it facilitates organized philanthropic efforts including meeting spiritual, psychological, financial, educational and basic humanitarian needs such as food, housing, and shelter. Black churches are also involved in organizing and providing volunteers to the community and in civil and human rights activism."

If the black church has not historically matched the endowment and special-giving levels of other faiths, Reverend Tom Watson, pastor of the Greater New Orleans Council of Black Ministers, suggests that it is only because the members of its congregations have lagged commensurately in individual wealth. "We still have a long way to go," he notes, in terms of overall economic disparity.

Reviewing the keystone role played by black churches, Reverend Watson also notes how it has served as a path to leadership for many notable African Americans, including, of course, Dr. Martin Luther King. "We didn't own a lot of businesses," says Watson, "except, perhaps, for the occasional franchise, so the institution we relied on as our wedge into large-scale political participation was the black church."

As African Americans do, increasingly, join the ranks of the American middle and upper class, the role of the black church in terms of charity and philanthropy seems to be changing as well. "The strongest black churches," notes Watson, "are led by the black middle and upper classes, which have become larger and more educated. These institutions have strong constituencies, and their congregations understand the role played by philanthropy because the economy has allowed them to participate in it."

Should African Americans Give More?

Dr. Alvin F. Poussaint, the civil rights champion-turned-Harvard-academic (he is professor of psychiatry and faculty associate dean for student affairs at Harvard Medical School, as well as director of the Media Center of the Judge Baker Children's Center in Boston) told me about a fundraiser given in his honor and chaired by Bill Cosby. It netted about $170,000—a tidy sum considering that the donors were far from wealthy, and that their average gift was $1,000. This was certainly an example of generous giving—but at the same time, Dr. Poussaint said that he felt torn. In his mind, at least, African Americans can and should be doing much more on the front lines of philanthropic giving.

Dr. Poussaint says he sometimes thinks that "African Americans don't have enough commitment to charitable giving, even though it works in their behalf. There's also a trace of suspicion: 'Will my money be used right?' And then there's the reluctance to hand over money that might be better used for something else."

When I asked Dr. Poussaint to diagnose the current state of African American philanthropy in America, he said, "It has to improve, because right now, it's not sufficient to support our organizations. We can do much, much better. Indeed, it's crucial for African Americans to give more." In his opinion, many programs meant to benefit blacks show an over-reliance on corporate support, as opposed to the sort of grassroots funds that might be raised from the black community. He draws an analogy to black businesses that fail in the black community because the latter neglects to support the former.

Especially damaging, said Poussaint, is when scandals enter the picture—when some major religious figure gets convicted for embezzling funds from his own church, for example. "People read about scandals like that and worry about whether their money was simply paying that official's fat salary."

"People like to see results," Poussaint continues. "What did you accomplish? What victories have you had? What are you going to use this money for in the future? Some people prefer programs in which their money funds 'general operating expenses,' but that sounds just unacceptably vague to me." Where should African Americans concentrate their giving, then? "The needs in the black community are so great," Poussaint answers, "that in the beginning you should help take care of your own."

Pouissant's detractors might well disagree, pointing out that giving takes many forms within the African American community. Though some are perhaps not nearly generous enough—a charge often leveled at black athletes and entertainers raking in millions of dollars—others are generous to a fault. And, as noted earlier in this article, many blacks whose income is hardly even near the "wealthy" range tend to be steady and dedicated givers.

Generation Next: The Future of Philanthropy

Mention the name "Vernon Jordan" and not everyone will call to mind his wife, Ann Dibble Jordan. Yet she is a powerhouse in her own right, chairing or sitting on the boards of corporations and nonprofits alike—among them, the National Symphony Orchestra, public television station WETA (Washington D.C.'s PBS affiliate), the Washington Area Women's Foundation, Sasha Bruce Youthwork, and Catalyst. This year, Jordan retired from the boards of Citigroup, Johnson & Johnson, and ADP, after long years of service.

Some observers see Ann Jordan as a "philanthropic influential"—someone who can wield her fiscal expertise to benefit select worthy causes; a person strategically positioned to broker connections between donors and recipients. She doesn't deny it. "You have to use what resources you can," she said to me, laughing. "We all reach out to our friends, who we think can help us or introduce us to other people in pursuit of a worthwhile cause."

*See: http//www.learningtogive.org/papers/index.asp?bpid=47.

Corporate America has become a stakeholder in African American philanthropy, Jordan believes, but at the same time "we always want to see more." Looking forward ten years, she sees African-American philanthropy as part of the mainstream. "All of these young people you see doing so well have sound philanthropic instincts," she notes. "Young people focus on their return on investment, which is a smart way to do it. They want to know what percentage of funds raised go directly to the cause versus what percentage goes to administrative costs. When I think about the intelligence they are applying to the process, I feel optimistic about the future of charitable support for community organizations."

Why Tavis Is Smiling

One recent event not to miss for those interested in African American giving was the Sixth National Conference on Black Philanthropy, held in Washington, D.C. over three days in July 2007 and sponsored by the National Center for Black Philanthropy. The symposium explored how African American philanthropy in particular can help solve the problems facing many black Americans.

The touchstone throughout the conference was Tavis Smiley's searingly honest essay collection, The Covenant with Black America (Third World Press, 2006), which takes a hard look at the array of social and economic circumstances confronting African Americans. Attendees were challenged to come up with new ways of identifying potential donors, as well as new ways of welcoming young people into the philanthropic fold.

The first thing you notice about Tavis Smiley is, in fact, his smile. Perhaps it's the occupational legacy of the countless television shows on which he has appeared, including his current platform: a late-night television talk show, as well as his radio program, The Tavis Smiley Show, which is distributed by Public Radio International (PRI). Smiley has also written an autobiography, What I Know for Sure: My Story of Growing Up in America (Doubleday, 2006).

What people may not know for sure is that Smiley directs one of the most successful charitable foundations around. The mission of the Tavis Smiley Foundation is to "enlighten, encourage and empower youth by providing leadership skills that will promote the quality of life for themselves, their communities and the world." It all began when Smiley became the mentor of a young boy whose mother was seeking influences that would shield her son from gang recruitment in their Atlanta neighborhood. "Many young black men around the country face that challenge," Smiley says. The mother asked Tavis if her son could shadow him for a day, and Tavis decided to extend their time together to a week. For a while, the boy traveled everywhere Smiley's work took him, including on a business trip to Canada. Smiley described their growing bond of trust during one of his commentaries on the nationally syndicated radio program, The Tom Joyner Morning Show.

That's when the floodgates opened up. "Every mother in the country, it seemed, wanted me to do this," Smiley explains. He also received—and answered—an avalanche of mail from young people seeking his advice about some fairly profound intersections in their lives. So dynamic was this feedback—and so dramatic was Smiley's positive effect on his "mentee"—that in 1999 he created his eponymous foundation to try to continue the work on a wider basis.

In forming the foundation, Smiley sought out a council of experts who had trod these paths before. They advised him how to set up the foundation, how to manage the finances, and how to be crystal-clear about the mission. "From the very beginning," Smiley recalls, "we knew exactly what we wanted—and that's half the battle right there." Still, Smiley doesn't hesitate to admit to mistakes. Among the early painful lessons Smiley and his team had to learn were these:

- When a grant comes in, you can't simply spend what has been given to you.
- Backers need to know what you've done with their money.
- Reports not filed on time can cause problems.
- Someone who is an ace at programming can make a lousy bookkeeper. You need someone strong in that position so you don't find yourself spending money you don't have.
- It's never a good idea to blow the deadline on submitting the results of an internal audit.

Because Smiley's name was on the foundation, he wanted to be intimately involved in every aspect of its work. That commitment has enabled him to engage with young people, which in turn has made him increasingly hopeful about the future. Each year he spends time speaking with students at the foundation's annual Leadership Institute, a five-day conference held during the summer on a college campus. Since its inception, more than 6,000 youths ages 13 to 18 have participated in the foundation's Youth 2 Leaders program. "A lot of bright, talented, ambitious young people out there want to make a meaningful contribution to their community and country," Smiley says.

> "What truly lives on is the work you do for young people, because they're going to pass it on to other young people, in turn," says Tavis Smiley. He adds, "I never realized that giving could feel so good."

Blinkered by the intensity of his drive to reach the pinnacle of his profession, Smiley explains that he had no clue his one-on-one work with kids would emerge as the most rewarding aspect of his work with the foundation. "That's going to be my focus going forward," he says, "and I hope it will be my lifetime legacy, as well. The TV show, the radio show, a book in print after I'm gone—none of that matters. What truly lives on is the work you do for young people, because they're going to pass it on to other young people, in turn." He adds, "I never realized that giving could feel so good."

A Last Word

Clearly, African Americans have a long tradition of philanthropy, giving not only their money but also their time and other personal resources to a variety of organizations and causes, which are by no means confined to the black community. They have proven time and time again that they are committed and consistent givers in a wide range of areas such as humanitarian causes, institutional development—including schools and churches—and they give to advance social issues, education, political causes and to promote the arts and cultural enrichment. The habit of being philanthropic may, in fact, be so deeply ingrained in the African American community that many don't even regard themselves as being particularly generous, even when they have to stretch their own resources to assist others. For many, that's just the way they were brought up. The new crop of wealthy black Americans, it seems, are therefore simply carrying on the traditions passed on to them down the generations—but each, in his or her own way, has found an individual philanthropic path for addressing the issues they care about. That's a form of personal expression that is surely satisfying to the giver, but the benefits to society are potentially, limitless.

PONCHITTA PIERCE is a journalist, television host and producer, writer, and editor who has been a special correspondent for CBS News, reporting for CBS *Morning News* and CBS *Evening News*. At WNBC-TV she co-hosted a Sunday morning magazine series, *The Prime of Your Life*. She also hosted and co-produced WNBC TV's *Today in New York*. In addition, she has written about politics, social issues, health and finance for national publications such as *Modern Maturity, Family Circle, Newsday, Ladies Home Journal, Ebony, Reader's Digest, Parade* and *McCall's*.

For Black Politicians, a Rocky Road but a Steady Climb

KAREN YOURISH

If Hawaii shaped Barack Obama, it is fitting that Illinois helped make him the country's first black presidential nominee. The history of African American participation in U.S. politics is closely tied to the state: Illinoisan Abraham Lincoln led the Union to victory in the Civil War and abolished slavery, paving the way for African Americans to vote. And Illinois voters have sent 16 black politicians to Congress—more than any other state. African Americans elected to legislative offices have helped weave the fabric of American history for some time. Gains made after the Civil War slipped away after Reconstruction, only to return in the middle of the century. Should Obama win in November, his presidency would write this history into the most powerful office in the land.

1865–1877: Reconstruction

In the decade after the Civil War, African Americans played a significant role in the politics of several Southern states. Hundreds were elected to local and state offices, and 16 came to Capitol Hill, including two senators. All of the black U.S. legislators were Republican and from the South, where blacks made up a large proportion of the population. African Americans largely supported the "Party of Lincoln" over Southern Democrats, who tended to favor pre-emancipation policies.

1877–1928: Steps Backward

When the federal government pulled its troops from the South, it marked an end to federal efforts to protect black Americans' civil rights until the middle of the 20th century. Democrats

regained control of the state legislatures and passed laws restricting the right of blacks to vote, despite the passage of the 15th Amendment.

An Uncertain Outcome

Despite the gains made by blacks in public office, it remains to be seen whether Americans are ready for a black president. Exit polls from the Democratic primaries indicate that Obama's support is strongest among blacks and younger whites.

DEMOCRATIC PRIMARY VOTE

Hillary Clinton   **Obama**

▼ Among blacks: ▼

| 15% | 82% |

Among whites:

| 55% | 39% |

Among whites age 18–29:

| 41% | 53% |

Among whites age 65+:

| 59% | 34% |

1866 Confederate veterans in Tennessee form the first Ku Klux Klan. Members wanted to restore white supremacy.

1868 The 14th Amedment, intended to provide black Americans with the protection of citizenship, is adopted.

1868 A black politician from Louisiana, John W. Menard, is elected to the House of Representatives, but the House Committee on Elections refuses to seat him.

1870–1901 Eight states had at least one African American in Congress during this time.

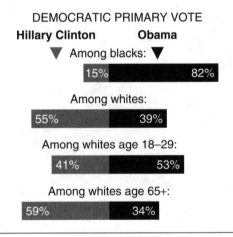

1900 90% of African Americans live in the South.

1902–1928 No African Americans in Congress.

1920 The 19th Amendment grants women the right to vote.

1963 The Rev. Martin Luther King Jr. delivers his "I Have a Dream" speech.

1969 The Congressional Black Caucus, originally called the democratic Select Committee, is created.

A 20th-Century First

A nearly three-decade stretch without blacks in Congress ended when Illinois elected Chicagoan Oscar S. DePriest (R) to the House in 1928.

1930s: Party Shift

After 70 years of solidly backing the Republican Party, many black voters—attracted to the policies embodied by President Franklin D. Roosevelt's New Deal programs—decided to become Democrats.

Massive Migration

From 1910 to 1970, the election of African Americans to Congress spread north and west as about 7 million blacks left the South. By the mid-1960s, an overwhelming majority of black voters were registered as Democrats. The Voting Rights Act of 1965 reversed nearly a century of various state efforts to prevent blacks from voting.

1990s: Redistricting

Until 1992, most black House members were elected from inner-city districts in the North and West. After the 1990 census, the courts ordered Congress to redraw congressional districts to create more with African American majorities. As a result, a record 17 black freshman members—several from the South for the first time since Reconstruction—were elected to the 103rd Congress.

Out of Proportion

Although the numbers of African Americans in Congress have grown, the totals fall short of reflecting the black population of the country.

Percentage of Americans who are black: **13%**
Number of blacks in the **House: 42** (10%)
14 more needed to equal 13%
Number of blacks in the **Senate: 1** (1%)
12 more needed to equal 13%

□ **25 states have never had an African American in Congress,** including Obama's home state of Hawaii

Historical photos courtesy of The Library of Congress; Graphic by *The Washington Post*

African Americans in Congress Today: 43.

UNIT 6

Hispanic/Latina/o Americans

Unit Selections

Key Points to Consider

- What does the debate about the use of the words Hispanic and Latino/a suggest about cultural agendas of minority groups?

- Do television programs, films, and other entertainment adequately address our understanding of pluralism within the Hispanic and Latino cultures?

- When do ethnic and racial issues foster understanding? Does the charge of racialism within the Hispanic/Latino community expose the limits of solidarity? How about the existence of color consciousness that is present in the population? Does the historical anti-immigrant position of African Americans explain this matter, or does such an argument simply fuel allegations of discrimination?

- In what respects is Hispanic/Latino American culture becoming part of mainstream American culture? What can be expected of relationships between Hispanic ancestry populations and the newest immigrants from Spanish-speaking countries?

- Hispanic voters are concentrated in California, Texas, Florida, and New York. How significant or crucial to electoral success are these states for presidential elections? Explain.

Student Web Site
www.mhcls.com

Internet References

Latino American Network Information Center (LANIC)
   http://lanic.utexas.edu
National Council of La Raza (NCLR)
   http://www.nclr.org

The following collection of materials on Hispanic/Latino Americans is a composite of findings about ethnicities. The clustering of these ethnicities and nationalities, as well as their relationship to the Spanish language, seems to be sufficient evidence of the commonalities that constitute the shared expression of this complex past and contemporary politics. Yet the use of "Hispanic" and "Latino" that differentiates them from Anglo-American foundations, and their social expression as they search for a cultural and political terrain, are but the surface of the process of inter-group dynamics in the United States. Are Portuguese-speaking groups Hispanic?

The articles in this unit propose angles of vision that enable us to view the process of accommodation and change that is articulated in political practice, scholarship, advocacy, and art. The issues presented provocatively shift traditional perspectives from the eastern and midwestern mindset toward the western and southwestern analysis of U.S. immigration patterns.

The Immigration Act of 1965 induced a process not unlike the period of large-scale eastern and southern European immigration between 1880 and 1924. This immigration includes scores of various ethnic groups. Cultural/geographic descriptions are not the clearest form of ethnic identity. Hispanic/Latino Americans are not a single ethnic group. The designation of various ethnic populations, whose ancestry is derived from Spanish-speaking countries by the words "Latino" and "Hispanic," is a relatively recent phenomenon in the United States. Hispanic was used in the 1970s, and Latino was added to the U.S. Census in 1990. The cultural, economic, and political differences and similarities of various Hispanic/Latino communities, as well as the wide dispersal of these communities, suggest the need for care in generalization about Latino and Hispanic American populations. Does geographic location in the United States significantly influence personal and group issues?

The realities of these groups—whether they are political refugees, migrant workers, descendants of residents settled prior to territorial incorporation into the United States, long-settled immigrants, recent arrivals, or the children and grandchildren of immigrants—present interesting and varied patterns of enclave community, assimilation, and acculturation, as well as isolation and marginalization. Hispanic/Latino American linkages to Central and South American countries and Spain, the future of their emerging political power, and their contributions to cultural

© BananaStock/age fotostock

and economic change within the United States are interesting facets of the Hispanic/Latino American experience. This Hispanic/Latino experience is a composite of groups seeking unity while interacting with the larger arena of ethnic groups that constitute American society. Convergent issues that bridge differences, as well as those that support ideological and strategic differences, bode well for a future of both cooperation and conflict.

What issues bind Hispanic or Latino groups? What values cause cleavages among these populations? What does bilingualism mean? Is bilingualism a freedom-of-speech issue? Is bilingualism a concern of non-Spanish-speaking persons in the United States? What are the implications of establishing an official public language policy?

Competition and conflict over mobility into mainstream leadership positions are aspects of American society that may be exacerbated by the misuse of ethnic indicators. Nonetheless, indicators of social cohesion and traditional family bonds are apparently noncompetitive and nonconfrontational dimensions of robust ethnic experiences. Thus, fears that Hispanic/Latino Americans may not relish competitive pressures are assuaged by the capacities of the family and community to temper the cost of any such failure. This dynamic personal and group interaction is a fascinating and fruitful topic for a society seeking competitiveness and stronger community bonds. Cast in this fashion, the American dilemma takes on a new and compelling relevance.

Inventing Hispanics
A Diverse Minority Resists Being Labeled

AMITAI ETZIONI

Thirty years ago immigrants from Latin America who settled in the United States were perceived in terms of their home nation—as, for example, Cuban Americans or Mexican Americans, just as European newcomers were seen as Italian Americans or Polish Americans. Today the immigrant flow from Central and South America has grown substantially, and the newcomers are known as Hispanics.

Hispanics are particularly important for understanding the future of diversity in American society.

Some observers have expressed concern that efforts to make Hispanics a single minority group—for purposes ranging from elections to education to the allocation of public funds—are further dividing American society along racial lines. But attempts, both incidental and ideological, to forge these American immigrants into a strongly defined minority are encountering an unanticipated problem. Hispanics by and large do not see themselves as a distinct minority group; they do see themselves as Americans.

Hispanics and African Americans

Hispanics are particularly important for understanding the future of diversity in American society. Already they have overtaken African Americans to become the nation's largest minority, and immigration patterns ensure that the number of Hispanics will continue to grow more rapidly than that of African Americans.

U.S. race relations have long been understood in terms of black and white. Until recently, many books on the subject did not even mention other races, or did so only as a brief afterthought. Now recognition is growing that Hispanics are replacing blacks as the primary minority. But whereas blacks have long been raising their political consciousness, Hispanics have only just begun to find their political legs.

Recent increases in minority populations and a decline in the white majority in the United States have driven several African-American leaders, including Jesse Jackson and former New York City Mayor David Dinkins, along with a few Hispanics, such as Fernando Ferrer, a candidate for the 2002 mayoral election in New York City, and some on the white left (writing in *The American Prospect*) to champion a coalition of minorities to unseat the "white establishment" and become the power-holders and shapers of America's future. The coalition's leaders are systematically encouraging Hispanics (and Asian Americans) to see themselves as victims of discrimination and racism—and thus to share the grievances of many African Americans. Whether they will succeed depends much on how Hispanic Americans see themselves and are viewed by others.

Hispanics and the Census

For several decades now, the Census Bureau has been working to make Hispanics into a distinct group and—most recently—into a race. In 1970, a 5 percent sample of households was asked to indicate whether their origin was Mexican, Puerto Rican, Cuban, Central or South American, or other Spanish. But it was only in 1980, that "Hispanics" became a distinct statistical and social category in the census, as all households were asked whether they were of "Spanish/Hispanic origin or descent." Had no changes been made in 1980, we might well have continued to think of Hispanics as we do about other white Americans, as several ethnic groups, largely from Mexico and Cuba.

The next step was to take Hispanics, who were until recently multiple ethnic groups that were considered racially white, and make them into a unique, separate group whose members, according to the census, "can be members of any race." This unusual status has had several notable results. One is the flurry of headlines following the release of new census data in March 2001 announcing that "California Whites Are a Minority"—even though 59.5 percent of Californians, including many Hispanics, chose white as their race. The only way for whites to be proclaimed a minority in California is for no Hispanics to be counted as white—even those 40 percent, or more than four million people, who specifically marked white as their race on the census form. Another curious result is the awkward phrase "non-Hispanic whites," by which the media now refer to the majority of Americans.

Because of their evolving status in the census, Hispanics are now sometimes treated not as a separate ethnic group but as a distinct race. (Race marks sharper lines of division than ethnicity.) Often, for example, when national newspapers and magazines, such as the *Washington Post* and *U.S. News and World Report,* graphically depict racial breakdowns on various subjects, they list Hispanics as a fourth group, next to white, black, and Asian. Much less often, but with increasing frequency, Hispanics are referred to as "brown" Americans, as in a *Newsweek* article that noted a "Brown Belt" across America. The result is to make the country seem more divided than it is.

Should one mind the way the census keeps its statistics? Granted, social scientists are especially sensitive to the social construction of categories. But one need not have an advanced degree to realize that the ways we divide people up—or combine them—have social consequences. One may care little how the census manipulates its data, but those data are what we use to paint a picture of the social composition of America. Moreover, the census categories have many other uses—for college admissions forms, health care, voting, and job profiles, government budget allocations, and research. And the media use the census for guidance. In short, the census greatly influences the way we see each other and ourselves, individually and as a community.

This is not to suggest that the Census Bureau has conspired to split up the nation. The recategorizations and redefinitions reflect, in part, changes in actual numbers (large increases in the nation's Hispanic population might arguably justify a separate category); in part, efforts to streamline statistics (collapsing half-a-dozen ethnic groups into one); and, in part, external pressures to which all government agencies are subjected. To be sure, the Census Bureau is a highly professional agency whose statistics are set by scientific considerations. But there is as yet no such thing as a government agency that has a budget set by Congress, that needs public cooperation for carrying out its mission, and that is fully apolitical. Likewise, the Office of Management and Budget, which sets the racial categories, is among the less political branches of the White House, yet still quite politically attuned.

Hispanics in Their Own Eyes

How do Hispanics see themselves? First of all, the vast majority prefer to be classified as a variety of ethnic groups rather than as one. The National Latino Political Survey, for example, found that three out of four respondents chose to be labeled by country of origin, rather than by "pan-ethnic" terms such as "Hispanic" or "Latino." Hispanics are keenly aware of big differences among Hispanic groups, especially between Mexican Americans (the largest group) and Cuban Americans, the latter being regarded as more likely to be conservative, to vote Republican, to become American citizens, and so on.

America has, by and large, dropped the notion that it will tell you what your race is, either by deeply offensive blood tests

or by examining your features and asking your neighbors (the way the census got its figures about race until 1950). We now allow people to indicate which race they consider themselves to be by marking a box on a census form. Many Hispanics resist being turned into a separate race or being moved out of the white category. In 1990, the census allowed people to buy out of racial divisions by checking "other" when asked about their racial affiliation. Nearly 10 million people—almost all of them Hispanics—did so.

When the Census Bureau introduced its "other" category, some African-American leaders objected because, as they correctly pointed out, the resulting diminution in minority figures both curtails numerous public allotments that take race into account and affects redistricting. So the 2000 census dropped "other" and instead allowed people to claim several races (but not to refuse to be racially boxed in). The long list of racial boxes to be checked ended with "some other race," with a space to indicate what that race was. Many of the 18 million people who chose this category, however, made no notation, leaving their race as they wanted it—undefined.

Of those who chose only "some other race," almost all (97 percent) were Hispanic. Among Hispanics, 42.2 percent chose "some other race," 47.9 percent chose white (alone) as their race, 6.3 percent chose two or more races, and 2 percent chose black (alone). In short, the overwhelming majority of Hispanics either chose white or refused racial categorization, clearly resisting the notion of being turned into a separate race.

A Majority of Minorities

As I have shown in considerable detail in my recent book, *The Monochrome Society,* the overwhelming majority of Americans of all backgrounds have the same dreams and aspirations as the white majority. Hispanic and Asian immigrants and their children (as well as most African Americans) support many of the same public policies (from reformed health insurance to better education, from less costly housing to better and more secure jobs). In fact, minorities often differ more among themselves than they do with the white majority. Differences among, say, Japanese Americans and Vietnamese Americans are considerable, as they are among those from Puerto Rico and Central America. (Because of the rapid rise of the African-American middle class, this group, too, is far from monolithic.)

Intermarriage has long been considered the ultimate test of relationships among various groups in American society. Working together and studying together are considered low indicators of intergroup integration; residing next to one another, a higher one; intermarriage—the highest. By that measure, too, more and more Hispanic (and Asian) Americans are marrying outside their ethnic group. And each generation is more inclined to marry outside than the previous ones.

In the mid-1990s, about 20 percent of first-generation Asian women were intermarried, as compared with slightly less than 30 percent of the second generation and slightly more than 40 percent of the third generation. Hispanic intermarriage shows a similar trend. More and more Americans, like Tiger Woods, have relatives all over the colorful ethnic-racial map, further binding America into one encompassing community, rather than dividing it along racial and ethnic lines.

In short, there is neither an ideological nor a social basis for a coalition along racial lines that would combine Hispanics, Asians, and African Americans against the white majority to fashion a radically different American society and creed.

Diversity within Unity

Immigrants to America have never been supra-homogenized. Assimilation has never required removing all traces of cultural difference between newcomers and their new homeland. The essence of the American design—diversity within unity—leaves considerable room for differences regarding to whom one prays and to which country one has an allegiance—as long as it does not conflict with an overarching loyalty to America. Differences in cultural items from music to cuisines are celebrated for making the nation, as a community of communities, richer.

Highly legitimate differences among the groups are contained by the shared commitments all are expected to honor: the Constitution and its Bill of Rights, the democratic way of government, peaceful resolution of conflict, and tolerance for differences. These shared bonds may change as new Americans join the U.S. community, but will do so in a largely gradual, continuous, and civil process rather than through rebellion and confrontation. I write "largely" because no country, the United States included, is completely free of troublesome transitions and we have had our share.

No one can be sure what the future holds. A prolonged downward turn in the economy (a centerpiece of most radical scenarios) would give efforts to enlist new immigrants into a majority-of-minorities coalition a better chance of succeeding. But unlike some early Americans who arrived here as slaves, most new immigrants come voluntarily. Many discover that hard work and education do allow them to move up the American economic and social ladders. That makes a radicalization of Hispanics (and Asian Americans) very unlikely. As far as one can project the recent past into the near future, Hispanics will continue to build and rebuild the American society as a community of communities rather than dividing it along racial lines.

AMITAI ETZIONI is author of *The Monochrome Society*.

Hispanic Heritage Month and **Cinco de Mayo**

Hispanic Heritage Month 2008: Sept. 15–Oct. 15

I n September 1968, Congress authorized President Lyndon B. Johnson to proclaim National Hispanic Heritage Week, which was observed during the week that included Sept. 15 and Sept. 16. The observance was expanded in 1988 to a monthlong celebration (Sept. 15—Oct. 15). America celebrates the culture and traditions of those who trace their roots to Spain, Mexico and the Spanish-speaking nations of Central America, South America and the Caribbean. Sept. 15 was chosen as the starting point for the celebration because it is the anniversary of independence of five Latin American countries: Costa Rica, El Salvador, Guatemala, Honduras and Nicaragua. In addition, Mexico and Chile celebrate their independence days on Sept. 16 and Sept. 18, respectively.

Population

45.5 million
The estimated Hispanic population of the United States as of July 1, 2007, making people of Hispanic origin the nation's largest ethnic or race minority. Hispanics constituted 15 percent of the nation's total population. In addition, there are approximately 3.9 million residents of Puerto Rico.[1]

About 1
. . . of every two people added to the nation's population between July 1, 2006, and July 1, 2007, was Hispanic. There were 1.4 million Hispanics added to the population during the period.[2]

3.3%
Percentage increase in the Hispanic population between July 1, 2006, and July 1, 2007, making Hispanics the fastest-growing minority group.[3]

132.8 million
The projected Hispanic population of the United States on July 1, 2050. According to this projection, Hispanics will constitute 30 percent of the nation's population by that date.[4]

22.4 million
The nation's Hispanic population during the 1990 Census—less than half the current total.[5]

2nd
Ranking of the size of the U.S. Hispanic population worldwide, as of 2007. Only Mexico (108.7 million) had a larger Hispanic population than did the United States (45.5 million). (Spain had a population of 40.4 million.)[6]

64%
The percentage of Hispanic-origin people in the United States who are of Mexican background. Another 9 percent are of Puerto Rican background, with 3.4 percent Cuban, 3.1 percent Salvadoran and 2.8 percent Dominican. The remainder are of some other Central American, South American or other Hispanic or Latino origin.[7]

About 50 percent of the nation's Dominicans live in New York City and about half of the nation's Cubans in Miami-Dade County, Fla.[8]

27.6 years
Median age of the Hispanic population in 2007. This compares with 36.6 years for the population as a whole.[9]

107
Number of Hispanic males in 2007 per every 100 Hispanic females. This was in sharp contrast to the overall population, which had 97 males per every 100 females.[10]

States and Counties

48%
The percentage of the Hispanic-origin population that lives in California or Texas. California is home to 13.2 million Hispanics, and Texas is home to 8.6 million.[11]

16
The number of states with at least a half-million Hispanic residents. They are Arizona, California, Colorado, Florida, Georgia, Illinois, Massachusetts, Nevada, New Jersey, New Mexico, New York, North Carolina, Pennsylvania, Texas, Virginia and Washington.[12]

44%

The percentage of New Mexico's population that is Hispanic, the highest of any state. Hispanics also make up more than a quarter of the population in California and Texas, at 36 percent each, Arizona (30 percent) and Nevada (25 percent).[13]

4.7 million

The Hispanic population of Los Angeles County, Calif., in 2007—the largest of any county in the nation. Maricopa County, Ariz. (home of Phoenix) had the biggest numerical increase in the Hispanic population (60,700) since July 2006.[14]

97%

Proportion of the population of Starr County, Texas, that was Hispanic as of 2007, which led the nation. In fact, each of the top 10 counties in this category was in Texas.[15]

308,000

The increase in Texas' Hispanic population between July 1, 2006, and July 1, 2007, which led all states. California (268,000) and Florida (131,000) also recorded large increases.[16]

20

Number of states in which Hispanics are the largest minority group. These states are Arizona, California, Colorado, Connecticut, Florida, Idaho, Iowa, Kansas, Massachusetts, Nebraska, Nevada, New Hampshire, New Jersey, New Mexico, Oregon, Rhode Island, Texas, Utah, Washington and Wyoming.[17]

Businesses[18]

1.6 million

The number of Hispanic-owned businesses in 2002.

Triple

The rate of growth of Hispanic-owned businesses between 1997 and 2002 (31 percent) compared with the national average (10 percent) for all businesses.

$222 billion

Revenue generated by Hispanic-owned businesses in 2002, up 19 percent from 1997.

44.6%

. . . of all Hispanic-owned firms were owned by Mexicans, Mexican-Americans and Chicanos.

29,168

Number of Hispanic-owned firms with receipts of $1 million or more.

- Nearly 43 percent of Hispanic-owned firms operated in construction; administrative and support, and waste management and remediation services; and other services, such as personal services, and repair and maintenance. Retail and wholesale trade accounted for nearly 36 percent of Hispanic-owned business revenue.
- Counties with the highest number of Hispanic-owned firms were Los Angeles County (188,422); Miami-Dade County (163,187); and Harris County, Texas (61,934).

Families and Children

9.9 million

The number of Hispanic family households in the United States in 2006. Of these households, 62 percent included children younger than 18.[19]

67%

The percentage of Hispanic family households consisting of a married couple.[20]

44%

The percentage of Hispanic family households consisting of a married couple with children younger than 18.[21]

66%

Percentage of Hispanic children living with two married parents.[22]

24%

Percentage of total population younger than 5 that was Hispanic as of July 1, 2007.[23]

Spanish Language

34 million

The number of U.S. residents 5 and older who speak Spanish at home. Spanish speakers constitute 12 percent of U.S. residents.[24]

29%

Percentage of Texas residents 5 and older who speak Spanish at home, which leads all states. (The percentage for Texas is not significantly different from that of New Mexico, however.) This compares with the national average of 12 percent.[25]

78%

Percentage of Hispanics 5 and older who speak Spanish at home.[26]

Income, Poverty and Health Insurance

$38,679

The median income of Hispanic households in 2007, statistically unchanged from the previous year after adjusting for inflation.[27]

21.5%

The poverty rate among Hispanics in 2007, up from 20.6 percent in 2006.[28]

32.1%

The percentage of Hispanics who lacked health insurance in 2007, down from 34.1 percent in 2006.[29]

Education

60%

The percentage of Hispanics 25 and older who had at least a high school education in 2007.[30]

13%

The percentage of the Hispanic population 25 and older with a bachelor's degree or higher in 2007.[31]

3.3 million

The number of Hispanics 18 and older who had at least a bachelor's degree in 2007, up from 1.7 million a decade earlier.[32]

811,000

Number of Hispanics 25 and older with advanced degrees in 2007 (e.g., master's, professional, doctorate).[33]

11%

Percentage of all college students in October 2006 who were Hispanic. Among elementary and high school students combined, the corresponding proportion was 19 percent.[34]

Educational attainment levels are higher among certain Hispanic groups than among others. For example, among Cubans 25 and older, 75 percent were at least high school graduates, and 26 percent had a bachelor's degree or higher.[35]

Jobs

68%

Percentage of Hispanics 16 and older who are in the civilian labor force.[36]

17%

The percentage of Hispanics 16 or older who work in management, professional and related occupations. Roughly the same percentage work in construction, extraction, maintenance and repair occupations (although this percentage is significantly lower than for those in management, professional and related occupations). Approximately 24 percent of Hispanics 16 or older work in service occupations; 22 percent in sales and office occupations; 2 percent in farming, fishing and forestry occupations; and 18 percent in production, transportation and material moving occupations.[37]

82,500

Number of Hispanic chief executives. In addition, 46,200 physicians and surgeons; 53,600 postsecondary teachers; 43,000 lawyers; and 5,700 news analysts, reporters and correspondents are Hispanic.[38]

Voting

7.6 million

The number of Hispanic citizens who reported voting in the 2004 presidential election. The percentage of Hispanic citizens voting—about 47 percent—did not change statistically from four years earlier.[39]

5.6 million

The number of Hispanic citizens who reported voting in the 2006 congressional elections. The percentage of Hispanic citizens voting—about 32 percent—did not change statistically from four years earlier.[40]

Serving Our Country

1.1 million

The number of Hispanic veterans of the U.S. armed forces.[41]

Notes

1. Source: Population estimates http://www.census.gov/Press-Release/www/releases/archives/population/011910.html and http://www.census.gov/Press-Release/www/releases/archives/population/011109.html

2. Source: Population estimates http://www.census.gov/Press-Release/www/releases/archives/population/011910.html

3. Source: Population estimates http://www.census.gov/Press-Release/www/releases/archives/population/011910.html

4. Source: Population projections http://www.census.gov/Press-Release/www/releases/archives/population/012496.html

5. Source: The Hispanic Population: 2000 http://www.census.gov/prod/2001pubs/c2kbr01-3.pdf

6. Source: International Data Base http://www.census.gov/cgi-bin/ipc/idbrank.pl http://www.census.gov/ipc/www/idbsum.html and population estimates http://www.census.gov/Press-Release/www/releases/archives/population/011910.html

7. Source: 2006 American Community Survey http://www.census.gov/acs/www/Products/users_guide/index.htm

8. Source: 2006 American Community Survey http://www.census.gov/acs/www/Products/users_guide/index.htm

9. Source: Population estimates http://www.census.gov/Press-Release/www/releases/archives/population/011910.html

10. Source: Population estimates http://www.census.gov/Press-Release/www/releases/archives/population/011910.html

11. Source: Population estimates http://www.census.gov/Press-Release/www/releases/archives/population/011910.html

12. Source: Population estimates http://www.census.gov/Press-Release/www/releases/archives/population/011910.html

13. Source: Population estimates http://www.census.gov/Press-Release/www/releases/archives/population/011910.html

14. Source: Population estimates http://www.census.gov/Press-Release/www/releases/archives/population/012463.html

15. Source: Population estimates http://www.census.gov/Press-Release/www/releases/archives/population/012463.html

16. Source: Population estimates http://www.census.gov/Press-Release/www/releases/archives/population/011910.html

17. Source: Population estimates http://www.census.gov/Press-Release/www/releases/archives/population/011910.html

18. Source for statements in this section: *Hispanic-owned Firms: 2002* http://www.census.gov/csd/sbo/hispanic2002.htm

19. Source: Families and Living Arrangements http://www.census.gov/Press-Release/www/releases/archives/families_households/009842.html

20. Source: Families and Living Arrangements http://www.census.gov/Press-Release/www/releases/archives/families_households/009842.html

21. Source: Families and Living Arrangements http://www.census.gov/Press-Release/www/releases/archives/families_households/009842.html

22. Source: Families and Living Arrangements http://www.census.gov/Press-Release/www/releases/archives/families_households/009842.html

23. Source: Population estimates http://www.census.gov/Press-Release/www/releases/archives/population/011910.html

24. Source: 2006 American Community Survey http://www.census .gov/acs/www/Products/users_guide/index.htm

25. Source: 2006 American Community Survey http://www.census .gov/acs/www/Products/users_guide/index.htm

26. Source: 2006 American Community Survey http://www.census .gov/acs/www/Products/users_guide/index.htm

27. Source: *Income, Poverty, and Health Insurance Coverage in the United States: 2007* http://www.census.gov/Press-Release/ www/releases/archives/income_wealth/012528.html

28. Source: *Income, Poverty, and Health Insurance Coverage in the United States: 2007* http://www.census.gov/Press-Release/ www/releases/archives/income_wealth/012528.html

29. Source: *Income, Poverty, and Health Insurance Coverage in the United States: 2007* http://www.census.gov/Press-Release/ www/releases/archives/income_wealth/012528.html

30. Source: Educational Attainment in the United States: 2007 http://www.census.gov/Press-Release/www/releases/archives/ education/011196.html

31. Source: Educational Attainment in the United States: 2007 http://www.census.gov/Press-Release/www/releases/archives/ education/011196.html

32. Source: Educational Attainment in the United States: 2007 http://www.census.gov/Press-Release/www/releases/archives/ education/011196.html

33. Source: Educational Attainment in the United States: 2007 http://www.census.gov/Press-Release/www/releases/archives/ education/011196.html

34. Source: School Enrollment—Social and Economic Characteristics of Students: October 2006 http://www.census .gov/Press-Release/www/releases/archives/education/011921.html

35. Source: 2006 American Community Survey http://www.census .gov/acs/www/Products/users_guide/index.htm

36. Source: 2006 American Community Survey http://www.census .gov/acs/www/Products/users_guide/index.htm

37. Source: 2006 American Community Survey http://www.census .gov/acs/www/Products/users_guide/index.htm

38. Source: Upcoming *Statistical Abstract of the United States: 2009,* Table 596 http://www.census.gov/compendia/statab/

39. Source: *Voting and Registration in the Election of November 2004* http://www.census.gov/Press-Release/www/releases/ archives/voting/004986.html

40. Source: *Voting and Registration in the Election of November 2006* http://www.census.gov/Press-Release/www/releases/ archives/voting/012234.html

41. Source: 2006 American Community Survey http://www.census .gov/acs/www/Products/users_guide/index.htm

Editor's note—The preceding data were collected from a variety of sources and may be subject to sampling variability and other sources of error. Facts for Features are customarily released about two months before an observance in order to accommodate magazine production timelines. Questions or comments should be directed to the Census Bureau's Public Information Office: telephone: 301-763-3030; fax: 301-763-3762; or e-mail: pio@census.gov.

Cinco de Mayo

Cinco de Mayo celebrates the legendary Battle of Puebla on May 5, 1862, in which a Mexican force of 4,500 men faced 6,000 well-trained French soldiers. The battle lasted four hours and ended in a victory for the Mexican army under Gen. Ignacio Zaragoza. Along with Mexican Independence Day on Sept. 16, Cinco de Mayo has become a time to celebrate Mexican heritage and culture.

28.3 million
Number of U.S. residents of Mexican origin in 2006. These residents constituted 9 percent of the nation's total population and 64 percent of the Hispanic population.

17.86 million
Number of people of Mexican origin who lived either in California (10.84 million) or Texas (7.02 million). People of Mexican origin made up more than one-quarter of the residents of these two states. (The unrounded total for California and Texas combined is 17,866,191.)

25.7
Median age of people in the United States of Mexican descent. This compares with 36.4 years for the population as a whole.

630,000
Number of Mexican-Americans who are U.S. military veterans.

1.2 million
Number of people of Mexican descent 25 and older with a bachelor's degree or higher. This includes about 350,000 who have a graduate degree.

37%
Among households where a householder was of Mexican origin, the percentage of married-couple families with own children younger than 18. For all households, the corresponding percentage was 22 percent.

4.1
Average size for families with a householder of Mexican origin. This compares to 3.2 people in all families.

14%
Percentage of employed civilians 16 and older of Mexican heritage who worked in managerial, professional or related occupations. In addition, 23 percent worked in service occupations; 20 percent in sales and office occupations; 19 percent in construction, extraction, maintenance and repair occupations; and 20 percent in production, transportation and material moving occupations.

$37,661
Median household income in 2006 for households with a house-holder of Mexican origin.

23%
Poverty rate in 2006 for people of Mexican heritage.

69%
Percentage of civilians 16 and older of Mexican origin in the labor force. The percentage was 65 percent for the population as a whole. There were 13 million people of Mexican heritage in the labor force, comprising 9 percent of the total.

51%
Percentage of householders of Mexican origin who owned the home in which they lived.[42]

Trade with Mexico

$347.3 billion
The value of goods traded between the United States and Mexico in 2007. Mexico was our nation's third-leading trading partner, after Canada and China.[43]

Businesses

701,078
Number of firms owned by people of Mexican origin in 2002. They comprised almost 45 percent of all Hispanic-owned firms. Among these Mexican-owned firms, 275,896 were in California and 235,735 in Texas. The Los Angeles-Long Beach-Riverside, Calif., combined statistical area had 174,292.

$96.7 billion
Sales and receipts for firms owned by people of Mexican origin in 2002.[44]

Mexican Food

$100.4 million
Product shipment value of tamales and other Mexican food specialties (not frozen or canned) produced in the United States in 2002.[45]

337
Number of U.S. tortilla manufacturing establishments in 2005. The establishments that produce this unleavened flat bread employed nearly 14,000 people. Tortillas, the principal food of the Aztecs, are known as the "bread of Mexico." About one in three of these establishments was in Texas.[46]

Notes

42. Source for the preceding statements: 2006 American Community Survey http://www.factfinder.census.gov/

43. Source: Foreign Trade Statistics http://www.census.gov/foreign-trade/www/

44. Source for statements in this section: Hispanic-Owned Firms: 2002 http://www.census.gov/prod/ec02/sb0200cshisp.pdf

45. Source: 2002 Economic Census http://www.census.gov/econ/census02/guide/INDRPT31.HTM

46. Source: County Business Patterns: 2005 http://www.census.gov/Press-Release/www/releases/archives/county_business_patterns/010192.html

---

Editor's note—The preceding data were collected from a variety of sources and may be subject to sampling variability and other sources of error. Facts for Features are customarily released about two months before an observance in order to accommodate magazine production timelines. Questions or comments should be directed to the Census Bureau's Public Information Office: telephone: 301-763-3030; fax: 301-763-3762; or e-mail: pio@census.gov.

From *U.S. Census Bureau*, 2008.

Minority-Owned Firms More Likely to Export

MONO PLACY

The Minority Business Development Agency shows America's competitiveness and economic growth in the global market will increasingly depend on the growth and expansion of minority owned businesses.

The report, *Characteristics of Minority Businesses and Entrepreneur: An Analysis of the 2002 Survey of Business Owners,* analyzes minority businesses to identify trends that may have impacted their performances in 2002. According to the report, minority-owned firms were twice as likely to export (2.5 percent of firms) compared to non-minority-owned firms (1.2 percent of firms). Accelerated growth of the minority population, which is expected to reach 50 percent of the Nations population by 2050, is a key factor in helping to position minority firms as increasingly important players in America's business sector.

"U.S. minority firms are a great American asset and the time is right for them to seize the opportunity to expand and export their goods internationally, said Ronald N. Langston, national director of the Minority Business Development Agency at the U.S. Department of Commerce. "Doing so will not only grow their business but strengthen the national economy and create jobs in minority communities."

More than 70 percent of the world's purchasing power—and 95 percent of its population—is beyond U.S. borders. Langston points to President Bush's trade agenda and free trade agreements as pro-business policies that are creating new business opportunities for minority businesses to grow.

"Free trade agreements, along with the ease of global transportation and the Internet continue to simplify the export process. Together, these are great tools to help all U.S. companies maintain their competitive advantage," said Langston. "We need to do everything we can to encourage more minority firms to engage in exporting and global expansion. They are vital to America's economic success."

The report confirms that minority firms have a competitive export advantage over all firms due in part to language capabilities, ancestral ties, cultural compatibility and potentially great agility and nimbleness because of their size.

With free trade partners in Asia, Africa, Latin American and the Caribbean, U.S. businesses continue to increase their sales abroad. In 2007, U.S. exports to countries where there was a free trade agreement in effect exceeded $472 billion, accounting for roughly 41 percent of U.S. exports.

Challenges for Minority Firms

To fully realize their growth potential, however, minority businesses must overcome some unique challenges. For example, the MBDA report examines obstacles minorities face in growing their businesses such as using adequate capital to start and expand the business.

Access to adequate capital remains a problem for most minority-owned firms. Minority-owned firms were more likely to use credit cards and less likely to use bank loans to start or acquire their businesses compared to non-minority-owned firms. One way MBDA and its network of centers is addressing this challenge is to facilitate traditional commercial loans, government guaranteed loans and in some instances, private equity for minority firms. In fiscal year 2006 MBDA produced $407 million in financial transactions and nearly $1.2 billion in procurement opportunities for its minority business clients.

"Access to capital and the marketplace are essential to fostering the growth of minority firms," said Langston. "Our programs and services are assisting thousands of minority business clients with securing the capital they need to realize their business potential."

The report also outlines other opportunities for minorities to grow their businesses.

Minority firms that have a diverse customer portfolio—other businesses/organizations, the federal government and international customers—are at an advantage to increase their bottom line. Large minority firms with receipts of $500,000 or more were already capitalizing on this market of opportunity. The report finds the larger the company in terms of receipts size, the more likely it sold goods and services to businesses or organizations, the federal government and globally.

Other characteristics of minority businesses include:

- Minority firms were more likely to operate as franchises compared to non-minority firms. Many franchised businesses provide managerial and marketing training to franchise operators. This training can help close the gap in educational attainment among minorities.

- Minority business owners attained lower educational levels compared to non minority business owners. Targeted educational programs are necessary to address the educational gap of minority entrepreneurs and support the growth and expansion of minority businesses.
- Average gross receipts for firms with employees increased by 5 percent between 1997 and 2002, as opposed to a decrease in those of all minority firms.

A full copy of the new MBDA report, *Characteristics of Minority Businesses and Entrepreneur: An Analysis of the 2002 Survey of Business Owners,* can be found at the Agency's website at www.mbda.gov.

The *2002 Survey of Business Owners* is part of the Economic Census and includes results from a questionnaire conducted by the U.S. Census Bureau. The survey was distributed by mail to a random sample of 2.3 million businesses selected from a list

of all U.S. firms operating during 2002 with receipts of $1,000 or more. About 81 percent of the 2.3 million firms responded to the survey.

About the Minority Business Development Agency, U.S. Department of Commerce

Established in 1969 and headquartered in Washington DC, the Minority Business Development Agency (MBDA) is part of the U.S. Department of Commerce. MBDA is the only federal agency created specifically to foster the establishment and growth of minority-owned business in this Nation. The Agency actively promotes the strategic growth and competitiveness of large, medium and small minority business enterprises by offering management and technical assistance through a network of approximately 50 local business centers throughout the United States.

Helpful business resources for minority entrepreneurs are available at www.mbda.gov.

UNIT 7

Asian Americans

Unit Selections

Key Points to Consider

- Examine the origin and sources of misinformation about Asian Americans.

- Does public attention to the activities of Asian Americans associated with Islamic countries seem to be increasing?

- The public passion generated during World War II have subsided, and anti-Japanese sentiment is no longer heard. Do you agree or disagree with this statement? Why? Is this phenomenon related to current perceptions of Arab Americans? Can current detainments be analogized to the Japanese internment camps?

Student Web Site
www.mhcls.com

Internet References

Asian American Studies Center
http://www.aasc.ucla.edu/default.asp
Asian Americans for Equality
http://www.aafe.org
Asian-Nation
http://www.asian-nation.org/index.shtml

The Asian American context discussed in this unit provides perspectives on immigrants' adjustment and their reception in various regimes and cultures. Asian Americans are engaged in the ongoing issue of cultural formation, the recovery of tradition, and the incorporation of new ethnicities from Asian into mainstream cultural entertainment. The political and economic forces that frame relationships at the personal and cultural levels pose dilemmas.

The growth of the Asian American population since the immigration reform of 1965, the emergence of Japan and other Asian nations as international fiscal players, and the image of intellectual and financial success of Asian Americans have heightened interest in this ethnic group in the United States. The variety of religious traditions that Asian immigrants bring to America is another dimension of cultural and moral importance. In what respect are non-Judeo-Christian/Islamic faith traditions issues of consequence? The details of familial and cultural development within Asian American communities compose worlds of meaning that are a rich source of material from which both insights and troubling questions of personal and group identity emerge. Pivotal periods of conflict in the drama of the American experience provide an occasion for learning as much about ourselves as about one of the newest clusters of ethnicities—the Asian Americans.

The following collection of articles on Asian Americans invites us to reflect on the fact that the United States is related to Asia in ways that would seem utterly amazing to the worldview of the American founders. The expansion of the American regime across the continent, the importation of Asian workers, and the subsequent exclusion of Asians from the American polity are signs of the tarnished image and broken promise of refuge that America extended and then revoked. The Asian world is a composite of ethnicities and traditions ranging from the Indian subcontinent northeastward to China and Japan.

To Be Asian in America

ANGELA JOHNSON MEADOWS

C. N. Le barely remembers fleeing Vietnam for the United States when he was 5. Sketchy images of riding a cargo ship to Guam, having his documents processed and boarding a plane that would take him to Arkansas are all that remain of the life-altering experience.

But the reason for leaving his war-ravaged homeland is crystal clear. After military pressure from communist North Vietnam caused the South Vietnamese government to collapse in 1975, Le's family was in jeopardy.

"The U.S. government knew that those who worked for the U.S. military were going to be persecuted pretty harshly if they stayed back in Vietnam," says Le, whose parents both were U.S. military workers. "So [the U.S. government] made arrangements for their Vietnamese employees and their families to be evacuated."

Le and his family spent their initial days in the United States at Fort Chaffee, an Arkansas military base that served as a processing center for Vietnamese refugees.

"We had a little playground there that kids would play on, so in a lot of ways my experience was more of a typical kid's experience . . . than a refugee experience," recalls Le, a visiting assistant professor at the University of Massachusetts Amherst.

"Adults who had more of a recognition of what was going on would probably tell you, like my parents have said, it was a pretty traumatic experience for them, having to leave their country, leave everything behind and try to start life in a whole new country," Le says.

Le's status as a refugee is different from that of Chinese, Asian Indians, Japanese and some other Asians who have come to America, yet regardless of country of origin or mode or time of arrival, the majority of these immigrants share a common goal—a better life. For some, that means educational or professional opportunities they were denied in their homelands; for others, it's escaping political turmoil; and for others still, it's sacrificing the comforts of middle-class life to provide better chances for their children. It is the quintessential U.S. immigrant story.

"We spoke Chinese in the home and ate Chinese food in the home. The home life was one thing, but going out into the regular world, you have to fit in; there is a certain amount of biculturalism."

—Lora Fong, Greenbaum, Rowe, Smith & Davis

There are nearly 12 million people of Asian heritage living in the United States. Asian Americans (a term used by *DiversityInc* to describe both immigrant and American-born Asians) represent East Asian nations such as China, Japan and Korea; South Asian countries including India, Pakistan and Nepal; and Southeast Asian nations such as Thailand, Vietnam and Malaysia.

Still only 4.6 percent of the U.S. population, the Asian-American segment is experiencing astronomical growth. Between 2000 and 2050, the population is expected to surge 213 percent, according to the U.S. Census Bureau. The projected general-population growth during the same time? A paltry 49 percent.

But this growth isn't a 21st-century phenomenon. Historians have traced their presence in the land that evolved into the United States of America as far back as 1763, when Filipinos traveling aboard Spanish galleons jumped ship in New Orleans to escape imprisonment and fled into the Louisiana bayou to establish the first recorded Filipino settlement in America. Some argue their history in the United States dates back to the 1400s.

The Chinese were the first group of Asians to arrive in great numbers, appearing in the mid-1800s. The lure? The potential economic prosperity of the 1848 California Gold Rush and job opportunities associated with agriculture and the building of the intercontinental railroad.

Asian Americans were recruited as laborers—mostly men who were enticed by the opportunity to earn money to support their families or indentured servants who were sent to work off the debts of other Asians back home.

"These people were often deceived," says Gary Okihiro, director of the Center for the Study of Ethnicity and Race and a professor of international and public affairs at Columbia University. "Although these [work and payment] conditions were spelled out to them, they were oftentimes unfulfilled."

Many planned to return to their homelands when their contracted work period ended, but were prevented by U.S. immigration laws.

"They locked those that were here in the U.S.," says Okihiro. "Their remittances were crucial for the sustenance of their families back in Asia, so they were oftentimes trapped into remaining in the U.S."

Subsequent Asians came in waves, with the largest population arriving after the 1965 passage of the Immigration and Nationality Act. Immigrants and their offspring from China, the Philippines, India, Vietnam, Korea and Japan now account for the largest Asian populations in the country.

A Brave New World

W.E.B. DuBois once described the African-American experience as one of a double-consciousness, rooted in the need to navigate between one's own culture and that of the mainstream. It is an experience that rings true for Asian immigrants and their descendants as well.

"When they arrive, they begin to realize that they're different," says John Kuo Wei Tchen, the founding director of the A/P/A Studies Program and Institute at New York University. "Identities get challenged and they have to deal with what it means to be American or resident alien."

Some Asian Americans relied on assimilation as a means of blending in with American society and as an attempt to escape anti-Asian sentiments that heightened during World War II. "This question about how much they wanted to or did assimilate is a question of how much they were permitted to assimilate," says Okihiro.

Today, ties to home remain strong for new Asian immigrants; however, many families experience acculturation—the process of assimilating new ideas into an existing cognitive structure—with U.S.-born generations.

"Parents would like to think their children are going to be very embracive and very welcoming of the parents' own culture," says Franklin Ng, a professor in the anthropology department at California State University–Fresno. "Parents may have these kinds of supportive mechanisms, encouraging them to go to a temple, or ethnic church, so their children will become familiar with their ethnic culture . . . [but] the youth are having their own trajectory."

Growing up in a Southern California suburb, Le struggled with his Vietnamese name. By the time he reached high school, racial and ethnic tensions had set in and Le decided to go by the name Sean. "At that age, you just want to fit in and be like everyone else," he says.

But a college course on race and ethnicity changed his thinking. "That's when I became more socially conscious . . . and really began to see that my identity . . . was a source of strength . . . rather than a source of embarrassment. I wanted to go back to my Vietnamese name. The name Sean didn't really fit my identity," says Le, who is also the founder of Asian-Nation.org, an online resource for Asian-American historical, demographic, political and cultural issues.

Today, Le uses his first and middle initials, a way to keep his Vietnamese name—Cuong Nguyen—without having to face the pronunciation problems of non-Asians.

This balancing act isn't limited to language issues. Many struggle with the expectations of both their family and mainstream society.

"We were raised in the family to be in a very consistent way with the traditional Chinese culture," says Lora Fong, a third-generation Chinese American. "We spoke Chinese in the home and ate Chinese food in the home. The home life was one thing, but going out into the regular world, you have to fit in; there is a certain amount of biculturalism."

When Fong's father died in 1984, her Chinese and American worlds collided. She was working at IBM at the time, a company that often assisted employees in making funeral arrangements for loved ones.

"I was a team leader, I was frequently running projects and giving assignments and keeping people on task," says Fong, now an attorney at Greenbaum, Rowe, Smith & Davis in Woodbridge, N.J. Fortunately, Fong had a Chinese-American supervisor who understood that her professional persona was in stark contrast to her status within her traditional Chinese family.

"He knew that I could not take on a role of being in charge [in my family]," Fong recalls. "He just said, 'She's the daughter. She's the youngest. She's not running things. The company does not have a role there, so just back off.' And that was really antithetical to the way the company took on a role in an employee's personal life. That was such a dichotomy."

Striving for Success

Despite viewing America as the proverbial land of opportunity, the path to a better life has not been without roadblocks, particularly for those who arrived prior to 1965. Chinese in the United States were denied citizenship in the late 1800s, while immigration of all Asians, except for Filipinos (whose residence in a U.S. territory gave them the status of nationals), was halted in 1924 through the National Origins Act. It wasn't until the Immigration and Nationality Act of 1965 that Asian Americans were accepted into the country in larger numbers. The gates to the United States were opened, particularly to those with expertise in the medical, science and technology fields, explaining in part the proliferation of Asian Americans in those disciplines today.

In the face of language barriers, cultural adjustments and government and societal oppression, Asian Americans as a whole appear to have done quite well in America. A look at demographic data shows that Asian Americans as a group surpass all other racial and ethnic groups in the country in median household income and education levels. And while many marketers are turned off by the small size and myriad languages of the population, the buying power of Asian Americans is projected to jump 347 percent between 1990 and 2009, compared with a modest 159-percent increase for the overall population.

For aspirational Asian Americans, social mobility is a priority and education often is viewed as the method of achievement. This focus contributes to the group's economic success.

"Researchers suggest that one legacy of Confucianism in many Asian countries (notably China, Korea, Japan and Vietnam) is the notion that human beings are perfectible if they work to improve themselves," write Yu Xie and Kimberly A. Goyette, authors of *Demographic Portrait of Asian Americans*. "Given this cultural heritage, some Asian Americans may be more likely than whites to believe that hard work in school will be rewarded."

"In China, you have a kind of high-stakes testing," adds Tchen, referring to the country's civil-service system. "The emperor constantly recruits the best to come to the capital or to work . . . It's not so odd for higher education to be seen as the modern variation of that practice."

Mia Tuan's mother and father encouraged higher learning.

"Even though my parents knew nothing about the U.S. educational system . . . it was always assumed that I would go to college," says Tuan, an associate professor of sociology at the University of Oregon.

How They Score Class of 2003 SATs

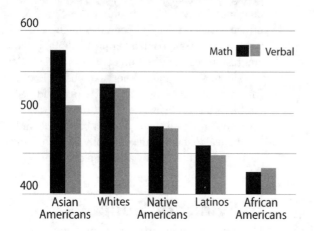

U.S. Asian Population

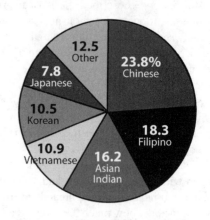

Educational Attainment
People 25 years and older, 2004

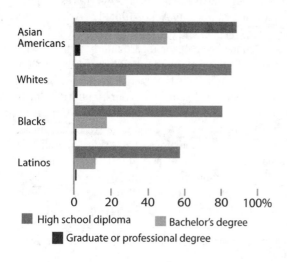

Median Family Incomes
In U.S. Population 25+

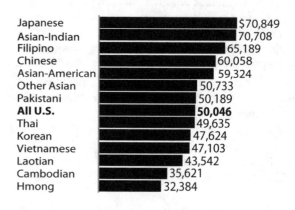

Japanese	$70,849
Asian-Indian	70,708
Filipino	65,189
Chinese	60,058
Asian-American	59,324
Other Asian	50,733
Pakistani	50,189
All U.S.	**50,046**
Thai	49,635
Korean	47,624
Vietnamese	47,103
Laotian	43,542
Cambodian	35,621
Hmong	32,384

Asian-American Buying Power
Projected rate of increase 1990–2009

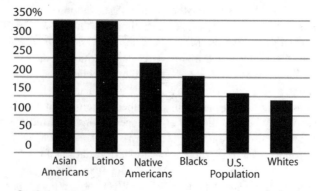

Figure 1 Asian-American Statistics.

Sources: College Board, U.S. Census Bureau, University of Georgia's Selig Center for Economic Growth.

Tuan's mother wanted her daughter to be the next Connie Chung. "Connie opened that door and parents encouraged us to go through that same door," says Tuan.

"I chose to not be the next Connie Chung, but a whole cohort of Asian-American women did hear that call and answered that call . . . When I told them I was going into sociology, they didn't know what the hell that was, but it was a Ph.D., so that counted for something."

But educational attainment isn't a priority for all Asians in America.

"If you come from a rural society where schooling and education was not such a benefit to your ability to raise crops . . . your emphasis on education would be different," says Tchen. "That would be true for Hmong or Southeast Asians . . . They don't necessarily relate to higher education as a way to better themselves."

This is played out in the educational statistics of Asian Americans. For example, in 2000, 76 percent of Asian Indians and 67 percent of Chinese Americans between the ages of 25 and 34 had a college degree or higher, compared with 43 percent of Filipino Americans and 27 percent of Vietnamese Americans.

The Model Minority and Other Myths

While the myths of universal affluence and intelligence among Asian Americans are just that, it hasn't stopped society from pinning them with the "model minority" label. They are seen as smart, wealthy and successful, and on the surface, it appears to be a positive perception.

"My parents' generation? They liked the model minority stereotype," says Tuan. "In their mind, it has served us well . . . They saw it as the price you pay for being an outsider and it was a price they were willing to pay."

But a look behind the stereotype and its implications reveals a troubling story.

"A lot of these [income] statistics can be misleading," says Le. "Family median income is mainly inflated because Asian-American families tend to have more workers . . . They're more likely to live in urban areas where salaries are higher, but the cost of living is also higher."

Per capital income for Asian Americans in the 2000 census measured $20,719, compared with $21,587 for the overall population.

A look at Fortune 500 companies illustrates that an intense focus on education really doesn't guarantee professional success. Despite high education levels, Asian Americans represent less than 1 percent of senior-management ranks or corporate boards.

"Everybody cites the success of Asian Americans, yet if you compared the level of education and position with that of white people, they come below white people," says Okihiro. "Their investment in education does not pay off. There's a glass ceiling for them."

Tuan's father was a diplomat with the Taiwanese government; however, after the U.S. office closed, he found it wasn't easy to translate his skills. He ended up opening a pizza shop.

"They lost a lot of status," says Tuan of her parents, whose migration to the United States erased the prestige of their

advanced degrees. "That put pressure on the next generation to make it worthwhile."

The belief that Asian Americans can succeed on their own dilutes the notion that some could benefit from programs ranging from Medicaid to affirmative action. Thirteen percent of all Asian Americans live in poverty. Twenty-three percent of Asians outside of the six largest groups are impoverished, rivaling the 24 percent of blacks of this economic status.

> **"My parents' generation? They liked the model minority stereotyype. In their mind, it has served us well . . . They saw it as the price you pay for being an outsider and it was a price they were willing to pay."**
>
> —Mia Tuan, University of Oregon

"With this spotlight on the talented tenth, there is neglect of those who may be in the lower tiers," says Ng.

Tuan recalls a meeting with faculty members and graduate students in her department.

"At one point [during the meeting] a graduate student said, 'We take issue with the fact that the department isn't hiring minorities,' " says Tuan, who was one of three recently hired Asian Americans in the department. "I was stunned when the student said that, and I said, 'So, do we not count?' And his answer was basically [that] we didn't, that Asians were this middle category . . . In his mind a minority hire would have been Latino, African American and Native American."

> **"Everybody cites the success of Asian Americans, yet if you compared the level of education and position with that of white people, they come below white people. Their investment in education does not pay off. There's a glass ceiling for them."**
>
> —Gary Okihiro, Columbia University

In addition to not being viewed as a traditional minority, Asian Americans also have an imposed identity as "eternal foreigners." Many American-born Asians have at least one story of being asked about their origins. A reply such as Fresno or Washington, D.C., is often met with the incredulous response of: "No, where are you *really* from?"

Even high-profile American-born Asians can't escape the stereotype. When Tara Lipinski defeated Michelle Kwan in the 1998 Winter Olympics figure-skating competition, MSNBC ran a headline that read: "American beats out Kwan." Kwan, who was born in Torrance, Calif., is just as American as Lipinski.

This misconception has some basis in truth, says Le. Approximately two-thirds of Asian Americans are immigrants. "But the social implications are that when someone is judged to be a foreigner, it is easier for that person to be treated as if they're not a real American . . . It becomes easier to deny them the same rights and privileges that are given to real Americans."

Asian Americans also face the perception that they are all the same. When Ng first settled in Fresno, Calif., he was taunted by a group of teenagers who ordered him to "Remember Pearl Harbor Day," an allusion to Japan's attack on the United States. As a child growing up in a Chicago suburb during the Korean War era, Tchen received the label of "gook," a disparaging term for Southeast Asians. Both Ng and Tchen are Chinese.

> **"The experience of being treated as foreigners, exotics, outsiders, hordes, dangerous, those kinds of images that are recycled in American media . . . perpetuate some kind of basis for people of different backgrounds to come together."**
>
> —John Kuo Wei Tchen, New York University

But perhaps the most notable misidentification occurred in 1982, when 27-year-old Vincent Chin visited a suburban Detroit strip club to celebrate his impending nuptials. While there, Chin encountered a couple of disgruntled autoworkers, one of whom had recently been laid off. The autoworkers hurled insults at Chin and blamed him for the demise of Detroit's auto industry. After Chin left the club, the two men met up with Chin in front of a fast-food restaurant and beat him with a baseball bat. Chin, who was Chinese—not Japanese, as his attackers had assumed—slipped into a coma and died five days later.

The Asian-American Identity in America

Asian Americans represent nearly 25 countries and speak at least as many languages; however, it is the challenges stemming from stereotypes, misconceptions, discrimination and exclusion that help this disparate group to unite under the umbrella term of "Asian American."

"The experience of being treated as foreigners, exotics, outsiders, hordes, dangerous, those kinds of images that are recycled in American media . . . perpetuate some kind of basis for people of different backgrounds to come together," says Tchen.

"A pan-Asian orientation is useful as sort of an instrument for coalition building for political advancement," adds Ng. "Asian Americans are ignored in the corridors of power, and collectively they can have more impact and can address issues that are more common."

Although Fong identifies first as a Chinese American, she's also concerned about broader Asian-American issues.

"We are all sharing a unique experience in terms of people's pre-conceived notion of who we are and what we should or shouldn't be doing in this society," says Fong, who is a past president of the Asian Pacific American Lawyers Association of New Jersey.

In addition to fighting shared struggles, Asian Americans have been able to collectively celebrate the accomplishments of Asian Americans of various backgrounds. Norman Mineta, U.S. Secretary of Transportation, and Elaine Chao, U.S. Secretary of Labor, are two of the highest-ranking Asian Americans in the Bush administration. Andrea Jung, chairman of the board and CEO of Avon Products, and Indira Nooyi, president and chief financial officer at PepsiCo, are just a few people who have broken what career consultant Jane Hyun describes as the "bamboo ceiling" of corporate America. And the presence of Asian Americans in sports and entertainment continues to flourish.

"When I was growing up . . . there was not exactly a wide range," says Tuan. "But if you were to ask—and I do ask these questions of the students—to name five prominent Asian-American public figures, they can come up with them now . . . I can only see that as being a good thing, because it shifts this notion of what's possible or who or what an Asian American is or what they're capable of. That's very powerful to me."

Lands of Opportunity

Many Chinese are leaving behind their homeland's booming economy for the brand of freedom offered in Maryland and the rest of America.

GADY A. EPSTEIN AND STEPHANIE DESMON

It was a quintessentially American scene: a split-level house in the suburbs, with a tree-shaded lawn and burgers on a gas-fired grill for friends and family gathered to congratulate a new college graduate.

The graduate, Kelly Li, citizen of China and future citizen of the United States, was about to go to work for one of the richest corporations in the world, Exxon Mobil.

This party in Lutherville wasn't just a celebration of an American dream realized; it marked the culmination of a plan that began taking shape in Guangzhou, China, some 17 years ago, when Kelly's parents began contemplating an American future for their only child.

Yet from the time Wenhui and Miaolian Li decided they wanted to leave China until they were given permission to do so five years ago, the dynamics had changed. They were leaving behind a new, surging China—departing what is quickly becoming this century's land of opportunity. At a time when the Chinese economy is expanding at a pace of about 10 percent a year, some legal immigrants like the Lis are taking a calculated step down the ladder of opportunity in coming to the U.S.

The Lis traded their white-collar office jobs and middle-class lives in China for blue-collar jobs in the Baltimore area—Mr. Li drives a truck for a company that supplies Chinese restaurants, Mrs. Li packs fruits and vegetables for a business that provides produce to Giant supermarkets. They sacrificed their place on the ladder to secure their daughter's.

For all of the progress in China, some of its citizens still see the U.S. as a better place—for economic reasons, political reasons, educational reasons. History matters, too. To families like the Lis, whose prospects and freedom were cut short by one Communist political campaign after another, America is a place for the next generation to have everything they could not.

Sometimes the reality doesn't match the promise of a nation seemingly brimming with opportunity and freedom. The future can be uncertain. Yet despite the sacrifices most make in taking the leap to a nation that is foreign to them in every way, they continue to come.

Even as prospects improved in China, the number of legal immigrants from there nearly doubled during the 1990s, according to census figures, from 530,000 to 989,000. The small Chinese population in Maryland grew as well.

America's appeal is so compelling that a large number of Chinese who can't wait or don't qualify for visas come anyway, sometimes paying huge sums to shadowy characters who help them enter illegally. Hundreds of thousands may have come this way in the past quarter-century. These immigrants may never realize all their hopes, however, as they face high barriers to success in a country that does not officially welcome them. Often they toil in lives lived mostly underground, as restaurant workers, as housekeepers or nannies to legal Chinese immigrants.

The flow of Chinese into the U.S. shows no sign of abating. Yet a new, albeit small, trend has emerged. In recent years, China's economic boom has enticed back an increasing number of its citizens who have American degrees. For them, moving back to China is the way to move up quickly.

As political leaders in the U.S. argue over immigration policy, they are re-enacting a great historical debate about what it means to be an American, and about who deserves to become one.

The debate today is focused mostly on the impoverished Spanish speakers who sneak across the U.S.-Mexican border. But it often overlooks the question embodied in the Chinese phenomenon: why, even as globalization spreads opportunity, so many people still want to become Americans.

People such as Yaming Luo, Kelly's uncle, who is among the revelers at her graduation celebration. Once a manager of a company in Guangzhou, Luo works in a windowless kitchen in the back of a sushi restaurant in Baltimore County, part of an isolated life lived entirely in the language of his home country. He dreams that one day, years from now, his payoff will come when his grandson—not yet conceived when Luo moved to Lutherville—can immigrate to the United States to study.

Nearby stand Jie and Daisy Zhang, friends of the Li family, who left behind memories of violent repression in China. After tanks rolled into Beijing in 1989 in a crackdown on student

Figure 1

protesters in Tiananmen Square, killing hundreds on the orders of the government, Daisy resolved to leave the country. The Zhangs came to the United States to study. They ended up building fairly typical suburban lives with well-paying jobs, a house on an Ellicott City cul-de-sac and three children, whom they have given the gift of U.S. citizenship.

What the children do with their lives here is up to them. "I never put my mind to my children," Jie Zhang said. "They are American people. They'll decide based on their judgments."

The first Chinese known to have arrived on the East Coast landed as accidental immigrants in Baltimore. In 1785, the trading ship Pallas reached Baltimore from Guangzhou. Three Chinese crew members ended up stranded.

Chinese immigration since then has ebbed and flowed, at times based on the politics of the United States, at others on the politics of China. The largest wave began after the death of Mao Zedong 30 years ago, when Communist China began to modernize and finally open itself to the world. The unlocked doors set off an exodus.

"The political constraints, the difficulty of people leaving, the ideological negative attitude toward the West and all that, all of a sudden all of these things were let loose," said Peter Kwong, a Hunter College professor who is an authority on Chinese immigration. "So there is this tremendous force . . . just wanting to get out of China, and thinking in terms of not just themselves but also their children."

As more people in China developed the financial means to emigrate, immigration to the United States—both legal and illegal—flourished.

Even more Chinese long to leave for the U.S.

Untold numbers of Chinese are regularly turned down for student and tourist visas for fear that they lack sufficient ties to their homeland and may try to stay permanently. Others don't have appropriate connections in the U.S. and can't get visas to immigrate, either because they don't have close relatives abroad, can't get employment or aren't accepted into American colleges. While officials no longer call them quotas, there are complicated, per-country limits for the number of immigrants allowed into the U.S. in any given year.

Those who can navigate the thicket of different visas and who can afford to pack up one life for another are typically those who make the journey halfway around the world. The poorest of the poor in China's vast countryside often lack the means to escape the depth of their poverty.

Legal avenues to the U.S. have broadened significantly in the past 15 years, with new kinds of visas aimed at elite workers and

entrepreneurs. But, as it undergoes a historic transformation, China also is bidding to keep them from leaving. Why so many still choose immigration can be traced in part to a history that present-day China cannot transform, no matter how much the country tries to forget.

Family Targeted

If not for China's Communist revolution 57 years ago, Miaolian Li would have been born into privilege. But by the time she was born, in 1954, she was fated to have a much harder life.

She was the daughter of what Chinese of the time called a "big capitalist," the owner of a textile factory in pre-revolutionary Guangzhou. In Communist China, this was a status to be rued, not celebrated. For as in Stalin's Soviet Union, Mao Zedong's China turned its former elites into political fodder. Communist ideology first took away your money and status, then your pride and dignity. Finally, it might take your life. Your children would suffer, too, for the misfortune of having parents who were capitalists or landlords or intellectuals.

For Miaolian and countless others her age, the reckoning was the Cultural Revolution launched by Mao in 1966. Mao turned the normal hierarchy of society upside down, violently setting workers against bosses, students against teachers and, most cruelly, children against parents.

Just 12 in 1966, Miaolian was too young to participate in the worst of the early atrocities. But her family was a target. A slight, often cheerful woman, Miaolian summoned these dark memories as she sat in the Lis' two-bedroom apartment in Catonsville. It's a cozy walk-up with hardwood floors, a 30-inch television, pictures of the Lis and their daughter on the walls and the smell of rice cooking in the kitchen. The year 1966 in southern China might seem most of a lifetime ago, but the act of remembering brought tears to Miaolian's eyes.

"My dad [died] during the Cultural Revolution because he was a capitalist, so I don't like to talk about it," she said. "He was attacked, because most of the landlords and capitalists were attacked during the Cultural Revolution, so my father got very scared, so he committed suicide."

Not long after Miaolian's father jumped from a building to his death, the schools all over China closed, and Miaolian was later sent off to toil in the countryside, along with millions of others with suspect backgrounds.

She stayed there for several years, and because she was a target as a capitalist, she felt the need to become an ardent young Communist, rising to party secretary of her local chapter of the Communist Youth League, asking to join the party that she blames for the death of her father and being rejected because of her capitalist roots. Later, as an adult, when she was working in a Guangzhou factory, she would be invited to join the party—a ticket to a better, privileged life—and she refused.

"I just wanted to do the right thing, and you don't have to be a party member to do the right thing," she said, tears again welling up in her eyes. "In China, if you wanted to have a good career and make lots of money, you had to join the Communist Party and become a party member."

America, Miaolian said, was different, was free and democratic. And in America, her daughter could get the best college education, she said, something the decade-long Cultural Revolution had denied her in China.

"During the Cultural Revolution, we didn't really go to school," Miaolian said. "So we wasted most of our youth."

'Don't Have Fun Here'

Yaming Luo and his family applied for visas to leave China in 1989, when his daughter was about 12 years old. Luo, now 57, wanted just what his relatives the Lis wanted—education, employment and wealth for his only child. But by the time the visas came 12 years later, it was too late for his daughter. She was too old to qualify for a visa. She would have to stay behind.

Her parents still came. In China, Yaming Luo was a supervisor with a transportation company, dispatching trucks on major highway construction projects. His wife, Janet Ji-Hong Li, was an accountant. In Maryland, they are restaurant workers. She makes salad and sushi at the Hunt Valley Japanese restaurant once owned by her sister Fenny Lay. He labors in its kitchen. They work 5 1/2 days a week.

Their lives haven't been broadened by the move from China, only narrowed.

They don't speak English. They have no plans to learn it. They're too old to bother, he says. Besides, behind the heavy swinging doors of the kitchen, they have no interaction with customers, so they don't have much chance to practice the little they know.

They live with Lay in her Lutherville home. They have a car, and sometimes they will venture on an off day into downtown Baltimore, to a Chinese restaurant where they can drink tea and sample some of the dishes. They don't meet people who aren't relatives or in their small circle.

"We just wanted to try out the American experience," Yaming Luo said through a translator. But, he said, "we don't really have fun here. . . . The biggest difficulty for us is we don't understand the language."

There is no real hub of the Chinese community in the Baltimore area.

Of the approximately 1 million Chinese legally living in the U.S. who were born in mainland China, 22,700 live in Maryland, according to census figures, including 3,500 in Baltimore County and under 1,700 in the city.

There was once a Chinatown in Baltimore, centered near Park Avenue and Mulberry Street, but that all but disappeared by the 1970s, as the suburbs opened to people of all races and ethnic backgrounds. Some churches and Chinese schools can be found, but life in the Baltimore area for a new Chinese immigrant can be an isolating experience.

Yaming Luo knows that. But he's here to stay anyway. He figured if he couldn't provide a life in the United States for his daughter, he could provide one for his grandchildren—though Luo had none yet when he left China. Now Luo waits for his U.S. citizenship, which would allow him to apply and wait more years yet to bring over his daughter, now 28, and his grandson, who was born last year.

Now Luo's hopes are not for the next generation but for a generation twice removed, that of this toddler who took his first steps in Guangzhou.

Returning to China

For the many Lis and Luos who make the difficult move to the United States for the next generation, there is a small but growing number of families choosing to return to China for opportunity now, for this generation.

Lu Lin, 40, and his wife Fang Yuxia, 38, recently left Baltimore County, trading a suburban existence, slower pace and quality public schools for the urban fast track and private schools of Beijing. Lu, an ambitious researcher of drug abuse, is among the elite of an already-elite class, the highly educated Chinese who in the past 20 years have come to the United States to study and advance their careers.

Arriving in the Baltimore area in 2001, he worked for the National Institutes of Health at its Johns Hopkins Bayview Medical Center offices and conducted research that led to a major paper in the field of drug abuse research.

If he had come to the U.S. five years earlier, anyone, including Lu himself, would have predicted he would stay in this country. There's more funding here and there are more labs for research than anywhere else in the world.

But Lu is also at the crest of another wave of elites, those who return to China from the United States. Contemplating the prospect of a junior faculty position at a top U.S. college—prestigious but lacking in the space and funding to do major research—he accepted a job as director of China's top drug abuse research institute, at the Harvard of China, Peking University.

Now Lu runs the institute in its six-story building, with a faculty of about 100. The university is constructing an entire floor of laboratory space for him, in addition to a smaller, 500-square-foot molecular biology lab above his office that on its own would be the envy of his former colleagues. "Only a big professor could have that" in the United States, he said.

Using a substantial research budget and his influence as the country's preeminent drug abuse researcher, Lu is supervising several studies, which could enable him to publish more papers in the next couple of years than he could have in the United States.

When he goes home, it is in a chauffeured car supplied by the university, to a spacious apartment (also provided by the university), where he might find his 10-year-old daughter, Siqi,

Table 1   Chinese Immigration

Foreign-born Chinese living legally* in the United States:

Year	Population
2000	988,857
1990	529,837
1980	286,120
1970	172,132

*An unknown number of undocumented Chinese also live in the U.S.
Source: U.S. Census Bureau.

studying Chinese after coming home from an international school (half the tuition paid by the university). "That's why so many people come back to China, to realize their dream," said Fang, Lu's wife. "Here they are a real master. China is their homeland."

But as the couple relax in their Beijing living room with their toddler son in front of the family's big-screen TV, and explain what feels good about being back in their native country, their daughter, Siqi, can't help eavesdropping from her room. She stops doing her homework to yell into the living room, "I feel worse."

"The environment is bad. There's too much dust. I have to clean every day. And there's too much homework," Siqi goes on, just warming up. "It's very noisy. And when you're tired, you can't sit on grass. No grass."

Her parents sigh, saying their daughter "doesn't know China."

The China of today bears no visible signs of the physical and psychic wreckage left 30 years ago, when the Cultural Revolution ended. An estimated 200 million people have risen out of poverty since then, cities of glass and steel have risen from fields and dust, and urban centers like Beijing and Shanghai have been torn down brick by brick and remade office tower by office tower.

China is indeed a land of opportunity, a place where almost every tangible indicator of progress seems to go up every year: the Gross Domestic Product, the average urban salary, the number of private businesses, the number of private cars on the road, the number of college graduates, the number of people using the Internet.

The countryside has lagged far behind—utterly neglected by more than a quarter-century of market-oriented policies that favor city dwellers and polluting businesses over farmers and the environment—but that does not change the fact that there are big opportunities in the big cities as never before.

Try explaining those nuances to a 10-year-old. Siqi, after several years in Baltimore County, doesn't feel at home amid the pollution and the culture in Beijing. Even the food seems alien. No mozzarella dippers, no veggie burgers and no pizza. "I hate Chinese food," she says.

Breathing Free

For all of China's recent advancements, some people would leave China and stay away not only to pursue a job or an education, and not just to escape the polluted air or the crowded cities. They leave for freedom.

The Zhangs of Ellicott City decided to leave Guangzhou, at the southern tip of China, after hearing only pieces of information about what happened at Tiananmen Square in Beijing on June 4, 1989. The official, government-sanctioned news said little about the events of that day. But there were purloined tidbits here and there, including from Voice of America, and what Daisy Zhang figured out changed the course of her life.

"I just had this impression—the world is not what they're telling you," she said.

So Zhang, at the time a 25-year-old college graduate working as a computer programmer at the Bank of China, bought a Peterson's college guide and sought out universities with graduate programs that accepted international students.

She ended up somewhere she had never heard of: Virginia Commonwealth University in Richmond. Before the fall semester of 1991, with two suitcases in hand, Zhang arrived there at midnight, starting classes toward her master's degree in biomedical engineering at 7 the next morning. Her newlywed husband was still in China.

She arrived having learned British English in school—a help, but not enough to prepare her for the speed at which Americans can speak. Add to that the Southern accents she encountered in Virginia, and it was a recipe for confusion and isolation. She didn't know any of the basics—how to apply for a Social Security number, how to open a bank account, how to get financial aid.

"My mom kept saying, 'If you don't like it for any reason, come back,'" Zhang said.

But Daisy Zhang, now 42, never turned back. Weary of the China she left behind, where the government can put unexpected obstacles in your way, Zhang believed that in America, if you worked hard, you would succeed. So she worked hard. She learned to keep up with her classes by taping the lectures and replaying them back in her room on her headphones.

And by mid-terms, her professors noticed her academic prowess. They got her a waiver for the $11,000-a-year tuition and found her a part-time job as a research assistant to pay for living expenses. Her husband gave up his job in China, as chief medical examiner in Guangzhou, to join her and start over again with the same diligence.

Life wasn't bad in China, but there wasn't freedom—the freedom to speak your mind, to own your home, to have as many children as you want. No matter how much things have improved in China, it remains a Communist country at its core, and that, to Jie Zhang, means something short of the self-determination he found in the United States, something short of being able to build a deck on your house with simply a permit and a bunch of supplies from Home Depot.

"As long as you work, you can get what you deserve," he said.

The Zhangs ended up in the Baltimore area with good jobs, he working in biostatistics at Johns Hopkins University, she as a senior software engineer in Columbia. They bought a two-story house in Ellicott City in 1998, and in 2002 they became U.S. citizens. Now they have three children, who know only a life of abundant plastic toys and bicycle rides and the consumer society into which they were born.

"I already tell my kids: 'You are lucky,'" said Jie Zhang, 43. "'Don't compare yourself to your generation. Compare to Mommy and Daddy's generation.'"

American Girl

Kelly Li embodies the new generation in every way, a fresh start without the burden of past hardship.

It was difficult at first in Maryland. Kelly's English was so poor when she arrived that she was placed in ninth grade, though she was just months from high school graduation in China.

But now she is armed with a chemical engineering degree from the University of Maryland, College Park, and a job at Exxon Mobil, where she started in Fairfax, Va., in July.

She hangs out with friends, likes to travel, keeps up on her e-mail and doesn't spend much time assessing how she came to be here. She has little to say about Tiananmen or the Cultural Revolution. Her least favorite subject in school was history.

She is not a political creature. She is Kelly Li, born Li Jiayan 23 years ago in Guangzhou, China, celebrating her graduation in the suburbs, working at the most profitable company in the world, and her parents couldn't be prouder.

She is not quite yet a citizen, but in every other sense, she's an American.

Asian/Pacific American Heritage Month and Revenues for Asian-Owned Firms Up 24 Percent

Asian/Pacific American Heritage Month: May 2008

In 1978, a joint congressional resolution established Asian/Pacific American Heritage Week. The first 10 days of May were chosen to coincide with two important milestones in Asian/Pacific American history: the arrival in the United States of the first Japanese immigrants (May 7, 1843) and contributions of Chinese workers to the building of the transcontinental railroad, completed on May 10, 1869. In 1992, Congress expanded the observance to a monthlong celebration. Per a 1997 Office of Management and Budget directive, the Asian or Pacific Islander racial category was separated into two categories: Asian and Native Hawaiian and Other Pacific Islander. Thus, this Facts for Features contains a section for each.

Asians

14.9 million
The estimated number of U.S. residents in July 2006 who said they were Asian alone or Asian in combination with one or more other races. This group comprised about 5 percent of the total population.[1]

5 million
The Asian population in California, the state that had the largest Asian population (either alone or in combination with one or more other races) on July 1, 2006, as well as the largest numerical increase from 2005 to 2006 (114,000). New York (1.4 million) and Texas (882,000) followed in population. Texas (43,000) and New York (34,000) followed in numerical increase. In Hawaii, Asians made up the highest proportion of the total population (56 percent), with California (14 percent) and New Jersey and Washington (8 percent each) next.[2]

3.2%
Percentage growth of the Asian population (either alone or in combination with one or more other races) between 2005 and 2006, the highest of any race group during that time period. The increase in the Asian population during the period totaled 460,000.[3]

3.6 million
Number of Asians of Chinese descent in the U.S. Chinese-Americans are the largest Asian group, followed by Filipinos (2.9 million), Asian Indians (2.7 million), Vietnamese (1.6 million), Koreans (1.5 million) and Japanese (1.2 million). These estimates represent the number of people who are either of a particular Asian group only or are of that group in combination with one or more other Asian groups or races.[4]

Education

49%
The percentage of single-race Asians 25 and older who have a bachelor's degree or higher level of education. This compares with 27 percent for all Americans 25 and older.[5]

86%
The percentage of single-race Asians 25 and older who have at least a high school diploma. This compares with 84 percent for all Americans 25 and older.[6]

20%
The percentage of single-race Asians 25 and older who have a graduate (e.g., master's or doctorate) or professional degree. This compares with 10 percent for all Americans 25 and older.[7]

The Asian population comprises many groups who differ in languages spoken and culture, which is reflected in the demographic characteristics of these groups. For instance, 69 percent of Asian Indians 25 and older had a bachelor's degree or more education, and 36 percent had a graduate or professional degree. The corresponding numbers for Vietnamese-Americans were 26 percent and 7 percent, respectively. (These figures represent the single-race population. The percentage of Vietnamese-Americans who had a bachelor's degree or higher was not significantly different from 27 percent, the percentage for all Americans.)[8]

Income, Poverty and Health Insurance

$64,238

Median household income for single-race Asians in 2006, the highest among all race groups.[9]

Median household income differed greatly by Asian group. For Asian Indians, for example, the median income in 2006 was $78,315; for Vietnamese-Americans, it was $52,299. (These figures represent the single-race population.)[10]

10.3%

Poverty rate for single-race Asians in 2006, statistically unchanged from 2005.[11]

15.5%

Percentage of single-race Asians without health insurance coverage in 2006, down from 17.2 percent in 2005.[12]

Businesses

Source for the statements referenced in this section, unless otherwise indicated: Asian-Owned Firms: 2002.

1.1 million

Number of businesses owned by Asian-Americans in 2002, up 24 percent from 1997. The rate of increase in the number of Asian-owned businesses was about twice that of the national average for all businesses.

More than $326 billion

Receipts of Asian-American-owned businesses in 2002, up 8 percent from 1997. An estimated 319,468 Asian-owned businesses had paid employees, and their receipts totaled more than $291 billion. There were 49,636 Asian-owned firms with receipts of $1 million or more, accounting for 4.5 percent of the total number of Asian-owned firms and nearly 68 percent of their total receipts.

In 2002, more than three in 10 Asian-owned firms operated in professional, scientific and technical services, as well as other services, such as personal services, and repair and maintenance.

2.2 million

Number of people employed by an Asian-owned business. There were 1,866 Asian-owned firms with 100 or more employees, generating nearly $52 billion in gross receipts (18 percent of the total revenue for Asian-owned employer firms).

46%

Percentage of all Asian-owned firms that was either Chinese owned or Asian Indian owned.

Nearly 6 in 10

Proportion of all Asian-owned firms in the United States in California, New York, Texas and New Jersey.

112,441

The number of Asian-owned firms in New York, which led all cities. Los Angeles (47,764), Honolulu (22,348) and San Francisco (19,639) followed.

28%

Proportion of Asian-owned businesses that responded to the 2002 Survey of Business Owners that they were home based. This is the lowest proportion among minority respondent groups.[13]

Languages

2.5 million

The number of people 5 and older who speak Chinese at home. After Spanish, Chinese is the most widely spoken non-English language in the country. Tagalog, Vietnamese and Korean are each spoken at home by more than 1 million people.[14]

Serving Our Nation

292,100

The number of single-race Asian military veterans. About one in three was 65 and older.[15]

Jobs

47%

The proportion of civilian employed single-race Asians 16 and older who work in management, professional and related occupations, such as financial managers, engineers, teachers and registered nurses. Additionally, 23 percent work in sales and office occupations, 16 percent in service occupations and 10 percent in production, transportation and material moving occupations.[16]

Counties

1.4 million

The number of Asians (alone or in combination with one or more other races) in Los Angeles County, Calif., in 2006, which tops the nation's counties. Santa Clara County, Calif. (home of San Jose) was the runner-up (556,000).[17]

17,600

Santa Clara County's Asian population increase from 2005 to 2006, the largest in the nation. Los Angeles (15,700) followed.[18]

59%

Percent of the population of Honolulu County, Hawaii, that was Asian in 2006, which led the country. One other county— Kauai, Hawaii—was also majority Asian. San Francisco County, Calif., led the continental United States, with 34 percent of its population Asian.[19]

Age Distribution

35.2

Median age, of the single-race Asian population in 2006. The corresponding figure is 36.4 years for the population as a whole.[20]

The Future

33.4 million

The projected number of U.S. residents in 2050 who will identify themselves as single-race Asians. They would comprise 8 percent of the total population by that year.[21]

213%

The projected percentage increase between 2000 and 2050 in the population of people who identify themselves as single-race Asian. This compares with a 49 percent increase in the population as a whole over the same period of time.[22]

Native Hawaiians and Other Pacific Islanders

1 million

The estimated number of U.S. residents in July 2006 who said they are Native Hawaiian and Other Pacific Islander, either alone or in combination with one or more other races. This group comprised 0.3 percent of the total population.[23]

Hawaii had the largest population (275,000) in 2006 of Native Hawaiians and Other Pacific Islanders (either alone or in combination with one or more other races), followed by California (260,000) and Washington (49,000). California had the largest numerical increase (3,400) of people of this group, with Texas (2,000) and Florida (1,500) next. In Hawaii, Native Hawaiians and Other Pacific Islanders comprised the largest proportion (21 percent) of the total population, followed by Utah (1 percent) and Alaska (0.9 percent).[24]

1.7%

Percentage growth of the Native Hawaiian and Other Pacific Islander population (either alone or in combination with one or more other races) between 2005 and 2006, the highest of any race group except for Asians.[25]

Education

14%

The percentage of single-race Native Hawaiians and Other Pacific Islanders 25 and older who have at least a bachelor's degree. This compares with 27 percent for the total population.[26]

84%

The percentage of single-race Native Hawaiians and Other Pacific Islanders 25 and older who have at least a high school diploma. This matches the corresponding percentage for the total population.[27]

4%

The percentage of single-race Native Hawaiians and Other Pacific Islanders 25 and older who have obtained a graduate or professional degree. This compares with 10 percent for the total population this age.[28]

Income, Poverty and Health Insurance

$49,361

The median income of households headed by single-race Native Hawaiian and Other Pacific Islander but did not report any other race.[29]

11.4%

The three-year average (2004–2006) poverty rate for those who reported their race as Native Hawaiian and Other Pacific Islanders.[30]

21.7%

The three-year average (2004–2006) percentage without health insurance single-race Native Hawaiian and Other Pacific Islanders.[31]

Businesses[32]

28,948

Number of Native Hawaiian- and Other Pacific Islander-owned businesses in 2002, up 49 percent from 1997. The rate of growth was more than three times the national average. The 3,693 Native Hawaiian-and Other Pacific Islander-owned businesses with a payroll employed more than 29,000 and generated revenues of $3.5 billion.

2,415

Number of Native Hawaiian- and Other Pacific Islander-owned firms in Honolulu, the most of any city in the nation.

$4.3 billion

Receipts for Native Hawaiian- and Other Pacific Islander-owned businesses in 2002, up 3 percent from 1997. There were 727 Native Hawaiian- and Other Pacific Islander-owned firms with receipts of $1 million or more. These firms accounted for 2.5 percent of the total number of Native Hawaiian- and Other Pacific Islander-owned firms and 66.8 percent of their total receipts.

In 2002, nearly 21,000 Native Hawaiian- and Other Pacific Islander-owned firms operated in health care and social assistance; other services (such as personal services, and repair and maintenance); retail trade; administrative and support, and waste management and remediation services; professional, scientific and technical services; and construction.

28

Number of Native Hawaiian- and Other Pacific Islander-owned firms with 100 or more employees. These firms generated $698 million in gross receipts—19.9 percent of the total revenue for Native Hawaiian- and Other Pacific Islander-owned employer firms.

53%

Percentage of all Native Hawaiian- and Other Pacific Islander-owned firms in Hawaii and California. These two states accounted for 62 percent of business revenue.

Serving Our Nation

27,700

The number of single-race Native Hawaiian and Other Pacific Islander military veterans. About one in six was 65 and older.[33]

Jobs

20%

The proportion of civilian employed single-race Native Hawaiians and Other Pacific Islanders 16 and older who work in management, professional and related occupations, such as financial managers, engineers, teachers and registered nurses. Meanwhile, 28 percent work in sales and office occupations, 23 percent in service occupations and 16 percent in production, transportation and material moving occupations.[34]

Counties

177,000

Native Hawaiian and Other Pacific Islander population (alone or in combination with one or more other races) in Honolulu County, Hawaii, in 2006, which led the nation. Los Angeles County, Calif., (59,000) was second. Hawaii County, Hawaii, and Clark County, Nev. (home of Las Vegas) had the largest numerical increases in this race since July 2005, around 900. Hawaii County had the highest percentage of people of this race: 29 percent.[35]

Age Distribution

29.9

The median age of the single-race Native Hawaiian and Other Pacific Islander population in 2006. The median age was 36.4 for the population as a whole.[36]

Editor's note—The preceding data were collected from a variety of sources and may be subject to sampling variability and other sources of error. *Facts for Features* are customarily released about two months before an observance in order to accommodate magazine production timelines. Questions or comments should be directed to the Census Bureau's Public Information Office: telephone: 301-763-3030; fax: 301-763-3762; or e-mail: pio@census.gov.

Revenues for Asian-Owned Firms Surpass $326 Billion; Number of Businesses Up 24 Percent

The number of Asian-owned businesses grew 24 percent between 1997 and 2002, approximately twice the national average for all businesses. The 1.1 million businesses generated more than $326 billion in revenues, up 8 percent from 1997. This is according to a new report, Survey of Business Owners: Asian-Owned Firms: 2002 [PDF], released today by the U.S. Census Bureau.

"The robust revenues of Asian-owned firms and the growth in the number of businesses provide yet another indicator that minority entrepreneurs are at the forefront as engines for growth in our economy," said Census Bureau Director Louis Kincannon.

Nearly half (47 percent) of all Asian-owned firms were Chinese-owned (290,197) and Asian Indian-owned (231,179). Korean-owned firms were the third largest at 158,031, followed by Vietnamese- (147,081), Filipino- (128,223) and Japanese-owned firms (86,863).

Almost 1-in-3 of all Asian-owned firms had paid employees. These 319,300 businesses employed more than 2.2 million people and generated revenues of nearly $291 billion.

Other highlights:

- In 2002, slightly more than 3-in-10 Asian-owned firms operated in professional, scientific and technical services, as well as other services such as personal services, and repair and maintenance. These firms accounted for 6 percent of all such businesses in the United States.
- Wholesale and retail trade accounted for 47 percent of all Asian-owned business revenue.
- There were 49,578 Asian-owned firms with receipts of $1 million or more. These firms accounted for 4.5 percent of the total number of Asian-owned firms and nearly 68 percent of their total receipts.
- There were 1,863 Asian-owned firms with 100 employees or more, generating nearly $52 billion in gross receipts (18 percent of the total revenue for Asian-owned employer firms).
- California and New York accounted for 59 percent (170,547) of all Chinese-owned firms, 37 percent (86,494) of all Asian Indian-owned firms and 46 percent (73,466) of all Korean-owned firms.
- California and Texas accounted for 51 percent (74,634) of all Vietnamese-owned firms.
- California and Hawaii accounted for 54 percent (69,061) of all Filipino-owned firms and 65 percent (56,490) of all Japanese-owned firms.

States with the Largest Number of Asian-Owned Firms: 2002

State	Firms (number)	Percent of Total	Receipts (Billion Dollars)	Percent of Total
California	371,415	33.6	125.6	38.5
New York	145,519	13.2	30.4	9.3
Texas	77,980	7.1	20.6	6.3
New Jersey	51,948	4.7	18.5	5.7
Hawaii	44,969	4.1	12.6	3.9
Illinois	44,480	4.0	14.6	4.5
Florida	41,278	3.7	11.2	3.4

Counties with the Largest Number of Asian-Owned Firms: 2002

County	Firms (Number)	Receipts (Billion Dollars)
Los Angeles County, Calif.	140,411	52.5
Queens County, N. Y.	48,241	5.5
Orange County, Calif.	46,015	11.3
Honolulu County, Hawaii	35,376	9.8

Cities with the Largest Number of Asian-Owned Firms: 2002

City	Firms (number)	Receipts (billion dollars)
New York, N. Y.	112,853	22.0
Los Angeles, Calif.	47,714	19.5
Honolulu, Hawaii	22,394	7.1
San Francisco, Calif.	19,639	5.4
San Jose, Calif.	16,233	6.1
Houston, Texas	15,966	5.5

Asian Ownership of Firms by Detailed Group: 2002

Group	Firms (Number)	Percent of Total	Receipts (Billions of Dollars)	Percent of Total
Asian-owned firms	1,104,189	(X)	326.4	(X)
Chinese	290,197	26.3	106.3	32.6
Asian Indian	231,179	20.9	89.0	27.3
Korean	158,031	14.3	46.9	14.4
Vietnamese	147,081	13.3	15.7	4.8
Filipino	128,223	11.6	14.6	4.5
Japanese	86,863	7.9	30.6	9.4
Other Asian	71,439	6.5	20.3	6.2

- Forty-nine percent (35,224) of all other Asian-owned firms were located in California, New York and Texas.
- Los Angeles County, by far, had the largest number of Asian-owned firms in 2002 with 140,411 or 13 percent of all Asian businesses. These businesses generated $52.5 billion in receipts. Queens County, N. Y., was second (48,241), followed by Orange County, Calif., (46,015) and Honolulu County, Hawaii (35,376).
- For cities, New York led the nation with 112,853 Asian-owned businesses with revenues of $22 billion. Los Angeles was second, with less than half as many firms at 47,714, followed by Honolulu (22,394), San Francisco (19,639), San Jose, Calif., (16,233) and Houston (15,966).

The 2002 Survey of Business Owners (SBO) defines Asian-owned businesses as firms in which Asians own 51 percent or more of the stock or equity of the business. Separate reports on additional minority-owned firms, including a new report on businesses owned by native Hawaiians and other Pacific islanders (previously included in the report on Asians), will be issued over the next two months.

The SBO is part of the 2002 Economic Census and combines survey data from a sample of more than 2.4 million businesses with administrative data.

Data for 2002 are not directly comparable to previous survey years because of several significant changes to the survey methodology. See "Comparability of 2002 and 1997 SBO Data" at http://www.census.gov/econ/census02/text/sbo/sbomethodology.htm#comparability.

The data collected in a sample survey are subject to sampling variability as well as nonsampling errors. Sources of nonsampling errors include errors of response, nonreporting and coverage.

Notes

1. Source: Population estimates.
2. Source: Population estimates.
3. Source: Population estimates.
4. Source: 2006 American Community Survey.
5. Source: 2006 American Community Survey.
6. Source: 2006 American Community Survey.
7. Source: 2006 American Community Survey.
8. Source: 2006 American Community Survey
9. Source: Income, Poverty, and Health Insurance Coverage in the United States: 2006.
10. Source: 2006 American Community Survey.
11. Source: Income, Poverty, and Health Insurance Coverage in the United States: 2006.
12. Source: Income, Poverty, and Health Insurance Coverage in the United States: 2006.
13. Source: Characteristics of Businesses: 2002.
14. Source: 2006 American Community Survey.
15. Source: 2006 American Community Survey.
16. Source: 2006 American Community Survey.
17. Source: Population estimates.
18. Source: Population estimates.
19. Source: Population estimates.
20. Source: 2006 American Community Survey.
21. Source: Population projections.
22. Source: Population projections.
23. Source: Population estimates.
24. Source: Population estimates.
25. Source: Population estimates.
26. Source: 2006 American Community Survey.
27. Source: 2006 American Community Survey.
28. Source: 2006 American Community Survey.
29. Source: 2006 American Community Survey.
30. Source: Income, Poverty, and Health Insurance Coverage in the United States: 2006 unpublished.
31. Source: Income, Poverty, and Health Insurance Coverage in the United States: 2006.
32. Source for the statements referenced in this section: Native Hawaiian- and Other Pacific Islander-Owned Firms: 2002..
33. Source: 2006 American Community Survey.
34. Source: 2006 American Community Survey.
35. Source: Population estimates.
36. Source: 2006 American Community Survey.

Editor's Note—The report can be accessed at http://www.census.gov/prod/ec02/sb0200csasian.pdf.

From *U.S. Census Bureau*, 2008.

UNIT 8

European and Mediterranean Ethnics

Unit Selections

Key Points to Consider

- The era of ethnic data collection began with the 1980 Census. A considerable shift toward self-identification began, which allowed persons to claim specific and/or multiple categories. Does the earlier scheme of designating groups have any scientific or political merit? Does personal identification trump all other considerations? How does ethnicity of an earlier era suggest the tension between worlds of meaning discussed in this section?

- What lessons can be learned from the experiences of eastern and southern Europeans?

- Discuss the ways ethnic groups are portrayed in films. What are the limits of ethnic comedy?

- Are you surprised by the variety, diversity, and intensity of opinions and positions on public policy found within and among various ethnic populations?

Student Web Site

www.mhcls.com

Internet References

Africa News Online
http://www.africanews.org
Cultural Survival
http://www.culturalsurvival.org
The North-South Institute
http://www.nsi-ins.ca/ensi/index.html
Order Sons of Italy in America
http://www.osia.org
The National Italian American Foundation
http://www.niaf.org
The Chicago Jewish News Online
http://www.chicagojewishnews.org
Polish American Congress
http://www.polamcon.org
Polish American Journal
http://www.polamjournal.com

In a very provocative book by Michael Novak, *The Rise of the Unmeltable Ethnics,* written at the very beginning of the 1970s, he makes the following observation: The eyes of others, Hegel noted, are mirrors in which we learn our own identity. The first eyes into which the immigrants from southern and eastern Europe looked were Nordic eyes, the eyes of old Americans or nativists. Two forms of prejudice stamped the immigrants. Both had a peculiar northern quality: one was racial and the other progressive. According to one view, it was his race and religion that made the southern European inferior. According to the other, it was his social and political backwardness. Though acknowledgment of ethnicity and cultural pluralism emerged as an intellectual and cultural force in the mid 1960s, its origins were formed even before the period of massive Mediterranean and Eastern European immigration to America.

The American experience from 1870 to 1924 addressed the influence of these groups, and in so doing, shifted American consciousness of itself. Even one hundred years later, America's public mind continues to identify and divide

its history as an immigrant-receiving country into two periods: The Old Immigration, meaning Northern Europeans and the New Immigration, meaning Others—The Mediterranean and Eastern European as well as Asian and Hispanic populations. One marker of this division can be found in the Report of The Dillingham Commission (1910), a Congressional and Presidential Blue Ribbon panel, which warned America that the Eastern European and Mediterranean character was less capable of Americanization than the Nordic and Tuetonic groups that had peopled America, and that these new immigrants had inborn, and socially inadequate qualities and undemocratic habits that could not be remedied by public education. The closing of immigration was required to protect the gene pool of the "Great American Race" from decline. But the popular and public mind of America was also concerned about imported religious traditions that varied from America's Protestant Christianity and enlightenment Deism. Fear and dread of Jews, Catholics, Muslims, and Orthodox Christians and their pre-reformation faiths evidences what Lydio Tomasi, a historian of immigrant religiosity, argues was a widely held 19th century pattern of the American public mind. A view he found critically expressed in 1855 by Abraham Lincoln in a letter to Joshua Speed: "As a nation, we began by declaring that 'all men are created equal'! We now practically read it. . . . All men created equal except Negroes, and foreigners and Catholics." Thus, Mediterranean and Eastern European immigrants and their religious traditions entered an industrializing economy, which required their labor much like plantation production in an earlier period of economy development required the indentured and the slave, but they also meet a cultural and political climate of potent challenges to and denials of their integrity and existence. As John Higham saw it, these "strangers in the land" discovered that the American public mind included both traditionalist and progressives, and that both were proponents of anti-Catholicism, anti-semitism, anti-urbanism, and anti-unionism. These ideological forces and popular passions grew, as did membership in the KKK and other nativist associations that lobbied vigorously and rallied ceaselessly in the streets against Negroes, Catholics, Irish, and the immigration policy. They lead the political struggle to amend the U.S. Constitution to prohibit the sale of alcohol and even contributed to limiting electoral participation of immigrants by manipulating electoral districts in municipalities and the states, as well as the size of the U.S. House of Representatives. Disregarding the 1920 Census by not reapportioning the number of Presidential Electors until 1932 is an enduring feature of this Post-Civil-War regime.

More than four decades later, Moynihan and Glazer's *Beyond The Melting Pot* (1964), The Report of the Kerner Commission, and findings of the National Center for Urban Ethnic Affairs confirmed that ethnicity was a salient factor and that the descendants of Mediterranean and Eastern European immigrants—even into the fourth generation—were just barely moving toward the middle class and that they were absent in the professions, rarely admitted to prestigious universities or colleges, and more specifically, Italians and Poles, notwithstanding the absences of affirmative action and legal recourse, were no less likely than Blacks and Hispanics/Latinos to be excluded from executive suites and boardrooms of America's largest corporations, regulated public bodies, and philanthropies. The emergence of interest in retracing the pathways of these immigrant groups and assessing their participation in inter-group relations in America are topics of many scholarly disciplines, and such findings are appearing in popular venues. The inclusion of the following articles presents but a peek behind the curtain of this neglected dimension of race and ethnic relations in America. Apropos of the selection of articles and our attempt to understand and direct current attention to this persistent cluster of ethnic Americans (the descendants of Mediterranean and Eastern European groups, which have been ignored and neglected, mislabeled white-ethnics and/or Euro-ethnics) is Noel Ignatiev's provocative book, *How The Irish Became White*. The Irish immigrants, though not part of a Mediterranean nor an Eastern European American ethnic group, had a parallel and a not dissimilar experience in America of being different from and perceived as racially apart from the American regime owing to their conquered status in the British Empire.

Because of the considerable fluidity of the immigrant experiences as well as the complex processes of cultural identity and political use of cultural symbols such as race and ethnicity, the search for more analytical rigor in this field is far from complete. Ethnicity for these groups is a modern American identity, which has blended localism and inherited symbols into a method of negotiating its existence between pluralistic and porous boundaries of institutions that constitute contemporary civil society.

The contributions and concerns of various ethnic immigrant groups over many generations provided a deep weave and pattern to the material and social history of America. Today we see a consciousness of ethnic tradition and the practice of multiethnic food preferences, exasperation and anger about stereotypes, and efforts to institutionalize attention to groups. Change and ethnicity are not contradictory, for each generation creates anew its ethnicity, which, alongside other affinities, affiliations, and loyalties constitutes the fabric of civil society. Present concerns of these ethnic groups include language preservation, fair hearings for homeland interests, enclave neighborhoods, inclusion in ethnic studies, and the rearticulation of historical American expressions of fairness, justice, and equity and the collection of accurate information and data among all ethnic groups in America. Perhaps the most obvious characterization of these ancestry-conscious persons and groups is their oscillation between self-celebration of achievements and anguished concern about their marginality. Their uncertain relationships with their ancestral homelands and their long-standing love affair with America and its promise of liberty and justice for all is inspired by their inheritance of this legacy from energetic, risk-taking, forbearers who left Europe in search of the American Dream—to own land and houses in a better economy, freer polity, and less status-bound culture. These values are thoroughly patterned into their worldview and their appropriation of the expansive promise of the American icon—The Statue of Liberty. After all, it was this icon of the American promise that resonated in their hearts and mind in 1965, when a bipartisan, northern coalition of Mediterranean and Eastern Americans in support of the immigration reform proposed by President Kennedy that ended the quota system, as well as in support of the 1965 Voting Rights Act that assured fair elections for the disenfranchised, especially Blacks in the South.

After the assassination of President Kennedy, this legislative coalition could only have been forged by Lyndon Johnson. It accomplished through deliberative democracy, not the mandate of the Supreme Court or ukase of administrative regulation, a fundamental change that significantly altered the terms of race and ethnic relations, and renegotiated the bonds of political union in a form of inclusive pluralism that echoed the deepest hopes of the American promise of liberty and justice for all without regard to race, religion or nationality. Some anticipated consequences of such legislation were foreseen by President Johnson, who is quoted by Bill Moyers as recognizing that though the Voters Rights Act was the right thing to do; it would probably cost the Democratic Party to lose the South for a generation. In fact in 1968, Republican electoral entrepreneurs seized this opportunity to reintroduce the long-entrenched tradition of racial divisiveness and wedge issues in American discourse. The George Wallace candidacy and Richard Nixon's Southern strategy, and the politics of massive resistance and direct action significantly heightened race and ethnic relations. Nixon's managerial fiat, OMB Directive 15, established five categories of governmental data collection and civil rights enforcement: American Indian or Alaskan Native, Asian or Pacific Islanders, Black, Hispanic, and White. This policy divisively fragmented the civil rights coalition into designated and privileged categories. Thirty years later this crucial moment, the full impact of this development is yet to be sufficiently clarified, this manifests itself in the waning discussion of affirmative action. Owing in part to the international politics and the eclipse of attention to domestic social policy, ethnic and ideological claims regarding foreign policy and salient ethnic features appear throughout the political horizons from Greece and Turkey to the Middle East, Middle Europe, and Asia, and to Ireland and the UK; it also appear in anti-apartheid and the Islamic dimensions of nation-building strategies. The massive migration of peoples during this thirty-year period, which included significantly large Mediterranean and Eastern European populations, has reengaged the immigrant factor in American politics and the ethnic factor among all Americans. This is patently clear to all analysts of human order. The search for understanding as well as managing such conflicts and fashioning remedies for ethnic and race passions have become the ongoing issues. Thus either through hope or fear, the ongoing use of such categories and symbols of personal and group identification has become a hallmark of domestic and international orders. Ethnicity is not a form of diminished existence for Mediterranean and Eastern European ethnics. It is one of the many ways of being themselves and an American; they are "Americans Plus"—Americans with a multicultural affinity and competencies in more than one culture.

The emergence of interest in retracing the pathways of these immigrant groups and assessing their participation in inter-group relations in America are topics of many scholarly disciplines. The inclusion of the following articles is but a peek behind the curtain of this neglected dimension of race and ethnic relations in America.

The massive migration of peoples during the past 40 years, which has included significantly large Mediterranean and

eastern European populations, has reengaged the immigrant factor in American politics and the ethnic factor among all Americans. Should ethnic populations be denied their distinctiveness through absorption into society, or can their distinctiveness accompany them into mainstream modern American identities? This is the pivotal issue of American pluralism.

Not surprisingly, most Americans, but especially the children and grandchildren of immigrants, in the process of becoming more conscious of the limiting effects of race in America, began to discover their ethnicity and became increasingly knowledgeable of the roots of their ethnic identities and curious about the group and personal identity that are interwoven in the construction of a pluralistic society. This new perspective on personal and group identity was fashioned from necessity and cultivated within a fresh moral imagination, which was grounded in the recognition that human rights included the various culture and civilizations articulated throughout the world, which were transplanted and then rearticulated in the social process that transformed American from its origin within the orbit of Anglo-conformity into the reluctant cosmopolitan it has become today. Immigration and the new demography of America are defining characteristics, and stunning facts of racial and ethnic realities.

The accelerated search for explanations of diversity among and within societies falsify the claims, and forecasts that sustained perspectives and social practices about society and its universal determinants derived from the Enlightenment and its sense of common humanity. Unlike these structural causes and determinants, current social practice appears to be motivated by a new horizon and aspiration.

The enormity of the educational effort that is required as we attempt to move beyond the ethnocentrism and racism that bred hatred and destructive relationships between persons and communities is revealed in a number of ways. Philosophic and theological reflection on the foundations of anthropological and epistemological issues, associated with explaining human variety, and the characteristics of human consciousness is important in this time of national and world crisis. It is precisely at this intersection of social philosophy and science, and its grappling with evil uses of power that the crucial breakthroughs in understanding are likely to appear.

Miracle

American Polonia, Karol Wojtyła and the Election of Pope John Paul II

JOHN RADZIŁOWSKI

Creating lists of the greatest events of the past is usually viewed as a somewhat facile exercise. For all that, however, "great events" are a common way of periodizing and organizing history, certainly for the general audience, but also for most scholars, whether they admit it or not. In considering the 150-year history of American Polonia, however, few great events are apparent. Polonia's historians have rarely thought of their subject in such terms. However, one candidate for the greatest single event to have affected Polonia was the election of Karol Cardinal Wojtyła of Kraków as Pope John Paul II in October 1978.

This event has heretofore not been covered by Polonia scholars. It was a very recent event, occurring within our own lifetime. The literature on John Paul II's pontificate in English, not to mention his impact in the United States, is large, but curiously there is almost no attempt to understand his impact on American Polonia.[1] This article is an early, tentative effort to survey the impact of Karol Cardinal Wojtyła on American Polonia in the 1970s and after his elevation as pontiff, the impact of the first years of his pontificate on Polish Americans.

Although the "ethnic revival" of the 1970s helped to spark new interest in things Polish, the 1970s were not an easy time for Polish Americans. The problems of urban neighborhoods worsened, further harming many traditional Polonia communities, eroding their geographic centers, and dispersing their members to suburbs where ethnic culture was strongly discouraged. A yet greater problem emerged from the American media and popular culture. With racist jokes directed at African Americans becoming increasingly unacceptable in polite discourse, Polish Americans provided a ready target for attack.[2] From the mid to late 1970s onward, Polonia faced growing anti-Polish sentiment from the media, the entertainment industry, and some quarters of academe. Polonia's organizations themselves faced serious problems in the form of a gradually declining and aging membership. In the larger world, despite some liberalizing trends, the Polish homeland remained under Soviet domination, behind an Iron Curtain that from the outside looked as eternal as the Great Wall of China. These depressing factors did not bode well for Polonia and, as in times past, some predicted its imminent demise, all of which made the events of October 16, 1978 all the more improbable, unexpected, and even providential.

On September 28, 1978, after a short pontificate, Pope John Paul I died in Rome. Eighteen days later, the College of Cardinals elected the first non-Italian Pope in over 400 years: Karol Cardinal Wojtyła of Kraków.

As the word spread to an incredulous world, reaction in major Polonia centers like Chicago was immediate as an account from the *Chicago Tribune* shows:

Just down the street . . . the women of [the] Polish Roman Catholic Union were working when one of them put down the phone and began to shout.

"We have a Polish Pope. My God. We have a Polish Pope!" And all the women began to cry.

"We cried," one says, "because of what it means for all of us. It has taken so long. One thousand years [the] Polish have been faithful Catholics and now one of our sons has been chosen for the highest honor in the world. We all had the feeling that nothing will ever be the same again for Poland."[3]

Reaction in other Polish-American communities was equally strong. "The election of a Polish Pope is a miracle," said Cleveland activist Ben Stefanski. Richard Jablonski, President of the Union of Poles in America, stated that the news was "so staggering it baffles the mind."[4]

For many Polish Americans the moment would live forever in their memories. Rev. Anthony Iwuc was in Poland with other priests on a bus tour when he heard the news: "I ran to the bus and with goose pimples all over my body, I joyfully shouted 'Cardinal Wojtyła is our new Pope.' Everyone aboard burst into tears, cheers, and song."[5] "I was speechless," wrote *Naród Polski* columnist Sabina Logisz, who had even described Cardinal Wojtyła as a possible papal candidate in 1976. "My first reaction was one of genuine sorrow that my deeply religious mother at whose knee I learned my first prayers—in Polish—and, who frequently reminded me of Grandpa Józef Roszkowski's exemplary Catholicism and patriotism—how he even died on Polish Constitution Day—was not here to share . . . this moment. Then stupor enveloped me and so I remained."[6]

John Paul II's election was one of the few times reporters from the mainstream media in the United States paid attention to

Polish-Americans. Requests for interviews from print and electronic media poured into Polish organizations and institutions, especially the Polish center at Orchard Lake. Polish-American community leaders joined National Security Advisor Zbigniew Brzeziñski and Sen. Edmund Muskie in the official White House delegation to the papal installation.[7] A large number of ordinary Polish Americans—perhaps 4,000 or more—also made a special journey to Rome for this event.[8] For once, Polish-Americans were pleased with the press coverage they received.[9] The reaction of Polonia's own press was jubilant.[10] One exception to this were the publications of the Polish National Catholic Church, which, while pleased, gave the story little coverage.[11]

Polish-American reactions took two forms. One was a desire to reconnect with both the Catholic and Polish wellsprings of ethnic identity. A letter from a reader, published in journal *Perspectives,* stated "I have never placed much weight upon my origin, taking my Polishness for granted. Yesterday, when in tears, on my knees before my TV set . . . accepting Pope John Paul II's blessing . . . I realized how deeply rooted in me is my Polish nationality."[12]

Many of those interviewed predicted a new era for Polish Americans and especially an end to the hateful anti-Polish "jokes" that were prevalent.

"The Poles have been downtrodden, treated like dogs, but that's over now, I'll tell ya," says feisty Marie Bykowski. . . . "He is going to be good for us, too. Maybe now people will walk a little taller. . . . Maybe they won't be so quick to change their names so they can get a good executive job. Maybe some won't try to hide that they are Polish."

The women behind her serving rolls and pouring hot coffee into big metal pitchers, nodded in agreement.

"That's right," one said, "maybe now they'll stop all those darn jokes."

"They'll stop," another one said. . . . "It's end of the Polish jokes now."

"The Polish," said Geri Kowalski, stopping. "They came here. They worked hard, stayed quiet, minded their own business. They built their own churches, they bought their little houses, they educated their kids.

"But they were put down. They never got the respect they deserved. That won't happen now. . . . We won't be laughed at anymore."

"It means so much to the older people," says Marie, who is 70 and doesn't look it. "It puts a tear in your eyes. For it's like a final reward for us."[13]

Msgr. Stanisław Grabowski was quoted in *Gwiazda Polarna* saying "now we can look forward to GOOD Polish humor."[14] A Polish activist in Minnesota, Edmund Lukaszewski, told a local paper: "I am so sick of those screwy Polack jokes that I said a Hail Mary (prayer) that for once this stupid Polack thing can come to rest because now there is an internationally respected Polish official . . . we finally made it."[15] Many non-Polish newspaper columnists suddenly discovered the admirable qualities of the Poles.[16]

One of the most crucial factors in Polonia's reaction to John Paul II was that he was relatively well known in Polonia prior

to 1978. He was well acquainted with Polonia's leading clergy, including members of the Felician Sister, the Congregation of the Resurrection, and prelates such as John Cardinal Krol of Philadelphia and Bishop Alfred Abramowicz of Chicago. In 1969 and 1976, as Cardinal-Archbishop of Kraków, the new Pope undertook extensive visits in the United States and met at length with Polish-American religious and secular leaders.[17] The future Pope's 1976 visit was particularly important since he spent a great deal of time addressing matters directly related to Polonia.[18]

During the 1976 visit, Cardinal Wojtyła participated in two events, a conference at Orchard Lake and a symposium at the KoŠciuszko Foundation, in which there was an important exchange on the relationship of Polonia to the American Catholic Church. At the KoŠciuszko Foundation, its president, Dr. Eugene Kusielewicz, along with Professors Thaddeus Gromada, Stanislaus Blejwas, Joseph Wieczerzak and Daniel Buczek were able to air complaints about the lack of representation in the American hierarchy.[19] The Cardinal responded to these by asking what Polonia and its clergy were doing to prepare themselves for greater responsibility within the church and pointing out the failure of many traditional Polonia organizations to encourage intellectual and academic achievement.[20] Hard work and patience would eliminate prejudices against Polish Catholics in the United States. "The situation of being penalized because you are Polish will not last," he stated emphatically.[21] He went on to note:

You can expect much cooperation from us in Poland. But you must yourselves do what you have a right to do. You must be insistent! . . . Polonians must be considered of great value to the church in America. . . . [T]he pastorate must continue to be Polish. Language alone is not the decider. It is the inheritance of culture. The new language can be used but the old one should not be forgotten.[22]

At Orchard Lake, the future Pope stated:

American and Canadian Polonia is near and dear to our hearts. We look upon you, we the Polish bishops, as an integral part of our responsibility, of our pastoral vocation, of our priestly service. And so that's why we turn to our brother bishops, your American shepherds . . . laying before them your particular needs which came from the common spiritual heritage as ours, as well as from the particular cultures and traditions which you and your forefathers brought with you from your native land.

We therefore ask you to remain faithful to this two-fold heritage. We commend to your special interest and concern the Seminary and School at Orchard Lake. . . . Even though circumstances in the Polonia have changes through the years, this Seminary and these Schools continue to be necessary even though their activities have been extended beyond the limits of bygone decades. . . . During our visit in America we were the guests of many parishes of the Polonia. . . . May they continue to be the guardians of the spiritual heritage of the Catholic Polonia.[23]

Because he was known to Polonia and knew Polonia, the new Pope's election raised tremendous hopes. Some of those hopes were unrealistic. Anti-Polish feelings did not disappear overnight and there were several prominent Americans who felt the new Pope was good material for more "polack jokes." Nevertheless, the new Pope's very public witness and the generally positive coverage he received during the first few years of his papacy made anti-Polonism more difficult to sustain and easier to fight.[24] This was further reinforced by the Holy Father's highly publicized visits to Poland and the United States in 1979, both of which refocused attention on Polish affairs, Polonia, and the remarkable personal charisma of the man himself.[25]

The question of Poles in the American Catholic hierarchy was not resolved to the satisfaction of community leaders, perhaps misunderstanding the role of the Papacy in church governance. Eugene Kusielewicz restated his points, made in the 1976 symposium, in an "Open Letter to Pope John Paul II," just prior to the Pope's visit to the United States in October 1979. It was published in many Polish-American periodicals. "Our hierarchy treats us with contempt," Kusielewicz wrote. "We are treated as if we do not exist." He concluded:

> Your Holiness, I pray that Your forthcoming visit to the United States will make our hierarchy aware of the injustices we are suffering; and not merely our people, but other ethnic groups within the Church. . . . I pray that Your visit will help remedy these injustices; but even more, may Your visit motive an interest in Poland, the country from which we both have come.[26]

For Polish American Congress (PAC) President Aloysius Mazewski the election of a Polish Pope meant new roles for Polonia's leading organizations.

> It was a great and unprecedented honor, but [it] also places upon our shoulders new responsibilities in all our organizational activities which must be conducted with dignity, certain decorum, and a deep sense of history and our responses to it [sic].

> Because the Vicar of Christ is of our ancestral roots, we must deport ourselves in such a manner as to bring credit and comfort and to the man who stature, greatness and world wide responsibilities light our pathways of living. . . . The time of greatness has arrived for Polonia and for Americans of Polish origin and heritage. This is amply reflected in steadily increasing requests . . . for information and explanation about Poland and Polonia.

> To satisfy this urgent need which will keep increasing with the growing status and prestige of Polonia, the Polish American Congress must establish a research and information center which will become the source and depository of all information sought about us and about the land of our ancestry.

> Our efforts and attainment in this area have been sporadic and rather poorly correlated [sic] and without corrective and expanding efforts we may lose a chance of a lifetime to place Polonia and Americans of Polish origin in proper historical, sociological and cultural perspective. . . . Such [a] research center . . . should be high on our priority.[27]

At the same time, it should be noted, Mazewski effectively vetoed a chance to reform the PAC, also citing the selection of John Paul II.[28]

Polonia's leaders invested a great deal of hope in John Paul II, assuming that he would be like a magic talisman that would solve Polonia's most pressing problems. Of all Polonia leaders, Mazewski seems to have best understood the need for Polonia to undertake some significant response to take advantage of the opportunities that presented themselves. Yet, little seems to have been done to create an information and research center as Mazewski envisioned. Two institutions that should have benefited the most from this unprecedented event were Orchard Lake and Polish Roman Catholic Union of America (PRCUA). At Orchard Lake, a small center to collect information and memorabilia about John Paul II was formed.[29] In the PRCUA, a number of new societies were organized and named after the new pontiff.[30] In neither institution, however, was there an effort to make significant changes or to change the way they presented themselves to Polonia or to the public at large. Why nothing happened on these fronts deserves a fuller discussion than cannot be provided here, but two possible explanations are that even at this stage Polonia was too weak institutionally to undertake major change or that the election of a Polish Pope merely confirmed for some their essential virtue as Poles and thus obviated any need to do things differently.

It is too soon to fully assess the continuing impact of John Paul II's remarkable pontificate. For Polonia, the impact on institutions seems relatively small.[31] There has been no major move to develop new initiatives, find inspiration in the voluminous writings of John Paul II, or to undertake some serious self-assessment. For ordinary Polish Americans, the picture is harder to frame and certainly more complex. The deep connection between being Polish-American and being Catholic was clearly strengthened by the witness of John Paul II and there is some evidence, both in old Polonia parishes and in those founded by newer immigrants, of a more serious devotional life. Although anti-Polish "humor" has not disappeared and hatred of the Pope as a Pole, as expressed in the major media in the years prior to his death in 2005 was also evidence. Nevertheless, anti-Polonism of the kind familiar in the 1970s has declined and is much rarer now than before and the election of John Paul II played a big role in that change.

John Paul II played a major role—*the* major role—in ending communism in Poland and east central Europe. Thus, his greatest impact on American Polonia may be indirect. The fall of communism has created a very new situation for Polonia, one to which it has yet to fully adjust.[32] If and how it does manage to adjust will help determine the true impact of the first Polish Pope on American Polonia.

Notes

1. Much of the biographical literature is of rather poor quality. The best biography of the Holy Father is George Weigel, *Witness to Hope: The Biography of Pope John Paul II* (New York: HarperCollins, 1999).

2. On the matter of Poles as a stand-in for blacks, see Thomas J. Napierkowski, "The Image of Polish Americans in American Literature," *Polish American Studies,* Vol. 40, No. 1 (Spring 1983), 5–44.

3. *Chicago Tribune,* October 18, 1978, 1, 18.

4. *Cleveland Press,* October 17, 1978, A1, A4. See also, for Minneapolis, Jim Adams, "'Nordeast' Jubilant over Polish

Pope," *Minneapolis Star,* October 17, 1978, 1A–2A; for Detroit, see August Gribbin, "Orchard Lake School Recalls Pope's Visits," *Detroit News,* October 17, 1978, 1A, 15A; "Pope John Paul II Brings Special Joy to Area Poles," *Hamtramck Citizen,* November 19, 1978. More generally, see "Cardinals' Choice Delights U.S. Poles" (AP story), *St. Paul Pioneer Press,* October 17, 1978, 2; *Time,* October 30, 1978, 30; and *Duluth News Tribune,* October 17, 1978.

5. *Naród Polski,* November 9, 1978, 2, 6.

6. *Naród Polski,* 2, 5. See also *ibid.,* September 9, 1976.

7. "Remembrances of the Papal Inauguration," undated publication of the John Paul II Center, Orchard Lake, Michigan (copy in the author's possession). This contains a complete list of the U.S. delegation.

8. John Funk, "Poles Here Scurry for Rome Flight," *Cleveland Press,* October 18, 1978, A4; Rick Vernaci, "Local Poles Revel in Audience with Pope," *Oakland Press* (MI), October 24, 1978.

9. Polish American Congress (Illinois Division) newsletter, November–December 1978, 1–2.

10. See, for example, *Gwiazda Polarna,* October 28, 1978, 2–3; *Zgoda,* November 1, 1978, 1–2; *Zgoda,* November 15, 1978, 1–2; "Habemus Papam Polonicum!" *Perspectives,* Vol. 8, No. 6 (November–December 1978), 1. For a devotional periodical see *Ave Maria* (Buffalo), Vol. 56, No. 595 (January–February 1979), 3–4. Polonia was also inundated with Papal memorabilia. See *Polish American Journal,* issues from December 1978 through 1979.

11. See, for example, "Historyczne Wydarzenie—Polak Papieżiem," *Rola Boža,* October 28, 1978, 20. One curious and now overlooked story that appeared briefly was that the new Pope had actually been married at one time. According to mainstream press reports, "this rumor seemed to have originated in the Polish community in the United States." (See New York Times News Service/Associated Press, supplementary item, October 18, 1978, 46, microfilm copy. The *New York Times* did not publish that week due to a strike, but the report is available on microfilm.) Exactly who in Polonia would have concocted this story and then fed it to the world media is not clear, but the story's details are similar to secret police provocations used against priests in Poland deemed unfavorable to the regime. It is possible that further research in as yet unopened Polish government archives may reveal additional details of this matter.

12. Editorial, *Perspectives,* Vol. 8, No. 6 (November–December 1978), 2.

13. *Chicago Tribune,* October 18, 1978, 18.

14. *Gwiazda Polarna,* October 28, 1978, 3 (emphasis in original).

15. *Minneapolis Star,* October 17, 1978, 2A.

16. Frank Hruby, "Poland Gives the World More than Jokes," *Cleveland Press,* October 18, 1978; *Polish American Journal,* January 15, 1979, 1, and February 12, 1979, 1.

17. See Rev. Adam Boniecki, ed., *Kalendarium žycia Karola Wojtyły* (Kraków: Znak, 2000), 294–99, 576–80; Weigel, *Witness to Hope,* 222, 225–26; *Naród Polski,* September 9, 1976; *Pope John Paul II Center Newsletter,* August–September–October 1985, 4–7. Not only did the new pope know Polonia, but he was well-known by Polonia. Rev. Chester Klocek of Rochester, N.Y., stated after the pope's election: "This man is as well prepared for the job as any man could be," a point later made very strongly by the pope's biographer, George Weigel. See *Polish American Journal,* November 1978, 2.

18. This included participation in a conference on Polonia at Orchard Lake. Other participants included Władysław Cardinal Rubin, Rector Rev. Walter Ziemba, and Msgr Zdzisław Peszkowski. See *Polish American Journal,* November 1978, 2.

19. *Polish American Journal,* November 1978, 2 (reprint from September 1976); Jimmy Breslin column, *Detroit News,* October 29, 1978.

20. *Polish American Journal,* December 1978, 3.

21. Breslin, *Detroit News,* October 29, 1978.

22. *Polish American Journal,* November 1978, 2.

23. "Farewell Letter of Cardinal Wojtyla," *Pope John Paul II Center Newsletter,* August–September–October, 1985.

24. Robert Strybel, "Pope's P.R. Gift to Polonia," *Polish American Journal,* September 1979, 2. See also *Polish American Journal,* December 18, 1978, 1.

25. These visits got wide coverage in Polonia media. See, for example, *Polish American Journal* and *Perspectives.*

26. Eugene Kusielewicz, "Open Letter to Pope John Paul II," *Perspectives,* November–December 1979, 527. Although Polish National Catholic Church periodicals published relatively few items on the new Pope compared to mainstream Polonia publications, this letter was, not surprisingly, one of the items that was printed. See Straž, October 11, 1978, 1.

27. *Zgoda,* December 1, 1978, 1, 7; *Polish American Journal,* December 18, 1978, 1.

28. *Zgoda,* December 1, 1978, 1.

29. *Polish American Journal,* December 18, 1978, 1.

30. See John Radzilowski, *The Eagle and the Cross. A History of the Polish Roman Catholic Union of America, 1873–2000* (New York: Columbia University Press, 2004), chapter 8.

31. One possible exception is the Polish American Priests Association. See *A Pastoral Plan for Polonia in the USA* ([Buffalo]: PAPA, n.d. [1995]).

32. See John Radzilowski, "Ostanie ofiary zimny wojny?" *Glaukopis,* Vol. 1, No. 1 (2003).

From *Polish American Studies,* Spring 2006, vol. LXII, no. 1, pp. 79–87. Copyright © by Polish American Historical Association. Reprinted by permission.

This Writer's Life: Gay Talese

In a recent interview, acclaimed author Gay Talese talks about his craft, his experiences as an Italian American, and the need for increased support of Italian-American authors.

MICHAEL LUONGO

Seventy-four-year-old Gay Talese's newest book, "A Writer's Life," was published in 2006 by Alfred A. Knopf. He was born Gaetano Talese on February 7, 1932 in Ocean City, New Jersey to parents who hailed from the southern Italian region of Calabria. Both worked in the clothing industry; his mother ran a dress shop and his father was a tailor.

Along with authors Tom Wolfe and Truman Capote, Talese is considered a founder of "new journalism," a 1960s writing movement in which the journalist becomes part of the story and the article's tone resembles fiction. Talese worked for The New York Times from 1956 to 1965, and anchored his fame in 1966 with two Esquire magazine articles—one about Frank Sinatra and the other on Joe DiMaggio, two of the most famous Italian Americans at the time. Both articles exemplified new journalism's narrative style, now common in many long magazine pieces.

Talese has authored 11 books, including "The Kingdom and the Power", "Honor thy Father", and "Unto the Sons." He lives with his wife, Nan Talese, a senior vice president and editorial director for Doubleday, in New York City. They married in 1958 and have two children: Catherine, 41, photography director at Absolute magazine and Pamela, 38, a painter.

In April of last year, writer Michael Luongo met Talese at the Italian American Writers Association's 15th Anniversary reading. In June, he sat down with Talese in the author's Upper East Side townhouse to discuss his new book, "A Writer's Life"; a portion of that interview was published by Bloomberg News. Here Luongo shares an excerpt of that interview with *Ambassador.*

Luongo's writing and photography have appeared in Bloomberg News Muse Division, The New York Times, the Chicago Tribune, Conde Nast Traveler, and National Geographic Traveler among other publications.

M.L.: Early in your career, you did profiles of Joe DiMaggio and Frank Sinatra. Did these two men fascinate you because, like you, they were Italian-American men who became famous at a time when it was difficult to do so?

G.T.: Yes, I became interested in learning about myself from the men who experienced more than I had about going public. They were public figures . . . I was interested in what it was like to go [to that] from the insular life of an Italian American. In the 1940s, most of the Italians who were in the headlines regularly were gangsters, and I was, and my father also was, very defensive about that fact.

So what did you celebrate? Well maybe you celebrated [Fiorello] LaGuardia . . . a couple of prize fighters, and . . . besides LaGuardia, there were some ethnic politicians, but there wasn't much in the mainstream of America, except for DiMaggio and Sinatra, that really broke out. And so when it came, when I had an opportunity, of course, I got to write about them. I got to see them to a degree. One of them, Sinatra, wouldn't even see me. But that's alright, because it didn't make any difference . . . I had the story in me that he would give me.

That was really my story as much as his because I was talking about a lot of people who worked around him in a sort of inferior position—his lackeys, his gofers, his valet, his, you know, people . . . who were not famous but played in a band that Sinatra would sing in front of, but they were my kind of people. You know when I wrote "Writer's Life," it's about the same kind of people . . . Sinatra's world was all these people around this *padrone,* this major figure.

M.L.: . . . What we might call the entourage today. One of the things you brought up in "Frank Sinatra Has a Cold" is growing up in an Irish-Catholic community where Sinatra's mother, even more than his father, fought for recognition from Irish Americans.

G.T.: Yes, she did, and in addition to what you said, she was also politically active. You see many—not many, most, the great majority—of the Italians who came to America to stay, were not politically aware.

M.L.: Well, most were from the South of Italy, which tended to be poor.

G.T.: That's right, they tended to be poor and they tended to have no system beyond the family. The family was the extent of their loyalty or identity. And while they came from Southern Italy as you say, even that was more defined by their region, by their area. My forebears came from Calabria, that's the most southern tip of the peninsula.

M.I.: The part kicking Sicily.

G.T.: Yeah, the part being kicked by Sicily I think, too. But nevertheless, they were Calabrians or they were from Puglia or they were from Naples, Neapolitans, or they were from Sicily or other parts. So we were small—really, all of us had a village mentality. And this village mentality actually was brought to the New World by the old Italians. So they'd settle in a mining town in Pennsylvania, or maybe a mining town in Ohio, or a farming part of South Jersey . . . and they'd cluster together, repeating the language of their homeland for a while, for a generation or so.

They settled among their own kind, so to speak, and continued their traditions as much as they could, as outsiders or minority people, and the next generation, which would have been Frank Sinatra, he had this mother that was unusually . . . engaged in local politics. It was she [who] pushed her husband to be promoted in the fire department to a higher position and it was she who pushed her son—not that she needed to push him too much in the area of singing—but to be a little bit more antisocial and respectable. She dressed him, she wanted to make him, you know, [have] a good appearance, [la] *bella figura*. She was a person that had ambitions; she wasn't going to be a peasant all her life in Hoboken, New Jersey.

M.L.: What I wanted to ask you also is, we started talking a little about the war [on terror] today. . . So, do you relate that with what's going on now with terrorism and with Arabs and with Muslims?

G.T.: Absolutely . . . My background [is] a son of a foreigner— and my mother was also a daughter of foreigners, Italians who settled in the early part of the 20th century in the United States. Now it's more than 50 years since I saw myself as an ethnic, when during the [1940s] I sometimes thought of myself as more Italian than American, though I did not and do not speak the language of Italy. I grew up speaking English only because my parents did want to assimilate to the degree that they could. It [wasn't] their desire so much as the desire of others to accept them.

M.L.: There was a sense of shame at that time?

G.T.: Well, there's a sense of being on the wrong side of the war. In 1940 that was pretty big because [Benito Mussolini] led the nation [of Italy], and . . . fascism was associated with Nazism, and the Japanese were a third force in that axis.

To be an Italian American then was almost like what being a Muslim is today, you know, if you are of the Arab world and have a different look . . . people look at you and think, 'This guy could be a terrorist, this guy could throw a bomb. Watch out! Watch out!' . . . I don't mean [the Italians] were ever on that level, [but] certainly during World War II they were considered part of the enemy until the collapse of fascism, and

that wasn't until the end of the war. Mussolini was strung up but that wasn't until the end of the war.

The Italians in America were kept for a while in a camp, not as bad as the Japanese, but there was a period, until the collapse of the Italian army and the collapse of the Italian government in the latter part of the mid 1940s . . . I think there was a camp [at Fort Missoula in Montana] that held many Italian Americans, as suspects. You know, it's like our Guantanamo today. You know there are hundreds of people in Guantanamo, [and] there might be a certain hard-core group that have a record, if you want to put it that way, but the overwhelming majority are just people that the American government doesn't know quite what to do with.

I'm 74. I'm probably among the last people that remember what it is like to have parents who carried the burden of . . . [being] newly arrived Americans, and carrying the additional burden of being suspect as citizens. The Italians looked different, a dark complexion, and they spoke broken English, many of them. They didn't learn English very well—it's a hard language for one generation to absorb and you always have an accent, even if you do adapt pretty well to the language. Also . . . because they didn't have much of an education, they didn't have good jobs. They were out there building the subways or paving the streets or sweeping the streets or collecting the garbage. The Italians have come a long way, but they also have a remembrance, especially if they have my memory.

M.L.: Growing up, I was told you don't talk about the mob. You wrote a whole book on the mob, "Honor thy Father." Were you ever afraid to do so? And were you ever even asked to join the mob when you were young?

G.T.: . . . I never saw that as an opportunity for me. My father was . . . very defensively law abiding, I think not wanting to be singled out as a suspected person. He was very careful—never got a parking ticket, never did anything in public, or in private for all I knew, that would single him out as an unworthy citizen of the United States. But, that partly is the result of being born as I was in a town where there was a majority Protestant rulership. Protestant, white-bread Americans dominated this town.

M.L.: When I read parts of the "Frank Sinatra Has a Cold" piece, I am reminded of detectives in film noir movies, and can almost hear Humphrey Bogart narrating it. Did detective movies and the like ever have any impact on your writing, especially with the notion of investigating a topic?

G.T.: I think it could be. I never thought of it in terms of that particular kind of film. But the Italian experience in the artistic community is much represented in the film business. There are very few writers of my generation who are Italian-American; however, there are so many people who chose to exhibit their abilities either as film directors or film actors, or maybe as singers, popular singers. Writing is a solitary occupation, and I think the Italians are more naturally expressive as verbal communicators, as singers, or as visual communicators. If they're not actors, then maybe directors, who are . . . like painters on film.

183

But . . . I always heard my voice as one that was trying to tell a story . . . and I heard my voice sometimes in the remembrance of where I come from, that is the outsider, or the boy in the store, where I first became interested in story-tellers, story-telling.

M.L.: We met at the Italian American Writers Association's 15th Anniversary reading. And I know you do a lot for [the National Italian American Foundation] and they even have a writing program named for you. Tell my why you think it's important to bring more Italian-American voices into the public.

G.T.: Because the Italian voice, I'm not saying it's been suppressed, it just hasn't been expressed, because the Italians have not been able to find a way to be heard. And the reasons they have not is because they haven't found control of language yet. In order to be able to be heard or to be read, you have to be able to communicate in a way [with which] people will identify.

The Italian writer, or the Italian journalist, or the Italian agent, or the Italian publisher is underrepresented when you figure there are 15 million Americans of Italian ancestry . . . Why? I think the Italians have been the victims of their own sense of privacy and the reluctance to be sharers of secrets. The Italians weren't people who came over here to reveal themselves.

First published in *Ambassador,* Vol. 19, No. 1, Winter/Spring 2007, pp. 18–22; written by Michael Luongo and edited by Monica Soladay at the National Italian American Foundation (NIAF). Copyright 2007 by Michael Luongo/The National Italian American Foundation. Reprinted by permission of the author and *Ambassador,* a publication of the National Italian American Foundation. www.niaf.org

Forces That Shape Ethnic Opinion
What Ethnic Americans Really Think

JAMES J. ZOGBY

Different patterns of self-definition and political thinking do appear to exist among the several ethnic groups in our survey. In the last chapter, we saw how each of the six communities was impacted by several demographic variables.

To obtain an even closer look at the impact of each of these factors, we reorganized the data from Chapter Four in order to compare how the ethnic identification and political ideology of each community is shaped by place of birth, education, religious observance, income, gender and age.

A. Ethnic Pride
1. Compared by Place of Birth

While Arab American immigrants are more conservative than native-born Arab Americans, they are also more inclined than native-born Arab Americans to identify with the Democratic party. As in the case of other groups,

high school graduate Arab Americans lean more toward the Democratic party than college-educated, and Arab American women, more than Arab American males, are identified as Democrat, while younger Arab Americans are much less inclined toward the Republican party than older Arab Americans.

The degree of pride in ethnicity and the importance of ethnic heritage are clearly impacted by place of birth, but the impact varies from group to group. Quite logically, ethnic heritage appears to be more important for immigrants in all of our ethnic groups than it is for their native-born counterparts. But the similarity ends there.

In addition to ethnicity being more important to their self-definition, immigrant Italian and Arab Americans also feel more pride in their ethnic heritage than native-born Italian and Arab Americans. Jewish and Asian American immigrants, on the other hand, feel substantially less pride in their heritage than their native-born counterparts.

Generally speaking, most groups report that their immigrants form friendships outside of their ethnicity to a lesser degree than their native-born counterparts. The only exception to this pattern is African American immigrants. The legacy of racial separation and its impact on native-born African Americans appears to be the reason here.

2. Compared by Education Level

Table 1   Pride in Ethnic Heritage

	Italian	African	Hispanic	Jewish	Asian	Arab
U.S.-Born	78.5	91.5	81.5	86.5	83.0	88.5
Immigrants	85.5	90.0	86.5	79.5	78.5	92.5

Table 2   Importance of Ethnic Heritage

	Italian	African	Hispanic	Jewish	Asian	Arab
U.S.-Born	29.5	62.0	53.5	46.0	41.5	41.0
Immigrants	47.0	69.0	76.5	66.5	58.5	73.0

Table 3   Friendships Outside Ethnic Groups

	Italian	African	Hispanic	Jewish	Asian	Arab
U.S.-Born	97.5	79.0	91.5	90.5	98.0	96.0
Immigrants	91.5	84.5	70.0	87.5	81.0	83.0

Table 4   Pride in Ethnic Heritage

	Italian	African	Hispanic	Jewish	Asian	Arab
High School	89.0	90.0	85.5	92.0	78.5	92.5
College	75.5	95.5	86.5	83.0	80.5	88.5

Table 5   Importance of Ethnic Heritage

	Italian	African	Hispanic	Jewish	Asian	Arab
High School	38.0	69.5	74.0	54.5	67.0	73.0
College	27.5	57.5	57.0	44.5	53.0	38.5

Table 6 Friendships Outside Ethnic Groups

	Italian	African	Hispanic	Jewish	Asian	Arab
High School	96.0	74.5	71.0	72.5	71.0	90.0
College	99.0	86.5	93.0	94.0	88.5	96.5

There is a clear pattern here. The higher the level of education, the lower the emphasis on ethnic heritage—both pride in heritage and its importance to self-definition. The only exception is in the case of African Americans, for whom pride in heritage increases as they become more educated.

All groups, to varying degrees, reveal that the college-educated among them have a higher percentage of friendships outside their ethnicity than those with high school degrees.

3. Compared by Frequency of Religious Observance

Without exception, there is a direct correlation between pride in heritage and the importance of ethnic heritage and attendance at religious services. Those who say they attend services weekly are more likely to indicate, to a greater degree, pride in their heritage and the importance of heritage in self-definition. The degree is most significant among Jewish Americans.

Table 7   Pride in Ethnic Heritage

	Italian	African	Hispanic	Jewish	Asian	Arab
Weekly	82.0	92.0	87.0	83.0	80.5	90.0
Never	61.5	85.5	75.0	64.0	72.0	87.0

Table 8   Importance of Ethnic Heritage

	Italian	African	Hispanic	Jewish	Asian	Arab
Weekly	36.0	67.0	70.0	76.5	57.5	54.5
Never	23.0	52.0	39.5	25.5	52.0	34.0

Table 9   Friendships Outside Ethnic Groups

	Italian	African	Hispanic	Jewish	Asian	Arab
Weekly	97.5	75.5	74.5	81.0	87.5	91.0
Never	97.0	82.0	91.0	97.0	90.5	96.5

Table 10 Pride in Ethnic Heritage

	Italian	African	Hispanic	Jewish	Asian	Arab
$25–50,000	81.5	93.5	82.0	89.0	82.0	89.5
$75,000	74.0	93.0	86.0	88.5	80.0	90.0

Table 11 Importance of Ethnic Heritage

	Italian	African	Hispanic	Jewish	Asian	Arab
$25–50,000	28.5	60.4	66.5	48.0	54.0	54.0
$75,000	24.0	55.5	51.0	42.0	43.0	48.5

Table 12 Friendships Outside Ethnic Groups

	Italian	African	Hispanic	Jewish	Asian	Arab
$25–50,000	98.0	80.5	84.5	87.0	80.0	96.5
$75,000	98.0	88.0	93.0	95.5	88.0	99.0

4. Compared by Income Level

Income is less of a determinant in ethnic pride than the other factors explored in this survey—but it does have an impact on some groups.

The general pattern that emerges is that ethnicity becomes slightly less important in self-definition as ethnics earn more income. And most ethnic groups in the higher income bracket report a slight increase in friendships outside their groups.

5. Compared by Gender

Table 13 Pride in Ethnic Heritage

	Italian	African	Hispanic	Jewish	Asian	Arab
Male	77.5	91.5	87.0	83.0	80.0	89.0
Female	80.5	91.5	86.0	89.0	79.5	90.5

Table 14 Importance of Ethnic Heritage

	Italian	African	Hispanic	Jewish	Asian	Arab
Male	22.0	62.0	60.0	35.5	49.0	42.5
Female	38.5	63.0	69.0	60.0	60.0	61.0

Table 15 Friendships Outside Ethnic Groups

	Italian	African	Hispanic	Jewish	Asian	Arab
Male	97.5	82.5	83.5	93.0	80.0	94.5
Female	97.5	76.5	75.5	88.0	90.0	89.0

Ethnic heritage is vastly more important to Italian, Jewish and Arab American women than it is to men in those three ethnic communities. To a somewhat lesser degree, gender plays a similar role for Asian and Hispanics. There are no gender differences among African Americans with regard to the importance of ethnicity in self-definition.

Slightly more African, Hispanic, Jewish, Asian and Arab American males report having friendships outside their ethnic groups than their female counterparts. The notable exception here is Asian American females, who report ten percent more external friendships than Asian American males.

6. Compared by Age

The age of some of our respondents does impact their attitudes toward their ethnic community. Older Italian Americans, and to a lesser extent older Asian and African

Table 16 Pride in Ethnic Heritage

	Italian	African	Hispanic	Jewish	Asian	Arab
18–34	70.5	89.5	86.5	86.0	76.0	91.0
55–69	85.0	94.5	84.5	87.5	83.5	91.0

Table 17 Importance of Ethnic Heritage

	Italian	African	Hispanic	Jewish	Asian	Arab
18–34	26.0	55.5	65.0	43.5	50.0	52.0
55–69	36.0	70.5	70.5	48.5	49.0	59.0

Table 18 Friendships Outside Ethnic Groups

	Italian	African	Hispanic	Jewish	Asian	Arab
18–34	98.5	85.0	79.5	83.0	87.5	92.0
55–69	97.0	75.0	71.0	93.5	82.5	91.0

Americans, feel greater degree of ethnic pride than their younger ethnic counterparts.

But the importance of ethnic heritage in forming the self-definition of our respondents increases among older ethnic Americans in almost all our groups. The most significant increases are among African Americans and Italian Americans.

A lower percentage of older African Americans, and Hispanic and Asian Americans, than their younger counterparts, report friendships outside their ethnic communities. Only among older Jewish Americans do these external friendships increase.

B. Political Identification
1. Compared by Place of Birth

Italian, Hispanic, Jewish and Arab American immigrants tend to be less liberal and more conservative than their native-born counterparts. Asian Americans, on the other hand, move in the opposite direction, with Asian American immigrants appearing to be somewhat more liberal and less conservative than native-born Asian Americans.

Native-born Italian and Jewish Americans tend to identify more with the Democratic party and less with the Republican party than their immigrant counterparts. The opposite is true for Asian and Arab American immigrants whose identification with the Republican party is lower than it is for native-born Asian and Arab Americans. African and Hispanic American immigrants also tend to identify slightly more with the Republican party, but overall identification with the Democratic party remains quite high among both groups.

Table 19 Ideology—Liberal/Conservative

	Italian	African	Hispanic	Jewish	Asian	Arab
U.S.-Born	28.5/33.0	41.5/25.0	40.5/26.0	50.0/19.5	29.5/32.5	26.5/36.5
Immigrant	22.0/38.0	43.0/23.5	32.5/33.5	37.0/28.0	35.5/26.0	16.5/40.5

Table 20 Party—Democrat/Republican

	Italian	African	Hispanic	Jewish	Asian	Arab
U.S.-Born	38.0/32.0	78.0/6.0	56.5/17.0	67.5/15.0	33.5/31.0	35.7/38.5
Immigrant	26.5/59.0	76.5/15.0	57.5/27.0	53.0/20.5	36.0/23.5	39.0/30.0

Table 21 Ideology—Liberal/Conservative

	Italian	African	Hispanic	Jewish	Asian	Arab
High School	28.5/30.5	31.5/32.5	38.5/33.0	36.5/32.0	26.5/29.0	24.5/41.5
College	29.0/33.5	49.5/12.5	38.0/25.0	51.5/75.5	24.5/28.5	22.5/37.0

Table 22 Party—Democrat/Republican

	Italian	African	Hispanic	Jewish	Asian	Arab
High School	49.5/26.0	79.5/7.0	57.0/20.5	60.0/22.0	30.0/32.5	49.0/30.5
College	33.5/37.0	74.9/9.5	53.5/23.5	69.0/14.0	32.0/26.5	35.5/38.5

2. Compared by Education Level

Their level of education appears to have a significant impact on the political outlook of African and Jewish Americans, with college-educated members of both groups appearing to be notably more liberal and substantially less conservative than their high school-educated counterparts.

Education had a similar but less substantial impact on the political philosophy of Hispanic and Asian Americans. It appears to have no impact on Italian and Arab Americans. Education levels appear to have only a slight impact on the party identification of African, Hispanic and Asian Americans. As Italian and Arab Americans become college educated, they tend to identify more than their high school counterparts with the Republican Party. The opposite holds true for Jewish Americans.

The impact of religious observance on the political philosophy of our surveyed ethnic Americans is substantial and consistent across the board. In all groups, those who are religiously observant tend to be more conservative and less liberal than those who are non-observant.

The same holds true, but to a slightly less degree, with party identification. The only exception here is with

3. Compared by Frequency of Religious Observance

Table 23 Ideology—Liberal/Conservative

	Italian	African	Hispanic	Jewish	Asian	Arab
Weekly	24.5/34.0	39.5/26.0	33.5/36.5	34.0/32.0	25.5/38.5	17.5/47.5
Never	37.5/26.0	44.5/14.5	41.0/26.5	58.0/15.0	38.5/24.5	32.0/22.5

Table 24 Party—Democrat/Republican

	Italian	African	Hispanic	Jewish	Asian	Arab
Weekly	36.5/42.0	78.0/6.0	57.0/23.5	59.0/21.0	24.5/28.0	36.0/40.5
Never	44.5/25.5	50.0/9.5	60.5/16.0	73.5/11.0	40.5/27.0	29.5/29.0

non-observant Arab Americans, who tend to be both Democratic and less Republican than Arab Americans who attend weekly religious services.

4. Compared by Income Level

Income plays a role in determining the political philosophy of our ethnic groups, but not in the way one might expect. As Italian, Jewish, Asian and Arab Americans earn more income, they identify less with a conservative political outlook. Among African and Hispanic Americans, the impact of income appears to be slight.

The impact of income on party identification, on the other hand, presents a more complex picture. Italian, African, Hispanic and Asian Americans become more Republican and less Democratic as they report larger incomes. Both Jewish and Arab Americans who earn more than $75,000 a year show a slight drop in identification with the Republican Party.

Only among Italian Americans does gender appear to play a significant role in influencing political philosophy and party identification. Italian American women are more liberal, less conservative, more Democrat and less Republican than Italian American men.

In the other ethnic communities in our study, the results are less clear. Asian American men, for example, are more liberal and only slightly more Democratic than Asian American women. The reverse is true for Arab Americans. Jewish women are more Democratic than Jewish men, but they are both equally Liberal.

5. Compared by Gender

Table 25 Ideology—Liberal/Conservative

	Italian	African	Hispanic	Jewish	Asian	Arab
$25–50,000	26.0/39.0	48.0/20.5	40.0/31.0	49.5/24.0	26.5/32.0	20.0/42.5
$75,000	27.0/26.5	50.0/23.0	28.5/34.5	50.0/17.0	39.0/30.0	32.0/22.5

Table 26 Party—Democrat/Republican

	Italian	African	Hispanic	Jewish	Asian	Arab
$25–50,000	36.0/26.0	80.0/65.0	62.0/24.0	64.0/19.0	43.5/19.5	35.5/44.5
$75,000	35.0/37.0	69.0/9.5	41.0/37.5	66.0/15.5	22.5/34.0	33.5/39.0

Table 27 Ideology—Liberal/Conservative

	Italian	African	Hispanic	Jewish	Asian	Arab
Male	24.0/36.5	44.0/24.5	36.0/33.0	49.0/19.0	38.5/26.5	23.0/40.0
Female	32.0/30.0	39.0/25.0	35.5/29.0	48.5/20.0	29.5/28.5	24.0/34.5

Table 28 Party—Democrat/Republican

	Italian	African	Hispanic	Jewish	Asian	Arab
Male	35.0/39.5	73.5/7.0	55.0/24.0	62.5/15.0	36.0/24.5	36.5/38.0
Female	39.5/27.5	82.0/6.0	59.0/18.5	69.5/16.5	34.5/27.0	39.5/33.0

Table 29 Party—Democrat/Republican

	Italian	African	Hispanic	Jewish	Asian	Arab
18–34	26.5/29.5	73.0/5.5	49.0/17.0	61.5/18.0	47.0/20.5	40.0/24.5
55–69	44.0/34.0	83.0/7.5	55.5/26.5	67.5/16.5	23.5/30.5	39.0/35.5

6. Compared by Age

Older Italian, African, Hispanic and Jewish Americans have a greater affinity toward the Democratic party. Older Asian and Arab Americans are more Republican. Of the other groups, only younger Asian Americans are more Democratic than their older counterparts.

Final Observations

Even after five chapters and ninety-four tables of data, it is safe to say that we have only just scratched the surface of this study. When printed in full, a complete set of cross-tabulations from Zogby International's "culture polls" contains over 2,000 pages of tables. What we have presented here is a synopsis of that data—its essence—in an effort to determine how ethnic Americans define themselves and how they think about issues.

What we have found is that ethnicity is a factor in shaping many people's self-definition and outlook. Clearly, most ethnic Americans, event those who are first, second and third generation native-born Americans, remain proud of their heritage. And this heritage, and the shared sense of history, culture and concerns that it represents, does, in fact, have a measurable impact on attitudes.

When four in five or more say that they are proud of their heritage, and when one-third to two-thirds of all of our respondents say that this heritage is *very* important to their self-definition—then we must pay attention to this factor.

How the impact of this factor makes itself felt may vary from group to group, and may increase in intensity from issue to issue. It is, for example, well-known that each ethnic community has some specific issue of concern, oftentimes foreign policy matters, that defines a key part of their political agenda.

While we measured the importance of many of these issues in polling our six individual ethnic communities, in this book we focused on the attitudes of ethnic Americans toward a more general set of issues that all have in common.

We found some areas where responses were quite similar. We also found some areas where striking differences exist between our groups and even their component subgroups. We found, for example, that of all of our groups, ethnic pride and the importance of ethnicity are strongest among African Americans, and to a different extent, immigrant Jewish and Arab Americans—groups that have experienced a degree of discrimination.

Though ethnic pride and identification are strongest among immigrants and only somewhat less strong among college-educated and wealthier native-born Americans, the pull of this force remains quite strong. More than 50% of all of our respondents retain a "strong emotional tie to the land of their "heritage," and almost 20% of those surveyed send money to family in the countries of their background.

We also found evidence in our study of the effects of discrimination. Although we seek to become "one America," almost half of our respondents reported experiencing discrimination because of their ethnic heritage, and more than 15% of our respondents noted that they do not have close personal friendships with individuals of other ethnic communities.

We also noted a connection between ethnic pride, religiosity and political philosophy. We found, for example, that the pull of ethnicity is most deeply felt among those who are the most religiously-observant in their respective communities. More than 50% of all of our respondents attend religious services at least weekly. And this group, by and large, appears to be more conservative in political outlook.

On the whole, however, we found that it is difficult to apply traditional labels to the positions that these ethnic Americans take on important current issues. In fact, if the combined set of positions supplied by all six ethnic communities were bundled together as a package, they contradict a central tenet of contemporary conventional political wisdom. While many self-styled "moderates" in both political parties have come to define the "new" political center as fiscally conservative and socially liberal, what we have found in our study, is that on many key issues, our groups are both fiscally liberal and socially conservative.

All of this should give pause to policymakers and provide material for further research for analysts. Our "culture polls" represent only a beginning of this study—a benchmark against which we intend to measure the results of future surveys. Much more can and should be done. We invite those who are interested to investigate our complete cross tabulations to make their own comparative studies.

Neither Natural Allies Nor Irreconcilable Foes

Alliance Building Efforts between African Americans and Immigrants

ANDREW GRANT-THOMAS, YUSUF SARFATI, AND CHERYL STAATS

African American–immigrant relations have been under increased scrutiny by a range of stakeholders, including researchers, community organizers, policy makers, and philanthropic leaders. From gang violence to political representation, from labor concerns to negative stereotypes, black Americans and immigrants face a variety of challenges. In some communities, in certain arenas, each group regards the other as a rival. A pervasive media storyline that underscores instances of conflict while all but ignoring signs of cooperation only exacerbates the difficulties. Nevertheless, opportunities to unite are present, and some community organizers are working actively, and successfully, to form strong alliances between the groups. In this article, we briefly outline some of the key challenges, opportunities, and strategies that define these alliances.

Numerous barriers confront those who try to forge constructive relationships between African American and immigrant communities. Structural challenges include the socioeconomic marginalization that marks many African American and immigrant communities and often leads members of each group to live in close proximity to each other, sometimes provoking tensions over the allocation of limited resources. Whether at the federal, state, or local government level, or at the community level, most immigrants receive little help with integrating socially, economically, or politically into their new communities. Conversely, the members of receiving communities typically receive little help anticipating or accommodating the community changes that often accompany the new arrivals, creating fertile ground for inter-group friction. These strains are compounded by the unfavorable perceptions that African Americans and immigrants too often harbor about each other, the existence of an anti-immigrant wedge movement, and the prevalence of a conflict narrative in the mainstream media that encourages a zero-sum mentality among both groups.

These and other significant challenges notwithstanding, opportunities to unite and to achieve important relationship-building and policy successes exist. A great many African Americans and immigrants share the need for education reform in low-opportunity neighborhoods, for better workplace safety measures and wage reforms, for an end to racial profiling practices, and so on. Many progressives regard the two communities as core constituents within any viable, broad-based movement for expanded social justice in the United States. Current alliance-building efforts may yet prove to be the seedbed for such a movement.

From our conversations with dozens of organizers representing a wide range of social justice organizations and alliances, we identified a set of approaches based on alternative logics around which African American-immigrant alliances are formed: *intercultural relationship-building, issue-based organizing,* and *workplace-based organizing.* These three do not exhaust the range of alliance-building efforts in the field; nor are they mutually exclusive.

Community organizers who espouse an intercultural relationship-building approach aspire to build strong multicultural communities. For them, establishing healthy relationships among people of color is an important value in itself. Insofar as relationship-building reshapes identities and interests, it is also seen as a prerequisite for effective issue campaigns. These organizers suggest that interpersonal trust between the communities needs to be established first, and can be done only by addressing commonly held misconceptions through the deliberate re-education of each community. Without the trust born of solid relationships, racial and xenophobic tensions invariably emerge, and partnership development becomes episodic at best. Re-education measures can range from preparing simple cultural exchange events to engaging in specialized curriculums and trainings.

While acknowledging the importance of relationship building, issue-based organizers argue that the best way to build solidarity across lines of race, ethnicity, and nativity is through appeals to shared "bread and butter" interests. Trust develops most surely as a byproduct of common struggle, preferably one that yields tangible successes. In contrast, these organizers claim that inter-group relationship challenges, as such, provide uncertain motivation for partnerships, especially among poor and working-class people likely to have more pressing concerns. "Issue-first" alliances are typically formed between organizations, rather than within particular organizations.

Finally, in some sectors of the economy, especially in low-paying jobs, African Americans and immigrants work side by side, making workplaces the frontlines of negotiations and *de facto* solidarity between the groups. These sectors include construction work, the hotel industry, restaurants, and the meat-packing industry. Some workplaces are home to initiatives that operate in the absence of formal coalitions. Unlike initiatives shaped by the first two approaches, these initiatives mobilize constituents not around their identities as "African Americans," "immigrants," or people of color, but around their common identity as workers. In other words, the goal of the organization is not to support immigrant or African American issues, as such, but to promote worker issues. The goal is presented in a color-blind manner, and the organizers try to emphasize the salience of associational rather than communal identities.

No matter which strategy or combination of strategies community organizers use, ongoing efforts and existing opportunities for further collaboration offer grounds for hope about the future of African American – immigrant alliance building work. Creating alliances that endure and prosper is a challenging task, but the potential benefits make such efforts worthwhile. Cooperation between African Americans and immigrants in the United States is crucially important for creating an inclusive pluralistic democracy in which people of different races and cultures thrive by recognizing both their differences and similarities and working for common goals.

The Study of Jewish American History and Dutch American History in Several Settings

The Study of American Jewish History: In the Academy, In the Community

HASIA R. DINER

As an enterprise the scholarly study of American Jewish history serves, metaphorically, two masters. On the one hand, it has thoroughly embedded itself into America's universities and into the professional domain of American history. Its practitioners see themselves as needing and wanting to conform to all the obligations of the academic world, particularly those which demand a degree of scholarly aloofness from the topic in order to see, as free as possible from personal biases, patterns at work in the past. Yet, at the same time, as a field of endeavor, it depends greatly on American Jewry's historical consciousness and on the beneficence of donors, on the interest of Jewish communal institutions, and as such on non-scholarly concerns.[1]

This state of affairs has been productive in the sense that scholars of American Jewish history have access to both the benefits of the larger scholarly world and those particular to the ethnic communal context. Yet the reality that American Jewish historians do, and believe that they must, also engage with popular audiences has consequences. Each interaction with the lay public involves an expenditure of time and energy, and raises historians' own anxieties about the dilution of their scholarly rigor.

They truly respond to two sets of demands and face two sets of opportunities. They hold university positions, train a constantly growing number of graduate students, and have access to the most prestigious publishing houses for their books. At the same time, they also have a Jewish constituency which provides funding, audiences, and a range of other benefits for those who have decided to study the American Jewish past. They as well can be said to have the advantages of access to multiple sets of colleagues. They hope to speak to their Americanist peers, and do so, at the same time that they maintain dense and constant conversations with scholars of modern Jewish history in the

United States, Israel, and Europe, making their work inherently international.

From the point of view of other ethnic historical associations and ethnic historical projects, this no doubt would appear to be an ideal state. Well-funded, institutionally rich, and throbbing with scholarly activity, American Jewish history has since the 1980s entered into a period of fruitful growth, with a fine future ahead of it, as more and more students apply to graduate school to study it, making it possible to see the field as continuing to develop in years to come.

This condition, which may seem to be an almost embarrassment of riches has a history and did not represent the inevitable outcome of the field's founding and early years. The history of the field of American Jewish history offers a window into this present state of affairs, and also sheds some light on the dilemmas of in fact serving two purposes, one academic and university-based and one communal, that is, facing the American Jewish public.

The study of the American Jewish past came into being at the end of the nineteenth century. In the 1890s, in the United States and in Great Britain, the small Jewish communities and their well-off, acculturated elites faced two interrelated challenges. Increasing numbers of east European Jewish immigrants flooded both countries, not only numerically overwhelming the small resident Jewish populations, but increasingly these newcomers drew public attention to Jews, Judaism, and the linkages between Jewishness and foreignness. At the same time in both countries anti-Semitism emerged as a new and ugly fact of life, as a matter of rhetoric, and popular representation and policy. Infused with the tropes of scientific racism, the anti-Semitism of the 1890s questioned the moral and mental capabilities of the Jews and certainly questioned their fitness for citizenship. Exclusion of Jews in places of leisure and employment, for example, began to confront Jewish women and men, relatively unused to such practices in their heretofore liberal, tolerant nations. Both nations began to discuss the need to restrict immigration and for Jewish communal leaders, this meant that the Jews of the Czarist lands, suffering increased impoverishment and escalating violence, would have no places of refuge.

The study of American and British Jewish history emerged from this moment in time. The American Jewish Historical Society founded in 1892, by a group of Jewish communal notables, some of whom a decade later would establish the American Jewish Committee, a body constituted to defend Jewish rights at home and abroad, included no historians. These highly interested lay people saw history as a way to defend the Jews, both those already in America and those who would be immigrating in the decades to come.[2]

They had a particular point to make about Jews in America. Jews, they sought to prove, had been there from the beginning and had participated in every war, had contributed to every development which had made the nation great. Without the Jews, their articles implied, the United States could not have achieved its greatness. Beneath that statement lay a contemporary message. Do not think of Jews as foreigners outside of the national experience. Today's Jewish newcomers will also integrate and they too will enhance the United States.

Notably the first large scale public history program sponsored by American Jews and the American Jewish Historical Society took place in 1905, to commemorate the 250th anniversary of Jewish settlement in North America. Ostensibly staged to recall the 1654 landing of a group of 23 Jews in the unfriendly environment of New Amsterdam where they had been met by Peter Stuyvesant who sought to expel them and bar Jews from dwelling in what would become New York, the celebration in actuality functioned in a deeply political context. That year and the two previous ones had witnessed bloody pogroms against Jews in Kishinev other places in the Ukraine and Bessarabia. The organizers of the 250th anniversary programs, including the one held in New York's Carnegie Hall featuring a speech by former President Grover Cleveland and words of solidarity from then President Theodore Roosevelt, had their eyes trained on the mass emigration from eastern Europe, the passage of the Aliens' Act in Great Britain, and their own deeply felt responsibility to labor to keep America's doors open to Jews fleeing eastern Europe.

Such use of history as group defense and apologia continued through the first decades of the twentieth century as Jewish communal leaders marshaled history and historical projects to prove the Jews' worthiness. By the middle of the century a new element entered into the practice of American Jewish history. By the 1950s the American Jewish Historical Society and the American Jewish Archives, founded in 1948, shifted the focus. By that point in time Jews could be said to have achieved a high level of integration into American society, and although barriers persisted into the 1960s, they fell one by one in the immediate postwar years. In 1945 the state of New York passed a civil rights act which benefited Jews, among others, and by 1947 opinion polls for the first time showed a steep decline in anti-Semitism in America. Young Jews had access to American higher education at a rate which exceeded that of nearly all other Americans,

particularly as compared to the children and grandchildren of the other immigrants who had accompanied them to the United States in the decades from the 1870s through the 1920s.

Now, American Jewish history came to serve a second purpose. No longer fretful about the behavior and attitudes of their non-Jewish neighbors, Jewish leaders, communal organizations, and probably the rank-and-file of American Jewry began to articulate fears about the vitality of Judaism and Jewish culture in America. By the end of World War II a grim reality confronted them. The virtual disappearance of European Jewry at the hands of the Germans and their allies during the war meant that American Jewry constituted the only large and economically robust Jewish collectivity in the world. They contemplated with worry the idea that American Jews did not have the cultural and communal wherewithal to basically replace the slaughtered Jews of Europe as the producers of Jewish culture.

Their worries stemmed from some of the basic characteristics of post-World War II America, including the drop in anti-Jewish attitudes and the banning of many of those practices which had until recently excluded Jews, suburbanization, the increasingly hospitable climate of this "age of affluence" in which young Jews, in particular, saw themselves as not so very different than their white, middle class, neighbors. Rabbis, Jewish educators, and the staffs of many of the Jewish communal bodies turned to American Jewish history as one tool in their kit to try to instill a sense of distinctiveness and group pride in the face of integration.

Jews, they wanted to show, wherever the settled in the United States had built and sustained their communities, even as they experienced integration. In this vein, over the course of the 1950s and 1960s a slew of American Jewish communal biographies got written. In fact the American Jewish Committee, the American Jewish Historical Society, the Jewish Theological Seminary, and other communal organizations participated in shepherding these projects through to publication. The histories of the Jews of Rochester, Syracuse, Utica, Baltimore, Philadelphia, Cleveland, Milwaukee, and numerous other cities saw the light of day, written by either Jewish academics, specialists in other fields, with no particular training in either American history, urban history or Jewish history. In a few cases congregational rabbis, some with doctorates in history, also participated in chronicling the history of their community. Whoever the author, they took upon themselves this specific practice of history to foster the vitality of Jewish community life and make possible, they hoped, Jewish cultural retention.[3]

Indeed so much did the study of American Jewish history come to be defined as a crucial element of post-war American Jewish life that in 1948 the Hebrew Union College in Cincinnati, the rabbinical seminary of the Reform movement, inaugurated the American Jewish Archives and launched the journal of the same name. Under the guidance of Jacob Rader Marcus, trained as a medieval Jewish historian, the American Jewish Archive in particular took as its mission collecting the documents and stimulating research on the history of American Jewish communities in the midwest, the south, and the other hinterlands of New York, American Jewry's undisputed capital.

The year 1954 offers a good and useful moment in time to look at this particular use of American Jewish history. In that year the Jews of the United States celebrated the 300th anniversary of that 1654 landing in Manhattan which had, in 1905 been staged to tell Americans how much Jews had contributed to the rise of the nation. For sure the 1954 festivities, more elaborate, extensive, and widespread than anything held at the beginning of the century, addressed and involved non-Jewish notable Americans. President Eisenhower attended the grand banquet which heralded the beginnings of the Tercentenary year and other important non-Jewish political, civic, and religious leaders played their part.[4]

But in 1954 the message targeted Jews much more than non-Jews and targeted them more than the turn-of-the-century programs had. Pedagogic projects, speakers, publications, films, radio broadcasts, and numerous other endeavors all sought to show the Jews of the United States that Jewish life had been successfully transplanted to America. There it had taken root, germinated, and flowered in directions different than what had existed in European Jewry, but still products of the same deep source. The history of American Jewry, Tercentenary texts asserted, represented a continuation of the great chain of Jewish history, but one which represented a perfect fusion or synthesis between that great tradition and the beneficence of America.

The year 1954 represents a watershed year in the relationship between the public practice of American Jewish history and its scholarly manifestations in another way. That year Harvard historian Oscar Handlin published a landmark book, *Adventures in Freedom.*[5] The author of the Pulitzer Prize winning *The Uprooted* and of *Boston's Immigrants,* the first Jew to receive tenure in Harvard's vaunted History Department, turned his attention in the 1954 book the history of the Jews of the United States. The title revealed the book's analytic frame, that life in America, for all its manifestations of anti-Semitism, for all of the scurrilous rhetoric, had been for Jews an experience *sui generis* in their long and tragic diasporic history.

One one level Handlin's publication of *Adventures in Freedom* stood as an anomaly in his lengthy and productive career as an American historian. Nearly everything he wrote, including the classic *The Uprooted* had nothing to do with Jews and the tone of that book, like that of *Boston's Immigrants,* expressed negativism and pessimism. They stressed conflict and the absence of synthesis. Yet he cast *Adventures in Freedom* in a decidedly positive tone which depicted as positive the meeting between America and the Jews. Likewise Handlin from the late 1940s contributed many lengthy pieces and small books to Jewish communal projects, writing for the Anti-Defamation League, the American Jewish Committee, the American Jewish Historical Society, and other organizations, and using his considerable scholarly skills and reputation to further a series of Jewish tasks. His articles appeared in the *American Jewish Yearbook,* a publication of the American Jewish Committee, and in its monthly magazine, *Commentary.* Handlin researched and developed policy statements for American Jewish organizations on civil rights, immigration reform, and numerous other liberal causes of the mid-twentieth century.[6]

His career as such in this middle of the 1950s and beyond provides one way in which American Jewish historians balanced between the demands of the community and the demands of the scholarly world. Handlin in essence bifurcated himself, maintaining two separate selves, one the communally active

Jew who employed his reputation and talents as an historian to write for the Jewish public and the leadership of the community, and the other, the American historian who, while he happened to be a Jew, only in one instance wrote scholarly works which took as their subject the experience of the Jews in the American context. As an American historian he presented himself devoid of his Jewish self, as it were, tackling a range of social and political matters with no reference to Jews in them.

Handlin's notable career offers one more important element in the professionalization of American Jewish history. He played a key role in articulating a desideratum that the study of American Jewish history needed scholars well trained in American history. Along with Columbia University's Salo Baron, the only professor of Jewish history in a general American university at mid-century, Handlin helped organize several conferences on the imperative of nurturing such a cadre of historians and he played his part in turn by supervising the dissertation of Moses Rischin, one of the first graduate students at Harvard to turn his attention to the American Jewish past. His dissertation became a now classic book, *The Promised City,*[7] a study of east European Jewish immigrants to New York at the end of the nineteenth and early twentieth centuries. That Harvard University Press published Rischin's book attested to its excellence, to Handlin's influence and to the emerging professional status of the field.

One more word is in order before moving on to the professionalization of the sub-discipline of American Jewish history and the way it stands mid-way between the academy and the community. In 1960s, at the time that Rischin's book appeared and at the earliest stage of the flourishing of American Jewish history, the field occupied a somewhat marginal place in the larger study of Jewish history. Those who engaged in the study of Jewish history, whether in the scholarly realm or the communal, regarded the European Jewish past most important, and American Jewish history as a fairly minor sideshow. They thought this way for two reasons, both of which placed America and its Jews decidedly on the sidelines of significance. When either scholarly and community audiences considered Jewish history they focused first and foremost on the history of suffering and persecution. Not surprising in the decades surrounding the rise of Nazism and the perpetration of the vast slaughter of European Jewry, this "lachrymose" view of Jewish history, the phrase coined by Baron, meant that America, with relatively mild history of anti-Semitism and its absence of persecution, particularly of state origins, mattered little. Similarly, a long tradition in Jewish scholarship valorized the study of Jewish ideas, the tradition of rabbinic commentary, and the emergence of great intellectual breakthroughs. In this historical paradigm the United States again had little to offer. The migration to American had involved some of the least learned of European Jewry, and their activities in the United States as peddlers, garment workers, labor organizers, and community builders offered little in terms of furthering the cannon of "real" Judaic knowledge.

Those who, from Rischin onward until the 1990s, study American Jewish history tended to be viewed as a bit softer as scholars, less dependent on acquiring multiple languages to do their research. They seemed to be treating subjects somehow, less important than victimization and the creation of the scholarly canon. But whatever scholars of European Jewish history may have thought of the enterprise of American Jewish history, it took off in earnest in the late 1960s and 1970s as discrimination against Jews in the American academy melted, as Jewish studies itself began to enter into American universities, and as those institutions of higher learning transformed and opened themselves up to a variety of ethnic projects. Starting in the early 1970s graduate students in American history programs, scattered throughout the country, although Columbia University produced the lion's share of them, started producing dissertations which focused on aspects of American Jewish past. They looked at Jewish community formation and Jewish interactions with other Americans, both in and outside of the political sphere. Many of these dissertations then became books, which in turn served as the first building blocks of a genuinely scholarly literature on the subject. These works, their authors hoped, would perform several tasks at one and the same time. They expected to show European Jewish historians that American Jews had a past too, one worthy of study and to demonstrate to their Americanist colleagues that the presence of Jews had made a difference to America as it developed over time. In an age when social history dominated the profession and when social historians sought to identify more and more groups whose experiences could complicate the master narrative of American history, American Jewish historians found themselves in the right moment in time to start creating their body of literature.[8]

By the 1980s American Jewish history as a field can be said to have come into its own as measured by the volume of books, articles, and doctoral dissertations it produced, and continues to produce.[9] It entered into a fruitful period, which continues apace into the early twenty-first century in terms of the number of students applying to the best graduate schools to study this and the prestige of the publishers under whose aegis their books come out.[10]

By the late 1980s so many academicians engaged in the study of American Jewish history struck out from the American Jewish Historical Society and created a separate unit within it. Through this Academic Council, American Jewish historians have for almost two decades held a biennial conference, the Scholars Conference in American Jewish History, which attracts dozens of panelists from around the country and from abroad. As of 2007 the Academic Council has a membership of 142, all professors, archivists, and professional librarians who focus exclusively or primarily on American Jewish history in their work.[11] In addition, a growing number of scholars of European Jewish history, a scholarly cadre long disdainful of American Jewish history, treating its as a minor intellectual stepchild of the weightier parent body, have now decided to write in American Jewish history themselves, and to add it to their repertoire of academic interests.

This turn of events has certainly encouraged American Jewish historians in their work. Yet while all these developments have taken place, as the number of scholars grows and the field blossoms, many of its practitioners who sit in history departments, feel a degree of marginality from their Americanist colleagues. As those who teach American Jewish history in universities see it, their peers who study other aspects of American history, do not consider Jewish history particularly important or relevant to the departmental mission. American Jewish historians basically

read the same journals and books, rely upon the same scholarly paradigms, engage with the same themes, and employ the same idioms, as other historians. Yet from the vantage point of the Jewish historians, they occupy a quite marginal status within their departments and the profession. By and large—and it would require systematic collection of data to prove the point definitively—most American Jewish historians do not feel utterly integrated into the practice of American history, not from their side but from what they perceive to be the attitudes and prejudices of the profession as a whole.

To chronicle the gap between how American Jewish historians see themselves and their work and the impact of that work on the larger practice of American history involves negative evidence. There have been, for example, nearly no articles on the topic of American Jewish history, by any of its practitioners in the *Journal of American History* or the *American Historical Review.* No American Jewish historian has been elected to office in the Organization of American Historians or sat on any of its committees. When the Organization of American Historians put together a roster of distinguished historians to lecture to public audiences on American history in its many manifestations, it included no American Jewish historians. The American Historical Association has never issued a pamphlet on the study and teaching of Jewish history, American or otherwise, in it excellent series of publications on the state of the art of various historical subjects. Most papers on American Jewish history appear at the annual meeting of the Organization of American Historians or the American Historical Association on what might be viewed as "ghetto" panels, that is, panels dedicated to some aspect or another of American Jewish history and rarely on thematic panels which look at a variety of subjects, built around a common problem. The list could go on, but the basic sense, whether accurate or not, American Jewish history, despite the richness of its development and the gravitas of its work, plays a very minor role in the field of American history.

If the scholars of American Jewish history find their relationship to other Americanists less than full and satisfying, they maintain at the same time, a complicated and extensive set of interactions with the larger non-scholarly Jewish public. These historians do not consider their relationship with the Jewish community a particular priority in their selection of topics, deriving as they do the impetus for their work from the academic world and its scholarly concerns. But the community has profoundly made itself felt and as such provided American Jewish historians with their second master, a master which provides much to them as scholars, but which in turn asked much of them.

The rise of Jewish studies in American universities indeed cannot be disentangled from the workings of Jewish communal life in America. Jewish studies came to the American university not by way of student protest, as Black studies did, or by the work of Jewish faculty who organized themselves to show administrators that a subject exist, like women's studies had. Rather Jewish studies entered the "halls of ivy" from the outside as Jewish donors, variously representing foundations, individuals, or organized Jewish communal bodies, offered universities funding to make courses on Jewish history, literature, and thought available to students. To some degree their largess reflected a worry that as universities started offering Black studies, Chicano studies, Asian American studies, and the like, Jews would be left out of the increasingly ethnicized campus. Only they, as a group, would have no department or program to represent their experience in the curriculum. Jewish studies in the general American university emerged as an innovation of the 1970s and a solution to the problem of Jewish academic invisibility.

Probably though, and this subject deserves a full length study, the increasing fear of Jewish communal leaders, that the American Jewish youngsters who received decreasing levels of Jewish education before college, would drift away from communal involvement once they became young adults. Fears of intermarriage, a major topic in Jewish publications, sermons, and the reports of Jewish organizations from the 1980s onward, propelled a quest of "continuity," the launching of numerous projects to forestall a mass defection from Judaism and Jewish life. While many who participated in this conversation did so in hyperbolic and gloom-and-doom terms, they did cast about for various ways to engage with Jewish youth.

The lavish funding of Jewish studies on campuses across the country represented one such approach. In addition on university campuses, public and private, including a number under Catholic auspices, with few Jewish students, local Jewish philanthropists have also endowed chairs in Jewish studies as a way to reach out the overwhelming non-Jewish majority and teach them something about Judaism and Jewish culture. In the last half decade or so, donors have offered handsome sums to various American universities, usually through Jewish studies departments, to showcase the teaching of Israel. In an era of intense debate, on and off campus, about the Middle East and Israel, donors have hoped that chairs and programs in Israel studies, would provide a balance to what they see as a tilt among academics towards the Arab position.

The universities on their part had much to gain from this largess. Jewish studies provided much needed resources and particularly in state universities which received declining amounts of support from legislatures, donations in the millions from philanthropists willing to endow Jewish studies became, as the colloquialism goes, a "cash cow." Universities also saw the entry of endowed Jewish studies programs to their campus as a way to upgrade the applicant pool. Whether rightly or wrongly, schools across the country worked on the assumption that more Jewish students on campus would help raise their academic standing, and that would consequently attract even more support from Jewish donors.

The academic study of Jewish topics, American Jewish history among them, as such became a potential weapon in a war for the Jewish future on the one side, and in the quest for higher rankings and increased financial resources, on the other. This meant, for the Jewish historians who worked in American universities, the development of a somewhat complicated relationship with the donors and by extension with the communities. While only in the rarest cases have donors attempted to exert any kind of influence on the content of the work being done by the beneficiaries of their gifts, or indeed which professors should teach the courses, sit on the endowed chairs, and the like, for the scholars, an unstated expectations exists that they would maintain some kind of relationship with the community. Whether

being asked to speak to community audiences, write something for a local Jewish newspaper, help in working on a local Jewish museum exhibition, teach an adult Jewish education course, or consult with a local community project, Jewish studies scholars, and American Jewish historians in particular, find themselves called upon to participate on the community level and to engage with popular audiences.

For sure, they can refuse to participate, but given the degree to which they hold positions that would not exist but for the bounty of the community, they live with a clear sense that turning their backs on the community would be less than graceful. These invitations to lecture, consult, and write for lay audiences come quite often with handsome remuneration, often beyond what other historians might receive from more general community sources and those honoraria surely function as rewards or lures to seduce American Jewish historians, and others, to turn to the public.

The emergence of Jewish studies in American universities has been viewed by local Jewish community members as a new source of learning and communal programming, as an additional source of adult Jewish education, existing in part to supplement the courses and lectures at synagogues, Jewish community centers, and the like. Conferences, for example, called by Jewish studies departments, on a vast array of historical, literary, and philosophic subjects, tend to bring out sizable community audiences. The organizers of the conference conceptualize themes around intellectually meaningful issues, invite scholars on the basis of the academic quality of their work, and structure the proceedings along conventional scholarly lines. But, when they look out at those seated in front of them, they will see, as likely as not, not other scholars—although some definitely show up—but interested members of the Jewish community. Jewish studies conferences in the main serve the participant scholars who surely learn from each other, but take place to benefit also the laity who come out in large numbers to such programs. No one has assessed the ways in which such a skewed balance between scholarly presenters with their academic agendas, and lay audiences eager to soak up something about Jewish culture and history impacts upon the intellectual rigor of the proceedings. But, whatever the impact, scholars participating understand fully that their jobs and the resources at their command depend in large measure upon the interest and support of those "ordinary" Jewish women and men who embrace Jewish learning, but by necessity at a level different than that of academics.

While this kind of engagement encompasses nearly all academics in Jewish studies departments, scholars of American Jewish history, have felt this particularly sharply. After all, the local community in which they work is an American one, and the women and men who make up the Jewish population of their town or city, live out their Jewish lives in an American context. The demand for and interest in American topics seems to be nearly insatiable. American Jewish historians can be said to have, in greater or lesser degree depending upon the size of the community in which they find themselves, almost second careers as speakers at synagogues, including as weekend length "scholars-in-residence" at congregations, as organizers of adult Jewish education programs in community centers and other Jewish venues, consultants to federations (the overarching Jewish fundraising and allocations bodies), planners of Jewish museums and oral history projects, and other kinds of endeavors, all of which take time but simultaneously bring with them remuneration and audiences.

Nothing demonstrated this more clearly than the hundreds of programs around the country held in 2004 and 2005 dedicated to celebrating the 350th anniversary of American Jewish settlement. From one end of the country to another, and with some spots overseas, American Jewish historians experienced a long banner year as they delivered their "350th" talks to multiple community audiences, interested in basically the subject of how to account for the uniqueness of the American Jewish experience. In a decade when mounting Jewish concern focused on the reemergence of anti-Semitism in Europe, particularly in France, and the linked demonization of Israel, the American Jewish polity in essence wanted to know why none of this seemed to be cropping up in the United States. These 350th programs whether in the form of lectures, symposia, films, radio, and television programs, provided American Jewish historian with more opportunities to share something about the contours of the American Jewish past than they ever had before. These programs, despite their time consuming nature, provided American Jewish historians with audiences that I venture to say would thrill any academic, in terms of size and interest level.

In addition, scholars of American Jewish history can expect that local and national Jewish newspapers and magazines will review their books, bringing these scholarly works wider attention than most conventional books in American history get. The publishers of their books, for their part recognize that these publications function as attractive venues for advertising. Nearly all Jewish communities hold an annual Jewish book fair every November as part of a national project in existence for decades, Jewish Book Month. Scholars of American Jewish history, just like novelists, journalists, compilers of Jewish cookbooks, and other authors of books on Jewish themes, make the Book Month circuit hosted by far-flung communities. These talks further expand the readership for books with Jewish themes, including those written from within the context of the academy.

In all of this, from the endowed chairs through the well-attended and nicely funded conferences, from the named centers, programs and departments to the fairly robust sales of books and the attention in the Jewish press to academic works, American Jewish historians confront a public engaged with them. They have a lay audience which sees them as partners in telling the narrative of their own past, as custodians of the community's memory.

Despite the excitement of having such audiences and the real rewards that come from them, such a cozy relationship can at times seem too close. At times, audiences want a particular version of that past, and they make it very clear that what the scholarly lecture or the academic book has laid out, jars with their idea of what happened and why. Audience members, usually among the most Jewishly committed individuals in a local community, come to the lecture or conference with deep passions about the American Jewish past and with their already fixed ideas about those developments, why they took place, and what they meant. Since the laity has not received scholarly training

and has not donned the mantle of objectivity, however problematic the nature of that construct as a goal or as a reality, they tend to see history as a matter of praising heroes and blaming villains. They want the past to have played itself out in a particular way and can become quite outspoken when the visiting lecturer, for example, points out that certain developments or phenomena appear quite different when subjected to empirical analysis.

The community audiences by definition function from a very particularistic perspective. While it would be unfair to describe their interests as insular, they come to the lecture, participate in the oral history project, or read the books because they see themselves as actors in the history being retold. They employ the pronoun "we," even if talking about Jews in the America in the eighteenth or nineteenth centuries. To them American Jewish history serves to confirm identity and shore up communal solidarity.

The historian, on the other hand, has a stake in maintaining a degree of distance, in fact, hopes to chip away at romantic and nostalgic ideas about the past. The historian opts for the pronoun "they" when talking or writing about the women and men they study. After all, historical scholarship maintains that the details and developments in the past must be seen as contingent on circumstances no longer operative and in existence. Therefore "we" cannot work. In addition most American Jewish historians, trained in American history, constantly have their eyes trained on the larger American narrative and on the experiences of other immigrant, ethnic, and religious groups in the United States, whose histories served as both points of convergence with those of Jews and whose activities played a not insignificant role in shaping the circumstances which Jews faced. The historians' training in essence takes them away from particularism.

The scholars who come to the community setting as such have to walk a fine line between sharing with the audiences their best understanding of historical matters, based not on comfortably familiar narratives but on historically accurate data, and at the same time providing a popular audience with a meaningful experience. Scholars of American Jewish history engage in a balancing act where they negotiate the "we" of the laity's perspective and the "they" orientation which professionalism demands of them.

What price strings come attached to this efflorescence of public interest in American Jewish history? To what degree do American Jewish historians see themselves as beneficiaries of communal interest or its hostages? Answering this question would no doubt vary from historian to historian, but in the largest sense, I predict that most would concur that they have a responsibility to serve that master, to show up, participate, give it their time, but not to give the Jewish public the stories that make it feel good, just because they conform to expectations.

Ironically historians of American Jewish history went into their work not because a popular audience existed for their endeavors, but because they hoped to function within the academy, in history departments in conversation with other Americanists. Yet the largest group of constituents who consume their works, beyond the circle of other professional scholars of American Jewish history, have been made up of not others in

American history, but from the large Jewish public hungry for learning and willing to support such work. American Jewish historians have benefited from this hunger but yet still hope to win the respect of their colleagues for the rigor of their scholarship. They yearn for approval from the other master.

Notes

1. For a more complete statement on the history and current situation of American Jewish historical studies see, Hasia R. Diner, "American Jewish History," in Martin Goodman, ed., *The Oxford Handbook of Jewish Studies* (Oxford: Oxford University Press, 2002), 471–490.

2. Jeffrey Gurock, "From Publications to American Jewish History: *The Journal of the American Jewish Historical Society* and the Writing of American Jewish History," *American Jewish History,* Vol. 81, No. 2 (1993–1994), 155–270.

3. Among many of this genre see Morris Gutstein, *A Priceless Heritage: The Epic Growth of Nineteenth Century Chicago Jewry* (New York: Bloch Publishing, 1953); Charles Reznikoff and Uriah Z. Engelman, *The Jews of Charleston: A History of an American Jewish Community* (Philadelphia: Jewish Publication Society of America, 1950); Selig Adler and Thomas E. Connolly, *From Ararat to Suburbia: The History of the Jewish Community of Buffalo* (Philadelphia: Jewish Publication Society of America, 1960); Louis J. Swichkow and Lloyd P. Gartner, *The History of the Jews of Milwaukee* (Philadelphia: Jewish Publication Society of America, 1963); Stuart E. Rosenberg, *The Jewish Community in Rochester, 1843–1925* (New York: Columbia University Press, 1954); Solomon J. Kohn, *The Jewish Community of Utica, New York, 1847–1948* (New York: American Jewish Historical Society, 1959); Hyman Grinstein, *The Rise of the Jewish Community of New York, 1654–1860* (Philadelphia: Jewish Publication Society of America).

4. For a discussion of the Tercentenary and the performance of American Jewish history, see, Arthur Goren, *The Politics and Public Culture of American Jews* (Bloomington: Indiana University Press, 1999).

5. Oscar Handlin, *Adventures in Freedom* (New York: McGraw-Hill, 1954).

6. Oscar Handlin, "New Paths in American Jewish History: Afterthoughts of a Conference," *Commentary* (April, 1949), 388–394.

7. Moses Rischin, *The Promised City: New York's Jews, 1870–1914* (Cambridge: Harvard University Pess, 1962).

8. Leonard Dinnerstein, *The Leo Frank Case* (New York: Columbia University Press, 1968); Arthur Goren, *New York Jews and the Quest for Community: The Kehila Experiment* (New York: Columbia Univesity Press, 1970); Jeffrey Gurock, *When Harlem Was Jewish* (New York: Columbia University Press, 1979); Hasia R. Diner, *In the Almost Promised Land: American Jews and Blacks, 1915–1935* (Westport, CT: Greenwood Press, 1977).

9. It would be nearly impossible to cite here the many books published since the 1980s in American Jewish history. Just three of the most recent worthy of mention include, Daniel Soyer, *Jewish Immigrant Associations and American Identity in New York, 1880–1939* (Cambridge: Harvard University Press, 1997); Tony Michel, *A Fire in their Hearts: Yiddish Socialists in New York* (Cambridge: Harvard University Press, 2005); Cheryl Greenberg, *Troubling the Waters: Black-Jewish Relations in the American Century* (Princeton, NJ: Princeton University Press, 2006); Eric Goldstein, *The Price of Whiteness: Jews, Race, and American Identity* (Princeton, NJ: Princeton University Press, 2006). Indeed by the late 1980s so much new and intellectually solid work had come out that Johns Hopkins University Press in conjunction with the American Jewish Historical Society issued a five-volume series, *The Jewish People in America.* Volumes in that series include, Eli Faber, *A Time for Planting: The First Migration, 1654–1820;* Hasia R. Diner, *A Time for Gathering: The Second Migration, 1820–1880;* Gerald Sorin, *A Time for Building: The Third Migration, 1880–1920;* Henry Feingold, *A Time For Searching, Entering the Mainstream: 1920–1945;* Edward Shapiro, *A Time for Healing: American Jewry Since World War II.*

10. Two one volume histories of American Jewry appeared in 2005, the year of the 350th anniversary of Jewish settlement in North America. See, Hasia R. Diner, *The Jews of the United States, 1654–2000* (Berkeley: University of California Press, 2005); Jonathan Sarna, *American Judaism* (New Haven: Yale University Press, 2005).

11. The American Jewish Historical Society continues to have a lay orientation as well. It maintains a mailing list of something between 16,000–18,000 individuals. It stages major exhibitions at its home in the Center for Jewish History, which opened in 2000.

Dutch American History in Several Settings: The AADAS and Other Visions

SUZANNE M. SINKE

In *Ethnic Options* Mary Waters suggested that for many U.S. citizens of European descent, to be "ethnic" is a choice, embraced in some settings and ignored in others.[1] There may be some limitations to that statement, but whether to join an ethnic history organization or not is definitely a choice.

Ethnic history organizations offer members the opportunity for cultural and sometimes linguistic exploration, and a venue for in-depth studies that might be rejected or overlooked in other settings. Though such groups typically welcome participation by anyone, in practice, many participants trace their ancestry at least partially to the ethnicity in question.[2] An ethnic history association serves, then, as a venue where one's ethnicity matters. This intense focus on one form of group identity to the (near) exclusion of others, reinforces a form of nationalism that scholars of migration challenge in many ways.[3] It can also obscure the importance of race to ethnic history for European groups.

The case of Dutch American ethnic historical organizations illustrates another element to this story, because there is no single Dutch American group, but rather a number of organizations highlighting the history of people calling themselves Dutch who arrived (and departed) at various times in North American history. I begin then with an overview of the history of one Dutch American historical society, of which I am the president. Beyond that I describe some of the related organizations that dot the North American landscape with scholarship on Dutch Americans. The persistence of divisions related to chronology, audience, and degree of attachment to history as opposed to other areas of research are three key features of this story.

Association for the Advancement of Dutch-American Studies

The Association for the Advancement of Dutch-American Studies—AADAS—was founded in 1979 with the goal of encouraging research on North American Dutch immigrants and those of Dutch ancestry. It had its genesis among the members of a group called the Dutch American Historical Commission, which included persons affiliated with the Netherlands Museum, Calvin College, Hope College, Calvin Seminary, and Western Seminary, all institutions located in west Michigan, and all associated with the Dutch migration of the mid-nineteenth century through the turn of the twentieth century, and particularly with branches of Reformed Protestantism.[4] AADAS took advantage of surging interest in immigration to fill a niche.

Dutch migration to North America existed from the colonial era through the present, but it divides into major migration movements with peaks in three separate centuries, with significant lulls featuring little migration between. These three peaks created populations that (at least in my view) share more in common with other contemporaries from Western Europe than with earlier or later migrant populations from the Low Countries. In other words, the invention of ethnicity finds evidence in the discontinuities of the descendants of the colonial Dutch with those who came later. "Dutch" can mean the descendants of: colonial elites, nineteenth century industrial workers and farm hands, or recent migrants who move their enormous dairy farms to less-regulated pastures.[5] AADAS reflects that tension, for at times it includes a few devotees of colonial descendants, but more often it concentrates on the nineteenth and early twentieth century migrants and their descendants. For example, at least nineteen of twenty-three presentations at the 2005 conference and twenty-one of twenty-seven in the 2007 conference dealt with the nineteenth/early twentieth century group or its descendants.[6] The post-World War II migration gains sporadic attention as well, though not nearly as sustained.

A second artifact of AADAS' foundation is the stress on Protestant Dutch life. This in part reflected the demographic distribution of the migrant group, because though the population of the Netherlands was more closely divided between Protestants and Catholics, Protestants were a significant majority of the nineteenth/early twentieth century migration to North America, and held a disproportionate role in developing Dutch American institutions in that era.[7] AADAS institutional connections to two major Reformed denominational colleges and seminaries also meant the stress would come from those directions, as well as from the personal beliefs of some of the participating scholars. Though AADAS members have researched Catholic and Jewish Dutch individuals and settlements in North America, the balance is decidedly tipped towards Protestantism.[8] Likewise, Dutch migrants and their descendants in Canada tend to get short shrift compared to those in the United States, though the demographics of migration would warrant more research above the border.[9] The group announced plans to meet in Canada in 2009 in part to address this lacuna.

A third artifact of the timing of AADAS' foundation is the focus on one European ethnic group in the context of what people understood as immigration history at the time. Just as ethnic studies sought to challenge patterns of study by using race as the key variable, scholars of the Dutch, like most of those concerned with European migrations, looked to one another for ideas about migration and adaptation. Because much of immigration history examined the migrations to North America from the late nineteenth and early twentieth centuries, AADAS fit into the general framework of the field. As scholars who read ethnic studies picked up the theme of race and the scholarly literature on whiteness grew, only the most academically inclined among AADAS tended to utilize the vocabulary and perspectives of white privilege. The tales of hard times in the log cabin in the woods or the sod house on the prairies, of working countless hours to succeed in business, of pious ministers and hardworking folks, left out many of the advantages that came with white skin and with the acceptance of Dutch colonial antecedents as one part of American heritage.

A fourth artifact of initial organization of AADAS is the stress on conferences and book-length publications. Because the affiliated organizations already sponsored museum exhibits, collected materials, and housed archives, AADAS concentrated more on writing history, and disseminating that information. Calvin College's Heritage Hall, which had major collections on Dutch Americans, began publishing *Origins* in 1983, shortly after AADAS began. This periodical centered on Dutch American life, particularly that associated with the Christian Reformed Church, and targeted a more general rather than a specifically scholarly audience. This became a publication outlet for many AADAS members.

AADAS took on the role of organizing biennial conferences open to all comers, and publishing a newsletter. To this day, these have remained the primary focus of the organization, though the publication record of the group has been spotty at times. In recent years both ongoing functions and publications gained a boost from the Van Raalte Institute, founded in 1993, as part of Hope College (the Reformed counterpart to Calvin).

The Van Raalte Institute, with a bit of help from a former fellow, handled the selection, editing, and dissemination of the AADAS 2007 conference volume.

From the outset, AADAS meant to encourage scholarship, not just by university-trained historians, but also by others, from amateur historians to genealogists. Hence the mission statement included the call to "serve as a clearing house for persons who have a mutual interest in these subjects." University-affiliated scholars typically form the majority of the presenters at conferences, though by no means all. The immediate past president, for example, is an amateur historian who does regular archival research and publishes in local and regional venues. The audience at AADAS conferences is more mixed. At least for some of the plenary sessions and tours it will include a significant number of educated older Dutch Americans, folks who want to know more about great-uncle Gerrit. The audience includes those from the local area, scholars from various parts of the United States and to a lesser degree Canada, and recently a few individuals from the Netherlands.

Geography shaped AADAS as well. AADAS organized its first meeting in Pella, Iowa, and the second in Holland, Michigan, the two founding communities for nineteenth century Dutch immigration. Other cities related to the migration followed: in Iowa, Illinois, and Michigan. Two additional conferences, one in Middelburg in the Netherlands, and one in Holland, Michigan, gained the co-sponsorship of AADAS. In general, funding for conferences came primarily from registration funds and the current treasury, though at times the organizers obtained money from private firms as well as state and local humanities organizations. There has (as yet) not been any sustained fundraising for the group.

AADAS conferences typically ran for two days, with at least one tour of Dutch-American highlights in the landscape, a reading by a Dutch-American writer, and perhaps a genealogy session as part of the program, not to mention a reception featuring wine and Dutch cheese. In early years there were no competing sessions, though recently organizers opted for two parallel sessions for at least part of the conference. Holland, Michigan typically drew the largest audiences, in large part because of ongoing activities of the local historical groups who would then publicize the conference. At their height, conference sessions might draw 175 people, though thirty was more common. The organizers typically chose a theme and tried to solicit contributions around it with an eye towards publication, but other research could easily become part of the program as well.

After the conference the group disseminated—copied in early years—the presentations and sent them to members. Little if anything in the way of editing took place initially, and to this day there is no formal referee process in place. In more recent years, the papers were put together somewhat more professionally thanks to the computer technology at the Joint Archives of Holland or Heritage Hall at Calvin College, and the efforts of their staffs. The most recent volume editors also selected contributions around the conference theme and edited them more systematically for format and style. The volumes now include an index as well.

The *AADAS Newsletter* underwent a similar technological and content transformation. After a hiatus due to the retirement of the editor in the 1990s, it returned in better form, and now appears on a biannual basis. It continues to publish bibliographic notes on works of interest, notices of upcoming conferences, as well as AADAS calls for papers. Recent issues also profiled board members and some of the key related institutions. Reports or reviews of new books and organizational business fill out the pages.

In 2006, after much planning, AADAS launched a website, aadas.net. The conference paper compilations are now coming online, albeit in rather rough form. The group also produced a new brochure to help publicize the organization and its activities. Outreach, in other words, occupied the board's thoughts in recent years. To further that goal, in 2007 AADAS cosponsored a lecture by a well-known Dutch author, Geert Mak, in Grand Rapids, Michigan. Board members started considering more advertising. Needless to say, fund raising may become more important in the group's existence as these programmatic initiatives increase.

Organizationally, the AADAS executive board manages the ongoing activities of the group, though rarely, except at our biennial conference, do we meet. Initially the group had a president, vice-president, one person who served as both secretary and treasurer, and two members at large. A newsletter editor came on board quickly as well. To these posts the group has added a membership secretary. Four members-at-large now round out the list. The board nominates a group of candidates, and the membership, in a meeting that is part of the biennial conference, elects their choices. In practice, the staff at the Dutch heritage programs of the two denominational colleges do much of the clerical work that allows the organization to function.

AADAS has worked sporadically with other Dutch American groups, both history and interdisciplinary groups, as well as Dutch American cultural groups such as the Dutch Immigrant Society, which regularly reports on our activities, but AADAS has not worked effectively with pan-ethnic organizations such as the Immigration and Ethnic History Society. This, I see as one of the challenges for the future. Neither have we cosponsored museum exhibitions, sessions at other conferences, or other similar opportunities. But then, we are a small group.

AADAS went from 55 dues-paying members in 1981 to 98 members in 1982. The numbers continued to climb for a time, and then fluctuated, contracting and expanding slightly depending on the success of the latest conference. In any case membership has held steady for a number of years somewhere between 150 and 200. As of mid-2007 there were approximately 165 members. Thus the group remained one of the smaller ethnic history organizations. Because the institutions with which we are associated have deep pockets and strong staffs, we are unlikely to face extinction soon, but without them we could be in deep trouble quickly. The strength of the group relies heavily on the board members. On the other hand, if the submissions for the 2007 biennial conference and for that of 2006 are any indication, there is a group of younger scholars now in the pipeline who want to promote what our new slogan reads: "sound scholarship to research and preserve our common history."

Other Dutch American Organizations

AADAS was never alone in its charge to promote the history of Dutch Americans. The focus on the migrations of the last two centuries, however, distinguished AADAS from groups interested in those of Dutch ancestry from the colonial era, such as the Holland Society, which boasted a much older pedigree, from 1885.[10] Both groups shared an interest in locating and disseminating information about their respective topics, and both included a significant contingent of amateur historians and genealogists in addition to academics. Apart from the time period of interest, AADAS shared some similarities with the current Holland Society, but it also differed in important ways.

A major difference between the groups is that membership in the Holland Society in New York was and still is limited to those who are descendants in a "direct male line of an ancestor who lived in New Netherland before or during 1675."[11] As Dutch scholar Jacob van Hinte wrote in 1928, this was not just an historical society "for they set up a class organization whose membership was drawn from those in the higher ranks."[12] At least in recent years the Holland Society provided a category of "Friends" that made it possible for others to gain access to the publications, genealogical assistance, and other benefits of association, though not to voting membership. This group made a point of including official representatives of the current Dutch government, from the queen to the local consul, in the Friends category.

Other local variations of the Holland Society, such as the Philadelphia chapter which began in 1892, also required colonial Dutch blood lines, as did the Society of Holland Dames, of the same period.[13] The elitism, but not the colonial connections, became part of chapters elsewhere, including the Holland Society of Chicago, which began in 1895. For the Chicago group, Dutch ancestry from any time period was sufficient, and it attracted some of the most prominent descendants of nineteenth-century migration as well.[14] The requirement for proving ancestry meant the group promoted genealogy. As was common for the era around the turn of the twentieth century, this chapter also advocated for a positive image of the Dutch in United States history. The core New York Holland Society constituency continued its outreach of promoting Dutch American history throughout the twentieth century and beyond, even as other chapters such as that in Chicago waned.

A second major difference between the Holland Society and AADAS related to size, as some chapters of the Holland Society are close to the entire membership of AADAS. The Holland Society chapters illustrate a much more social function in many locations in recent years, with yacht races, winery tours, and concerts interspersed among reports of attending lectures on Dutch heritage, Dutch language instruction, or discussions with the Dutch consul in a particular location. Not surprisingly the Midwest chapter of the Holland Society most reflects the nineteenth-century connection, with members attending a local Dutch festival to watch wooden shoe dancers and street scrub-

bers.[15] Attention to promoting Dutch American history more broadly, however, remains a secondary or even non-existent goal for some chapters. The New York chapter, on the other hand, embraced this goal from its outset, and has continued this into the present.

In the early years, from 1886 to 1929, the New York chapter of the Holland Society sponsored yearbooks on colonial Dutch topics. This organization began publishing *De Halve Maen,* a journal "illuminating the Dutch contribution to American history" in 1922.[16] The glossy quarterly serves as an outlet for historical and folkloric information about the colonial Dutch presence. Articles on aspects of material culture, such as architecture, decorative arts, and agriculture, intertwine with scholarship on individuals and organizations of New Netherland, particularly those related to the Reformed Church and its luminaries. Later collections reprinted some of this information, in addition to adding other topics.[17]

In 1974 the Holland Society partnered with the Library of the State of New York in Albany in the New Netherland Project. Under the direction of Dr. Charles Gehring, the project sought to translate and publish all seventeenth-century Dutch documents held in the Archives. The goal was both to make this information available to scholars of colonial history who did not read Dutch, as well as to make it accessible to a general public, in hopes this would "demonstrate the impact of the Dutch in American colonial history."[18] Volume after volume rolled off the presses as the project participants worked their way through the voluminous papers.

The New Netherland Project added another dimension with the formation of the New Netherland Institute, a group designed to create interest in the project, disseminate information about the publications, and raise funds. The group published a quarterly newsletter, *De Nieu Nederlandse Marcurius,* with information on upcoming lectures and conferences on colonial Dutch topics.[19] The New Netherland Project gained National Endowment for the Humanities support, and together with the New Netherland Institute continued in the task of disseminating colonial Dutch material to a wide audience through a web site.

The public outreach of the New Netherland Project (and AADAS) contrasts with another organization, the American Association for Netherlandic Studies (AANS), formed in 1982, around the same time as AADAS. AANS traced its origins to a group of Dutch language scholars who began meeting at the annual Modern Language Association meetings in the 1960s. The group started publishing a newsletter in 1975, and sponsored its first interdisciplinary conference in 1982.[20] These two activities, the newsletter and conferences (with related publications), remain key components of AANS activities. AANS was and is more closely tied to an academic audience. As its website states: "AANS is a university-level organization that promotes the study of the language, literature, history, art history and general culture of the Low Countries."[21] In contrast to the centrality of history to AADAS, AANS is more interdisciplinary, serving in particular as a mouthpiece for scholars of Dutch language and literature.

The AANS *Newsletter* reflects this audience, regularly presenting book reviews, exhibition reports, scholarship opportunities, news of summer Dutch language study programs, and reports of related conferences, in addition to news of its own interdisciplinary conference. Ethnic history, in other words, is peripheral at best. The same is true for the book-length publications. In the proceedings of the third interdisciplinary conference, for example, three of twenty-five articles dealt with Dutch American history, nine explored Dutch language issues, and ten handled questions of Dutch literature.[22] In the subsequent volume, only one of twenty-five articles focused on the Dutch American history.[23] AANS by no means discouraged participation by historians, but history as a discipline remained a minor part of most programs and publications.

The Canadian counterpart of AANS, the Canadian Association for the Advancement of Netherlandic Studies/Association canadienne pour l'avancement des études néerlandaises (CAANS/ACAEN), had its origins in the 1960s, gaining official incorporation in 1971, just before its U.S. counterpart. Because all the Canadian learned societies in the humanities and social sciences meet concurrently on an annual basis, CAANS could organize its annual meeting sessions in this context and thus coordinate interdisciplinary activities somewhat more easily than its U.S. counterpart. In addition, however, local chapters of CAANS organized topical conferences, most often on literary themes.[24] In 1980 CAANS began a semiannual publication, the *Canadian Journal of Netherlandic Studies,* which continues to this day. This journal provides articles on literature and art as well as North American and European History. As with AANS, the balance in terms of contents tends towards language and linguistics. In addition the group publishes a Newsletter, available primarily in electronic format since 2007.[25]

Like AANS, CAANS sought to promote the teaching of Dutch language and culture in Canada, but in addition it fostered outreach through local chapters in various cities around the country. To this purpose, the local chapters often sponsored a variety of activities. In Montreal in the first half of 2005, for instance, the chapter organized a historical lecture by a scholar, another lecture by someone who had lived through the assault on Arnhem in the Second World War, a report on the experience of a prisoner of war in a Japanese work camp during the Second World War, a lecture on the current nominees for a poetry prize in the Netherlands, a film evening featuring a documentary in Dutch, and the annual chapter meeting in the form of a dinner at one member's home.[26] The local chapters often united those of Dutch ancestry for a variety of activities. While the Dutch departments at U.S. universities sometimes organized similar activities, the scope of such activism in the CAANS chapter groups illustrated a different organizational model and the consequences in terms of public participation.

Yet another organization that shows some interest in the Dutch in North America is the Association for Low Country Studies (ALCS) in Great Britain and Ireland. This group began publishing *Dutch Crossing: A Journal of Low Country Studies* in 1977. The multidisciplinary journal with a scholarly focus presented articles in English about the Netherlands and Belgium, and the relationship of those countries to the English-speaking world.[27] Twice a year *Dutch Crossing* would provide a mix of language, literature, history, and a variety of other subjects. The inclusion of translations, research reports, and other news, made this a rather mixed venue. Conference papers from the biennial conference of the ALCS constituted a regular feature. The Nederlandse Taalunie, or Dutch Language Union in the Hague, assisted with funding this publication, as it did with various activities related to language in North America (meaning both AANS and CAANS). In addition to *Dutch Crossing,* the ALCS published *Crossways: Occasional Series,* for books, and a biannual newsletter. ALCS sponsored an annual essay prize contest, with undergraduate and postgraduate categories, as well as research grants.[28] It helped coordinate the "Student Days" where students at the nine universities in the U.K. and Ireland where Dutch was taught could come together and enjoy speakers and tours.[29] Once again, Dutch American history might appear sporadically in these venues.

The Dutch colonial past also fell within the purview of the Society for Netherlandic History (SNH), a group that formed in the United States around the beginning of 2000. The SNH characterized its aim as providing a "forum where specialists of Dutch and Belgian history can present their work and exchange ideas."[30] It sponsored three biennial conferences, with themes to promote discussion.[31] At least one of the conferences resulted in a publication.[32] As the name implied, however, the emphasis was on history in Europe more than in the colonial setting. The nineteenth-century past remained outside this purview.

This overview by no means exhausts the groups which have at least passing interest in Dutch American ethnic history. Overall, AADAS fills a particular niche for the descendants of nineteenth and twentieth-century Dutch American migrants and those who study this group. Several other groups work to promote Dutch language and culture in other ways, with a minor role for ethnic history as part of this. The Dutch government provides at least supplementary funds most consistently for language and literature studies. The Holland Society, despite its strong genealogical emphasis in early years, has become closer to a counterpart for AADAS in recent years with its promotion of Dutch North American colonial history, though it shows little interest in broadening that emphasis to Dutch migrants of later years. AADAS continues to rely heavily on the denominational colleges associated with Dutch American migrants of the nineteenth century. How long that focus can remain as many descendants of the fourth, fifth, and later generations come to the fore, will remain an important question. Some suggest that only the religious ties will remain, particularly because Dutch ethnicity remains an optional identity for many of those who could embrace it. Others see the optional identities tied to ethnic histories as one part of multicultural worlds.

Notes

1. Mary C. Waters, *Ethnic Options: Choosing Identities in America* (Berkeley: University of California Press, 1990).

2. A rather negative impression of this connection appears in Paul Spickard, *Almost All Aliens: Immigration, Race, and Colonialism in American History and Identity* (New York: Routledge, 2007), p. xix.

3. See for example Dirk Hoerder, "Historians and Their Data: The Complex Shift from Nation-State Approaches to the Study of People's Transcultural Lives," and Matthew Frye Jacobson, "More 'Trans'; Less 'National' " both in *Journal of American Ethnic History,* Vol. 25, No. 4 (Summer 2006), 85–96 and 74–84 respectively.

4. *AADAS Newletter,* Vol. I, July 1980, p. 1.

5. Werner Sollors popularized the term "invention of ethnicity" in his book of the same name, published in New York by Oxford University Press in 1989. Research on both colonial Dutch and nineteenth-century workers is extensive. That on Dutch dairy farmers is only now coming into view: One paper at the 2007 AADAS conference dealt with this phenomenon. It remains largely the purview of non-historians.

6. AADAS conference brochures, 2005, 2007.

7. This stress on Protestantism remains a major puzzle for audiences in the Netherlands. Hans Krabbendam used the continuing strength of Dutch American Protestant religious institutions compared to absence of similar "Dutch" Catholic continuation as justification for this emphasis in his *Vrijheid in het Verschiet: Nederlandse emigratie naar Amerika 1840–1940* (Hilversum: Verloren, 2006), introduction.

8. See Yda Saueressig-Schreuder, *Dutch Catholic Immigrant Settlement in Wisconsin, 1850–1905* (New York: Garland, 1989); Robert P. Swierenga, *The Fore-runners: Dutch Jewry in the North American diaspora* (Detroit: Wayne State University Press, 1994).

9. The placement of a book session on the 2005 AADAS program for the publication of a revised and translated version of Johan Stellingwerff's *Iowa Letters: Dutch Immigrants on the American Frontier* (Grand Rapids, MI: William B. Eerdmans, 2004), but no comparable session on Donald Sinnema's *The First Dutch Settlement in Alberta: Letters from the Pioneer Years 1903–14* (Calgary: University of Calgary Press, 2005) hints at the division.

10. Information from the Holland Society home page, http://www. hollandsociety.org/, accessed June 29, 2007.

11. "Membership," http://www.hollandsociety.org/membership .html, accessed January 3, 2008.

12. Jacob van Hinte, *Netherlanders in America,* trans. by Adriaan de Wit (Grand Rapids, MI: Baker Book House, 1985 [Reprint, 1928],) p. 71.

13. Annette Stott, *Holland Mania* (Woodstock, NY: Overlook Press, 1998), pp. 206–207.

14. Robert P. Swierenga, *Dutch Chicago* (Grand Rapids, MI: William B. Eerdmans Publishing Company, 2002), pp. 529, 533.

15. "Calendar of Branch Activities," http://www.hollandsociety .org/branch_activities.html, accessed January 3, 2008.

16. "Publications of the Holland Society," http://www. hollandsociety.org/pub.html, accessed June 29, 2007.

17. For example Records of the Reformed Dutch Church of Bergen, NJ, appeared in several yearbook issues and then was reprinted in 1976 by Genealogical Publishing Co.

18. "About the New Netherland Project," http://www.nnp.org/nnp/ index.html, accessed June 27, 2007.

19. "De Nieu Nederlandse Marcurius," http://www.nnp.org/nni/ Marcurius/index.html, accessed January 3, 2008.

20. William Z. Shetter, "20 Years of AANS," *AANS Newsletter,* Vol. 58 (October 2002), 2–3.

21. http://polyglot.lss.wisc.edu/aans/, accessed January 5, 2008.

22. Ton J. Broos, ed., *Publications of the American Association for Netherlandic Studies: Papers from the Third Interdisciplinary Conference on Netherlandic Studies* (Lanham, MD: University Press of America, 1988).

23. Margriet Bruijn Lacy, ed., *Publications of the American Association for Netherlandic Studies, 3: The Low Countries: Multidisciplinary Perspectives* (Lanham, MD: University Press of America, 1990).

24. A. P. Diereck, "History," http://www.caans-acaen.ca/Who/ index.html, accessed January 5, 2008.

25. Basil Kingstone, "Editorial," *CAANS/ACAEN Newsletter,* December 2006.

26. "Reports from Chapters," *CAANS/ACAEN Newsletter,* August 2005.

27. "Dutch Crossing: A Journal of Low Country Studies," http://alcs.group.shef.ac.uk/publications/Dutchcrossing.htm, accessed June 29, 2007.

28. "Research Grants," http://alcs.group.shef.ac.uk/grantsandprizes/ grants.htm, and "The ACLS Prize for Low Country Studies," http://alcs.group.shef.ac.uk/grantsandprizes/prize.htm, accessed June 29, 2007.

29. "Student Days," http://alcs.group.shef.ac.uk/studentdays/ studentdays.htm, accessed June 29, 2007.

30. "News: Society for Netherlandic History," *De Nieu Nederlandse Marcurius,* Vol. 16, No. 1 (February 2000), p. 1.

31. "Society for Netherlandic History," http://homepages.udayton .edu/ CarlsoMB/snh.htm, accessed June 29, 2007.

32. Wayne te Brake and Wim Klooster, eds., *Power and the City in the Netherlandic World* (Leiden: Brill, 2006).

UNIT 9

The Presidential Election 2008

Unit Selections

Key Points to Consider

- Certainly a variety of issues and positions about public policy, presentations of self and competency, as well as other affinities and attractions will drive the decisions of voters in this election. Yet each of these aspects may include a ethnic and race sub-text. What did voters report as most determinative of the choice?

- What issues were particularly important?

- What is the central argument and appeal of Barack Obama's speech on race in America?

- How important is ethnic identity?

- Are race and ethnicity limited to symbolic politics and marginal to the central issues of America foreign and domestic policy?

- What does playing the race card mean? What is a wedge issue?

- How do identity politics and issues politics address representation, consent to be governed, and the universal aspirations of democracy?

- How extensively were ethnically and racial charged advertisements used? Were they effective or did they produce backlashes?

- What explains different levels of ethnic group interest and mobilization?

- Does anyone really reveal that their choice was based on race and ethnicity?

- What do you make of concentrated ethnic settlements and voting patterns in such locations?

- What techniques of voter mobilization seem especially effective in this campaign?

- Are party affiliation, and ethnicity, or issue orientation drivers of electoral behavior?

- What occurs at the intersection of ethnicity and gender in American politics?

- In what respects are ethnic factors in national elections and local elections different from each other?

- Is ideology related to race and ethnicity? How? Why?

- In what respect is regionalism important and related to ethnic and race relations?

Student Web Site

www.mhcls.com

Internet References

CNN Election Headquarters
   http://www.cnn.com/ELECTION/2008/
President-Elect Obama's Web Site
   http://change.gov/

A generation ago amid significant ethnic turbulence and considerable expansion of electoral eligibility, Levy and Kramer's *The Ethnic Factor: How America's Minorities Decide Elections* attempted to clarify conflicting claims regarding advocacy, resistance, and denial that ethnic group political behavior was relevant and salient. Since that time, the revolutions in data collection have revealed fine-grain patterns of ethnic group settlement, and have significantly expanded our knowledge of political mobilization strategies, the impact of voter turnout, and the connection of these variables to ethnicity and race.

Levy and Kramer argued that fallacious claims about the decline of ethnic politics were posited on the notion that race and ethnicity were divisive and unworthy of the American regime and its grounding in individual rights. Normative political science under the influence of Enlightenment universalism, and the positivistic expectation regarding the waning of ethnicity fashioned and civics education popularized this critique of ethnicity and ethnic saliency. Claims that ethnic politics were visceral and emotional, and thus without standing, were challenged by the emergence of identity politics and particularistic realism of ongoing cultural pluralism, and the revivals of ethnicity as meaning producing technique. The overwhelming evidence of cultural and social organization rooted in ethnicity characterize all human orders at the local level of experience. Such patterns of meaning are prior to more complex forms of social, economic, and political orders. Such complex forms of order may in fact deepen ethnic and racial segmentations. In fact, all existing political orders must account for the persistence and ongoing malleability of ethnicity as a form of social experience, cultural invention, and personal identities, as well as the wellspring of images and narratives that can be incorporated into political ideologies.

Levy and Kramer's pioneering work came at a time when few acknowledged the importance of the ethnic factor except for local political practitioners, which their experience, commonsense, and political success would not allow them to deny. Levy and Kramer applied such perception as well as existing polling data to argue the following theses concerning national elections:

- a serious independent, black presidential candidate would assure the defeat of any Democratic Party candidate;

- Italian-Americans did not follow the Republican Party as strongly as conventional wisdom held;

- an Italian-American on either Party's ticket was good political sense;

- Jewish Americans were among the most liberal;

- Myths of a backlash notwithstanding, Polish-Americans continue to vote for the Democratic Party;

- Hispanic voters are at a political takeoff point, which could determine the outcome of presidential elections in California and Texas; and

- Irish-Americans are assimilated and middle class, but vote 2 to 1 Democratic.

© The McGraw-Hill Companies

The 2008 presidential election and the successes of Barack Obama in Democratic caucuses, primary elections, his nomination at the Democratic National convention, and his victory over John McCain produced a plethora of analysis and interpretation about the race factor and its distribution in the electorate, the impacts of Obama's genealogy and style, and the forms of campaign strategies and tactics that were employed. The analysis of such factors now that the election is a part of history will continue to be tabulated and will serve future candidates in their quest for office. Such macro findings will be spatially disaggregated and correlated with ethnic and race patterns. Pre-election polling data and exit polls will add further information, which the reader should add to the articles found in this edition. Thus, with the prospective views found in this collection of articles and the post election perspectives of the ethnic and race factor, you are invited to contribute some insight into our understanding of this singularly interesting and history-making event in race and ethnic relations. Articles in this unit are designed to explore race and ethnic relations through the various lenses of their authors. The Presidential Election of 2008 includes the candidacy of the son of an immigrant from Kenya, whose mother was from Kansas, whose formative years included living abroad in another culture and later in one of the newest and geographically distant states to join the United States of America. This election has already contributed a massive amount of discussion of race in America. The outcome of this new period of political change will call further attention to the ways in which the personal and political intersect race and ethnic relations in our time.

Transcript of Obama's Speech

The following is a transcript of Sen. Barack Obama's speech, as provided by Obama's campaign.

We the people, in order to form a more perfect union. Two hundred and twenty one years ago, in a hall that still stands across the street, a group of men gathered and, with these simple words, launched America's improbable experiment in democracy.

Farmers and scholars; statesmen and patriots who had traveled across an ocean to escape tyranny and persecution finally made real their declaration of independence at a Philadelphia convention that lasted through the spring of 1787.

The document they produced was eventually signed but ultimately unfinished. It was stained by this nation's original sin of slavery, a question that divided the colonies and brought the convention to a stalemate until the founders chose to allow the slave trade to continue for at least 20 more years, and to leave any final resolution to future generations.

Of course, the answer to the slavery question was already embedded within our Constitution—a Constitution that had at its very core the ideal of equal citizenship under the law; a Constitution that promised its people liberty, and justice, and a union that could be and should be perfected over time.

And yet words on a parchment would not be enough to deliver slaves from bondage, or provide men and women of every color and creed their full rights and obligations as citizens of the United States.

What would be needed were Americans in successive generations who were willing to do their part—through protests and struggle, on the streets and in the courts, through a civil war and civil disobedience and always at great risk—to narrow that gap between the promise of our ideals and the reality of their time.

This was one of the tasks we set forth at the beginning of this campaign—to continue the long march of those who came before us, a march for a more just, more equal, more free, more caring and more prosperous America.

I chose to run for the presidency at this moment in history because I believe deeply that we cannot solve the challenges of our time unless we solve them together—unless we perfect our union by understanding that we may have different stories, but we hold common hopes; that we may not look the same and we may not have come from the same place, but we all want to move in the same direction—towards a better future for our children and our grandchildren.

This belief comes from my unyielding faith in the decency and generosity of the American people. But it also comes from my own American story.

I am the son of a black man from Kenya and a white woman from Kansas. I was raised with the help of a white grandfather who survived a Depression to serve in Patton's Army during World War II and a white grandmother who worked on a bomber assembly line at Fort Leavenworth while he was overseas.

I've gone to some of the best schools in America and lived in one of the world's poorest nations. I am married to a black American who carries within her the blood of slaves and slaveowners—an inheritance we pass on to our two precious daughters.

I have brothers, sisters, nieces, nephews, uncles and cousins, of every race and every hue, scattered across three continents, and for as long as I live, I will never forget that in no other country on Earth is my story even possible.

It's a story that hasn't made me the most conventional candidate. But it is a story that has seared into my genetic makeup the idea that this nation is more than the sum of its parts—that out of many, we are truly one.

Throughout the first year of this campaign, against all predictions to the contrary, we saw how hungry the American people were for this message of unity.

Despite the temptation to view my candidacy through a purely racial lens, we won commanding victories in states with some of the whitest populations in the country. In South Carolina, where the Confederate Flag still flies, we built a powerful coalition of African-Americans and white Americans.

This is not to say that race has not been an issue in the campaign. At various stages in the campaign, some commentators have deemed me either "too black" or "not black enough."

We saw racial tensions bubble to the surface during the week before the South Carolina primary. The press has scoured every exit poll for the latest evidence of racial polarization, not just in terms of white and black, but black and brown as well.

And yet, it has only been in the last couple of weeks that the discussion of race in this campaign has taken a particularly divisive turn.

On one end of the spectrum, we've heard the implication that my candidacy is somehow an exercise in affirmative action, that it's based solely on the desire of wide-eyed liberals to purchase racial reconciliation on the cheap.

On the other end, we've heard my former pastor, Rev. Jeremiah Wright, use incendiary language to express views that have the potential not only to widen the racial divide, but views that denigrate both the greatness and the goodness of our nation—that rightly offend white and black alike.

I have already condemned, in unequivocal terms, the statements of Rev. Wright that have caused such controversy. For some, nagging questions remain.

Did I know him to be an occasionally fierce critic of American domestic and foreign policy? Of course. Did I ever hear him make remarks that could be considered controversial while I sat in church? Yes. Did I strongly disagree with many of his political views? Absolutely—just as I'm sure many of you have heard remarks from your pastors, priests or rabbis with which you strongly disagreed.

But the remarks that have caused this recent firestorm weren't simply controversial. They weren't simply a religious leader's effort to speak out against perceived injustice.

Instead, they expressed a profoundly distorted view of this country—a view that sees white racism as endemic, and that elevates what is wrong with America above all that we know is right with America, a view that sees the conflicts in the Middle East as rooted primarily in the actions of stalwart allies like Israel, instead of emanating from the perverse and hateful ideologies of radical Islam.

As such, Rev. Wright's comments were not only wrong but divisive, divisive at a time when we need unity; racially charged at a time when we need to come together to solve a set of monumental problems—two wars, a terrorist threat, a falling economy, a chronic health care crisis and potentially devastating climate change; problems that are neither black or white or Latino or Asian, but rather problems that confront us all.

Given my background, my politics, and my professed values and ideals, there will no doubt be those for whom my statements of condemnation are not enough. Why associate myself with Rev. Wright in the first place, they may ask? Why not join another church?

And I confess that if all that I knew of Rev. Wright were the snippets of those sermons that have run in an endless loop on the television and YouTube, or if Trinity United Church of Christ conformed to the caricatures being peddled by some commentators, there is no doubt that I would react in much the same way

But the truth is, that isn't all that I know of the man. The man I met more than 20 years ago is a man who helped introduce me to my Christian faith, a man who spoke to me about our obligations to love one another; to care for the sick and lift up the poor.

He is a man who served his country as a U.S. Marine, who has studied and lectured at some of the finest universities and seminaries in the country, and who for over thirty years led a church that serves the community by doing God's work here on Earth—by housing the homeless, ministering to the needy, providing day care services and scholarships and prison ministries, and reaching out to those suffering from HIV/AIDS.

In my first book, "Dreams From My Father," I described the experience of my first service at Trinity.

"People began to shout, to rise from their seats and clap and cry out, a forceful wind carrying the reverend's voice up into the rafters . . . . And in that single note—hope!—I heard something else; at the foot of that cross, inside the thousands of churches across the city, I imagined the stories of ordinary black people merging with the stories of David and Goliath, Moses and Pharaoh, the Christians in the lion's den, Ezekiel's field of dry bones.

"Those stories—of survival, and freedom, and hope—became our story, my story; the blood that had spilled was our blood, the tears our tears; until this black church, on this bright day, seemed once more a vessel carrying the story of a people into future generations and into a larger world.

"Our trials and triumphs became at once unique and universal, black and more than black; in chronicling our journey, the stories and songs gave us a means to reclaim memories that we didn't need to feel shame about . . . memories that all people might study and cherish—and with which we could start to rebuild."

That has been my experience at Trinity. Like other predominantly black churches across the country, Trinity embodies the black community in its entirety—the doctor and the welfare mom, the model student and the former gang-banger.

Like other black churches, Trinity's services are full of raucous laughter and sometimes bawdy humor. They are full of dancing, clapping, screaming and shouting that may seem jarring to the untrained ear.

The church contains in full the kindness and cruelty, the fierce intelligence and the shocking ignorance, the struggles and successes, the love and yes, the bitterness and bias that make up the black experience in America.

And this helps explain, perhaps, my relationship with Rev. Wright. As imperfect as he may be, he has been like family to me. He strengthened my faith, officiated my wedding, and baptized my children.

Not once in my conversations with him have I heard him talk about any ethnic group in derogatory terms, or treat whites with whom he interacted with anything but courtesy and respect. He contains within him the contradictions—the good and the bad—of the community that he has served diligently for so many years.

I can no more disown him than I can disown the black community. I can no more disown him than I can my white grandmother—a woman who helped raise me, a woman who sacrificed again and again for me, a woman who loves me as much as she loves anything in this world, but a woman who once confessed her fear of black men who passed by her on the street, and who on more than one occasion has uttered racial or ethnic stereotypes that made me cringe.

These people are a part of me. And they are a part of America, this country that I love.

Some will see this as an attempt to justify or excuse comments that are simply inexcusable. I can assure you it is not. I suppose the politically safe thing would be to move on from this episode and just hope that it fades into the woodwork.

We can dismiss Rev. Wright as a crank or a demagogue, just as some have dismissed Geraldine Ferraro, in the aftermath of her recent statements, as harboring some deep-seated racial bias.

But race is an issue that I believe this nation cannot afford to ignore right now. We would be making the same mistake that Rev. Wright made in his offending sermons about America—to simplify and stereotype and amplify the negative to the point that it distorts reality.

The fact is that the comments that have been made and the issues that have surfaced over the last few weeks reflect the complexities of race in this country that we've never really worked through—a part of our union that we have yet to perfect.

And if we walk away now, if we simply retreat into our respective corners, we will never be able to come together and solve challenges like health care, or education, or the need to find good jobs for every American.

Understanding this reality requires a reminder of how we arrived at this point. As William Faulkner once wrote, "The past isn't dead and buried. In fact, it isn't even past." We do not need to recite here the history of racial injustice in this country.

But we do need to remind ourselves that so many of the disparities that exist in the African-American community today can be directly traced to inequalities passed on from an earlier generation that suffered under the brutal legacy of slavery and Jim Crow.

Segregated schools were, and are, inferior schools; we still haven't fixed them, fifty years after Brown v. Board of Education, and the inferior education they provided, then and now, helps explain the pervasive achievement gap between today's black and white students.

Legalized discrimination—where blacks were prevented, often through violence, from owning property, or loans were not granted to African-American business owners, or black homeowners could not access FHA mortgages, or blacks were excluded from unions, or the police force, or fire departments—meant that black families could not amass any meaningful wealth to bequeath to future generations.

That history helps explain the wealth and income gap between black and white, and the concentrated pockets of poverty that persists in so many of today's urban and rural communities.

A lack of economic opportunity among black men, and the shame and frustration that came from not being able to provide for one's family, contributed to the erosion of black families—a problem that welfare policies for many years may have worsened.

And the lack of basic services in so many urban black neighborhoods—parks for kids to play in, police walking the beat, regular garbage pick-up and building code enforcement—all helped create a cycle of violence, blight and neglect that continue to haunt us.

This is the reality in which Rev. Wright and other African-Americans of his generation grew up. They came of age in the late fifties and early sixties, a time when segregation was still the law of the land and opportunity was systematically constricted.

What's remarkable is not how many failed in the face of discrimination, but rather how many men and women overcame the odds; how many were able to make a way out of no way for those like me who would come after them.

But for all those who scratched and clawed their way to get a piece of the American Dream, there were many who didn't make it—those who were ultimately defeated, in one way or another, by discrimination.

That legacy of defeat was passed on to future generations—those young men and, increasingly, young women who we see standing on street corners or languishing in our prisons, without hope or prospects for the future. Even for those blacks who did make it, questions of race, and racism, continue to define their worldview in fundamental ways.

For the men and women of Rev. Wright's generation, the memories of humiliation and doubt and fear have not gone away; nor has the anger and the bitterness of those years.

That anger may not get expressed in public, in front of white co-workers or white friends. But it does find voice in the barbershop or around the kitchen table. At times, that anger is exploited by politicians, to gin up votes along racial lines, or to make up for a politician's own failings.

And occasionally it finds voice in the church on Sunday morning, in the pulpit and in the pews. The fact that so many people are surprised to hear that anger in some of Rev. Wright's sermons simply reminds us of the old truism that the most segregated hour in American life occurs on Sunday morning.

That anger is not always productive; indeed, all too often it distracts attention from solving real problems; it keeps us from squarely facing our own complicity in our condition, and prevents the African-American community from forging the alliances it needs to bring about real change.

But the anger is real; it is powerful; and to simply wish it away, to condemn it without understanding its roots, only serves to widen the chasm of misunderstanding that exists between the races.

In fact, a similar anger exists within segments of the white community. Most working- and middle-class white Americans don't feel that they have been particularly privileged by their race.

Their experience is the immigrant experience—as far as they're concerned, no one's handed them anything, they've built it from scratch. They've worked hard all their lives, many times only to see their jobs shipped overseas or their pension dumped after a lifetime of labor.

They are anxious about their futures, and feel their dreams slipping away; in an era of stagnant wages and global competition, opportunity comes to be seen as a zero sum game, in which your dreams come at my expense.

So when they are told to bus their children to a school across town; when they hear that an African-American is getting an advantage in landing a good job or a spot in a good college because of an injustice that they themselves never committed; when they're told that their fears about crime in urban neighborhoods are somehow prejudiced, resentment builds over time.

Like the anger within the black community, these resentments aren't always expressed in polite company. But they have helped shape the political landscape for at least a generation.

Anger over welfare and affirmative action helped forge the Reagan Coalition. Politicians routinely exploited fears of crime for their own electoral ends. Talk show hosts and conservative commentators built entire careers unmasking bogus claims of racism while dismissing legitimate discussions of racial injustice and inequality as mere political correctness or reverse racism.

Just as black anger often proved counterproductive, so have these white resentments distracted attention from the real culprits of the middle-class squeeze—a corporate culture rife with inside dealing, questionable accounting practices and short-term greed; a Washington dominated by lobbyists and special interests; economic policies that favor the few over the many.

And yet, to wish away the resentments of white Americans, to label them as misguided or even racist, without recognizing they are grounded in legitimate concerns—this too widens the racial divide, and blocks the path to understanding.

This is where we are right now. It's a racial stalemate we've been stuck in for years. Contrary to the claims of some of my critics, black and white, I have never been so naive as to believe that we can get beyond our racial divisions in a single election cycle, or with a single candidacy—particularly a candidacy as imperfect as my own.

But I have asserted a firm conviction—a conviction rooted in my faith in God and my faith in the American people—that working together we can move beyond some of our old racial wounds, and that in fact we have no choice if we are to continue on the path of a more perfect union.

For the African-American community, that path means embracing the burdens of our past without becoming victims of our past. It means continuing to insist on a full measure of justice in every aspect of American life.

But it also means binding our particular grievances—for better health care, and better schools, and better jobs—to the larger aspirations of all Americans, the white woman struggling to break the glass ceiling, the white man whose been laid off, the immigrant trying to feed his family.

And it means taking full responsibility for own lives—by demanding more from our fathers, and spending more time with our children, and reading to them, and teaching them that while they may face challenges and discrimination in their own lives, they must never succumb to despair or cynicism; they must always believe that they can write their own destiny.

Ironically, this quintessentially American—and yes, conservative—notion of self-help found frequent expression in Rev. Wright's sermons. But what my former pastor too often failed to understand is that embarking on a program of self-help also requires a belief that society can change.

The profound mistake of Rev. Wright's sermons is not that he spoke about racism in our society. It's that he spoke as if our society was static; as if no progress has been made; as if this country—a country that has made it possible for one of his own members to run for the highest office in the land and build a coalition of white and black, Latino and Asian, rich and poor, young and old—is still irrevocably bound to a tragic past.

But what we know—what we have seen—is that America can change. That is the true genius of this nation. What we have already achieved gives us hope—the audacity to hope—for what we can and must achieve tomorrow.

In the white community, the path to a more perfect union means acknowledging that what ails the African-American community does not just exist in the minds of black people; that the legacy of discrimination—and current incidents of discrimination, while less overt than in the past—are real and must be addressed.

Not just with words, but with deeds—by investing in our schools and our communities; by enforcing our civil rights laws and ensuring fairness in our criminal justice system; by providing this generation with ladders of opportunity that were unavailable for previous generations.

It requires all Americans to realize that your dreams do not have to come at the expense of my dreams; that investing in the health, welfare and education of black and brown and white children will ultimately help all of America prosper.

In the end, then, what is called for is nothing more, and nothing less, than what all the world's great religions demand—that we do unto others as we would have them do unto us. Let us be our brother's keeper, Scripture tells us. Let us be our sister's keeper. Let us find that common stake we all have in one another, and let our politics reflect that spirit as well.

For we have a choice in this country. We can accept a politics that breeds division, and conflict, and cynicism. We can tackle race only as spectacle—as we did in the O.J. trial—or in the wake of tragedy, as we did in the aftermath of Katrina—or as fodder for the nightly news.

We can play Rev. Wright's sermons on every channel, every day and talk about them from now until the election, and make the only question in this campaign whether or not the American people think that I somehow believe or sympathize with his most offensive words.

We can pounce on some gaffe by a Hillary supporter as evidence that she's playing the race card, or we can speculate on whether white men will all flock to John McCain in the general election regardless of his policies.

We can do that.

But if we do, I can tell you that in the next election, we'll be talking about some other distraction. And then another one. And then another one. And nothing will change.

That is one option. Or, at this moment, in this election, we can come together and say, "Not this time." This time we want to talk about the crumbling schools that are stealing the future of black children and white children and Asian children and Hispanic children and Native American children.

This time we want to reject the cynicism that tells us that these kids can't learn; that those kids who don't look like us are somebody else's problem. The children of America are not those kids, they are our kids, and we will not let them fall behind in a 21st Century economy. Not this time.

This time we want to talk about how the lines in the emergency room are filled with whites and blacks and Hispanics who do not have health care, who don't have the power on their own to overcome the special interests in Washington, but who can take them on if we do it together.

This time we want to talk about the shuttered mills that once provided a decent life for men and women of every race, and the homes for sale that once belonged to Americans from every religion, every region, every walk of life.

This time we want to talk about the fact that the real problem is not that someone who doesn't look like you might take your job; it's that the corporation you work for will ship it overseas for nothing more than a profit.

This time we want to talk about the men and women of every color and creed who serve together, and fight together, and bleed together under the same proud flag.

We want to talk about how to bring them home from a war that never should've been authorized and never should've been waged, and we want to talk about how we'll show our patriotism by caring for them, and their families, and giving them the benefits they have earned.

I would not be running for president if I didn't believe with all my heart that this is what the vast majority of Americans want for this country. This union may never be perfect, but generation after generation has shown that it can always be perfected.

And today, whenever I find myself feeling doubtful or cynical about this possibility, what gives me the most hope is the next generation—the young people whose attitudes and beliefs and openness to change have already made history in this election.

There is one story in particular that I'd like to leave you with today—a story I told when I had the great honor of speaking on Dr. King's birthday at his home church, Ebenezer Baptist, in Atlanta.

There is a young, 23-year-old white woman named Ashley Baia who organized for our campaign in Florence, South Carolina. She had been working to organize a mostly African-American community since the beginning of this campaign, and one day she was at a roundtable discussion where everyone went around telling their story and why they were there.

And Ashley said that when she was 9 years old, her mother got cancer. And because she had to miss days of work, she was let go and lost her health care. They had to file for bankruptcy, and that's when Ashley decided that she had to do something to help her mom.

She knew that food was one of their most expensive costs, and so Ashley convinced her mother that what she really liked and really wanted to eat more than anything else was mustard and relish sandwiches. Because that was the cheapest way to eat.

She did this for a year until her mom got better, and she told everyone at the roundtable that the reason she joined our campaign was so that she could help the millions of other children in the country who want and need to help their parents, too.

Now Ashley might have made a different choice. Perhaps somebody told her along the way that the source of her mother's problems were blacks who were on welfare and too lazy to work, or Hispanics who were coming into the country illegally. But she didn't. She sought out allies in her fight against injustice.

Anyway, Ashley finishes her story and then goes around the room and asks everyone else why they're supporting the campaign. They all have different stories and reasons. Many bring up a specific issue. And finally they come to this elderly black man who's been sitting there quietly the entire time.

And Ashley asks him why he's there. And he does not bring up a specific issue. He does not say health care or the economy. He does not say education or the war. He does not say that he was there because of Barack Obama. He simply says to everyone in the room, "I am here because of Ashley."

"I'm here because of Ashley." By itself, that single moment of recognition between that young white girl and that old black man is not enough. It is not enough to give health care to the sick, or jobs to the jobless, or education to our children.

But it is where we start. It is where our union grows stronger. And as so many generations have come to realize over the course of the two-hundred and twenty one years since a band of patriots signed that document in Philadelphia, that is where the perfection begins.

Public Domain, March 18, 2008.

Pulling the Race Card from the Deck

Stanford's Richard Thompson Ford looks at black and white and sees gray.

PETER SCHMIDT

It's just before noon, and Sam's Grill rapidly fills with the power-lunch crowd. The clientele of this venerable Financial District eatery are unmistakably old-school, graying white men in business suits who order Manhattans and veal chops from tuxedo-clad waiters. Even here in San Francisco, a guy in line for a table jokes loudly about a gay acquaintance being "light in his loafers." Richard Thompson Ford steps in out of a drenching Pacific storm, one of few men in the room with dark skin and no necktie.

He is not at his table more than a few minutes when his chair gets pushed violently by some guy being seated behind him. No "Excuse me" or "May I please?" Just his chair hurtling forward so quickly and unexpectedly his face briefly signals alarm, as a voice behind him mumbles something in midshove about needing more space.

A lot of people would have taken the shove personally, and reacted with anger as they seized upon some explanation for the perceived slight.

Ford clearly noticed the shove; he could recall it three weeks after the fact. But he chose at the time to let it roll off of him, continuing his conversation. Later, explaining his reaction, he says he feels comfortable at Sam's. He frequented the place in a past job as a lawyer working nearby, and he knows it gets crowded. He sees getting jostled as just part of the Sam's dining experience. No big deal.

Considering the broader context of real and potential conflict is something Ford does a lot these days.

A law professor at Stanford University, Ford has taken it upon himself to analyze many of the high-profile racial controversies that have divided Americans in recent decades, mulling over the Tawana Brawley incident, the O.J. Simpson trial, and the accusations of racism surrounding the federal government's botched handling of Hurricane Katrina.

He published his assessment of race relations in America in a book, *The Race Card* (Farrar, Straus and Giroux), released late last month. And the conclusions he reached have been winning him praise as a fresh voice among black scholars, a critical race theorist willing to skewer the identity-politics movements of the left while challenging conservative opponents of affirmative action and those who prescribe personal responsibility as the cure for what ails black America.

His bottom-line conclusion is that many allegations of racism—as well as other forms of discrimination—are not just false but counterproductive. The behaviors the accusers attribute to discrimination are actually due to something else, usually broader societal problems. And the back and forth of accusation and denial set in motion by such discrimination complaints sidetracks discussions of how to solve bigger problems, and sometimes even keeps us from realizing those problems exist.

"The assumption is that if there is a racial inequity, there is a racist to blame for it," Ford said when interviewed at Sam's. Conversely, he said, "if there is no racist, people think there is no problem." The reality, he said, is that "we can have a lot of racial problems in our society even when there aren't any racists to blame for them."

In his book (subtitled *How Bluffing About Bias Makes Race Relations Worse*), Ford calls for a different approach to remedying most racial injustice. Rather than thinking of it much as we think of crime—as the product of wrongdoing by individuals who may or may not ultimately be held accountable—we should instead approach it as we do air pollution, as an urgent social problem that is better solved through collective action than by trying to affix the blame.

So far, at least, Ford's book has been well received by both scholars and pundits. In a review in *The New York Times,* the Harvard sociologist Orlando Patterson praised *The Race Card* as the work of "an exquisitely subversive mind," offering "a vigorous and long-overdue shake-up of the nation's stale discourse on race." Stuart Taylor Jr. of the *National Journal* called it "a lively new book" with "a wealth of perceptive insights." Writing for *The New York Sun,* John H. McWhorter, a senior fellow at the Manhattan Institute, said that Ford "is not the contrarian that the book's title and publicity have been crafted to imply," but that his basic point "remains valuable."

It is hard to imagine Ford's book escaping any sort of backlash, however, given the many fights he picks in it. He accuses several popular black figures—including Al Sharpton, Oprah Winfrey, and Cornel West—of making allegations of racial bias that were unsubstantiated or hollow. In a chapter called "Wild Card: Racism by Analogy," he roams well beyond the field of race relations in search of targets. He mauls People for the Ethical Treatment of Animals for comparing animal husbandry to human slavery and racist lynching. He pokes fat-acceptance advocates for equating racial discrimination and discrimination against the overweight, contending that "fat is not the new black" and that, for most people, losing weight is "only moderately challenging." Drawing upon his scholarly interest in an area tangential to the book—gay rights—he argues that advocates of same-sex marriage err in labeling their opponents as bigots, and that they might achieve more if they focused on seeking the legalization of domestic partnerships and same-sex civil unions.

Lashing right, he says Clarence Thomas "shamelessly played the race card" in describing his confirmation hearing as a high-tech lynching, and finds "ostrichlike obliviousness" in Ward Connerly's failed 2003 California ballot initiative to severely limit when state agencies could classify people based on race.

Paul Campos, a professor of law at the University of Colorado at Boulder and author of *The Obesity Myth* (Gotham, 2004), challenges Ford's assertion about the ease of losing weight as "just nonsense" in light of medical research on the subject. And, he argues, the "enormous amount of discrimination focused on people today who are heavier than average" makes comparing weight discrimination to racial discrimination appropriate, even if the analogy may be somewhat imprecise.

But Richard Delgado, a professor of law at the University of Pittsburgh, says he believes Ford "is quite right" in asserting that the victims of various nonracial forms of discrimination—such as Hispanic people who endure ethnic bias rooted in their historical status as the subjects of conquest—need to stake out their own justifications for legal protection, apart from the body of law prohibiting discrimination based on race. Ford's argument on this point "should strike a responsive chord for leading Latino scholars," Delgado says.

Working in favor of *The Race Card* is remarkable timing. Nearly two years in the works, it managed to hit the bookstores just before last month's South Carolina Democratic presidential primary, when it seemed that race cards were being played like ace-king combinations at a blackjack tournament. With the real possibility that Barack Obama and Hillary Rodham Clinton will still be battling for the Democratic presidential nomination at convention time, and Ward Connerly seeking to get bans on affirmative-action preferences on the ballot in five states, issues of race and gender are likely to remain hotly debated throughout much of the year.

O n a personal level, Ford, 42, has spent much of his life negotiating predominantly white environments and achieving considerable success within them.
He was raised mostly in Fresno, Calif., where his father was dean of the school of health and social work at the local campus

Excerpts from *The Race Card*

Taking every racial issue personally can blind us to the many racial injustices for which no one is to blame. If every racial injustice entitles its victims to lambaste the person nearest to hand, then when there is no racist to blame, it follows that there must be no injustice. As racial politics increasingly focuses on trivial slights, innocent slips of the tongue, and even well-intentioned if controversial decisions, the most severe injustices—such as the isolation of a largely black underclass in hopeless ghettos or even more hopeless prisons—receive comparatively little attention because we can't find a bigot to paste to the dartboard.

The notion that civil-rights law should forbid employers from discriminating on the basis of *behavior* underlies a flood of new claims of racism by analogy. If, as the legal multiculturalists claim, racism is a failure to tolerate nonmainstream norms and practices, then the loser of almost any social or political conflict can claim to be the victim of racism-like bias. . . .

Even as the nation has become increasingly conservative and skeptical of social-justice claims, multiculturalists blithely advance a radical agenda that would force employers and businesses to effectively subsidize cultural nationalism—a worldview most Americans find abhorrent. This is a grave tactical mistake. The multiculturalists assume that if they can tie their agenda to civil rights, the nation will have to accept it. In fact, with the two bound together, the nation would have a choice—accept both civil rights and its multicultural sidecar or send them both to the wrecking yard.

Post-racism is an inexact term. But it's a useful catch-phrase for the ambiguous examples of bigotry that I've addressed in this book. Post-racism has emerged because legal rules and social norms against overt prejudice have succeeded. Black entertainers can afford to flirt with racial stereotypes because social activists, civil-rights lawyers, and brave ordinary citizens have made it anathema to advance those stereotypes seriously. Because working people like Rosa Parks risked all to stand up to unabashed bigots who were backed by social convention and the force of law, celebrities such as Oprah Winfrey and Jay-Z have the luxury of complaining of minor and ambiguous slights from professional snobs. Because earlier generations had the guts to call racism by its name when the shape of society depended on their actions, professional intellectuals can now write books about playing the race card with the comfort of tenure and air-conditioned offices at elite universities. We all stand on the shoulders of, if not giants, then people who met admirably the challenges they faced at a moment in history that demanded much more of them than ours does of us.

We owe it to them and their legacy to at least meet the milder—if more subtle—challenges of our day. . . . We need to advance the civil-rights agenda by tailoring it to fit the circumstances of today.

of California State University. He recalls that Central Valley city as a place where people seemed decent but unenlightened. He was always one of just a few black children in his classes at its public schools.

Ford earned his bachelor's degree in political science from Stanford in 1988. He then enrolled at Harvard Law School, becoming a housing-policy consultant for the City of Cambridge during his final year. His work on housing policy got him interested in the study of race relations and segregation and helped shape his perspective on such matters. He says he frequently encountered neighborhood segregation "in the absence of discriminatory intent." The cause, rather than existing racism, he says, was often a combination of historical discrimination and the self-interested behavior of people who simply saw integration as hard on home values.

After graduating from Harvard Law in 1991, Ford worked for about a year and a half as a litigation associate at a San Francisco law firm; was awarded a 16-month fellowship at Harvard studying political geography, race relations, and urban law; and then took a position on the faculty of Stanford Law School. His wife, Marlene, works in San Francisco as a trademark lawyer, and he commutes to Stanford from their home in the city's Sunset District.

Ford has published one other book on race relations, *Racial Culture: A Critique* (Princeton University Press, 2005). In it he challenged those scholars of multiculturalism who advocate the use of civil-rights laws to protect certain cultural practices so that, for example, refusing to hire someone because he wears his hair in dreadlocks would be viewed in much the same light as refusing to hire someone based on his ethnic background. Ford argued that enshrining "cultural rights" in law would be a mistake, and harmful to the intended beneficiaries, because it would result in rigid, limiting definitions of how the members of certain social groups are expected to behave.

When interviewed last month, Ford said he was well aware that cultural differences could be a source of societal conflict, with people coming under pressure from others to comply with certain norms. "But," he said, "better to have the conflicts worked out in the rough-and-tumble of real life than to have the outcomes dictated by the courts."

Other legal scholars did not wholeheartedly embrace *Racial Culture* and the positions Ford took in it. In the *Duke Journal of Gender Law & Policy,* Barbara J. Flagg, a professor of law at Washington University in St. Louis, called Ford's critique of "rights to difference" proponents "little more than a disappointing caricature," and said he had presented her views on the subject in a manner she found "infuriatingly misleading." When Ford initially staked out his position in 2000 in an essay published in the *UCLA Law Review,* Leti Volpp, then an assistant professor of law at American University, praised the article as "largely persuasive and extremely insightful" but argued that Ford underestimated how often discrimination against certain cultural traits is "an expression of racial hostility."

Ford revisits his critique of multiculturalism in *The Race Card.* He writes, "The proponents of multicultural rights are inspired by a worldview and commitments that few Americans of any race share" and "blithely advance a radical agenda that would force employers and businesses to effectively subsidize ethnic and racial nationalism." In tying their agenda to civil rights, he says, multicultural-rights advocates imperil both because the laws prohibiting discrimination in employment, housing, and public accommodations are acts of Congress that "can be amended, watered down, or even repealed" if rendered unpopular through such linkages.

Most of his new book's barbs are not aimed at multiculturalists, however, but at prominent African-Americans whom he sees as too hasty to level charges of racial discrimination.

Take Cornel West, the prominent Princeton University religion professor and author of the widely read book *Race Matters* (Beacon Press, 1993). In his book, West recounted parking his "rather elegant" car in "a safe parking lot" in New York City and waiting at the corner of 60th Street and Park Avenue to catch a cab to meet a photographer in East Harlem. "After the ninth taxi refused me, my blood began to boil," West wrote.

Ford sees the cab drivers who refused West as motivated by a fear of crime, rather than racism, and poses the question: If West won't risk taking his car into East Harlem, why should he expect a cab driver to risk his livelihood, and maybe even his life, to go there? (West could not be reached for comment.)

Oprah Winfrey comes under Ford's microscope for alleging racism when an exclusive Hermès leather-goods store in Paris refused to let her in to shop 15 minutes after closing time. Michael Jackson gets taken to task for blaming a "racist conspiracy" at Sony Music for the tanking of one of his albums.

Of the many examples cited by Ford to make his point, perhaps the most illustrative does not involve a specific person, but a place: New Orleans. Yes, he says, racism did play a role in the suffering of that city's residents after Hurricane Katrina. But it was the past racism that left the city's black residents congregated in low-lying neighborhoods and created a cycle of poverty that left many unable to afford homes elsewhere or cars to flee quickly when the levees broke. The Bush administration's handling of the disaster betrayed shortsightedness, incompetence, perhaps even indifference to a constituency it did not view as politically supportive. But "there is little evidence George Bush cares less about poor black people than poor whites," Ford says.

Ford sees himself as on the political left, despite his criticisms of many other thinkers found there. He characterizes American society as "in many ways inequitable and in need of reform." And he rejects the view of many conservative black scholars that promoting personal responsibility will fix problems that have plagued black Americans for generations. "When you are confronting social problems, what you need are social solutions," he says.

Ford predicts many such problems will not be remedied cheaply or easily, and some of the solutions he offers are likely to make conservatives cringe. He suggests, for example, that the single best solution to ghetto poverty may be the creation of a public-sector jobs program, similar to the Works Progress

Administration created by Franklin Delano Roosevelt during the Great Depression.

Among the other policies Ford advocates is affirmative action in college admissions, though not for the sake of what he calls "the questionable pedagogy of diversity." The point, he argues, should be the racial integration of colleges. And just as he believes people should be willing to endure a modest amount of racial profiling by law-enforcement agencies when it is a practical necessity, he thinks white and Asian-American college applicants should be willing to risk longer admissions odds to help integrate the institutions they wish to enter. Those who respond by complaining of "reverse racism," he says, are themselves playing the race card.

In Ford's thinking, all of American society should learn this lesson from New Orleans: Pointing fingers at racists won't hold back the water. It's time to work together to shore up the levees.

PETER SCHMIDT is a senior writer at *The Chronicle*.

Polonia and the Elections: Why We Matter?

DOMINIK STECULA

The presidential elections of 2008 are approaching at a fast pace. Through the lengthy process of the primaries, both major parties elected their candidates, based on their stance on multiple important issues, "electibility", and a variety of other factors. We saw candidates catering to the voters, taking positions that would make them more popular with different groups, trying to appeal to the widest possible base. What we didn't see, however, were the candidates making a special appeal to the Polish-American vote. We heard a lot about, and from, Latinos, Arabs, Jews, and other ethnic groups, but somehow the Polish voice was not heard or listened to in the public debate.

It is very unfortunate that the fifth largest ethnic group in the country is virtually nonexistent on the political map of the United States. We are invisible. Yet in 2006, 10,024,683 Americans declared Polish ancestry. Assuming at least a 10 percent undercount, 3.7 percent of the population of the USA is of Polish background. We are smaller in numbers only to the German, Irish, English, and Italian ancestries. It is worth noting that those groups are "old immigrations," already assimilated to the American culture, with a relatively small amount of "new blood" coming from Europe annually, unlike Poles, who consistently keep coming in relatively large numbers. Tens of thousands have continued to come each decade. Since 1918, about 533,310 Poles have arrived as immigrants, while 297,855 others came as refugees and asylum seekers between 1940 and 1992.

Despite acculturation, Poles are still one the largest groups in the country that continues to speak the ancestral language at home. Millions into the fifth generation still maintain and practice Polish customs and traditions. Around 500,000 of Poles currently in America were born in Poland, which accounts for about 5 percent of the Polish population in the United States. But even the Poles born in the United States oftentimes speak Polish at home, as demonstrated by the fact that around 8 percent of Poles in the USA speak Polish at home.

Despite the fact that the Polish population is, in general, very much attached to the Polish culture, Poles are functioning well indeed in American society. In most aspects, Poles are doing better than the average American. Poles are more educated than average Americans (30 percent of Poles have a Bachelor's degree or higher, compared to 24 percent of the average Americans).

About Piast Institute

The Piast Institute, a national institute for Polish and Polish-American affairs, is the only independent Polish, American think tank and research center in the United States. We strongly believe that Polonia is not a fading remnant of a European culture, but a dynamic, new creation by Polish immigrants and their progeny in the United States. Our major goal is to build the new Polonia of the 21st Century. We immediately recognized Polonia Votes 2008 as an initiative worth supporting and helping to expand. As one of 59 official U.S. Census Information Centers in the United States, and the only one in the nation dedicated to a European-American population, we can provide the necessary demographic and socio-economic, as well as historical information that might help the Polonia Votes 2008 initiative. We encourage other organizations and individuals to get interested in the initiative and help it grow. For more information on the Piast Institute, please visit our work-in-progress website at: piastinstitute.org or read about us on Wikipedia. You can also contact us at: (313)664-0321 or via e-mail at: cic@piastinstitute.org.

Our median household incomes, median family incomes, and per capita incomes are all significantly higher than average. Our homes are worth more than the average American home, and we are more likely to own a house than other Americans. We are also 50 percent less likely to live below the poverty level compared to the average in America.

Historically speaking, Poles in America were always involved politically. Poles were active both locally and nationally. In local politics, ethnic loyalty often superseded party affiliation (In heavily Democratic Polish Buffalo, for example, the Polish vote went Republican twice to support Polish mayoral candidates). At the beginning of the twentieth century, Poles nationally supported the Democratic Party. Support was around 60 percent, soaring in 1928 in support of Governor Al Smith, Catholic and veteran, for president. Poles chose the Democrats party because of its traditional importance of economic, political, and social support in their eyes, the state and society had to the community. Main objectives of public policy, therefore, should be to alleviate poverty and social distress. Polls consistently showed that until the 1980s when Polish-Americans showed the highest support from any other major ethnic group, for the idea that government should do all in its power to eradicate poverty. After 1980, polling by ethnic group on such questions virtually ceased. The "family wage" was a policy that was very popular with Polish-Americans reflecting both an economic as well as social policy orientation. The Democratic Party platform expressed similar opinions, resulting in large support from the Polish community until the 1970s. After 1968, the Democratic Party made a major strategic decision to reconstitute its coalition within which Catholic ethnic voters were no longer to play a key role. Gradually, the Democratic Party also adopted the libertarianism of the Republicans in social matters, moving away from the more communitarian approach that Polish-Americans found culturally and religiously attractive.

The Republican Party, on the other hand, was historically seen as a vessel of profit-driven industrialists, Drys, and Protestants, whose philosophy was laissez-faire capitalism and libertarian individualism, with little regard for the role of the community. However, after World War II, loyalties switched. Many Poles felt that President Roosevelt betrayed Poland. Angered by Yalta Conference, many members of Polonia were attracted by the Republican strong anti-Communism movement although, in the mid-1980s majority of Polish-Americans disapproved of the Reagan welfare cuts. However, the Republican adoption of the older communal values under the name of "family values" did attract Polish-American votes, at least at the national level.

Generally speaking, the majority of the Polish vote since 1932 at the national level, except in the elections of 1956 (Eisenhower), 1972 (Nixon), 1984 (Reagan), and 2004 (Bush), went to the Democratic Party. At the local level and in Congressional elections the majority of the Polish vote still goes Democratic, Currently, however, the Polish vote does not have a safe home. About 45–50 percent seems loyal to the Democrats, with about 10–15 percent swing between the parties, with the reminder having, moved into the Republican column. This is the result of the demographic changes in Polonia, indifference of the parties to the Polish vote, and philosophic changes in the parties' platforms, as noted above.

In terms of elected officials, we currently have six representatives (from Ohio, Michigan, Illinois, Pennsylvania, and Indiana) in the 110th Congress and three Senators (from Maryland, Alaska, and Nevada). The highest representation of Polish-Americans was achieved in 1958, with 15 representatives. In terms of Senate, the current representation is the highest ever. Only one other Polish-American senator was elected, that being Edmund Muskie, in 1958, from Maine.

With this upcoming election, we can finally grow in importance again, to the level that we deserve. The first step is to appear prominently in the public arena and to have coherent positions on issues, especially those that deal with the life of our communities in America. We also need to be able to raise funds to support candidates and policies we favor. It is only then that we can expect the candidates to meet with our leaders and discuss our issues.

To start, we need to let people know we have votes and we can mobilize them. Campaigns will soon be selling and distributing, "Polish-Americans for Obama," or "Polish-Americans for McCain," bumper stickers. It is time for them to fight for our votes. With the initiative like Polonia Votes 2008, we can make history happen. Many Polish-Americans already pledged to vote in the November elections, and the official race has barely begun. Our community has the potential and the political drive. We also have one other critical factor that the candidates care about—geographical location. Our heaviest concentrations are in New York, Michigan, Illinois, Pennsylvania, New Jersey, Wisconsin, California, Florida, Ohio, and Massachusetts. Many of those states are considered crucial swing states. Together, they make up 43 percent of the Electoral College. With all that on our side, and a great initiative like Polonia Votes 2008, all we have to do as Polonia is live up to our potential.

White Seniors Energize McCain Campaign

PAUL WEST

I f Barack Obama's mother were alive today, she'd be 65. In other words, she'd be part of his problem.

Obama's problem is with older white voters. He's been wooing them for months and still has little to show for it.

During the primaries, they swung solidly behind Hillary Clinton. Now they're backing John McCain.

Among white voters 65 and older, McCain leads by 15 points, according to a recent Greenberg Quinlan Rosner survey for Democracy Corps. The Democratic firm found that McCain is running four points better among white seniors than President Bush did four years ago.

McCain is running four points better among white seniors than Bush did four years ago, according to a recent survey.

"White seniors," then, may be the solution to a puzzle that's perplexed some people, namely, why are the national polls so close, given the built-in advantages for a Democratic candidate this year?

Answer: Because McCain's popularity among older whites is offsetting enthusiasm for Obama among their children and grand-children.

Generational Divide

If McCain can build on this advantage, the generational divide could turn out to be the defining dynamic of the '08 election. Of course, it's still relatively early, and many voters aren't tuned in yet to the presidential contest.

For Obama, women could be the key to fixing his problem with seniors, since they are more likely to vote Democratic than men. At the moment, though, white women 65 and older favor McCain over Obama by double-digit margins, according to a recent national survey of female voters.

"It makes the Republican strategy pretty clear," says Democratic consultant Celinda Lake, who helped conduct the poll for Life-time television.

"If you get the women who are 50 to 64 to join the women who are over 65, you've got a strategy for beating Obama."

Older white women are worried about Obama's age (he's 47), which feeds into their doubts about his qualifications and inexperience at the national level, Lake says. Older women voters do want change, she adds, but they also believe there is both good change and bad change.

"Some of it is race," she says. But older white women "are nervous about Obama not just because he's African-American, but because he's new in so many ways."

Republican pollster Kellyanne Conway, who collaborated on the Lifetime survey, says McCain can gain strategically if he's able to extend his lead among older whites. It would free him to spend less time defending a Republican-leaning state, like Florida, and put more into pinning Obama down in senior-rich Pennsylvania, which the Democrat would like to put away early.

The Republican advantage among white voters isn't new. President Lyndon Johnson was the last Democrat to carry a majority of the white vote, more than 40 years ago.

But seniors had been a different story—more Democratic than the rest of the electorate—until fairly recently.

Now they're steadily crossing over to the Republican side. In 2004, voters ages 65 and up went Republican for the first time in years, backing Bush more heavily than the rest of the electorate.

That's partly because the generation with roots in Franklin Roosevelt's New Deal is passing away. Today's seniors increasingly identify with Reagan conservatism, according to analysts in both parties, and they're better off financially than the Roosevelt seniors (at least in part because of government programs enacted by Democrats).

McCain could extend, or even accelerate, this Republican trend. In his campaign, McCain has tried to shift the debate away from controversial Republican proposals to partially privatize Social Security, which he supported in the past. And neither candidate has made much of an appeal for senior votes.

"When was the last time you saw a campaign run on Social Security and Medicare?" asked Tony Fabrizio, a Republican pollster. "I expect you'll see McCain do well with older voters, not because of his age, but because of his politics."

McCain, who turns 72 this month, will be the oldest presidential nominee since Bob Dole, 73 in 1996.

But in a strange twist, McCain—a generation older than his Democratic rival—is the candidate whose mother, now 96, has a prominent campaign role (to counter the age issue).

Obama can't help it that his mother died of cancer in 1995. But he has used her image in campaign commercials to make the point that he was raised by a (white) single parent.

Telling the Story

That life story is still unfamiliar to many voters, including seniors he needs to reach.

Bill Clinton used his nominating convention to dispel a widespread misimpression that he came from a wealthy family. Obama has a similar opening this month in Denver to make voters—including skeptics from his mother's generation—more comfortable with the idea of him as president.

"The convention's a major opportunity," says Lake. "Obama has an incredibly compelling story to tell women in terms of his background, his own economic struggle, his single mom, going to school, relating to their concerns."

The other day, at a campaign event in Ohio, a woman identified as a 78-year-old retired teacher had question for Obama: "Who is spreading that vicious rumor that women my age, white-haired and all, don't support you?"

With a laugh, Obama replied that it was, indeed, "a vicious rumor," and untrue.

At least for now, those women are supporting McCain, however, and keeping the Republican in the game.

Where their votes end up may well determine whether the presidential election is a nailbiter or a blowout.

Is Obama the End of Black Politics?

Matt Bai

Forty-seven years after he last looked out from behind the bars of a South Carolina jail cell, locked away for leading a march against segregation in Columbia, James Clyburn occupies a coveted suite of offices on the second and third floors of the United States Capitol, alongside the speaker and the House majority leader. Above his couch hangs a black-and-white photograph of the Rev. Martin Luther King Jr. speaking in Charleston, with the boyish Clyburn and a group of other men standing behind him onstage. When I visited Clyburn recently, he told me that the photo was taken in 1967, nine months before King's assassination, when rumors of violence were swirling, and somewhere on the side of the room a photographer's floodlight had just come crashing down unexpectedly. At the moment the photo was taken, everyone pictured has reflexively jerked their heads in the direction of the sound, with the notable exception of King himself, who remains in profile, staring straight ahead at his audience. Clyburn prizes that photo. It tells the story, he says, of a man who knew his fate but who, quite literally, refused to flinch.

On the day in early July when Clyburn and I talked, Barack Obama, who is the same age as one of Clyburn's three daughters, had recently clinched his party's nomination for president. Clyburn, who as majority whip is the highest-ranking black elected official in Washington, told me that on the night of the final primaries he left the National Democratic Club down the street about 15 minutes before Obama was scheduled to speak and returned home to watch by himself. He feared he might lose hold of his emotions.

"Here we are, all of a sudden, in the 60th year after Strom Thurmond bolting the Democratic Party over a simple thing, something almost unheard of—because he did not want the armed forces to be integrated," Clyburn said slowly. "Here we are 45 years after the 'I have a dream' speech. Forty years after the assassinations of Kennedy and King. And this party that I have been a part of for so long, this party that has been accused of taking black people for granted, is about to deliver the nomination for the nation's highest office to an African-American. How do you describe that? All those days in jail cells, wondering if anything you were doing was even going to have an impact." He shook his head silently.

This time, however, a lot of the old activists stood in the path of an African-American's advancement rather than blazing it. While Democratic black voters embraced Obama by ratios of 8 or 9 to 1 in a lot of districts, the 42 House members in the Congressional Black Caucus, for a time, split more or less down the middle between Obama and Hillary Rodham Clinton, and the country's leading black ministers and mayors trended toward the Clinton camp. Clyburn himself declined until the very end to endorse a candidate in this year's primaries, saying that his leadership role required him to remain neutral, but he made no effort to disguise his relief at having been able to invoke that excuse. "Being African-American, sure, my heart was with him," Clyburn told me. "But I've got a head too. And in the beginning my head was with Clinton. The conventional wisdom was that this thing was going to be over in February."

He then recalled a moment, just after the Georgia primary in early February, when he ran into John Lewis, the legendary civil rights leader and Georgia congressman, on the House floor. Lewis was in anguish over the primaries. He had endorsed his friend Hillary Clinton, but his constituents had gone heavily for Obama, and he was beginning to waver. As Clyburn remembered it, Lewis told his old friend sadly that after all these years, they were finally going to see history yield to the forces they had unleashed. "And I'm on the wrong side," Lewis said. (Later, after weeks of public vacillating, he would switch his allegiance.)

It is hard for any outsider to fully understand the thinking that led many older black leaders to spurn the candidacy of a man who is now routinely pictured, along with '60s-era revolutionaries like Angela Davis and Malcolm X, on the T-shirts sold at the street-corner kiosks of black America. ("You'd be real embarrassed if he won and you wasn't down with it," the comedian Chris Rock joked to a Harlem audience while introducing Obama last November. "You'd say: 'Aww, I can't call him now! I had that white lady! What was I thinking?'") Conversations like those I had with Clyburn and Lewis, however, begin to illuminate just how emotionally complicated such internal deliberations were.

On a surface level, those who backed Clinton did so largely out of a combination of familiarity and fatalism. If you were a longtime black leader or activist at the end of 2007, you probably believed, based on your own life experience, that no black man was going to win the nomination, let alone the presidency. ("If anybody tells you they expected this result, they're not being honest with you," Clyburn cautioned.) You knew the Clintons personally, or at least you knew their allies in the community. Who was this Obama, really, aside from the resonant voice and the neon smile? As Charles Rangel, Harlem's powerful representative and a strong Clinton ally, told me recently, "Of course I would support someone I knew and had liked and had worked with, versus someone I'd never heard of."

But maybe it wasn't only what you didn't know about Obama. What did he know about you? Obama was barely 2 years old when King gave his famous speech, 3 when Lewis was beaten about the head in Selma. He didn't grow up in the segregated South as Bill Clinton had. Sharing those experiences wasn't a prerequisite for gaining the acceptance of black leaders, necessarily, but that didn't mean Obama, with his nice talk of transcending race and baby-boomer partisanship, could fully appreciate the sacrifices they made, either. "Every kid is always talking about what his parents have been through," Rangel says, "and no kid has any clue what he's talking about."

For black Americans born in the 20th century, the chasms of experience that separate one generation from the next—those who came of age before the movement, those who lived it, those who came along after—have always been hard to traverse. Elijah Cummings, the former chairman of the Congressional Black Caucus and an early Obama supporter, told me a story about watching his father, a South Carolina sharecropper with a fourth-grade education, weep uncontrollably when Cummings was sworn in as a representative in 1996. Afterward, Cummings asked his dad if he had been crying tears of joy. "Oh, you know, I'm happy," his father replied. "But now I realize, had I been given the opportunity, what I could have been. And I'm about to die." In any community shadowed by oppression, pride and bitterness can be hard to untangle.

The generational transition that is reordering black politics didn't start this year. It has been happening, gradually and quietly, for at least a decade, as younger African-Americans, Barack Obama among them, have challenged their elders in traditionally black districts. What this year's Democratic nomination fight did was to accelerate that transition and thrust it into the open as never before, exposing and intensifying friction that was already there. For a lot of younger African-Americans, the resistance of the civil rights generation to Obama's candidacy signified the failure of their parents to come to terms, at the dusk of their lives, with the success of their own struggle—to embrace the idea that black politics might now be disappearing into American politics in the same way that the Irish and Italian machines long ago joined the political mainstream.

"I'm the new black politics," says Cornell Belcher, a 38-year-old pollster who is working for Obama. "The people I work with are the new black politics. We don't carry around that history. We see the world through post-civil-rights eyes. I don't mean that disrespectfully, but that's just the way it is.

"I don't want in any way to seem critical of the generation of leadership who fought so I could be sitting here," Belcher told me when we met for breakfast at the Four Seasons in Georgetown one morning. He wears his hair in irreverent spikes and often favors tennis shoes with suit jackets. Barack Obama is the sum of their struggle. He's the sum of their tears, their fights, their marching, their pain. This opportunity is the sum of that.

"But it's like watching something that you've been working on all your life sort of come together right before your eyes, and you can't see it," Belcher said. "It's like you've been building the Great Wall of China, and you finally put that last stone in. And you can't see it. You just can't see the enormity of it."

The latest evidence of tension between Obama and some older black leaders burst onto cable television last month, after an open microphone on Fox News picked up the Rev. Jesse Jackson crudely making the point that he wouldn't mind personally castrating his party's nominee. The reverend was angry because Obama, in a Father's Day speech on Chicago's South Side, chastised black fathers for shirking their responsibilities. To Jackson, this must have sounded a lot like a presidential candidate polishing his bona fides with white Americans at the expense of black ones—something he himself steadfastly refused to do even during his second presidential run in 1988, when he captured more votes than anyone thought possible.

Most of the coverage of this minor flap dwelled on the possible animus between Jackson and Obama, despite the fact that Obama himself, who is not easily distracted, seemed genuinely unperturbed by it. But more interesting, perhaps, was the public reaction of Jesse Jackson Jr., the reverend's 43-year-old son, who is a congressman from Illinois and the national co-chairman of Obama's campaign. The younger Jackson released a blistering statement in which he said he was "deeply outraged and disappointed" by the man he referred to, a little icily, as "Reverend Jackson." Invoking his father's most famous words, Jesse Jr. concluded, "He should keep hope alive and any personal attacks and insults to himself."

This exchange between the two Jacksons hinted at a basic generational divide on the question of what black leadership actually means. Black leaders who rose to political power in the years after the civil rights marches came almost entirely from the pulpit and the movement, and they have always defined leadership, in broad terms, as speaking for black Americans. They saw their job, principally, as confronting an inherently racist white establishment, which in terms of sheer career advancement was their only real option anyway.

For almost every one of the talented black politicians who came of age in the postwar years, like James Clyburn and Charles Rangel, the pinnacle of power, if you did everything right, lay in one of two offices: City Hall or the House of Representatives. That was as far as you could travel in politics with a mostly black constituency. Until the 1990s, even black politicians with wide support among white voters failed in their attempts to win statewide, with only one exception (Edward Brooke, who was elected to the U.S. Senate from Massachusetts in 1966). On a national level, only Jesse Jackson was able to garner a respectable number of white votes, muscling open the door through which Obama, 20 years later, would breezily pass.

This newly emerging class of black politicians, however, men (and a few women) closer in age to Obama and Jesse Jr., seek a broader political brief. Comfortable inside the establishment, bred at universities rather than seminaries, they are just as likely to see themselves as ambassadors to the black community as they are to see themselves as spokesmen for it, which often means extolling middle-class values in urban neighborhoods, as Obama did on Father's Day. Their ambitions range well beyond safely black seats.

Artur Davis, an Alabama representative and one of the most talked-about young talents on Capitol Hill, recently told me a story about his first campaign for Congress, in 2000, when he challenged the longtime black incumbent Earl Hilliard. Davis was only 32 at the time, a federal prosecutor who graduated from Harvard Law School, and he saw Hilliard as the classic example of a passing political model—a guy who saw himself principally as a spokesman for the community rather than as an actual legislator.

After a debate in which Davis pounded the incumbent for being out of touch with the district, Hilliard took him aside. "Young man, you have a good political future," Davis recalled Hilliard telling him. "But you've got to learn one basic lesson. You're trying to start at the top, and you can't start at the top in politics."

"With all due respect, Congressman," Davis replied, "I don't think a group with 435 members can be the top of anything."

Davis lost that race, but he won in a rematch two years later. Now he's weighing a run for governor.

One telling difference between black representatives of Davis's generation and the more senior set in Washington is how they initially viewed the role of race in this year's primaries. Older members of the Congressional Black Caucus assumed, well into the primary season, that a black candidate wouldn't be able to win in predominantly white states. This, after all, had been their lifelong experience in politics. Not only did Davis, who grew up in post-segregation Montgomery and supported Obama, reject this view, but he also wouldn't concede when we talked that Obama's race was, on balance, a detriment.

"Race was a factor in the contest between Obama and Clinton," he told me. "There's no question race will be a factor with Obama and McCain. But I'm not sure it plays out as neatly as people think. There's no question that some young cohort of white voters were drawn to Obama because they like the idea of a break with the past. A young, white politician from Illinois might not have gotten that support. So race probably cost Obama some votes. And it probably won him some votes. That's the complex reality we're living in."

When I met last month with Cory Booker, the mayor of Newark who at 39 is already something of a national sensation, he told me that he had just finished reading, belatedly, Obama's memoir "Dreams From My Father." He said passages about Obama's youth in Hawaii had reminded him of his own experience with subtle racism in the affluent, mostly white suburb of Harrington Park, New Jersey "You know, what it's like growing up every single day and having people ask to touch your hair because they've never seen hair like that," Booker said. "To have the entire class laugh and giggle when somebody pronounces 'Niger' as 'nigger.' The constant bombardment of that kind of thing really affects your spirit, and it's every single day. Like when people want to come back from a vacation and compare their tan to yours and joke about being black."

No doubt these were searing experiences for Booker, and I had to wince as he ticked them off, recognizing too much of myself and my white classmates from the 1980s in the imagery. But as Booker himself noted, they are a world away from the reality that was pounded into civil rights activists like his parents, to whom racism meant dogs and hoses and segregated schools and luncheonettes. You can imagine what James Clyburn—still haunted by the vivid memory of the moment he found out that his erudite father had never been allowed to graduate from high school—would make of the lifelong trauma caused by suburban kids asking to feel your hair.

A Rhodes scholar who graduated from Stanford and Yale Law, Booker won his office in 2006 after first running unsuccessfully in 2002 against the incumbent, Sharpe James, who governed Newark for an astounding 20 years (and was sentenced last month to prison time on federal corruption charges). James was the very model of the Black Power mayor, a defiant spokesman for his community and a deft conjurer of America's racial demons. James derided Booker as a suburban outsider and questioned his blackness. ("You have to learn how to be African-American," James said in a speech directed at Booker, "and we don't have time to train you.") Booker famously took up residence in a city housing project, but his relationship to Newark's black community was, and still is, more tenuous and complicated than his predecessor's.

When I asked Booker if he considered himself a leader of the black community, he seemed to freeze for a moment. "I'm Popeye," he replied finally. "I am what I am." He paused again, then tried to explain.

"I don't want to be pigeonholed," he said. "I don't want people to expect me to speak about those issues." By this, presumably, he meant issues that revolve around race: profiling by police, incarceration rates, flagging urban economies. "I want people to ask me about nonproliferation. I want them to run to me to speak about the situation in the Middle East." Since the mayor of Newark is rarely called upon to discuss such topics, I got the feeling that Booker does not see himself staying in his current job for anything close to 20 years. "I don't want to be the person that's turned to when CNN talks about black leaders," he said.

Even so, Booker told me that his goal wasn't really to "transcend race." Rather, he says that for his generation of black politicians it's all right to show the part of themselves that is culturally black—to play basketball with friends and belong to a black church, the way Obama has. There is a universality now to the middle-class black experience, he told me, that should be instantly recognizable to Jews or Italians or any other white ethnic bloc that has struggled to assimilate. And that means, at least theoretically, that a black politician shouldn't have to obscure his racial identity.

"So Obama's the first one out there on the ice," Booker told me. "This campaign is giving other African-Americans like myself the courage to be themselves."

Given this generational perspective, it is easy to understand why Obama's candidacy was greeted coolly by much of Washington's black elite. Obama joined the Congressional Black Caucus when he arrived in 2005, but he attended meetings only sporadically, and it must have been obvious that he never felt he belonged. In part, this was probably because he was the group's only senator and thus had little daily interaction with his colleagues in the House. But to hear those close to Obama tell it, it was also because, like Booker and other younger black politicians, he simply wasn't comfortable categorizing his politics by race. One main function of the black caucus is to raise money through events, because many of the members represent poorer districts. Obama, already a bestselling author by the time he was sworn in, should have been a huge fund-raising draw, but he never showed much interest in headlining caucus events, and he was rarely asked.

Jesse Jackson Jr. warned his colleagues in the black caucus of the risks of shunning Obama's candidacy, reminding them of the political aftermath of Jesse Jackson Sr.'s campaigns in the 1980s. Back then, too, most black congressional Democrats sided with the white presidential candidates, and Jackson carried many of their districts in 1984 and virtually all of them in 1988, driving up voter registration in the process. A result, over the next few election cycles, was a flurry of primary challenges, the retirement or defeat of several incumbents and the arrival in Washington of a new class of black congressmen, including James Clyburn. Jackson's message was clear: even if Obama lost, there could be a cost for opposing him.

Still, most in the caucus didn't take Obama all that seriously as a potential nominee, and neither did the Clinton campaign. They calculated that he would need a huge share of black votes to wrest the nomination from Hillary, and her advisers, white and black, considered that a near impossibility. "There was an arrogance and a complete dismissiveness in our campaign against Obama, that he was a lightweight, that he couldn't get black support," one senior Clinton aide told me recently. "A lot of the black leaders didn't know him, didn't think he was black enough, didn't think he was of the civil rights movement." This point about whether Obama was "black enough," a senseless distinction to most white voters, came up often in my discussions. It referred to the perception among some black leaders that not only had Obama not shared their generational experience, but also that he hadn't shared the African-American experience, period. Obama's father was a Kenyan academic; his family came to America on scholarship, not in chains.

Internally, Clinton's strategists set a goal of receiving half the black vote in the Southern primaries, though they calculated that they needed as little as 30 percent in order to beat back Obama. It seemed like a sure bet. Last fall, as the primaries neared, their own polls had them winning more than 60 percent of black voters.

Within hours of Obama's victory in Iowa, however, Clinton's black support began to crumble. Black voters, young and old, simply hadn't believed that a black man could win in white states; when he did, a wave of pride swept through African-American neighborhoods in the South. Nor did those voters apparently have the deep affection for Hillary Clinton that many of their ministers and local pols did. Carol Willis, a Clinton aide from the Arkansas days who was leading the campaign's outreach to black voters, told me, "I always heard people saying: 'I know Bill Clinton. I don't know Hillary Clinton. So I'll give Barack Obama a closer hearing.'" Internal polling in both campaigns after Iowa showed Obama suddenly garnering closer to 75 or 80 percent of the black vote in primary states.

From then on, the Democratic nomination fight sometimes took on the feel of one of those contentious diversity workshops, with every word parsed for its racial undertone and every emotion rising to the surface. What did Bill Clinton mean by "naïve" and "fairy tale"? Was it an accident that Hillary Clinton used the word "spadework" to deride her opponent's record? Clyburn and Bill Clinton had long and tense phone conversations because of several comments the former president had made. The one that bothered Clyburn the most, he told me, came when he read in a South Carolina newspaper that Clinton had referred to Obama as a "kid." "I grew up in the South, where men like Barack Obama, who right now is older than Bill Clinton was when he ran for president, were called 'boy,'" Clyburn told me. "And that's what a kid is—a boy." The most damaging moment for Bill Clinton, though, came just after the South Carolina primary, when he waved away the victory by comparing it with Jesse Jackson's wins there in 1984 and 1988. "There was something about the condescension on his face when he said it and the dismissiveness in his voice," Artur Davis recalled. "It was a verbal pat on the head."

In March, shaken by the persistent controversy over comments pulled from the sermons of the Rev. Jeremiah Wright, an icon in Chicago's black community and Obama's former pastor, Obama gave his now famous speech on race. It was aimed, for the most part, at reassuring white voters over the Wright controversy, but it also marked the first time that he publicly addressed the generational divide his own campaign had exposed among black Americans. "For the men and women of Reverend Wright's generation," Obama said, "the memories of humiliation and doubt and fear have not gone away, nor has the anger and bitterness of those years. . . . At times, that anger is exploited by politicians, to gin up votes along racial lines or to make up for a politician's own failings." Some older black politicians may have recognized themselves in Obama's subtle criticism, but those I spoke to said they took pride in seeing a black candidate articulate their experience to white America.

A lot of black incumbents who supported Clinton now find themselves trying to explain how they ended up so disconnected from their constituents, and many are preparing for their strongest primary challenges in years. (In a primary last month, John Lewis, who had run unopposed since 1992, had to beat not one but two primary opponents, including a 31-year-old minister named Markel Hutchins who designed his campaign to look just like Obama's, right down to renting the same office space and using a red, white and blue logo in the shape of an "O.") So far, incumbents facing insurrection over their endorsements of Clinton have easily dispatched their challengers, leading to a collective exhalation inside the black caucus in Washington. But then, as Jesse Jackson Jr. tried to remind his colleagues, the history of black politics is that such challengers are often heard from again.

On the first Tuesday in July, I traveled to Philadelphia, the site of Obama's landmark speech on race, to see the city's mayor, Michael Nutter. Known as a reformer during a 14-year stint on the City Council, Nutter played a central and intriguing role in this year's presidential contest, emerging as the black face of Hillary Clinton's campaign in Pennsylvania at a time when she desperately needed—and got—a solid victory in the state. Nutter certainly wasn't the only visible black politician to campaign for Clinton deep into the primary season, but he was, in some ways, the least likely. Nutter is only four years older than Obama, Ivy League-educated, bookish and doggedly unemotional. He is, in short, the very prototype of the new generation of black political stars. But unlike Cory Booker or Artur Davis or Deval Patrick, the governor of Massachusetts, Nutter sided with Clinton, and he enthusiastically campaigned for her.

I was curious to know whether Nutter, who was elected to a four-year term just last fall, was bracing for the consequences of that decision. About 9 of every 10 black voters in Philadelphia pulled the lever for Obama, according to exit polls, and I heard at least one black Obama backer in

Washington vow to make Nutter pay for his apostasy. On the day that I visited him at City Hall, his aides had been reviewing the video of a sermon from last fall in which a prominent black minister in the city suggested that Nutter might have a "white agenda."

It was late in the day when Nutter and I sat down at a long conference table in his office, accompanied by the sounds of subway trains rumbling underneath and R & B music piped in from mounted speakers. He told me that he had made his decision methodically and had felt no pressure at all from his constituents.

Nutter said he sat down with both Clinton and Obama after his election as mayor and quizzed them about urban issues like housing, education and transportation. Race, he said, hadn't entered into this thinking. He understood, he said, why the prospect of a black president after hundreds of years of discrimination was "powerful stuff" for a lot of his constituents, but he had a greater responsibility, and that was to run the nation's sixth-largest city. "In the context of what I do for a living, I've not figured out a black or white way to fill a pothole," he said, in a way that made me think he had said this many times before. Nutter was a delegate for Bill Clinton way back in 1992, and he said that the former first lady had shown a "depth of understanding" of what cities like Philadelphia were facing. It probably didn't hurt that Obama endorsed one of Nutter's opponents in last year's mayoral primary, either.

Nutter said he wasn't bothered by comments that the Clintons or their surrogates made during the campaign that had so incensed other black officials. "I think there was a lot of sensitivity, some warranted and some unwarranted," he said. "It's based on your life experience, and it's generational. You know, if you have a sore on your arm, you don't necessarily have to touch the sore to feel the pain. You can touch another part of your arm. You've still got a certain sensitivity to it. So if race is the sensitive thing, then anything that even gets close to it—sounds like it, looks like it, feels like it—is it."

I asked Nutter if, during his private conversations with Obama early in the campaign, the subject of race and the historic nature of his candidacy came up. He stared at me for a moment. "Um, I knew he was black," he said finally. "I'd really kind of picked up on that."

Later, when I mentioned that it could be hard for a white journalist to understand all of the nuances of race, he looked over at his press secretary, who is black, and interrupted me. "He's not black?" Nutter deadpanned, motioning back at me. "You guys told me it was a skin condition. I thought I was talking to a brother." Nutter is known to have a dry sense of humor, but I also had the sense that he was tweaking me in these moments, watching with some amusement as I tried to navigate subjects that white and black Americans rarely discuss together. He seemed to think I was oddly preoccupied with race.

In fact, Nutter seemed puzzled by the very notion that he should be expected to support a candidate just because they both had dark skin. "Look, I never asked anybody to be for me because I was black," he said. "I asked people to be for me because I thought I was the best candidate when I ran for City Council and when I ran for mayor. I'm proud of the votes I received. I'm proud I received the votes of the majority of the African-American community and the majority of the vote from the white community. But I never asked anybody to give me anything because I was black. I asked people to give me a chance because I thought I was the best."

For most black Americans, Obama's candidacy represented a kind of racial milestone, the natural next phase of a 50-year movement. But for Michael Nutter, the reverse was also true: not supporting Obama's candidacy marked a kind of progress, too. The movement, after all, was about the freedom to choose your own candidate, white or black. In a sense, you could argue that it was Nutter—and not those black politicians who embraced Obama because they so closely identified with his racial experience—who represented the truest embodiment of Obama-ism. Here, perhaps, was a genuine postracial politician, even if that meant being, as John Lewis put it, on the wrong side of history.

I asked Nutter if he found it insulting to have me come barging into his office, demanding to know why he didn't pick the black guy.

"It's not insulting," he answered. "It's presumptuous. It demonstrates a continuation of this notion that the African-American community, unlike any other, is completely monolithic, that everyone in the African-American community does the same thing in lockstep, in contrast to any other group. I mean, I don't remember seeing John Kerry on TV and anybody saying to him, 'I can't believe you're not for Hillary Clinton.' Why?"

It's inspiring to hear Michael Nutter say that governing a city isn't about race, that there's no black or white way to fill a pothole. And yet, it's also true that in any given American city there are likely to be more potholes in black neighborhoods than in white ones—along with more violence, more unemployment and more illiteracy. Having grown up in West Philadelphia, Nutter knows well that while the decisions he makes as a mayor have no racial antecedents, rarely do they affect the races equally. "The challenge there is never forgetting where you came from," he told me. "So, yes, I am mayor of all Philadelphia, but I am quite well aware of, and raise on a regular basis, the fact that the majority of people who are killed in Philadelphia are African-American, that the overwhelming majority of people who have health-care challenges are African-American, that education has tremendous disparity gaps. Unemployment, incarceration, poverty, homelessness, housing—all affect the African-American community at a disproportionate level as opposed to everyone else."

In this way, post-Black Power politicians like Nutter and Booker embody the principal duality of modern black America. On one hand, they are the most visible examples of the highly educated, entrepreneurial and growing black middle class that cultural markers like "The Cosby Show" first introduced to white Americans in the 1980s. According to an analysis by Pew's Economic Mobility Project, almost 37 percent of black families fell into one of the three top income quintiles in 2005, compared with 23 percent in 1973. At the same time, though, these black leaders are constantly confronted in their own cities and districts by blighted neighborhoods that are predominately black, places where poverty collects like standing water, breeding a host of social contagions.

That both of these trend lines can exist at once poses some difficult questions for black leaders and institutions. Back in the heyday of the civil rights movement, the evils and objectives were relatively clear: there were discriminatory laws in place that denied black Americans their rights as citizens, and the goal was to get those laws repealed and to pass more progressive federal legislation at the same time. You marched and you rallied and—if you had the bravery of a James Clyburn or a John Lewis—you endured blows to the head and to the spirit, and eventually the barriers started to fall. Things become more complicated, and more confounding, however, when those legal barriers no longer exist and when millions of black Americans are catapulting themselves to success. Now the inequities in the society are subtler—inferior schools, an absence of employers, a dearth of affordable housing—and the remedies more elusive.

This confusion over the direction of the movement has all but immobilized the nation's premier civil rights group, the NAACP Synonymous with the long journey toward racial equality since its founding by W. E. B. Du Bois and others in 1909, the organization has, in recent years, lost much of its cachet with younger black Americans. In 2005, the NAACP's unwieldy 64-member board hired Bruce Gordon, a former Verizon executive, to retool the organization. Gordon's premise was that civil rights was no longer simply about protesting discrimination—that African-Americans were now stymied not only by institutional barriers but also by conditions in their communities. He proposed that a new N.A.A.C.P step into this breach, organizing services that might include SAT prep classes or training for new parents. He also created a new class of online members who didn't have to pay any dues, adding more than 100,000 members to a group whose paying membership had declined, in Gordon's estimate, to under 300,000.

Gordon's agenda was always controversial among the NAACP's board members ("Most of them are older than me," the 62-year-old Gordon told me), and after a little more than 19 months in the job, Gordon resigned. In May, after a highly contentious process that divided the board once again, the NAACP hired the youngest president in its history, 35-year-old Benjamin Todd Jealous, the chosen candidate of Julian Bond, the civil rights leader and the NAACP's board chairman.

You might expect Jealous, a native of mostly white Monterey County, California, and a Rhodes scholar, to have shared the racial experience of other emerging black leaders. But generational lines are rarely that neatly drawn, and when we met for breakfast on Independence Day, I was surprised to find that Jealous spoke about race not like Booker or Nutter but much like his heroes of an earlier era. The NAACP's main job, he told me, was to be the place where African-Americans could turn when institutional racism assaulted their communities. He mentioned the racially charged arrests of six black teenagers in Jena, Louisiana, in 2006, as well as the suspicious death, just a few days earlier, of an accused cop killer in his suburban Maryland jail cell.

"It's still a human rights struggle," Jealous told me. "This isn't a struggle that began in the 1930s or 1960s. It's a struggle that began in 1620. It's a struggle against slavery and its children."

Jealous's main difficulty in rejuvenating the NAACP, though, may have less to do with the racist power structure than with a new class of black competitors online. And in this way, what's happening among the black grass roots mirrors what's been happening in the Democratic Party over the last several years, as loyalty to institutions and leaders has given way to a noisy conversation about how to better hold them accountable. A new generation of black activists is now focused on reforming institutions, namely the Congressional Black Caucus and the NAACP, that they say have become too mired in the past and too removed from their constituents. And as in the rest of the political world, this rebellion is happening on the Internet, driven by ordinary Americans with laptops and a surprising amount of free time.

"The African-American voting population is very much online," Cheryl Contee, who in 2006 helped found the blog Jack and Jill Politics, told me. Contee, who is an owner of a digital consulting business, blogs under the pseudonym Jill Tubman, and hers is one of a number of sites that have emerged in just the last year as part of what's often called the "Afrosphere." "One of the things I talk to clients about is that the digital divide has changed," Contee said. "It's no longer along racial lines like it was in 1996 and 2000. Now it's more economic and educational." In other words, after lagging for a time, college-educated African-Americans are now organizing online in the same way as their mostly white counterparts at Daily Kos and MoveOn.org started doing several years ago.

One of most vibrant voices in this debate belongs to Color of Change, a Web site designed to replicate the MoveOn model among black Web surfers. Two Bay Area activists, Van Jones and James Rucker, founded Color of Change in 2005, a week after the images of devastated black neighborhoods began streaming back from New Orleans. The group now boasts about 425,000 members, about half of whom are white. The bulk of the membership is between the ages of 35 and 55 and probably falls into the categories of middle class or affluent—in other words, the very people who were once the NAACP's base of support. Those members pay no dues but contributed about $250,000 during a three-month period in 2007 to pay the legal fees of the defendants in Jena.

As in the liberal online community at large, there is not a lot of ideological coherence among the emerging "black roots." There is no clear action plan for how to bridge the divide between middle-class black families and the millions left behind, aside from the same basic antiwar, anticorporate ethos that permeates the rest of the digital left. But there is a strong sense that the leaders of the civil rights generation need some kind of retirement plan, and soon. "Victims don't make things happen," says Rucker, who previously worked for MoveOn. "Things are changing from where they were 30 years ago. The fights are changing. And you have an infrastructure that's not producing results. Look at the incarceration rates, the difference between whites and blacks. What are the old organizations accomplishing?"

Most of all, the black roots make it clear to elected officials and civil rights advocates that being black doesn't, by itself, make you a leader. Online activists have attacked the Congressional Black Caucus for, among other things, standing by William Jefferson, the black representative accused of stuffing a freezer with cash bribes. They have harshly criticized several caucus members, some for having endorsed Clinton and others, like Artur Davis, for not being sufficiently liberal. Some bloggers went after the Rev. Al Sharpton and the NAACP for reflexively coming to the defense of four black teenagers in West Palm Beach who were charged with taking part in an unusually horrific rape of a mother and her 12-year-old son. (Sharpton and the local NAACP claimed that the boys were being treated differently from accused white rapists in a separate case, who were freed on bail.) Color of Change claims to have raised more than $10,000 and some 50 volunteers for Donna Edwards's successful Web-supported primary campaign against Representative Albert Wynn, a black incumbent who voted for the Iraq war.

"There are some members who need to go or to update and be accountable," Rucker told me. "It's not about getting rid of the NAACP or our members of Congress. It's just wanting to be proud of our leaders."

For some black operatives in the Clinton orbit—people who have functioned, going back to Jesse Jackson's campaigns in the 1980s, as Democratic Washington's liaisons to black America—the fallout from an Obama victory would likely be profound. "Some of them will have to walk the plank," an Obama adviser told me bluntly. In their place, an Obama administration would empower a cadre of younger black advisers who would instantly become people to see in Washington's transactional culture. Chief among them is Valerie Jarrett, a Chicago real estate developer who is one of Barack and Michelle Obama's closest friends. "She's poised to be one of the most influential people in politics, and particularly among African-Americans in politics," Belcher told me. "She may be the next Vernon Jordan." In fact, the last time I saw Clyburn, he told me he had just spent two and a half hours at breakfast with Jarrett.

Then there are operatives like Belcher himself; Michael Strautmanis, Obama's former chief counsel and de facto younger brother, who first met Michelle Obama when he was working as a paralegal at her law firm; Matthew Nugen, a political aide who is Obama's point man for the Democratic convention; and Paul Brathwaite, a 37-year-old lobbyist who used to be the executive director of the black caucus and who might act as a bridge between black congressmen and an Obama White House.

Should they win in November, Obama and these new advisers will confront an unfamiliar conundrum in American politics, which is how to be president of the United States and, by default, the most powerful voice in black America at the same time. Several black operatives and politicians with whom I spoke worried, eloquently, that an Obama presidency might actually leave black Americans less well represented in Washington rather than more so—that, in fact, the end of black politics, if that is what we are witnessing, might also mean the precipitous decline of black influence.

The argument here is that a President Obama, closely watched for signs of parochialism or racial resentment, would have less maneuvering room to champion spending on the urban poor, say, or to challenge racial injustice. What's more, his very presence in the Rose Garden might undermine the already tenuous case for affirmative action in hiring and school admissions. Obama himself has offered only tepid support for a policy that surely helped enable him to reach this moment. In "The Audacity of Hope," he wrote: "Even as we continue to defend affirmative action as a useful, if limited, tool to expand opportunity to underrepresented minorities, we should consider spending a lot more of our political capital convincing America to make investments needed to ensure that all children perform at grade level and graduate from high school—a goal that, if met, would do more than affirmative action to help those black and Latino children who need it the most."

Then there are the issues that Ben Jealous and others might raise: black men incarcerated at more than six times the rate of white men, black joblessness more than twice as high as the rate for white Americans. Just talking about such disparities as systemic problems could be harder for an African-American president—for any African-American, really—than it was before. "If Obama is president, it will no longer be tenable to go to the white community and say you've been victimized," Artur Davis told me. "And I understand the poverty and the condition of black America and the 39 percent unemployment rate in some communities. I understand that. But if you go out to the country and say you've been victimized by the white community, while Barack Obama

and Michelle and their kids are living in the White House, you will be shut off from having any influence."

As a candidate, Obama has outlined an agenda for "civil rights and criminal justice," aimed primarily at urban African-Americans. His platform includes refocusing the Justice Department on hate crimes, banning racial profiling by federal law-enforcement agencies and reforming mandatory minimum sentences (which disproportionately affect black men, especially those convicted on crack-cocaine charges). Obama's black advisers caution, however, that no one should expect him to behave like a civil rights leader, marching alongside Al Sharpton to protest the next Jena or putting black causes ahead of anyone else's. "It's a very interesting question, but as a black person, you should feel confident that he will focus on your injustices and know that all the other injustices in other communities affect you too," Valerie Jarrett told me. "There have been wounds in all the communities, not just in the black community. There are plenty of wounds to go around."

If there is any American who can offer a glimpse of what it would be like for Obama as president, it's probably Governor Deval Patrick of Massachusetts. While most of the younger black politicians know one another only from the occasional encounter or phone call, Patrick and Obama shared a cup of coffee, at the suggestion of a mutual friend, in the mid-1990s and developed a close friendship. (The senator even borrowed some of Patrick's oratory during the primaries, which led the Clinton camp to charge plagiarism.) Patrick was Coca-Cola's general counsel and the assistant attorney general for civil rights in the Clinton administration before he became, in 2006, only the second black man to be elected governor in American history, following L. Douglas Wilder in Virginia in 1989.

When we talked recently, Patrick explained for me some of the inherent pressures that come with being a black executive in a state with a history of friction among the races. "You're constantly tested by a whole host of factors to see whether you're speaking for the entire Commonwealth or just for one community," Patrick told me. "I don't fit in any box, and I think that's what the electorate has had to learn about me."

Black ministers were slow to embrace Patrick after he supported gay marriage as a candidate and refused to back down. After a black child was shot and killed in Boston last year, Patrick told me, he sent a note to the family and prepared to attend the funeral service, but relatives held a news conference at which they criticized him for not coming by to pay his respects. (Patrick later grew close to the family.) I remarked that it was usually the city's mayor who was expected to comfort victims of urban crime.

"Yes, but it's not good enough for me to have the reaction that you just did, to say I'm the governor, not the mayor," Patrick told me. "They expect more." In other words, he was expected not only to be a governor but also to fill the traditional role of the black politician—that of spokesman, minister and conduit to the white establishment.

Patrick and I spoke just a week after Jesse Jackson was caught wishing Obama bodily harm. "You wouldn't believe how many times in the last few days people have stuck microphones in my face to ask my opinion about Jesse Jackson's comments," he said, sounding a little exasperated. He had declined to offer one. "I don't have to be the black oracle," Patrick told me. "All I have to be is as good a human being and as good a governor as I can be, and the rest will take care of itself." If Obama's day comes, he might want to think about borrowing those words too.

UNIT 10

Understanding International Aspects of Ethnic Relations

Unit Selections

Key Points to Consider

- Will the ethnic and religious conflict that is emerging in Iraq overshadow the American formulation of its future as a free market and democracy?

- What can and should be done about genocidal violence? By whom?

- Does China run a parallel risk as it attempts to extend the influence of the central government into its western regions, where Islamic populations and a range of ethnic groups seem to be intent on maintaining their autonomy?

- Are political solutions to pluralism and military/economic regimes in support of free markets and democracy compatible?

- Do regional organizations and/or international organizations such as the United Nations have the capacity and the rightful authority to intervene in ethnic group conflicts? Or to prevent the wholesale destructions of ethnic groups within countries? Why or why not? Are there human rights that are beyond the claims of sovereignty? Explain.

- Are religious affiliations and state citizenship as well as a single ethnic tradition, a defensible goal and a worthy political objective? In what ways are religious representation and participation related to public affairs and social policy?

- How will increased immigration, technological advances, and more competitive world markets affect the relationships between religious and ethnic groups?

Student Web Site
www.mhcls.com

Internet References

Yale University Guide to American Ethnic Studies
   http://www.library.yale.edu/rsc/ethnic/internet.html
American Indian Ritual Object Repatriation Foundation
   http://www.repatriationfoundation.org
Center for Research in Ethnic Relations
   http://www.warwick.ac.uk/fac/soc/CRER_RC
The International Center for Migration, Ethnicity, and Citizenship
   http://www.newschool.edu/icmec

The articles in this section invite us to pursue the search for fresh insight into the social and symbolic formation of cultures. The debate regarding the relationship of various ways of knowing invites us to search for understanding and particular skills, competencies, and rules for dialogue among religious, ethnic, and political traditions. Support of civilization and peaceful means of resolving differences are clearly imperative. While the situation of these issues is worldwide, understanding and action in this arena is nearly always local and specific to the particularly social history and interaction of cultures and political leadership.

The winds of political change in the Middle East, and the movement of new populations into Eastern and Central Europe reveal the saliency of ethnicity and the varied textures of group relations. In America, the ongoing affinity of ethnic populations to the nations of their origin is expressed in subtle as well as obvious ways. These articles explain the transmission of ethnic tradition in music and suggest linkages between religion and ethnicity. The story of the interaction of ethnicity and religion is curiously exposed in the etymology of the Greek word *ethnikos* (i.e., the rural, Gentile, or pagan people of the ancient Mediterranean world). Though such philological roots no longer drive our principal understanding of ethnicity, the experience of social affinity and cultural affiliation elaborated in the following articles about ethnics deepens our awareness and understanding of ethnicity—as changing yet persistent aspect of human identity and social cohesiveness. As Eric Voegelin noted, the self interpretation of a society does not wait for the social scientist. Societies in historical existence are not merely facts and events and external locations; they are "little worlds of meaning, *cosmions,* illuminated with meaning from within by human beings who continuously create and bear it as the mode and condition of their self-realization . . . relations between its members and groups of members, as well as its existence as a whole, transparent for the mystery of human existence . . . members of a society experience it more than as an accident or a convenience; they experience it as of their human essence."

The process of better understanding the multiethnic character of larger countries and the world involves the coordinated efforts of formal and informal education, which are influenced by public and private institutions and the community-based voluntary associations that are the building blocks of society. This collection of articles addresses resistance to the challenges that are embedded in passionately held and politically potent traditions of ethnic opposition. The persistence of confusion, uncertainty, insensitivity, and violence toward and among ethnic groups is a sobering and stunning fact. Strategies for dealing with the tension and reality of bias are examined in this unit. Hatred and prejudice are frequently based on conscious manipulation of powerful images that profoundly shape personal and group identity. Exploring other societies is often a way of gaining fresh perspective on the American reality; differences and commonalities

of the situations described in this unit are worth pondering.

Examination, for example, of the legacy of the civil rights laws crafted during the 1960s, and the process of shaping a society grounded in exclusionary habits and institutions involves assessment on many levels—the social, the political, the ideological, and the economic. Even on the most basic level of public perception, most agree that progress has been made toward a society of equality and social justice, with increased hopes for decreased segregation in schools and neighborhoods. Yet disparities of these views among ethnic and racial groups indicate that uniformity and a shared sense of the past and present are not generally common. Attempting to overcome such gulfs of understanding before they lead to more serious forms of conflict is among the great challenges of the present.

Since the breakup of the Soviet empire, ethnicity has reoriented the international arena. New national claims as well as the revival of ancient antagonisms are fragmenting Europe. War, the systematic expression of conflict, and its aftermath are also occasions for the use and misuse of ethnically charged political rhetoric. The presence of a politically relevant past and the invocation of religious warrants for group conflict have indicated the need for new approaches to peacekeeping, and educational strategies for meeting and transcending group differences. The critiques challenging multiculturalism, the educational controversy regarding which should be the dominant expressions of our human commonality, and the various values and virtues found in all ethnic traditions pose challenges for economically and socially turbulent times. Whether these moments are crises of growth or decline will be measured by a host of indicators. Which of these indicators are the most salient is, of course, another question, whose answer depends on our selective invocation of historical materials and ethnic symbols as guides for contemporary analysis.

Ethnic relations have erupted into warfare in Africa, where conflicts have shattered emerging states and thus challenged the hopeful myth of postcolonial renewal as well as the racial/ethnic myth of black solidarity. But Africa's emerging countries are not alone: The Middle East, Central Europe, Canada, Ireland and the Northern Counties, and the Balkans and Caucasus are additional venues of destructive conflict. Each of these simmering cauldrons—not melting pots—illustrates the stakes and consequences of unresolved conflict and distrust concerning land, religion, culture, leadership, and economic production and distribution. Each also shows the rewards and recognitions that fuel human passions, ambitions, and the will to dominate and to govern the affairs and destinies of various peoples that cohabit contiguous regions. Thus, the dramas of regional ethnic struggle and the growth of worldwide ethnic challenges to the constitution of human order itself are increasingly marked by episodes of blatant bigotry and intolerance. Fanaticism and zealotry impose themselves on the stage of history, which is rushing toward a new millennium. The threshold of hope that it promises for those who can recover and embrace the mystery of diversity waits to define the human condition in the twenty-first century.

In The United States of America, generations of slaves and their descendants were not considered, nor legally warranted rights, as persons. American legal and political entities supported a race-conscious culture that sustained its economy. This fundamental pattern continued even as a more complex web of cultures and economic development changed the social composition of the population. Aided by an open immigration policy that sought the benefits of large-scale population growth, industrialization, and urbanization, America began to transform itself. The transformation yielded American ethnicities and a new free-associational form of religiosity—a tradition alien to the dominant Protestant churches. When Catholicism and Judaism become socially effective, new claims were woven into the deep structures of a changing cultural and social fabric.

The theory and practice of developing a new political culture and an inclusive constitutional tradition drew its energy and inspiration from a wellspring of hope articulated in the American aspiration to "liberty and justice for all," as manifested in the Declaration of Independence. In the United States, after nearly a century of social and regime construction and reconstruction, our understanding of pluralism, at best, yields the following finding: Ethnicity is one of the modern identities developed by the largely peasant migrants who poured into the United States during the last two centuries.

For most immigrants, their ethnicity became a cultural modality that emerged as they became Americans, and their religious faith and institutions were influenced by the new dynamics of American development. This new notion of personhood replaced loyalty to village or region as the reference point around which they organized their sense of life, located the place of their family in the moral and physical universe, and shaped their community. The long-term misreading of meanings indicates the current need for critical reformulation of approaches to race and ethnic relations. Concrete strategies for improving this situation call upon both the public and the private sectors in areas of relief, institution building, education, employment, and training. The emergence of new findings and scholarly contentions in genetics and its applications to medicine are intersecting race, ethnicity, and religion. The outcome of this great debate may establish new horizons for which our understanding of the human condition, in an era of science and human rights, may enable us to perceive the wonders of pluralism with deepened insight and respect for its awesome complexity and profound unity.

Obama & Israel
A Missed Opportunity

Don Wycliff

Barack Obama's brilliant Philadelphia speech on race has been eclipsed by his complete break last month with the man he was trying to explain and avoid breaking with, Rev. Jeremiah Wright. Yet, for all the Philadelphia speech's brilliance and wisdom, one aspect of it left me profoundly sad and troubled.

Early in the speech, as Obama recited a list of questions raised about him as a result of the Wright video snippets, he said: "Did I strongly disagree with many of his political views? Absolutely—just as I'm sure many of you have heard remarks from your pastors, priests, or rabbis with which you strongly disagreed."

Obama is too smart and his campaign too efficient for the omission of any reference to Islamic clergymen—"your imams," perhaps—to have been accidental. That it wasn't became clear just a few sentences later when Obama characterized Wright's as "a profoundly distorted view of this country," and included among his distortions "a view that sees the conflicts in the Middle East as rooted primarily in the actions of stalwart allies like Israel, instead of emanating from the perverse and hateful ideologies of radical Islam."

With all due respect—and I think Obama is due a lot of it—if that is to be his approach to the nation's most difficult, persistent, and intractable foreign-policy challenge, then we might as well not bother to change leadership. I want to believe that Obama was simply doing what a Democrat must to win the party's nomination: pledge undying support for Israel to avoid getting crosswise with Jewish voters. He could not afford to do less in a contest with Hillary Clinton, who never misses a chance to underscore her support for Israel. Witness her recent pledge to "obliterate" Iran if that nation staged a nuclear attack on Israel. John McCain has done much the same by attempting to tie Obama to Hamas.

Obama probably also figured that, with a substantial chunk of the electorate still laboring under the misimpression that he is a Muslim, speaking kindly of Muslims and Islam while defending himself in the Wright matter would have been like trying to put out a fire by dousing it with gasoline. Still . . .

Part of the promise that people see in Obama is that, as a nontraditional president from a nonwhite minority background, he may enable the rest of the world to look at America in a different way from the one it has become accustomed to doing during the Bush-Cheney-Rumsfeld-neocon era. I first heard this hope expressed by a high-school classmate, Kathy Alexander, over dinner at her home in Terre Haute, Indiana, last September. Since then I've heard it numerous times from Americans of all racial and political stripes. But Obama won't do that if he enters the White House committed to the view of the situation in the Middle East he expressed in Philadelphia.

No, Israel is not the root of all evil in the Middle East, and the U.S. commitment to its security must remain nonnegotiable. In a succession of speeches and interviews over the last month, Obama has gone out of his way to underscore his belief in that commitment. But if Obama seriously believes that Israel's forty-plus-year occupation of the West Bank and Gaza is not an open sore constantly oozing pus into this country's relationship with virtually every Islamic country in the world . . . well, he's not half as intelligent as I think he is.

The fact of the matter is that the condition of the Palestinians is that of serfs: they effectively have no rights that any Israeli is bound to respect. Rev. Wright may have overstated the matter when he characterized Israel's occupation as "state terrorism," but it certainly bears a strong resemblance to some of the more morally egregious human-rights violations in the world.

Yes, Iran is under the sway of homegrown Islamic theocrats. Al Qaeda and its adherents certainly subscribe to a "perverse and hateful" species of "radical Islam." And without question, Hamas officially clings to an implacable opposition to Israel's very existence as a nation. But the majority of Palestinians seem to me to be intent mainly on getting the boot of Israeli military occupation off their necks, gaining control of their own territory, eliminating the daily insults of checkpoints and settlements on their land, and of Israeli settlers occupying land that, legally, isn't Israel's to give.

It would be interesting to see how soon a peace could be concluded if we had a president with the gumption to be even-handed in the Israel-Palestine dispute and to give the impression he genuinely cares about the Palestinian people. If Obama sees only "the perverse and hateful ideologies of radical Islam" as the source of unrest and violence in the Middle East—and not also the legitimate grievances of the Palestinian people—then, at least in this key area of foreign policy, he'll be no improvement on the current regime.

It would furthermore be interesting to see what a Palestinian-Israeli peace would do to all the other conflicts in the Middle East. How much venom and anger would be drained if there were not a daily diet of images of soldiers shooting at rock-throwers and of homes being bulldozed? How much harder would it be for Islamic radicals to fill their ranks without such provocations?

Obama's Philadelphia speech—especially the part in which he spoke of the racial resentments of whites—showed him to be a careful listener with an understanding heart. I hope he has listened to the Palestinians and understood their complaints. Some of his recent remarks suggest that he has. I hope he has listened to his own speech, and understood how worrying his remarks about the Middle East were. And I hope the view of things he expressed in that speech was not fully reflective of his understanding of the forces at play in that region.

DON WYCLIFF, a former journalist, lives and writes in South Bend, Indiana.

American Self-Interest and the Response to Genocide

ROGER W. SMITH

For 20 years, I taught a course on genocide: What is "genocide," why does it happen, who is responsible for it, and how could this ultimate crime be prevented? I told students that genocide—intentional acts to eliminate in whole, or in substantial part, a specific human population—had claimed the lives of some 60 million people in the 20th century, 16 million of them since 1945, when the watchword was "Never again." Genocide has, in fact, been so frequent, the number of victims so extensive, and serious attempts to prevent it so few, that many scholars have described the 20th century as "the age of genocide." Some have wondered if genocide is not itself a product of modernity, the dark energy of civilization.

But what my students wanted to know was: Why had the nations of the world, and particularly the United States, which they thought of as both powerful and just, not prevented the killing of millions of innocent people? Where was American power and moral commitment when a million Armenians were being slaughtered in Turkey in 1915, six million Ukrainians starved to death by Stalin in 1932–33, two million Bengalis murdered by Pakistan in 1971? What was America doing when still more millions were killed in Cambodia, Bosnia, and Rwanda, not because of what they had done, but because of who they were? And, of course, there was the much-discussed question of whether more could have been done to prevent the Holocaust.

My students also wanted to know why it had taken the United States 40 years to ratify the Genocide Convention, which the United Nations endorsed unanimously in 1948, with strong U.S. support. The convention defined genocide and declared it a crime against international law. Why, as soon as the United States finally did ratify the convention, in 1988, did it support Saddam Hussein's regime despite evidence that the dictator had committed genocide against the Kurds in Iraq in 1987–88?

Today we continue to hear about genocide. As before, however, few Americans pay much attention. What is happening in Sudan? In Congo? With indigenous peoples in many other regions? Can you tell me? My students' questions—and my own—are increasingly important to all of us, both morally and politically.

Unfortunately they are not easy to answer. Sometimes the response hinges on factual information, but more often on

Key Works Discussed in This Essay

Arguing About War, by Michael Walzer (Yale University Press, 2004).

The Burning Tigris: The Armenian Genocide and America's Response, by Peter Balakian (HarperCollins, 2003).

A Century of Genocide: Utopias of Race and Nation, by Eric D. Weitz (Princeton University Press, 2003).

Genocide: Its Political Use in the Twentieth Century, by Leo Kuper (Yale University Press, 1982).

The New Killing Fields: Massacre and the Politics of Intervention, edited by Nicolaus Mills and Kira Brunner (Basic Books, 2002).

"A Problem From Hell": America and the Age of Genocide, by Samantha Power (Basic Books, 2002).

"Provoking Genocide: A Revised History of the Rwandan Patriotic Front," by Alan J. Kuperman, in the *Journal of Genocide Research,* Vol. 6, No. 1, March 2004:61–84.

The Specter of Genocide: Mass Murder in Historical Perspective, edited by Robert Gellately and Ben Kiernan (Cambridge University Press, 2003).

judgment, an assessment of competing responsibilities, and context. At the outset we can reject claims that relieve all bystanders, whether states, organizations, or individuals, of responsibility for attempting to prevent or mitigate genocide. One argument, coming from perpetrators, is that victims of genocide (although the term is avoided) bear responsibility for their own destruction, having brought it upon themselves through provocation. Genocide is strictly an internal matter, this argument goes. Outside powers should mind their own business. Two immediate objections arise: First, provocations, when they exist at all, stem from a minority of the group of victims. Most of those who will be killed are innocent. Second, genocide is seldom without international consequences, ranging from a vast outpouring of refugees, with the need for large amounts of humanitarian aid, to regional instability and war.

Some have wondered if genocide is not itself a product of modernity, the dark energy of civilization.

A recent article in the *Journal of Genocide Research* provides a chilling variation on the argument about the responsibility of victims. In "Provoking Genocide: A Revised History of the Rwandan Patriotic Front," Alan J. Kuperman states: "In most cases of mass killing since World War II—unlike the Holocaust—the victim group has triggered its own demise by violently challenging the authority of the state." Kuperman adds that he does not use provocation to excuse genocide. Nor does he deny that there is an international responsibility to prevent genocide. But the obligation takes a bizarre turn: Intervention by third parties should not be directed against those we perceive as perpetrators; they, after all, are only defending themselves. Rather, intervention should be aimed at changing the behavior of the victims. In other words, in the Rwandan genocide of 1994, the international community should have ignored the Hutu preparations for genocide and focused, instead, on the intended Tutsi victims. The upshot of that *Alice in Wonderland* argument is that the victims become the perpetrators.

Claims are also made that genocides are inevitable, the result of ancient hatreds, conflict over scarce resources, or the advance of progress. A version of the inevitability thesis that found favor with some international planners in the 1960s was that genocide is simply a byproduct of development, and benefits to the surviving group outweigh the costs to the group that is decimated, or perhaps eliminated. Over the years that argument has been applied not only to the elimination of indigenous peoples (the Yanomami in Brazil, the Chittagong Hills tribesmen in Bangladesh), but also to the destruction of the Armenians in Turkey, which, we are told by some historians, paved the way for a more unified and stronger nation, one allied with the United States during the cold war.

Genocide, however, is never inevitable: It is always the result of choice. And surely lives are not interchangeable.

Another argument is that genocides should be allowed to run their course: It is best to let the violence complete itself, reducing the chance for further violence and, hence, any need for intervention. That proposition, devoid of even animal pity, was advanced to me by a student in international relations after I mentioned that Rwanda had had recurrent genocides. Had the killers not been restrained, he asserted, unity and peace would have been established. When I asked him if he would maintain his position if he were a member of the group slated for victimization, he replied that he lived in the United States, and that therefore the question wasn't relevant. That was shortly before September 11.

The field of genocide studies itself is relatively new, dating to the late 1970s. Several factors were involved: a growing emphasis on the protection of human rights, the frequency of genocide in the 1960s (Rwanda, Indonesia) and 1970s (Bangladesh, Burundi, Cambodia), a rediscovery of the Armenian genocide and a new awareness of how it had been denied. Not last: a disenchantment with the emphasis in the social sciences on methodology at the expense of substance.

One of the best works is still Leo Kuper's 1982 *Genocide: Its Political Use in the Twentieth Century,* which discusses the nature and history of genocide, its treatment under international law, the conditions that promote it, and the inability of the United Nations to suppress it. But since the book's publication, new genocides have been committed, extensive research on genocide has been conducted, and explanations of why genocides occur have taken on new sophistication. Three recent books provide essential, updated information about genocide in the 20th century.

The first, *The New Killing Fields: Massacre and the Politics of Intervention,* edited by Nicolaus Mills and Kira Brunner, is perhaps the narrowest, yet the most contemporary, focusing on four cases of genocide: Cambodia, Bosnia, Rwanda, and East Timor. Most of the essays are by journalists, some of whom were present as genocide was taking place around them. Their accounts, mostly descriptive and personal, provide a wealth of information. *The New Killing Fields* also includes two essays, by Michael Walzer and Samantha Power, that suggest how we can begin to evaluate international responses to genocide. When, where, how, and at what cost should outside states intervene? More on that later.

Eric D. Weitz's *A Century of Genocide: Utopias of Race and Nation* also concentrates on four cases of genocide in the 20th century: the Soviet Union, Nazi Germany, Cambodia, and Bosnia/Kosovo. Systematic in his comparisons, Weitz concludes that those genocides were the result of "ideologies of race and nation, revolutionary regimes with vast utopian ambitions, moments of crisis generated by war and domestic upheaval." What is distinctive about his thesis is that he maintains that genocide has a dual character: It is organized by states but is possible on a vast scale, as in the 20th century, only with widespread participation by the population. The book is also strong in its emphasis on the rituals of degradation and cruelty that occur in genocide. Its weakness is that it omits the Rwandan genocide altogether, and its concentration on the Soviet Union gets bogged down in party purges and political repression, which Weitz admits are not examples of genocide. (Many of those sent to the gulag were released, and Soviet officials often thought they were pursuing "reform" rather than annihilation, he notes.) On the other hand, the Stalin-induced famine in the Ukraine in 1932–33, intended to destroy the kulaks as a class, end Ukrainian nationalism, and force peasants into collective farms, receives virtually no attention, though most scholars regard it as genocide.

If the other books are selective in the cases of genocide they focus upon, *The Specter of Genocide: Mass Murder in Historical Perspective,* edited by Robert Gellately and Ben Kiernan, strives to be comprehensive. It discusses the Armenian genocide, the Holocaust, and genocides against indigenous peoples in Africa, North America, and Australia, and is particularly strong on its coverage of genocides in the post-1945 period: Indonesia, Cambodia, Ethiopia, Bosnia, Rwanda,

East Timor, and Guatemala. The cumulative impact of the book is to demonstrate just how prevalent state-sponsored mass murder has been in the 20th century. Rather than an aberration, genocide has been commonplace, occurring in most parts of the world. Oddly, however, at least two major examples are omitted: the mass killing in East Pakistan, and Saddam Hussein's gassing of the Kurds. Those are important in their own right, but also, as we shall see, in terms of the U.S. response to them.

Almost from the beginning, the field of genocide studies has been concerned with two questions: Not just, Why does genocide take place?, but also, How can it be prevented? One early idea seemed to offer great promise: a "genocide early-warning system." Comparative analysis would provide indicators to predict where imminent threats of genocide existed; intervention could follow immediately. Naïvely, scholars assumed that individual states or international organizations would act on evidence of when and where genocide was likely to occur. It didn't take long to realize that the problem wasn't about knowing, but about doing. It was a matter of political will.

Inaction and political will became the major topics of discussion in genocide studies as of the mid-'80s. But as often happens in academic life, we were talking mainly to each other. There was little attempt to engage either policy makers or the public in a dialogue. Nor was there an effort to provide a comprehensive account of American policy toward genocide over the course of the 20th century. Some of us thought about doing such a study, but the idea seemed so huge that it was shelved. Then in 2002, the book did appear and, significantly, addressed not so much the academy as the public and the political establishment.

Samantha Power's *"A Problem From Hell": America and the Age of Genocide* won a Pulitzer Prize for its thorough documentation of the dark history of the American inaction to stop genocide in the 20th century and its explanation of why the United States had failed to act. Only rarely did the U.S. government even condemn the killing as it was taking place. For Power, "What is most shocking is that U.S. policy makers did almost nothing to deter the crime." Of course, there were individuals, both in government and in society, who sought to change policy, but, Power notes, their efforts failed. The United States, on the other hand, has been both generous and effective in providing humanitarian aid after a people has been decimated.

It is not just a question of inaction. Power tells us that on several occasions, the United States "directly or indirectly aided those committing genocide." We provided $500-million in agricultural and manufacturing credits to Iraq as that country was destroying thousands of Kurdish villages and gassing Kurds. After Vietnam had ousted Cambodia's Pol Pot regime, the United States, in an effort to deny Vietnam influence in that country, took the lead in the United Nations in recognizing the genocidal Khmer Rouge as the legitimate government of Cambodia. The United States also led the arms embargo against the Bosnian Muslims, even though it was clear that doing so would prevent them from defending themselves. And it did everything in its power to remove U.N. peacekeepers from Rwanda and prevent their return. Some 800,000 persons died as a result; the violence also spilled over into neighboring countries, setting off local and regional wars. Other examples pile up.

How can we explain the U.S. response to genocide? Those who made the decisions not to act typically argued that they didn't know what was going on, that the facts were unclear, that any effort to stop the killing would have been futile, that the United States lacked the means to do so, that intervention would have made the situation even worse. Power rejects such claims: "Simply put, American leaders did not act because they did not want to. They believed that genocide was wrong, but they were not prepared to invest the military, financial, diplomatic, or domestic political capital needed to stop it." On the other hand, when it seemed to be in the national interest, those same policy makers could collaborate in genocide either by giving permission (East Timor) or by active support (Indonesia, Guatemala).

For the most part, genocide in the 20th century seemed to be something that happened to other people, in other parts of the world, with little effect on American interests, narrowly defined. It was seldom a subject of public debate. There has been, Power says, a mutual failure in the democratic process: An uninformed public makes no demands for the suppression of genocide, and politicians, having done what they can to silence the public, cite the lack of public demand as a basis for inaction as genocide claims its victims.

There has always been, however, a problem about how public opinion is related to public policy. I would argue that relatively small, well-organized lobbying groups are more likely to be effective in moving policy makers to act against genocide than broad, but somewhat amorphous, public opinion. Public opinion may be reported, but it doesn't get direct access to policy makers the way human-rights lobbyists sometimes can. Moreover, human-rights groups have the expertise to be persuasive and the commitment to stay with the issue as public opinion—easily manipulated by those with power and an ideological agenda—waxes and wanes.

But the reverse is also true: Farm and manufacturing interests were able to defeat the legislation that would have prohibited credits to Iraq after the gassing of the Kurds. Nearly 25 percent of American rice production annually went to Iraq, along with a million tons of wheat, insecticides, fertilizers, tractors, and so on. Agricultural lobbyists argued that Iraq was not an enemy, but an opportunity. Suspending credits would not punish Iraq—other countries would supply Saddam Hussein. American businesses would be the real victims. The Reagan administration, also claiming that "engagement" with Iraq would allow a gentler dictator to emerge, seconded those arguments.

We can see the impact of public opinion, and its limitations, in Peter Balakian's important book, *The Burning Tigris: The Armenian Genocide and America's Response.* There are several interrelated themes and narratives in *The Burning Tigris.* First, there are the detailed, heart-wrenching accounts of the Turkish massacres of some 200,000 Armenians in the 1890s, and of the genocide, beginning in 1915, that claimed the lives of at least a million Armenians. At the same time, the author describes the dedication and courage of American diplomats, who tried, with little support from the State Department, to end the carnage. But there is also the story of a broadly based American humanitarian movement that sought to provide relief to the Armenians in their desperate condition, and that demanded that the U.S. government protect them from further violence. Balakian, however, shows that by the beginning of the 1920s there was a growing conflict between public opinion, which strongly supported an independent Armenia, and a Congress and White House that had other interests. In his final chapter, he documents Turkey's continuing denial of the Armenian genocide and its efforts, largely successful, to enlist the White House and State Department in defeating Congressional resolutions that would publicly recognize the genocide.

But the point to emphasize here is that while public support was crucial for the relief efforts and helped save many lives, it was not able to carry the day politically. The United States did not declare war on Turkey in World War I, even though Turkey and Germany were allies. An influential group of missionaries and their supporters argued that their colleges and schools would be seized by Turkey, and that relief supplies would not be allowed in the country. After World War I, although the public strongly supported an American mandate to protect the fragile Armenian state, a growing isolationism in Congress put an end to the project. From 1920 on, where Armenia was concerned, it was through the voice not of the people, but of big oil. As one Senate critic summarized the Harding administration's attitude: "Show this administration an oil well, and it will show you a foreign policy." Shades of the past continue. Did Iraqi oil help blunt criticism of what was happening to the Kurds?

Whether the issue is about taxes or human rights, elites and their interest groups tend to prevail. In part that is because most human-rights organizations in the United States have small budgets. And in part because the major humanitarian organizations have differing agendas: Amnesty International focuses on individuals, Human Rights Watch on policy and institutions. Other groups focus on humanitarian aid once the slaughter has commenced. As a result resources and efforts are scattered. What recent scholarship helps us see is that those who want the United States to take a more active stance against genocide have no choice but to create organizations that can lobby more effectively than they have in the past.

In addition, it is crucial that policy makers redefine "national interest" to include the prevention of genocide abroad. How such a conceptual revolution can come about is problematic, but without it, we can expect only more of the same: the deaths of hundreds of thousands of people while Uncle Sam takes a hike. The case for an expanded understanding of the national interest is not new. It has had a prominent place in scholarly discussions for at least the past 20 years, but it has either been ignored or viewed with skepticism by most in power.

The argument rests on two elements. The first is moral: Genocide is a crime committed upon a particular people, but by its very nature, it is also a crime against humankind, permanently diminishing the biological and cultural possibilities of human existence. It is an outrage to our sense of justice. Since when can we support, allow, defend the mass killing of the innocent? The second reason: Genocide leads to war, regional and international instability, disruption of trade, an enormous outflow of refugees,

and if not stopped, sends a message to would-be perpetrators that they can go ahead with impunity. Further still, as Power reminds us, survivors of genocide may become a threat in the future, harboring a thirst for vengeance and having learned that violence is an acceptable way to "solve" social and political problems. In that sense, the case for the prevention of genocide is rooted in enlightened self-interest.

A major barrier to an expanded notion of national interest or, more generally, a willingness to prevent or mitigate genocide, is that "intervention" is widely thought to mean solely military intervention. That is, in fact, how the political theorist Michael Walzer understands the term in his essay in *The New Killing Fields*. He would limit military intervention to cases of genocide and ethnic cleansing; other violations of human rights, however egregious, would be left to the local population. Whether he would approve of Britain's recent military intervention in Sierra Leone is uncertain.

Moreover, Walzer insists that the task of intervention is limited: "Once the massacres and ethnic cleansing are really over and the people in command are committed to avoiding their return, the intervention is finished." He notes that "when intervention is understood in this minimalist fashion, it may be a little easier to see it through." But in his new book, *Arguing About War,* Walzer supports intervening countries' staying for the long term: "Humanitarian intervention radically shifts the argument about endings, because now the war is from the beginning an effort to change the regime that is responsible for inhumanity." That position may be logical, but it also suggests the difficulties that make countries and international organizations unwilling to commit themselves.

There are other ways of thinking about intervention. Actual military intervention may sometimes be necessary to stop a continuing genocide, as it was in East Pakistan in 1971 and East Timor in 1999. In some cases intervention may prevent genocide: Gen. Roméo Dallaire, the U.N. commander in Rwanda, thought that 5,000 troops would have been adequate to thwart the impending genocide. But nations can also respond to genocide, or the likelihood of genocide, short of military intervention, with all of its human and political risks. The options are not confined to either doing nothing or waging full battle with the genocidal regime.

The war against terrorism is taking center stage, helping to push genocide to the back of our consciousness.

Part of the problem is to identify in advance the countries most likely to commit genocide and take steps to mediate conflicts; to transform, as much as possible, the conditions that give rise to genocide; and to use a variety of incentives and threats to affect decisions in the potentially genocidal regime. Once genocide begins, there are also steps that intervening nations or groups can take. Samantha Power provides a compelling list of such actions. She urges countries to "respond to genocide with a sense of urgency, publicly identifying and threatening the perpetrators with prosecution, demanding the expulsion of representatives of genocidal regimes from international institutions such as the United Nations, closing the perpetrators' embassies in the United States, and calling upon countries aligned with the perpetrators to ask them to use their influence." Other actions might include economic sanctions, freezing financial assets, and, to prevent incitement of genocide, jamming radio and televisions channels that spew out messages of hate. Ultimately, military intervention may nevertheless be necessary, although that would not have to be undertaken by just one nation.

Multilateral intervention provides greater legitimacy, reducing the perception that action has more to do with self-interest than with humanitarianism, and thus helps to securely establish the right to intervene to stop mass killing. It also distributes the burden of intervention. But intervention by a single state may be justified, as when India used force in adjacent East Pakistan in 1971.

Yet, if the U.S. government has a dismal record on responding to genocide, there have been signs in the past 10 years of possible change. After a very late start a U.S.-led NATO force intervened in Bosnia, first with air power, then with the orchestration of the Dayton Accords; that was followed by military intervention in Kosovo. Then in 1999, the United States supported U.N. intervention in East Timor to protect the right to self-determination and what was left of a people still under assault by militias and the Indonesian army. For several years a joint CIA-State Department genocide early-warning system has been in place.

At present the State Department is discussing whether the mass killing, razing of villages, and burning of crops in the Darfur region of Sudan, by government-supported Arab militias against non-Arabs who live in the region, constitutes genocide. (However, possible sanctions mentioned publicly, like freezing the killers' assets in the United States, are more symbolic than likely to have a real impact.)

But there have also been countersigns: the steadfast refusal to recognize the International Criminal Court that could try, as a last resort, persons accused of war crimes, crimes against humanity, and genocide. Moreover, the war against terrorism is taking center stage, once more helping to push genocide to the back of our consciousness.

Even if the political will to prevent genocide suddenly appears, another problem exists. Most genocide scholars and human-rights advocates believe that, unless the United States takes the lead, other countries will stay on the sidelines, as they have in the past. But American power is not enough. To enlist others in the effort to prevent genocide, moral authority is required. Therein lies the issue: What is left of America's moral credibility after Iraq?

ROGER W. SMITH is a professor emeritus of government at the College of William & Mary and a former president of the Association of Genocide Scholars.

Never Underestimate the Power of Ethnicity in Iraq

AMY CHUA AND JED RUBENFELD

Sick to death of "identity politics" at home, Americans ironically find themselves dealing with a tinderbox of ethnic division in Iraq. We may be the least well-equipped nation in the world to manage the kinds of group hatreds that threaten Iraqi society today. Because of our beliefs in the "melting pot" and the United States' own relatively successful—though halting and incomplete—history of assimilation, Americans don't always understand the significance of ethnicity, both at home and especially abroad. In Iraq, our obliviousness to the realities of group hatred was on display from the first days of the occupation, when U.S. officials appointed former members of the almost-exclusively-Sunni Baath Party to the highest government and police positions, apparently unaware that these appointments would provoke the fury of Iraq's Shiites, Kurds and others, who make up more than 80 percent of the population. The outraged reactions forced the Americans to rescind the appointments.

British colonial governments, by contrast, were fastidiously conscious of ethnic divisions. But their policies are a dangerous model. When it was the British Empire's turn to deal with nation-building and ethnicity, the British engaged in divide-and-conquer policies, not only protecting but favoring minorities, and simultaneously aggravating ethnic resentments. As a result, when the British decamped, time bombs often exploded, from Africa to India to Southeast Asia.

The U.S. government's ethnic policy for Iraq has essentially been to have no policy. The Bush administration's overriding goal is the transfer of power by the end of next June from the U.S.-led coalition to a new Iraqi government selected, in theory, through some kind of democratic process. The administration seems strangely confident that Iraq's ethnic, religious and tribal divisions will dissipate in the face of rapid democratization and market-generated wealth. In President Bush's words, "freedom and democracy will always and everywhere have greater appeal than the slogans of hatred."

Unfortunately, recent history suggests just the opposite. Rapid democratization has been attempted in many poor, ethnically divided societies in the last two decades, and the results are sobering. Democratic elections in the former Yugoslavia produced landslide victories for the hate-mongering Franjo Tudjman in Croatia and the genocidal Slobodan Milosevic in Serbia. In Rwanda in the early 1990s, democratization fomented ethnic extremism, yielding the majority-supported Hutu Power movement and the ensuing ethnic slaughter of Tutsis. In Indonesia in 1998, sudden democratization after the fall of Suharto's 30-year dictatorship produced a wave of anti-Chinese demagoguery and confiscations, leading to the devastating flight of more than $40 billion in Chinese-controlled capital.

It is impossible to predict who would win free and fair elections in Iraq, but given the demographic and economic conditions, it is extremely unlikely that such elections in the near future would produce a secular, pro-American outcome.

Iraq's ethnic and religious dynamics involve conflicts that cut across and among Kurds, Turkmens, Shiites, Christians and Sunnis; many horrendous massacres; wholesale confiscations; and deep feelings of hatred and the need for revenge. Iraq's Shiites represent a 60 percent majority, which has suffered cruel oppression at the hands of the Sunni minority. While Iraq's Shiites are far from homogeneous, liberation has already fueled religious demagoguery among vying Islamic clerics and unleashed powerful fundamentalist movements throughout the country. Needless to say, these extremist movements are intensely anti-American, anti-secular, anti-women's rights and illiberal. Meanwhile, Iraq's 20 percent Kurdish minority in the north, mistrustful of Arab rule, represents another source of profound instability. Finally, as many have pointed out, Iraq's oil could prove a curse, leading to massive corruption and a destructive battle between groups to capture the nation's oil, its main source of wealth.

None of this is democracy's fault. The blame for Iraq's current group hatreds rests largely with the fascistic regime of Saddam Hussein, which systematically terrorized and murdered Shiites and Kurds. In addition, Hussein's sadistic secularism spurred the growing fundamentalism among Iraq's Shiites.

Blaming Saddam, however, does not alter the facts. Given the conditions today in Iraq—conditions created by colonialism, autocracy and brutality, not to mention the historical schism between Shiite and Sunni Muslims—hasty national elections could very well produce renewed ethnic radicalism and violence; an illiberal, Islamist regime in which women are murdered by their relatives for the crime of being raped (already happening in Shiite Baghdad); and an anti-American government determined to oust U.S. firms from Iraq's oil fields. Any of these results would create, at best, an awkward moment for the Bush administration. Combined, they could be catastrophic for American interests, for the Middle East and for Iraq.

Perhaps for these reasons the Bush administration is trying to create a "democratic" government by June without popular elections.

What is to be done? Retreating from democracy is not an option. Unfortunately, few good models exist to guide U.S. ethnic policy in Iraq. The British strategy might have been to pit Shiites against Sunnis, and perhaps Kurds against both. But if we want an Iraq not divided and conquered, but united and self-governing, the way forward will be considerably harder.

The polar opposite of no ethnic policy would be a plan for explicit ethnic and religious power-sharing. For example, a new Iraqi constitution could contain a Dayton-style formula guaranteeing Sunnis and Kurds major government posts. Such a plan might have salutary short-term effects, but enshrining ethnicity and religious division in the constitution would be a perilous strategy. It could harden group identity at the cost of national unity. The one thing potentially worse than rushing to national Iraqi elections might be rushing to such elections while clumsily manipulating combustible ethnic dynamics that few in the United States even understand.

All this suggests a very different alternative: Put the brakes on national democracy, and focus much more energy and resources on local democracy. To date, astonishingly, there have been virtually no city or town elections anywhere in Iraq. Apparently, U.S. policy calls for implementing national self-government first and worrying about local self-government later. The order of priority should be exactly the opposite.

Democracy at the national level will essentially pit the Shiite majority against the hated Sunni minority and autonomy-seeking Kurds in a battle for control over the country's destiny and oil wealth. By contrast, many Iraqi towns and cities are relatively less divided along ethnic and religious lines, and the electoral stakes there would be much lower. In elections for city councils and other municipal positions, the competing candidates and parties would have much less incentive to define themselves along sectarian lines or to engage in ethnic demagoguery.

Local democracy is the best instruction for national democracy. British and American democracy started locally, not nationally. The message of the U.S.-led coalition to Iraqis should be: We are turning over governance to you, right now, in every one of your neighborhoods, towns and cities. Although oil and certain other national policy matters would be taken off the table—they could not possibly be decided at the town level—local self-government would still represent an enormous transfer of sovereignty. Most of the Iraqi reconstruction effort will be local: providing water; restoring electricity; building and staffing schools; fostering commerce; establishing town courts; and of course policing. Billions of dollars will be spent on these things over the coming years; crucial policy decisions will be made about priorities, jobs for women, and the distribution of goods and services.

To its credit, after the war, the U.S. military created district and town councils to assist in local governance all over Iraq. Coalition officials refer to these councils as "inclusive" and "democratically selected," but there is a big difference between selected and elected. In fact, the councils appear to have been selected by U.S. military authorities. As one U.S. official candidly acknowledged, "In terms of actual elections, we are not focused on that in our assistance at this point." An October poll indicated that half of all Iraqis did not even know the councils existed.

To be sure, some Iraqi towns might elect fundamentalist clerics as their lawmakers. The coalition must not try to suppress such results. Let Iraqis see their decisions respected. Let them see some towns where fundamentalism reigns and some where it does not. The hopes of a democratic Middle East may depend on it.

Local self-government will not be easy to achieve. Ethnically diverse cities such as Baghdad and Kirkuk could present special challenges. But local governance is a far more realistic goal than trying in the next six months to establish national, democratic government. Instead of premature national elections, the coalition should pursue an interim Iraqi constitution establishing the framework for immediate local self-government. During the ensuing period, coalition authorities would have the job of ensuring fair elections, a free press and freedom of movement (so that Iraqis can also "vote with their feet"). Because they would also retain control over Iraq's oil for an additional year or so, coalition forces must credibly demonstrate that they are keeping the country's oil wealth in trust for the Iraqi people. National elections would be postponed until Iraqis agreed on a permanent constitution, a process that would profit enormously from actual experience with local democracy.

Before she was assassinated, Iraqi Governing Council member Akila Hashimi warned against top-down efforts to remake her country. "Culture creates laws, not the other way around," she said. If democracy is to flourish in Iraq—and elsewhere in the Middle East—it must spread from the bottom up.

To sow the seeds of democracy, better to think locally.

AMY CHUA is a professor at Yale Law School and author of *"World on Fire: How Exporting Free Market Democracy Breeds Ethnic Hatred and Global Instability"* (Anchor Books). **JED RUBENFELD** is also a professor at Yale Law School and a U.S. observer at the Council of Europe.

From *The Washington Post,* January 4, 2004. Copyright © 2004 by The Washington Post Writers Group. Reprinted by permission via PARS International.

Is Ethnic Conflict Inevitable?

Better Institutions, Not Partition

JAMES HABYARIMANA ET AL.

Jerry Muller ("Us and Them," March/April 2008) tells a disconcerting story about the potential for ethnic diversity to generate violent conflict. He argues that ethnic nationalism—which stems from a deeply felt need for each people to have its own state—"will continue to shape the world in the twenty-first century." When state and ethnic-group boundaries do not coincide, "politics is apt to remain ugly."

Muller points to the peace and stability in Europe today as evidence of the triumph of "the ethnonationalist project": it is only because of a half century of violent separation of peoples through expulsions, the redrawing of state boundaries, and the outright destruction of communities too weak to claim territories of their own that Europe today enjoys relative peace. Elsewhere, the correspondence between states and nations is much less neat, and there Muller seems to agree with Winston Churchill that the "mixture of populations [will] . . . cause endless trouble." He advocates partition as the best solution to this difficult problem.

If correct, his conclusion has profound implications both for the likelihood of peace in the world and for what might be done to promote it. But is it correct? Do ethnic divisions inevitably generate violence? And why does ethnic diversity sometimes give rise to conflict?

In fact, ethnic differences are not inevitably, or even commonly, linked to violence on a grand scale. The assumption that because conflicts are often ethnic, ethnicity must breed conflict is an example of a classical error sometimes called "the base-rate fallacy." In the area of ethnic conflict and violence, this fallacy is common. To assess the extent to which Muller falls prey to it, one needs some sense of the "base."

How frequently does ethnic conflict occur, and how often does it occur in the context of volatile mismatches between ethnic groups and states? A few years ago, the political scientists James Fearon and David Laitin did the math. They used the best available data on ethnic demography for every country in Africa to calculate the "opportunities" for four types of communal conflict between independence and 1979: ethnic violence (which pits one group against another), irredentism (when one ethnic group attempts to secede to join co-ethnic communities in other states), rebellion (when one group takes action against another to control the political system), and civil war (when violent conflicts are aimed at creating a new ethnically based political system). Fearon and Laitin identified tens of thousands of pairs of ethnic groups that could have been in conflict. But they did not find thousands of conflicts (as might have been expected if ethnic differences consistently led to violence) or hundreds of new states (which partition would have created). Strikingly, for every one thousand such pairs of ethnic groups, they found fewer than three incidents of violent conflict. Moreover, with few exceptions, African state boundaries today look just as they did in 1960. Fearon and Laitin concluded that communal violence, although horrifying, is extremely rare.

The base-rate fallacy is particularly seductive when events are much more visible than nonevents. This is the case with ethnic conflict, and it may have led Muller astray in his account of the triumph of European nationalism. He emphasizes the role of violence in homogenizing European states but overlooks the peaceful consolidation that has resulted from the ability of diverse groups—the Alsatians, the Bretons, and the Provençals in France; the Finns and the Swedes in Finland; the Genoese, the Tuscans, and the Venetians in Italy—to live together. By failing to consider the conflicts that did not happen, Muller may have misunderstood the dynamics of those that did.

Of course, ethnic divisions do lead to violent conflict in some instances. Violence may even be so severe that partition is the only workable solution. Yet this extreme response has not been required in most cases in which ethnic divisions have existed. Making sense of when ethnic differences generate conflict—and knowing how best to attempt to prevent or respond to them when they do—requires a deeper understanding of how ethnicity works.

Muller offers one explanation for why ethnic identities figure so centrally in political conflict. Corresponding as it does to "enduring propensities of the human spirit," he argues, ethnonationalism "is a crucial source of both solidarity and enmity." This explanation echoes a fairly conventional account of ethnic conflict according to which people tend to prefer members of their own group and, in some cases, have active antipathy toward out-group members, making conflict the inevitable result. This is an appealing narrative. It helps outsiders make sense of the seemingly gratuitous violence of Africa's bloodiest conflicts. It resonates with the demonization of immigrants and the threats of ethnic domination that politicians around the world invoke in election campaigns. It appears consistent with demands for greater autonomy and self-government by ethnic enclaves in eastern Europe and the former Soviet Union. If ethnic diversity generates antipathies so deep that they cannot be realistically resolved, separation becomes the obvious and, perhaps, only feasible antidote, as Muller concludes. But positive feelings toward in-group members and antipathies for out-group members might not be the correct explanation for why political action is often organized along ethnic lines.

Indeed, recent research points to at least two alternative explanations. One argument suggests that members of the same group tend to work together to achieve collective ends not because of their discriminatory preferences but because of efficiency: they speak the same language, have access to the same types of information, and share social networks. In environments with scarce resources, they may even choose to work together against other groups, whether or not they care for or even like their peers. Thus, political coalitions form along ethnic lines not because people care more for their own but simply because it is easier to collaborate with their ethnic peers to achieve collective ends.

A second account emphasizes the norms that may develop within ethnic groups. Even when people see no efficiency gains from working with their co-ethnics and have no discriminatory preferences, they may still favor their own simply because they expect them to discriminate in their favor as well. Such reciprocity is most likely to develop in environments that are devoid of the institutions and practices—for example, enforceable contracts and impartial state institutions—that protect people from being taken advantage of by others. In such cases, reciprocity is a protection against being cheated.

Distinguishing these different theories is important because each one suggests a starkly different strategy for dealing with ethnic conflict. If the problem is tribal or national antipathies, there may well be some utility in separating groups. But if it stems from the technological advantages that accrue to members of the same ethnic group, then initiatives that break down barriers to cooperation (for example, Julius Nyerere's introduction of Swahili as a common language in Tanzania in the 1970s) are more likely to bear fruit. If instead discrimination in favor of one's ethnic peers is a coping strategy that individuals employ to compensate for the absence of functional and impartial state institutions, then the best response may be greater investment in formal institutions so that individuals are assured that cheating will be punished and that cooperation across ethnic lines will be reciprocated.

To discern these competing perspectives, we set out to study ethnicity and conflict using experimental games. We put people in strategic interactions with members of their own and other ethnic groups and examined the decisions they made. We carried out our research in Uganda, where differences between ethnic groups have been a basis for political organization and the source of persistent national political crisis and violent conflict since independence.

Remarkably, we found no evidence that people care more for the welfare of individuals from their own ethnic groups than for the welfare of those from other groups. Given the opportunity to make anonymous donations of cash to randomly selected partners, individuals were just as generous to out-group members as they were to their co-ethnics. One could easily tell a story that links Uganda's decades of ethnic conflict to tribal antipathies (and many have), but our research provided no evidence of such antipathies at work among a diverse sample of Ugandans.

We also found only weak evidence that impediments to cooperation across group lines explain the ethnic dynamics of Ugandan politics. In another set of experiments, we randomly matched participants with a partner and confronted the pairs with tasks that put a premium on successful communication and cooperation. We found no relation between the success in completing these tasks and the ethnic identities of the participants; success rates were just as high when individuals were paired with members of their own ethnic groups as when they were paired with people outside their ethnic groups. Hence, efficiency gains alone cannot easily account for the propensity of political coalitions to take on an ethnic character.

Instead, our studies suggested that patterns of favoritism and successful collective action within ethnic groups should be attributed to the practice of reciprocity, which ensures cooperation among group members. Our subjects showed no bias in favor of in-group members when given the opportunity to make cash donations anonymously, but their behavior changed dramatically when they knew that their partners could see who they were. When they knew that other players would know how they behaved, subjects discriminated strongly in favor of their co-ethnics. This shows, at least in our sample of Ugandans, that ethnic differences generate conflict not by triggering antipathy or impeding communication but by making salient a set of reciprocity norms that enable ethnic groups to cooperate for mutual gain.

Our experimental findings—from a setting quite different from the European context that Muller treats but in which ethnic divisions run equally deep—reveal that what might look from the outside like an intractable problem of discriminatory preferences may instead reflect norms of reciprocity that develop when individuals have few other institutions they can rely on to police the behavior of others.

Of course, ethnicity may not work in Uganda today the same way that it does in other parts of the world or that it did at other points in history. But our results do point out a need to consider seriously the possibility that the conventional view is at best an incomplete and at worst an incorrect explanation for why ethnic nationalism generates conflict when and where it does.

If ethnic hatreds are not at work, separating groups may not make much sense as a strategy for mitigating the corrosive effects of ethnic divisions. It might be far more important to invest in creating impartial and credible state institutions that facilitate cooperation across ethnic lines. With such institutions in place, citizens would no longer need to rely disproportionately on ethnic networks in the marketplace and in politics. In this respect, modernization may be the antidote to ethnic nationalism rather than its cause.

JAMES HABYARIMANA is Assistant Professor of Public Policy at Georgetown University. **MACARTAN HUMPHREYS** is Assistant Professor of Political Science at Columbia University. **DANIEL POSNER** is Associate Professor of Political Science at UCLA. **JEREMY WEINSTEIN** is Assistant Professor of Political Science at Stanford University.

Separatism's Final Country

RICHARD ROSECRANCE AND ARTHUR STEIN

Muller argues that ethnonationalism is the wave of the future and will result in more and more independent states, but this is not likely. One of the most destabilizing ideas throughout human history has been that every separately defined cultural unit should have its own state. Endless disruption and political introversion would follow an attempt to realize such a goal. Woodrow Wilson gave an impetus to further state creation when he argued for "national self-determination" as a means of preventing more nationalist conflict, which he believed was a cause of World War I.

The hope was that if the nations of the Austrian, Ottoman, and Russian empires could become independent states, they would not have to bring the great powers into their conflicts. But Wilson and his counterparts did not concede to each nation its own state. They grouped minorities together in Hungary, Italy, and Yugoslavia, and the Soviet Union ultimately emerged as a veritable empire of nationalities. Economists rightly questioned whether tiny states with small labor forces and limited resources could become viable, particularly given the tariffs that their goods would face in international trade.

More important, the nationalist prospect was and remains hopelessly impractical. In the world today, there are 6,800 different dialects or languages that might gain political recognition as independent linguistic groups. Does anyone seriously suggest that the 200 or so existing states should each, on average, be cut into 34 pieces? The doctrine of national self-determination reaches its reductio ad absurdum at this point.

Furthermore, the one-nation, one-state principle is unlikely to prevail for four good reasons. First, governments today are more responsive to their ethnic minority communities than were the imperial agglomerations of yesteryear, and they also have more resources at their disposal than their predecessors did. Many provinces populated by discontented ethnic groups are located in territories adjacent to national capitals, not overseas. And many governments in this era of globalization have annual budgets equivalent to nearly 50 percent of their GDPs, much of which is spent on social services. They can—and do—accommodate the economic needs of their states' differentiated units. They also respond to those units' linguistic requests. Basques, Bretons, Punjabis, Québecois, and Scots live quite well inside the bonds of multinational sovereignty and in some cases better than residents of other provinces with no claims of being a distinct nation.

Second, the achievement of separate sovereignty today depends on external recognition and support. Prospective new states cannot gain independence without military assistance and economic aid from abroad. International recognition, in turn, requires the aspiring nationalist movement to avoid international terrorism as a means of gaining attention. If a separatist group uses terrorism, it tends to be reviled and sidelined. If an ethnic group does not have enough support to win independence by peaceful electoral means inside its country, its resorting to terrorism only calls into question the legitimacy of its quest for independence.

Recognizing this, the Québecois abandoned the terrorist methods of the Quebec Liberation Front. Most Basques castigate Basque Homeland and Freedom (known by its Basque acronym ETA). Enlightened Europeans have withdrawn their support for the Chechen rebels. And the continued terrorist shelling of Israeli cities from a Hamas-dominated Gaza might undermine the previous international consensus in favor of a two-state solution to the Palestinian problem, or at least warrant an exceptional approach to Gaza.

With the possible exception of the Palestinians, the notion that any of these peoples would be better off in smaller and weaker independent states in a hostile neighborhood is unrealistic. Occasionally, dissidents make the case that if they were to leave the state unit, they would be taken into the comforting embrace of the European Union or the North American Free Trade Agreement, thereby gaining access to a large market. But that would depend a great deal on outsider support for their cause. The United Kingdom might not wish to see Scotland in the EU and would be in a position to veto its membership. The United States and Canada might not agree to let an independent Quebec join NAFTA. The belief that when a tiny nation is born it falls automatically into the loving hands of international midwives is questionable. The truth varies from case to case.

Third, although globalization initially stimulated ethnic discontent by creating inequality, it also provides the means for quieting discontents down the road within the fold of the state political system. Distributed economic growth is a palliative for political discontent. Indonesia, Malaysia, Singapore, and Thailand contain different ethnic groups that have largely profited from the intense economic resurgence of their states stimulated by globalization. Northern and southern Vietnam are culturally different, but both have benefited from the country's economic growth. Cambodia has a diverse population, but it has gained greatly from China's move to externalize some of its production.

Fourth, a discontented population may react to ethnic discrimination, but it also responds to economic need, and whatever its concerns, it does not always have to seek independence to alleviate them. It has another safety valve: emigration to another country. The state of Monterrey has not sought independence from Mexico; rather, many of its inhabitants have moved, legally or illegally, to the United States. The huge emigration from the Maghreb to France and Italy reflects a similar attitude and outcome; the dissatisfied populations of North Africa can find greater welfare in Europe. And when Poles move to France or the United Kingdom, they do not secede from the mother country but demonstrate greater satisfaction with French or British rule. Emigration is the overwhelming alternative to secession when the home government does not sufficiently mitigate economic disparities.

Even where the central government has used force to suppress secessionist movements, it has offered carrots at the same time that it has yielded sticks. The province of Aceh has been coaxed, even as it has been subjected to threats, to remain inside the Indonesian republic. Kashmir, facing a balance of restraints and incentives, is unlikely to emerge as an independent state in India. And the Tamil Tigers have lost the sympathy of the world by their slaughter of innocent Sinhalese.

The recent formation of an "independent" Kosovo, which has not yet been recognized by various key countries, does not foretell the similar arrival of other new states. It is unlikely that Abkhazia or South Ossetia, although largely autonomous in fact, will gain full and formal independence from Georgia or that the Albanian areas of Macedonia will secede. Rather, prospective secessionists, dissuaded by both central governments and the international community, are likely to hold back. Indeed, the most plausible future outcome is that both established states and their international supporters will generally act to prevent a proliferation of new states from entering the international system.

Much empirical work, which shows that a province's aspirations for sovereign status can be confined within a state if the province has access to monies from the central government and is represented in the governing elite, supports this conclusion. The Sikh party Akali Dal once sought Punjab's independence from India, but to little effect, partly because Punjabis are heavily represented in the Indian army and because fiscal transfers from New Delhi quieted dissidence in the region. The Québecois benefit from financing from Ottawa, elite connections, flows of private capital into Quebec, and the Canadian government's acceptance of bilingualism in the province. Chechnya remains poor, but if it seeks to remedy its relative neglect through a strategy of terrorism, it will undercut its own legitimacy. Lacking external support, and in the face of Russia's continued firmness, Chechnya has settled into a degree of political stability. In all three cases, the maintenance of the existing national boundaries seems likely, and so, too, does it seem likely in other cases.

The apostles of national self-determination would do well to consider a still more important trend: the return to bigness in the international system. This is happening not only because great powers such as China, India, and the United States are now taking on greater roles in world politics but also because international economics increasingly dwarfs politics. To keep up, states have to get bigger. The international market has always been larger than the domestic ones, but as long as international openness beckoned, even small powers could hope to prosper and attain some degree of economic influence. In the past decade, however, the tariff reductions proposed in the Doha Round of international trade negotiations have failed, industrial duties have not fallen, and agriculture has become even more highly protected than it was in the nineteenth century.

Globalization has clearly distributed economic boons to smaller countries, but these states still require greater political scale to fully realize globalization's benefits. To generate scale, states have negotiated bilateral and multilateral trade preferences with other states regionally and internationally, thereby gaining access to larger markets. The EU has decided to make up in the enlargement of its membership and a bigger free-trade area what it lacks in internal economic growth. The 27 countries of the EU currently have a combined GDP of over $14 trillion, besting the United States' $13 trillion, and the union's expansion is not over yet.

Europe never faced the limits on "manifest destiny" that confronted the United States—the shores of the Pacific Ocean. Charles de Gaulle was wrong when he heralded a "Europe from the Atlantic to the Urals": the EU has already expanded into the Caucasus. And with at least eight new members, it will proceed into Central Asia. As the borders of Europe approach Russia, even Moscow will seek de facto ties with the increasingly monolithic European giant.

In Asia, current tensions between China and Japan have not prevented proposals for a free-trade zone, a common currency, and an investment bank for the region. Chinese in Indonesia, Malaysia, the Philippines, Singapore, Taiwan, and Vietnam draw their adopted countries toward Beijing. China will not expand territorially (except titularly when Taiwan rejoins the mainland), but it will move to consolidate an economic network that will contain all the elements of production, except, perhaps, raw materials. Japan will adjust to China's primacy, and even South Korea will see the writing on the wall.

This will leave the United States in the uncomfortable position of experiencing unrealized growth and the possible failure of new customs unions in the Western Hemisphere. NAFTA may have been deepened, but a Free Trade Area of the Americas now seems beyond reach because of opposition from Argentina, Bolivia, Brazil, and Venezuela. U.S. politics has also turned, temporarily at least, against such ventures. South American nations have, in recent years, been far more responsive to China and Europe than to the United States. The U.S.—Central American Free Trade Agreement, now in the making, may be the only likely new string to the current U.S. bow.

Some economists contend that great size is not necessary in a fully open international economic system and that even small countries can sell their wares abroad under such conditions. But the international economic system is not open, and the future resides with broad customs unions, which substitute expanded regional markets for restricted international ones. China is seeking bilateral preferential trade arrangements with several other states, and so is the United States. Prospective secessionists will not prosper under such circumstances. They have to depend on international assistance, membership in trade pacts, and the acquiescence of their mother countries. They may have none of these, and they will fail if they use terrorism to advance their causes.

Under the present circumstances, secessionists will generally be better off remaining inside existing states, if only because the international system now advantages larger agglomerations of power. Economies of industrial scale are promoting economies of political size. In U.S. politics, the problem of outsourcing gets much political attention, but how is it possible to prevent that activity when national production and the national market are too small? Only larger political entities can keep production, research and development, and innovation within a single economic zone. Big is back.

RICHARD ROSECRANCE is Adjunct Professor of Public Policy at the John F. Kennedy School of Government and Senior Fellow at the Belfer Center for Science and International Affairs, both at Harvard University. ARTHUR STEIN is Professor of Political Science at UCLA. They co-edited *No More States? Globalization, National Self-Determination, and Terrorism* (2006).

Muller Replies

My essay is not agenda-driven or prescriptive. It is meant to suggest that the power of ethnic nationalism in the twentieth century has been greater than is generally recognized and that the probability of its ongoing global impact is greater than is generally appreciated. I argue that Americans often have a distorted sense of substantial areas of the world because they tend to generalize on the basis of their own national experience or, rather, a truncated and idealized version of that experience. Of course, ethnicity (and its conceptual cousin, race) has long played a role in American life and continues to do so, as reflected in everything from residential patterns to voting behavior.

But by and large, ethnic identification in the United States tends to erode across generations, and the notion that different ethnic groups ought to have their own political entities is marginal. (Voting districts drawn along racial lines echo conceptions of ethnic nationalism. And the Chicano vision of the reconstitution of Aztlán—a lost nation of indigenous Americans said to include Mexico and much of the American Southwest—would qualify as ethnonationalist but seems to have limited appeal.) Thus, Americans have a hard time imagining the intensity of the desire that many ethnic groups abroad have for a polity of their own or the determination of others to maintain the ethnic structure of existing polities. If Poles and Ukrainians get along tolerably well in Chicago, why not Sunni Arabs, Kurds, and Turkmen in Kirkuk?

I further argue that this misperception also occurs among educated western Europeans, who project the cooperative and pacific model of the EU onto the rest of the world while losing sight of the history of ethnic disaggregation that seems to have served as a precondition for the comity of contemporary Europe. The propensity to impose on the rest of the world one's own categories and idealized conceptions of one's historical and current experiences leads to a kind of misleading universality, apt to result in misunderstanding and miscalculation.

There are categories of self-definition that are unfamiliar or uncomfortable to some people's sensibilities—including ethnonational identity, caste (common in India), or tribe (common in much of Africa and the Muslim world). But the fact that some people may find these categories unreal (since they know that beneath the skin humans are ultimately the same: put them in a room together with a game to play, and see how little they differ) does not make them any less real to those who do believe in them.

The problem of taking seriously the diverse ways in which people in different parts of the world define themselves is

exacerbated by the universalizing and scientistic pretensions of some streams of academic political science. "Scientism" refers to the endeavor to apply the methods and criteria of the natural sciences to all realms of human experience—although for some they are inappropriate. This includes the effort to explain all phenomena with simplified theories of human motivation and the attempt to replicate the hard sciences by using laboratory conditions to study political science. History provides a useful source of data with which to study the range and complexity of human behavior. It is a highly imperfect laboratory, where both the data and their interpretation are influenced by the methodological and ideological predispositions of the investigator. But it is often superior to the alternative: apparently scientific forms of explanation.

My claim is not that the violence of the European experience will repeat itself but a more modest one: that ethnic tensions are likely to be exacerbated, rather than eliminated, by the occurrence of similar processes of modernization in other parts of the world. Contrary to what James Habyarimana, Macartan Humphreys, Daniel Posner, and Jeremy Weinstein claim, nowhere do I argue that "ethnic divisions inevitably generate violence." And while I quoted Churchill, I did not endorse his views as a general policy prescription.

What I actually wrote, toward the end of my article, was this:

> Sometimes, demands for ethnic autonomy or self-determination can be met within an existing state. . . . But such arrangements remain precarious and are subject to recurrent renegotiation. In the developing world, accordingly, where states are more recent creations and where the borders often cut across ethnic boundaries, there is likely to be further ethnic disaggregation and communal conflict. And as scholars such as Chaim Kaufmann have noted, once ethnic antagonism has crossed a certain threshold of violence, maintaining the rival groups within a single polity becomes far more difficult.
>
> . . . When communal violence escalates to ethnic cleansing, moreover, the return of large numbers of refugees to their place of origin after a cease-fire has been reached is often impractical and even undesirable.
>
> . . . Partition may thus be the most humane lasting solution to such intense communal conflicts.

Habyarimana, Humphreys, Posner, and Weinstein continue their misrepresentations by claiming that I attribute ethnic tension merely to "enduring propensities of the human spirit"; in fact, I attribute ethnic tension to "some enduring propensities of the human spirit that are heightened by the process of modern state creation." My explanation, drawn largely from the sociologist Ernest Gellner, is actually echoed by the four co-authors, albeit in a different vocabulary, when they write that members of the same ethnic group tend to come together because "they speak the same language, have access to the same types of information, and share social networks." As so often happens in the social sciences, here is an attempt at product differentiation through rebranding—recasting known insights in a new vocabulary.

More novel is the authors' belief that their quasi-scientific experiments in Uganda provide useful new avenues for public policy. They say that their game-playing experiments provide insights as to how the diverse ethnic actors would behave when freed of the social and political contexts in which their actions are known to others. Perhaps, but it is precisely the nature of the real world that this would never be the case.

Moreover, their conclusion that the problem lies in a weak institutional environment characterized by an "absence of functional and impartial state institutions" is both true and misleading, for it fails to consider that the very multiplicity of ethnicities is among the major sources of this institutional environment. A reading of Chinua Achebe's 1960 novel, *No Longer at Ease*—about the plight of an idealistic young civil servant who tries to embody the ethos of impartiality in a setting in which such norms are at odds with the understanding of his co-ethnics, who regard his bureaucratic position as a form of group property—would cast more light on the situation than hundreds of experimental games.

This is not the place for a full critique of the much-cited calculations of Fearon and Laitin on the incidence of interethnic violence in Africa from 1960 to 1979. If one lives in a neighborhood where three in a thousand interactions result in violence and one has three interactions per day, one is violently attacked only three times a year. But is that a safe neighborhood or a dangerous one? The assertion that "with few exceptions, African state boundaries today look just as they did in 1960" is also both true and misleading. It attests as much to the ability of the dominant ethnic coalitions to suppress attempts at rebellion as to the absence of ethnic conflict.

The Biafran War (1967–70) counts as only one incident of interethnic violence in Fearon and Laitin's data and resulted in no change of borders. The million or so lives lost do not register in their calculations. Had Fearon and Laitin repeated their computations for the years since 1979, the murder of some 800,000 Rwandans (mostly Tutsis) would also have appeared as a matter of small statistical consequence.

The claim by Richard Rosecrance and Arthur Stein that the ethnonationalist ideal of a separate state for each cultural unit has been a source of instability is true or, at least, a half-truth. That is what a good part of my article is about. But the fact that ethnonationalism is destabilizing has not diminished its appeal or impact. The other half-truth is that the fulfillment of the ethnonationalist ideal has had a stabilizing effect, at least for large groups.

However, as my article notes and as Rosecrance and Stein emphasize, not every ethnonational aspiration can be realized, and ethnonational aspirations for autonomy and self-determination can be realized within larger political units through federalism—the devolution of power and income to subnational units. As such, federalism represents a form of "semi-partition," as the political scientist Donald Horowitz has noted. It has the very real advantage of permitting participation in larger political and economic units. But, as Horowitz has also noted, "federalism is not cheap. It involves duplication of facilities, functions, personnel and infrastructure" and often entails jurisdictional disputes. Moreover, "states that could benefit from federalism typically come to that realization too late, usually after conflict has intensified."

Rosecrance and Stein may be right that a greater pool of income can alleviate ethnonational aspirations. But it is worth recalling that the government is in a position to distribute sums equivalent to 50 percent of their GDPs are in Europe, whereas the ethnic groups in potential conflict are in Africa, Asia, and Latin America, where there is less wealth and so less GDP available for redistribution. Moreover, massive government redistribution through taxation may itself inhibit economic growth or make capturing the state apparatus too enticing a prize compared with other pursuits.

Various claims by Rosecrance and Stein are questionable, if not clearly mistaken. The authors assert that mass emigration can serve as an "alternative to secession when the home government does not sufficiently mitigate economic disparities." First, this assumes that all discontents are ultimately expressions of individually conceived economic interest, a radical simplification of human motivation that ignores the desire of some people to share a common culture and their perception that protecting that culture requires political autonomy. For example, throughout much of the first half of the twentieth century, French Canadians emigrated from Canada to the United States, where over time they assimilated into the larger population. Québecois nationalism represents a rejection of that path.

Second, the authors' emigration-as-safety-valve strategy ignores the fact that in contrast to the earlier era of globalization (from the late nineteenth century through World War I), the current era of globalization is characterized by governments better able and more inclined to police their borders and, hence, by the comparatively limited mobility of people across national borders. Moreover, discontent in the relatively wealthy states of the West with some recent streams of immigration has already led to pressures for governments to exercise greater control over the movement of people from particular regions. It is far from clear that emigration from the Maghreb to France, for example, will be allowed to continue indefinitely.

Rosecrance and Stein's assertion that a new era of bigness in international economic affairs is here is truer than the implications they draw from it. The economic advantages of the division of labor do expand with the extent of the market, as Adam Smith explained over two centuries ago. But it is simply not true that "to keep up, states have to get bigger." States can negotiate treaties and other forms of association that allow for freer international trade. As the authors note in passing, smaller nations have opted for inclusion in transnational markets and have often prospered as a result.

In short, Rosecrance and Stein assume that a rational economic calculus governs international activity. This simplification of human motivation has the advantage of methodological elegance. But their predictions conflate three very different circumstances: what global actors would do if they rationally calculated their utilities based on a set of preferences much like those of American professors of political science; what global actors would do if they rationally calculated their utilities based on their actual preferences, which may diverge substantially from those of American political scientists; and what may actually happen given the unlikelihood that either American political scientists or global actors would rationally calculate their utilities. That is to say, Rosecrance and Stein have purchased methodological elegance at the expense of explanatory power by radically reducing the range of relevant motivations and interactions.

For a historian, the authors' assertion that "international economics increasingly dwarfs politics"—like so much of their response to my essay—is eerily resonant of a British best-seller of a century ago. In 1910, Norman Angell published *The Great Illusion,* which explained on economic grounds why an extended war between great powers was impossible under the contemporary economic conditions. His argument was logically compelling but wrong. In 1933, Angell published a new edition of his book, in which he suggested that nations could not enrich themselves by conquering their neighbors and that war was therefore futile. He was awarded the Nobel Peace Prize, but his message seems not to have reached all the relevant parties. I fear that the predictions of Rosecrance and Stein about the future of ethnic nationalism will meet the same fate.

Still, Rosecrance and Stein do raise an important issue that I did not explore in my article: the question of external recognition and support for potential new states. What ought to be the response by external countries, such as the United States, to ethnonationalist claims for independence? If one takes seriously the forces leading to the enduring power of ethnonationalism—rather than dismissing them as archaic, illusory, or subject to elimination by good governance conjured out of the blue—the implications for policy are by no means self-evident.

I leave aside the purely legal and philosophical issues, since the "right" to self-determination, like so many others, often conflicts with other purported rights. Representatives of existing states are strongly disposed against the redrawing of borders and the formation of new states. They see self-interest in maintaining the international status quo, which may or may not be justified by prudence. To recognize that national self-determination does provide satisfactions of its own and may well result in viable states is not to say that the endless creation of new states is either viable or desirable. Yet there are dangers both in supporting ethnonationalist claims and in denying them prematurely.

One danger of the international recognition of insurgent ethnonationalist claims to sovereignty is that it may lead to unilateral secession (as in the recent case of Kosovo) as opposed to mutually agreed separation. Secession without ethnic partition usually means that the new political entity will include a substantial minority of people whose co-ethnics dominate the state from which the new state has seceded. This provides a ready source for new ethnic tensions within the new state and international tensions between the new state and the old. Mutually agreed partition that separates the rival ethnic groups may be preferable in order to minimize the likelihood of future conflict. Another danger of a greater international willingness to recognize ethnonationalist movements is that it may create an incentive for the governments of existing countries to violently crush incipient ethnic political movements before they can organize.

There are perils, however, in a blanket refusal of the international community to recognize the claims of legitimate ethnonationalist movements. For having deemed secession an impossibility, governments may feel no incentive to respond to the desire of ethnic groups for greater power and self-determination within the confines of the current states. To recognize the enduring power of ethnic nationalism is not to support it or provide a ready recipe for action but to offer a more realistic appreciation of the dilemmas that will continue to arise in the twenty-first century.

Test-Your-Knowledge Form

We encourage you to photocopy and use this page as a tool to assess how the articles in *Annual Editions* expand on the information in your textbook. By reflecting on the articles you will gain enhanced text information. You can also access this useful form on a product's book support Web site at *http://www.mhcls.com*.

NAME: DATE:

TITLE AND NUMBER OF ARTICLE:

BRIEFLY STATE THE MAIN IDEA OF THIS ARTICLE:

LIST THREE IMPORTANT FACTS THAT THE AUTHOR USES TO SUPPORT THE MAIN IDEA:

WHAT INFORMATION OR IDEAS DISCUSSED IN THIS ARTICLE ARE ALSO DISCUSSED IN YOUR TEXTBOOK OR OTHER READINGS THAT YOU HAVE DONE? LIST THE TEXTBOOK CHAPTERS AND PAGE NUMBERS:

LIST ANY EXAMPLES OF BIAS OR FAULTY REASONING THAT YOU FOUND IN THE ARTICLE:

LIST ANY NEW TERMS/CONCEPTS THAT WERE DISCUSSED IN THE ARTICLE, AND WRITE A SHORT DEFINITION:

We Want Your Advice

ANNUAL EDITIONS revisions depend on two major opinion sources: one is our Advisory Board, listed in the front of this volume, which works with us in scanning the thousands of articles published in the public press each year; the other is you—the person actually using the book. Please help us and the users of the next edition by completing the prepaid article rating form on this page and returning it to us. Thank you for your help!

ANNUAL EDITIONS: Race and Ethnic Relations 09/10

ARTICLE RATING FORM

Here is an opportunity for you to have direct input into the next revision of this volume.
We would like you to rate each of the articles listed below, using the following scale:

1. **Excellent: should definitely be retained**
2. **Above average: should probably be retained**
3. **Below average: should probably be deleted**
4. **Poor: should definitely be deleted**

Your ratings will play a vital part in the next revision.
Please mail this prepaid form to us as soon as possible.
Thanks for your help!

RATING	ARTICLE	RATING	ARTICLE
	1. Cambridge Makes History		26. Tribal Philanthropy Thrives
	2. Chicago and the Irish		27. Black History Month: February 2008
	3. 'Bursting with Pride' in Little Italy		28. Who Is an African American?
	4. Parishes in Transition: Holding on While Letting Go and Old Order Changing on South Bend's West Side		29. That's a Bare-Knuckles Kiss
			30. African American Philanthropy
	5. In Manassas, the Medium Is the Issue		31. For Black Politicians, a Rocky Road but a Steady Climb
	6. In Brooklyn, an Evolving Ethnicity		32. Inventing Hispanics: A Diverse Minority Resists Being Labeled
	7. Mélange Cities		
	8. The Hotel Africa		33. Hispanic Heritage Month and Cinco de Mayo
	9. The Fixer		34. Minority-Owned Firms More Likely to Export
	10. Racial Restrictions in the Law of Citizenship		35. To Be Asian in America
	11. Dred Scott v. Sandford		36. Lands of Opportunity
	12. Brown et al. v. Board of Education of Topeka et al.		37. Asian/Pacific American Heritage Month and Revenues for Asian-Owned Firms Up 24 Percent
	13. How the GOP Conquered the South		
	14. 'Bakke' Set a New Path to Diversity for Colleges		38. Miracle: American Polonia, Karol Wojtyła and the Election of Pope John Paul II
	15. Shaare Tefila Congregation v. Cobb and Saint Francis College v. Al-Khazraji		39. This Writer's Life: Gay Talese
			40. Forces That Shape Ethnic Opinion: What Ethnic Americans Really Think
	16. Historical Discrimination in the Immigration Laws		
	17. The Diversity Visa Lottery—A Cycle of Unintended Consequences in United States Immigration Policy		41. Neither Natural Allies Nor Irreconcilable Foes: Alliance Building Efforts between African Americans and Immigrants
	18. Ancestry 2000: Census 2000 Brief		42. The Study of Jewish American History and Dutch American History in Several Settings
	19. Minority Population Tops 100 Million and More than 300 Counties Now "Majority-Minority"		
			43. A More Perfect Union
	20. Irish-American Heritage Month (March) and St. Patrick's Day (March 17) 2008		44. Pulling the Race Card from the Deck
			45. Polonia and the Elections: Why We Matter?
	21. A Profile of Today's Italian Americans: A Report Based on the Year 2000 Census Compiled by the Sons of Italy		46. White Seniors Energize McCain Campaign
			47. Is Obama the End of Black Politics?
			48. Obama & Israel
	22. Polonia in Numbers: How Many of Us Are out There?		49. American Self-Interest and the Response to Genocide
	23. Still Unmelted after All These Years		50. Never Underestimate the Power of Ethnicity in Iraq
	24. Who Is a Native American?		
	25. American Indian and Alaska Native Heritage Month: November 2008		51. Is Ethnic Conflict Inevitable?

ABOUT YOU

Name

Date

Are you a teacher? ❏ A student? ❏
Your school's name

Department

Address

City

State

Zip

School telephone #

YOUR COMMENTS ARE IMPORTANT TO US!

Please fill in the following information:
For which course did you use this book?

Did you use a text with this ANNUAL EDITION? ❏ yes ❏ no
What was the title of the text?

What are your general reactions to the Annual Editions concept?

Have you read any pertinent articles recently that you think should be included in the next edition? Explain.

Are there any articles that you feel should be replaced in the next edition? Why?

Are there any World Wide Web sites that you feel should be included in the next edition? Please annotate.

May we contact you for editorial input? ❏ yes ❏ no
May we quote your comments? ❏ yes ❏ no